Global Marketing

Global Marketing provides students with a truly international treatment of the key principles that every marketing manager should grasp.

International markets present different challenges that require a marketer to think strategically, and apply tools and techniques creatively in order to respond decisively in a fiercely competitive environment. Alon et al. provide students with everything they need to rise to the challenge:

- Coverage of **small and medium enterprises**, as well as **multinational corporations**, where much of the growth in international trade and global marketing has occurred.

- A shift toward greater consideration of **services marketing** as more companies move away from manufacturing.

- A focus on **emerging markets** to equip students with the skills necessary to take advantage of the opportunities that these rapidly growing regions present.

- Chapters on **social media, innovation, and technology** teach students how to incorporate these new tools into their marketing strategy.

- New material on **sustainability, ethics, and corporate social responsibility**; key values for any modern business.

- Short **cases and examples** throughout the text show students how these principles and techniques are applied in the real world.

- **Longer cases** provide instructors and students with rich content for deeper analysis and discussion.

Covering key topics not found in competing books, *Global Marketing* will equip students with the knowledge and confidence they need to become leading marketing managers.

A companion website features an instructor's manual with test questions, as well as additional exercises and examples for in-class use.

Ilan Alon is a Professor of Strategy and International Marketing at the University of Agder, Norway, as well as a visiting scholar at Georgetown University, USA. The author of several books, Alon has taught at top business schools globally, and consulted in marketing and international business for multinational corporations and government organizations.

Eugene Jaffe is a Professor of Marketing at the School of Economics and Business Administration, Ruppin Academic Center, and Emeritus Professor at the Graduate School of Business Administration, Bar-Ilan University, both in Israel. He has authored seven books, and published in several journals, including the *Journal of Marketing Research, Journal of World Business, International Marketing Review*, and *International Business Review*.

Christiane Prange is a Professor of Global Strategy and Marketing at Tongji University, China. She has been a visiting professor at top international business schools and has consulted multinational companies on marketing and internationalization strategies, global innovation management, and corporate agility. She has published five books and several journal articles.

Donata Vianelli is a Professor at the University of Trieste, Italy, where she teaches international marketing and international business. She has authored four books and has published in a range of international journals. She researches global distribution and cross-cultural consumer behavior with a focus on Europe and Asia.

Global Marketing
Contemporary Theory, Practice, and Cases

Second Edition

Ilan Alon, Eugene Jaffe, Christiane Prange, and Donata Vianelli

Routledge
Taylor & Francis Group

NEW YORK AND LONDON

Please visit the companion website at www.routledge.com/cw/alon

Second edition published 2017
by Routledge
711 Third Avenue, New York, NY 10017

and by Routledge
2 Park Square, Milton Park, Abingdon, Oxon OX14 4RN

Routledge is an imprint of the Taylor & Francis Group, an informa business

© 2017 Taylor & Francis

The right of Ilan Alon, Eugene Jaffe, Christiane Prange, and Donata Vianelli to be identified as authors of this work has been asserted by them in accordance with sections 77 and 78 of the Copyright, Designs and Patents Act 1988.

First edition published by McGraw-Hill Higher Education 2012

Library of Congress Cataloging in Publication Data
A catalog record for this book has been requested

ISBN: 978-1-138-80787-7 (hbk)
ISBN: 978-1-138-80788-4 (pbk)
ISBN: 978-1-315-75089-7 (ebk)

Typeset in ITC Stone Serif
by Servis Filmsetting Ltd, Stockport, Cheshire

MIX
Paper from
responsible sources
FSC® C014174

Printed and bound in the United States of America by Sheridan

Dedications

To my wife
—Ilan Alon

To my wife Liora
—Eugene Jaffe

To M.A.
—Christiane Prange

To my sons Marco, Alessandro, and Alberto
—Donata Vianelli

Contents

15   *Designing and Controlling Global Marketing Systems*   604

Figures

Geo Maps

Tables

Boxes

PART I

Global Marketing Environments

CHAPTER 1

Understanding Global Markets and Marketing

Marketing is not a function, it is the whole business seen from the customer's point of view.

Peter F Drucker, US management consultant

LEARNING OBJECTIVES

After Reading This Chapter, You Should Be Able to:

- Understand the history of globalization and how it impacts marketing strategy.
- Define what is meant by "global marketing."
- Identify major trends of the past and the future that influence global marketing.
- Understand the general discussion of adaptation versus standardization.
- Adapt global marketing for high-technology firms.
- Understand how to adapt global marketing to emerging market countries (4As).
- Adopt a Global Marketing Management framework that helps structure decisions.

GLOBAL MARKETS TODAY

Africa's economic performance has improved greatly since the turn of the century, leading to notable gains in gross domestic product (GDP) per capita and lower levels of poverty. Several African countries are expected to be among the fastest growing countries in the world over the next decade. The following countries are expected to have the most potential for luxury goods demand expansion: Angola, Egypt, Ethiopia, Ghana, Kenya, Morocco, and Nigeria. The baseline expectation is that economic activity will expand by more than 5 percent per annum (p.a.) in all selected countries except Egypt by 2020. While on the aggregate, the African luxury good sector remains in its infancy, taking into account the demographic dividend and rising per capita GDP levels, the potential for expansion remains vast.[1] Especially, small African companies have the ambition to introduce luxury products to the outside world. Often, these products have a strong link to their home country and also want to sell the African spirit or experience (Figure 1.1).

FIGURE 1.1
Images of Africa
Source: www.pixabay.
com (Free Pictures,
Compiled by Author)

For instance, African company YSWARA, founded in 2013 by entrepreneur Swaady Martin-Leke, is a South African boutique that first focused on selling tea and now also sells candles of soy wax and essential oils that can be used as a moisturiser once they have melted. Some 13,000 tins of tea and more than 3,000 candles have been sold at outlets in 10 countries, from Nigeria to Norway and Kenya to Sierra Leone, mainly to hotels and other businesses but also directly to retail customers. The company's strategy for the future is to expand the product range to include honey, chocolate and other gourmet items that would have a distinctly African feel.[2] YSWARA is a luxury brand and delivers little pieces of Africa every day. Founder and CEO Swaady Martin-Leke explains that "we have a worldly and soulful approach that encompasses a prevailing monthly theme such as 'identity', 'love', 'passions and dreams', 'knowledge and learning' and happiness. Through these themes we will explore meaningful topics under the 4 main categories of style, art and culture, travel and soul." She goes on to say that "many people perceive luxury brands in a materialistic sense, but true luxury brands have deeper meanings and aims; they are vital for culture's survival and renewal."[3]

Increasing luxury demand is also present in other countries. Just have a look at one of the Prada shops in Beijing's major shopping streets. The increasing interest of Asian customers in luxury products is more than a shallow indicator of how the purchasing power in different parts of the world changes. Especially Chinese customers are increasingly exposed to luxury goods through the Internet, overseas travel, and first-hand experience. As a result, they have become more discerning. Once a country has a middle class, luxury in the form of status symbols will sell. In fact, China accounted for about 20 percent, or 180 billion renminbi ($27 billion[4]), of global luxury in 2015, according to new McKinsey research.[5] There are many other examples outside the luxury sector that illustrate how the world's largest companies have reconsidered their major target markets and how they have been forced to compete with companies from emerging markets, such as China, Russia, Brazil, India, and others. For instance, Brazil's JBS and Cosan are the global number one in food processing and biofuels respectively. Or take Russia's Gazprom as number one in energy (excluding oil) and India's Infosys and Wipro, both number five in information and outsourcing services. And finally, have a look at the Chinese automotive market, where traditional US-American and European brands like Ford, Daimler, VW, Audi and others are fiercely competing for market share. As Ford reports, China sales surged to about 840,000 vehicles in the first 11 months in 2014, up more than 50 percent from a year earlier amid an effort to double production capacity in the country by 2015. The carmaker has said it introduced 15 new models in China between 2011 and 2015, including for the luxury brand Lincoln and the classic Mustang muscle car.

It seems that products are selling everywhere, with consumers becoming similar in preferences, life-style, and aspirations. Kenichi Ohmae calls this the "Californization of Need."[6] In essence, it means that whatever their nationality, global citizens get the same information and want the prestige that comes with certain kinds of consumer products—fashion, international cuisine, electronics, entertainment, and news. Furthermore, outside the luxury segments, they often want the products for the lowest prices which emerging market multinationals are more likely to offer given their favorable labor conditions. That is, global competition is becoming tougher in a world without boundaries.

Local Preferences in Global Markets

However, there is another, seemingly opposite trend. Consider this: In Copenhagen, 18-year-old Hanna logs on to a Canadian website, orders the latest CD recorded by Madonna, and pays for it in kroner, using a Danish credit card issued by her local bank. Her cousin Jacques, visiting from France, logs on to a consumer electronics site, where he notices an advertisement for a new recording gadget developed in Japan but not available in European stores. Jacques enters a search engine and finds that the gadget is available for sale in Macau. He orders the gadget from a Macau dealer, has it sent to his home address in Paris, pays for it in euros, and receives a receipt for payment sent to his e-mail address. These transactions represent global marketing that permits buyers and sellers the world over to meet and do business online in virtually any language and currency, with ease, precision, security, and reliability. Why is this? Because companies face consumer needs that are, despite all global harmonization, different across countries, religions, peer groups and cultures; marketing channels vary, preferred means of payment are not the same, and language choice is important for customer satisfaction. Even more, **the identification of local preferences can lead to true innovations.** Take a look at the Swiss company Nestlé. Product "taste adaptation" is something the company is already implementing in China and is now employing in West Africa as well. Nestlé's local markets are supplied by imported base ingredients, such as onion powder, wheat flour as well as chillies grown in Europe. The R&D centre in Abidjan is looking at ways to prepare Nestlé products using locally sourced ingredients, such as cassava, sorghum, and millet. In addition, it is creating new and improved products that access a previously untapped market—consumers who prefer local products. If these products are successful, they will also create a new market for African farmers.[7] In each corner of the world, there are inherent characteristics that need to be respected.

In this textbook, we will place a **major focus on emerging markets**, both as a target market for Western companies, and as a driver of innovation and competitiveness in its own right, based on new rules and principles that emerging market firms have introduced in less than a decade. Many emerging market firms have managed to enter the global landscape because they have developed new and unconventional products or business models, often with the help of new technologies or the Internet. These new developments cannot be understood without a thorough appreciation of the underlying technologies. Learning from emerging markets instead of adopting a predominantly Western mantra is our proposition. In addition, there are many other trends that shape our global business landscape.

For instance, **global ethics and social responsibility** have turned into very important subjects. Many international MBA programs have already included an ethics module in their course plan. The reason is obvious. For instance, France's Société Général, or Germany's Siemens (SI), have admitted to nearly $2 billion in bribes, leading to the resignations of both its board chairman and its CEO in 2007. It is even more critical for companies and individual managers to develop a set of global values and a global code of conduct. Operating ethically requires much more than a code of conduct. The CEO and top management must engage with employees around the world to insist on transparency and compliance. Otherwise, they will never know what's going on. The company must have a closed-loop system of monitoring and auditing local marketing practices. The "don't look, don't tell" approach is bound to destroy your company's reputation. High standards must be enforced with a zero tolerance policy.[8] While it is certainly not easy to teach ethics at a business school, it is necessary to sharpen one's mind about any kind of fraud, corruption or a combination of pressure one is exposed to. This is especially the case when individual managers need to decide against short-term profits and socially responsible behavior, like for instance, the refusal of animal testing (or specific conditions that accompany this procedure) or the initial use of drugs in emerging market countries, where there is no shortage of people willing to receive free treatment despite the risks (Box 1.1). While this tendency may be true for several countries, Africa is a very pertinent case because of its many countries below the poverty line.

The preceding examples illustrate that the global market place exhibits several characteristics and is not always easy to analyze and classify. As a result, many

Box 1.1 Country-in-Focus: South Africa

Drug Testing in South Africa

While many countries have set ethical standards for clinical trials, this is not a guarantee they will be respected by those who perform the trials. "The problem is implementing these [ethical] guidelines and the imperialistic attitude of researchers and sponsors who come to the country and frequently disregard our process," Ames Dhai, director of the Steve Biko Centre for Bioethics at the University of Witwatersrand, South Africa adds.

By 2008, for example, there were three times as many developing countries participating in clinical trials registered with the US Food and Drug Administration than there were in the entire period between 1948 and 2000, with many "transitional" countries, such as Brazil, China, India, Mexico and South Africa, taking part.

The main incentive for developing countries is the promise of advanced medical science and access to the latest medications. However, the process of putting in place a legal and ethical framework to protect participants is not going at the same pace in many of these countries, the meeting heard.

According to Sonia Shah, author of *The Body Hunters: Testing New Drugs on the World's Poorest Patients*, up to 80 percent of patients recruited in some developing countries are not informed about the nature of the study they are taking part in. In addition, many of them do not feel free to quit the trial, because they think that they or their children will lose out on good healthcare or treatment if they abandon it.

Sources: SciDevNet, The Guardian.com, Monday July 4, 2011, http://www.theguardian.com/global-development/2011/jul/04/ethics-left-behing-drug-trials-developing [Accessed: January 15, 2015]; Wemos Foundation (2013). 'The clinical trials industry in South Africa: Ethics, rules, and realities.'; Fahsi, M. (2013). 'Medical neocolonianism: Big pharma outsources unethical clinical trials to South Africa.' Mint Press News, July 22, 2013.

business organizations must choose a global marketing strategy to enable them to win market share and capture and retain current and prospective customers. Marketing is becoming more important as organizations around the world strive to develop products and services that appeal to their customers and aim to differentiate their offering. Global marketing is by no means an easy approach to develop a profitable company but we believe that global marketing strategy is the key to attaining global competitive advantage. Therefore, the objective of this book is to show how a successful global marketing strategy can be developed and sustained.

In this introductory chapter, we will discuss the following questions in detail: How does technology support globalization? What exactly is globalization and how does it affect global marketing? What are the trends that have influenced global marketing so far and what are future developments? How can you develop global marketing strategies, both in developed and in emerging markets?

TECHNOLOGY AIDS GLOBALIZATION

Technology Drives Emerging Market Growth

With many emerging market players becoming global, issues such as co-creating companies' products together with world consumers (i.e. joint idea development, or co-manufacturing), marketing innovative and/or high-tech products, entering new markets with new technologies and managing the digital revolution become top priorities. In 2012, the Internet contribution to a country's revenues (iGDP) was significantly higher for developed countries, with Sweden leading the ranking. But emerging countries, especially in Africa, are catching up. For instance, Senegal and Kenya, though not the continent's largest economies, have Africa's highest iGDPs, and governments in both countries have made concerted efforts to stimulate Internet demand (Figure 1.2). Consulting firm McKinsey says that by 2025, Africa's iGDP should grow to at least 5 to 6 percent, matching that of leading economies such as Sweden, Taiwan, and the United Kingdom. However, if the Internet achieves the same kind of scale and impact as the spread of mobile phones in Africa, iGDP could account for as much as 10 percent, or $300 billion, of total GDP while producing a leap forward in economic and social development. Under this scenario, increased Internet penetration and use could propel private consumption 13 times higher than current levels.

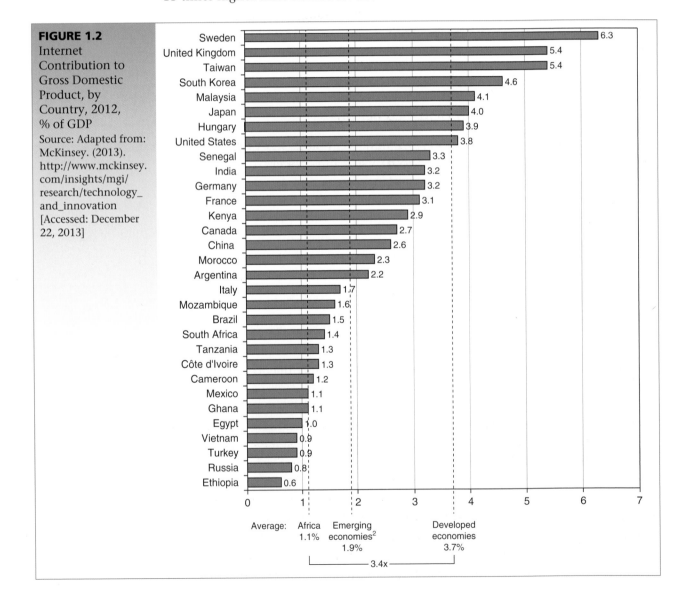

FIGURE 1.2
Internet Contribution to Gross Domestic Product, by Country, 2012, % of GDP
Source: Adapted from: McKinsey. (2013). http://www.mckinsey.com/insights/mgi/research/technology_and_innovation [Accessed: December 22, 2013]

The impact of technology on the global markets is also manifested in the vitality index of products, i.e. the percentage of current year sales coming from new products. For instance, 3M's financial performance is driven by products based on its 46 technology platforms, and its product vitality index is currently at a healthy 33 percent. A glimpse into the future was presented at the International Consumer Electronics Show in Las Vegas in 2014, where self-driving shuttles and solar cars were on display. And while smartphones and tablets are leading spending in the consumer electronics space, consumer electronics is effectively entering the third industrial revolution, which will be based around mass customization. 3D printing, is a nascent market, as well as wearable high tech, or ultra HD TV. What all these products have in common is that nobody imagined them a couple of years ago—today they start revolutionizing the tech industry. Technological innovations are by no means limited to developing countries. For instance, India is fast emerging as a global powerhouse economy. Its leading companies are major players on the world stage, and India exhibits several success stories in innovation including green energy, clean technology, smart cities, sustainable food, and water supplies.

High-Tech as the Backbone for Global Competitiveness

Creating, exploiting and commercializing new technologies is essential in the global race for competitiveness and high-tech sectors and enterprises are key drivers of economic growth, productivity and social protection, and generally a source of high value-added and well-paid employment. High-tech can be defined according to three different approaches:[9]

- **the sector approach** looks at the high-tech manufacturing sector, medium high-tech manufacturing sector, and high-tech knowledge-intensive service sector, focusing on employment, and economic indicators;

- **the product approach** considers whether a product is high-tech or not and examines trade in high-tech products;

- **the patent approach** distinguishes high-tech patents from others.

If we take the first approach, in 2010, the European Union had almost 50,000 enterprises in high-tech manufacturing. High-tech manufacturers were most numerous in Germany, the United Kingdom, Italy and the Czech Republic, all together accounting for around 55 percent of the high-tech sector in the EU-27.[10] The United Kingdom displayed the greatest number of enterprises in the high-tech knowledge-intensive services (KIS) sector (139,017), followed by Italy and France. As for the product approach, we can have a look at the high-tech sector of solar photovoltaic[11] and the export development share across countries (Figure 1.3). Chinese companies, including Suntech, JA Solar and Yingli have become major technology producers, with the largest share of their output exported. The solar photovoltaic (PV)

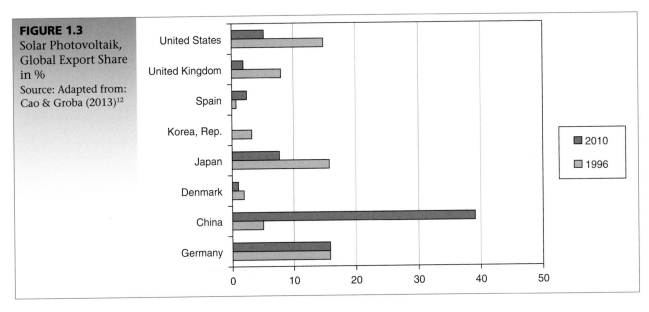

FIGURE 1.3
Solar Photovoltaik, Global Export Share in %
Source: Adapted from: Cao & Groba (2013)[12]

module producing industry is extremely prosperous with double digit growth rates since 2000 and became the largest producer in 2010.

There are numerous other examples of how technological leadership and innovation drive emerging market growth, such as Brazilian Embrapa (Geo Map 1.1) that employed traditional techniques to boost vitamin content in banana, beans, corn, manioc, and squash. It also used gene splicing to increase disease resistance in papaya and beans, and up the energy content of sugar cane, Brazil's ethanol source. Recently, Embrapa launched a Brazil–Africa partnership to share agricultural technology.

Finally, a patent approach can be used as a proxy for a country's innovativeness and technology orientation. It is well known that Israel's high-tech sector is widely regarded as a hotbed of cutting-edge technologies, and as the growth engine of the Israeli economy in the nineties and beyond. If you look at the number of patent applications, Israel maintains its position as the top country in the Middle East

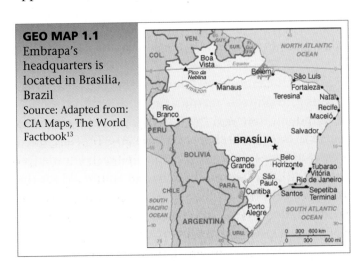

GEO MAP 1.1
Embrapa's headquarters is located in Brasilia, Brazil
Source: Adapted from: CIA Maps, The World Factbook[13]

filing for overall patents and ranks in the top 20 countries globally. The majority of the patents are for medical technology, such as biotechnology and pharmaceuticals. Other fields with a large number of patents include telecommunications and semiconductors.

Taken collectively, many companies from emerging markets or located at the periphery have been catching up in product quality and technology development. However, when it comes to their global reputation and branding, they often lag behind. Globalization has affected countries and companies in a different way and it is important to understand how competitiveness can be increased.

GLOBALIZATION: THE WORLD IS BECOMING SMALLER

Globalization—the trend toward a single integrated and interdependent world—is driven by international trade and made possible largely by information technology. But international trade has already existed in ancient times. In Greece and the wider Aegean, local, regional, and international trade exchange existed from the Bronze Age. The earliest written sources of Homer and Hesiod attest to the existence of trade (emporia) and merchants (emporoi) from the eighth century B.C. International trade grew from 750 B.C., driven by social and political factors such as population movements, colonization of interstate alliances, the spread of coinage, the gradual standardization of measurements, warfare, and safer seas following the determination to eradicate piracy.[14]

Globalization has grown over the past hundreds of years in various forms and may be understood by different perspectives. To the economist, globalization refers to the emergence of global markets. On the other hand, sociologists see globalization as the convergence of life-styles and social values. To the political scientist, globalization reduces national sovereignty. While aspects of globalization have been around for more than a hundred years, one of the first to recognize it as such was Marshall McLuhan. He coined the term "global village," wherein people who are physically separated by time and space are interconnected by electronic media. This linkage, while having positive benefits, also carries responsibilities on a global level.[15] A look back into the past illustrates the different facets and implications.

History of Globalization

Whether one can precisely determine when globalization began has been fiercely debated within various globalization experts. Some authors suggest that globalization began as early as the discovery of America, while others claim that it did not actually begin until the Industrial Revolution in the latter part of the eighteenth century.[16] Among those who argued for a world where all competitors have an equal opportunity and historical and geographical distances become increasingly irrelevant is Thomas Friedman with his international bestselling book, *The World Is Flat: A Brief History of the Twenty-First Century,* in which he analyzes globalization in the beginning of the twenty-first century. However, it should be noted that this approach has not been uncriticized. Pankaj Ghemawat, for instance, is the major proponent who supports the so-called "Ten-Percent Presumption," arguing that the world is by no means flat. He illustrated this by looking at a variety of international activities, such as telephone calls, tourists, foreign direct investment, and showed that the internationalization level of those activities was rather ten than 100 percent.[17]

Other authors date globalization back to the first circumnavigation of the Earth in 1519–21, the expansion of European capitalism in the sixteenth century or the heyday of international trade and investment before the convulsions of World War I and the Great Depression. For instance, Jeffrey Williamson[18] classified the years between 1820–1914 as the first great globalization era, and the period since World War II as the second. Facilitated by the international financial order, which sought to restore the volume of world trade, international trade relations have continued to grow. International business activities skyrocketed due to several reasons. First, firms' strategic imperatives, which motivated globalization, and second, environmental changes, which facilitated it.[19] The motives which compelled firms to extend their operations beyond local markets were comparatively simple. They wanted to leverage home market competences into foreign markets, acquire resources at low cost, beat rivals, and meet the local unavailability of raw materials. For example, in order to overcome the problem of domestic market saturation, the American firm Gillette expanded to Indonesia in the late 1990s. Gillette was founded in Boston

---

Box 1.2   Person-in-Focus: Thomas Friedman

Thomas Friedman's *The World Is Flat*

Thomas Friedman (born July 20, 1953) is an American journalist, columnist, and author. He has written extensively on foreign affairs including global trade, the Middle East, globalization, and environmental issues, and has won the Pulitzer Prize three times.

In his bestselling book, *The World Is Flat*, he takes a fresh look at the interconnectedness of the modern world, and explores the implications of the changes brought on by huge improvements in communications technologies. By the phrase "The World is Flat" he means that "the global competitive playing field is being leveled … It is now possible for more people than ever to collaborate and compete in real time with more other people on more different kinds of work from more different corners of the planet and on a more equal footing than at any previous time in the history of the world" (p. 8). He also points to several other causes, from the fall of the Berlin Wall to the rise of the Internet, as sources of this flatness — developments that are making it easier with every passing day for people all over the world to work together … or compete against each other. Taken collectively, Thomas Friedman demystifies the brave new world for readers, allowing them to make sense of the often bewildering global scene unfolding before their eyes.

Throughout all of the interviews and anecdotes, Friedman's optimism shines through. He clearly wants to tell us how exciting this new, flatter world will be. But he also wants us to understand that we're going to be trampled if we don't keep up with it, and take ownership of this great challenge.

Sources: Friedman, T.L. (2005). *The World Is Flat: A Brief History of the Twenty-First Century*. New York: Farrar, Straus and Giroux; Gulyani, A. (2013). 'The World Is Flat by Thomas L. Friedman – Book Review & My Cliff Notes', http://gulyani.com/the-world-is-flat-by-thomas-l-friedman-book-review-my-cliff-notes/; http://www.thomaslfriedman.com [Accessed: January 22, 2014].

to provide hygienic resources, and especially razors, to consumers. The company's original belief was that greater demand for razors would result from an improvement of the educational system and increasing exposure to the Western style of living. Consequently, they first launched the product in bigger and wealthier cities and subsequently triggered information campaigns in rural areas.

The second driver, environmental changes, clearly initiated the fastest phase of globalization in the second half of the nineteenth century, when transportation and communication technologies as well as political liberalization blossomed. International business became more feasible and attractive than ever before. Also, political conditions favored the rise of globalization, especially as trade barriers were reduced and investment was encouraged. Especially the principles established in the General Agreement on Tariffs and Trade (GATT) in 1947 and its successor, the World Trade Organization (WTO) largely opened the world to economic relations to be conducted on the basis of non-discrimination. In terms of political change, it goes without saying that the emerging new political landscape after the collapse of European communism largely impacted the way business was conducted. Central and Eastern Europe today is as important a market space and economic success story as are the new winners in Asia, like for instance South Korea, or Latin America, especially Brazil.

Box 1.3   Company-in-Focus: VW Versus Toyota

How Globalization Challenges Companies

For many Japanese firms, survival may depend on overseas expansion, given the stagnant home market. For instance, Toyota doesn't think it will sell as many cars in Germany as it originally hoped for 2014 as it has failed to keep up with demand for its hybrid-powered cars in the country. Toyota had been too slow in delivering the battery packs needed for hybrid cars from Japan. Sales of Toyota vehicles fell 9 percent in the first ten months in Germany to 62,009, according to data from the country's federal transport authority (KBA). This gave the carmaker a market share of 2.5 percent.

These tendencies are characteristic for several Japanese firms. But even Japanese companies with established global businesses face stronger competition and must rejuvenate their overseas business models. Building a globalized company will require many Japanese executives to think in new and unfamiliar ways about their organization, marketing, and strategy. What has worked long back in the past—replication—will no longer suffice to succeed in foreign operations. Japan's companies have undertaken a bold move to cope with globalization, moving to English as the corporate language and recruiting non-Japanese executives. Many Japanese companies understand the benefits of globalization, but their executives may lack a compelling "globalization story" for employees—global goals, aspirations, and value propositions. Are these widely understood and properly communicated in a way that excites and energizes the organization while addressing the anxiety that comes with big changes in direction? Spending time and effort developing such messages may seem trivial, but a globalization effort won't get far unless employees are on board.

Many Japanese companies should be global leaders, given their manufacturing and technological prowess and overall size and scale. While the automotive sector is already quite global, this is not the case for other sectors. Many executives of Japan's largest consumer companies privately acknowledge that they have fallen behind the likes of Apple, P&G, Samsung, and Unilever in their efforts to ensure shopper-focused rather than R&D lab-centric product development.

Meanwhile, foreign competitors have penetrated Japan's once-insular market, taking advantage of the Japanese consumer's new openness to foreign products. In many ways, these consumers, long touted as unique, behave increasingly like their counterparts in Europe and the United States: what they want is value. In a Japanese context, value means products that look attractive or stylish. For instance, VW, the German car manufacturer, wants to double its Japan sales by 2018. VW is bullish on Japan, despite hurdles to imports and despite the moribund domestic market's perpetual state of decline. A basic explanation is its truly global approach in developing the best products using the best technology.

Sources: Iwatani, N., Orr, G., and Salsberg, B. (2011). 'Japan's Global Imperative', http://www.mckinsey.com/insights/strategy/japans_globalization_imperative [Accessed: September 12, 2014]; http://www.autonews.com/article/20120920/BLOG06/120929989/japan-a-closed-market?-don%92t-tell-vw [Accessed: September 12, 2014]; http://europe.autonews.com/article/20131114/ANE/311149983/toyota-lowers-car-sales-goal-in-germany-due-to-hybrid-shortages [Accessed: September 12, 2014].

Definitions and history aside, globalization is a rather fragmented and contradictory phenomenon. In order to understand it better, let's first look at today's manifestations.

Globalization does not occur as a single phenomenon but affects many facets of our life. One of the most obvious signs is visible whenever we travel as a tourist and look at large-scale "ambient media" that cover whole buildings.

Cultural Globalization

Look, for instance at the Red Square in Moscow, where one finds Rolex and McDonald's advertisements covering the old and famous architecture. Or else, the quest of language purists who, especially in France, wanted to keep their language free from any Anglo-Saxon influence, have now relinquished their claims and accept words like laptop, hard disk, revenues, hobbies and flat screen intruding into the French world of Rousseau and Montesquieu. These manifestations of cultural globalization show that it is clearly more than just commerce. Changes in the economy are linked with other aspects of society, like social and economic structures, preferences and beliefs, patterns of consumption, and the repertory of cultural expressions. However, there have also been ethnocentric concerns that culture is becoming too global, in the sense of becoming too homogenized. These concerns typically go along with the fear that cultural globalization implies Americanization and the uniformity of mass culture leads to a demise of national cultural heritage. These concerns may not be completely wrong. If we look at the "intrusion" of American thought, we may take the examples of Hollywood films, which account for roughly 95 percent of screen time in Canada while France, through extensive subsidies, manages to keep the market share down to around 70 percent.[20] The fear of being overwhelmed by the output of Hollywood is greatest in Europe while, at the same time, the demand for these films is rising. If we look at globalization as a Westernization process, we face a dilemma as many countries aspire to be globalized yet not Westernized, most notably the People's Republic of China. The Chinese government is attempting to reap the benefits of open markets without the unwanted side effects of Westernization. China's current and effective Internet filtering regime characterizes its concerted attempt to ensure globalization that does not lead to Westernization and subsequent democratization—a reflection of the political grip on power of the Chinese Communist Party.

However, the issue is not simply the protection of a country's culture, although this is perhaps the best emotional argument. Cultural protectionism actually becomes difficult if we look at new content production that is becoming more easily shared through the Internet than it has been for years. Another example of cultural globalization is the fact that McDonald's restaurants are meanwhile present in most countries of the world, which gives rise to nutritional concerns and labor conditions, and children who may have never seen a hoop can identify Michael Jordan or the logo of the NBA. Cultural manifestations of globalization are manifold, and whether they incur a loss of local values or enrich people's minds towards multifaceted global perspectives and the interchange of knowledge and ideas remains a question of balance.

Financial Globalization

If we look at aspects of financial globalization, some of the largest changes manifest themselves in 24-hour availability of information and trading potential. For instance, CMC Markets PLC, established in 1989, is a global leader in online financial trading. They make available over 3,000 instruments across 18 global markets as well as easy access to equities, indices, forex, commodities and treasuries, 24 hours a day from one single account. Increased transparency does not only benefit the professional trader but has also helped to establish international financial centers where loans can be negotiated at better costs than restricting oneself to local banks. Thus, more efficient global allocation of resources, sustained trade balance, and the prevention of national shocks may just be some of the presumed benefits. On the other hand, critics have remarked that the interconnectedness of world financial markets may also increase the exposure to real shocks and to risks that sudden capital reversals may translate into large-scale economic disruptions. This can be most clearly evidenced by looking at the changes of major stock indices and their interdependent moves both upwards and downwards.

Technological Globalization

Also, the technological manifestations of globalization are by no means negligible in their controversial impact. For instance, the events of September 11, 2001 could not have taken place before the current global era. Communication and transportation systems have facilitated access to information, but are also at the disposal of terrorists, money launderers, and internationally operating criminals. In contrast, the collapse of the Iron Curtain would probably not have been possible without an extended and well-functioning system of modern communication technologies. Today, we are used to consuming international news, wherever we are and whatever

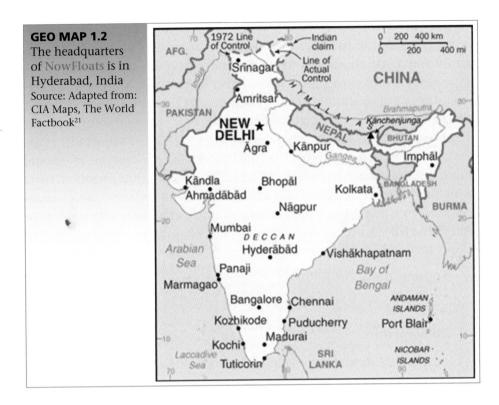

GEO MAP 1.2
The headquarters of NowFloats is in Hyderabad, India
Source: Adapted from: CIA Maps, The World Factbook[21]

we do. Progress in technology and communication has also benefited poorer countries. For example, India is playing an increasing role in information technology innovation and major US multinationals rely on their Indian employees to design software platforms and next generation features.[22] Currently, Microsoft Ventures is in talks with a Hyderabad-based startup, NowFloats, which if successful will mark the first investment in India by the early stage investment arm of the global software maker.[23]

The flip side of the coin, however, becomes evident when large multinationals recruit world-class talent at a fraction of what they would have had to pay in their own country and that the dislocation of human resource activities is not without problems for the value-generation of firms.

Educational and Sociological Globalization

Educational and sociological manifestations of globalization go hand in hand. There clearly is a large issue of labor mobility, induced by the downfall of boundaries, especially but not exclusively within Europe. Take, for example, the increasing mobility of researchers and students across different countries with the dominant attracting nations being the UK, France, and Germany. Student flows in and out of countries are typically uneven by nation and vary in character. Choice of destination seems to be largely affected by the language of use, and by global rankings which are believed to impact future careers. Thus, business schools around the world are fiercely competing not only for qualified personnel but also for the brightest students. As for the movement of researchers, the major flows have been towards the US with possible earnings and career perspectives being the primary considerations. Recently, Asian labs in Singapore and also in China have proliferated and joined the global fight for talent. Also, South Korea has intensified its international recruitment efforts in offering university positions to be exclusively filled with foreigners. Indeed, companies and nations will have to look for their future leaders on a global scale or, in the words of Jack Welch, "Globalization has changed us into a company that searches the world, not just to sell or to source, but to find intellectual capital – the world's best talents and greatest ideas."[24] But there is also a downturn associated with increasing family dislocation that results from permanent commuting, lack of identity and social boundaries due to multiple homes and "global" citizens.

Economic Globalization

Economic aspects of globalization are clearly the most often and most controversially discussed ones and the major issue has always been the reduction of poverty. The surest route to sustained poverty reduction is clearly economic growth. For instance, the Heritage Foundation/Wall Street Journal Index of Economic Freedom clearly shows that the economies of countries that open their markets grow at a faster pace than the economies of countries that open their markets less or not at all. Of the 142 nations whose economies have been observed during the seven-year period between 1997 and 2004, those that opened their markets the most grew twice as fast as those that opened them the least. A growing economy, so the argument runs, increases the demand for goods and services, and as demand increases, more businesses start and expand their operations. Such expansion leads to the creation of more, better-paid jobs. The same is true when the market expands beyond borders. Gaining free access to other markets opens up new business opportunities, encouraging investment and fostering job creation.

Positive and Negative Aspects of Globalization

Building on the previous arguments, there is a large heterogeneity of views as to the positive and detrimental effects of globalization and no consensus has yet been reached. Clearly, wealth has increased for the rich nations, but poverty reduction has also succeeded while critics say globalization has failed to relieve the debts of poorer countries increasing their dependence on international organizations. A provocative reformulation of these issues was offered by Peter Singer, a renowned professor of bioethics at Princeton University and co-author of the path-breaking book *One World—The Ethics of Globalization*. He asked the following simple questions to increase reflections on moral issues:

Suppose you want to look at the gap between the poorest third and the richest third. The answer seems to be that that gap has narrowed and that the poorest third have become significantly better off ...And so you see that values come into whether you think this is a good or a bad thing now. If someone tells you that the gap between the poorest third and the richest third has narrowed and the poorest third are better off than they used to be, but the gap between the poorest tenth and the richest tenth has widened and the poorest tenth are no better off than they used to be, is that something that you welcome or deplore? That is where you have to look at your own values about what is important about issues in justice.[25]

Activists responded to the increasing inequality by mounting large street protests at major meetings of the key international organizations—the WTO in Geneva (1998) and Seattle (1999), the IMF and World Bank in Prague and Washington, DC (2000), the G8 in Genoa (2001) or Heiligendamm (2007). Anti-globalization movements have sprung up worldwide. At global summit conferences in Genoa and Seattle major riots occurred which resulted in major damages. Companies are criticized for having greater power than nation states—they can switch headquarters to evade taxes, abide only to stock market rules rather than to stakeholders and are purely profit-driven.

A more recent development is Occupy Wall Street (OWS) a name given to a protest movement that began on September 17, 2011, in Zuccotti Park, located in New York City's Wall Street financial district, protesting against social and economic inequality worldwide.[26]

Globalization and Global Marketing

While globalization poses many challenges to global marketing, we must be aware that one of the major difficulties results from the non-linear, complex, and often ambiguous developments in the environment that yield unpredictable results. In chaos theory, this is called the "butterfly effect" when the sensitive dependency on initial conditions in which a small change in one place can result in large differences in a later stage.[27] Instead of simply extrapolating trends from the past, i.e. assuming that the population of selected countries will grow in the same way it did in the past and that this would lead to a realistic forecast of potential consumers, companies are required to learn, to change their knowledge base, and to innovate on a permanent basis. That is, when markets may be subject to changes that we cannot anticipate today, and where clear-cut guidelines may have worked in the past, firms today experience tensions between alternative roadmaps. They need to engage in the management of contradictory trends or paradoxes.

GLOBAL MARKETING—TENDENCIES OF THE PAST AND SCENARIOS FOR THE FUTURE

Challenges firms have to face are swirled around seemingly contradictory but interwoven forces. For instance, firms may cope with innovation tensions, i.e.

whether to focus on incremental or radical innovation; they face challenges as to whether they should enter proximate markets, or those that are far apart, but may yield richer potential; they need to modify existing internal resources to remain competitive while, at the same time, explore new business models and tap into unknown sources of knowledge. Finally, both managers and firms need to continuously update their knowledge while being open to relearn and challenge previously acquired recipes and managerial tools. This requires that they engage in processes of single- and double-loop learning[28] with the former reconfirming existing mindsets and the latter questioning them. Challenges also elaborate calls in practitioner literature for paradoxical "both/and" instead of "either/or" approaches to management.[29]

For a global firm, this implies general objectives for global reach and skills that transcend any particular country. Indeed, a firm may enter a country because of its vision and its advanced skill set can make more of that country's productive resources than local firms. For instance, kiloWattsol is one of the leading European independent technical advisors in the field of renewable energies, with worldwide expertise. Over the last 12 months (2013), the French start-up kiloWattsol has contributed to the construction of solar power plants situated on four continents. It applies its standardized technological expertise to make use of the specific infrastructure conditions of many emerging and developed markets. On the other hand, global firms are challenged by their comparative disadvantage in navigating many features of local markets. Success means adapting knowledge to particularities of individual countries, often to the extent that each country is treated as a singular market with differences in prices, products, preferences, and tastes.

A global approach requires the firm to focus its efforts worldwide, rather than developing marketing strategies on a country-by-country basis. The American Marketing Association defines global marketing as follows:

> 1. (global marketing definition) A marketing strategy that consciously addresses global customers, markets, and competition in formulating a business strategy. 2. (consumer behavior definition) An approach to international strategy that argues for marketing a product in essentially the same way everywhere in the world.[30]

Global marketing also requires the coordination and integration of production, marketing, and other functional activities across countries. For many firms, a global marketing strategy requires a centralized operation to leverage scale advantages and optimize resources and reduce costs. Specifically, the objective of global marketing is to attain worldwide coordination, rationalization, and integration of all marketing activities including target market selection, marketing-mix decisions, and organizational design and control mechanisms.[31] The worldwide integration of marketing activities includes the development of global products and brands and global communication and distribution strategies. However, even a global marketing strategy will need to account for some local adaptations and the existence of paradoxes.

The marketing literature has described these paradoxes as "the simultaneous existence of two inconsistent states, such as between innovation and efficiency, collaboration and competition, or new and old."[32] More generally, a paradox involves two opposing thoughts or propositions which, however contradictory, are equally necessary to convey a more imposing, illuminating, life-related or provocative insight into truth than either fact can muster in its own right. For instance, there is a need for both local adaptation and global synergy, slow and accelerated international market entry, geographical expansion and market penetration or local capability development and foreign exploration.[33] What makes it challenging for managers is the fact that they do not only need to identify the paradoxes posed by conflicting trends but also find solutions to solve them.

From Naisbitt to Juggling Janus[34]

When one of the major gurus of future research, John Naisbitt, formulated his "megatrends" some 25 years ago, he presented the most far-reaching developments, which painted a picture of our future at the turn of the millennium. He defined a megatrend as a general shift in thinking or approach affecting countries, industries, and organization. They impact different actors, such as governments, individuals and their consumption patterns, as well as companies and their strategies. A bestseller author, Naisbitt was seen as a trailblazer for social and economic trend research. Published in 1990, the #1 New York Times bestseller *Megatrends 2000*[35] described what was beginning to shape the twenty-first century, including the rise of the Pacific Rim, the dawn of the age of biology, the triumph of the individual, the emergence of the free market socialism, a religion revival, and cultural nationalism. In hindsight, some of his trend scenarios have lost nothing of their relevance.

- **Economic growth of Pacific Rim countries:** The Pacific Rim countries include those along the Pacific Ocean and they are continually gaining strength in the world economy. Four Pacific Rim countries have been coined "economic tigers" because of their economic progress: Hong Kong, Singapore, Taiwan, and South Korea. The rise of China is without question, though experts have started to discuss the declining speed of its future growth.

- **Capitalism in socialist countries:** Today, the opening of communist countries is a reality that started with Perestroika in the late 1980s in Russia where communism collapsed. Though the Russian development was not foreseen, a wide number of countries has adopted capitalist ideas and has introduced a market economy.

- **Women becoming leaders:** This prediction has gained a lot in importance with female CEOs, researchers, Margaret Thatcher as prime minister in the UK, and Angela Merkel as Chancellor of Germany. The introduction of quota systems and quests for equal payment both illustrate that governments have tried to promote women leadership.

- **Growth of biotechnology:** Consumers and companies alike are searching for eco-friendly sources of energy and more effort is being made to identify ways to harness them in an eco-friendly manner. Wind energy has come to the fore as the feasibility of newer sources of energy are being explored.

- **Similarities in individual lifestyles:** As the middle classes have become more, people have been able to fulfill their aspirations and become voracious consumers of luxury items. This has led many people to adopt Western life-styles and products.

What all these trends have in common is their almost linear development, which facilitated forecasts in the past. This is not to say that Naisbitt had an easy job back in the past, but he was not torn between the conflicting and paradoxical developments that people are facing today. The trends today are double-faced with positive and negative implications; they are paradoxical in the sense of Janus, the double-faced Roman god, with one face looking back into the past, the other one into the future.

Some of these trends refer to the paradox of prosperity versus poverty, the increasing power of multinational firms versus fragility of multinationals, and media reach versus fragmentation of media.[36] These paradoxes have important ramifications for managers and require them to be aware that decision-making is no longer a question of "right" or "wrong" but one of balance.

Rich Versus Poor

Take, for instance, the conflict between rich and poor. The global population of High Net Wealth Individuals (HNWIs), i.e. those individuals with US$1 million or more in investable assets, both increased substantially to reach record levels in 2012. After remaining flat in 2011, the population of HNWIs grew by 9.2 percent worldwide, increasing by one million individuals to reach 12.0 million.[37] As in between 2007 and 2011, North America continued to hold the greatest share of HNWI investable wealth, with US$12.7 trillion in 2012, compared to US$12.0 trillion for Asia-Pacific, US$10.9 trillion for Europe, and US$7.5 trillion for Latin America. Wealth growth was the strongest in Asia-Pacific at 12.2 percent, led by strong growth in many of the region's countries, followed by North America at 11.7 percent. Globally, from 2007 to 2012, HNWI investable wealth expanded at a modest compound annual growth rate (CAGR) of 2.6 percent, slightly above the real GDP CAGR of 1.6 percent over the same period. As a consequence, global marketing faces homogeneous consumer segments that are susceptible to high quality luxury products with prices being of lower interest.

On the other hand, the United Nations (UN) defines poverty as living on less than $2 a day and nearly half the world's population lives below or just barely above this poverty line.[38] With such limited incomes, people struggle to survive in the fight for food, water, and medicine. Especially rural areas account for three in

FIGURE 1.4
Discrepancy
Between Rich and
Poor
Source: www.pixabay.
com (Free Pictures)

every four people living on less than US$1 a day and a similar share of the world population suffering from malnutrition. In developing countries some 2.5 billion people are forced to rely on biomass—fuelwood, charcoal and animal dung—to meet their energy needs for cooking. In sub-Saharan Africa, over 80 percent of the population depends on traditional biomass for cooking, as do over half of the populations of India and China.[39] How then should a can of Coca-Cola for 1US$ or a T-shirt for 20US$ be marketed? It almost sounds sarcastic to even think about global marketing in these countries. But it is precisely here that other challenges arise that ask companies to engage in social marketing and/or change their marketing approach to cope with the requirements of these markets (see below for the 4As in emerging markets).

The gap between the two segments—the ultra-rich and the extremely poor (Figure 1.4)—is continuously widening, despite the emergence of an affluent middle class in countries like China, India, or Africa. However, it should be noted that probably very rich and very poor segments exist in most countries. For firms that want to be present on a global scale, this requires intense efforts to adjust their marketing strategies.

Power Versus Fragility

Take another paradox. We see many multinational companies (MNCs) gaining in power. In comparing their revenues against the GDP of countries, in 2012, 42 corporations would rank among the top-100 country list.[40] (Table 1.1 for a comparison between company revenues and country GDP). In addition, MNCs exert influence on governments to deal with subsidiaries or set standards that influence technological development or the institutional context, such as the legal or tax system. On the other hand, MNCs are becoming more fragile because many small competitors—both from emerging and developed markets—have entered the scene and occupy a global niche market. The so-called "hidden champions" are threatening the power of traditional multinational firms. Thus, global marketers need to consider the global competitiveness of other firms competing for scarce resources and customer attention.

Company Name	Country Code	Last Avail. Year	Turnover Thousand US$, Last Avail. Year	Number of Employees Last Avail. Year	
1 Wal-Mart Stores, Inc.	US	2013	476,294,000	2,200,000	**TABLE 1.1**
2 Royal Dutch Shell PLC	GB	2013	451,317,000	92,000	Transnational
3 China Petroleum & Chemical Corporation	CN	2013	440,751,001	368,953	Corporations and Countries: Top 8
4 Exxon Mobil Corp	US	2013	420,836,000	75,000	World Companies
Austria GDP			_394,458,000_		
5 BP PLC	GB	2013	379,631,000	83,900	
6 Saudi Arabian Oil Company (Aramco)	SA	2013	320,000,017	56,066	
Denmark GDP			_314,889,000_		
7 Vitol Holding B.V.	NL	2012	302,748,187	2,111	
8 Volkswagen AG	DE	2013	280,191,740	572,800	
Croatia			_56,447,000_		
Luxembourg			_55,143,000_		
Syria			_46,540,000_		
Slovenia			_45,380,000_		
Tunisia			_45,132,000_		
Costa Rica			_45,107,000_		

Source: Adapted from: ORBIS—Bureau VanDijk Database, https://orbis.bvdinfo.com/version-2015102/home.serv?product=orbisneo

Media Overload Versus Fragmentation of Media and Audiences

Also the role of and the access to media in our modern world poses a paradoxical trend for many companies. For instance, the top ten providers that offer social network communities in the world each have a minimum of 225 million (up to one billion users) (Table 1.2). The world turns into a "global village"[41] as communication costs decline owing to improvements in information technology. For example,

Rank	Name	Registered Users	Date of Statistic	Date Launched	Country of Origin	
1	Facebook	1+ billion	September 2013	February 2004	United States	**TABLE 1.2**
2	Tencent QQ	784+ million	September 2012	February 1999	China	Major Online
3	WhatsApp	400+ million	19 December 2013	June 2009	United States	Communities Worldwide
4	Google+	1+ billion	October 2013	June 2011	United States	
5	Twitter	500+ million	December 2012	March 2006	United States	
6	LinkedIn	259+ million	June 2013	May 2003	United States	
7	Tencent Qzone	597+ million	September 2012	2005	China	
8	Odnoklassniki	205+ million	April 2013	March 2006	Russia	
9	Skype	663+ million	January 2013	August 2003	Estonia	
10	Sina Weibo	500+ million	February 2013	August 2009	China	

Source: Data from Various Sources[42]

a three-minute phone call from New York to London cost $245 in 1930; the same call cost only $3 in 1990. Today, these costs are virtually negligible given flat rates and modern media like Skype.

Making a bank transaction by telephone costs about $0.55; making the same transaction in an ATM machine reduces the cost to $0.45, and by the Internet to less than $0.10. On the other hand, several countries are still excluded from the Internet. While some of them are catching up (see again Figure 1.2), others are still lagging behind. In addition, different age groups prefer different media. For arguments sake, just compare the use of MP3 players in your own generation to that of your grandparents. This gap between media access and media illiteracy, or idiosyncratic media channels, poses a huge challenge for global marketing.

What Is the Solution for Global Marketers?

How should marketers develop their strategies in a world of paradoxes and disruptions? There is benefit in addressing many global marketing phenomena in a non-exclusionary, "both-and" approach. Many phenomena are seemingly contradictory yet interrelated at the same time. Understanding paradox as a frame that encompasses opposites enables a more complicated comprehension of their coexistence and interconnections.[43] The philosopher Rosi Braidotti[44] speaks of the need to develop a map or cartography to cope with the "fluidity" of postmodern life. She envisages multiple maps, not one linear scheme or plan, and emphasizes the importance of context and movement. Paradox provides such a frame to interpret current trends in our environment.

DEVELOPING GLOBAL MARKETING STRATEGIES

In order for firms to successfully compete globally, they must achieve significant competitive advantage over their rivals. To do so, a firm must develop a global marketing strategy. This strategy is linked to the type of global mindset the firm adopts—the EPRG framework. It is based on management's worldview of the firm, which determines the way in which its foreign market activities are organized. According to the framework, there are four approaches or orientations by which a firm is managed in foreign markets. These approaches or orientations also reflect different stages in the internationalization of the firm, from solely a domestic player to a world competitor. Building on the mindset, a company needs to determine the degree of standardization or localization of its marketing strategy. The operational strategy of global marketing also deserves attention, as there will be changes from the traditional 4Ps to the 4As when applied to emerging markets. This is because some of the traditional marketing mix instruments (the 4Ps: Product, place, price, promotion) do not fully comply with the characteristics of emerging markets, where marketers need to reconsider their pricing to make sure that their products are *affordable*. They also need to attract people's attention to the product, which often implies using personal information campaigns focused on oral and direct communication (*awareness*); they have to select or create distribution channels that fit the infrastructure of the country (*availability*); and finally, they need to make sure that people accept products in a world where they use and reuse products over generations (*acceptability*). In most cases, the 4As will not substitute for but rather complement the 4Ps.

The EPRG Framework

The EPRG framework was developed by Perlmutter in 1969.[45] It is based on management's worldview of the firm, which determines the way in which its foreign market activities are organized. These approaches or orientations also reflect different stages in the internationalization of the firm, from solely a domestic player to a world competitor.

Ethnocentric Orientation

In this stage, the focus is on the home market. Firms holding this view believe that domestic strategies are superior to foreign ones, and therefore are applied in overseas operations as well. Overseas operations are considered secondary to domestic operations. No systematic marketing screening is made to search for foreign markets. Instead, products, tools, and procedures are applied in the same way abroad as at home. An example of this approach was the initial expansion of the American pharmaceutical company Eli Lilly into overseas markets. It established offices in key markets, hired local nationals to staff them, and maintained tight control by measuring each country on bottom-line profitability. Operations of foreign subsidiaries were limited to downstream activities required to support local sales, while marketing programs were developed at headquarters.[46]

An ethnocentric orientation often occurs in an early stage of a company's internationalization path or in conjunction with a strong country-of-origin effect,[47] which describes how consumers' attitudes, perceptions, and purchasing decisions are influenced by products' country of origin labeling, e.g. Vodka from Russia, Chocolate from Belgium, Watches from Switzerland. If the country excels in a certain product category, it seems like its benefits can be marketed in the same way internationally. While an ethnocentric version of marketing worked well for several companies back in the 1960s, today ethnocentrism is no longer a viable paradigm as differences in markets—however small—prevent companies' adopting a totally standardized marketing approach.

Polycentric Orientation

Unlike ethnocentric firms, those following this approach use decentralized management, allowing affiliates to develop their own marketing strategy. However, the mindset of management is focused on the host country in the belief that because country markets are dissimilar, marketing strategies must be adapted to the specific needs of each. There is little room in this orientation for standardized marketing. Overseas markets are screened individually. Each market operation functions independently without any meaningful coordination or integration between them. Marketing activities are organized and carried out country by country, modifying the marketing mix as necessary to meet the requirements of each market. This orientation is a "dream for the customer" because it is tailored to individual needs, but a "nightmare for companies" due to the duplication of functions and procedures. In terms of innovation, a polycentric approach takes into account that innovations should be developed in cooperation with national customers rather than in corporate headquarters which are far detached from national preferences and usability criteria. However, the decentralized organization has a major disadvantage, in that knowledge sharing between subsidiaries is typically slow. An example of this orientation was Ford's marketing of the Escort. The UK version was differentiated from the American model, not only because the steering apparatus had to be shifted from the right to the left side, but also because the engine displacement was greater in the United States, and styling was also different.

Regiocentric Orientation

A regiocentric orientation tries to overcome the disadvantages of a polycentric view by bundling countries into regions; a particular region is viewed as comprising a single market. Thus, regional trade areas such as the European Union and Mercosur may be the focus of marketing activities. The definition of a region is not easy as it draws from a mix of criteria, such as geographic distance, culture, language, historical similarity, etc. An attempt is made to develop and implement marketing strategy for all countries comprising an entire region. However, unlike the polycentric approach, emphasis is on coordination of marketing in the region and standardization whenever possible.

Most multinational companies today adopt a broad regional orientation. An example of a company organized along regiocentric lines is Toyota. About 45 percent of its sales revenues are generated in Japan, with another 39 percent originating in North America. Toyota's success in North America stems from its customer-driven new product development, aimed at this regional market. Also, Taiwanese Acer focuses the efforts of its main subsidiaries on the US and the Asian region (China and Singapore) with R&D-centers concentrated in China and Japan.

Geocentric Orientation

Firms adopting this approach view the world as a potential market. In these markets, an attempt is made to implement global marketing by integrating worldwide operations. Global products and brands are produced in large volumes in order to achieve scale economies. A standardized product, brand, image, and positioning (as well as standardized advertising whenever possible) with minimal adaptations are

Orientation	Mindset and Challenge	Strategy
Ethnocentric	What is produced at home is best and can be marketed exactly in the same way The world is not the same as home	Simply export whatever you a producing and doing at home
Polycentric	Every market follows its own rules and exhibits a different culture There is no synergy between markets	Follow a decentralized market approach and design marketing strategy for each market individ
Regiocentric	Several markets can be bundled into regions because they exhibit similar criteria (cultures, customer preferences, languages, etc.) Difficulty to define a region	Benefit from similarities between countries and use the same marketing strategy for several of them
Geocentric	Build on existing homogeneity of markets and offer global products Even standardization requires a certain extent of localization	Identify common denominator between markets and standardize as much as possible

Source: Adapted from: Perlmutter (1969)

offered in all markets. In both regiocentric and geocentric orientations, the ability to acquire and share knowledge (such as best practices) among the various components of the global, corporate network is maximized in order to attain and sustain competitive advantage. For example, the Tide brand of laundry detergent marketed in the United States by Procter & Gamble was first developed by its German subsidiary and then introduced in Germany (under the brand name Vizer) and later produced and marketed in several other European countries. The European and later Latin American introduction of Vizer/Tide was made possible by the experience and knowledge gained by German management that was shared with other subsidiaries of P&G.

Table 1.3 summarizes the different mindsets and approaches to strategy of a multinational firm under each of the above conditions.

What becomes obvious from the discussion of the four marketing orientations is that they are not clearly distinct but overlapping. There is no geocentric approach that follows a 100 percent standardization. Even a company like Coca-Cola that is presumed to be a 100 percent global company, needs to localize parts of its marketing strategy and/or business functions.

The Standardization Versus Localization–Adaptation School

If we could put together a seminar attended by marketing managers of multinational corporations, one of the main topics for discussion would be whether a standardized marketing approach to markets is preferable to a localized (differentiated) approach. A truly globalized marketing strategy would aim to standardize elements of the marketing mix in all markets served by the company. In 1983, Theodore Levitt's article in the *Harvard Business Review*, "The Globalization of Markets,"[48] paved the way for adopting standardized, high-quality world products and marketing them around the globe by using standardized advertising, pricing, and distribution. Levitt believed that accustomed differences in national or regional preferences were a thing of the past. If marketers could provide high-quality products at reasonable, low prices, they would appeal to consumers in different countries. The ability of manufacturers to do so, however, depends on three factors: (1) substantial economies of scale, (2) consumer sensitivity to price and quality above all other considerations, and (3) homogenization of consumer desires and tastes across national boundaries. Levitt's assumptions have been questioned, especially the second and third above. There are significant differences between national markets that require adaptation and customization in, if not all of marketing programs, then at least in some parts, such as product and promotional strategies. Whether consumers everywhere will prefer less expensive, standardized products over differentiated ones (remember Ford's Model T—"You can choose any color as long as it's black"?) has been largely discounted. Levitt himself toned down his vision and realized that companies had to balance persistent national cultural patterns with the general trend toward the embrace of global brands. Thus, he acknowledged tactics like McDonald's supplementing its standard menus with local fare like vegan meals in India, and Coca-Cola varying the sugar content of its soft drinks.

In reality, it is rare to find a completely standardized marketing mix. Some companies may be able to standardize products but have to localize advertising campaigns. Others may have to localize product strategy but are able to standardize advertising. The Dell Computer Company, for example, standardizes its direct sales strategy in all its markets but localizes advertising strategy.

Also, service providers typically localize their offers to a very high degree (e.g. educational service providers that need to tailor their services to local languages or customs, or lawyers that need to rely on local laws), but attempt to standardize their advertising campaigns as much as possible. Figure 1.5 depicts a framework that is called the Global-Integration vs. Local-Responsiveness Grid. Its four cells are organized around the needs for standardization or localization. While factors that drive adaptation are rooted in local consumer tastes, factors for global standardization are, for instance, short product life cycles, or high R&D investments. The Grid also illustrates that the degree of localization needed depends on the business function performed. Most marketing functions need some sort of adaptation across markets, whereas such functions, such as finance, need very little adjustment. Brand identity is a function that most companies want to standardize, in order to maintain a uniform image worldwide.

When is a standardized strategy preferable? There are several reasons why manufacturers and service providers prefer standardized marketing strategies on a global basis. These include gaining economies of scale in production and marketing, lowering costs—especially high R&D and development costs—and easing pressures

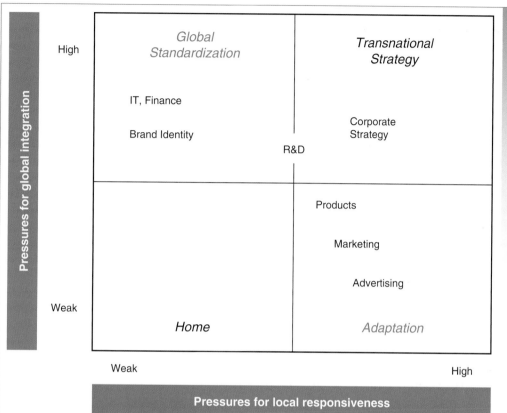

FIGURE 1.5
The Need for Localizing Value by Business Function (Global Integration Versus Local Responsiveness Grid)
Source: Adapted from: Prahalad, C.K. and Doz, Y.L. (1987). *The Multinational Mission, Balancing Global Integration with Local Responsiveness.* New York: Free Press; London: Collier Macmillan

exerted by global customers for the supply of uniform products. In industries that have high development and setup costs and rapid technological obsolescence, it is to their advantage to develop standardized products that can be rapidly introduced in a large number of markets in order to recoup investment. Likewise, in industries where learning curve advantages are important, standardization can lower costs. Global customers can also pressure their suppliers to offer uniform products to their various manufacturing facilities that are located in a number of countries. For example, global suppliers of paint products to global car manufacturers must provide a standardized product from their different plant locations to ensure that all cars will have the same exterior finish.

However, there are several factors working against the ability of firms to standardize marketing strategies: different tastes and customer preferences and performance requirements and standards across countries inhibit the ability to standardize. When Nestlé introduced its coffee products into China, it created a blend adapted to the particular tastes of Chinese consumers. Nestlé's wafer bar brand Kit Kat generates roughly $1 billion in sales worldwide. This product is adapted in many markets. For example, in Russia, its size is smaller than in Western countries and the chocolate is coarser, while in Japan the flavor is strawberry. Kenichi Ohmae[49] writes that "When it comes to product strategy, managing in a borderless economy doesn't mean managing by averages. It doesn't mean that all tastes run together into one amorphous mass of universal appeal. And it doesn't mean that the appeal of operating globally removes the obligation to mobilize products. The lure of a universal product is a false allure." However, in a revised edition,[50] Ohmae observes that "young people of the advanced countries are becoming increasingly nationality-less and more like 'Californians' all over the Triad countries—the United States, Europe, and Japan … ." The inference here is that this particular market segment of young people in developed countries may be targets for standardized products. We can think of some: Levi's jeans, iPods, and Timberland shoes. These are some examples of products that are standardized across borders.

Even when products are standardized, it may not be possible to standardize other elements of the marketing mix. A case in point was a Nescafé commercial aired in Chile. The commercial showed a house by a lake. Inside, the father tries to wake his son to go fishing, but the son prefers to stay in bed. Soon, the son wakes up and prepares a cup of coffee. Reinvigorated, he brings a cup of coffee to his father who is sitting by the lake, disappointed by his son's decision not to join him. However, father and son are reunited over a cup of coffee. The message is that coffee helped the relationship of both. However, the same commercial aired, for example, in Paris, might simply be viewed as an environmental statement. While coffee tastes may conceivably be the same in both countries, perception of the same advertising appeal might be quite different.

Another example of different perceptions of the same advertising message occurred when a television commercial produced for North American audiences was aired in several Latin American countries. The idea behind the message was to encourage the sale of additional telephone sets in two-story homes. A phone call for the husband was received by his wife who was working in the kitchen. The husband was on the second floor, without a telephone installation. The housewife shouted to her husband to come down right away and answer the phone. The ad was perceived negatively because the wife gave an order to her husband in a very masculine country, and she seemed to be impatient in a society where orientation to time and urgency were much different than in North America. One of the firms that successfully adopts a global advertising campaign is McDonald's ("I'm loving it"), but even this company is facing localization needs, as for instance the requirement to use Cyrillic letters in Russia (Figure 1.6).

Another more recent strategy is the **transnational strategy**,[51] where companies integrate aspects of learning, innovation, and knowledge development. Companies use a strategy of foreign countries that exploits location economies, leverages core competencies, and responds to key local conditions. In particular:

- The causes of interactive global learning and worldwide information sharing are championed.

- Value is created by the relentless renewal, enhancement, and exchange of ideas, products, and processes across functions and borders.

FIGURE 1.6
McDonald's in Malaysia and Russia
Source: © Author

- The transnational multinational enterprise (MNE) differentiates capabilities and contributions while finding ways to systematically learn and ultimately integrate and diffuse knowledge, thus developing more powerful core competencies.

This strategy is very often applied by companies in turbulent markets with high product innovations, e.g. BASF or Vestas Wind Energy.

Global Marketing in Emerging Market Countries—from 4Ps to 4As

As shown previously, world power and wealth is being redistributed. This involves the rise of emerging market multinationals. Emerging economies comprise more than half of the world's population, account for a large share of world output, and have very high growth rates; all indicators of enormous market potential.[52]

Importance of Emerging Markets

Many companies have increased their international activities in the last decades. Many new players have emerged on the scene while others have disappeared. The world's pecking order is changing with emerging market firms taking over the top positions in the world's most global firms. A comparison of the Forbes list of Global 2000 companies in 2004 and 2013 illustrates these changes (Table 1.4).

While it is not surprising to see mostly US-American companies in 2004, the list in 2013 tells a different story with companies from countries barely represented in the earlier list. Among them, China features most prominently with companies from the construction and utilities sectors. In the full list of 2013, we also have many firms from India, Russia, and South America. Many among them are global leaders in their sector, such as the Russian energy giant Gazprom (no. 21), the Brazilian energy company Petrobras (no. 25), the Industrial and Commercial

TABLE 1.4 Top-10 Firms in the Global Forbes List 2004 and 2013	Rank	2004	Country	Revenues US$ bn	2013	Revenues US$ bn	Country (GDP/US$ bn)
	1	Wal-Mart Stores Inc.	US	287.9	Wal-Mart Stores Inc.	476.2	US (16,768)
	2	BP	UK	285.0	Royal Dutch Shell	459.5	UK/NL (2,678/853)
	3	Exxon Mobile	US	270.7	Sinopec	457.2	China (9,181)
	4	Royal Dutch Shell	NL	268.6	China National Petroleum	432.0	China (9,181)
	5	General Motors	US	193.5	Exxon Mobile	407.6	US (16,768)
	6	Daimler Chrysler	Germany	176.6	BP	396.2	UK (2,678)
	7	Toyota	Japan	172.6	State Grid	333.386	China (9,181)
	8	Ford Motors	US	172.2	Volkswagen	261.5	Germany (3,730)
	9	General Electric	US	152.8	Toyota	256.4	Japan (4,898)
	10	Total	France	152.6	Glencore	232.6	Switzerland (685)

Source: Based on Data from: 'The Fortune Global 500,' http://money.cnn.com/magazines/fortune/global500/ [Accessed: October 20, 2014]

Bank of China (no. 29), high-technology firm Hon Hai Precision Industry from Taiwan (no. 30), or the Mexican Pemex Company, focused on mineral oil (no. 36).

Or take another example: While the Western world has been pushing forward research and development in many high-technology areas, Chinese firms have entered the global index with 96 companies in 2013 as compared to 16 firms in 2004. Emerging market multinationals, also from other countries, have become serious competitors and are likely to challenge Western firms. But what makes emerging markets and emerging market multinationals so special?[53]

- They are often strongly built around their founding characters and stories (for example, Stan Shih, the founder of Acer always figures strongly in the public press and in internal communications). That is, the original spirit serves as a strong motivator much more than in Western firms.

- They are less pressurized by financial market demands, including the publication of quarterly results and short-term gains. It is more a take it all mentality than stakeholder expectations to which Western firms succumb.

- Their strategies are built on quick learning and experience accumulation to catch up in terms of innovation and quality. That is, failure is seen as a necessary component of progress.

- They have a truly global approach. As they know about the difficulties of doing business in emerging markets, their expansion steps also include other emerging countries as well as developed markets. In contrast to Western firms, they are much better prepared to deal with institutional voids, weak financial markets, and other market insufficiencies. That is, they also find solutions where Western firms surrender to seemingly invincible barriers of bureaucracy.

Emerging markets have also become increasingly interesting as a target market for Western firms but they need to adapt their marketing strategies and their marketing mix.

4As in Emerging Market Marketing

Some of the traditional marketing mix instruments (the 4Ps: Product, place, price, promotion) do not fully comply with the characteristics of emerging markets. Therefore, they are often complemented or substituted by the 4As (Affordability, availability, acceptability, awareness).

Affordability

With the low income of many emerging market consumers, products need to be affordable, especially to the rural population, many of whom barely earn enough to make a living. Several companies have addressed the affordability problem by introducing small unit packs. For instance, Hindustan Lever was among the first companies to realize the potential of India's rural market, and has launched a low-price small package variant of its largest selling soap brand, Lifebuoy.

Availability

With a huge part of the poorer population living in rural areas, the question of physical availability becomes an issue. This is especially critical, if the geographic area spans over several millions of square meters, like for instance, in India or the Philippines. Access is often limited due to insufficient transportation or infrastructures. This is one of the reasons why IKEA initially failed in India because part of its business model is built on decentralized warehouses with consumers transporting items to their homes.

To increase availability, companies have adopted specific sales structures, direct selling, or syndicated distribution systems, to reach distant areas. For instance, Hindustan Unilever started Project "SHAKTHI" in partnership with self-help groups of rural women to whom they provide income generation opportunities to amplify the company's rural distribution network. Others, like Avon, use a specialized personal selling system in Brazil to be in close touch with the local population.

Acceptability

A further important issue for marketers is to have their products or services accepted. This is sometimes difficult given the extended product life cycles in emerging markets, where everything is fixed and reused across generations. In addition, several products are of no use because they require a technological infrastructure that is not given (e.g. electricity). This requires companies to adopt a creative approach and research the real needs of consumers. For instance, insurance companies in India offer low profile contracts for several years. Thereby, they increase brand awareness and benefit from consumers climbing up the financial ladder. A similar strategy is used by telecommunication providers in Africa, who sell mobile phones, but have wealthier siblings abroad paying for them. Acceptance rates are typically higher because these people have adopted a different life-style and can afford to buy the products.

Awareness

In countries where illiteracy is high, television is non-existent, and electricity is lacking, modern media is unlikely to survive. Creating awareness often means using word-of-mouth communication or advertising at the place of purchase. This is often done through local mom-and-pop shops where local sellers spread the news. Firms use product and brand ambassadors to inform or educate people, coming to their homes or preferred shopping sites.

Taken collectively, emerging market countries enter the global scene of competition at a path-breaking speed, and it is likely that Western firms will need to learn from them in the future. Rather than adopting a biased Western perspective to marketing, we here advocate a system of mutual learning and integration (Figure 1.7).

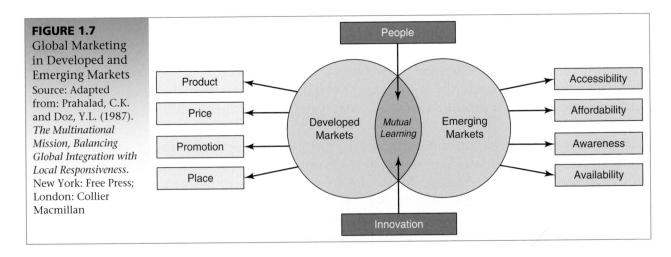

FIGURE 1.7
Global Marketing in Developed and Emerging Markets
Source: Adapted from: Prahalad, C.K. and Doz, Y.L. (1987). *The Multinational Mission, Balancing Global Integration with Local Responsiveness.* New York: Free Press; London: Collier Macmillan

A GLOBAL MARKETING MANAGEMENT FRAMEWORK

A number of researchers[54] argue that global marketing strategy influences a firm's global marketing performance. Global marketing strategy, in turn, is mediated by external market drivers and internal drivers, which are in effect internal characteristics of the firm. Studies in industrial economics have shown that a firm's external environment influences its strategy and hence its performance.[55] Those firms that are able to "read" and understand these drivers are more likely to perform well. It is imperative for firms operating globally to respond quickly and effectively to changes in the economy, competition, consumer requirements, and technology. The boycott of French wine in the United States briefly during 2003, owing to France's opposition to the invasion of American forces in Iraq, and the boycott against Danish products in Middle Eastern countries stemming from the Danish Mohammed cartoon crisis in 2005, demonstrate the importance of keeping an ear open to such changes. Likewise, a firm's success will depend upon the extent to which it develops internal capabilities and resources to implement its strategy. Needed are managers who both recognize the importance of internationalizing the firm and who succeed in implementing a global marketing strategy.

The elements of a global marketing strategy and its internal and external drivers are shown in Figure 1.8. Internal drivers are those that emanate from within the firm, and are thus controllable by management, such as a global vision and firm capabilities and the financing and international experience of executives. External drivers, on the other hand, are not controllable by the firm, but impact its ability to determine and execute a global strategy. Among these drivers are the global economy, culture, political/legal systems, and technology. As mentioned earlier, these drivers are increasingly based on paradoxical developments and are thus difficult to monitor. All of these drivers will be discussed in the chapters that follow.

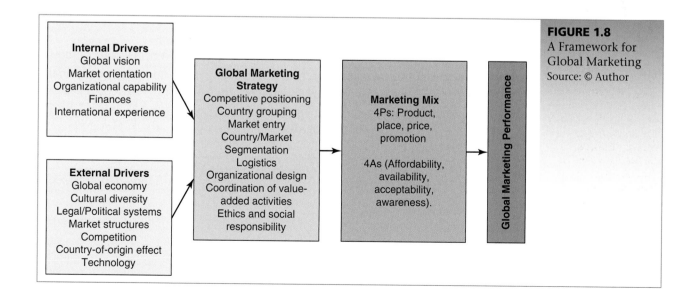

FIGURE 1.8
A Framework for Global Marketing
Source: © Author

We begin a discussion of the Global Marketing framework with attention to the dependent variable: Global Marketing Performance.

Global Marketing Performance

Ambler and Xiucun[56] (2003) suggest that marketing effectiveness or performance can be measured within four dimensions of business activity. While financial outcomes measure overall firm performance, market and consumer-oriented metrics are better indicators of marketing success. If global marketing strategy takes into consideration external globalizing drivers, there should be a significant impact on the firm's global performance.[57] Moreover, there is evidence of a positive relationship between the development of customer knowledge, new product advantage, and market performance.[58]

SUMMARY

- This chapter has explored how global marketing is strongly influenced by technological developments.
- We discussed the origin of globalization, its many facets, and implications for global marketing strategy.
- We defined what is meant by global marketing and global marketing strategy and how they may be implemented, either in a standardized or in a locally adapted way.
- We highlighted trends from the past and the future and showed that they are increasingly non-linear and ambiguous. Thus, companies need to cope with paradoxes and awareness of ethical issues.
- Traditional marketing mix instruments—the 4Ps—need to be complemented by the so-called 4As, especially when dealing with the lowest consumer segment levels in emerging markets.
- The international performance of companies can be determined by a variety of indicators. We have suggested a number of measures to determine performance based on the consumer, product development, and financial returns.
- We have suggested a framework for global marketing strategy that will serve as the agenda for topics discussed in the chapters that follow.

OUTLINE OF THE BOOK

This book addresses students of Master or EMBA-classes but is also of interest for managers who want to keep up with current trends.

   Throughout the book, we will focus on emerging markets, innovation and sustainability, encompassing both the multinational companies and the small and medium enterprises

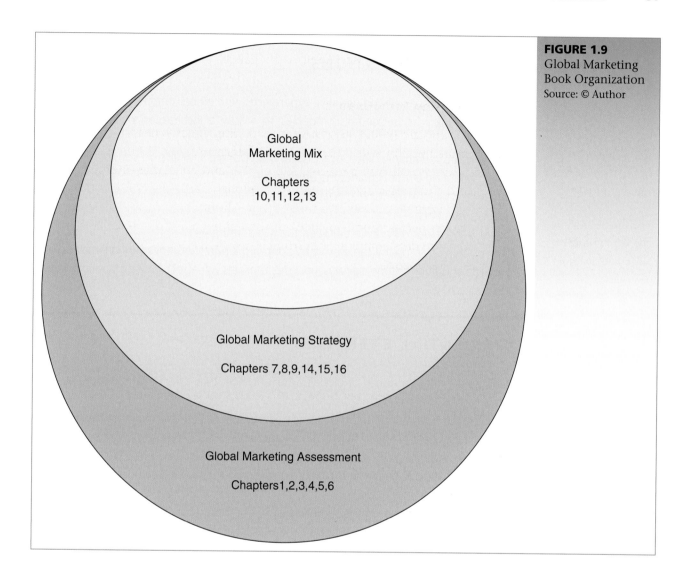

FIGURE 1.9
Global Marketing
Book Organization
Source: © Author

Global
Marketing Mix

Chapters
10,11,12,13

Global Marketing Strategy

Chapters 7,8,9,14,15,16

Global Marketing Assessment

Chapters1,2,3,4,5,6

(SMEs), and taking into consideration the shift from a manufacturing to a service economy. We believe that marketing strategy is the key to attaining competitive advantage in the global marketplace. Therefore, the objective of this book is to show how a successful global marketing strategy can be developed and sustained.

The book is organized around three global marketing activities: assessment, strategy, and the marketing mix. These three steps are shown in Figure 1.9. Before entering global markets, an assessment must be made of their economic, political, and cultural environments. After making the assessment, the next step in the determination of global marketing strategy concerns selecting markets and market entry strategies. Finally, a marketing mix and product, promotion, distribution, and pricing strategies are determined for each market. Figure 1.9 shows the sequence of chapters for each of the three activities.

DISCUSSION QUESTIONS

1. What are your positive and negative experiences with globalization?
2. Do you think it is better for companies to follow a localization or a globalization approach?
3. If you look at companies like Coca-Cola and McDonald's, where do you think the limits are to adopting a global marketing approach?
4. What do you think the list of global companies (Table 1.4) will look like in 2020? Provide some arguments.
5. What is the major difference between the 4Ps and the 4As?
6. Do you think a company can survive by adopting a purely ethnocentric orientation?
7. How do you think technological issues (the Internet) will affect future global marketing strategies?

EXPERIENTIAL EXERCISES

1. Discuss the different forms of globalization and how they affect your personal/business life.
2. Do research on the Internet and identify companies that seem to almost totally standardize/adapt their products across global markets.
3. Have a look at the EPRG framework and discuss whether an ethnocentric orientation can still be valuable today. Try to find examples and show how the companies present themselves.
4. Identify two companies in the same industry, one from an emerging, the other from a developed country. Analyze whether there is any difference in their marketing. Then talk to consumers and identify whether they know and how they perceive the brand.
5. Imagine you are a manager of Apple iPods. Do you think you could develop Zambia as an interesting target market? Do you think Apple has adopted a standardization approach?

KEY TERMS

- Accessibility
- Affordability
- Availability
- Awareness
- EPRG framework
- Ethnocentric orientation
- Geocentric orientation
- Global marketing
- Global markets
- Globalization
- Hidden champions
- Industrialization
- Marketing performance
- Megatrends
- Paradox
- Polycentric orientation
- Regiocentric orientation
- Technology drivers

NOTES

1 KPMG. (2014), 'Luxury goods in Africa', http://www.kpmg.com/Africa/en/IssuesAndInsights/Articles-Publications/General-Industries-Publications/Documents/Luxury%20Goods%20in%20Africa.pdf [Accessed: March 10, 2015].

2 England, A. (2014), 'Trium graduate symbolises an entrepreneurial generation', *Ft.com*,http://www.ft.com/intl/cms/s/2/623c6e06-4d6e-11e4-bf60-00144feab7de.html#axzz3UNlUtVBo [Accessed: March 10, 2015].

3 Vivid Luxury (2013), 'Yswara Griot launches as Africa's first true cultural infusion blog', http://thevividluxuryblog.co.za/?p=8391 [Accessed: March 10, 2015].

4 At the December 2010 exchange rates.

5 McKinsey. (2015), 'Digital inside: Get wired for the ultimate luxury experience', http://www.mckinsey.de/sites/mck_files/files/dle-2015-global-report.pdf [Accessed: January 2, 2015].

6 Ohmae, K. (1989), 'Managing in a borderless world', *Harvard Business Review*, May–June, pp. 152–61.

7 Nestlé. (2012), 'Developing products for local tastes, Côte d'Ivoire', http://www.nestle-cwa.com/en/csv/case-studies/AllCaseStudies/Developing-products-for-local-tastes-Côte-dIvoire [Accessed: November 10, 2014].

8 George, B. (2008), 'Ethics must be global not local', *Business Week/ Bloomberg*, February 12, 2008, http://www.bloomberg.com/bw/stories/2008-02-12/ethics-must-be-global-not-localbusinessweek-business-news-stock-market-and-financial-advice [Accessed: December 12, 2014].

9 Eurostat. (2013), 'Statistics explained', http://epp.eurostat.ec.europa.eu/statistics_explained/index.php/High-tech_statistics [Accessed: December 12, 2014].

10 The EU-27 countries with year of accession are: Austria (1995), Belgium (1952), Bulgaria (2007), Cyprus (2004), Czech Republic (2004), Denmark (1973), Estonia (2004), Finland (1995), France (1952), Germany (1952), Greece (1981), Hungary (2004), Ireland (1973), Italy (1952), Latvia (2004), Lithuania (2004), Luxembourg (1952), Malta (2004), Netherlands (1952), Poland (2004), Portugal (1986), Romania (2007), Slovakia (2004), Slovenia (2004), Spain (1986), Sweden (1995), United Kingdom (1973). Croatia entered as the 28th country in 2013.

11 Photovoltaic (PV) devices generate electricity directly from sunlight via an electronic process that occurs naturally in certain types of material, called semiconductors. Electrons in these materials are freed by solar energy and can be induced to travel through an electrical circuit, powering electrical devices or sending electricity to the grid. Solar Energy Industries Association. http://www.seia.org/policy/solar-technology/photovoltaic-solar-electric [Accessed: January 21, 2013].

12 Cao, J. and Groba, F. (2013), 'Chinese renewable energy technology exports: The role of policy, innovation, and markets', *Discussion Paper DIW-Berlin*, http://www.diw.de/discussionpapers [Accessed: 20 December, 2013].

13 The World Factbook. (2015), https://www.cia.gov/library/publications/the-world-factbook/docs/refmaps.html [Accessed: August 1, 2015].

14 Cartwright, M. (2012), 'Trade in ancient Greek', *Ancient History Encyclopedia,* http://www.ancient.eu.com/article/115/ [Accessed: January 3, 2014].

15 McLuhan, M. (1964). *Understanding media*. New York: Mentor.

16 Al-Rodhan, N.R.F. and Stoudtmann, F. (2006). *Historical milestones of globalization*. Geneva Centre for Security Policy, New York; Friedman, T.L. (2005). *The world is flat: A brief history of the twenty-first century*. New York: Farrar, Straus and Giroux.

17 Ghemawat, P. (2007). *Redefining global strategy*. Cambridge, MA: Harvard Business School Press.

18 Williamson, J. (2002), 'Winners and losers over two centuries of globalization', *NBER Working Paper*, No.9161.

19 Pustay, M.W. and Griffin, R.W. (2007). *International business*. New Jersey: Prentice-Hall, p.12.

20 Feigenbaum, H.B. (2002). *Globalization and cultural diplomacy*. Center for Arts and Culture: The George Washington University, Washington D.C.

21 The World Factbook. (2015), https://www.cia.gov/library/publications/the-world-factbook/docs/refmaps.html [Accessed: August 1, 2015].

22 Lison, J. and Akanksha, P. (2013), 'Indian companies set sights on software outsourcing deals worth $50 billion in 2013', *The Economic Times*, http://articles.economictimes.indiatimes.com/2013-01-21/news/36463209_1_software-exporter-hcl-technologies-information-technology [Accessed: November 10, 2014].

23 Gooptu, B. (2014), 'Microsoft ventures may invest in Hyderabad startup NowFloats for India foray', *The Economic Times*, http://articles.economictimes.indiatimes.com/2014-06-18/news/50678741_1_microsoft-ventures-seed-fund-blume-ventures [Accessed: November 10, 2014].

24 General Electric. (2013), 'Annual Report', http://www.ge.com/ar2006/util_downloads.htm [Accessed: January 10, 2015].

25 Singer, P., Pogge, T., and Wenar, L. (2003), 'One world: The ethics of globalization', Peter Singer (New Haven: Yale University Press, 2002) and 'World Poverty and Human Rights', Thomas Pogge (Cambridge: Polity, 2002) http://www.carnegiecouncil.org/publications/journal/17_2/reviews/1028.html [Accessed: October 15, 2014].

26 The Occupy Solidarity Network. http://occupywallst.org/about/ [Accessed: July 20, 2014].

27 Lorenz, E. N. (1963), 'Deterministic nonperiodic flow', *Journal of the Atmospheric Sciences,* 20(2), pp. 130–41.

28 Argyris, C. and Schoen, D.A. (1978). *Organizational learning: A theory of action perspective.* Reading, MA: Addison-Wesley Publishing Company.

29 Collins, J.C. and Porras, J. I. (1994). *Built to last.* New York: HarperCollins.

30 Definition provided by the American Marketing Association. http://www.marketingpower.com/_layouts/dictionary.aspx?dLetter=G [Accessed: December 15, 2013].

31 Dole, I. and Lowe, R. (2012). *International marketing strategy.* London: Cengage.

32 Eisenhardt, K. M. (2000), 'Paradox, spirals, ambivalence: The new language of change and pluralism', *Academy of Management Review*, 25(4), pp. 703–5.

33 Prahalad, C.K. and Doz, Y. (1987). *The multinational mission: Balancing local demands and global vision.* New York: Free Press; Schmid, S. and Kotulla, T. (2011), '50 years of research on international standardization and adaptation – From a systematic literature analysis to a theoretical framework', *International Business Review*, 20(5), pp. 491–507; Casillas, J. C. and Acedo, F.J. (2013), 'Speed in the internationalization process of the firm', *International Journal of Management Reviews*, 15(1), pp. 15–29; Hashai, N. (2011), 'Sequencing the expansion of geographic scope and foreign operations of 'Born Global' firms', *Journal of International Business Studies,* 42(8), pp. 994–1015.

34 Pitt, L.F. and Schlegelmilch, B.B. (2008), 'Juggling Janus – strategy for general managers in an age of paradoxical trends', *Journal of General Management*, 33(3), 69–84.

35 Naisbitt, J. (1990). *Megatrends 2000. Ten new directions for the 1990's.* New York: William & Morrow Company, Inc.

36 Pitt, L.F. and Schlegelmilch, B.B. (2008), op.cit.

37 Cap Gemini/RBC Wealth Management. (2013), 'World Wealth Report', https://www.capgemini.com/resource-file-access/resource/pdf/wwr_2013_0.pdf [Accessed: July 10, 2014].

38 Population Reference Bureau. (2009), 'World Population Data Sheet', http://www.prb.org/pdf09/09wpds_eng.pdf> [Accessed: July 10, 2014].

39 UN Millennium Development Report. (2007), http://www.un.org/millenniumgoals/pdf/mdg2007.pdf [Accessed: July 10, 2014].

40 Herz, N. (2003). *The silent takeover: Global capitalism and the death of democracy.* New York, NY: Harper Collins Publishers; The Worldbank. http://databank.worldbank.org/data/download/GDP.pdf [Accessed: January 22, 2014]; Global Fortune-500 firms. http://money.cnn.com/magazines/fortune/global500/2012/full_list/ [Accessed: January 22, 2014].

41 McLuhan, M. (1964), op.cit.

42 CNN money. http://money.cnn.com/gallery/technology/2012/09/10/china-social-media.fortune/index.html; Statistica (2014). http://www.statista.com/statistics/274050/quarterly-numbers-of-linkedin-members/; www.

linkedin.com; www.tencent.com; www.google.com; Lunden, I. (2012), 'Twitter may have 500M+ users but only 170M are active, 75% on Twitter's own clients', http://techcrunch.com/2012/07/31/twitter-may-have-500m-users-but-only-170m-are-active-75-on-twitters-own-clients; Tan, V. (2013), 'Sina Weibo enters Twitter's turf in Southeast Asia. Suicidal or genius? (Startup Asia preview)'. techinasia.com. http://www.techinasia.com/sina-weibo-sea-startup-asia-preview. [All Accessed: January 20, 2014].

43 O'Driscoll, A. (2008), 'Exploring paradox in marketing strategy: Managing ambiguity towards synthesis', *Journal of Business and Industrial Marketing*, 23(2), pp. 95–104.

44 Braidotti, R. (2005). *Transpositions: On nomadic ethics.* Cambridge: Polity Press.

45 Perlmutter, H. (1969), 'The tortuous evolution of the multinational corporation', *Columbia Journal of World Business,* 4(1), pp. 9–18.

46 Malnight, T. (1995), 'Globalization of an ethnocentric firm: An evolutionary perspective', *Strategic Management Journal,* 16(2), pp. 119–41.

47 Aichner, T. (2014), 'Country-of-origin marketing: A list of typical strategies with examples', *Journal of Brand Management*, 21(1), pp. 81–93.

48 Levitt, T. (1983), 'The globalization of markets', *Harvard Business Review,* 61, pp. 92–102.

49 Ohmae, K. (1989), 'Managing in a borderless world', *Harvard Business Review,* 67(3), pp. 152–61.

50 Ohmae, K. (1991), 'The boundaries of business: The perils of protectionism', *Harvard Business Review*, 69(4), pp. 128–30.

51 Prahalad, C.K. and Doz, Y. (1987), op.cit.

52 See also the Market Potential Index. (2013), http://globaledge.msu.edu/mpi.

53 Guillén, M. F. and García-Canal, E. (2013). *Emerging markets rule: Growth strategies of the new global giants.* New York: McGraw-Hill, pp. 7–8.

54 Porter, M. (1986), 'Changing patterns of international competition', *California Management Review,* 28(2), pp. 9–40; Ohmae, K. (1989), 'Managing in a borderless world', *Harvard Business Review, 67,* pp. 152–61; Yip, G. (1995). *Total global strategy: Managing for worldwide competitive advantage.* Englewood Cliffs, NJ: Prentice-Hall; Zou, S. and Cavusgil, T. (2002), 'The GMS: A broad conceptualization of global marketing strategy and its effect on firm performance', *Journal of Marketing,* 66(4), pp. 40–56; Townsend, J.D., Yeniyurt, S., Deligonul, S. and Cavusgil, S. (2004), 'Exploring the marketing program antecedents of performance in a global company', *Journal of International Marketing*, Winter 2004, 12(4), pp. 1–24.

55 Porter, M. (1980). *Competitive strategy.* New York: The Free Press.

56 Skinner, R. (2014), 'All marketing leaders need to measure the success of their content', *The Guardian*, http://www.theguardian.com/media-network/media-network-blog/2014/feb/10/marketing-measure-success-content-metrics [Accessed: February 1, 2015]; Farris, Paul W., Bendle, Neil T., Pfeifer, Phillip E. and Reibstein, David J. (2006). *Marketing metrics: 50+ metrics every executive should master.* Philadelphia, Pennsylvania: Wharton School Publishing.

57 Zou, S. and Cavusgil, T. (2002), op.cit.

58 Li, T. and Cavusgil, S. (2000), 'Decomposing the effects of market knowledge competence in new product export: A dimensionality analysis', *European Journal of Marketing,* 34(1/2), pp. 57–79.

CASE 1.1 EVALUESERVE—MANAGING INTERNATIONAL SERVICES MARKETING

At the end of its annual evaluation review, the management expressed satisfaction at Evalueserve's performance and progress in the past years. Since its foundation in late 2000, Evalueserve has taken decisive and effective steps in attracting and managing growth. However, the management was fully cognisant of its responsibility to keep its eyes and ears open for spotting future opportunities in the fast-changing environment of the nascent Knowledge Process Outsourcing (KPO) industry and building on them. In this context, they realised the importance of constantly reviewing the company's strategy to garner more business.

Evalueserve is a pioneer in the knowledge process outsourcing (KPO) industry. The company has come a long way in this industry in a very short time. Founded in 2000, the management of Evalueserve has managed to grow from a four-employee company up to 1,200 in early 2006. It has not only witnessed an increase in the scope of services offered but also continuously requires a higher 'knowledge' input. To keep pace with these developments, Evalueserve has also expanded its service offerings over the years to make them among the most comprehensive in the industry. The company has executed projects in more than 192 countries and has worked in more than 65 languages. The company's client portfolio comprises over 500 clients from across the world. These include 20 global consulting firms, 40 Fortune 500 companies, 50 market research firms and 400 small and medium enterprises.

Evalueserve has the most comprehensive line-up of services across all the companies in the industry. The company offers services in the following five lines of business:

1. Business Research

2. Investment Research

3. Market Research

4. Intellectual Property

5. Financial and Data Analytics

Evalueserve's unique advantage over other competitors in this industry is its capability to serve its clients through its comprehensive service bouquet. The main feature of these service offerings is that they are customised to suit specific client needs. By interacting closely with clients and fully understanding their requirements, Evalueserve is able to deliver high quality output at a reasonable price due to its well strategically located delivery centres in India and China. The company does not believe in offering products such as syndicated reports; instead, it maintains a competitive edge by customising solutions to suit client needs. Most other KPO companies offer services in one, two or three business lines. On the other hand,

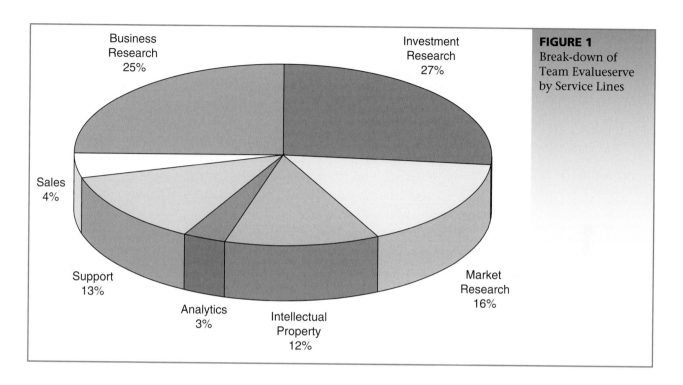

FIGURE 1
Break-down of Team Evalueserve by Service Lines

Evalueserve, apart from working on individual business lines, also uses its synergy within these to execute projects that require strong cross-domain expertise.

The management was quick to realise the importance of client engagement managers in selling the company's services. These managers were required to understand client needs and accordingly suggest appropriate services to them. The company currently has a team of 30 Client Executives (CEs) operating worldwide, up from 8 in 2001. CEs act as intermediaries between clients and project teams, ensuring a smooth flow of activities between the two. Using their rich and varied experience, CEs offer valuable guidance to analysts by offering suggestions on research activities, methodologies and content. In Evalueserve's business model, a great deal of importance is attached to the role played by CEs. They not only supplement existing client relationships, but also sell the company's services to prospective clients. Their role includes convincing clients on outsourcing their tasks to obtain high-quality, timely and value-added offerings from Evalueserve. In the process, CEs enable clients to gain a dual advantage: implementing cost saving and freeing their personnel to concentrate on their core activities within their firms and leaving secondary activities to Evalueserve. The critical role played by CEs contributes significantly to the growth of the company. Initially, the team of CEs was primarily composed of people with general experience. However, over time, the company has endeavoured to change the composition of the CE team by hiring personnel for specific service lines.

Evalueserve also has a sales team that assists and complements the marketing and selling efforts of CEs. The sales team provides the support required by CEs to foster healthy client relationships. It also assists CEs in identifying potential clients

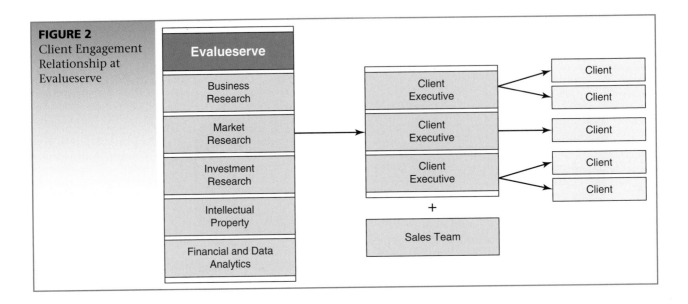

FIGURE 2
Client Engagement
Relationship at
Evalueserve

and opportunities. Figure 2 outlines the relationship between the different parties involved in the interaction between Evalueserve and the clients.

The CE model is perhaps one of Evalueserve's direct approaches of marketing its services. Since the company believes in the power of direct and indirect marketing efforts, it employs several such efforts. Evalueserve regularly also publishes papers about current or emerging "hot" topic ranging from an industry to a promising start-up to venture capital scenarios as for example the recent paper about the "Impact of Skype on Telecom Service Providers". Such papers are widely quoted and circulated not only in the press and business magazines but also by academia and current and prospect clients. These circulations act as a very powerful marketing tool for the company as well. Evalueserve has co-authored reports in collaboration with industry representative bodies such as Nasscom. The exposure received by Evalueserve through co-branding goes a long way in showcasing its capabilities. Certain reports co-authored by Evalueserve has set benchmarks in industry dynamics; an example is the one on the KPO industry. In addition, the company publishes two weekly newsletters, CommNow and GlobalSourcingNOW, which focus on the telecommunications and global outsourcing industries, respectively. These newsletters act as powerful marketing tools for showcasing the company's expertise in these industries.

The company's unique and successful business model was validated when it received in 2006 the Red Herring Top 100 Asia Award. The company is today ready to take purposeful strides, thanks to the management's vision and the employees' efforts. To progress in this direction, it is imperative that Evalueserve continues to retain the competitive advantage that it possesses. By retaining its core advantages of offering quality services at lower prices and implementing faster turnaround times on all its projects, Evalueserve will enable it to better market its services to its clients worldwide.

The management is currently engaged in examining future strategies to identify ways and means for enhancing greater growth. It is fully aware that this growth can be chiefly achieved only through the contributions of a strong team of client executives (CEs) and direct as well as indirect marketing efforts.

QUESTIONS

1. Can a wide bouquet of service offerings become a hindrance for Evalueserve in future as it may divert the focus of the company?
2. Should Evalueserve use advertising for marketing its services?
3. How can Evalueserve sustain the advantage of its association in the KPO Industry?

DISCLAIMER

Professor Marc Fetscherin from Rollins College, and Mr. Ashish Thakre, Mr. Vishal Suri, Mr. Gaurav Sharma and Ms. Nidhi Seth from Evalueserve prepared the original version of this case, 'Evalueserve – Managing International Services Marketing'.

Certain figures and detail have been disguised and do not reflect the actual operations of Evalueserve. This case has been developed solely for class discussion. Cases are not intended to serve as endorsements, sources of primary data, or illustrations of effective or ineffective management.

CHAPTER 2

Assessing the Global Marketing Environment—The Global Economy and Technology

If GM had kept up with technology like the computer industry has, we would all be driving 25$ cars that got 1,000 mpg.

Bill Gates

LEARNING OBJECTIVES

After Reading This Chapter, You Should Be Able to:

- Understand the current situation of economic growth and world trade.
- Understand how to analyze balance of payment and balance of trade figures.
- Learn about different economic systems and stages of economic development.
- Realize the potential of emerging global giants.
- Conduct a thorough environmental analysis using a variety of tools.
- Demonstrate the importance of high technology and environmentalism.
- Show how marketing strategies adopt an environmental perspective.

Many companies enter unfamiliar markets around the globe. The concept of doing business in these markets requires significant changes in the way commercial activities are carried out. For instance, risk managers have to make sure that overseas representatives do not offer bribes to obtain lucrative contracts. Or that engineers sent to carry out tests at a highway construction site in a developing country are covered with a kidnap and ransom insurance policy that includes a provision for a local crisis team trained to deal with such situations. Some countries are more closely linked to home markets through former colonial ties, common history, or similar political developments. For instance, Tunisia is a new emerging market set to make an impact in the immediate future. This Mediterranean country is very closely linked to Europe, which makes it today a platform for investment as well as for production and trade. Especially tourism is a strategic sector and thanks to an extensive and diversified tourism base Tunisia has enjoyed an

FIGURE 2.1
A Typical Tourist
Hotel in Tunisia
Source: © Authors

increase in numbers of tourists (Figure 2.1 for a typical tourist hotel in the country). Diversification of the offer was further consolidated by an increasingly developed infrastructure. Tunisia's property market may just be in its early stages, but with its strong economy and tourist sector, large-scale property investment by Middle East developers, and low-entry prices, Tunisia looks well set to become one of the most interesting emerging markets. As the economy recovers, Tunisia is bringing budget and current account deficits under control, shoring up the country's financial system, bringing down high unemployment, and reducing economic disparities between the more developed coastal region and the impoverished interior. GDP in 2014 amounted to US$47 billion with GDP per capita US$4,226. Overall, there is a positive outlook with expected new business and consumer confidence that led to growth of 3.9 percent in 2015.[1]

To succeed in emerging market countries, even more than in developed markets, responsible managers must collect a variety of data, preferably in a systematic and clearly structured manner rather than on an ad hoc basis. To date, many studies focus on a selection of underlying factors that should be considered for doing business abroad.

In this book we will focus on criteria mainly from the external environment though clearly consumer research and internal analysis should not be neglected. In this and the following chapters, we will learn about the global marketing environment, which includes political, economic, sociological, technological,

Factor	Possible Factors for Study	Examples	
Political	Local and national government structure, government stability, internal politics that affect business, international relations, terrorist activity.	Crisis in the Ukraine, which leads to political instability.	**TABLE 2.1** A PESTEL Analysis of the Macro-Global Environment
Economic	Regional economic growth indicators, exchange rates, trade and trade policy, government intervention in the economy, taxation, consumption, employment/unemployment, inflation, balance of payments.	Economic growth of emerging market countries has multiplied in the last decade.	
Social	Demographics, lifestyle, education, living standards (health and welfare), immigration/emigration.	In 2012, the Austrian government changed its national anthem to account for gender issues.	
Technological	Technological infrastructure, including market opportunities in the electronics, high-tech markets, development of biotechnology and information technology industries, and clean technology markets.	The email celebrated its 30th anniversary in 2014 and it has completely changed the way we communicate with each other.	
Environmental/ Legal	Environmental regulations, global warming, pollution, green marketing, legal systems, business legislation, consumer protection, intellectual property issues.	Huge pollution problems and intellectual property protection issues in China that pose a threat to doing business.	

Source: Compiled by Authors

environmental, and legal determinants of global marketing strategy. These environmental factors relate to the macroenvironment and form the acronym PESTEL, which helps to systematically guide the analysis and can be used as a framework for the audit of a company's external environment. Its findings can be used as a major input for a multiple-decision-criteria-analysis where you weigh a set of criteria and support strategic marketing planning. To help the decision-maker, a PESTEL analysis should include examining these and similar factors included in Table 2.1.

In addition to PESTEL, it is also important to analyze the industry environment and the level of competitors; that is to conduct a Five-Forces Analysis and a Strategic Group Analysis. A Five-Forces Analysis identifies the competitive forces in the industry to assess its attractiveness: the threat of new entrants, rivalry among existing firms, the bargaining power of suppliers, the bargaining power of buyers, and the threat of substitute products or services. According to the "market positioning" school, of which Michael Porter is the leading exponent, the fundamental determinant of a firm's profitability is industry structure and the rules of competition are embodied in the five forces.[2] However, firms can adopt different strategies within the same industry, e.g. they can focus on premium versus low-cost products, they can adopt a broad scope or focus on a niche market, they can offer an international or a local product. The concept of strategic groups looks at groupings of firms within an industry and has been defined as "a cluster of firms within an industry following the same or similar strategy."[3] A strategic group is therefore a way of making sense of different types of competitors and different competitive strategies within the same industry. This is an important insight because some companies in the same industry may not be direct competitors. For example, luxury jewelry does not compete with costume jewelry though they are in the same industry.

In addition, internal characteristics of the firm need to be taken into account to make sure that it has the necessary resources and capabilities to enter foreign markets and to develop product offers relevant to the identified target group. This investigation should include a Resource-Audit[4] and a Value Chain Analysis[5] to validate the company's internal match with its environmental challenges. For instance, since China opened up to foreign investment in the late 1970s, some of America's most powerful corporations have gone confidently into the People's Republic, only to stagger out a few years later, battered, confused, and defeated. In fact, large companies like Tesco have been struggling with big problems in China, not only because of external factors and cultural adaptation problems but also because of their inability to quickly adapt their internal resources and capabilities. For instance, e-commerce sites run by Jingdong, Alibaba and Tencent now carry many of the same items as traditional hypermarkets but for far less. What's more, most of those online names can often deliver goods on the same day, and a few are even trialing services that deliver in two hours or less—great achievement in terms of supply chain organization. And Tesco is hardly alone in its inability to compete successfully in China. Earlier in 2013, media reported that global retail giants Wal-Mart and Carrefour had similar problems. Also Best Buy, which entered China in 2006 by paying $180 million to take control of Five Star, China's fourth-largest electronics retailer failed.[6]

Taken collectively, a thorough analysis of both internal and external factors (possibly comparing them in a SWOT analysis = strengths, weaknesses, opportunities, and threats) should precede any foreign business involvement.

This chapter provides insight into how to examine the external environment of the global economy with an emphasis on high-tech markets. According to the PESTEL model, it explicitly adds insights on ecological and technical issues (see last sections). Chapter 3 covers the social environment, including the role of culture and cultural distance, and Chapter 4, the political and legal environment.

THE GLOBAL ECONOMY

Economic Growth and World Trade

The major trends that occurred at the turn of the last century include increased economic liberalization and integration. One of the best examples is the European Union (EU). The meanwhile 28 member countries are so integrated with regard to a monetary policy, technological advances, and global trade that exceed domestic growth. However, there are also drawbacks of this tight union, which were evident during the financial crisis in 2008 when weaker countries, such as Greece, began to develop severe financial problems that quickly spread over to other countries. But economic liberalization is generally thought of as positive and desirable, especially for emerging and developing countries. The goal is to have unrestricted capital flowing into and out of the country in order to boost growth and efficiencies within the home country. The effects following liberalization are what should interest investors as they can provide new opportunities for diversification and profit. Tables 2.2 and 2.3 show the trends in world trade depicting major exporters and importers of merchandise and services. Services are the fastest growing sector of world trade and include, among others, education, engineering, accounting, travel and entertainment, etc. What is noteworthy is the increase of exports from emerging market countries (China, Russian Federation) and the drop in figures of Germany, one of the export champions in 2009. In terms of imports, the United States remains the major player with increasing annual percentages.

While China is the leading exporter of merchandise, it lags behind in terms of exporting services. With regards to imports, China and India have changed their position with an annual increase of 18 percent and 3 percent respectively for services between 2011 and 2012. Other emerging countries, like Brazil (no. 22 and 29 on the list of exporters of merchandise and services respectively), have increased their ranking in the list. For countries like Brazil, very often restrictions apply, which need to be overcome in order to increase their export rates as Box 2.1 illustrates.

Rank	Exporters	Value	Share	Annual Percentage Change	Rank	Importers	Value	Share	Annual Percentage Change	
1	China	2049	11.1	8	1	United States	2336	12.6	3	**TABLE 2.2** Leading Exporters and Importers in World Merchandise Trade, 2012 (Billion US$ and Percentages)
2	United States	1546	8.4	4	2	China	1818	9.8	4	
3	Germany	1407	7.6	−5	3	Germany	1167	6.3	−7	
4	Japan	799	4.3	−3	4	Japan	886	4.8	4	
5	NL	656	3.6	−2	5	UK	690	3.7	2	
6	France	569	3.1	−5	6	France	674	3.6	−6	
7	Korea, Republ.	548	3.0	−1	7	NL	591	3.2	−1	
8	Russian Federation	529	2.9	1	8	Hong Kong China	553	3.0	8	
9	Italy	501	2.7	−4	9	Korea Republ.	140	2.8	−1	
10	Hong Kong China	493	2.7	8	10	India	490	2.6	5	

Source: WTO International Trade Statistics, 2013, www.wto.org/statistics [Accessed: November 15, 2014]

TABLE 2.3 Leading Exporters and Importers in World Services, 2012 (Billion US$ and Percentages)	Rank	Exporters	Value	Share	Annual Percentage Change	Rank	Importers	Value	Share	Annual Percentage Change
	1	United States	621	14.3	6	1	United States	411	9.9	4
	2	UK	280	6.4	−3	2	Germany	293	7.1	−1
	3	Germany	257	5.9	−1	3	China	280	6.7	18
	4	France	211	4.8	−6	4	Japan	175	4.2	5
	5	China	190	4.4	8	5	UK	174	4.2	0
	6	Japan	142	3.3	0	6	France	172	4.1	−9
	7	India	141	3.2	3	7	India	127	3.1	3
	8	Spain	136	3.1	−4	8	NL	119	2.9	−1
	9	NL	131	3.0	−3	9	Singapore	118	2.8	3
	10	Hong Kong, China	123	2.8	5	10	Ireland	112	2.7	−3

Source: WTO International Trade Statistics, 2013, www.wto.org/statistics [Accessed: November 15, 2014]

Box 2.1   Country-in-Focus: Brazil

Forget About Football—Brazil's Move to Confectionery Exports

Brazilian confectionery manufacturers are forced to commit up to 15 percent of export costs towards resolving bureaucratic problems that hinder their sales abroad, according to the Brazilian confectionery industry association (ABICAB). These export expenditures mainly occur to resolve red tape related problems and often delay exports for more than six months.

Brazil is the third largest confectionery producer in the world. Brazilians average an annual per capital chocolate consumption of 2.5 kg per year. The rate of consumption is far greater than in other emerging markets such as China (1.2 kg) and India (0.7 kg), however lower than in Russia (5.9 kg). Nestlé leads the Brazilian chocolate market with a value share of 41.6 percent through brands such as Garoto, Especialidades and Alpino.

The strategy of the majority of Brazilian confectioners is to focus on the key US, South America and Africa markets. But exports dropped in 2013. It exported 30.000 metric tons of chocolate in 2013 vs. 32.000 metric tons in 2012 respectively. The poor results are in part blamed on the economic crisis in Argentina, one of Brazil's largest commercial partners. Despite the drop in exports, some companies are attempting to regain lost stakes in foreign markets through a range of capacity-building projects by investing in sophisticated packaging, new flavors, and consumer-pleasing formats. First, since 2009, the Brazilian sweet and chocolate industry has invested more than $350 million in modernizing and expanding production capabilities. As the world's eighth largest economy with a population of nearly 191 million people, Brazil has both the natural resources and the consumer base to support a healthy confectionery marketplace.

Sources: http://www.confectionerynews.com/Regulation-Safety/Brazilian-confectionery-exports-hampered-by-red-tape; http://www.confectionerynews.com/Markets/Premium-chocolate-samba-in-Brazil; http://www.candyindustry.com/articles/brazil-an-emerging-powerhouse; http://www.just-food.com/news/confectioners-focus-on-key-export-markets-for-growth_id121921.aspx [All Accessed: December 12, 2014].

Balance of Payments and Balance of Trade

The **balance of payment** (BOP) is a statistical statement for a given period and records the payments and receipts of the residents of the country in their transactions with residents of other countries.[7] If all transactions are included, the payments and receipts of each country are, and must be, equal. Any apparent

	2008	2009	2010	2011	2012	
Current Account	421	243	238	202	214	**TABLE 2.4**
Capital and Financial Accounts	40	198	287	221	−117	China's Balance of Payments (2008–12), in US$ bn
Net Errors and Omissions	19	−41	−53	−35	–	
Change in Curreny Reserves	480	400	472	388	97	
Currency Reserves at Year's End	1,946	2,399	2,847	3,181	3,312	

Source: China's State Administration of Foreign Exchange (SAFE), http://www.safe.gov.cn/wps/portal/english/ [Accessed: March 10, 2014]

inequality simply leaves one country acquiring assets in the others. For example, if China buy automobiles from Germany, and have no other transactions with Germany, the Germans must end up holding dollars (or the currency in which the transaction was executed), which they may hold in the form of bank deposits. The payments of China to Germany for automobiles are balanced by the payments of Germans to Chinese individuals and institutions, including banks, for the acquisition of financial assets. Put another way, Germany sold China automobiles, and China sold Germany dollars or currency-denominated assets such as treasury bills or office buildings.

Although the totals of payments and receipts are necessarily equal, there will be inequalities—excesses of payments or receipts, called **deficits** or **surpluses**—in particular kinds of transactions. Thus, there can be a deficit or surplus in any of the following: merchandise trade (goods), services trade, foreign investment income, unilateral transfers (foreign aid), private investment, the flow of gold and money between central banks and treasuries, or any combination of these or other international transactions.[8] In 2008, for the first time, more money leaves China than enters it. China's current account is still in surplus because its exports exceed its imports. China is also attracting lots of foreign direct investment (FDI). But both these inflows were outdone by a record of outflows of other capital, amounting to a minus of US$117 billion in 2012. This left China's overall balance of payment in deficit. Table 2.4 also shows the currency reserves at the end of the year and annual changes.

The BOP is divided into three main categories: the **current account**, the **capital account** and the **financial account**.[9]

The Current Account

The current account is used to mark the inflow and outflow of goods and services into a country. The current account also includes goods such as raw materials and manufactured goods that are bought, sold or given away (possibly in the form of aid). Services refer to receipts from tourism, transportation (like the levy that must be paid in Egypt when a ship passes through the Suez Canal), engineering, business service fees (from lawyers or management consulting, for example), and royalties from patents and copyrights. When combined, goods and services together make up a country's **balance of trade (BOT)**. The BOT is typically the biggest

TABLE 2.5		Balance of Trade	Balance of Payment
Comparison Between Balance of Trade and Balance of Payment	Definition	The difference between the export and import of goods and services.	The flow of cash between domestic country and all other foreign countries. It includes not only import and export of goods and services, but also financial capital transfer.
	Calculation	BOT = net earning on export – net payment for imports	BOP = BOT + (net earning on foreign investment – payment made to foreign investors) + cash transfer + capital account + or – balancing item
	Favorable or Unfavorable	If export is more than import, at that time, BOT will be favorable. If import is more than export, at that time, BOT will be unfavorable.	Balance of payment is favorable, if there is a surplus in current account for paying all past loans in the capital account. Balance of Payment will be unfavorable, if there is a current account deficit and the country takes more loans from foreigners, including interests.
	Affected by	a) cost of production b) availability of raw materials c) exchange rate d) prices of goods manufactured at home	a) conditions of foreign lenders b) economic policy of Govt. c) all the factors of BOT
	Meaning of Credit and Debit	Credit means total export of different goods and services and debit means total import of goods and services in current account.	Credit means inflow of cash both to current and capital account, and debit means total outflow of cash both to current and capital account. Difference between debit and credit will be net balance of payment.

Source: Adapted from: http://www.svtuition.org/2011/04/difference-between-balance-of-trade-and.html [Accessed: July 1, 2014]

bulk of a country's balance of payments as it makes up total imports and exports (Table 2.5 compares the two). If a country has a balance of trade deficit, it imports more than it exports, and if it has a balance of trade surplus, it exports more than it imports.

The Capital Account

The capital account is where all international capital transfers are recorded. This refers to the acquisition or disposal of non-financial assets (for example, a physical asset such as land) and non-produced assets, which are needed for production but have not been produced, like a mine used for the extraction of diamonds. The capital account is broken down into the monetary flows branching from debt forgiveness, the transfer of goods, and financial assets by migrants leaving or entering a country, the transfer of ownership on fixed assets (assets such as equipment used in the production process to generate income), the transfer of funds received to the sale or acquisition of fixed assets, gift and inheritance taxes, death levies and, finally, uninsured damage to fixed assets.

The Financial Account

In the financial account, international monetary flows related to investment in business, real estate, bonds and stocks are documented. Also included are government-owned assets such as foreign reserves, gold, special drawing rights (SDRs) held with the International Monetary Fund (IMF), private assets held abroad and direct foreign investment. Assets owned by foreigners, private and official, are also recorded in the financial account.

While China and the United States are the biggest importers and exporters, both carry deficits of their balance of payment (BOP). A country can run a trade deficit, but still have a surplus in its balance of payments. How? Foreigners invest in the country's growth by loaning to businesses, buying government bonds, and hiring workers from that country. If the other components of the balance of payments are in a large enough surplus, a trade deficit can be completely offset. Needless to say, countries strive to have a positive balance of trade, and it is imperative upon governments to do as much as possible to boost the country's income and, at the same time, decrease the country's expenditures. A **deficit** generates a decrease in aggregate income and its associated measures, especially consumption, savings, investment, and tax revenue. However, for some countries, an increase in economic growth and aggregate income will result in higher domestic consumption expenditures, including the purchase of imports from foreign countries. In this case, the increase in imports, which may widen the trade deficit, is actually a result of a prosperous economy. Therefore, the trade deficit should not be labeled "unfavorable."

Gross National Happiness

The term "gross national happiness" (GNH) was coined in 1972 by Bhutan's fourth Dragon King, Jigme Singye Wangchuck, who opened Bhutan to the age of modernization. GNH has only been officially used in Bhutan, where a Gross National Happiness Commission is charged with reviewing policy decision and allocation of resources.[10] In recent years, a few rich-world leaders have pushed efforts to study whether a happiness statistic could prove useful. For example, Canada, France, and Britain have jumped on the happiness bandwagon by adding measures of citizen happiness to their official national statistics. However, measuring happiness could be questionable as results may differ according to measurement approaches. In July 2011, the UN General Assembly passed a resolution inviting member countries to measure the happiness of their people and to use this to help guide their public policies. On April 2, 2012 this was followed by the first UN High Level Meeting on "Happiness and Well-Being: Defining a New Economic Paradigm."

A recent article in *The Economist*[11] asked the question of "how can the French, who invented joie de vivre, the three-tier cheese trolley and Dior's jaunty New Look, be so resolutely miserable?" If you look at the emblem of love, the Eiffel

Tower in Paris, and the many luxury brands along the Champs-Élysées, you may wonder why France doesn't rank at the top of the happiness index (no. 25 on a list of 85 countries, with the ranking led by Denmark, Norway, Switzerland, The Netherlands and Sweden[12]). Actually, polls suggested that the French are more depressed than Ugandans or Uzbekistanis, which rank significantly lower in GDP, and are more pessimistic about their country's future than Albanians or Iraqis, which have undergone serious political troubles. What can be the reason for this attitude?

Apparently, the French are even unhappier than people in Belgium and Canada, so language could not be the issue, even though the French language has lost the prominence it had in earlier diplomatic times. Actually, unhappiness seems to be something about being French. If we look at France's history, we might find some explanations. In the period from the fall of the *Ancien Régime* in 1789 to 1814, France overthrew a monarchy, endured the terror, and lost an empire. Afterwards, melancholy dominated, infused with nostalgia and bourgeois values. Indeed, melancholy is seen as a noble state, a higher aesthetic condition as famous French writers like Baudelaire or Hugo express it. This trend finds itself reiterated in the mid-twentieth century in the work of existentialists Albert Camus and Jean-Paul Sartre. And in addition, France today is contemplating its diminishing status it once had in the world of high culture. There is a profound pessimism that France has become a country like any other and this is difficult to digest. Results from a recent WIN-Gallup poll confirm these perceptions of happiness or unhappiness and expectations for future development.[13]

EXPLANATIONS OF INTERNATIONAL TRADE

Differences in international trade have also been analyzed by different theories, which deal with the question of how and why international trade improves the welfare of countries. To understand them, it is important to examine the criticism of classical trade theory and examine alternative viewpoints of which business and economic forces determine trade patterns between countries. Table 2.6 gives an overview of the major theories we deal with in this section. Knowledge about these theories is important for marketers because they need to understand developments on the country level to evaluate potential attractiveness as target markets.

The Beginning of Free Trade

With the two landmark publications, *Wealth of Nations* (1776) by Adam Smith and David Ricardo's *Principles of Economics* (1821), the formulation of a theory of free trade was heralded. Classical trade theory dictates that the extent to which a country exports and imports relates to its trading patterns with other nations. For Smith, the **division of labor** provided the base for lowering labor costs, which

Name	Origin	Basic Idea	
Absolute Advantages	Adam Smith	Each country should specialize in the production and export of that product, which it produces most efficiently, that is, with the fewest labor hours.	**TABLE 2.6** Overview of Major Trade Theories
Comparative Advantages	David Ricardo	Even if a country was most efficient in the production of two products, it must be relatively more efficient in the production of one product. It should then specialize in the production and export of that product in exchange for the import of the other product.	
Factor Proportion Theory	Eli Heckscher and Bertil Ohlin	A country that is relatively labor abundant (capital abundant) should specialize in the production and export of that product which is relatively labor intensive (capital intensive).	
Leontief Paradox and Differences in International Taste	Wassily Leontief	The test of the factor proportion theory which resulted in the unexpected finding that the United States was actually exporting products that were relatively labor intensive, rather than the capital intensive products that a relatively abundant country should, according to the theory.	
Product Life Cycle Theory	Raymond Vernon	The country that possesses comparative advantages in the production and export of an industrial product changes over time as the technology of the product's manufacture matures.	
National Competitive Advantage	Michael Porter	International competitive advantage stems from a combination of conditions: demand conditions, related and supporting industries, firm strategies, structures and rivalry. Competitive advantage is also established through geographic "clusters" or concentrations of companies in different parts of the same industry.	
New Trade Theory	Paul Krugman	Economies of scale, and network effects, can be so significant that they outweigh the more traditional theory of comparative advantage.	

Source: Compiled by Authors

ensured effective competition across countries. He observed the production process of the early stages of the Industrial Revolution in England and recognized the fundamental changes that were occurring in production. Economic advantages or disadvantages may also arise from country differences in factors such as resource endowments, labor, capital, technology or entrepreneurship. Possible dilemmas in terms of the need for monetary adjustments for countries having a continuous trade surplus (with absolute advantage in all traded goods) could be shelved aside by relying on the automatic adjustment, in terms of price-mechanisms, the theory offered by Smith's contemporary, David Hume, around the same time.

From Absolute to Relative Advantages

David Ricardo in his *Principles of Political Economy* (1817) extended the free trade argument by proposing that efficiency of resource utilization leads to more productivity. In the England of Ricardo's time, industrial capitalism was at a relatively advanced stage as compared to what it was in Smith's time, both with rapid growth of large-scale industries and captive markets in overseas colonies. The country attributed a special role to the import of goods (e.g. corn) to cheapen prices and hence labor cost. Ricardo's cost calculations, despite his concerns for the introduction of machinery on a large scale, were based on labor hours, which were treated as a single homogeneous input with production subject to constant costs. It was *comparative* and not absolute advantage, which was considered both necessary, as well as sufficient, to ensure mutually gainful trade across nations, warranting complete specialization in the specific commodity with a comparative advantage in terms of labor hours used per unit of output. For instance, Hollywood or Bollywood film production creates a comparative advantage for the US and India respectively, as do textiles in Guatemala or consumer electronics in South Korea. While countries focus on the production of these products, they may import others.

Factor Proportion Theory (Heckscher–Ohlin)

Factor Proportion Theory, developed by the Swedish economist Eli Heckscher and later expanded by his former student Bertil Ohlin[14] aims at explaining differences in advantages exhibited by trade countries in another way. The main argument is that there are two factors of production, labor and capital. Technology determines the way they combine to form a good. Different goods require different proportions of the two factors of production. At heart, the Heckscher–Ohlin model seeks to mathematically explain how countries should operate when resources are not distributed equally around the world. For example, some countries have ample oil reserves but little gas, while other countries have access to precious metals but not agriculture. The model goes beyond tradable commodities by also including other factors of production, such as labor. Because global labor costs vary, countries with cheap labor should focus on goods that are too labor-intensive in other countries.

The model emphasizes how countries can benefit from international trade by exporting what they have in abundance. By not having to rely solely on internal markets, countries are able to take advantage of more elastic demand. As countries develop and labor costs increase, their marginal productivity declines. By trading internationally, they are able to shift to capital-intensive goods, which could not occur if they can only sell internally. More precisely, a country that is relatively labor abundant should specialize in the production of relatively labor-intensive goods. It should then export those labor-intensive goods in exchange for capital-intensive goods. A country that is relatively capital abundant should specialize in the production of relatively capital-intensive goods. It should then export those capital-intensive goods in exchange for labor-intensive goods.

Leontief Paradox and Differences in International Taste[15]

The first serious attempt to test the Heckscher–Ohlin model was made by Professor Wassily W. Leontief in 1954. Leontief reached a paradoxical conclusion that the US—the most capital abundant country in the world by any criterion—exported labor-intensive commodities and imported capital-intensive commodities. This result has come to be known as the *Leontief Paradox*. Leontief himself suggested an explanation for his own paradox. He argued that US workers may be more efficient than foreign workers. Perhaps US workers were three times as effective as foreign workers. Note that this increased effectiveness of the American workers was not due to a higher capital–labor ratio, because we assume that countries have identical technologies and hence identical capital–labor ratios. It means that the average American worker is three times as effective as he would be in the foreign country. Given the same capital–labor ratio, Leontief attributed the superior efficiency of American labor to superior economic organization and economic incentives in the US. Kreiner (1965)[16] tried to empirically prove this and conducted a survey of engineers and managers, and tested whether an average American worker is three times as effective as a foreign worker. A realistic difference in effectiveness between the representative workers in the US and those in the foreign countries was about 20–25 percent. Obviously, this difference does not explain the Leontief Paradox.

Difference may be rather attributed to trade patterns and differences in tastes in a market economy and a command economy, and this explanation may be more important. Also, modern technology is available to Russians, but production in the former Soviet Union is still inefficient due to lack of incentives. Thus, managerial behavior and workforce motivation are other important sources of differences.

Product Life Cycle Theory

A different explanation was offered by Raymond Vernon (1966),[17] drawing attention to what was observed as the "product life cycle" (PLC) of technology-driven foreign investment and trade flows. Vernon focused on the product rather than the country. He observed that innovations, which led to adoption of new technology in the lead advanced country led to "new" products that were produced, consumed, and exported to the rest of world. With the "maturing" of product innovation, technology as well as capital was supposed to move to the rest of advanced countries and to produce similar goods, which in turn are exported back to the lead, advanced nation. Less-developed countries import these goods from the respective producing advanced country/countries during the first two stages of production. However, production gradually starts in the least-developed country as well as the product is "standardized," thus completing the life cycle of the product. Technology at this stage of the PLC has already traveled, along with capital, initially from most advanced to other advanced nations, and finally to these least-developed countries that now export the product to advanced nations.

With product specifications (new, maturing, standardized) and the initial control over the market by advanced countries, the PLC theory of technology-driven trade incorporates both product differentiation and market imperfections. A similar emphasis was laid on technology-driven trade flows and its pattern in models that interpreted the "technological gap" among nations in terms of "demand-lag" on the part of consumers and "reaction-lag" on the part of producers in the home country, as well as the "imitation-lag" on the part of producers in the foreign country.

In hindsight, the PLC model seems to have provided a platform for an integrated approach to trade, technology, and FDI, while introducing product differentiation as well as market imperfection. Compared to the earlier approaches, which were primarily location-specific (comparative cost, resource endowments), PLC theory has introduced product-specific (new, mature, standardized) characterizations and also organization-specific factors. Critique pertains to Vernon's main assumption that the diffusion process of new technology occurs slowly enough to generate temporary differences between countries in their access and use of new technologies. By the late 1970s, he recognized that this assumption was no longer valid. Income differences between advanced nations had dropped significantly, competitors were able to imitate products at much higher speed than previously envisioned, and MNCs had built up an existing global network of production facilities that enabled them to launch products in multiple markets simultaneously.

Theory of National Comparative Advantages

As trade theory evolved, it shifted its focus to the industry and product level, leaving the national-competitiveness question somewhat behind. Attention has focused on the question of how countries, governments and even private industries can alter the conditions within a country to aid the competitiveness of firms. Michael Porter[18] is one of the major proponents of this theory and argues that a firm must avail itself to four dimensions of competition, which he calls the diamond model of national competitiveness. Factor conditions relate to the factors of production to compete successfully in an industry, e.g. skilled labor, research institutes. Demand conditions relate to the degree of health and competition the firm must face in its original home market. That is, if competition is strong in the home market, firms can learn and improve their products and services. Related and supporting industries are another vital factor and relates to the need of constant and close interaction with suppliers and partners to guarantee timeliness and close working relationships. Finally, firm strategy, structure, and rivalry either hinder or aid the firm's creation of international competitiveness. This relates to ownership structures, managerial decision-making as well as to a firm's operational strategies.

Countries should be exporting products from those industries where all four components of the diamond are favorable, while importing in those areas where the components are not favorable.

New Trade Theory

New trade theory (NTT) is a collection of economic models in international trade, which focuses on the role of increasing returns to scale and network effects, which were developed in the late 1970s and early 1980s. Paul Krugman was a leading academic in developing new trade theory. He was awarded a Nobel Prize (2008) in economics for his contributions in modeling these ideas. New trade theorists relaxed the assumption of constant returns to scale, and some argue that using protectionist measures to build up a huge industrial base in certain industries will then allow those sectors to dominate the world market.

Economies of scale, and network effects, can be so significant that they outweigh the more traditional theory of comparative advantage. In some industries, two countries may have no discernible differences in opportunity cost at a particular point in time. But, if one country specializes in a particular industry then it may gain economies of scale and other network benefits from its specialization. Another element of new trade theory is that firms who have the advantage of being an early entrant can become a dominant firm in the market. This is because the first firms gain substantial economies of scale meaning that new firms can't compete against the incumbent firms. This means that in these global industries with very large economies of scale, there is likely to be limited competition, with the market dominated by early firms who entered, leading to a form of monopolistic competition. This means that the most lucrative industries are often dominated in capital-intensive countries that were the first to develop these industries. Therefore, being the first firm to reach industrial maturity gives a very strong competitive advantage.

New trade theory also becomes a factor in explaining the growth of globalization. It means that poorer, developing economies may struggle to ever develop certain industries, because they lag too far behind the economies of scale enjoyed in the developed world. This is not due to any intrinsic comparative advantage, but more the economies of scale the developed firms already have. While the implication for marketers may be that it is not worth targeting developing countries in certain industries, growth rates and the increasing speed of their transition to developed economies with increasing middle-market segments speak another language.

ECONOMIC SYSTEMS

Four Basic Economic Systems

The world's economic systems fall into one of the four main categories: traditional economy, market economy, command economy, and mixed economy, and several variations of these. An economic system must define what to produce, how to produce it, and for whom to produce it.[19] Other questions include: What is the standard of living? Is it changing? Why? Are there institutions, i.e. organizations, processes, procedures, and laws that a nation has that affect the economy? For example, what laws govern contracts and exchange? What rights do buyers, workers, sellers, lenders, or borrowers have? How are these rights enforced? What type of organization exists? How are these organizations governed? The nation's institutions also affect the evolution of its ideologies. The prevailing ideology and institutions will determine the degree of trade and integration and industrialization.

1. Traditional Economic System

A traditional economic system is the most ancient type of economy in the world. These economies still produce products and services that are a result of their beliefs, customs, religion, etc. Countries that adopt this system typically belong to rural, second- or third-world areas closely tied to an agrarian landscape. In this system, each new generation retains the economic position of its parents and grandparents. Tradition decides what an individual does for his living. Examples of those systems are Aborigines, Amazon tribes, or mostly any subsistence economy. The advantages of such a system are that every member knows exactly what to do. There is a strong social network that governs behavior and that helps to embed the individual in society. Typically, positions and tasks are already established and life is generally stable, predictable, and continuous. However, there are also disadvantages in that this type of society is rather slow to change and does not take advantage of technological advancements. There is relatively little intellectual and scientific promotion and typically the provision of goods and services is insufficient. In addition, there is insufficient use of skill in relation to the factors of production.

2. Market Economic System

A market-based economic system is based on individual or consumer-related consumption. Consumers decide which products they desire and companies decide which products to produce to meet the demand. The state has relatively little influence in determining the rules of this system apart from promoting competition and ensuring consumer protection. Complete market economies do not utilize price controls or subsidies and prefer less regulation of industry and production. Arguably, the biggest advantage to a market economy is the separation of the market and the government. This prevents the government from becoming too powerful by reducing its impact on controlling resources.

While capitalist countries, such as the US, Japan, and Western Europe, practice a market-based approach, there are still differences among them. For instance, Japanese companies are tightly controlled by what has come to be known as "Japan Inc." that is a system of interlocking relationships between companies, banks, and other stakeholders that govern the way business is organized. A disadvantage of the market economic system may be that it emphasizes growth and prosperity over social relationships and ethics. In today's world of harsh profit making and repeated firm collapses, a recurrence on trust and morals may indeed be an important issue of discussion.

3. Command Economic System

A command system is characterized by a centrally controlled economy where the government takes all the decisions. The state decides which goods are produced and consumers can only buy what is available. Communism is a typical example of such a system, where the government owns companies or entire industries and where the market plays little to no role in production decisions. As a consequence, these economies are less flexible than market economies and react slower to changes in consumer purchasing patterns and fluctuations in supply and demand. Over time, the system also creates unrest among the general population that demands more and other things than those on offer.

Currently, we see the influence of the state changing in various countries. For one, active support in opening the economy and driving internationalization can be seen in countries like China, or even Cuba, a long-time communist-dominated country. In other countries like, for instance, North Korea, the collapse of communist governments around the world in 1991, forced the North Korean economy to realign its foreign economic relations. However, basic adherence to a rigid centrally planned economy continues, as does its reliance on fundamentally non-pecuniary incentives. North Korea remains as one of the world's poorest and least developed countries, in sharp contrast to South Korea, which has one of the largest and most diversified economies in the world.

4. Mixed Economic System

A mixed economic system, also called a dual economy, primarily refers to a mixture of market and command economy. Many variations exist, with some economies being primarily free markets and others being strongly controlled by the government. In most mixed economies, state ownership is very low or non-existent except for a few areas, which comprise education or transportation, for example. While all these industries also exist in the private sector in the United States, this is not always the case for a mixed economy.

In general, the mixed economy is characterized by the private ownership of the means of production, the dominance of markets for economic coordination, with profit-seeking enterprises, and the accumulation of capital remaining the fundamental driving force behind economic activity. But unlike a free-market economy, the government would wield indirect macroeconomic influence over the economy through fiscal and monetary policies designed to counteract economic downturns and capitalism's tendency toward financial crises and unemployment, along with playing a role in interventions that promote social welfare.

There are also disadvantages of a mixed economy. Sometimes, government regulation requirements may cost a company so much that it puts it out of business. In addition, unsuccessful regulations may paralyze features of production. This, in return, can cause the economic balance to shift. Another negative is that the government decides the amount of tax on products, which leads to people complaining about high taxes and their unwillingness to pay them. Moreover, lack of price control management can cause shortages in goods and can result in a recession.

Changing Economic Systems: From Socialism to Capitalism

The current economic systems as we experience them today have been strongly influenced by a decline of communism, a development that started in Eastern Europe.

Fall of Communism in Eastern Europe[20]

On November 9, 1989, thousands of jubilant Germans brought down the most visible symbol of division at the heart of Europe—the Berlin Wall (Figure 2.2). For two generations, the Wall was the physical representation of the Iron Curtain, and East German border guards had standing shoot-to-kill orders against those who tried to escape. But just as the Wall had come to represent the division of Europe, its fall came to represent the end of the Cold War and of communism in several parts of the world. Not even the most optimistic observer of President Ronald Reagan's 1987 Berlin speech calling on Soviet General Secretary, Mikhail Gorbachev, to "tear down this wall" would have imagined that two years later the communist regimes of Eastern Europe would collapse like dominoes. By 1990, the former communist leaders were out of power, free elections were held, and Germany was whole again.

FIGURE 2.2
Parts of the Former Wall in Berlin
Source: © Authors

However, the fall of communism did not start in Germany but was pre-shadowed by a variety of historical events in Eastern Europe. While Soviet troops encountered strong resistance already in East Berlin in June 1953, again in Hungary in 1965, followed by riots in Czechoslovakia in 1968, the 1980s were a period of strong rhetoric emphasizing new leadership in the Soviet Union. Especially, Mikhail Gorbachev's policies of perestroika (restructuring) and glasnost (transparency) further legitimized popular calls for reform from within (Box 2.2). On February 6, 1989, negotiations between the Polish Government and members of the underground labor union, Solidarity, opened officially in Warsaw. The results of the "Round Table Talks," signed by government and Solidarity representatives on April 4, included free elections for 35 percent of the Parliament, free elections for the newly created Senate, a new office of the President, and the recognition of Solidarity as a political party. By August 24, ten years after Solidarity emerged on the scene, Tadeusz Mazowiecki became the first non-communist Prime Minister in Eastern Europe.

In Hungary, many changes also influenced the political landscape. Free associations were allowed and the country's borders with the West were opened. On June 16, 1989 the country ceremoniously reinterred Imre Nagy, the reformist communist leader of the 1956 Hungarian Revolution. In East Germany, the collapse became evident, forcing the government to allow inhabitants to emigrate. The East German leader Erich Honecker was asked to resign. On November 9, as the world watched on television, the East German Government announced the opening of all East German borders. In a fluid situation, the Berlin Wall came down. Then

---

Box 2.2   Person-in-Focus: Mikhail Gorbachev

Mikhail Gorbachev and the Fall of Communism

Mikhail Gorbachev was born March 2, 1931, in Privolye, Stavropol kray, Russia, U.S.S.R. He was general secretary of the Communist Party of the Soviet Union (CPSU) from 1985 to 1991 and president of the Soviet Union in 1990–91. His efforts to democratize his country's political system and decentralize its economy led to the downfall of communism and the breakup of the Soviet Union in 1991. In part because he ended the Soviet Union's postwar domination of Eastern Europe, Gorbachev was awarded the Nobel Prize for Peace in 1990.

In 1987–88 Gorbachev proceeded to initiate deeper reforms of the Soviet economic and political system. Under his new policy of *glasnost* ("openness"), a major cultural thaw took place: freedoms of expression and of information were significantly expanded; the press and broadcasting were allowed unprecedented candor in their reportage and criticism; and the country's legacy of Stalinist totalitarian rule was eventually completely repudiated by the government. Under Gorbachev's policy of *perestroika* ("restructuring"), the first modest attempts to democratize the Soviet political system were undertaken: multicandidate contests and the secret ballot were introduced in some elections to party and government posts.

The failing Soviet economy, the ability of citizens to criticize, and the new political freedoms all weakened the power of the Soviet Union. Soon, many Eastern bloc countries abandoned Communism and many republics within the Soviet Union demanded independence. With the falling of the Soviet empire, Gorbachev helped establish a new system of government, including the establishment of a president and the end of the Communist Party's monopoly as a political party. Facing pressures from other groups who wanted more democratization, Gorbachev resigned his post as president of the Soviet Union on December 25, 1991, a day before the Soviet Union officially dissolved.

Sources: http://www.britannica.com/EBchecked/topic/238982/Mikhail-Gorbachev; http://history1900s.about.com/od/people/p/gorbachev.htm; http://www.biography.com/people/mikhail-sergeyevich-gorbachev-9315721#synopsis [Accessed 1 February, 2014]

dominoes started falling at a quickened pace. A new, non-communist government took Prague's reins on December 5, and on December 29, Václav Havel, the famed playwright and dissident, was elected President. In Bulgaria, protests lead to the removal of Todor Zhivkov, the long-time leader of the Bulgarian Communist Party, and his replacement with reformist communist, Petar Mladenov. The new government quickly announced free elections in 1990.

By the summer of 1990, all of the former communist regimes of Eastern Europe were replaced by democratically elected governments (Geo Map 2.1 for the countries in Europe). In Poland, Hungary, East Germany, and Czechoslovakia, newly formed center-right parties took power for the first time since the end of World War II. In Bulgaria and Romania, reformed communists retained control of the governments, but new center-right parties entered parliaments and became active on the political scene. The course was set for the reintegration of Eastern Europe into Western economic, political, and security frameworks.

GEO MAP 2.1
Map of Europe
Source: Adapted from: CIA Maps, The World Factbook[21]

For many companies, the new Eastern countries seemed to be the *eldorado* for Western firms. But actually, countries are still in the process of catching up with GDP/capital still below that of Western countries in Europe.

Catch-Up Policies of Eastern Countries

Many companies consider Eastern Europe as an important target market. But the markets in Central and Eastern Europe do not only offer opportunities, they also entail risks that the international economic crisis has further intensified. There is further imbalance between the individual countries. For instance, Poland, Slovakia, Latvia, and Lithuania have boosted their per capita gross domestic product by 40 percent, while Estonia is next with a 30 percent gain. However, even with those gains, living standards are only half of Western European levels. In Romania and Bulgaria, which were admitted to the EU in 2007, the situation is worse. These poorest EU states lag far behind. Others, like Bosnia and Herzegovina, or Moldova are far beyond the European average.

Differences are still evident when you travel through individual countries or consider the choice of companies' headquarters in individual countries. For instance, Vienna in Austria has become the Eastern European hub for many multinational companies that target their international marketing strategies at the surrounding countries. A precise evaluation of Europe's development gap can be found by looking at the Catch Up Index,[22] which looks at four different kinds of indicators: economy, democracy, governance, and quality of life. Each of these categories aggregates a basket of measurements that includes everything from GDP per capita (for economy) and Transparency International's Corruption Perception Index (for governance) to the Gini coefficient measuring inequality (for quality of life) and the Press Freedom Index from Reporters without Borders (for democracy).

The latest Catch Up Index, published in January, 2014, has no overall surprises. Scandinavia remains on top, and the Balkans are still on the bottom. But some of the details are important. The economic crisis, for instance, is bringing about a minor convergence between rising Eastern European countries (Poland, Czech Republic) and falling Western European countries (Ireland, Spain, Italy). Also, the Czech Republic and Slovakia as well as Estonia have gained ground and now rank in the middle. As a consequence, rankings may influence companies' location choices as well as their selection of target markets. While forecasts pertain to up to 60 years for Eastern countries to catch up,[23] countries on other continents, especially Asia and Africa, are yet in different stages of their development.

Transition Countries in Asia[24]

In Asia, several countries can be characterized as first-tier or second-tier newly industrialized countries (NIEs). Among the first-tier NIEs (newly industrialized economies)—the Republic of Korea, Taiwan Province of China, Singapore and Hong Kong (China Special Administrative Region)—in East Asia, the Republic of Korea's interventionist policies in the 1960s and 1970s relied heavily on close interaction between state and business leader, and very large diversified corporate conglomerates, so-called *chaebols*. This closely resembled the Japanese situation with *keiretsu* business groups. A *keiretsu* is a set of companies with interlocking business relationships and shareholdings. In contrast, the state–business relationship in Taiwan Province of China, particularly in its formative years, was more distant and fragmented, largely due to strained relations between the transplanted political structures (bureaucracy and military) from the mainland and the indigenous business elites. As a result, large state-owned enterprises (SOEs) in some key sectors coexisted with smaller firms elsewhere.

The second-tier NIEs in Southeast Asia (Indonesia, Malaysia, and Thailand) have been faced with typically complex class structures, and they have tended to rely on the continuing importance of resource production. Their natural resource wealth has given rise to agro-based leading sectors in their economies. In comparison with Japan and the Republic of Korea, they have initiated their development with a far more modest role for the state. It is pointed out that the second-tier NIEs have generally adopted a much less demanding policy regime (i.e. less interventionist industrial policy), and concentrated on more conservative macroeconomic management. In comparison with Japan and the Republic of Korea, they have also pursued more liberal trade and FDI policies.

In China, the role of the State in industrialization has been historically larger than in Japan and the first-tier NIEs. In the years following the communist revolution in 1949, all industrial firms were brought under public ownership. Initially, economic policy followed the example of the Soviet Union. National Five-Year Plans were introduced, with the physical production goals for all industrial sectors being predetermined and laid down. As in many economies in East Asia, China succeeded in high levels of savings, but unlike others, all investment in China was done via the public sector. The choice of heavy industrial sectors and the role of the state were linked. In December 1978, China announced a policy shift, which involved some economic liberalization. It started with a liberalization of the agricultural sector (including the abolition of the commune system), which led to an explosive growth in agricultural production. More far-reaching were the creation of special economic zones (SEZs) and the identification of some areas that have been granted special priority for FDI. When the SEZs were established in 1979 there were strong controls by the State, but since the mid-1980s some policies of market reforms have been progressively introduced, which included more autonomy for firms, and a greater openness to foreign trade.

MARKET DEVELOPMENT AND GLOBAL GEOGRAPHICS

All countries tend to go through roughly the same pattern when transforming from a poor economy to a rich one. The countries of Western Europe, Canada, and the United States followed this pattern when they transformed their poor economies

Income	Cutoff Income	Region Average Income	Country Examples	BRIC Countries	TABLE 2.7 Gross National Income Per Capita, 2013, US$
High Income	$12,746 or more	Euro area 38,336	e.g. South Korea, G8 countries: (Japan, US, Germany, France, Britain, Canada, Italy, Russia), Australia, Singapore	Russia	
Upper Middle Income	$4,126 to $12,745	Latin America & Caribbean 9,536	Colombia, Mexico, Panama, Turkey, South Africa	China, Brazil	
Lower Middle Income	$1,046 to $4,125	Sub-Saharan Africa 1,615	Indonesia, Philippines, Egypt, Ukraine	India	
Low Income	$1,045 or less		Afghanistan, Bangladesh, Guinea, Mali, Zimbabwe		

Source: World Bank. (2014), http://databank.worldbank.org/data/download/GNIPC.pdf [Accessed: July, 2014]

into rich ones during the nineteenth and twentieth centuries. Many of the previously impoverished markets in Asia, including Taiwan and South Korea, would later follow this pattern to become equally wealthy as the nations of Europe. Typically, several stages are distinguished by different criteria. One of the most pertinent classifications is the one by the World Bank that uses gross national income (GNI) per capita as a criterion (Table 2.7).[25] It is argued that the impoverished country moves up from one stage to the next just like a person climbing up the rungs of a ladder, gradually achieving more and more prosperity.

- **A high-income economy** is typically an advanced, developed, and industrialized country with a GNI per capita above 12,746 US$. Here, most parts of society live in prosperity and persons living in this society are offered both abundance and a multiplicity of choices. Countries have a high command of infrastructure and knowledge-based business with a dominant service sector. Apart from most Central European Countries, the US, and Japan, some of the Eastern European countries, like the Czech Republic and the Slovak Republic and Croatia belong to this group. Also, South Korea features prominently within the high income country group. In a region of fast growth, since the 1960s the country has increased its per capita GNI more quickly than any of its neighbors. In 2009, the electronics company, Samsung, ranked 19th on Interbrand's Best Global Brands list. Samsung's rise in ranking over the last decade was the fastest among any of the top 100 brands. It has even surpassed rival Sony, which now ranks 29th. Hyundai Motor Company and LG Electronics are making similar dramatic progress.

- An **upper-middle income economy** is an industrializing or developing country with a GNI per capita ranging from 4,126–12,745 US$. There is a strong move towards the industrial sector and population movement towards the urban areas.

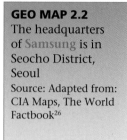

GEO MAP 2.2
The headquarters of Samsung is in Seocho District, Seoul
Source: Adapted from: CIA Maps, The World Factbook[26]

Countries that belong to this group are rapidly accelerating their economy, have rising wages, highly developed public sector institutions with a particular focus on education and rising literacy. For instance, in 2014, the economy of Malaysia was the third largest economy in South East Asia behind more populous Indonesia and Thailand, and the 29th largest economy in the world. It is considered a newly industrializing country. Malaysia today is a middle-income country with a multi-sector economy based on services and manufacturing. Malaysia is one of the world's largest exporters of semiconductor components and devices, electrical goods, solar panels, and information and communication technology (ICT) products.[27]

- **Lower-middle income economies** are those with a GNI per capita between 1,046 and 4,125 US$. These countries mainly benefit from low labor costs and an attractive infrastructure for Western companies which often makes them an interesting place for outsourcing or subsidiary locations focusing on standardized labor, e.g. textiles, manufacturing. However, these countries very often do not have stable infrastructures or institutions and investment may be impeded by political developments. For instance, Ukraine received a pre-crisis annual average foreign direct investment of almost $8 billion a year, according to United Nations body UNCTAD. But this more than halved last year to $3.7 billion and has almost certainly evaporated further in 2014 as the standoff with Russia has intensified.

- **Low income economies** have a GNI per capita below 1,045 US$. In these countries, very often, basic supply in terms of food, health care, infrastructure, education, etc. is missing. Even the most optimistic analyses accept that many low-income countries (LICs) will remain low income for some time to come. Consequently, when assessing the policy options available to LICs, it is important to take a long-term view. Key limitations to overcome are the infrastructure deficit, public debt, the role of the government, the size of the state, and taxation.[28] For many companies, marketing their products to these target markets poses a particular challenge as traditional marketing instruments cannot be applied but need to be adjusted to consumers (see again Chapter 1).

Developing Countries as Important Target Markets

Today, emerging markets figure high in prominence when companies discuss their expansion strategies. However, both definitions and challenges of emerging markets differ hugely. A common reference is made to the so-called BRIC-countries (Brazil, Russia, India, and China). These four countries are supposed to be key players in the future, albeit with different speed and power on the world market (Table 2.7). A more general definition of emerging markets is the one provided by the International Finance Corporation (IFC) in 1981, which was initially used to describe stock markets in developing countries that are considered either low- or middle-income as defined by the World Bank, or that have low investable market capitalization relative to GDP (IFC, 1999). Today, emerging markets have come to represent entire countries rather than stock markets and, in particular, those countries that hold the promise of high rates of economic growth.

Emerging market countries are also interesting to marketeers because of their sheer population number and growth. Population demographics in general are changing. As the twenty-first century began, the world population included approximately 600 million persons over 60 years of age—triple the number recorded 50 years earlier. By mid-century, there will be some two billion older persons—once again, a tripling of this age group in a span of 50 years. Population aging is profound, having major consequences and implications for all facets of human life. According to United Nations estimates, nearly one-third of Japan's population, one-quarter of the European Union's population, and one-fifth of the United States population will be over 60 years old by 2015.[29] In the economic area, population aging will have an impact on economic growth, savings, investment and consumption, labor markets, pensions, taxation, and intergenerational transfers. Note that the relatively younger population of Asia means that these nations should have abundant labor necessary to sustain the high levels of growth recently attained (Figure 2.3). Western European countries and the United States will have to maintain immigration from Third World countries to provide the workforce needed to

FIGURE 2.3
Aging Population
Source: Adapted
from: 'Asia's Role
in the World
Economy', *Finance and
Development IMF.* June
2006, 43(2)

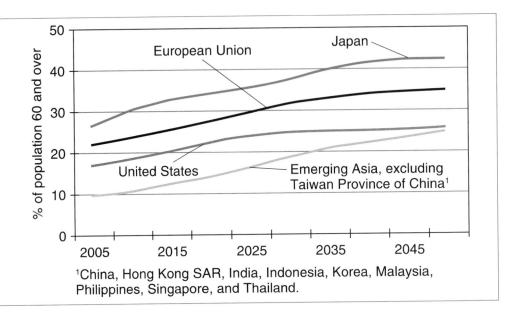

¹China, Hong Kong SAR, India, Indonesia, Korea, Malaysia,
Philippines, Singapore, and Thailand.

sustain economic growth. In the social sphere, population aging affects health and healthcare, family composition and living arrangements, housing, and migration.

The world population stands at about 6 billion. Of importance to global marketing is the estimate that nearly a billion new consumers will enter the marketplace in the next decade. By 2025, more than half of the world's population will have joined the consuming classes, driving annual consumption in emerging markets to $30 trillion.[30] This is most likely the case for transition countries with huge growth rates.

In the next sections, we follow the PESTEL analysis and add insights on technological and ecological factors.

HIGH-TECH PRODUCTS LEAD WORLD TRADE

High-tech products are produced by research-intensive industries using the most advanced technology available. In the past, high-tech products were mainly driven by advanced economies but increasingly, emerging market giants are entering the global competition (see below). High-tech products include aerospace, pharmaceuticals, computers, electronics, and communications equipment. In most economies, the high-tech manufacturing sector has shown the fastest growth. The global market for high-tech products has grown twice as fast as that for other manufactured goods. Nearly 65 percent of revenues for the leading United States high-technology companies are generated from sales outside United States borders.

The rapid rate of *globalization* is made possible by the development and expansion of the Internet economy, which in turn is fueled by the unprecedented growth of high-tech electronics manufacturing. In just one human generation, the high-tech revolution has spread out from its birthplace in Silicon Valley, California, to encompass vast sections of the globe. Scotland, Ireland, Israel, and Taiwan are important producers of high-tech products, most of which are exported. After the United States, which country is currently registering the largest number of new high-tech companies? Great Britain? France? Japan? Germany? Wrong! It is Israel—and that's in terms of actual numbers, not as a proportion of the country's population. Although only half the size of Switzerland, Israel boasts over 3,000 high-tech companies, four-fifths of which are less than ten years old.

Increased uses of technology will affect the way people interact with one another. Both global and domestic businesses are increasing their use of IT applications for knowledge generation and communication, and for producing and marketing finished products or services. Advanced technology and statistical control devices enable management to utilize sophisticated software programs to run their organizations. New developments in fields, such as, nanotechnology and biotechnology are being harnessed by business. Some of the industries that are most likely to be affected by nanotechnology are electronics (Kodak EasyShare providing brighter and less-energy-consuming displays), fashion (Maui Jim sunglasses having better anti-reflection capabilities) and cosmetics (L'Oréal having better skin moisturizing properties). As a result of significant public and private investments in nanotechnology during the past decade and an expanding array of commercial applications, the field of nanotechnology has matured to the point of showing significant potential to help societies achieve the shared goal of improving efficiencies and accelerating progress in a range of economic sectors, including medicine, manufacturing, and energy.[31]

Biotechnology has led to a wide field of industrial applications, ranging from health care, pharmacological products, and cosmetic materials to marine applications and medical imaging diagnostics. Despite the Great Recession over the last five years, California remains the national leader with more than 2,300 biomedical companies and nearly 153,000 workers in 2011.[32] However, more and more pharmaceutical companies are offshoring their research to China, India, and Eastern Europe. Within the next decade, Asia is expected to overtake Europe in pharmaceutical sales, driven by growth in key emerging markets. For example, China is predicted to be the second largest pharmaceutical market after the United States by 2015. Such observations help to explain why many large pharmaceutical companies have increased their presence in emerging markets in recent years—in particular in China, but also in other countries including India, Brazil, Russia, Korea, and Mexico. Notably, this growing presence is increasingly moving beyond the use of contract research organizations and marketing of established products to include early-stage research aimed at specific medical needs of patients in these regions.[33]

Many high-tech products are manufactured from components made in several countries. For example, a typical computer now contains components manufactured and assembled all over the world—semiconductor chips made in New Mexico, Scotland, or Malaysia; a disk drive made in Singapore or Thailand; a CRT (cathode ray tube) monitor made in Japan; circuit boards made in China and assembled in Mexico or Costa Rica. Emerging markets are indeed redrawing the map of global trade in high-tech goods with several countries in Asia vaulting up

TABLE 2.8
High-Tech Exports Globally
Source: Adapted from: HSBC

Rank	Country	2000	Country	2013	Country	2030
1	USA	29.9	China	36.5	China	51.1
2	Japan	7.0	HK	13.0	HK	10.1
3	Germany	6.7	USA	9.6	USA	6.6
4	UK	6.6	Singapore	6.8	Korea	5.7
5	HK	6.5	Japan	6.6	Mexico	4.5
6	China	6.5	Korea	6.1	Singapore	4.5
7	Singapore	5.9	Mexico	5.7	Japan	4.0
8	Canada	5.2	Germany	4.4	Malaysia	3.7
9	Mexico	5.1	Malaysia	3.3	Germany	2.3
10	Malaysia	4.6	France	1.5	Vietnam	1.8
11	Korea	4.3	UK	1.3	Poland	0.9
12	France	4.0	Vietnam	1.1	France	0.8
13	Ireland	1.9	Canada	0.9	Indonesia	0.8
14	Australia	1.4	Poland	0.9	UK	0.8
15	Brazil	1.3	Indonesia	0.6	India	0.8

Source: http://blogs.ft.com/beyond-brics/2014/03/18/china-leads-em-surge-in-high-tech-exports/ [Accessed July 2, 2014]

the global ranking in terms of exports of high-tech products (Table 2.8). China's total share of world exports of high-tech goods increased to 36.5 percent in 2013, from a mere 6.5 percent in 2000. The US, by contrast, saw its share of total high-tech exports fall to 9.6 percent from 29.2 percent in the same period. Also South Korea, Malaysia, and Indonesia figure higher in 2013. Together seven of the countries that classify as emerging markets—China, South Korea, Mexico, Malaysia, Vietnam, Poland, and Indonesia, account for over 53 percent of the world's trade in high-tech products.

How could a developing country be a top exporter of electronics despite having very limited technological capabilities? The basic idea is that electronics components—as intermediate inputs—can be imported for the assembly of final products to serve domestic and foreign markets or for processing in the country to be re-exported. Companies such as General Electric and Intel have large manufacturing plants in the Philippines, while IBM and Siemens have plants in China. Many lower-income countries have high imports of electronics components for the processing of components, or their assembly into final products is based on the employment of lower-wage workers rather than technological capabilities.

Characteristics of High-Technology Markets

What characterizes high-tech markets? High-tech markets are:

(1) Highly dynamic, (2) Complex, (3) Risky

As a result, markets tend to mature rapidly. They are fast moving and expensive, owing to technological advances, intense competition, and demanding consumers.[34] A major difference between high- and low-tech product markets is that the former are production- rather than consumer-oriented. Because these markets are very competitive, manufacturers rush to market, sometimes without proper preparation or consumer research.

In many cases, consumers cannot visualize future demand for high-tech products. Supply determines demand for most consumer products, rather than the other way around. Therefore, high-tech product developers must anticipate consumer needs even before consumers are aware of them. High-tech marketers rely on a product focus, which is driven by technology rather than customer needs. However, there are abundant examples in which high-tech consumer products could not generate sufficient demand. Among the well-known consumer product failures include Sony's Betamax video tape player and Philips's CD-i (compact disk home entertainment system). Steve Jobs, the CEO and co-founder of Apple, was asked what sort of market research the company did before launching the iMac. He answered that little was done because "for something this complicated, it's really hard to design products by focus groups … . people don't know what they want until you show it to them."[35] The disregard for consumer choice was also evident in the failures of the Betamax and CD-i products.

In order to reduce the risk of market failure in the introduction of high-tech products, Rosen, Schroeder, and Purinton (1998)[36] suggest that the following steps be taken:

- Determine whether "first-mover" advantage is necessary, or whether it is best to be as sure as possible that there is sufficient interest in the product.

- Rethink the value of market research before launching the product.

- Target the market carefully, carefully identifying the consumers most likely to purchase the product.

- Exploit the innovators and early adopters.

Another critical issue in high-tech marketing concerns the market entry choices of startup companies in high-technology industries. Global supply chain performance is also critical, especially as manufacturing expands beyond traditional locations into new regions and countries. As high-tech manufacturers are subject to intense customer demands for service and delivery, the fact that component manufacture is performed in several countries, as pointed out earlier, complicates control over the supply chain. Therefore, manufacturers need to effectively manage global trade operations. That is, technology in processes and operations becomes vital.

GLOBAL COUNTRIES AND EMERGING GIANT COMPANIES

Both countries and companies can be typed according to the extent to which they are global. For example, the KOF Globalization Index classifies countries according to the three main dimensions of globalization: economic, social, and political. While there are not many differences between 2013 and 2014, a few interesting facts remain. For instance, The Netherlands, as a small country, is very much dependent on global trade, which is also shown in its openness to foreigners and the bilingual policy with almost everybody speaking English fluently. The UK lost a few ranks probably due to its internal political debates around the European Union. Overall, it is mostly small countries with several national languages or identities that are more open to globalization.

The term global economy expresses the fact that most of the world's nations have become increasingly interconnected. Economies have expanded beyond national borders, and an increasing amount of production is being accounted for by transnational corporations (TNCs). In short, production, finance, marketing, communications, and labor forces have become globalized. The number of transnational corporations in the world has increased from about 8,000 in 1975 to 40,000 in 2005. It is estimated that more than one-third of the world's private assets are owned by TNCs and that one-third of all international trade occurs in intra-TNC transactions. While global in reach, nearly all of these corporations' headquarters are concentrated in industrialized countries. More than half are headquartered in France, Germany, the Netherlands, Japan, and the United States. But despite their growing numbers, their resources are highly concentrated; i.e. the 300 largest corporations account for approximately one-quarter of the world's productive assets (Table 2.9).

Not only are TNCs highly globalized, they possess significant economic power. The economic strength or size of several transnational companies equal that of many developed countries. This can be visualized by comparing transnational corporate sales with the GDP of countries (see again Chapter 1), with Walmart's sales being higher than the GDP of many developed countries such as Norway, Denmark, or Austria.

In the last 20 years, that story—and the multinational map of corporate power—has undergone a fundamental shift: away from established companies in the developed world and toward ambitious upstarts in the developing world. Emerging market economies grew at a remarkable pace from the late 1990s until the onset of the global financial crisis in 2008–09. With some exceptions, activity in emerging market and developing economies rebounded much more strongly in 2009–10 than in advanced economies.

In their book, *"Emerging Markets Rule: Growth Strategies of the New Global Giants,"*[37] Wharton management professor Mauro Guillen and co-author Esteban Garcia-Canal shine light on the importance of the giants coming from emerging markets. When Forbes first published its Global 2000 list in 2003, the United States, Japan, and the United Kingdom dominated. Today, emerging markets have broken that stronghold in a big way. Emerging market multinationals (EMMs) are now at the top of markets as varied as household appliances, ready-mix concrete, seamless tubes for oil drilling, regional jets, meat, bread, and candy (Box 2.3, Alibaba). In 2010, for example, the Chinese battery and electric automaker, BYD, topped

TABLE 2.9 The World's Top 20 Non-Financial TNCs in 2013

Corporation	Home Country	Industry	Assets		Sales		Employment		TNI[a]
			Foreign Assets	Total	Foreign Sales	Total	Foreign Employment[b]	Total	(percent)
General Electric Co	United States	Electrical & electronic	331 160	656 560	74 382	142 937	135 000	307 000	48.8
Royal Dutch Shell plc	United Kingdom	Petroleum	301 898	357 512	275 651	451 235	67 000	92 000	72.8
Toyota Motor Corporation	Japan	Motor vehicles	274 380	403 088	171 231	256 381	137 000	333 498	58.6
Exxon Mobil Corporation	United States	Petroleum	231 033	346 808	237 438	390 247	45 216	75 000	62.6
Total SA	France	Petroleum	226 717	238 870	175 703	227 901	65 602	98 799	79.5
BP plc	United Kingdom	Petroleum	202 899	305 690	250 372	379 136	64 300	83 900	69.7
Vodafone Group plc	United Kingdom	Telecommunications	182 837	202 763	59 059	69 276	83 422	91 272	88.9
Volkswagen Group	Germany	Motor vehicles	176 656	446 555	211 488	261 560	317 800	572 800	58.6
Chevron Corporation	United States	Petroleum	175 736	253 753	122 982	211 664	32 600	64 600	59.3
Eni SpA	Italy	Petroleum	141 021	190 125	109 886	152 313	56 509	83 887	71.2
Enel SpA	Italy	Electricity, gas and water	140 396	226 006	61 867	106 924	37 125	71 394	57.3
Glencore Xstrata PLC	Switzerland	Mining & quarrying	135 080	154 932	153 912	232 694	180 527	190 000	82.8
Anheuser-Busch InBev NV	Belgium	Food, beverages and tabacco	134 549	141 666	39 414	43 195	144 887	154 587	93.3
EDF SA	France	Utilities (Electricity, gas and water)	130 161	353 574	46 979	100 364	28 975	158 467	34.0
Nestlé SA	Switzerland	Food, beverages and tabacco	124 730	129 969	98 034	99 669	322 996	333 000	97.1
E.ON AG	Germany	Utilities (Electricity, gas and water)	124 429	179 988	115 072	162 573	49 809	62 239	73.3
GDF Suez	France	Utilities (Electricity, gas and water)	121 402	219 759	72 133	118 561	73 000	147 199	55.2
Deutsche Telekom AG	Germany	Telecommunications	120 350	162 671	50 049	79 835	111 953	228 596	61.9
Apple Computer Inc	United States	Electrical & electronic	119 918	207 000	104 713	170 910	50 322	84 400	59.6
Honda Motor Co Ltd	Japan	Motor vehicles	118 476	151 965	96 055	118 176	120 985	190 338	74.3

[a]TNI, the Transnationality Index, is calculated as the average of the following three ratios: foreign assets to total assets, foreign sales to total sales and foreign employment to total employment.

[b]Employment data refers to revised 2012 figures, as data were not yet available.

Source: Adapted from: UNCTAD. (2014), http://webcache.googleusercontent.com/search?q=cache:b7QrRi5ULRoJ:unctad.org/Sections/dite_dir/docs/WIR2015/WIR14_tab28. xls+&cd=1&hl=de&ct=clnk&gl=de [Accessed: August 10, 2014]

Box 2.3 Company-in-Focus: Alibaba

A Tremendous Success of an Emerging Market Firm

Alibaba is China's—and by some measures, the world's—biggest online commerce company. Its three main sites—Taobao, Tmall, and Alibaba.com—have hundreds of millions of users, and host millions of merchants and businesses. Alibaba handles more business than any other e-commerce company.

The group began in 1999 when Jack Ma founded the website Alibaba.com, a business-to-business portal to connect Chinese manufacturers with overseas buyers. In 2012, two of Alibaba's portals handled 1.1 trillion yuan ($170 billion) in sales. The company primarily operates in the People's Republic of China (PRC), and at closing time, on the date of its historic initial public offering (IPO), 19 September 2014, Alibaba's market value was measured as US$231 billion.

Alibaba's consumer-to-consumer portal, Taobao, similar to eBay.com, features nearly a billion products and is one of the 20 most-visited websites globally. The Group's websites accounted for over 60 percent of the parcels delivered in China by March 2013, and 80 percent of the nation's online sales by September 2014. Alipay, an online payment escrow service, accounts for roughly half of all online payment transactions within China.

Sources: www.alibaba.com; 'E-commerce in China: The Alibaba phenomenon', *The Economist,* March 23, 2013, http://www.economist.com/news/leaders/21573981-chinas-e-commerce-giant-could-generate-enormous-wealthprovided-countrys-rulers-leave-it; Baker, L.B., Toonkel, J., and Vlastelica, R. (2014), 'Alibaba surges 38 percent on massive demand in market debut.' *Reuters,* September 19, 2014, http://www.reuters.com/article/2014/09/19/us-alibaba-ipo-idUSKBN0HD2CO20140919 [All Accessed: October 10, 2014].

GEO MAP 2.3
The headquarters of BYD are in Shenzhen, China
Source: Adapted from: CIA Maps, The World Factbook[38]

Bloomberg Businessweek's Tech 100 list. BYD is located in Shenzhen, Guangdong Province, China (Geo Map 2.3).

American businessman, Warren Buffett, was so impressed that he took a 10 percent stake in the company. Yet a March 2012 search of the previous year turned up only one mention in The New York Times, while the 98th-ranked firm, California-based VMWare, showed 1,100 results for the same period.[39]

Based on their 20-year study of EMMs, Guillen and Garcia-Canal have distilled an important "axiom" that for them defines the twenty-first century way of global business: *"Execute, Strategize, Then Execute Again."* These simple words imply one of the book's central themes: that execution is of primary importance and that the best strategy emerges organically from practical experience on the ground. Among old-guard companies, the authors argue, strategizing has become both a ritual and a crutch. Not only do managers "agonize" over formulating the perfect strategy; once they think they've found it, they become infatuated with it, clinging to it even in the face of rapidly changing circumstances. By contrast, EMMs are quick to formalize and re-orient their strategy as markets demand. In addition, these firms are not only first movers in nascent domestic sectors, but are also latecomers to globally mature industries that are dominated by world-class competitors. In learning from them and accelerating capability building, EMMs, combine their traditional advantages, e.g. vision, risk tolerance, flexibility, and speed, with the more "Western" capabilities, such as, brand building and quality improvement.

THE GREEN ECONOMY

The green economy is an economy that results in reducing environmental risks and ecological scarcities, and that aims for sustainable development without degrading the environment.[40] The green economy seeks to optimize the synergy among three sets of values: social (people), environmental (planet), and financial (profit). This is most often referred to as the "triple P" or "triple bottom line." By definition, the green economy is:

- Environmentally sustainable, based on the belief that our biosphere is a closed system with finite resources and a limited capacity for self-regulation and self-renewal. We depend on the earth's natural resources, and therefore we should create an economic system that respects the integrity of ecosystems and ensures the resilience of a life-supporting system.

- Socially just, based on the belief that culture and human dignity are precious resources that, like our natural resources, require responsible stewardship to avoid their depletion. We should create a vibrant economic system that ensures all people have access to a decent standard of living and full opportunities for personal and social development.

- Locally rooted, based on the belief that an authentic connection to place is the essential precondition to sustainability and justice. The green economy is a global aggregate of individual communities meeting the needs of its citizens through the responsible local production and exchange of goods and services.

Increasing energy and commodity costs and consumer demands for a more sustainable environment have led to a push for a green economy in industries such as energy and utilities, construction, transportation, and manufacturing. Understanding the green economy and the opportunities it provides worldwide is of critical importance to global marketers. Part of the green economy entails the adoption of "clean technologies." There is no standard definition of clean technology, but it is believed to comprise products, services, and processes that use renewable materials while conserving natural resources. Representative clean tech industries include wind power, solar energy, hydropower, and biofuels. Today, South Korea and China are the major investors in clean technology, followed by the United States.

Especially, China is a forerunner in developing renewable energy technologies, greening industry, and promoting the environmental goods and services sector. This is partly due to the fact that China has had huge environmental costs. It is the world's largest producer of greenhouse gas (GHG) emissions, more than 90 percent of its urban water bodies are thought to be polluted and outdoor air pollution is estimated to contribute to over a million premature deaths per year in China. The investment into clean technologies is creating jobs, economic growth, and improved well-being for citizens.

In the last decade, China has witnessed growth in a wide range of sectors that have contributed to a green economy transition—from wind, solar and other renewable energies, to the environmental industry. China sees an opportunity to firmly anchor the environmental dimensions of sustainable development into the social and economic agenda of the country, and pave the way for further in-depth assessment to illustrate how a transition towards an inclusive green economy can accelerate the attainment of national development goals. China pursues several objectives towards becoming a green economy: It already has the world's largest installed capacity of wind farms. It is the world's leading manufacturer of solar photovoltaic modules, and it produces more hydroelectricity than any other country. In 2012, renewable energy investment in China stood at US$67.7 billion, the highest in the world, and double the level of investments in 2009. Following the onset of the global financial crisis, the Chinese government launched a large-scale investment programme to avert an economic slowdown. An estimated 5 percent of the stimulus, or RMB 210 billion, was directly spent on the environmental industry. China also plans to produce 15 percent of its energy from non-fossil fuel sources by 2020.[41]

The Green Economy Market Size

How large is the green economy? Since the mid-1990s, the scope of the market for green goods and services has broadened to embrace the economy as a whole, and its growth rate has progressively converged with that of global GDP. Growth rates for the global market for green goods and services is expected to more than double from €1,400 billion in 2007 to €3,100 billion in 2020.[42] The fastest-growing sectors will be the new markets in eco-technologies such as renewable energies, energy efficiency, and clean technologies. More mature segments such as water and waste management, along with air and ground pollution abatement are expected to grow more slowly, yet even these sectors will continue to grow.[43]

According to the market research company, IRI,[44] consumers are increasingly embracing natural and organic products, and often they are as concerned about

FIGURE 2.4
Green and Healthy Products
Source: © Authors

what is not in the products they buy, especially food, as much as what is in it. Today, there is even a tendency to market **products that lower cholesterol** naturally, that are exceptionally nutritious, packed with protein and phytochemicals, and will boost your immune system and give you energy all while tackling your cholesterol and triglycerides (Figure 2.4).

To help companies, they came up with a new and unique segmentation of the total US population, which focuses on how shoppers think about, purchase and use natural/organic/eco-friendly products. Two shopper segments, "True Believers" and "Enlightened Environmentalists," offer outsized opportunities for manufacturers and retailers. Each group represents 9 percent of the US population, but together account for 46 percent of all natural/organic product sales.

- **True Believers**—These shoppers are passionate about staying fit and healthy. They are focused on trying new things, serving as strong role models for their children, and are strong believers in the benefits of natural/organic products. True Believers enjoy a median income of $65,000, have an average age of 40, attended college and, in some cases, embarked on post-graduate studies.

- **Enlightened Environmentalists**—This segment is passionate about the environment and making good choices to support it. These shoppers are making a real effort to make healthier choices and will go out of their way to shop at stores that carry natural/organic products. Enlightened Environmentalists are older than True Believers, averaging 63 years old, attended graduate school, and have a median income of $57,000.

The following five segments comprise the remaining 54 percent of sales. A brief description of each is below:

- **Strapped Seekers**—This group likes to try new things and live a healthy lifestyle, but knows they should make healthier choices than they do. With a median income of $45,000 and median age of 45, these shoppers represent all levels of education.

- **Healthy Realists**—Being healthy and fit and making exercise a priority is important to these shoppers. They are often the first among their friends to try something new, but can have difficulty deciding whether to buy healthy or traditional products. Their average age is 39, they have attended college, and earn a median income of $65,000.

- **Indifferent Traditionalists**—Leading a simple life with few passions, they may try healthy products but do not consider themselves on the leading edge of change. With a median income of $46,000 that skews under $25,000, these shoppers are aged 65 on average and have a high school education.

- **Struggling Switchers**—These shoppers are focused on staying within their budgets, have suffered during the last recession, but know they should be eating healthier and getting more exercise. With a median income of $56,000, they are aged 39 on average and attended all levels of school.

- **Resistant Non-Believers**—With very little desire to explore other options for things to buy, Resistant Non-Believers stay loyal to the products they know. They have completed high school, have an average age of 52, and a median income of $48,000.

People are realizing that their current behavior in the marketplace has consequences for the future generation. Some research suggests that sophisticated media reports of environmental issues have helped people realize that their personal consumption affects production around the globe.[45] People are interested in what companies are doing to help the environment and how their business operations impact the environment.

Because of the relatively higher costs to develop green products, it is essential to see how consumers behave, especially in their attitudes towards green and environmentally-friendly products. From a more academic side, there are several segmentation approaches. For instance, Straughan and Roberts (1999) provided an early classification by segmenting college students based on ecologically conscious consumer behavior and stated that younger individuals were likely to be more sensitive to environmental issues.[46] The results of their study indicated that the demographic variables such as age and sex were significantly correlated with ecologically conscious consumer behavior when considered individually, and that income lacks significance. **Green purchase intention correlates positively with age and income except for education.**[47]

Some consumers are ready to focus on the intrinsic value of goods and services, rather than simply the materialistic or egocentric value. Making each purchase count is especially important in an economy where consumers must think twice about how they spend their money. Choice justification comes into play when the purchase of green products pull at individuals' sense of responsibility and people are intrinsically motivated to reduce cognitive conflict or dissonance.[48]

Research by Hjelmar[49] showed a growing trend in the type of consumer behavior in which price and convenience take a back seat to giving more importance to personal and societal concerns, specifically in the purchase of organic food products. This consumer behavior can be motivated by life events that cause consumers to react emotionally. Life events can range from having children to viewing unsettling world events presented in the mass media. To avoid cognitive dissonance, consumers must process the life events or new information in a way to find consistency between emotional impulses and rational beliefs and align their consumer behavior accordingly. Thus, consumer image and cognitive dissonance can play into the success of marketing green products. Other researchers uncover socially oriented motives as a powerful impetus behind green purchases.[50] Being environmentally conscious can generate a prosocial reputation. Having the reputation of caring about the environment can be helpful in a person's social sphere because environmentally conscious people are seen as trustworthy and loyal. Green marketing messages that appeal to a person's reputation or status are effective. Status motives lead people to buy green products rather than self-serving products.[51] The environmentally conscious segment can be an aspirational group that people aspire to join. This group is seen as exhibiting collectivism rather than individualism.

However, while more and more firms experience the desire of consumers to be environmentally friendly, many firms have not experienced the expected financial gains. The reason why consumers fail to live in a way that is congruent with their values may be attributed to two reasons:[52] First, the consumer may not feel enough social pressure to buy green. Second, given the vast scope of the problem, many individuals do not believe that one person can have a tangible effect. Apart from these more generic aspects, green products are also quite often perceived to be of lower quality, which stems from inferior performance associated with products from the 1980s and 1990s. Other reasons include lack of awareness, lack of ecological knowledge, as well as inauthentic messages from companies, high prices, and low availability.[53] In order to solve these issues, several managerial activities and public policy implications have been suggested[54] (Table 2.10).

TABLE 2.10	**Activities**	**Explanation**
Managerial Guidelines and Policy Implications for Improving the Profitability of Green Products	Overcome apathy, convenience, and price elasticity.	Emphasize the positive aspects of green consumerism.
	Provide more information.	Consumers need to be educated about the firm's green offerings. Also authenticity is very important.
	Distinguish the benefit of product types.	A company should position the product as more than *just* green; that is the additional benefit should be mentioned.
	Balance price and quality.	Green products need to perform at least as good as other products if not better. Determining the price elasticity is paramount.
	Public policy implications.	Consumers find it difficult to be green. Therefore, incentives should be given to pursue a green lifestyle.

Source: Adapted from: Gabler, C.B., Butler, T.D., and Adams, F.G. (2013), 'The environmental belief-behavior gap: Exploring barriers to green consumerism', *Journal of Customer Behavior*, 12(2/3), pp. 159–176

SUMMARY

- The PESTEL model is a useful framework for scanning the macro-global environment. A PESTEL analysis measures market potential, particularly indicating growth or decline, and market attractiveness, business potential, and whether market access should be attempted.

- Global trade has outpaced economic growth in most industrialized and emerging countries. China is the leading exporter of merchandise, followed by the US and Germany. In services, however, China only ranks fifth in the list which is headed by the US.

- Eastern Europe has become an important trade region, but differences are still huge between individual countries. Catching up with the average GDP/capita in Europe will still take several years.

- Technological exports and imports dominate world trade, especially among developed countries. The global market for high-technology goods is growing at a faster rate than that for other manufactured goods, and high-technology industries are driving economic growth around the world.

- Emerging market multinationals (EMMs) have increasingly entered global rankings like the Fortune 500. They utilize different strategies than companies from advanced economies because of their need of catching up in terms of branding and technology.

- There is a large potential for employment and income creation in the green economy. Examples of green economy employment throughout the world include China, where 600,000 people are already employed in solar thermal making and installing products such as solar water heaters; Nigeria, where a biofuel industry based on cassava and sugar cane crops might employ 200,000 people; and India, which could generate 900,000 jobs in biomass gasification by 2025, of which 300,000 would be in the manufacturing of stoves and 600,000 in areas such as processing briquettes and pellets for the fuel supply chain. These figures show that the global market potential for green and clean tech products and services could become one of the fastest-growing economic sectors.

DISCUSSION QUESTIONS

1. Can a nation have a favorable balance of trade and an unfavorable balance of payments?
2. How do you consider the risks of investing in a low income country?
3. What are the different challenges to design your marketing strategy for a high income and a lower-middle income country?
4. It is argued that high-tech products will dominate trade in the twenty-first century. Does this mean emerging market countries will be left out of this development?
5. Does the Green Economy pose more challenges or more threats to a global marketer?

EXPERIENTIAL EXERCISES

1. Select any country you wish (except your own) and apply the PESTEL model for any analysis of the environment for solar water heaters.
2. Go to the Internet and look up on Newsweek's website the "10 best countries to live in." Does this index have any relevance for global marketing? (Hint: Look at how the scores are calculated.)

KEY TERMS

- Diamond model of national competitiveness
- Economic systems
- Emerging market multinationals
- Balance of payment
- Balance of Trade
- European Union
- Fall of Communism
- Global Happiness Index
- Green Economy
- Gross National Income
- High Tech Products
- PESTEL
- Regional trade
- TNCs

VIDEO MATERIAL

Balance of Payments versus Balance of Trade (Video and Quiz) http://www.econedlink.org/interactives/index.php?iid=222&type=student

NOTES

1 Economic Outlook Tunisia. Market Research.com, http://www.marketresearch.com/Business-Monitor-International-v304/Tunisia-Business-Forecast-Q1-8538200/ [Accessed: January 30, 2015].

2 Porter, M. (1980). *Competitive strategy: Techniques for analyzing industries and competitors*. New York: The Free Press.

3 McGee, J. (1985). Strategic groups: A bridge between industry structure and strategic management? In: Thomas, H. and Gardner, D. (eds.). *Strategic marketing and management*. Chichester: Wiley.

4 Grant, R.M. (2012). *Contemporary strategy analysis. Concepts, techniques, applications*. 8th ed. Chichester: John Wiley.

5 Porter, M.E. (1985). *Competitive strategy: Techniques for analysing industries and competitors*. New York: The Free Press.

6 Riley, J. (2013), 'Abandoned shopping carts: Why did Tesco and Best Buy fail in China?', *WOW Business*. Monday, September 23, 2013. http://www.tutor2u.net/blog/index.php/business-studies/comments/abandoned-shopping-carts-why-did-tesco-and-best-buy-fail-in-china [Accessed: June 15, 2014].

7 International Monetary Fund. (2014), 'Balance of payments manual', https://www.imf.org/external/pubs/cat/longres.aspx?sk=22588.0 [Accessed: March 1, 2014].

8 Examples taken from: *The Concise Encyclopedia of Economics*. (2014), http://www.econlib.org/library/Topics/HighSchool/BalanceofTradeandBalanceofPayments.html [Accessed: July 3, 2014].

9 Heakal, R. (2014), 'What is the balance of payments?', *Investopedia*, http://www.investopedia.com/articles/03/060403.asp [Accessed: July 3, 2014].

10 Cross National Happiness Commission Bhutan. (2015), http://www.gnhc.gov.bt [Accessed: February 10, 2015].

11 The Economist. (2013), 'Bleak chic', December 21, www.economist.com/news/.../21591749-bleak-chic [Accessed: March 3, 2014].

12 World Happiness Ranking: http://en.wikipedia.org/wiki/World_Happiness_Report [Accessed: February 12, 2015].

13 WIN-Gallup poll. (2012): http://www.wingia.com/web/files/news/38/file/38.pdf [Accessed: September 4, 2014].

14 Leamer, E.E. (1995), 'The Heckscher-Ohlin model in theory and practice', *Princeton Studies in International Finance*. Zurich, Switzerland: Gallup International. https://www.princeton.edu/~ies/IES_Studies/S77.pdf [Accessed July 1, 2014].

15 Leamer, E.E. (1980), 'The Leontief paradox reconsidered', *The Journal of Political Economy*, 88(3), pp. 495–503.

16 Kreiner, M.E. (1965), 'Comparative labor effectiveness and the Leontief scarce-factor paradox', *The American Economic Review,* 55(1/2), pp. 131–40.

17 Vernon, R. (1966), 'International investment and international trade in the product cycle', *The Quarterly Journal of Economics*, 80(2), pp. 190–207.

18 Porter, M. (1998), *The competitive advantage of nations*. New York: Free Press.

19 Gemma, W. (2014), 'The 4 types of economic systems explained', https://www.udemy.com/blog/types-of-economic-systems/ [Accessed: January 5, 2015].

20 US Department of State. Office of the Historians. 'Milestones 1989–1992', https://history.state.gov/milestones/1989-1992/fall-of-communism [Accessed: December 12, 2014].

21 The World Factbook. (2015), https://www.cia.gov/library/publications/the-world-factbook/docs/refmaps.html [Accessed: August 1, 2015].

22 The Catch Up Index: http://www.thecatchupindex.eu/TheCatchUpIndex/

23 Dabrowski, M. (2012), 'EU and central and eastern Europe: The catching up process', http://www.eif.oeaw.ac.at/dabrowski/index-en.php [Accessed: September 1, 2014].

24 See for the following: Kasahara, S. (2013), 'The Asian development state and the flying geese paradigm', http://unctad.org/en/PublicationsLibrary/osgdp20133_en.pdf [Accessed: February 12, 2015].

25 The World Bank, 'Country and lending groups', http://data.worldbank.org/about/country-and-lending-groups#High_income [Accessed: October 18, 2015].

26 The World Factbook. (2015), https://www.cia.gov/library/publications/the-world-factbook/docs/refmaps.html [Accessed: August 1, 2015].

27 US Department of State. (2015), 'US relations with Malaysia', http://www.state.gov/r/pa/ei/bgn/2777.htm State.gov. 14 July 2010 [Accessed: October 18, 2015].

28 United Nations University. (2013), 'Growth for low-income countries', http://unu.edu/publications/articles/growth-for-low-income-countries.html [Accessed: June 1, 2014].

29 United Nations. (2015), 'World population prospects', http://esa.un.org/unpd/wpp/Publications/Files/Key_Findings_WPP_2015.pdf [Accessed: October 1, 2015].

30 McKinsey. (2013), 'Winning the $30 trillion decathlon', http://www.mckinsey.com/features/30_trillion_decathlon [Accessed: June 1, 2014].

31 OECD. (2012), 'Washing symposium 2012', http://www.oecd.org/sti/nano/Washington%20Symposium%20Report_final.pdf [Accessed: June 10, 2014].

32 California Healthcare Institute/PriceWaterhouseCoopers. (2014), 'California biomedical industry report', http://www.pwc.nl/nl/assets/documents/pwc-california-biomedical-industry-2013.pdf [Accessed: February 2, 2015].

33 Nature Reviews Drug Discovery 9, 417–20 (June 2010), http://www.nature.com/nrd/journal/v9/n6/full/nrd3204.html [Accessed: August 1, 2014].

34 Mohr, J., Sengupta, S., and Slater, S. (2010). *Marketing of high-technology products and innovations.* 3rd ed. Upper Saddle River, New Jersey: Pearson Education, Inc.

35 Jobs, S, (1998, May 18), 'There's sanity returning', *Newsweek*, pp. 48–52.

36 Rosen, D., Schroeder, J., and Purinton, E. (1998), 'Marketing high-tech products: lessons in customer focus from the market place', *Academy of Marketing Science*, 6, pp.1–17.

37 Guillen, M.F. and Garcia-Canal, E. (2012). *Emerging markets rule: Growth strategies of the new global giants*. New York: McGraw-Hill.

38 The World Factbook. (2015), https://www.cia.gov/library/publications/the-world-factbook/docs/refmaps.html [Accessed: August 1, 2015].

39 (August 15, 2013), 'Emerging market giants assert global dominance', *Shanghai Daily,* http://www.shanghaidaily.com/Opinion/china-knowledge-wharton/Emerging-market-giants-assert-global-dominance/shdaily.shtml [Accessed: August 1, 2014].

40 (2015), 'United Nations Environmental Programme', http://staging.unep.org/greeneconomy/AboutGEI/WhatisGEI/tabid/29784/Default.aspx [Accessed: November 14, 2014].

41 Bloomberg New Energy Finance. (2013). *New investment in clean energy fell 11% in 2012.* [Press release, January 2013], http://about.bnef.com/press-releases/new-investment-in-clean-energy-fell-11-in-2012-2/ [Accessed: July 28, 2014].

42 United Nations Environmental Program. (2010), 'Green economy report: A preview', http://www.unep.org/pdf/GreenEconomyReport-Preview_v2.0.pdf [Accessed: October 1, 2015].

43 United Nations Environmental Program. (2015), www.unep.org [Accessed: November 14, 2014].

44 IRI. (2013). [Press release]. http://www.iriworldwide.com/NewsEvents/PressReleases/ItemID/1808/View/Details.aspx?utm_source=delivra&utm_medium=email&utm_campaign=Press%20Release%20Alert%20IRI%20and%20SPINS%20Create%20SPINS%20NaturaLink%20Segmentatio [Accessed: July 28, 2014].

45 Prothero, A., McDonagh, P., and Dobscha, S. (2010), 'Is green the new black? Reflections on a green commodity discourse', *Journal of Macromarketing*, 30(2), pp.147–59.

46 Straughan, R.D. and Roberts, J.A. (1999), 'Environmental segmentation alternatives: A look at green consumer behavior in the new millennium', *Journal of Consumer Marketing*, 16(6), pp. 558–75.

47 Soontonsmai, V. (2001). *Predicting intention and behavior to purchase environmentally sound or green products among Thai consumers: An application of theory of reasoned action.* [Unpublished doctoral thesis] Nova Southeastern University.

48 Qin, J., Kimel, S., Kitayama, S., Wang, X., Yang, X., and Han, S. (2011), 'How choice modifies preference: Neural correlates of choice justification', *NeuroImage*, 55(1), pp. 240–46.

49 Hjelmar, U. (2011), 'Consumers' purchase of organic food products: A matter of convenience and reflexive practices', *Appetite*, 56, pp. 336–44.

50 Van Vugt, M. (2009), 'Averting the tragedy of the commons: Using social psychological science to protect the environment', *Current Directions in Psychological Science*, 18, pp. 169–73.

51 Vladas, G., Tybur, J.M., and Van den Bergh, B. (2010), 'Going green to be seen: Status, reputation, and conspicuous conservation', *Journal of Personality and Social Psychology*, 98(3), pp. 392–404.

52 Gabler, C.B., Butler, T.D., and Adams, F.G. (2013), 'The environmental belief-behavior gap: Exploring barriers to green consumerism', *Journal of Customer Behavior*, 12(2/3), pp.159–76.

53 Lin, Y.C. and Chang, C.C.A. (2012), 'Double standard: The role of environmental consciousness in green product usage', *Journal of Marketing*, 76(5), pp. 125–34.

54 Gabler et al. (2013), op. cit.

CASE 2.1   MOBILE LANGUAGE LEARNING: PRAXIS MAKES PERFECT IN CHINA

Professor Ilan Alon and Allen H. Kupetz wrote this case solely to provide material for class discussion. The authors do not intend to illustrate either effective or ineffective handling of a managerial situation. The authors may have disguised certain names and other identifying information to protect confidentiality.

Ivey Management Services prohibits any form of reproduction, storage or transmittal without its written permission. Reproduction of this material is not covered under authorization by any reproduction rights organization. To order copies or request permission to reproduce materials, contact Ivey Publishing, Ivey Management Services, c/o Richard Ivey School of Business, The University of Western Ontario, London, Ontario, Canada, N6A 3K7; phone (519) 661-3208; fax (519) 661-3882; e-mail cases@ivey.uwo.ca.

Version: (A) 2010-03-29

I think we just approached it differently. We first started by looking for ways that technology could solve problems of the average language student here in Shanghai. From our research we found that students often spent more time traveling to/from class and waiting for class than they actually spent *in* class. This seemed like a big inefficiency to us and we speculated how things would change if students were able to listen to their instructional materials on the way to class and then use their actual class time more efficiently to practice.[1]

Hank Horkoff (2006)

Sitting in his office on the third floor in Shanghai near the ZhongShan Park and LouShanGuan Road subway stations, Hank Horkoff was contemplating the next moves for his company, Praxis Language. With the growth of its ChinesePod.com brand, Praxis led the field of mobile learning through the uniqueness of its business model, mobile learning solutions, and tailored content. Coupled with the explosive growth of smart phones in China, in 2006 the company experienced remarkable growth. What's more, the company had received considerable attention from international media that contributed to its fame and fortune. Chinese language education was coming of age and the advent of technology and globalization made this company a prominent innovator in the mobile language learning category. But Horkoff, a Richard Ivey School of Business alumnus, now faced the challenges of continuing Praxis's growth, capitalizing on its existing assets, fighting off imitators and maintaining its momentum. New competitors were coming online daily. Technology was creating new possibilities for teaching/learning Chinese. And the demand for both Chinese and English language education was on the rise.

ENTREPRENEURIAL OPPORTUNITIES OVERSEAS

After graduating from the University of British Columbia (UBC) in political science in 1996, Horkoff decided to explore opportunities overseas. While studying for his bachelor's degree, he also learned how to program and create web sites. The late 1990s had many opportunities for those who were computer savvy and Horkoff was keen on capitalizing on them. He learned how to program and was able to land a few small projects. This experience proved useful later on.

Leaving Canada, Horkoff decided to venture to Moscow. Russia in the 1990s was exciting. The market had just opened and opportunities for freelance work were available. While getting travel and work experience was fun, Horkoff felt that he wanted more. He wanted to learn more about business and be able to apply this knowledge in the international environment. The Richard Ivey School of Business, which had one of the leading MBA programs in the world, would allow him to obtain exactly these skills. He matriculated in the full-time MBA program and successfully graduated by 2001. After graduation, more international opportunities for business presented themselves.

Horkoff decided to go to Singapore next. There he associated with a bio-technology firm building business plans for various entrepreneurial companies. His knowledge of technology, coupled with his business education, made him especially apt for the position. The job, however, did not provide him with the kind of stimulation he was looking for. Shortly after starting the position, he met a friend who invited him to work as a business planning consultant for Samsung in Beijing. After working there for nine months, he quickly realized that the Beijing job was also not a good fit for him. He felt that working for somebody else, building someone else's business plans, was not what he was destined to do. He quit.

Next, Horkoff went to Shanghai, China's business center and the "land of opportunities." Drawing on his previous skills, he started doing some freelance work and started his own consulting firm doing web consulting and development, customer relations management systems (CRM), backend enterprise development, e-commerce and promotion, etc. Working in Shanghai doing consulting proved to be a life-changing activity.

Through a referral, he started doing some work for the Kaien Language school, which needed a new CRM system. *Kai En English Training Center* was a language school (named after its founders, Ken and Brian) under Western management that provided high-quality language teaching to English learners in Shanghai since 1996.[2] The school offered students the opportunity to improve their business English communication skills in a dynamic environment using modern communicative language teaching methods. The language trainers were qualified and experienced, with a strong interest in developing themselves professionally.

CRAWLING OUT OF THE POD

Praxis wanted to find a way to leverage technology to enhance language training. Horkoff realized that much of the time spent learning a language in crowded Shanghai was used traveling to and from the brick and mortar training center. And even outside Shanghai, there would be too much time spent listening to lectures and reviewing mundane information that could be replaced easily by podcasting. In early 2005, podcasting — digital audio and/or video media files that are made available for download via web syndication — was becoming increasingly popular as Internet use in China was surging exponentially.

The English language learning market in China was strong. International trade was growing rapidly along with foreign direct investment. Chinese employees who wanted an edge in the job market quickly realized that they needed to be competent in English to take advantage of the growth in international business. Praxis estimated the demand for English language instruction in China to be about 60 million adult learners, but the market was highly fragmented. The biggest competitor in the field, New Oriental, had only about five per cent of the market. New Oriental had 30 to 40 students per classroom and little personalization. In addition, in China there were about 50,000 private language schools, international academic institutions and freelance teachers.

Kai En English Language Training Center was well positioned in the marketplace. First, it was an early entrant, having started in Shanghai in 1996. Second, it was owned by two highly competent entrepreneurs with international experience in English as a Second Language (ESL) teaching. Brian McCloskey and Ken Carroll, the founders, were involved in managing language schools in Taiwan before relocating to Shanghai to establish Kai En. By 2007, there were five centers in Shanghai and more than 7,000 annual graduates. The teaching staff included a team of 60-70 full-time native speaking professional English-as-a-First-Language teachers and more than 20 additional Chinese ESL instructors. In short, Kai En was a powerful local brand with a strong reputation.

At first, the founders and Horkoff were keen on leveraging technology to teach English to grow their business. They realized that much of the time of learning a new language was not productive. The real learning happened during the communicative, interactive, and experiential portion of the class when the teacher and students were engaging one another in active speaking, listening, and responding. How can they use technology, they wondered, to maximize the active learning in the classroom?

One way was to shift the passive learning to an online platform. They took the cue from the Wall Street Institute School of English, which early on used computers to augment student learning in the classroom.[3] Wall Street in the 1990s augmented the physical classroom with computer programs to teach English and bundled it with traditional instruction to charge more for its services. Typical foreign language learning environment consisted of three hours a week. Online added another hour a week to engage — and charge — students. The business model was based on Chris Anderson's *freemium* model in which Praxis gave away audio podcast lessons, while charging for the five types of subscriptions (see Exhibit 1). At the end of 2009, Praxis had more than 10,000 customers paying between US$9-199 per month, resulting in annual income in excess of US$1 million with 50 per cent gross margins. Instructors were paid US$1,000 per month for roughly 160 hours of work. At the end of 2009, Praxis had 50 full-time and 10 part-time employees. It rented a 400 square meter space for US$8,000 per month.

Praxis identified three distinct segments in the English language learning segment in China: academic, enterprise and individual (see Exhibit 2). Praxis believed that each segment required a unique marketing strategy (see Exhibit 3).

EXHIBIT 1 Product Pricing	Price (US$)	Price (RMB)	Discount		Price (US$)	Price (RMB)	Discount
Basic				**Virtual School**			
1 Month	$9	¥60		3 Months	$249	¥1,668	
6 Months	$49	¥328	9.3%				
12 Months	$79	¥529	26.9%				
24 Months	$129	¥864	40.3%				
Premium				**Executive Plan**			
1 Month	$29	¥194		1 Month	$199	¥1,333	
6 Months	$149	¥998	14.4%	6 Months	$899	¥6,023	24.7%
12 Months	$249	¥1,668	28.4%	12 Months	$1,599	¥10,713	33.0%
24 Months	$399	¥2,673	42.7%	24 Months	$2,999	¥20,093	37.2%
Guided				**Praxis Pass**			
1 Month	$49	¥328		1 Month	$39	¥261	
6 Months	$249	¥1,668	15.3%	6 Months	$169	¥1,132	27.8%
12 Months	$429	¥2,874	27.0%	12 Months	$299	¥2,003	36.1%
24 Months	$699	¥4,683	40.6%	24 Months	$549	¥3,678	41.3%

Source: Company records.

EXHIBIT 2
Proposed Market Segmentation
Source: Company records.

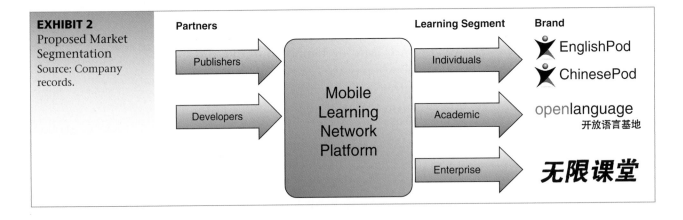

EXHIBIT 3 Marketing Segmentation Strategy	Academic	Enterprise	Individual
Market size (est)	US$125 million (2013)	US$1 billion (2013)	Billions
Competition	Dyned, Moodle, Blackboard	Wall Street, English First, Global English	Wall Street, Rosetta Stone, New Oriental
Revenue Model	School acts as reseller	Direct	*Freemium*
Marketing	Online, conferences, partnerships	Target HR and training departments	Online, business development

Source: Company records.

Praxis built three different web sites to target each of these markets:

Academic: http://openlanguage.com
Enterprise: http://wxclass.com
Individual: http://chinesepod.com (see Exhibit 4)

Eventually the Praxis management team decided that using technology as a differentiator was not enough to survive and grow given the intense competition for English language education. The partners decided to target an entirely new market: a Chinese language learning center for foreigners. Just as Chinese students saw English as a tool to increase accelerate their career advancement, so too would foreigners need to develop some level of Chinese to survive in their own organizations in the future against locals seeking employment with foreign firms. They could start a new category of business and be the ultimate innovators in this category by infusing technology in the learning/teaching of the language. The Chinese language education market was expanding rapidly, but sophisticated competitors were still largely non-existent.

The birth of ChinesePod.com in 2005 came from the convergence of the growing globalization of the Chinese language, which accompanied China's economic

★ ChinesePod	
Week Connencing: 10/09/2009	
Week 1	
1.	Intermediate - Ordering Office Supplies
2.	Intermediate - Traditional Chinese Medicine
3.	Intermediate - Tai Chi
4.	Intermediate - Opinions on Poetry
5.	Intermediate - Calligraphy
Week 2	
1.	Intermediate - Wang Tries to Excel at the Office
2.	Intermediate - Up-and-Comer in the Office
3.	Intermediate - A Firing A foot?
4.	Intermediate - Trimming the Fat at Wang's Office
5.	Intermediate - Lao Wang Plans Revenge
Week 3	
1.	Intermediate - Lao Wang Plans to Sue
2.	Intermediate - Lao Wang in the Doghouse
3.	Intermediate - Delivery Problems
4.	Intermediate - A Dodgy Opportunity for Lao Wang
5.	Intermediate - Requesting a Raise
Week 4	
1.	Intermediate - Job Interview
2.	Intermediate - Studying Chinese
3.	Intermediate - Using a Dictionary
4.	Intermediate - Dorm Life: Late For Class
5.	Intermediate - Signing up for Art Class

EXHIBIT 4
Sample Lesson Plan and Daily Lesson
Source: http://chinesepod.com.

growth, and the growing use of technology, particularly podcasting and interactive technologies, such as Skype. Furthermore, ChinesePod.com took the computer out of the classroom and put the programs online. This increased the possible engagement with the language learner from 4-5 hours per week to 8-10. Mobile interaction (lab and classroom) provided the potential for 24/7 interaction with the consumer.

The ChinesePod.com business model was fairly simple: offer free Chinese language podcasting for beginner Chinese language learners to draw them into the website. The podcasts were practical, useful, and short daily conversations about typical subjects such as eating out, making a cell phone call, using the metro, celebrating a birthday, etc. The lessons were divided into several levels: newbie, elementary, intermediate, upper intermediate, advanced, and media. Paid subscribers also had access to dialogue, vocabulary, and exercises. The idea was to break away from the traditional classroom experience and to give potential students a learning experience that was available when they wanted. The company motto was "Learning on Your Terms."

Praxis Language's *Mobile Learning Network* blended podcast lessons, social collaboration tools, classroom integration, mobile distribution and administration features. Different brands targeted the unique market segments of the market in China. (see Exhibit 5).

Different levels of paid subscriptions existed. The highest level also included a daily Chinese language teacher who would speak to the student for about 10

EXHIBIT 5
Sample Mobile Language Learning Lessons
Source: http://chinesepod.com/.

minutes relating to the podcasted lesson assigned for the day. Because the company used Skype internet telephone technology, a service that provided free computer-to-computer telephone communications for those who downloaded the program, the learner could be located anywhere in the world and still benefit from a native speaker residing in China. The time difference between China and the host country was a bit of a challenge, but that burden was placed on the teacher in China rather than the students.

TECHNOLOGY: THE LINGUA FRANCA

The iPhone is emblematic of a category of mobile devices generally called "smart phones," which actually have more in common with computers than phones in that their primary use is to send and receive data, rather than to talk to other users. Although smart phones were originally sold with hard drives ever-increasing in size, the latest trend pointed to devices that used the "Internet cloud" — large servers like those used by Google to store information. Mobile devices were projected to become little more than access devices, retrieving information and running applications that existed in the cloud. Synonyms for cloud-based computing included cloud computing, software as a service (SAAS), infrastructure as a service, and rent versus own computing.

China was not at the forefront of this cloud computing revolution, but was the world leader in mobile phone subscriptions with more than 700 million cell phone subscribers as of December 2009. According to BDA Limited, an analyst firm that tracked Asian markets, subscribers would grow to around 784 million by 2011, with almost 250 million Chinese accessing the Internet with their cell phone by 2011.[4] Smart phones were used by just a small per centage of Chinese subscribers due to the high cost of the device and the data service. But three of the biggest brands in smart phones, Research in Motion's Blackberry, Taiwan's HTC (running Google's Android software platform on a Linux operating system), and Apple's iPhone, were launched in China in 2006, May 2009 and October 2009, respectively. According to the Chinese Ministry of Industry and Information Technology, there were almost 10 million Chinese using third-generation (3G) services in October 2009.[5] 3G networks gave subscribers access to much faster data rates, meaning that more cloud computing and other commercial services that formerly could only be accessed by fixed/wired networks could now migrate to wireless devices (see Exhibit 6).

Praxis identified three technology keys to success in the mobile language learning space:

- using mobile interfaces to simplify access for students;
- using multiple online and offline tools to connect with students to maximize engagement;
- open (non-proprietary) platforms to collaborate with schools, publishers and developers.

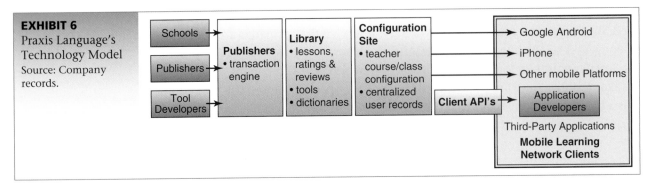

EXHIBIT 6
Praxis Language's Technology Model
Source: Company records.

Horkoff realized he could not use the technology immediately to address what remained the largest addressable market: English for native Chinese speakers. Most Chinese, while quick to adopt mobile phones, were still completely unfamiliar with podcasting. So Praxis decided to first use this technology to launch ChinesePod. com — Mandarin Chinese for native English speakers. ChinesePod.com offered a viable alternative to potential language learners who would not or could not take evening classes to learn Chinese or couldn't afford a set of books and CDs.

THE OPPORTUNITY AND CHALLENGES AHEAD

While ChinesePod.com was doing well, a need existed to examine opportunities for growth. Competitors were coming online daily and the concept had few barriers to entry, technical or otherwise. Should the company move to other language groups? And if so, which ones? Should it simply concentrate on Chinese language education and try to get more customers? Should the company return to its roots and further develop English language training in China? What other services could it add to the platform it had already built?

Two new technologies were coming online in China: the Google Android phone and Apple's iPhone. How could Praxis leverage these new systems? What risks did these and emerging technologies pose to the Praxis business model?

NOTES

1   Huw Collingbourne, "Podcasting Secrets — ChinesePod," Bitwise Magazine, August 18, 2006, www. bitwisemag.com/2/Podcasting-Secrets-ChinesePod.

2   http://career.kaien.net.cn/index.php?page=about.kaien.

3   www.wallstreetinstitute.com/students/overview.aspx, retrieved March 6, 2010.

4   "How many new cell phone accounts are opened in China a day?" http://news.cnet.com/8301-10784_3-9724502-7.html.

5   China's Information Technology and Internet, www.chinatoday.com/it/it.htm.

CHAPTER 3

Evaluating Cultural and Social Environments

When colouring in 800,000 pixels on a map of India, Microsoft coloured eight of them a different shade of green to represent the disputed Kashmiri territory. The difference in greens meant Kashmir was shown as non-Indian, and the product was promptly banned in India. Microsoft was left to recall all 200,000 copies of the offending operating system software, Windows, to try and heal the diplomatic wounds. It cost them millions.[1]

LEARNING OBJECTIVES

After Reading This Chapter, You Should Be Able to:

- Recognize the importance of culture to global marketing.
- Identify the components of culture.
- Apply cultural frameworks to understand consumer behavior.
- Segment countries by cultural similarities.
- Understand different models of culture and cultural distance.
- Employ cultural concepts to determine communication strategy.
- Understand the difference between verbal and non-verbal communication.

BIG BROTHER'S BIG CONTROVERSY[2]

"Racist Attacks Trigger Outrage" claimed *Hindustan Times*, "Big Brother India Backs Shilpa in UK" declared *The Asia Age*, and *The Economic Times* pronounced "Big Brother's Brown Shadow on Brown," referring to the visiting UK Chancellor of Exchequer Gordon Brown.

The event that spurred these headlines in the Indian press, and equally agitated ones in the UK press, was an episode of the "Big Brother" reality show aired on UK's Channel 4. What became known as "race row" in Britain, India and around the world, started with a series of negative comments directed towards Shilpa Shetty, a Bollywood star, by some of the contestants on the show's "Celebrity" edition, which followed the lives and interactions of 14 housemates as they were confined together and isolated from the rest of world for four weeks. Each week, at least one of the contestants, which included pop singer Jermaine Jackson (Michael's brother), and various other actors, singers and models, was voted out of the house by the rest.

The housemates' comments, seemingly meant to insult Shilpa's race and culture, prompted street protests in India, a discussion on the floor of the British Parliament, an awkward press conference moment for Chancellor Brown, a pullout from the show's main sponsor, and over 40,000 complaints by viewers.

An equally vigorous debate carried on in the global media on whether the housemates' comments were truly meant to disparage Shilpa's Indian heritage or if they were simply the angry outbursts of culturally ignorant people. Referring to Jade Goody, the model whose comments sparked the most outrage, Jermaine Jackson simply said: "...Shilpa is from another culture and they [Shilpa and Jade] don't fit." While Shilpa went on to win the Big Brother contest that season and managed to rise above the social tumult, the issue of cultural differences and people's inherent difficulties with it is destined to remain a subject of discussion in our globalizing world.

Marketers clearly have to be aware of subtle cultural differences between consumers. For instance, India is a country with many different social and cultural facets: While Hindi is the official language, there are 21 other languages in which business is being done, including Bengali, Telugu, Marathi, Tamil, Urdu, and Gujarati. English is widely used in national, political, and commercial communication. India also celebrates many national festivals, such as, Deepawali, Holi, Guru Nanak Jayanti, Raksha Bandhan, Christmas, Janmashtami, and Id-ul-Zuha. When it comes to doing business in the country, it is also important to recognize that business in India is relation-based and that personal contacts often count more than a straightforward offer or transaction (Figure 3.1).

In general, cross-cultural conflicts can result not only in breaking up relationships but also in the poor management of market entry, product adaptation, and customer analysis. They affect the functioning and success of companies and managers, as demonstrated in Box 3.1.

Culture, and all its obvious and hidden implications, plays a critical role in the business world. International marketers, in particular, stumble upon it every time they try to market their product or service to a target audience that does not share their own cultural heritage. This chapter discusses the reasons why cultural differences play such a big role in international business and marketing, and the ways business professionals can learn about and cope in social and cultural environments that are different from their own.

An understanding of culture is important because it can give insight into international markets and provide competitive advantage to global business leaders. Especially when entering foreign markets, firms frequently fall into a trap of the "self-reference" criterion,[3] which means that their business representatives might be unconsciously applying their own cultural experiences and values to marketing communication in another culture. What is equally dangerous is ethnocentrism,

FIGURE 3.1
Relationships
Matter in India
Source: © Authors

Box 3.1   Company-in-Focus: An Issue of Sub-Cultures

Why IKEA Took China by Storm and Home Depot Dramatically Failed

In 1998, IKEA started its retail operations in China. To meet local laws, it formed a joint venture. The venture served as a good platform to test the market, understand local needs, and adapt its strategies accordingly. It understood early on that Chinese apartments were small and customers required functional, modular solutions. The company made slight modifications to its furniture to meet local needs. The store layouts reflected the typical sizes of apartments and also included a balcony. In addition, transportation policies had to be changed. As Smedberg, marketing manager China explained, "Usually IKEA stores open relatively far out in the suburbs, but we knew China had to be different since, for example, only 20 percent of visitors in Shanghai have cars." Thus, IKEA has built its PRC stores near public transportation lines, offers local home delivery and long-distance delivery to major cities in China for a fee, and maintains taxi lanes.

IKEA, famous for its flat-pack furniture which consumers have to assemble themselves, realized that understanding the local culture is important—Chinese people hate the do-it-yourself concept. IKEA did well to adapt in China, although it took numerous changes to its strategies and more than 12 years for the company to become profitable in the Asian nation. In fact, sales have been growing faster in China than in the company as a whole.

So if the Chinese don't like do-it-yourself, why did IKEA succeed and why did Home Depot, another major retailer, fail so miserably? Home Depot is the largest US home-improvement retailer, which entered China in 2006 by acquiring 12 stores from Home Way, a Chinese company. But by September 2012, all Home Depot stores closed in China. The company struggled to gain traction in a country where cheap labor has stunted the do-it-yourself ethos and apartment-based living leaves scarce demand for products like lumber. Chinese customers need to be educated in decorating their home and they are very eager to learn from the West. When you go to Home Depot, you're asking for help to solve an existing problem that you have—you want to install a ceiling fan, you want to put new windows in, or you want to build a deck. The staff is helpful, and they'll help you figure out what you have to do for the project, but the project in itself isn't necessarily packed with Western culture. IKEA, on the other hand, teaches the consumer how to decorate their home, and thereby experience Western culture.

Retailers often don't realize how complex things are in China. There are so many subcultures and so many things beyond a company's control. For instance, most Chinese people live in condos and don't have garages to stockpile tools. And Chinese consumers, just like everywhere else, are fickle, mercurial, and unpredictable.

Sources: Miller, P. (2014), 'IKEA with Chinese Characteristics', http://www.chinabusinessreview.com/ikea-with-chinese-characteristics/; http://www.businessinsider.com/ikea-home-depot-china-failed-2012-9; Chu, V., Girdhar, A., and Sood, R. (2013), 'Couching Tiger Tames the Dragon', July 21, 2013, http://businesstoday.intoday.in/story/how-ikea-adapted-its-strategies-to-expand-in-china/1/196322.html [All Accessed: December 10, 2014].

i.e. the belief that one's own culture is superior to any other,[4] which will ruin marketing efforts. Being culturally mindful is vital for international marketing leaders to adapt their strategies to achieve business success in any society and culture. The concept of culture is complex. It has been the subject of extensive research in multiple fields of study that has added to the understanding of how cultural differences influence both business and consumer behavior.

CULTURAL DIVERSITY IN THE ERA OF GLOBALIZATION

Globalization has enabled us to overcome geographical and economic boundaries, creating borderless enclaves. Within this borderless world, the growth in the number of transnational corporations and the dissemination of information and ideas around the world, have all had an impact on individual cultures. While globalization is a strong force for the spread of ideas around the world, there still exists a great deal of cultural diversity among regions and individual countries and even within countries. For example, Table 3.1 lists countries measured by language and religious diversity. While English is the dominant language in the United States, spoken by 82 percent of the population, there are some 150–300 additional languages in use (some used only in tribal rituals).

The most widely spoken languages other than English are Spanish and Mandarin. In some areas, such as California and Texas, Spanish speakers comprise 35 percent of

TABLE 3.1 Countries with the Largest Cultural Diversity Indices	**Number of Languages**	**Number of Religions**
	India (several hundred)	India (40)
	United States (150–300)	South Africa (30)
	Philippines (170)	Taiwan (25)
	Russia (100)	United States (20)
	Mexico (62)	Canada (15)
	China (10)	United Kingdom (10)

Source: Wikipedia. (2014), https://en.wikipedia.org/wiki/Religions_by_country; World Religions. (2014), http://www.infoplease.com/ipa/A0855613.html [Both Accessed: June 1, 2014]

Country Name	Spanish Speaking Population	% of Spanish Speakers in World
Mexico	109,955,400	24.30%
Columbia	45,013,674	9.95%
United States	44,321,038	9.80%
Argentina	40,677,348	8.99%
Spain	40,491,051	8.95%
Peru	29,180,899	6.45%
Venezuela	26,414,815	5.84%
Chile	16,454,143	3.64%
Ecuador	13,927,650	3.08%
Guatemala	13,002,206	2.87%

FIGURE 3.2
Spanish-Speaking in the US and Top Spanish-Speaking Countries
Source: © Author's Photo; Adapted from: www.maps of world.com; www. Spanishlinguist.com

FIGURE 3.3
Learning Mandarin Has Increased in Attraction
Source: © Authors

the population. In Los Angeles alone, there are 22 Spanish-language radio stations, 17 audited weekly and daily newspapers, and eight TV stations. In some regions of the US, like for instance Florida, Spanish is actually the first language spoken by many people (Figure 3.2).

Mandarin is the third most common language spoken in New York and the fourth most common language spoken in California and Maryland. Not surprisingly, demand for language classes has increased across the world (Figure 3.3).

As well as the more obvious cultural differences such as language, eating habits, dress and traditions, there are also significant variations in the way societies organize themselves, in their shared conception of ethics, and in the ways they interact with their environment. According to UNESCO, some five countries monopolize the world cultural industries trade. In the cinema industry, for example, 88 out of 185 countries do not have the ability to produce their own films.

Companies such as Starbucks, McDonald's and KFC have changed eating habits in many countries; For example, McDonald's sells spicy French fries and a Shogun Burger (a pork bun served with Japanese teriyaki sauce and cabbage) in Hong Kong, while beef and pork products are not offered in India. Other variations are served in additional countries such as Japan and the Philippines. KFC offers Sichuan pickle and shredded pork chops in addition to chicken in China.

This chapter discusses the following issues: How useful is the study of culture in the determination of global marketing strategy? How have cultures been affected by globalization? To what extent have cultures remained diverse in the era of globalization? Before we tackle these questions, let us define what is meant by culture.

What is Culture?

Culture is a notoriously difficult term to define. In 1952, the American anthropologists, Kroeber and Kluckhohn,[5] critically reviewed concepts and definitions of culture, and compiled a list of 164 different definitions. For instance, a country's culture has been defined as "the collective programming of the mind that distinguishes the members of one group or people from another."[6] A broad view of culture is that it encompasses all value systems of a nation. It is what defines a human community, its individuals, social organizations and economic and political systems.[7] Culture is comprised of concepts such as religion, cuisine, social habit, music, arts, or symbols, etc. For instance, consider the following picture (Figure 3.4), where the stylized "S" is used both as the "S" in the word "Sparkasse" (savings bank) and at the same time for "stadt" (city) symbolizing the importance of savings banks in the capital city of Berlin. This play of words is only comprehensible to those who know the role of savings banks in Germany and are well aware that Berlin is the capital of Germany.

Others provide the following elements of culture and suggest analyzing them in detail:[8]

- National character

- Values

- Time orientation

- Space orientation

- Architecture

- Perception

FIGURE 3.4
The Stylized S-Symbol Is Used for the "S"parkasse (Savings Bank) and Here Also Serves as the "s" In Haupt"s"tadt (Capital City of Berlin, Germany)
Source: © Authors

- Thinking

- Language

- Colors

- Non-verbal communication

- Behavior

- Social groupings and relationships

Many of those cultural elements can be depicted as an "iceberg"; some are above the surface, ("surface culture"), the tangible aspects, those that can be seen, heard, and touched. We can see how people behave, how they dress, and how they speak. However, most elements of culture are below the surface ("deep culture"), such as values, orientation toward time and space, and non-verbal communication, such as facial expressions and posture ("body language"), many of which have hidden meanings, understandable only to cultural insiders. The large area below the water-line can only be suspected, estimated, or intuited.

For instance, you are invited to someone's home in a foreign country for tea. Is "tea time" at the end of a dinner, or served alone, say in mid-afternoon? You are invited for dinner at seven p.m. in a Latin American country. Should you arrive promptly at the specified time, or somewhat after? How do you greet people in another country? Shake hands, embrace with a hug, or keep a respectful distance?

FIGURE 3.5
Color Chart
Source: Adapted from: http://webdesign.about.com/od/colorcharts/l/bl_colorculture.htm [Accessed: July 2, 2014]

RED

Australian Aboriginals: Land, earth
Celtic: Death, afterlife
China: Good luck, celebration
India: Purity
South Africa: Color of mourning
Russia: Bolsheviks and Communism
North America: Danger, love, passion, excitement
Middle East: Luck, good fortune

BLUE

China: Immortality
Iran: Color of heaven and spirituality, mourning
North America: Trust, soothing
Scandinavia: Cleanliness
Ukraine: Good health
South Africa: Happiness
Israel: Holiness

GREEN

China: Green hats imply a man's wife is cheating on him, exorcism
India: Islam
Ireland: Symbol of the entire country, religious (Catholics)
Islam: Perfect faith
Japan: Life
Europe/US: Environmental awareness
Malaysia: Danger

YELLOW

China: Nourishing, royalty
Egypt: Mourning
India: Merchants
Japan: Courage
Italy: Summer
Mexico: Mourning
South Africa: Wealth

BLACK

Australian Aboriginals: Color of the people
China: Color for young boys
Thailand: Bad luck, unhappiness, evil
US/Europe: Mourning, death
Nigeria: Ominous

WHITE

China: Death, mourning
India: Unhappiness
Japan: White carnation symbolizes death
US/Europe: Marriage, peace, holiness
India: Unhappiness
Middle East: Status, peace

What color should your dress be? (Figure 3.5). White is probably not appropriate in Asia, where it symbolizes death. In turn, red is seen as the color of joyfulness and prosperity. Proper behavior in another culture depends upon understanding both the explicit and the implicit parts of culture. Making mistakes at the tip of the iceberg may not be serious, but mistakes below the surface can lead to communication failure, for instance if two parties use English as a business language but the meaning of "yes" and "no" is different across cultures.

A marketing example of communication failure is illustrated by the case of a North American telephone company TV advertisement in a Latin American country. The ad portrayed a home with only one telephone located on the ground floor. As the phone rang, the wife was on the second floor and shouted to her husband to answer. The theme of the ad was that it would be more convenient to have a phone on each floor. The ad was a failure because in a masculine oriented country, it was not the norm for the husband to be given what was perceived to be a command from his spouse. Other examples pertain to the way culture and language relate. For example, the Chinese translation proved difficult for Coke, which took two tries to get it right. They first tried "Ke-kou-ke-la" because when pronounced it sounded roughly like Coca-Cola. It wasn't until after thousands of signs had been printed that they discovered that the phrase means "bite the wax tadpole" or "female horse stuffed with wax," depending on the dialect. Second time around things worked out much better. After researching 40,000 Chinese characters Coke came up with "ko-kou-ko-le" which translates roughly to the much

FIGURE 3.6
Culture Embedded
in Architecture
(Germany and
China)
Source: © Author

more appropriate "happiness in the mouth."[9] Apart from gender stereotypes and language, culture is incorporated in a variety of global marketing elements. **Culture can also be embedded in the architecture a country prefers,** such as the pictures above illustrate (Figure 3.6). A country's culture has been identified as a key environmental characteristic underlying systematic differences in behavior.[10] As such, it is a powerful force that shapes consumer behavior.

Moreover, ignoring cultural differences between countries has been cited as one of the causes of many business failures.[11] Take the following incident, for example:

> An executive of Turbo Beer, a Scandinavian brewery, was sent on assignment to Eastern Europe as regional marketing manager. His task was to research the potential for, and then develop the market for his company's premium beer. Beer tastes and consumption are known to be influenced by culture. Therefore, the first step in the executive's plan was to determine whether the culture of the countries comprising the region were similar. Also, he wanted to know whether there were any similarities to beer drinking in these countries with his home country.

The executive in the above case needs some sort of model(s) that can show which cultures are similar and which are dissimilar, and in what aspects are the similarities and/or differences represented. In other words, what national cultural frameworks exist that can be relied on to provide the information that the beer executive needs for his project? This is why INSEAD (Institut Européen d'Administration des Affaires—a top French business school) professor, Erin Meyer, says that you need to spend a lot of energy learning how to adapt your style to work in different ways. Meyer calls this "authentic flexibility." Meyer tells the story of one Russian woman in her seminar who commented, "you know Americans on my team send me these emails. And they don't say 'Dear So and So'. They just get right to the content, and then they sign their names with their initials. And I just look at the email and think, 'don't you even care enough about me to write your name?'"[12]

The Concept of National Character

One such framework is the concept of national character. The concept assumes that each country has its own character; i.e. people from a given nation share common behavioral patterns that are distinct from other nations. For example President George W. Bush proclaimed "National Character Counts Week" in 2006. What values shape the American character? According to the President's proclamation they are supposed to be "integrity, courage, honesty, and patriotism." And what about the Asian, or more specifically, the Chinese character? As a Chinese said about his own culture: "Speaking of Chinese national character, an important point is collectivism. …we put a high value on cohesion within our nation, as if we were a family…. we prefer to pursue the harmony of a society, while western countries focus more on human rights."[13] Are these perceptions of the American and the Asian character generalizations based on personal experience or stereotypes that may have a "kernel of truth" or may they simply be inaccurate? It is important to note that there is a difference between a stereotype and a sociotype. While a stereotype has limited value, it is not entirely irrelevant. For example, the stereotypes Bangladeshis had about the piousness of members of different Bangladeshi tribes were found to be valid when compared with observations of the frequency of praying. However, most stereotypes reflect traits that are not reliably observed. If there is another source of data (e.g. ethnographic observation) in addition to individual perceptions, we talk about a sociotype. A sociotype is defined as a valid stereotype based on ethnographic work.[14] How then, may national character be determined?

Historically, the concept of national character or culture had its origins among philosophers beginning in the eighteenth century, among them d'Argens, Montesquieu and Jean-Jacques Rousseau. They debated what constitutes the national character of a nation, such as physical and spiritual factors and political institutions. D'Argens, for example, averred that the inhabitants of each country constitute a nation with a unique set of characteristics.[15] Nevertheless, d'Argen's descriptions of "nations" were generally stereotyped.[16] The Spanish were described as being shrewd, proud, vain, and jealous, while the British were intelligent, fair, industrious, but rude. For another example, see Darton's portrayal of national culture in Figure 3.7, published in 1790.

Studies of national culture have been criticized for two main reasons. First, some national cultural studies lack rigorous foundations that result in stereotyped findings that have little basis in fact. People in all cultures have shared perceptions about the personality characteristics of the typical member of their own culture and of typical members of other cultures. Perceptions abound of national character, such as "the Germans lack humor," "the Italians are excitable," the British are "fair players," and the Swedes are "introverted." However, the reliability of these perceptions has been widely criticized by Peabody.[17] He claimed that perceptions of national character are often based on indirect experience and therefore are inaccurate and are clouded by racism, ethnocentrism, and discrimination.

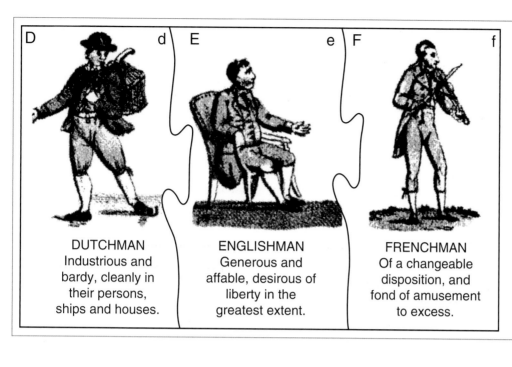

FIGURE 3.7
Early Conceptions of National Culture
Source: Darton, W. (1790). Inhabitants of the World

D | d | E | e | F | f

DUTCHMAN
Industrious and bardy, cleanly in their persons, ships and houses.

ENGLISHMAN
Generous and affable, desirous of liberty in the greatest extent.

FRENCHMAN
Of a changeable disposition, and fond of amusement to excess.

National character may not reflect actual personality traits, as was found in a study of 49 cultures.[18] Terracciano and fellow researchers asked respondents to describe their "national culture." They found that perceptions of national culture differed significantly from personality scores (characteristics) of fellow nationals. Therefore, perceptions of national character may be based more on stereotypes than on reality as the following illustrates:

> [A] characteristic of Swedish mentality is the urge to agree on things. Heated discussions are rare, and the best way to convince somebody in a matter is not to put maximum emotional energy into the discussion, but to give some good arguments. For this reason, foreigners sometimes think Swedish people [are] undercooled and formal. They probably have a point there, but it should be remembered that the tendency towards rationality and objectivity most of all is seen in public and professional life. Swedish people can be very emotional, too, especially after 2 a.m. in a bar.[19]

In addition, national character traits can be very difficult to detect, if people were raised in multicultural environments and work across national borders as Box 3.2 illustrates.

The Role of Subcultures

Marketers should also develop an understanding of the differences between national cultures and the various subcultures that operate within them. Subcultures develop around a shared characteristic that is different and unique within the predominant national culture. This shared quality among the members of a subculture can be

Box 3.2 Person-in-Focus: Carlos Ghosn

National Character Versus Global Citizen

Carlos Ghosn is a very exceptional manager, who is currently the chairman and CEO of Paris-based Renault and holds the same position at Japan-based Nissan, which together produces and sells cars worldwide. Born in Brazil, raised in Lebanon, educated in Paris, and fluent in four languages, Ghosn meets the challenges of modern leadership with aplomb. He spends approximately one-third of his time in France, one-third in Japan, and one-third traveling to Renault–Nissan operations throughout the world. For orchestrating one of the decade's most aggressive downsizing campaigns and spearheading the turnaround of Nissan from near bankruptcy in the late 1990s, Ghosn earned the nicknames "le cost killer" and "Mr. Fix It." After the Nissan financial turnaround, he achieved celebrity status and ranks as one of the 50 most famous men in global business and politics. His life has been chronicled in a Japanese manga comic book.

In today's world crossing cultures to communicate or do business with people whose identities are different from your own is now commonplace. Ghosn often mentions that leaders of the future will also need to have a lot more empathy and sensitivity—not just for people from their own countries, but also for people from different countries and cultures. They are going to need global empathy, which is a lot more difficult: "I would say even though the term today is not very popular, love the country and love the culture in which you are in. And try to learn about its strengths, don't focus on the weaknesses, and make sure that all the people you are transferring with you are of the same opinion."

He also stresses the importance of cultivating a certain mindset or character that truly enjoys the challenge of living in new environments: "If you have to work and particularly do something significant in a country it is much easier if somehow you connected with the country and you like the country and you respect the people and you are curious about the culture." When Ghosn went to Japan, he had some ideas about the culture, he says, such as the language and the food. But he found there were some concepts that were totally new to him—such as walking into an elevator before a woman. He says that while it would be considered "very gross" in a Western country, not to do so could be deemed to violate the code of Japanese culture. While his task was to help revive an icon of the Japanese car industry, he says, the experience wasn't simply about performing a job—it was about discovering a new culture and it was very rewarding.

Sources: Fonda, D. (2003). Motor trends: Le Cost Killer. *Time*, 19 May, 2003. [http://www.time.com/time/magazine/article/0,9171, 1004877,00.html]

INSEAD (2008). The transcultural leader Carlos Ghosn. CEO of Renault/Nissan [http://knowledge.insead.edu/leadership-management/operations-management/the-transcultural-leader-carlos-ghosn-ceo-of-renault-nissan-1904]

Berfield, S. (2008). Career advice from a comic book. Businessweek.com. 21 Feb, 2008. [http://www.businessweek.com/stories/2008-02-20/career-advice-from-a-comic-book]

Kirkland, R. (2012). Leading the 21st century: An interview with Carlos Ghosn. McKinsey & Company. [http://www.mckinsey.com/insights/leading_in_the_21st_century/an_interview_with_carlos_ghosn] [All accessed September 1, 2014].

anything from a different ethnic background, religion, language, or a demographic factor, such as age and gender, to a shared interest. For example, players of the popular online game Second Life form a subculture, as do fashionistas or vegetarians. What is often referred to as a company's "corporate culture," is also, in effect, a subculture that exists predominantly in the business world. For instance, corporate cultures in the same industry may hugely differ if you consider the way IBM, Google, HP, Microsoft organize their business activities. Or take regional subcultures like the ones in Switzerland being influenced by Italian, French, and German, customs and values. In a study on refrigerators, Baoku et al.[20] state that customers evaluate product attributes differently in various regions and markets. In the case of the refrigerator market, segmentation is very important.

It is important to note that subcultures often transcend national borders and cultures, especially in today's interconnected world. Users around the world who adopt a subculture's values and rules often adapt them to their own national cultural values and, unwittingly, become a part of the ongoing paradox of modern society where national culture and globalization are inextricably mixed. Think of the MySpace user in Ukraine who has accepted the value of individual expression (culturally associated with the US) by having a MySpace page, but has also customized that page to her own culturally-influenced values and sensibilities and who, in turn, has connected with other MySpace users from around the world who share her interest in the online community but not necessarily her national cultural values or tastes. Marketers who are trying to reach this hypothetical consumer, should then ask themselves whether their product or service would appeal to their national cultural values, the values of the subcultures of which they are a member, or both.

The criticisms of attempts to develop national character frameworks can be addressed by referring to those research approaches that are valid and theory-based for studying cross-cultural behavior. These approaches consist of empirical studies of national character based on personality traits such as "openness," "agreeableness," and "conscientiousness," and other elements.[21] Examples of such frameworks include Hofstede,[22] Schwartz,[23] Globe,[24] and others. Further, some question the relevance of national character to international marketing because it cannot explain individual consumer behavior. However, the concept is important to international marketing because it can be useful in explaining national differences in marketing phenomena. While national character studies do not explain or predict individual consumer behavior, they can explain *aggregate* consumer behavior, which can identify similar behavioral patterns cross-nationally. Moreover, there is evidence that national culture moderates individuals' value priorities.[25] Identifying value similarities and differences has become a useful method to studying cultures. While these similarities and differences operate at the group level, they are often internalized by individuals. For example, Moon et al.[26] found that the degree of national culture individualism affects attitudes towards purchase intentions of both groups and individuals. This information can be used to shape market segments and to determine regional or global marketing strategy.

HOFSTEDE'S SIX DIMENSIONS OF NATIONAL CULTURE

Hofstede's framework is the most used and cited in international marketing research. Already until 2001, Lenartowicz and Roth report that almost 10 percent of the articles published in ten renowned journals during 1996–2000 used culture as an independent variable.[27] **Hofstede originally identified four dimensions that are inherent in cultures**: Individualism (relationship of individuals in a group), Masculinity (implications of gender), Power Distance (social inequality), Uncertainty Avoidance (handling of uncertainty), and later added a fifth dimension of Long-Term versus Short-Term Orientation. In addition, the dimension Indulgence (enjoying life and happiness) was added. Each dimension is scaled on a continuum running from high to low.[28] The six dimensions are summarized in Table 3.2. His original database consisted of 116,000 questionnaires filled out by managers and workers of IBM subsidiaries in 66 Western countries from 1967 to 1973, replicated again during 1980 and 1983.

In the 2010 edition of the book, *Cultures and Organizations: Software of the Mind*, scores on the dimensions are listed for 76 countries, partly based on replications and extensions of the IBM study on different international populations and by different scholars.[29]

While considering employees of IBM-subsidiaries as representative of a nation's culture is problematical,[30] several researchers have replicated Hofstede's

TABLE 3.2 Hofstede's Cultural Dimensions	**Cultural Orientations**	**Contrasts Across Cultures**
	Concepts of the Self and Others Individualism Versus Collectivism	The relationship between an individual and the group. Efforts and achievement are best accomplished by the individual or solved by the group.
	Interaction *with* others or *for* others Masculinity Versus Femininity	Assertiveness and personal achievement are favored (masculinity) versus caring for others, adopting nurturing roles, and emphasizing quality of life (femininity).
	Dealing with Uncertainty Uncertainty Avoidance	Tendency to avoid risks (high uncertainty avoidance), to prefer stable situations, uncertainty reducing rules and risk-free procedures, which are seen as a necessity for efficiency. Or, conversely, a risk prone attitude (low uncertainty avoidance) where people as individuals are seen as the engine of change, which is perceived as a requirement of efficiency.
	Equality or Inequality in Interpersonal Interactions Power Distance	Hierarchy is strong, power is centralized at the top (high power distance); power is more equally distributed and superior and subordinates have a sense of equality as human beings (low power distance).
	Virtue Regardless of Truth Long-Term Versus Short-Term Orientation	Values associated with Long-Term Orientation are thrift and perseverance; those associated with Short-Term are respect for tradition, fulfilling social obligations and protecting one's "face".
	Facilitation of Human Needs Indulgence Versus Restraint	Indulgence stands for a society that allows relatively free gratification of basic and natural human drives related to enjoying life and having fun. Restraint stands for a society that suppresses gratification of needs and regulates it by means of strict social norms.

Source: Adapted from: Usunier, J. (2000). *Marketing Across Cultures*. Harlow: Pearson Education. http://www.geert-hofstede.com/

methodology more recently in various countries and have revalidated Hofstede's dimensions.[31]

For example, Søndergaard's paper[32] contains a review of over 60 replications of Hofstede's cultural model and concludes that Hofstede's dimensions are "largely confirmed." More recently, Alkailani et al. provided a replication study of Hofstede's scores in Jordan, but identified major differences between Hofstede's scores in Arab countries and their own investigation.[33]

In 1991, to compensate for overemphasis on Western cultures, Hofstede added a fifth dimension to his original four—Long-Term versus Short-Term Orientation—which was developed from surveys of students in 23, mostly Asian, countries, using a questionnaire developed by Chinese researchers. Values associated with the Long Term are thrift and perseverance and those associated with the Short Term are respect for tradition, fulfilling social obligations, and protecting one's "face." The concept of "face," means showing respect to someone in a way that acknowledges publicly his or her status. Berating a subordinate by a manager in front of other workers will cause the subordinate to lose face. Criticizing someone or pointing out mistakes or errors in public may make the person feel shamed or inferior. But a manager may also lose face because of the anger expressed in front of subordinates. For a person to maintain face is not unique to, but is very important in Asian social relations because face translates into power and influence and affects goodwill. Loss of face can result in a person losing honor and cause serious embarrassment. Moreover, if one person loses face, the whole group loses face, so the consequences may be very serious. Take for example, the following example:

> Imagine an office in a Shanghai skyscraper. The head of sales of a US-American multinational company meets with his local reports to discuss last month's target pitfalls. He questions him and asks for explanations. For the local manager this constant interrogation is painful but he silently nods and peers out the window. He leaves the meeting, avoids further discussion with the sales head, and never returns.[34]

In the above example, continued confrontation between home and host management was seen as a very damning indictment. The local manager felt that his pride was compromised and he lost respect. A more proactive way for foreigners is to actively give face, that is, to acknowledge status, showing appreciation and recognizing prestige. In the case of negative feedback, a loss of face is almost always inevitable, so Chinese managers and supervisors avoid this by simply not giving any. Balancing the need to drive high performance and while maintaining employee morale is very challenging. An interesting finding from neuroscience explains that the brain's pain receptors fire equally when stimulated by social pain or by physical pain. Only the effect of social pain remains much longer.[35]

Plotting countries using Hofstede's dimensions on two-dimensional maps or tables produces clusters or groups that are similar. As shown in Table 3.3, individualism is more pronounced in developed and Western nations, while collectivism is inherent in developing countries. Masculinity is high in Eastern European

TABLE 3.3 Hofstede's Cultural Dimensions (Based on Hofstede)	**Feminine, Collectivist**	**Collectivist, Masculine**
	Korea, Thailand, Chile, Costa Rica, Bulgaria, Russia, Portugal, Spain	China, Japan, Mexico, Venezuela, Egypt, Jordan, Syria, Greece
	Individualist, Feminine	**Individualist, Masculine**
	France, Netherlands, Scandinavian countries	Hungary, Poland, Slovenia, United States, UK, Australia, Germany, Austria
	Small PD, Weak UA	**Large PD, Weak UA**
	US, UK, Australia, Denmark, Sweden, Norway	China, India
	Small PD, Strong UA	**Large PD, Strong UA**
	Germany, Austria, Hungary, Israel	Egypt, Jordan, Syria, South Korea Japan, Latin America

PD = Power Distance, UA = Uncertainty Avoidance
Source: Compiled from: www.geert-hofstede.com [Accessed: June 10, 2014]

and German speaking countries. Uncertainty avoidance is high in Latin American countries and Japan. Power distance is high in Latin American, Asian, and African countries. Fitting marketing strategies to each country cluster because of cultural distances is necessary for products that are culturally bound, and for advertising messages, as we will see below and in further chapters.

Applying Hofstede's Model to Global Marketing

Cultural values affect many decisions inherent in the marketing mix, especially product and promotional considerations. Values affect the way a company can connect to its local customers. For example, when Google entered China, the Chinese logged onto Google.cn and typed in a vulgar term for breasts. Google Suggest offered links that displayed raw nudity, and more. The official typed in the word meaning "son," and one of the Google Suggest terms was "love affair between son and mother." The links to this term yielded explicit pornography. The woman serving tea in the conference room almost fainted at the spectacle.[36]

Lim and Park's study in South Korea and the United States[37] found that the impact of national culture on individual's innovativeness is evident. However, the direct effect of innovativeness on innovation adoption was only significant in the United States. Innovativeness was also found in weak uncertainty avoidance countries. Because innovativeness is related to tolerance for ambiguity, members of weak uncertainty avoidance cultures tend to be more innovative. A cluster of high individualistic and masculine countries include Austria, Belgium, Czech Republic, Germany, Hungary, Italy, Poland, and the United Kingdom. Among those countries that have relatively low uncertainty avoidance scores are Austria, Germany, Italy, and the United Kingdom. Innovative consumers attach more importance to values such as stimulation, creativity, and curiosity. Therefore, these values should be used in communicating new products to consumers in low uncertainty

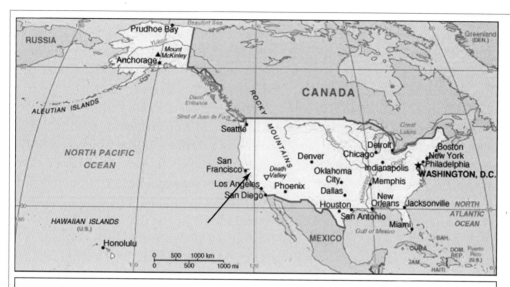

GEO MAP 3.1
Häagen-Dazs
Source: Adapted from:
CIA Maps, The World
Factbook[38]

The headquarters of **Häagen-Dazs** is located in Oakland, California, United States

avoidance countries. Häagen-Dazs is an example of a product that is positioned as originating in Scandinavia (although produced in the United States by Unilever) in order to invoke novelty and creditability to the brand.

The diffusion of innovation was originally researched by Everett Rogers.[39] A limited number of studies empirically explored diffusion on a cross-national basis. For instance, Dwyer et al.,[40] in focusing on technological innovations across 13 European countries, found that national culture explains a relatively sizeable amount of variation in cross-national diffusion rates. Especially, the dimensions of masculinity and power distance were positively associated with diffusion rates at national levels, whereas the dimensions of individualism and long-term orientation were negatively related to the diffusion rates. For marketing managers, there are important implications for market launch, which should begin in cultures that are high in collectivism, short-term oriented, high in masculinity, and high in power distance.

In another study, Steenkamp[41] calculated percentages of adoption categories for packaged goods in five European countries (France, Germany, Italy, Spain, and the United Kingdom). He found significant correlations between the adoption of these packaged goods and low uncertainty avoidance and high individualism cultures.

Researchers also looked at the relationship between culture and global branding and advertising. De Mooji and Hofstede[42] summarize research that uses the Hofstede model to explain differences in the concept of self, personality and identity, which in turn explain variations in branding strategy and communications. For instance, self and personality as developed in Western countries, include the person as an autonomous entity with a distinctive set of attributes, qualities or processes, which cause behavior. Personality, including ideal characteristics in collectivist countries, varies by social rules, and Easterners believe in the continuous shaping of personality traits by situational influence.[43] These differences affect the practice of attaching personalities to brands, which is typical of individualist cultures. For instance, Aaker defines a brand personality as a set of human characteristics associated with a brand. She illustrates it with the following example: "Absolut Vodka personified tends to be described as a cool, hip, contemporary 25-year old...."[44]

Several studies have found that brand personality factors are culture specific and represent human values.[45] For instance, a study of Korean brand personalities of well-known global brands like Nike, Sony, Levi's, Adidas, Volkswagen, and BMW, found two specific Korean brand personalities, labeled "passive likeableness" and "ascendancy."[46] Consumers also attribute different personalities to the same brand, e.g. consumers differ in what they attribute to the brand Red Bull, which nonetheless has been marketed with the same brand identity. The difficulty for marketers is that companies want to be consistent in their global messages worldwide, but consumers attribute personalities to such brands that fit their own cultural values, not the values of the producer of the brand. Thus, companies need to identify the values that are associated with human characteristics or traits in a society (see also Chapter 13 on Advertising).

The Schwartz Value Survey and Trompenaars' Dimensions

Schwartz's research has provided insight into the development and consequences of a diverse range of behavioral attitudes and orientations, such as religious belief, political orientation and voting, social group relations, consumer behavior, as well as the conceptualization of human values across cultures.[47] The cultural values framework was designed with the intent to overcome some of the limitations of Hofstede's approach. Schwarz initially identified 56 individual values and then investigated which of these values had an equivalent meaning across cultures. His framework is based on four dimensions: openness to change (autonomy vs. conformity), self-transcendence (self-direction), conservation (tradition) and self-enhancement (achievement, power). Some similarities between the Hofstede and Schwartz theories can be detected. Openness to change and self-transcendence are similar to Hofstede's individualism construct. The conservatism/autonomy value dimension bears considerable similarity to Hofstede's individualism/collectivism dimension. It also is closely linked to Hofstede's power distance dimension. The Schwartz Value Survey has been replicated in many countries and validated for measurement equivalence.[48] Schwartz's human values scale identifies ten motivationally distinct value orientations that are common to people in different cultures.

When examining differences between the two frameworks, Ng and colleagues[49] advocate that Schwarz's value dimensions have many advantages when compared to those of Hofstede. The former was theoretically derived, whereas the latter was empirically developed. In addition, Schwarz's framework represents a more comprehensive set of cultural dimensions. Researchers also found that in some countries, e.g. The Netherlands, Australia, a Schwarz-based cultural distance measure had greater explanatory power than the traditional Hofstede version.[50]

Another advantage to using the Schwartz Value Survey is that **it can measure individual value differences**. Schwartz and Bilsky[51] argued that the individualism–collectivism construct implicitly implies that different types of individualist values vary together consistently to form one type of value orientation that opposes that of collectivism. However, at the individual level personal and in-group interests may serve both individualist and collectivist values. Some values are collective but not those of the in-group (e.g. equality for all and social justice). Heterogeneity of individuals within a society means that not all individuals in a collectivist culture necessarily share a collectivist orientation. To overcome some of these limitations, Schwartz proposes exploring value orientations at the individual level in greater depth. Individual values are concerned with hedonism, achievement, self-direction, social power, and stimulation; collective values are pro-social, restrictive conformity, security and tradition, while maturity is classified as both an individual and collective value type. If the cultural values of participants had been measured in accordance with this paradigm, the importance of tradition for choice behavior could have been explored further and other relationships between value types and choice behavior may have been uncovered.

A number of researchers have utilized the Schwartz Value Survey to study consumer behavior, especially for market segmentation and advertising. Krystallis et al.[52] adapted the Schwartz Value system to identify organic food relevant surveys. A food-related lifestyle segmentation approach contributed to the identification of different consumer segments in eight European countries. Benevolence and universalism were found to form a joint factor reflecting the transcendence dimension of the Value theory. Overall, the study could explain consumer behavior in an organic food purchasing context for 81.5 percent of the European sample. Their study further confirmed the usefulness of using a value-based approach in different situations that are affected by human values. De Juan Vigaray and Hota[53] validated nine out of ten value types in Spain in the Spanish fashion apparel context. In addition they found three culturally unique Spanish value types: ecology, spiritualism, and self-direction. Likewise, a group of researchers found that value segmentation could be used to understand both differences and similarities across countries in Scandinavia, which some may consider to be homogeneous.[54]

Other models, like **The Seven Dimensions of Culture**, were identified by Fons Trompenaars and Charles Hampden-Turner in their 1997 book,[55] *Riding the Waves of Culture*. The authors developed the model after spending ten years researching the preferences and values of people in dozens of cultures around the world. As part of this, they sent questionnaires to more than 46,000 managers in 40 countries. They found that people from different cultures aren't just randomly different from one another; they differ in very specific, even predictable, ways. This is because each culture has its own way of thinking, its own values and beliefs, and different preferences, placed on a variety of different factors. Trompenaars and Hampden-Turner concluded that what distinguishes people from one culture compared with another is where these preferences fall in one of the following seven dimensions:

- Universalism versus particularism.
- Individualism versus communitarianism.
- Specific versus diffuse.
- Neutral versus emotional.
- Achievement versus ascription.
- Sequential time versus synchronous time.
- Internal direction versus outer direction.

Fletcher and Melewar[56] compared the fourteen least developed (i.e. emerging) with the fourteen most developed countries. This study found that with Hofstede's dimensions, emerging markets exhibit much greater degrees of both power distance and collectivism. With Trompenaars' dimensions, the study found that emerging markets tend to be particularist rather than universalist with obligations and particular circumstances taking precedence and that ascription played a greater role than achievement in such cultures. They also found that emerging markets were specific rather than diffuse and characterized by cultures that are highly focused on context. In such cultures, information is largely obtained from **personal information networks**. Also, Hofstede's sample of IBM employees did not include countries from the bottom of the pyramid. Knowledge of the cultural drivers of those at the BOP is necessary so as to appreciate their circumstances and underlying thinking when making purchasing decisions. This was the approach adopted by the Grameenphone company operation in Bangladesh (Geo Map 3.2) (leased mobile phones to housewives who rented usage by the minute to their friends and acquaintances) and with "barefoot banking" as exemplified by the Wau Microbank in Papua New Guinea (who created lending programs for BOP customers to enable them to establish small-scale businesses).[57]

These cultural drivers may be reflected in the social climate of communities at the BOP. For example, collectivism is manifest in India where it is not uncommon to engage in collective purchasing and common use of facilities, for instance when several families band together to buy a washing machine. Such collective activities also create an emphasis on the need to maintain relationships.

GLOBAL LEADERSHIP AND ORGANIZATIONAL BEHAVIOR EFFECTIVENESS[58]

The Global Leadership and Organizational Behavior Effectiveness (GLOBE) model uses a set of cultural values and practices to measure national culture. GLOBE was developed in response to Hofstede's call for good measurement and good theory in order to conduct rigorous cross-cultural research. The theory was developed from a proposition that attributes defining a specified culture are predictive of leadership styles and organizational practices. The theory also predicted that selected aspects

GEO MAP 3.2
Grameenphone
Source: Adapted from:
CIA Maps, The World
Factbook[59]

The headquarters of **Grameenphone** is located in
Basundhara, Baridhara, Dhaka-1229, Bangladesh.

Anglo	Arab	Confucian Asia	Germanic Europe	Eastern Europe	
England	Qatar	Taiwan	Austria	Hungary	**TABLE 3.4** Some Societal Clusters of Countries
Australia	Morocco	Singapore	Switzerland	Russia	
South Africa	Turkey	Hong Kong	Germany	Kazakhstan	
Canada	Egypt	South Korea	The Netherlands	Albania	
New Zealand	Kuwait	China		Poland	
Ireland		Japan		Greece	
USA				Slovenia	
				Georgia	

Source: Adapted from: Gupta, V. et al. (2002), 'Cultural clusters: Methodology and findings', *Journal of World Business*, 37(1), pp. 11–15

of cultural practices will account for the economic competitiveness of nations as well as the physical and psychological well-being of their members.

The GLOBE research group has clustered countries on the basis of shared similarities among social and psychological variables such as attitudes, values, and work goals. Sixty-one nations have been grouped into ten clusters (Table 3.4) on the basis of nine cultural dimensions (Table 3.5), five of which have similar definitions to those of Hofstede. Like Hofstede, respondents included middle managers. However, unlike Hofstede, these managers were selected from 825 organizations (rather than focusing on one organization) in the 61 countries sampled.

TABLE 3.5 GLOBE Cultural Dimensions	**Uncertainty Avoidance**	The extent to which members of an organization or society strive to avoid uncertainty by reliance on social norms, rituals, and bureaucratic practices to alleviate the unpredictability of future events.
	Power Distance	The degree to which members of an organization or society expect and agree that power should be unequally shared.
	Societal Collectivism	The degree to which organizational and societal institutional practices encourage and regard collective distribution of resources and collective action.
	In-Group Collectivism	The degree to which individuals express pride, loyalty, and cohesiveness in their organizations or families.
	Gender Egalitarianism	The extent to which an organization or a society minimizes gender role differences and gender discrimination.
	Assertiveness	The degree to which individuals in organizations or societies are assertive, confrontational, and aggressive in social relationships.
	Future Orientation	The degree to which individuals in organizations or societies engage in future-oriented behaviors such as planning, investing in the future, and delaying gratification. (Includes the future-oriented component of the dimension "Confucian Dynamism" of Hofstede and Bond (1988).
	Performance Orientation	The extent to which an organization or society encourages and rewards group members for performance improvement and excellence.
	Humane Orientation	The degree to which individuals in organizations or societies encourage and reward individuals for being fair, altruistic, friendly, generous, caring and kind to others. (Similar to the dimension "Kind Heartedness" by Hofstede and Bond (1988).

Source: Adapted from: House, R. et al. (2002), 'Understanding cultures and implicit leadership theories across the globe: An introduction to project GLOBE', *Journal of World Business*, 37(Special Issue), pp. 3–10

Are the GLOBE and Hofstede clusters similar? Taking the Anglo cluster as an example, we can compare the individual country ratings of both frameworks. However, there are differences in scale ratings between the two frameworks. Power Distance was rated higher in the GLOBE Survey, while Uncertainty Avoidance and Long-Term (future) orientation was rated lower in Hofstede's sample than by GLOBE. Other cultural measures were similar in the two frameworks. These differences stem from sample selection and the way questions were worded on the questionnaires.

CULTURE AND CULTURAL DISTANCE

While concepts of culture, especially Hofstede's, have not explicitly referred to cultural *distance* (CD), they are used to assess multifaceted and sophisticated differences between/across (national) culture systems. Based on Hofstede's identification of cultural dimensions, the **Kogut/Singh**[60] **index** soon became the paradigmatic measure of distance. However convenient their use, both the notion of distance and its measurement often involve problems in conceptualization and measurement. The reasons for inconsistencies in empirical results can be traced back to several reasons, including (1) methodological flaws and the narrow conceptualization of the culture distance construct; (2) illusion of linearity, symmetry, and stability; (3) illusion of discordance.[61]

- *Methodological flaws and narrow conceptualization:* Hofstede's country scores were developed through factor analysis of the means of nationally aggregated individual item responses, which were collected as part of IBM employee surveys.[62] The dimensions do not exist at the level of the individual, and thus national culture scores cannot be attributed to individuals living in the respective countries.[63] To assume similar relationships exist across levels has been labeled "ecological fallacy."[64]

- *Illusion of linearity, symmetry and stability*: Apart from methodological problems, previous conceptions of CD are often simplistic and neglect the depth, richness, and complexity of culture. Among the major limitations is the "illusion of linearity" which hints at the linear impact of CD on investments, entry mode, and performance, i.e. the higher the distance, the higher the problems. Another potential problem with reporting performance results relates to the presumed symmetry of distance concepts but perceived distances may largely differ from A to B and B to A. Finally, CD has often been considered as implicitly stable—an assumption, which is obviously unrealistic. Cultural values change as, for instance, recent developments in emerging markets show.

- *Illusion of discordance:* CD is perceived as a concept, which considers difference, dissimilarity, or diversity, as leading to a lack of fit and thus an impediment to successful interaction. This assumption underlies most market entry studies which suggest that the minimization of distance is likely to yield higher performance rates. However, this "illusion of discordance" ignores the possible beneficial outcomes of balancing seemingly opposed concepts or cultural dimensions, and there is sufficient evidence that diversity triggers performance.[65]

While Hofstede's cultural dimensions and their operationalization have remained the most used concepts in international business and marketing research, a couple of other concepts have been introduced to overcome some of their inherent difficulties. Table 3.6 provides an overview.

Notably, the idea of **cultural diversity** refers to cultural heterogeneity in a firm's global portfolio of business units or activities.[66] Indeed, there have been increased calls to look at the positive side of cultural distance and consider differences an asset not just a liability.[67] Researchers argue that greater cultural diversity is positively associated with various firm outcomes, such as increased innovation and learning benefits, better teamwork, and more successful marketing efforts.[68] With regard to market entry selection, cultural diversity emphasizes the potentially enriching and unique capabilities of foreign contexts, which can lead to new ways of doing business and to greater exploration of resources. Gaining sufficient diversity is often considered to be the driving force to expand and enrich a company's portfolio of restricted products, technologies, or industry segments.

TABLE 3.6 Comparison Between Different Concepts of Culture and Distance	Culture Concept	Explanation	Examples
	Cultural distance	Difference has a negative effect that poses a barrier to international business activities.	Entering new markets and designing new products for very distant countries implies larger difficulties in doing business and higher adaptation costs.
	Cultural diversity	Difference has a positive effect that enhances relationships and operations.	Product development efforts often benefit from cross-cultural teams where different ideas, values, and backgrounds benefit creativity.
	Cultural friction	Friction arises from situation-specific contact between organizations and does not yield positive or negative consequences per se.	Organizations may choose different forms of market entry modes, where joint ventures or mergers are likely to create higher friction than export-based forms of entry. However, higher friction may not automatically be detrimental but could also result in new businesses and strategies.
	Cultural positions	Organizations may have different positions on cultural dimensions (low-high) and these positions determine their relationship.	Managing headquarters-subsidiary relationships may be influenced on how partners' positions on their cultural dimensions are. For instance, if both score high on uncertainty avoidance, a stricter regulation and control system may be appreciated and executed.

Source: Compiled by Authors

Shenkar[69] talks about **cultural friction** and argues that friction indicates the actual cultural contact between exchanging organizations in an environment where multilevel, yet intertwined cultural differences simultaneously occur. Departing from the cultural distance concept, the friction concept captures cultural differences at multiple levels, such as national, organizational, team, and individual levels whenever they are in contact. In addition, cultural friction may not transform into a clash, or yield any positive or negative interaction effect until organizations truly interact. That is, friction is manifested through situation-specific contact and can be influenced through a variety of managerial mechanisms, such as communication, acculturation, socialization, entry speed, etc.

Drogendijk and Holm[70] suggest **cultural positions** by adopting a relational view of cultural differences. They are interested in how cultural characteristics of two organizational units, and the differences between them, affect the units' relationship. "Position" refers both to the "absolute" cultural characteristics of each party (in terms of scores or qualitative description) and to their relative content or value. For example, two organizations may both score high or low in terms of power distance. Overall, both scenarios result in low distance between them but both scenarios may have different consequences for the management of their relationship. This view challenges the assumption that cultural distance is always symmetric, i.e. the distance partner A perceives to B is the same that partner B perceives to A.

CULTURE AND COMMUNICATION

An important component of culture and means to overcome cultural distance is the way people communicate with each other. In addition to verbal communication, there is a variety of means by which people can transfer meaning. Remember the elements of culture, for instance, where architecture or the location of your office can communicate a lot more than you may have originally intended.

Verbal Versus Non-Verbal Communication

The spoken word, or verbal communication, is often believed to be the dominant form, yet it has been estimated that between 50 and 90 percent of communication is non-verbal. During the eighteenth century, many Europeans were educated in the art of elocution—how to use gestures, posture, dress, and proper diction to make speeches more dramatic and emotional. The first social scientific perspectives on non-verbal communication emerged in the nineteenth century. Most notably, in his book, *The Expression of Emotion in Man and Animals*, Charles Darwin (1872/1904) examined how non-verbal behavior communicates emotion in socially adaptive ways.

However, body language can be misunderstood and gestures have different meanings in different cultures (Figure 3.8). It is sometimes difficult to understand each other even with a common language, as the following examples of verbal communication that follow and in Box 3.3 illustrate.

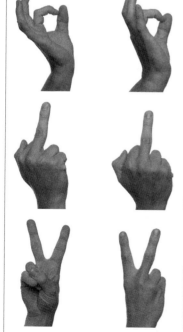

A circle means OK in the United States, but in Japan it signifies money, in Germany it is obscene, and it is impolite in Russia

The middle finger implies an insult in most Western countries.

The two fingers are often used to symbolize "victory" or success. However, they are also considered as insult or American dominance.

FIGURE 3.8
Example of Non-Verbal Communication
Source: www.pixabay.com (free photos)

Box 3.3   Technology-in-Focus: Lenovo

A multicultural product design team met at Lenovo's North Carolina office to develop a concept that would give the computers a "unique look and feel." However, cultural differences were apparent. "The Western-based people said that the Lenovo product line should have a consistent look and feel, or what it described as a 'common icon.' The design team from China disagreed … The Western team used the word 'common' as a synonym for universal, while the team from China understood the word 'common' as a synonym for ordinary." This example shows that many words may have different meanings across cultures. For example, "boot" in British English, "trunk" in American English; "mess kit" to the British army means the smart bow tie gear worn to a formal mess dinner. To the Americans, "mess kit" means a knife, fork, spoon, and tin plate. "Cheers" in South Africa means goodbye, while in the UK it means thanks; "just now" in South Africa means shortly, while in the UK it signifies right now.

Source: Adapted from: Rosenbusch, S. (2008, Spring). The developing world 101. *Wharton Alumni Magazine*, 15.

The meeting, planned over a number of weeks, was over in less than an hour. The German team was annoyed that their hard work was not recognized, the French team was anxious that their lack of preparation for the meeting would not be revealed. The real problem was concealed in the translation of one word. The Germans wanted a discussion of their Konzept. The French translation used the apparently similar French word, concept. Unfortunately, the words have different meanings. To the Germans, Konzept meant a detailed plan of a proposed new product; to the French, concept meant an opportunity to discuss, propose, and create a proposal that would eventually become the detailed plan. Unfortunately, the meeting never started with a firm mutually agreed framework. The result was a wasted meeting.[71] See also Box 3.3 for another example of how cross-cultural communication can fail.

High- Versus Low-Context Cultures

The anthropologist Hall (1966)[72] introduced the notion of high- and low-context cultures in order to understand their basic differences in communication styles. In high-context cultures (e.g. Asian and Arab countries), the communication style is influenced by close human relationships, a well-structured social hierarchy, and strong behavioral norms. The message is transmitted through the person and its context, with little information in the coded, explicit, transmitted part of the communication. Thus, the recipient is expected to read "between the lines" and to understand what remains unsaid. Moreover, members of high context cultures tend to place more focus on non-verbal communication such as body language. There is even an aphorism that expressly addresses this issue: He who knows does not speak; he who speaks does not know. In low-context cultures (e.g. Germany, France, UK, US), most information is included in the transmitted part of the message. A low-context culture is characterized by direct, linear communication, which is always explicit.

Research focusing on Hall's low-context country dimension has reiterated the difference in language use. For instance, Usunier and Roulin[73] analyze business websites and found that websites from low-context cultures tend to be more direct, offer more informative content, and are more transparent than their counterparts from high-context cultures. Communication in low-context cultures is precise, open, and based on true intentions. Generally, people from low-context communication cultures think that rational appeals for the products and services are important, and tend to employ direct, textual, factual, and analytical argumentation in advertising and marketing.[74] For instance, the IKEA Chinese website uses heavy graphics from daily life (balls) and is bright and colorful so as to induce children to play, the Dutch website is focused on the functionality of items and is visually very orderly and gives a lower impression on interactivity. Your task as a web designer or global marketer will be to create materials that appeal to the values of the respective target group. A large part of that is making sure your message resonates with your target group's cultural preferences and expectations.

Time Orientation

Hall's work has also been significant in his treatment of time. **Both high and low-context cultures can be distinguished by their relation to time.** Low-context cultures are generally **monochronic** ("doing one thing at a time"); time is important and regulates how things are done. For example, it is more important to stick to the agenda of a meeting, and use Gantt charts to plan and control projects. On the other hand, **polychronic** ("doing a number of things at the same time") cultures are much less time-oriented and therefore, less organized. Interrupting a speaker at a meeting is taken as a sign of interest, rather than rudeness. Arriving 10–15 minutes late for a meeting in a monochronic culture requires a slight apology, while the same sort of apology in a polychronic culture would be the thing to do only if one arrives an hour after the scheduled time (Table 3.7).

Some dimensions of time orientation for both monochronic and polychronic cultures are shown in Table 3.8. It should be kept in mind that in certain cultures, orientation to time may not be a dichotomy. For example, the Japanese tend to use both styles. In technology and dealings with foreigners they tend to be monochronic, while polychronic for personal relations.

	If late in a monochronic culture	If late in a polychronic culture	**TABLE 3.7**
Whisper an excuse	5–10 minutes	45–60 minute	What to Do If You Are Late
Make an apology	10–15 minutes	60+ minutes	
Prepare good excuse	15+ minutes	Over one hour	
Source: Compiled by Authors			

TABLE 3.8 Some Differences Between Monochronic and Polychronic Action	Factor	Monochronic Action	Polychronic Action
	Actions	Do one thing at a time.	Do many things at once.
	Focus	Concentrate on the objective or task.	Are easily distracted.
	Attention to time	Plan when things must be achieved.	What will be achieved is more important than when.
	Priority	The task comes first.	Relationship comes first.
	Respect for property	Seldom borrow or lend things.	Borrow and lend things often and easily.

Source: * Adapted from: Hall, E.T. (1959). *The Silent Language*. New York: Doubleday

Space and Distance

Another aspect of non-verbal communication is its relation to space. Hall recognized three types of space: fixed-feature and semi-fixed, and the way in which people organize things, such as homes and offices. Some people demand large homes, big cars, and spacious offices. Even the location of a parking space adjacent to an office building may be an indication of status. "Big" in these cases may signal status, power, and importance. In other cultures, big may not be as important. University classrooms for example, can be organized so that students sit in an oval shaped arrangement or in straight rows facing the lecturer. Moreover, classrooms can be level or banked, theater style. The way in which the classroom is designed will affect the interaction between students with each other and with the lecturer.

Another form of space relates to distances between people, or personal space. According to Hall,[75] the distance required between people depends not only on the culture, but also on the situation. Situational distances depend upon whether people meeting each other are acquaintances or strangers, whether the meeting is formal or informal. Generally, distances are greater between strangers during formal meetings. What is the permissible body contact in a given culture? In high-contact cultures such as those of Latin America and the Middle East, people maintain close distances between each other, as opposed to those of low-contact cultures, in which the opposite is true. An attempt by a Latin-American salesperson to greet a potential German customer with a bear hug would not be conducive for starting a fruitful relationship.

These cultural distinctions largely explain why Western social networks such as Facebook and Twitter were not successful in Japan. Mixi, the country's largest social network, was positioned as a tool for communicating at a distance through the use of diaries and communities to meet like-minded members. It was not positioned like Facebook; to make new friends or for self-representation.

GLOBAL CUSTOMERS

We learned previously that culture is a key to understanding consumer behavior. This part of the chapter looks at the characteristics of some of the major regional markets of the world, including China and India. In studying these markets, we focus on the processes by which buyers learn, evaluate, and adopt products, and the factors that affect their decisions.

China

Many Western companies view China as the world's largest market. Companies often tend to think of China in terms of a simplistic, arithmetic calculation. For example, if each of the 1.3 billion people will use a product once in a year, that will bring enormous sales to companies. In fact, no one should be so naïve as to think of the market in these terms. However, many marketers have overestimated the market in China. There is a real need to understand the market prospects as well as the complexity of the Chinese market.

China has long been known as the "factory of the world" with low-cost manufacturing and increasing export rates of cheap products. But policymakers in Beijing, looking to strengthen China's economy, are no longer satisfied with this positioning. They want to break China's dependence on foreign technology, moving from a model of *"made in China"* to one of *"innovated in China,"* accompanied by increasing labor and production costs. China is no longer the *eldorado* of entrepreneurs trying to earn money very quickly. Instead, the country demands a lot of energy, as the Chinese are loyal consumers but hard to satisfy.

Approaching China as one unified consumer market is wrought with danger. Today it is actually a collection of many different consumer archetypes, groups of consumers with different preferences and behaviors. In fact, China is very similar to the European Union in terms of its subtle but important differences in culture, language, and tastes, and the economic development of its different regional markets. For instance, urban Chinese consumers now exhibit the consumption patterns of a middle-class lifestyle. This means they are spending money on things and experiences that not long ago would have been considered luxuries. It also means spending more on goods that are perceived to be of higher quality. As a consequence, marketers are well advised to reflect on their segmentation, for instance, by differentiating between first-tier cities (e.g. Shenzhen, Shanghai, Guangzhou, Beijing), second-tier cities (Ningbo, Nanchang, Chengdu), and third-tier cities (Jilin, Weifang, Xuzhou).[76]

China's outdated transportation infrastructure and shaky commitment to scheduling, further give Western marketers, used to "just-in-time" operations, quite a challenge when it comes to distribution and logistics. Then there are the gender differences. According to one experienced advertising agency executive, Chinese women in the field are more honest, flexible, and quicker learners than the men, but they may often be in short supply as bigger and better offers from competing agencies often sway even the most loyal professionals. Finally, there's the most important difference for marketers: Chinese consumers rely on advertising for different information, depending on their level of marketing sophistication. The Chinese middle class, that is quickly acquiring the needs and wants of

Box 3.4   People-in-Focus: The Chuppies Are Here

Urban, young, and affluent Chinese professionals are dubbed "Chuppies." Many are successful entrepreneurs, business leaders, and employees of foreign companies based in China. While they comprise only a majority of the Chinese population (50 million), they are growing by 10 percent by year. Nevertheless, they comprise a significant potential consumer market. They are owners of iPods, use credit cards, are fashion conscious, dine out, and attend cultural events. They are much different than their parents when it comes to behavior and dress. They remain single longer, purchase their own home rather than rent, invest in stocks and bonds, and travel outside the country. Those born after 1960 did not experience the "Cultural Revolution" and its implication. They prefer the image of Mark Zuckerberg to Mao Zedong. Chuppies under the age of 30 dress the same as Chinese professionals living and working abroad.

Yet there are some differences between the Chuppies and their age class in Western countries. About half of the Chuppies save about 50 percent of their incomes, about 20 percent live with their parents, and the majority does not hesitate to buy fake branded products.

In short, Chuppies will continue to be an important consumer segment in China that exporters and those doing business in the country cannot afford to ignore.

Source: Adapted from: Robert Hsu (2010). *The Chuppie strategy*. Philips Investment Resources, LLC, [Newsletter to subscribers].

its counterparts around the world, is also more receptive to traditional product branding messages. The majority of Chinese consumers, however, expect to learn more basic information about a product from its ads and labels. Therefore, localizing product packaging and marketing campaigns becomes as important as ever in China. For instance, after nearly 14 years of working to persuade China to buy into its foreign coffee culture, Starbucks Corp. is aiming to become more Chinese as it plans a rapid expansion in the country. In terms of retail outlets, kiosk-sized stores work well in the US, where office workers grab bacon and Gouda sandwiches to go in the morning on the way to work. Starbucks has learned that Chinese consumers value space and couches on which to relax in the afternoons. It also plans to introduce new Chinese-inspired flavors, building on existing favorites like red bean frappuccinos.[77] Another aspect of Chinese culture that influences buyers' behavior is the reluctance to pioneer. The typical Chinese consumer does not want to be among the first to try a new product, but the discomfort of being "behind the times" may make them think that if the neighbors have tried it, they had better follow suit soon. The strong collective characteristic may imply that informal channels of communication are important in Chinese society, and that key opinion leaders play a vital role.

India

With a population of over one billion and a GNP of US$1856.5 billion, India's per capita GNI of US$1,550 in 2012 was one of the lowest in the region. Some population experts predict that India will overtake China, which had a one-child policy until recently, as the world's largest country by the middle of the century. Income within the country is polarized. India has hundreds of millions of poor people. Many of these people, an estimated 60 percent of the population, live close to or below the US$2 a day poverty line.[78] But India also has pockets of prosperity in cities such as Bangalore, the Indian Silicon Valley, where talented and computer-savvy young graduates are fueling the growth of the software industry in the country. Given this talent, the low salaries vis-à-vis the United States and the availability of real-time communication links, many US companies have sourced or opened offices in India for software development and export. In fact, India's software industry has been growing rapidly over the last few years and high-technology exports (percentage of manufactured exports) in India was last measured at 6.87 in 2011, according to the World Bank.

Based on this feverish economic growth, many compare India to the other emerging economic giant in Asia—China. However, there are some signs that India will have a harder time keeping pace with its rival. From signs of rising inflation, to dismal infrastructure, lacking public services, and corruption, India may be about a decade behind China in development.[79] Table 3.9 shows how India's infrastructure compares with China, and the United States. China is rapidly catching up to the United States in roadways and airports, while India lags far behind. However, while China's growth may seem impressive, do not forget about the relative sizes (distances and populations) of the countries. Parts of China are still backward compared to the United States.

Nevertheless, given India's enormous market size and its current relatively small, but growing middle class, marketers should consider its potential and the opportunities presented in this underserved market. However, major challenges such as widespread corruption, a large informal economy, which accounts for a big portion of the gross national product in some Latin American countries, and the widest income disparity in the world between the poor majority and the rich elite, still threaten to derail the progress made in recent years in the region.

C.K. Prahalad claims in his influential book, *The Fortune at the Bottom of the Pyramid*, that these developing markets provide one of the biggest opportunities for companies currently. The four billion people that live on less than $2

	India	China	United States	
				TABLE 3.9
Population (2014)	1,269,933,700	1,395,212,358	323,026,398	India's Infrastructure Compared to China and the United States
National expressways (2012, in million km)	4.1	4.24	6.58 (2014)	
Airport passengers (2011)	34,729,467 (New Delhi)	77,403,668 (Beijing)	92,365,860 (Atlanta)	
Nuclear power production (2012, in MW)	4,780	12,086	102,136	
Internet users (2014)	243,198,922	641,601,070	279,834,232	
Port shipments (2012, volume in million TEUs)	4.26 (Jawaharlal Nehru)	32.53 (Shanghai)	8.08 (Los Angeles)	
Source: Different Data from Various Sources[80]				

a day represent tomorrow's four billion consumers if only they are offered the right products. Surprisingly, marketers control many of the factors that can make these products a reality and thus, create the "capacity to consume" in these previously ignored target markets. According to Prahalad, the four Ps of marketing (product, price, promotion, and place) need to be modified and complemented by the four As (affordability, access, awareness, and availability) as mentioned in Chapter 1.

Developing markets in developing countries by designing products and services that fit the poor's special needs and purchasing patterns can mean opportunities not only for the underprivileged but also for the companies that are serving these markets. Today, with the spread of mobile phones and the rise of user-generated content (UGC) on the web, early adopters and influencers have more ways than ever to communicate with their social circle and the world at large. Blogs, podcasts, websites, and all other interactive tools available through Web 2.0 make such interactions exceedingly simple.

SUMMARY

- Perhaps the most striking fact about world markets and buyers is that for the first time in modern history, the entire world is growing. According to World Bank estimates, every world region including Africa will continue to grow, and for the most part the developing countries will grow faster than the rich.
- There are various ways of dividing the countries of the world into different regional markets. In effect, defining regional markets is an exercise in clustering countries so that similarities within clusters and differences between clusters will be maximized.
- The shortage of goods and services is the central problem of transitioning economies and low-income countries. While these countries may pose certain challenges for marketers, they represent potentially attractive markets for many consumer product companies. Marketers could apply basic marketing concepts to ensure that products are designed that fit the needs and incomes of these markets.
- All buyers go through a similar process in making a purchase decision. Thus, although buyers in different countries and world regions will go through a similar process in making their purchase decisions, they will make different purchases since they will respond to the unique economic, social and cultural, political and governmental, environmental, competitive, and personal factors that influence buyer decisions.
- The process that buyers go through is summarized in diffusion theory; a marketing universal. The pattern by which an individual adopts a new idea, described by sociologist Everett Rogers, comprises of three concepts that are extremely useful to global marketers: the adoption process, characteristics of innovations, and adopter categories.

DISCUSSION QUESTIONS

1. Think about different ways in which culture can be represented. What are the implications for managers?
2. Based on the information in Box 3.4, "The Chuppies Are Here," develop a market entry plan for a hypothetical wine label from Spain that is looking to enter the Chinese market.
3. Consumers in some countries, like Japan, are reluctant to accept "foreign" retailing institutions and imported products. Explain this behavior by using the models of culture contained in this chapter.
4. Do you agree with the statement "People do not buy products, they buy relationships"? Why or why not?

EXPERIENTIAL EXERCISES

1. Using the Hofstede framework, compare your home country with France and Indonesia. How would the framework help you to understand consumer behavior for culturally-bound products like furniture?
2. Compare the Hofstede clusters of countries with those of the GLOBE model. Which clusters have a common group of countries? Which do not? How do you account for the fact that some of the clusters of both frameworks do not overlap?
3. How well do you know the hidden language of color? Take the test here: http://www.aplustranslations.com/importance-of-colours-in-different-countries/

KEY TERMS

- Cultural distance
- Cultural diversity
- Cultural friction
- Cultural position
- Diffusion of innovation
- Ethnocentrism
- Global leadership
- High-context culture

- Hofstede's framework
- Kogut/Singh-Index
- Low-context culture
- Monochronic versus polychronic cultures
- National character
- Non-verbal communication
- Self-reference criterion
- Subculture

APPENDIX—SELECTED HOFSTEDE SCORES

APPENDIX 3.A Hofstede's Dimensions of Culture	COUNTRY	PD	IDV	UA	MAS	LT	IND
	Australia	36	90	51	61	31	71
	Canada	39	80	48	52	23	68
	Germany	35	67	65	66	31	40
	Great Britain	35	89	35	66	25	69
	Netherlands	38	80	53	14	44	68
	New Zealand	22	79	49	58	30	75
	Sweden	31	71	29	5	33	78
	USA	40	91	46	62	29	68
	Brazil	69	38	76	49	65	59
	China (mainland)	80	20	66	30	118	24
	Hong Kong	68	25	29	57	96	17
	Taiwan	58	17	69	45	87	49
	Japan	54	46	92	95	80	42
	South Korea	60	18	85	39	75	29
	India	77	48	40	56	61	26
	Philippines	94	32	44	64	19	42
	Singapore	74	20	8	48	48	46
	Thailand	64	20	64	34	56	45
	West Africa	77	20	54	46	16	-

Source: www.geert-hofstede.com [Accessed: January 2, 2015]

NOTES

1 http://www.kwintessential.co.uk/cultural-services/articles/cultural-sensitivity.html [Accessed: September 2, 2014].

2 Sources: BBC News; Indiapress.org; Channel 4.com.

3 Dudovskiy, J. (2012), 'Self-reference criterion: Introduction and illustrations', http://research-methodology.net/self-reference-criterion-introduction-and-illustrations/ [Accessed: September 3, 2014].

4 For one of the classic studies see: Shimp, T. A. and Sharma, S. (1987), 'Consumer ethnocentrism: construction and validation of the CETSCALE', *Journal of Marketing Research*, 24(3), pp. 280–9.

5 Kroeber, A.L. and Kluckhohn, C. (1952), 'Culture: A critical review of concepts and definitions', *Harvard University Peabody Museum of American Archeology and Ethnology Papers*, pp. 1–47.

6 Hofstede, G. (2001). *Culture's consequences: Comparing values, behaviors, institutions and organizations across nations*. 2nd ed. Thousand Oaks, CA: Sage.

7 Carpenter, J.M., Moore, M., Alexander, N., and Doherty, A.M. (2013), 'Consumer demographics, ethnocentrism, cultural values, and acculturation to the global consumer culture: A retail perspective', *Journal of Marketing Management*, 29(3–4), pp. 271–91.

8 Zimmermann, K.A. (2012), 'What is culture? Definitions of culture', *Life Science*, July 9, 2012, http://www.livescience.com/21478-what-is-culture-definition-of-culture.html [Accessed: August 31, 2014].

9 'Some humorous cross-cultural advertising gaffes', (from a brochure at a Tokyo car rental firm), http://www.takingontobacco.org/intro/funny.html [Accessed: August 12, 2014].

10 Yaprak, A. (2008), 'Culture study in international marketing: A critical review and suggestions for further research', *International Marketing Review*, 25(2), pp. 215–29.

11 Tian, K. and Borges, L. (2011), 'Cross-cultural issues in marketing communications: An anthropological perspective of international business', *International Journal of China Marketing*, 2(1), pp. 110–26.

12 See website of Erin Meyer for examples of the culture map and video: http://erinmeyer.com [Accessed: June 10, 2014].

13 Xiaozhu, Z. (2012), 'Before you talk politics with the Chinese', http://www.zess.uni-goettingen.de/wordpress/?p=779 [Accessed: July 14, 2014].

14 Mikulincer, M. and Shaver, P.R. (2014). *APA handbook of personality and social psychology*. Washington D.C.: American Psychological Association.

15 Kra, P. (2002), 'The concept of national character in 18th century France', www.fupress.net/index.php/cromohs/article/view/15716/14605 [Accessed: January 10, 2014].

16 d'Argens, Jean-Baptiste. (1738). *Lettres juives*. The Hague.

17 Peabody, D. (1985). *National characteristics*. Cambridge, UK: Cambridge University Press.

18 Terracciano, A. et al. (2005), 'National character does not reflect mean personality trait levels in 49 Cultures', *Science*, 310, 5745, pp.96–100; McCrea, R. and Terracciano, A. (2006), 'National character and Personality', *Current Directions in Psychological Science*, 15(4), pp.156–61. Actually, this is also one of the major criticism of Hofstede's and the GLOBE scores (see below).

19 'Absolutely Swedish – Outlining a national character', www.sverigeturism.se/smorgasbord/smorgasbord/culture/swedish/index.html. [Accessed: April 18, 2007].

20 Baoku, L., Lijuan, W., and Bingru, L. (2011), 'Demand attributes and market segmentation: An evaluation of refrigerator purchase behavior in rural China', *International Journal of China Marketing*, 1(2), pp. 13–33.

21 Terracciano, A. et al. (2005), 'National character does not reflect mean personality trait levels in 49 cultures', *Science*, 310, 5745, pp. 96–100.

22 Hofstede, G., Hofsted, J.G., and Minkov, M. (2010). *Cultures and organizations: Software of the mind*. 3rd ed. New York: McGraw-Hill.

23 Schwartz, S. (1994). Beyond individualism/collectivism: New cultural dimensions of value. In: Kim, U. et al. (eds.). *Individualism and collectivism: Theory, method and applications*. Thousand Oaks: Sage. pp. 85–119; Schwartz, S. H. and Boehnke, K. (2004), 'Evaluating the structure of human values with confirmatory factor analysis', *Journal of Research in Personality*, 38, pp. 230–55.

24 Javidan, M., House, R., Dorfman, P., Hanges, P., and de Luque, M. (2006), 'Conceptualizing and measuring cultures and their consequences: A comparative review of GLOBE's and Hofstede's approaches', *Journal of International Business Studies*, 37(6), pp. 897–914.

25 Fischer, R. and Schwartz, S. (2011), 'Whence differences in value priorities? Individual, cultural or artifactual sources', *Journal of Cross-Cultural Psychology*, 42(7), pp. 1127–44.

26 Moon, J., Chadee, D., and Tikoo, S. (2008), 'Culture, product type, and price influences on consumer purchase intention to buy personalized products online', *Journal of Business Research*, 61(1), pp. 31–9.

27 Soares, A.M., Farhangmehr, M., and Shohan, A. (2007), 'Hofstede's dimensions of culture in international marketing studies', *Journal of Business Research*, 60(3), pp. 277–84.

28 All value scores can be found on Hofstede's website, which also facilitates a comparison between several countries: www.geert-hofstede.com; see also Appendix 3.A for selected examples.

29 Hofstede, G., Hofsted, J.G., and Minkov, M. (2010), op.cit.

30 Shenkar, O. (2012), 'Cultural distance revisited: Towards a more rigorous conceptualization and measurement of cultural differences', *Journal of International Business Studies*, 43(1), pp.1–11.

31 Zhang, M., Chebat, J.-C., and Zourrig, H. (2012), 'Assessing the psychometric properties of Hofstede versus Schwarz's cultural values of Chinese consumers', *Journal of International Consumer Marketing*, 24(5), pp.304–19.

32 Søndergaard, M. (1994), 'Research note: Hofstede's consequences: A study of reviews, citations and replications', *Organization Studies* 15(3), pp. 447–56.

33 Alkailani, M., Azzam, I.A., and Athamneh, A.B. (2012), 'Replicating Hofstede in Jordan: Ungeneralized, reevaluating the Jordanian culture,' *International Business Research*, 5(4), pp. 71–80.

34 Adapted from: Vorhauser-Smith, S. (2012), 'When your employees lose face', *Forbes*, 5/29/2012, http://

www.forbes.com/sites/sylviavorhausersmith/2012/05/29/when-your-chinese-employees-lose-face-you-lose-them-2/ [Accessed: June 1, 2014].

35 Vorhauser-Smith, S. (2012), op.cit.

36 Levy, S. (2011), 'Inside Google's China misfortune', *Fortune*, April 15, 2011, http://fortune.com/2011/04/15/inside-googles-china-misfortune/ [Accessed: September 3, 2014].

37 Lim, H. and Park, L.S. (2013), 'The effects of national culture and cosmopolitanism on consumers' adoption of innovation: A cross-cultural comparison', *Journal of International Consumer Marketing*, 25(1), pp. 16–28.

38 The World Factbook. (2015), https://www.cia.gov/library/publications/the-world-factbook/docs/refmaps.html [Accessed: August 1, 2015].

39 Rogers, E.M. (1983). *Diffusion of innovation*. 3rd ed. New York: The Free Press.

40 Dwyer, S., Mesak, H., and Hsu, M. (2005), 'An exploratory examination of the influence of national culture on cross-national product diffusion', *Journal of International Marketing*, 13(2), pp. 1–28.

41 Steenkamp, J. (2002), 'Consumer and market drivers of the trial probability of new consumer packaged goods', *Working Paper, Tilburg University*.

42 De Mooji, M. and Hofstede, G, (2010), 'The Hofstede model. Applications to global branding and advertising strategy and research', *International Journal of Advertising*, 29(1), pp. 85–110.

43 Norenzayan, A., Choi, I., and Nisbett, R.E. (2002), 'Cultural similarities and differences in social influence: Evidence from behavioral predictions and lay theories of behavior', *Personality and Social Psychology Bulletin*, 28, pp.109–20.

44 Aaker, J. L. (1997), 'Dimensions of brand personality', *Journal of Marketing Research*, 34(3), pp. 347–56.

45 Torelli, C.J., et al. (2012), 'Brand concepts as representations of human values: Do cultural congruity and compatibility between values matter?', *Journal of Marketing*, 76(4), pp. 92–108.

46 Sung, Y. and Tinkham, S.F. (2005), 'Brand personality structure in the United States and Korea: Common and culture-specific factors', *Journal of Consumer Psychology*, 15(4), pp. 334–50.

47 Schwartz, S.H. (2012), 'An overview of the Schwarz theory of cultural values', http://scholarworks.gvsu.edu/cgi/viewcontent.cgi?article=1116&context=orpc [Accessed: July 10, 2014].

48 Schwartz, S. et al. (2012), 'Refining the theory of basic individual values', *Journal of Personality and Social Psychology*, 103(4), pp. 663–88; Bilsky, W., Janik, M., and Schwartz, S. (2010), 'The structural organization of human values: Evidence from three rounds of the European social survey (ESS)', *Journal of Cross-Cultural Psychology*, 42(5), pp. 759–76.

49 Ng, S.I., Lee, J.A., and Soutar, G.N. (2007), 'Are Hofstede's and Schwarz's value frameworks congruent?', *International Marketing Review*, 24(2), pp. 164–80.

50 Ng, et al. (2007), op.cit.; Drogendijk, R. and Slangen, A. (2006), 'Hofstede, Schwarz, or managerial perceptions? The effects of different cultural distance measures on establishment mode choices by multinational enterprises', *International Business Review*, 15(4), pp. 361–80.

51 Schwartz, S. and W. Bilsky (1990), 'Toward a theory of the universal content and structure of values: Extensions and cross-cultural replications', *Journal of Personality and Social Psychology*, 53(5), pp. 550–62.

52 Krystallis, A., Vassallo, M., and Chryssohoidos, G. (2012), 'The usefulness of Schwartz's "Values Theory" in understanding consumer behavior towards differentiated products', *Journal of Marketing Management*, 28(11–12), pp.1438–63.

53 De Juan Vigaray, M.D. and Hota, M. (2008), 'Schwarz values, consumer values and segmentation: The Spanish fashion appareil case', *Working paper, IESEG*.

54 Bjerke, R., Gopalakrishna, P., and Sandler, D. (2005), 'Cross-national comparison of Scandinavian value orientations: From value segmentation to promotional appeals', *Journal of Promotion Management*, 12(1), pp.35–56.

55 Meanwhile, the third edition is available: Trompenaars, F. and Hampden-Turner, C. (2012). *Riding the waves of culture: Understanding diversity in global business*. Colombus, OH: McGraw-Hill.

56 Fletcher, R. and Melewar, T.C. (2001), 'The complexities of communicating with customers in emerging markets', *Journal of Communications Management,* 6(1), pp. 9–23.

57   Fletcher, R. (unknown date), 'The impact of culture on marketing at the bottom of the pyramid – a relationship creation and network development approach', http://www.unice.fr/crookall-cours/iup_cult/_docs/_Fletcher%20-%20Cultural%20Differences%20marketing%205687.pdf [Accessed: March 10, 2015].

58   Javidan M., House R.J., Dorfman P.W., Hanges P.J., and Sully de Luque, M. (2006), 'Conceptualizing and measuring cultures and their consequences: A comparative review of GLOBE's and Hofstede's approaches', *Journal of International Business Studies*, 37(6), pp. 897–914.

59   The World Factbook. (2015), https://www.cia.gov/library/publications/the-world-factbook/docs/refmaps.html [Accessed: August 1, 2015].

60   Kogut, B. and Singh, H. (1988), 'The effect of national culture on the choice of entry mode', *Journal of International Business Studies*, 19(3), pp. 411–32.

61   Shenkar, O. (2012), 'Cultural distance revisited: Towards a more rigorous conceptualization and measurement of cultural differences', *Journal of International Business Studies*, 43(1), pp.1–11.

62   Hofstede, G. (2001), op.cit. p. 491.

63   Brewer, P. and Venaik, S. (2012), 'On the misuse of national culture dimensions', *International Marketing Review*, 29(6), pp.1–17.

64   Piantadosi, S., Byar, D., and Green, S. (1988), 'The ecological fallacy', *American Journal of Epidemiology*, 127(5), pp. 893–904.

65   Jian, R. J., Tao, Q. T., and Santoro, M.D. (2010), 'Alliance portfolio diversity and firm performance', *Strategic Management Journal*, 31(10), pp. 1136–44.

66   Gomez-Mejia, L.R. and Palich, L. (1997), 'Cultural diversity and the performance of multinational firms', *Journal of International Business Studies*, 28(2), pp. 309–35.

67   Stahl, G.K. and Tung, R.L. (2014), 'Towards a more balanced treatment of culture in international business studies: The need for positive cross-cultural scholarship', *Journal of International Business Studies*, 46(8), pp. 1–24.

68   Stahl, G.K., Maznevski, M.L., Voigt, A., and Jonson, K. (2010), 'Unraveling the effects of cultural diversity in teams: A meta-analysis of research on multi-cultural work groups', *Journal of International Business Studies*, 41(4), pp. 1–20.

69   Shenkar, O. (2012), 'Beyond cultural distance: Switching to a friction lens in the study of cultural differences', *Journal of International Business Studies*, 43(1), pp. 12–17.

70   Drogendijk, R. and Holm, U. (2012), 'Cultural distance or cultural positions? Analysing the effect of culture on the HQ-subsidiary relationship', *International Business Review*, 21(3), pp. 383–96.

71   The Guardian (March 15, 1993).

72   Hall, E.T. (1966). *The hidden dimension*. New York: Doubleday.

73   Usunier, J.C. and Roulin, N. (2010),'The influence of high- and low-context communication styles on the design, content, and language of business-to-business web sites', *International Journal of Business Communication,* 50 (July), pp. 253–77.

74   Liao, H., Proctor, R., and Salvendy, G. (2008), 'Content preparation for cross-cultural e-commerce: A review and a model', *Behaviour and Information Technology,* 27(1), pp. 43–61.

75   Hall, E.T. (1959). *The silent language*. New York: Doubleday.

76   All China Review. (2015), 'The allures and challenges of China's changing consumer market', July 3, 2015, http://www.allchinareview.com/the-allure-and-challenges-of-chinas-changing-consumer-market/ [Accessed: October 11, 2015].

77   Burkitt, L. (2012), 'Starbucks plays to local Chinese tastes', *WSJ*, November 26, 2012, http://online.wsj.com/news/articles/SB10001424127887324784404578142931427720970 [Accessed: July 1, 2014].

78   Singh, M.K. (2014), 'New poverty line: Rs 32 in villages, Rs 47 in cities', *The Times of India*, July, 2014, http://timesofindia.indiatimes.com/india/New-poverty-line-Rs-32-in-villages-Rs-47-in-cities/articleshow/37920441.cms [Accessed: September 3, 2014].

79   Wilson, W.T. (2014), 'India unleashed', *The National Interest*, June 16, 2014, http://nationalinterest.org/feature/india-unleashed-10667 [Accessed: September 3, 2014].

80 http://www.geohive.com; http://www.roadtraffic-technology.com/features/featurethe-worlds-biggest-road-networks-4159235/; http://www.theguardian.com/news/datablog/2012/may/04/world-top-100-airports; http://www.iaea.org/PRIS/WorldStatistics/OperationalReactorsByCountry.aspx; http://www.internetlivestats.com/internet-users/; http://www.worldshipping.org/about-the-industry/global-trade/top-50-world-container-ports [All Accessed: July 1, 2014].

CASE 3.1   THREE MULTICULTURAL MARKETING DIRECTORS WALK INTO A BAR: AND WHY IT WAS NO LAUGHING MATTER

Rochelle Newman-Carrasco, Walton Isaacson, USA

Three multicultural marketing directors walk into a bar. Sounds like the premise of a decent joke, but it's actually the trigger for a heated discussion about who really has the right to hold the multicultural marketing director title and why. And technically it was only two MMD's. The third was an unemployed senior-level marketer, looking for a multicultural marketing position, and getting nowhere fast.

I won't name names. I will only describe the players. The unemployed marketer, was a self-defined Chicano, a Mexican-American from the mid-West, the child of migrant farm workers and physically similar to Cesar Chavez in skin tone and features. Why is this physical characterization important? Bear with me. It is included with specific intent.

The first of our two MMD's was raised in Mexico City. Although I'm fairly certain he was not born there, he lived in Mexico for decades and was an alum of the prestigious American School. He is likely the son of non-Latino Americans and, therefore, in spite of his years South of the Border, is technically speaking, non-Hispanic white.

The second MMD is African-American. Not Black Hispanic. African-American. However, at an early age, he began speaking Spanish and subsequently pursued job opportunities that would enable him to live in Latin America and leverage his love for the language and the culture. Too look at him and to hear him speak Spanish, one would easily jump to the conclusion that he was a Black Hispanic, possibly of Dominican, Panamanian or Cuban descent, rather than an African-American with no known family or blood ties to Hispanic heritage.

What started as veritable pissing match about who spoke better Spanish, quickly devolved into a heated argument about Corporate America's hiring practices for multicultural marketing directors. The spark was lit by the unemployed marketer who voiced his anger at Corporate America for favoring African-Americans to fill the multicultural marketing slots at their organizations. This was followed by a similar accusation about the hiring of Hispanic MMD's, with the complaint being that when Hispanics were hired in these positions, they were almost always racially white Hispanics or white non-Hispanics with some cultural and linguistic skill-set. Asians were left out of the discussion altogether.

In short, the unemployed marketer was basically telling his colleagues that they fit the racial profiles of Corporate American preference for this position – a black executive and a white executive. Neither of the two MMD's disputed his assessment. It seemed to be an agreed upon insight. And perhaps I wouldn't be writing this blog if it had been left at that. But the frustrated unemployed marketer went on to suggest that neither of his two colleagues should have agreed to take positions that required Hispanic marketing involvement and that they were part of the problem. Needless to say, neither MMD took kindly to this shift from being critical of Corporate America to being critical of them as professionals and frankly, simply as people.

Certainly no one person is so diverse in and of themselves that they can represent each one of the cultural segments that their MMD job title might suggest they embrace. With interracial marriages and births on the rise, however, the day will most certainly come when a candidate will have been raised by a Hispanic-Asian mother and a Black-Jewish father, for example, making them one-quarter of each racial or cultural group. Even so, this candidate could still not lay claim to the title of "Perfect Multicultural Marketer 2010." There is, of course, no such thing. Which got me to thinking. What qualities would make for a close-to-perfect multicultural marketing director? Is it one's ethnic or racial background? Is it one's education or extra curricular activities? Is it someone single or married or someone with an urban or suburban lifestyle?

Short of being Pollyanna-ish, I think it starts with something no one can see or read on a resume. I believe it's all about what's in someone's heart.

In my mind the close-to-perfect multicultural marketer might be described as follows:

- A marketer first and foremost, but not just any marketer.

- They can be of any race, religion, gender, sexual orientation or ethnic heritage. That said, however, they need to have immersed themselves personally, professionally and even academically, in the area of cultural insights and the role of culture as relates to marketing and communications.

- While we all use our personal life experiences as a backdrop for our understanding of what goes on around us, a successful multicultural marketer will not rely on personal stories and experiences as the filter through which all consumer behavior is evaluated and even less so for how marketing decisions are made.

- They must know how to engage specialists who do have true depth of knowledge with those consumer segments of most importance to their brand's bottom lines. Once engaged, they must give those specialists the room, respect and resources to do their jobs and bring their specific insights to the table.

- They should, however, never relinquish their responsibilities as multicultural marketers by "trusting" any one specialist blindly simply because they may be of a certain culture or background. Of course, to some degree, when it comes to cultural understandings, trust becomes a necessity. Encountering cultural norms or nuances that have to be experienced - nuances that simply can't be described in words or explained in dry, rational ways - is part of an MMD's daily reality. However, "blind trust" is a form of abandoning one's professional responsibilities. An MMD should question, probe and do their best to find analogies or other such tools that assist with their understanding of any piece of information or hypothesis they find questionable or do not understand. "Trust me, I'm _____" is simply not enough.

- Finally, a Multicultural Marketing Director should be ready to get vocal or even quit if they don't have the support of the CEO, the CMO and the CFO (and not just when it comes to budgeting for Diversity Days or dinners celebrating "fill-in-the-blank" History month).

Too many multicultural marketing directors that I know are angry and frustrated and are all too clear that the companies that they are working for hired them under false pretenses. (Or perhaps it was just wishful thinking on their part that allowed them to miss all the warning signs.) They are all too clear that they have a title without teeth, and that the kind of impact they want to make only comes with real resources being allocated to prioritized programs that are measurable and for which they want to be and should be held accountable. Truth be told, there is many a multicultural marketing director out there who is tired of hearing about what great "potential" and how much "opportunity" their departments hold. They would prefer to be a priority. Potential and opportunity get discussed. Priorities get done.

So the next time three multicultural marketing directors walk into a bar, I truly hope it will be to toast their change-agent roles as relates to the transformation of a company's culture, regardless of what their own culture may be. The success stories are out there. The MMD's that have their leadership's ear and their wallet, and for all the right reasons. The MMD's that work on priorities not just projects. Regardless of what you may look like outside and specifically because of everything that is driving you inside, here's to you.

ENDNOTE

1 Reprinted with permission from author; originally published in *Advertising Age* (2010). The Editor wishes to thank Jean Boddewyn for pointing out this article for inclusion in *AIB Insights*.

Rochelle Newman-Carrasco (rnewman-carrasco@waltonisaacson.com) joined Walton Isaacson to lead the agency's Hispanic-marketing division, contributing to the agency's growth with clients such as Lexus, Hillshire Brands, Wells Fargo and others. Ms. Newman-Carrasco previously co-founded and managed Enlace Communications, a marketing-communications agency targeting the Hispanic market. She also led efforts on the P&G business as president of Grey Advertising's Hispanic division.

CHAPTER 4

Analyzing Political and Legal Environments

LEARNING OBJECTIVES

After Reading This Chapter, You Should Be Able to:

- Understand some of the legal barriers to using a global, standardized marketing mix.
- Identify legal issues of international marketing.
- Relate how the use of the Internet for the international sale of goods raises legal problems.
- Discuss how intellectual property disputes can be resolved.
- Understand the forms of political risk and how political risk can be managed.
- Discuss the efforts of the WTO to liberalize trade.

LEGAL/GLOBAL POLITICAL SYSTEMS

Global trade and marketing are subject to laws, rules, and regulations formulated by diverse legal systems. There are five different legal systems in the world. No one system dominates the world's legal landscape, but Common, Civil, and Muslim law are dominant. Only about 30 percent of the world's gross domestic product is generated in countries governed by civil and common law systems. Civil law systems are based mainly on Roman law heritage and are found in Europe, Asia, Central and South America. They consist of a comprehensive system of rules, or legislation, usually codified, that are applied and interpreted by judges. Common law, adopted in North America, is based on English custom, where court adjudications are the primary source of law, although governments pass statutes and legislation that are only seen as incursions into the common law and thus interpreted narrowly. Each case that raises new issues is considered on its own merits, and then becomes a precedent for future decisions on that same issue. Exceptions include the State of Louisiana in the United States, whose legal system is based on the *Napoleonic Code*, and Quebec, which adheres to civil law.

Both the common and civil law systems are fundamentally different with regard to concepts and legal method. However, common law countries such as the United States also have civil law and learn how to work with statutes. Also, Scots law is civil based such that UK attorneys are often exposed to a more European environment. However, today there are sufficient legal advisors who are versed in both systems.

Islamic Law

There are five types of conduct under Muslim law (*Sharia*): mandatory, recommended, permitted, recommended against, and banned. For example, engaging in commerce is recommended, but taking interest is banned. Money is considered to have no intrinsic value but rather is purely a medium of exchange. The Institute of Islamic Banking and Insurance[1] holds that a Muslim cannot lend or receive money that includes interest. There are areas where Islamic law is vague, such as how to treat intellectual property, which is neither prohibited nor mandated. As a result, intellectual property protection is left to the authority of the state as long as it is consistent with its power to regulate human society consistent with Islamic law. While this presents issues for international business dealings, however, many of the Islamic States have a set of codified corporate laws. So-called non *Sharia* law covers those areas needed to run a modern state.

Another example concerns employment practices. Multinational companies operating in Muslim countries face many challenges in the management of human resources. For example, the employment of women may be a problem, as in Saudi Arabia. Dress codes for both men and women must be followed. Although integration of the sexes and their employment in common areas such as meeting rooms is permissible in many Muslim countries, nevertheless an understanding of local regulations is necessary.

Given the intricacies of Islamic law, expert legal advice is a necessity in practically all areas of business behavior.

LEGAL ISSUES FOR GLOBAL MARKETING

Global marketers should be familiar with certain aspects of the legal systems in which they operate. Specifically, sales agent, distributorship agreements and other forms of doing business abroad, customs and international trade regulation, export incentives and controls, arbitration, intellectual property rights and international technology transfer should be consulted.

Consider some examples:

- Buyers in Peru didn't pay for a shipment of bearings from a small supplier in Houston, Texas. What is the recourse for the supplier?

- Consumers in France ordered books from a supplier in another country who falsely advertised the goods on the internet. Where can the buyers file their complaint, at home or in the seller's country (if identifiable)?

- Your branded products (for example Samsung cellular phones) are sold through authorized distributors in a certain country. You receive a call from one of your dealers informing you that these same products are being imported and distributed by an unauthorized distributor. What can you do about it?

- Is your product politically vulnerable in the target market?

As the global marketing manager for your company, you and your legal advisors must be able to answer these questions. In the first case above, breach of contract violations may be adjudicated under the United Nations Convention on Contracts for the International Sale of Goods (1980), to which both the United States and Peruvian governments are signatories. In the case of cross-border consumer fraud, the redress is dependent upon cross-border agreement and cooperation. The growing use of the Internet has led to fraud on a large scale across national borders. Fraudulent companies often set up shop in one country to target consumers in another. Most likely, consumers should turn to the country in which the fraud was committed. However, the ease of doing so is dependent upon whether the country in question has the evidence (the alleged fraud was committed in another country) necessary to prosecute and is willing to do so in the first place.

A sale of products through unauthorized distributors is a practice that is called "parallel importing" or gray market distribution. It occurs when identical products are sold without authorization from the owner of the brand and trademark, usually the manufacturer. In some countries parallel importing is illegal, in others it is legal.

The sale of politically vulnerable products should be avoided. Cigarettes and alcohol are examples. However, even food products may be vulnerable to political influence. Countries whose population suffer from "over nutrition," i.e. who have significant numbers of overweight people, may ban products that contain high amounts of so-called "trans" fats. Some defense-related products may be designated as crucial to the economy and their exportation limited or prevented altogether. The exportation of computers and peripheral equipment to Communist countries was banned by the United States and some Western countries who were members of the NATO (North Atlantic Treaty Organization). Military aircraft produced today by several countries, including the United States and France are not exported with the latest electronic technology in use. It is wise to determine the "political" status of products before introducing them into foreign markets. This determination is part of political risk analysis.

Additional legal issues include patents, trademarks and intellectual property protection, marketing mix regulations, consumer protection employment practices, and environmental regulations.

INTELLECTUAL PROPERTY ISSUES: TRADEMARKS, COPYRIGHTS, AND PATENTS

Trademarks and patents, like all *intellectual property*, are based on the principle of territoriality. Each state or country determines for its own territory, what is to be protected, who should benefit from such protection and for how long, and how the protection should be enforced.

Companies, particularly those which sell goods or services direct to the public, regard their trademarks (whether brand names or pictorial symbols) as being among their most valuable assets. Trademarks protect words, names, symbols, sounds, or colors that distinguish goods™ and services[SM], in other words, a brand name or an advertisement.[2] Trademarks, unlike patents, can be renewed forever as long as they are being used. The rights to a trademark are gained by registration in most countries, "first to file," or by their use "first to use," depending on country legislation. While globalization implies global recognition of trademarks, this is not necessarily the case. International trademark disputes may arise from a number of causes. For example, the same term regarded as distinctive in one country, may not be in another because of different consumer perceptions of a brand from one country to another. Another cause of disputes is the mistaken belief that a trademark covers

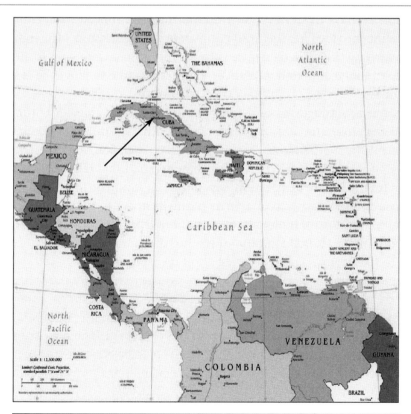

GEO MAP 4.1
Cuba
Source: Adapted from:
CIA Maps, The World
Factbook[3]

With diplomatic relations between the United States and
Cuba the trade embargo will be lifted.

similar products or services. For example, a Lenovo computer trademark may not cover Lenovo "sunglasses" in some countries, assuming the manufacturer extends its product line from its main line, computers to dissimilar categories as in the sunglasses example.

Changing international relations between states may present legal problems relating to intellectual property. Take the case of Cuba. Normalizing relations between Cuba and the United States may open a Pandora's box of legal problems. The General Cigar Co. Inc. of Richmond, Va., has sold Cohiba brand cigars in the United States since the 1990s. Cohiba is also Cuba's premier brand and was reportedly a favorite of Fidel Castro before he stopped smoking in the mid-1980s. But Habanos S.A., the state-owned tobacco company, never registered the Cohiba trademark in the United States. Even so, when General Cigar marketed its own Cohiba brand in 1997, Habanos sued. After a nine-year court battle, the US Supreme Court ruled in 2006 that the US trade embargo against Cuba barred such a trademark challenge. With trade restrictions lifted, this problem will have to be resolved.

Trademark Protection

A global arrangement for trademark protection is exemplified by the Madrid agreement administered by the International Bureau of the World Intellectual Property Organization (WIPO) in Geneva, Switzerland. Registration of a trademark under the Agreement provides for the legal equivalent of registration in member countries designated by the mark owner and affords the owner protection in all member countries for a ten-year period. Moreover, registration in one language is sufficient for all countries.[4]

Despite the advantages of registration through the Agreement, the US and several other major countries (e.g. Australia, Denmark, Finland, Greece, Iceland, Ireland, Japan, the Netherlands, Republic of Korea, Sweden, and the UK) are signatories only to the Protocol. This means that international registrations based on application for trademark registration, say in the US, would be limited to protection only in those countries who are members of the Protocol.[5]

Regional recognition of trademarks is exemplified by the Community Trademark Registration which affords unitary rights to their mark in all EU countries.

Box 4.1   Country-in-Focus: China

China has a first-to-file trademark system that requires no evidence of prior use or ownership, leaving registration of popular foreign trademarks open to anyone, including some well-known global brands such as Sony-Ericsson and even the coat of Britain's royal family! It is imperative that any foreign franchisor considering establishing a franchise in the PRC must take immediate action to register its trademark, domain names, and brands. If patents are involved they should be registered also. Failure to do so can have devastating consequences and may result in a lengthy court battle. Another option would be to buy back the trademark from its owner.

Source: The Author

Trademark protection is available throughout the EU by using the mark in only one EU country.

The importance of protecting one's trademark is illustrated by the following example. A lawsuit initiated by The Hershey Company prohibited a New Jersey, US-located company called Let's Buy British, from importing UK-made Cadbury chocolates. The reason for the lawsuit was that the imported product too closely resembled a similar product and package manufactured by Hershey in the US under license from Cadbury. The contention of Hershey was that there is a significant difference in the composition of the Cadbury (UK) and the Cadbury (US) products; while the two Cadbury packages look the same, the candy inside is not. In addition, the chocolate made in the UK contains a higher fat content. The Cadbury UK candy bar contains vegetable fats, while the Cadbury US product contains emulsifiers not used in the UK product.

The first ingredient shown on the UK-packaged product is "milk," while the first ingredient shown on the US-made product package is "sugar." Consumer tests of the two versions showed that the difference in ingredients resulted in a different taste sensation in favor of the Cadbury UK product.[6]

Box 4.2   Company-in-Focus: McDonald's

An Indian restaurant in Malaysia used the name "McCurry." McDonald's claimed its trademark was infringed and sued the restaurant, in spite of the fact that the only thing in common to both trademarks is the prefix "Mc." Nevertheless, McDonald's believes that the prefix is its intellectual property. A precedent occurred in Malaysia when McDonald's won a court case against two restaurants that called themselves "McBagel's" and "McDhamma's." However, in this case, the court ruled in favor of the local restaurant, enabling it to continue using the name "McCurry." Craig Fochler, a trademark lawyer, reflecting on this ruling, said "When you get a [trade]mark like McDonald's or Coca-Cola or 7-Eleven, it's a constant policing effort."

In Australia, the situation was different. There the court held that the prefixes "Mac" and "Mc" are the intellectual property of McDonald's. A small business in Tasmania used the "McBaby" brand for its children's clothing line. The court ruled that "McBaby" was too close to the trademark "McKid's" sold in Walmart stores under license by McDonald's.

Source: Adapted from: DKD Trade. (7 May 2009), 'Trademark battle lost by McDonald's', *Trademark News*; Eviatar, D. (2005), 'It takes a global village to protect McDonald's trademark', *IP Law & Business*.

Patents

A patent is a form of protection that provides a person or legal entity with exclusive rights for making, using, or selling a concept or invention and excludes others from doing the same for its duration. There are a number of international patent agreements, including the Patent Cooperation Treaty (PCT), the Eurasian Patent Office (EAPO) and the African Regional Industrial Property Organization (ARIPO).

The PCT is administered by the World Intellectual Property Organization. It addresses procedural requirements for obtaining a patent and aims to simplify filing, searching, and publication of international patent applications. The Patent

Cooperation Treaty provides the possibility to seek patent rights in a large number of countries by filing a single international application with a single patent office. All EU countries are members of the Treaty, but there is no EU-wide patent available. Generally, applicants first apply in their home country before applying elsewhere. The European Patent Convention (EPC) allows the filing of a single European patent application in one of three languages (English, French, and German); it is possible to obtain patents in all EPC countries. However, as it is in the case of trademarks, the decision to grant or reject a patent rests with each country authority. As of 2009, there were 36 member countries of the European Patent Organization with several more pending for admittance. Patents can be maintained for a maximum period of twenty years.

GEO MAP 4.2
Eurasian Patent Organization
Source: Adapted from: CIA Maps, The World Factbook[7]

The Eurasian Patent Organization members are Armenia, Azerbaijan, Belarus, Kazakhstan, Kyrgyzstan, Moldova, Russia, Tajikistan, and Turkmenistan.

The Eurasian Patent Organization (EAPO) members include Armenia, Azerbaijan, Belarus, Kazakhstan, Kyrgyzstan, Moldova, the Russian Federation, Tajikistan, and Turkmenistan. Under the Eurasian Convention a single patent application designating all of the member countries is filed in a single language (Russian) in a central patent office in Moscow. Administration of that application is similar to that of the European Patent Office. Maximum duration of a patent is twenty years.

Of all countries, the United States had the most patent applications in 2013 (Table 4.1), followed by Japan and China. There are a number of factors that account for the number of patent filings in a given country. Some of these are the amount of money invested in research and development (R&D) and education. Other indices measure the relative success of a country in producing patent applications. One such index is the number of patents per million people, which takes the size of country into consideration. Using this index, the United States was in third place after Japan and South Korea. In contrast, China was ranked third in number of patent applications, but tenth per million people while Sweden ranked tenth in number of patent applications, but sixth per million people.

Most patent filings in the United States, Japan, and Europe are for high-technology applications. The United States Patent Office had the highest share of patent applications in the high-technology fields, with 39 percent of all applications occurring in this area. Of this number, 55 percent were from domestic applicants. At the Japanese Patent Office, the share of high-technology applications decreased to 22 percent in 2007, and 86 percent of such applications were from domestic applicants. At the European Patent Office, the share of high-technology applications remained stable at 23 percent, with 37 percent coming from 39 member states and three applicants (Albania, Bosnia and Herzegovina, and Serbia).

In Africa, there are two intellectual property organizations: The African Regional Intellectual Property Organization (ARIPO) whose members are mainly English speaking and the African Intellectual Property Organization for French speaking nations. Each organization has 16 members. In ARIPO, membership is open to

Country	Rank	Number of Applications	Applications Per Million People	Rank	
USA	1	57,239	630	3	**TABLE 4.1** Patent Applications by Country (2013)
Japan	2	43,918	2,836	1	
China	3	21,516	51	10	
Germany	4	17,927	586	4	
Republic of Korea	5	12,386	2,814	2	
France	6	7,899	235	8	
UK	7	4,865	314	5	
Switzerland	8	4,367	251	7	
Netherlands	9	4,198	134	9	
Sweden	10	3,960	306	6	

Source: © Author; adapted from World International Property Organization, Patents, 2014, pp. 12, 28, 29. www.wipo.int/edocs/pubdocs/en/wipo_pub_941_2014.pdf

members of the United Nations Economic Commission for Africa or the African Union (AU). Both organizations centralize the registration of applications for patents and trademarks for all member countries which are then submitted to member states for consideration.

Copyrights

A copyright is a law that gives ownership to "original works of authorship," such as literary works, paintings, music, video games, and drama. In the United States, the Library of Congress registers copyrights for the life of the author, plus 70 years as is the case in the EU. Copyrights extend to other countries as long as the country in question is covered by an international copyright treaty, convention, or organization. In Canada, copyrights extend 50 years after the life of the author. One of the most contentious issues is the question of databases, digital recordings, and websites. The agreement also states that performers must also have the right to prevent unauthorized recording, reproduction, and broadcast of live performances (bootlegging) for no less than 50 years. Producers of sound recordings must have the right to prevent the unauthorized reproduction of recordings for a period of 50 years.

Software Piracy

Software piracy is the unauthorized reproduction and illegal distribution of software, whether for business or personal use. While software publishers have methods of countering illegal copyright infringement it is costly to do so. The most obvious is through lawsuits filed in civil court, or in pressuring authorities to file criminal charges. Software piracy is endemic throughout the word, but especially so in the emerging economies. As shown in Table 4.2, the piracy rate in the BRIC countries ranges from 53 percent in Brazil to 77 percent in China. While the piracy rate is much lower in developed countries it is still very costly to software developers and merchants. According to the BSA Global software Piracy Study, the commercial value of printed software piracy amounted to $63 billion worldwide, including $9.7 billion in the United States alone.

How can software be protected? The best way to protect software is to apply for a patent—but the software must have some novel application. A developer needs to prove that the software's processes or end-result constitutes a service that did not previously exist, fulfilling the technical condition of the patent. In the European Union, however, software protections through patents have been disallowed since 2003. Barring the ability to obtain a patent, the second-best solution is to obtain a copyright. The primary concern with copyrighting software is that it is not a literary work as such and it is better suited under the definition of a mathematical formula or algorithm, which ordinarily cannot be copyrighted. However, the advantages of a copyright in the case of software is that it is automatically applicable in the US and EU: once a program has been created on one's computer and afterwards recorded (disk, hard disk, USB flash, etc.), according to Article 2(2) of the Berne

Country	Pirated Value ($M)	Legal Sales ($M)	Piracy Rate (%)
USA	9,773	41,664	19
China	8,902	2,559	77
Russia	3,227	1,895	63
India	2,930	1,721	63
Brazil	2,848	2,526	53
France	2,754	4,689	37
Germany	2,265	6,447	26
Italy	1,945	2,107	48
UK	1,943	5,530	26
Japan	1,875	7,054	21
Indonesia	1,467	239	86
Mexico	1,249	942	57
Spain	1,216	1,548	44
Canada	1,141	3,085	27
Thailand	852	331	72
South Korea	815	1,223	40
Australia	763	2,445	23
Venezuela	668	91	88
Malaysia	657	538	55
Argentina	657	295	69

TABLE 4.2

Top 20 Economies in Commercial Value of Pirated PC Software, 2011

Source: Adapted from: http://globalstudy.bsa.org/2011/downloads/study_pdf/2011_BSA_Piracy_study-InBrief.pdf. [Accessed: November 2, 2014]

Convention (see below), it is already covered by copyright. Second, the copyright is relatively cheap and almost universally recognized.[8] According to agreements by the World Trade Organization (WTO) and the Trade-Related Aspects of Intellectual Property Rights (TRIP), any written software has an automatic copyright. The WTO defines intellectual property in much the same way as the Berne agreement (Berne Convention for the Protection of Literary and Artistic Works) but they have added computer programs and data to the list of protected works. In short, each of the contracting (member) countries provides automatic protection for works first published in other countries of the Berne union.

Trade Secrets

Trade secrets are information that companies do not wish to divulge in order to give them an advantage over their competitors; however they are not protected by intellectual property law the same way that trademarks or patents are. Protection for trade secrets is done by using non-disclosure agreements to insure that the information will be kept confidential. For example, a firm demands that its employees sign such an agreement not to disclose designs, instruments, or whatever is classified as a trade secret. The lack of formal protection, however, means that a third party is not prevented from independently duplicating and using the secret information once it is revealed.

Box 4.3   Technology-in-Focus: Trade Secret Protection

A trade secret is any device or information (such as a formula, database, method of operation or material) that is used in a business and that gives the owner an advantage over competitors who do not know or use it. Trade secret protection requires that reasonable steps must be taken to protect the secret, such as limiting access to the secret and obtaining signed nondisclosure agreements from individuals or entities to which the secret is disclosed. Many technology companies rely on trade secret law as one of the primary means of protecting their intellectual property. However, trade secrecy is the most fragile form of intellectual property protection, and companies that count on trade secrecy must be ever vigilant in guarding against disclosure. Trade secret protection also has significant limitations—it does not cover those who independently discover the secret, or legitimate reverse engineering efforts.

For example, where the chief technology officer (CTO) of a technology company leaves in the middle of a major new software rollout, and then goes to work for a competitor on exactly the same application, the company may be entitled to an immediate injunction walling off the former CTO from involvement in the competitive project.

Sources: *Patent Protection for High Technology and Life Sciences Companies*, Fenwick and West, LLP, 2005. www.Fenwick.com/docstore/Publications/IP/Patent _Protection.pdf. [Accessed: December 3, 2009]; Andrew B. Flake, Arnall Golden Gregory, LLP, (2007), Tasgonline.org. [Accessed: August 6, 2010].

TRADE REGULATIONS

From 1947 to 1994, the General Agreement on Tariffs and Trade (GATT) was the main international organization that codified rules for trade liberalization. It put order into a world trading system that had broken down during World War II. Its major goal was to work towards agreement to lower tariff restrictions. During the tenure of the organization, about half of all world trade was covered by subsequent agreements. One of the major problems of the GATT agreement was that services were not included even though they had become a significant component of overall world trade. Another problem was an increasing protectionist policy among many nations in order to subsidize their agricultural exports. These and other problems led to a decrease in the effectiveness of the GATT and to the formation of a new organization called the World Trade Organization (WTO). In 1995 the GATT was replaced by the World Trade Organization which functions to this day.

In its formative years (1947–73) the WTO concentrated on reducing tariffs through multilateral negotiations in so-called "trade rounds" (see Table 4.3). The Tokyo Round held intermittently during 1973–9 with 102 countries involved in the negotiations, was the first major attempt to deal with trade barriers other than tariffs. However, the Tokyo Round met with mixed success because few industrialized nations could agree to many of the proposals. The eighth, the Uruguay Round of 1986–94, was the last and most extensive of all. It led to the WTO and a new set of agreements including services, agriculture, and intellectual property, resulting in an average one-third cut in customs duties in the world's nine major industrial markets, bringing the average tariff on industrial products down to 4.7 percent. Another round took place in Doha, Qatar in 2001 and negotiations have continued in Cancun (2003), Geneva (2004), Hong Kong (2005), Geneva (2006), Potsdam

Year	Place/Name	Subjects Covered	Countries	
1947	Geneva	Tariffs	23	**TABLE 4.3**
1949	Annecy	Tariffs	13	GATT Trade Rounds
1951	Torquay	Tariffs	38	
1956	Geneva	Tariffs	26	
1960–1961	Geneva Dillon Round	Tariffs	26	
1964–1967	Geneva Dillon Round	Tariffs and anti-dumping measures	62	
1973–1979	Geneva Dillon Round	Tariffs, non-tariff measures, "framework" agreements	102	
1986–1994	Geneva Dillon Round	Tariffs, non-tariff measures, rules, services, intellectual property, dispute settlement, textiles, agriculture, creation of WTO, etc	123	
2001–	Doha, Qatar	Needs of developing countries, non-tariff barriers, and agriculture and industrial tariffs.		

Source: Adapted from: World Trade Organization, Selected Yearbooks

(2007) and Geneva again (2008). The negotiations in 2008 reached an impasse because of disagreement between developed and developing countries on the liberalization of agricultural trade, especially between the United States, India, and China. In particular, there was considerable disagreement between India and the United States over the special safeguard mechanism (SSM), a measure designed to protect poor farmers by allowing countries to impose a special tariff on certain agricultural goods in the event of an increase in imports or a fall in prices. However, in the series of discussions in Bali, agreement was reached on a small number of issues in December 2013.

Like the GATT, the World Trade Organization (WTO) is a forum for governments to negotiate trade agreements and to settle trade disputes. There are some 150 nations who are members of the WTO. About 75 percent of them are developing countries. Developing countries have been given some preferential treatment such as a longer period of time to meet tariff reductions required under the agreement. Unlike the GATT agreement, the WTO covers services, including intellectual property. In addition, non-tariff barriers such as discriminatory product standards are also included in the agreement.

Arbitration and Mediation

Trade disputes arise often as exemplified by the examples on pages 150–1. Disputes can arise between private parties such as businesses, between two countries, or between an individual and a country. There are three ways to settle a dispute: (1)

litigation through a court, (2) arbitration, or (3) mediation. Litigation can be very costly and time-consuming. Therefore, many prefer other alternatives.

What is the difference between arbitration and mediation? Arbitration is a course of action by which a dispute is submitted by the parties to one or more arbitrators whose decision is binding. This procedure is an alternative to going through the courts. Once arbitration commences, the parties cannot withdraw. The arbitrators' ruling is therefore binding on the parties and must be carried out within a reasonable amount of time. The advantages of arbitration are enforceability, confidentiality, technical expertise of the arbitrators, and that it's usually less expensive than litigation.

Mediation on the other hand, is non-binding. It is a process where two parties agree on a mediator who tries to guide them to a satisfactory settlement of the dispute. Even if mediation does not result in an agreement, the process itself defines the issues of a dispute that can later be used to prepare for arbitration if needed. Mediation may be the preferred procedure to take when the parties hope to preserve or renew their commercial relationship. Another advantage of mediation is the shorter amount of time it takes.

There are a number of international organizations that provide arbitration, mediation services, or both. Examples of arbitration centers include the International Center for Settlement of Investment Disputes (ICSID), the World Intellectual Property Organization (WIPO) Arbitration and Mediation Center, the London Court of International Arbitration (LCIA), and the International Chamber of Commerce (ICC). The following are examples of arbitration cases:

"A French pharmaceutical research and development company licensed know-how and patented pharmaceuticals to another French company. The license agreement includes an arbitration clause that provides that the dispute will be resolved under the WIPO Arbitration Rules by an arbitral consisting of three members in accordance with French law. Faced with the licensee's apparent refusal to pay the license fee, the R&D Company initiated arbitration proceedings."

"A US company providing data processing software and services and an Asian bank concluded an agreement regarding the provision for account processing services. The parties agreed that the US Company was to be the exclusive service provider for certain of the bank's affiliates in North America and Europe. The agreement stated that any dispute arising out of or in connection with the agreement would be resolved under the WIPO Expedited Arbitration Rules.

Four years after the conclusion of their agreement, the US Company alleged that the bank had violated the agreement by using processing services offered by third parties in the countries covered by the agreement. When the parties failed to settle the dispute, the US service provider commenced WIPO expedited arbitration proceedings claiming infringement of the agreement and substantial consequential damages.

The parties agreed upon a sole arbitrator who held a two-day hearing in New York City. Three months after the request for expedited arbitration, the arbitrator rendered a final award finding partial infringement of the agreement and granting damages to the US service provider."[9]

International Center for Settlement of Investment Disputes (ICSID)

Headquartered in Washington, D.C. the ICSID arbitrates investment disputes between nations and nationals of other nations (e.g. Continental Casualty Company v. Argentine Republic; EDF (Services) Ltd. v. Romania). A filing fee for arbitration is $25,000, which is non-refundable. There are 156 signatory States to the ICSID convention.

World Intellectual Property Organization (WIPO) Arbitration and Mediation Center

Based in Geneva, the Center provides arbitration and mediation services for settling disputes between private parties. The Center specializes in disputes involving technology, intellectual property and the internet and electronic commerce. The Center has handled disputes involving sums ranging from 20,000 to several hundred million US dollars.

The London Court of International Arbitration (LCIA)

The LCIA provides arbitration and mediation services for contractual disputes in international commerce, including telecommunications, insurance, oil and gas exploration, construction, shipping, aviation, pharmaceuticals, shareholders agreements, IT, finance and banking. It is a non-profit organization and covers its expenses by charging £1,500 for filing a request for arbitration and thereafter an hourly fee. It is managed by the City of London, the London Chamber of Commerce and Industry, and the Chartered Institute of Arbitrators. Its court of arbitrators has up to thirty-five members from major world trading areas, of which no more than six members are citizens of the UK.

MARKETING MIX REGULATIONS

Product Standards

Consumers all over the world expect that the products they buy will be safe and healthy, and conform to the claims of the manufacturer. In order to ensure these expectations, product and promotion regulations have often been necessary. The impact of worldwide legislation and regulations is a primary concern to both manufacturers of consumer and industrial products. The concern is owing to the possibility of different product regulations and standards on a global, regional, or national level. These differences mean that multinational manufacturers must plan product strategy on a global or regional basis, adapting products whenever necessary to fulfill required standards. Product planning is of three major types. First, end products must meet standards in each target country. Can a manufacturer design the product to allow acceptance by all the regulatory agencies? Second, how does a company efficiently and cost-effectively accomplish this task? How can you ensure that new products or new generations of older products will satisfy all of the regulations necessary to qualify for sale? The third challenge relates to the standards themselves. Do they represent an achievable goal, or will conformance cause undue hardship to manufacturers and customers alike? And how can changes to regulations be anticipated before the product is marketed?

While nearly all products are subject to some sort of regulation, industries such as pharmaceuticals, cosmetics, food, and electronics are more closely supervised. For example, the pharmaceutical industry has become one of the most legislated and regulated industries in the world. Worldwide regulations, although differing in scope and intensity, all target pharmaceutical development, testing, and manufacture of drug products.

For a multinational electronics manufacturer, selling products to countries all over the world means contending with an array of conformance standards that can vary significantly from one country to the next. The production, processing, distribution, retail, packaging, and labeling of food products are governed by a mass of laws, regulations, and codes of practice and guidance that differ from one country to another.

Achieving a worldwide or regional-wide agreement for product standardization is a difficult task. Many of you have traveled abroad with a laptop. Going from the UK to France and then to Switzerland requires three plug adapters. While this is a minor annoyance, there are more serious barriers, such as safety requirements for cars and trucks, and in some cases, machinery. All require adaptation of products to meet the specific requirements of a given country. In some cases, differentiating product standards is done to gain a competitive edge. Sony introduced its Betamax system in 1975. A year later, JVC launched its VHS (Video Home System). Manufacturers were divided between the two competing systems, with Japanese companies adopting either one or the other. However, a major difference between the two was recording time. Betamax could record only up to 60 minutes while VHS lasted up to three hours. By 2002, Betamax was history and today both systems have been replaced by digital technology.

There is no such thing as a worldwide standard for products. The EU has begun a process of harmonization of standards that will apply to all its members. The term "harmonization" refers to a process by which the technical requirements of various standards have been made equivalent or identical. An exception is the "principle of mutual recognition" of the EU. This principle holds that a product lawfully marketed in one member state should be allowed to be marketed in any other member state, even when the product does not fully comply with the technical rules of the member state of destination. However, a member state may refuse entry to any

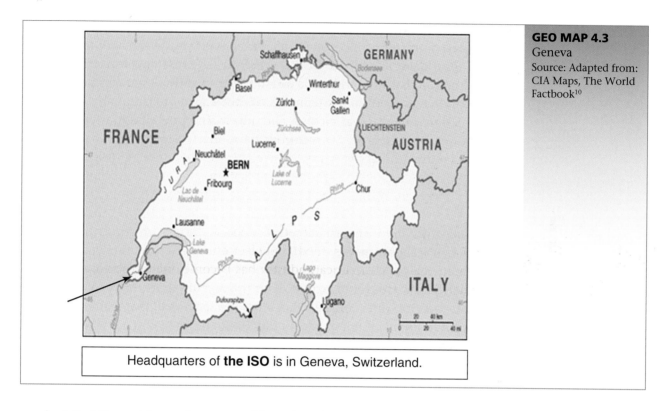

GEO MAP 4.3
Geneva
Source: Adapted from:
CIA Maps, The World
Factbook[10]

Headquarters of **the ISO** is in Geneva, Switzerland.

product that it considers a threat to public safety, health, or the environment.

The International Organization for Standardization (ISO)

The ISO is a non-governmental organization (NGO) headquartered in Geneva, Switzerland, consisting of a network of national standards institutes of over 160 countries. Its primary task is to develop international product standards based on consensus with its members. Compliance with ISO standards is voluntary. Member organizations may apply for certification of ISOs. Quality Management System ("QMS"), which includes top management commitment to quality, employee competence, process management (for production, service delivery, and relevant administrative and support processes), quality planning, product design, review of incoming orders, purchasing, monitoring and measurement of processes and products. Most well-known brands are ISO certified as complying with international standards, e.g. Adobe Systems' PDF (Portable Document Format), Bang & Olufsen, Samsung, Nokia, and HP.

REGULATION OF COMMUNICATION

Advertising regulations are nationally and locally determined. Every country determines how to regulate advertising that is perceived to be fraudulent or misleading. In the European Union, advertising is self-regulated. According to the European

Standards Advertising Alliance, self-regulation (SR) is a system by which the advertising industry actively polices itself. The three parts of the industry (advertisers, advertising agencies, and media) work together to agree on standards and to set up a system to ensure that advertisements which fail to meet those standards are quickly corrected or removed. While attempts have been made to harmonize especially sensitive advertising, such as alcohol and advertising to children, little has been accomplished. However, all EU countries have enacted legislation that regulates advertising in these areas.

Cyberlaw

Most people today have an email account or access the web on a daily basis. If you have an email account you have no doubt been inundated with "junk mail" (unsolicited commercial email), commonly known as *spam*. These messages offer products for sale, some that you would want in your home, but others that you would not. In any case, you can filter some but not all of the *spam* mail that comes your way. Mail that is not filtered is not only a nuisance but also has a cost, a higher monthly service fee resulting from the time it takes to delete unwanted mail. Unwanted mail also uses memory on both ends and can result in slowing down traffic on the web. While unsolicited commercial email is an international problem, there are difficulties in the regulation of cyberspace. A single transmission may involve regulations in three countries: (1) regulations of the country in which the recipient resides, (2) regulations of the country where the server is located, and (3) regulations of the country in which the transaction takes place. It is not out of the ordinary that these regulations may be at odds. Take for example, the Yahoo!™ vs. France case:

In 2001, Nazi memorabilia was offered for sale on the Yahoo!™ auction website in France. As the sale of such products was banned in France, a number of groups took legal action to have the memorabilia removed from the company's website. The French court ordered Yahoo!™ to remove the memorabilia from its website and failing to do so would incur a fine of F100,000 for each day of non-compliance. The company in turn held that as it was incorporated in the United States, the French court did not have jurisdiction over it. It requested the district court of California to overrule the French court's decision. The American court held that the French court's order was not enforceable in the United States and was in violation of the First Amendment of the United States Constitution. Thus, this case shows that the jurisdiction of a court in one country may not necessarily be enforceable in another country.

A step in the attempt to harmonize computer crime laws on the international level is the Council of Europe's Convention on Cybercrime signed by 38 countries including the United States. The convention is intended to outlaw computer intrusion, child pornography, commercial copyright infringement, and online fraud. In the words of former US Attorney, General Alberto Gonzales, the "treaty provides important tools in the battles against terrorism, attacks on computer networks and the sexual exploitation of children over the Internet, by strengthening U.S. cooperation with foreign countries in obtaining electronic evidence."[11] Both European and non-European countries are signatories of the treaty, such as the United States, Canada, Japan, and South Africa.

POLITICAL RISK

Businesses make a serious mistake when they ignore or underestimate political risk. Crises such as the Eurozone negotiations, the debt ceiling debate in the United States, and the Arab Spring protests had significant repercussions on the day-to-day operations of many multinational companies. Given that there is significant political risk in some countries, it cannot be ignored. However, while political risk cannot be eliminated, it can, in some cases, be reduced, or managed. The political risk management process consists of three stages: Identification of political risks, measurement of the risk, and managing the risk. These stages are discussed below.

Political risk may be defined as the probability that a set of unwanted events may occur. "Unwanted events" are those that can impact upon a firm's performance to the extent that they threaten the firm's value. Examples (Table 4.4) of such events include firm-specific risks (micro risk) that are directed at a particular company, and country-specific risks (macro risk) that are not aimed at a particular firm, but are nationwide, impacting all firms in a given industry. Examples of firm-specific risks include expropriation of the firm's assets, kidnapping employees, limits on the transfer of certain technologies, and breach of contract.

Country-level risks include limiting the repatriation of profits, civil unrest, currency inconvertibility, forced local shareholding, and nationalization of an industry (e.g. the government taking over the assets of all firms in a given industry, such as electricity production). For example, after Fidel Castro's government took control of Cuba in 1959, hundreds of millions of dollars' worth of American-owned assets and companies were expropriated. Unfortunately, most, if not all, of these American companies did not receive any compensation for their financial losses.

A major American retail clothing chain reports that the future performance of the company depends upon foreign suppliers and may be adversely affected by the following political and operating risk factors:

	Government Risks	Instability Risks	TABLE 4.4
Firm-Specific Risks	• Discriminatory regulations • "Creeping" expropriation • Breach of contract	• Sabotage • Kidnappings • Firm-specific boycotts	Categories (Identification) of Political Risk
Country-Level Risks	• Mass nationalizations • Regulatory changes • Currency inconvertibility	• Mass labor strikes • Urban rioting • Civil wars	

Source: Adapted from: Daniel Wagner. (2000), 'Defining "Political Risk"', International Risk Management Institute. www.irmi.com/articles/expert-commentary/defining-political-risk. [Accessed: March 21, 2007]

- Financial or political instability in any of the countries in which our merchandise is manufactured or the channels through which it passes;

- Currency and exchange risks;

- Inability of our manufacturers to comply with local labor, health and safety laws, or labor practices;

- Increased security and regulatory requirements applicable to imported goods;

- Imposition or increases of duties, taxes, and other charges on imports;

- Imposition of new legislation relating to import quotas or other restrictions;

- Impact of natural disasters and public health concerns on our vendor manufacturing operations;

- Delays in shipping due to port security considerations or labor disputes;

- Regulations under the United States Foreign Corrupt Practices Act;

- Increased costs of transportation.

Assessing political risk should be a major concern for companies that have:

- High ratios of international to domestic revenues;

- Significant amounts of capital invested abroad;

- Dependence on a global supply chain;

- Significant concentration of assets or operations in a single region or country;

- Dependence on international growth.

MEASURING POLITICAL RISK

The major issues that concern political risk are its measurement and management. Most observers of political risk agree that it is determined by the exercise of political power, either by government or groups such as unions and activists. The use (or misuse) of political power is usually an outgrowth of unrest caused by economic downturns, religious strife, etc. Therefore, the probability that political risk may occur can be measured by monitoring whether political unrest and instability may occur and eventually threaten the firm's performance. Political risk assessment is done by risk management experts employed in transnational firms, banks, or by consulting firms. Methods for assessing political risk range from comparative techniques of rating and mapping systems to analytical techniques such as expert systems and probability determination.

There are two approaches to measure political risk: (1) qualitative, based on expert (economists, union officials, politicians, local businessmen) analysis using

Delphi-type techniques, and (2) quantitative, which begins with the identification of quantifiable factors that affect political risk. Then a formula is used to determine numerical scores for each factor. A weighted average of the factors' numerical scores is the final score for the country. For example, the in-house staff at American Can uses the PRISM system (primary risk investment screening matrix—Strand Technology), which creates an index-based feedback from overseas managers and consultants on over 200 variables. While quantitative techniques seem more objective, they may not be more accurate than qualitative methods. It all depends upon the reliability and validity of the models and the databases used.

Two well-known providers of political risk assessment using quantitative methods are the Economist Intelligence Unit (the EIU model) and the Business Environment Risk Intelligence (BERI) model. The EIU composite risk rating includes political risk (22 percent of the composite), economic policy risk (28 percent), economic structure risk (27 percent) and liquidity risk (23 percent). The political risk component measures political stability (war, social unrest, orderly political transfer, politically motivated violence, and international disputes). The BERI model includes a Profit Opportunity Recommendation, which is a macro risk measure, based on an average of three ratings:

- Political Risk Index, composed of ratings on political and social variables.

- Operations Risk Index, composed of political, financial, and structural (economic) variables.

- R Factor, Remittance and Repatriation, a weighted index of the country's legal framework, foreign exchange, hard currency reserves and foreign debt.

The Economist Intelligence Unit provides measures of both political and operating risks as shown in Table 4.5. Here we have a comparison of ratings for example, of

Risk Rating	Brazil	Russia	India	China	France	
Overall Assessment	C	D	C	C	B	**TABLE 4.5** Political and Operating Risks, October 2014
Security Risk	C	D	C	B	B	
Political Stability Risk	B	D	A	C	B	
Government Effectiveness Risk	D	E	D	D	B	
Legal and Regulatory Risk	C	D	C	C	A	
Macroeconomic Risk	C	C	B	B	C	
Foreign Trade and Payments Risk	B	C	C	B	A	
Financial Risk	B	D	B	B	A	
Tax Policy Risk	C	C	E	B	B	
Labor Market Risk	C	C	C	C	B	
Infrastructure Risk	C	C	C	B	A	
Note: E=most risky						

Source: Adapted from: The Economist Intelligence Unit.
http://viewswire.eiu.com/index.asp?layout=RKCountryVW3&country_id=1350000135. [Accessed: October 12, 2014]

the BRIC countries and a developed country, France, taken during October 2014. These ratings are updated every quarter. You can log into the EIU and look up the current ratings.

Looking at the ratings in Table 4.5, which country do you believe has the most serious risks? Take political stability for example. Clearly, Russia is the most risky, followed by China. India has the highest rating (lowest risk) on this factor. Note that France has only a B rating. While the overall assessment is the same for three of the BRICs, some individual ratings differ. It is therefore important to look at those ratings that are most important for the firm's decision making. For example, "financial risk" might be more important in the case of an investment decision, while "foreign trade and payments risk" might be most important in the case of exporting.

It is imperative for each company to conduct a risk assessment, keeping in mind unique, industry-specific micro-political risks, in addition to operating and financial risks while at the same time taking into consideration the general macro-political risks. Table 4.6 proposes a simplified risk-assessment model using critical variables that have been discussed in this chapter. This table can serve as a matrix that every company can use to model a comprehensive political and operating risk assessment strategy. Firms should add the appropriate country-industry-project-specific variables to the micro-variables section. Assigning a weighting factor to each critical variable should reflect the respective firm's industry, location, risk tolerance, and general political-economic environment. Scores should then be assigned for each country in each category and multiplied by the weighting factor. The country scores are added, and the total scores for each country are then easily compared to assess the relative risk of each country.

The above discussion also drives home another very significant factor: the existence of country-specific or region-specific risks. For instance, while companies seeking to operate in the Middle East, South Asia, and certain parts of Africa face a heightened threat of terrorism and corruption, companies seeking to expand into the Scandinavian countries do not face a similar threat. Each nation or region must be looked upon as a unique operating environment. This suggests that companies must resort to risk-assessment strategies at multiple levels.

It is recommended that every company adopt political risk assessment at two or three levels. The assessment team at the corporate headquarters can be assigned the task of creating a general model that identifies broad macro-variables applicable for all international operations such as exchange-rate fluctuations, GDP growth rate, and threat of war, and broad, industry-specific micro-variables. On the other hand, assessment teams at each international location can create submodels that incorporate country-specific macro- and micro-variables. Large multinational corporations can take it a step further by creating region-specific models as well. In conclusion, every global company in today's world must consider adopting a comprehensive political risk-assessment strategy to ensure it invests in the right places and continues making the decisions necessary to outperform its competitors.

TABLE 4.6 A Political Risk Assessment Matrix

	MACRO-VARIABLES	WEIGHT	Country -1-	Country -2-	Country -3-	Country -4-
POLITICAL/ GOVERNMENTAL	War & Security Issues	0-10				
	Regime Stability	0-10				
ECONOMIC	Inflation	0-10				
	Exchange Rate Volatility	0-10				
	Economic Stability	0-10				
	GDP per captia	0-10				
	Balance of Payments	0-10				
	Real GDP growth rate	0-10				
	Currency Convertibility	0-10				
SOCIAL	Social Revolutions	0-10				
	Corruption	0-10				
	MICRO-VARIABLES	WEIGHT	Country -1-	Country -2-	Country -3-	Country -4-
POLITICAL/ GOVERNMENTAL	Industry Regulatory Bodies	0-10				
	(Appropriate Political Governmental Micro-variables)	0-10				
ECONOMIC	Energy Vulnerability	0-10				
	(Appropriate Economic Micro-Variables)	0-10				
SOCIAL	(Appropriate Social Micro-variables)	0-10				
	TOTAL					

Source: Adapted from: Alon, I., Gurumoothy, R., Mitchell, M., and T. Steen (2006), 'Managing micropolitical risk: A cross-sector examination,' *Thunderbird International Business Review*, 48(5), pp. 623–42

THE CASE OF TERRORISM

Terrorism has become a major threat to the stability of entire regions of the world (Middle East, Africa and parts of Latin America and Asia). Terrorism poses both direct and indirect threats to the operations of the firm. It represents a market imperfection that increases transaction costs and creates barriers to the free flow of goods, affecting potential gains that would occur in the presence of unhindered exchange. Terrorism reflects the risk or actual encounter of violent acts, whose goal is to engender fear, coercion, or intimidation.[12] Terrorism has impacted on tourist travel as well as overall trade. A Gallup poll of Americans taken in February 2014 found that 77 percent of respondents believed that international terrorism posed a critical threat, 19 percent believed it posed an important threat to the vital interests of the United States.[13] These perceptions are also held by the general public as evidenced by cancellations of travel plans whenever a threat of terrorism arises.

Nitsch et al.[14] studied bilateral trade flows of more than 200 countries over the period 1960 to 1993 and found that terrorist actions reduced the volume of trade. A doubling in the number of terrorist incidents was associated with a decrease in bilateral trade by about 4 percent. Costoiu also found a relationship between increased terror and a reduction in trade[15]. Given the association between terror and trade, the latter has become an important component of political risk analysis.

Terrorism can impact on many forms of business activity, including attacking tourists, kidnapping personnel, and damaging infrastructure, to name a few. Terrorism risk can be viewed as having three components: the *threat* to a target, the target's *vulnerability* to the threat, and the *consequences* should the target be successfully attacked. People and organizations represent threats when they have both the intent and capability to damage a target. The *threat* to a target can be measured as the probability that a specific target is attacked in a specific way during a specified period. Thus, a threat might be measured as the annual probability that a city's football stadium will be subject to attack with a radiological weapon. *Vulnerability* can be measured as the probability that damage occurs, given a threat. Damages could be fatalities, injuries, property damage, or other consequences; each would have its own vulnerability assessment. *Consequences* are the magnitude and type of damage resulting, given a successful terrorist attack. Risk is a function of all three components: threat, vulnerability, and consequences.[16]

In testimony before the US Congress, Professor Czinkota discussed the results of a survey undertaken to determine the perception of terrorism and readiness of managers in American business firms who were involved in some sort of international marketing.[17] The vast majority of respondents felt that there had not been a specific terrorism threat against their business, even though many more believed that their firm might be directly affected by a terrorist attack in the next ten years. However, many managers reported that their firms had no contingency plans to deal with terror. On a cost-benefit basis, many believed that the risk did not justify the investment required to manage it. Nevertheless, domestic companies having subsidiaries and/or affiliates abroad should consult with one or more of the many terrorism risk management firms to determine whether a threat exists and if so, what the extent of vulnerability is. The United States government, in particular, has enacted a Terrorism Risk Insurance Program which compensates insurance companies that have losses due to a recognized terrorism act. Prior to the September 11, 2001 terrorist attacks on the United States, coverage for losses from such attacks was normally included in general insurance policies without specific cost to the policyholders. Following the attacks, such coverage became very expensive if offered at all. Because insurance is necessary for a variety of trans-actions, it was feared that the absence of insurance against terrorism loss would have a wider economic impact. Terrorism insurance was largely unavailable for most of 2002, and some have argued that this had an adverse effect on parts of the economy. While the United States has not experienced much domestic terrorism, other countries have unfortunately been affected by it. Spain, for example, has experienced much terrorist activity by Basque separatist movements. As a result, the government has insured against acts of terrorism since 1954. As a result of the turmoil in Northern Island, The United Kingdom created Pool Re, a privately owned mutual insurance company with government backing, specifically to insure terrorism risk.

After the 09/11 attack on the World Trade Center, many foreign countries reas-sessed their terrorism risk and created a variety of approaches to deal with it. The UK greatly expanded Pool Re, whereas Germany created a private insurer with gov-ernment backing to offer terrorism insurance policies. Germany's plan, like TRIA in the United States, was created as a temporary measure. It has been extended since its inception, but like many temporary plans, it may be discontinued at any time. Not all developed countries have deemed it necessary to sponsor some sort of insur-ance against terrorism. The Canadian government, for example, considered such a plan but never adopted one.[18]

Can terrorism also be a threat to solely domestic companies that have little or no investment abroad? The answer is a definite yes. Take for example the case of supply chains. Domestic companies that rely on overseas supplies of raw materials, components and the like can have their production or sales affected if their supply is cut off. Many if not most of the clothing retailers in the United States outsource their merchandise in Asia and the Middle East. Terrorist attacks in these areas could cut off their production and of course, sales for a long period of time before they can replace their supply chain. Such companies must have alternate sources of supply in case such a development occurs.

How Accurately Can Political Risk Be Forecasted?

Sottilotta (2013) attempted to answer the question raised above by comparing three forecasting services, two of which are commercial (EIU and PRS) and one quasi-governmental (SACE). The Economist Intelligence Unit was described earlier. The Political Risk Services, or PRS Group, analyzes the possibility of political turmoil

TABLE 4.7	RANK	PRS	#	SACE	#	EIU
Top 10 High-Risk Countries	1	Somalia	1	Somalia	1	Zimbabwe
	2	Congo, D.R.	2	Iraq	2	Chad
	3	Iraq	3	Afghanistan	3	Congo, D.R.
	4	Sudan	4	Congo, D.R.	4	Cambodia
	5	Côte d'Ivoire	5	Zimbabwe	4	Sudan
	6	Haiti	6	Korea, North	6	Iraq
	7	Guinea	7	Sudan	7	Côte d'Ivoire
	8	Zimbabwe	8	Myanmar	7	Haiti
	9	Nigeria	9	Uzbekistan	7	Pakistan
	10	Myanmar	10	Liberia	7	Zambia
	10	Pakistan	11	Eritrea	7	Afghanistan

Source: Adapted from: Sottilotta, C.E., 'Political risk: Concepts, definitions, challenges', LISS School of Government, Rome, Italy, April 2013. www.sog.luiss.it

Note: PRS = Political Risk Services; SACE = Servizi Assicurativi per il Commercio Estero; EIU = Economist Intelligence Unit

and eleven types of government intervention that may affect the business climate. SACE, the Italian Export Agency, employs a model that measures expropriation risk (rule of law, property rights, government intervention, control of corruption), transfer risk (regulatory quality, monetary policy, investment freedom, financial freedom), and political violence risk (accountability, political stability and the rule of law). Using the three services, Sottilotta compared the rankings of fifteen of the highest risk countries (ten of which are shown in Table 4.7) reported by SACE in 2008, the EIU in 2009–10 and PRS in October 2010. The "Arab Spring" began in Egypt during December 2010 and then spread to Tunisia and Syria. What is evident from the data in Table 4.7 is that none of the countries that were about to experience dramatic political change were included in the "top ten" of political risk in the ranking provided by PRS, SACE, and EIU. Apparently, these sorts of models do not have the ability to take into account possible regional contagion effects; the effect that serious, destabilizing events which take place in one country, have on others in the region.

MANAGING POLITICAL RISK

For example, insurance against some political risks is offered by both governmental and private agencies. The Overseas Private Insurance Corporation (OPIC), an American government agency, offers insurance covering currency inconvertibility, expropriation, and political violence, and is available for investments in new ventures and expansions of existing enterprises. Similar insurance coverage is available from the Canadian government agency, Export Development Canada. Many other governments, and some private insurance carriers such as AIG, offer similar insurance policies.

Type of venture	Strategy	
Joint Business Ventures (Equity Sharing)	Partner with local company or individual who understands the local environment.	**TABLE 4.8** Risk Management Strategies
Licensing	A non-equity contract to manage production.	
Adaptation	Adjustments required to lessen the harmful impact of unwanted events.	
Flexible Supply Chain	Diversifying supply chains to respond to disruptions.	
Localization	Modification of the subsidiary's name, brands, to suit local tastes and to appear as a local, rather than a foreign firm.	
Dependency	Keeping the host nation dependent on the subsidiary by controlling distribution, assigning some key positions to host managers.	
Lobbying and Prominent Alliances	Legitimate influencing of government policy through trade associations or professional lobbyists.	
Community Initiatives	Contributing to local social endeavors such as education and health.	
Insurance	Policies covering risks of expropriation, political violence, etc.	

Source: Compiled by Author

Table 4.8 lists a number of risk management alternative strategies. One possibility is to share ownership with host country nationals such as through joint ventures. This alternative has a number of advantages. First, governments are less likely to take action that would be detrimental to local economic interests. Second, participation of local nationals can be a good bridge to host government and union representatives. Another method in which risk can be reduced is through participating in community projects such as promoting social welfare (schools, medical facilities) and rural development projects. An example of participation in social-welfare projects is the case of Nike's, micro-development project in Indonesia. In a five-year period, the Nike-funded project has provided nearly $1.8 million in small business loans, called micro-credit, to 11,500 Indonesian entrepreneurs. These collateral-free loans have enabled them to launch their own enterprises, lifting them out of chronic poverty.[19]

Entering markets via non-equity methods, such as licensing and franchising, reduces the financial risk of operating in high political risk countries. Dependency strategies include local sourcing of components and hiring resident managers as much as possible who can create goodwill toward the company rather than employing expatriates.

In short, it may be possible to do business in countries where at first glance political risk seems to be excessive. However, careful use of appropriate tools for the identification, measurement, and management of political risk can result in the selection of markets that otherwise might be overlooked.

SUMMARY

- Although there are five different legal systems in use around the world, common and civil law countries account for about 30 percent of the world's gross national product.
- Global marketers must be aware of the legal problems that can arise when doing business abroad. Specifically, these problems center on marketing issues such as the "4Ps"; product, place, price, and promotion.
- Intellectual property includes patents, trademarks, copyright and related rights, geographical indications, industrial designs, know-how and trade secrets. Intellectual property is an integral part of international trade, and its importance is increasing as the effective use of knowledge contributes ever more to national and international economic prosperity.
- Trade disputes can occur between countries, countries and business firms, and between business firms. The major agency dealing with trade disputes involving two or more countries is the World Trade Organization. However, while it deals with settling trade disputes, its main aim is to liberalize trade through the reduction or elimination of trade barriers such as tariffs and quotas.
- Doing business abroad may entail political risk. There are two types of risk: macro, or country risk that threatens an entire economic sector and micro, or firm risk that threatens individual companies. Political risk cannot be eliminated. Therefore, it is imperative for global firms to forecast what sort of risk they face and how it can be managed.

DISCUSSION QUESTIONS

1. How can intellectual property rights be protected in China?
2. Select four EU countries. Explain how the advertising of alcoholic beverages is regulated.
3. Explain some of the pitfalls faced by a multinational manufacturer when trying to have its products conform to a universal standard.
4. You are responsible for risk management in your firm. How would you go about forecasting the political risk for investment in emerging markets? How can a SME assess and manage political risk?

EXPERIENTIAL EXERCISES

1. Using whatever sources you can find, prepare a political risk analysis for China.

2. Select four EU countries. Explain how the advertising of alcoholic beverages is regulated in each.

KEY TERMS

- Arbitration
- Civil law
- Common law
- Country-specific risk
- Firm-specific risk
- GATT
- Intellectual property

- Mediation
- Parallel importing
- Patent treaties
- Political risk
- Product standards
- WTO

NOTES

1 http://www.islamic-banking.com
2 The familiar symbol ® designating a trademark can only be used in the United States following registration.
3 The World Factbook. (2015), https://www.cia.gov/library/publications/the-world-factbook/docs/refmaps.html [Accessed: August 1, 2015].
4 However, some legal experts suggest registration in the local language as well, e.g. China, Muslim countries.
5 For a list of members of the Agreement and Protocol, see www.wipo.int
6 Schollberg, T. (2015), 'After a deal, British chocolates won't cross the pond', *The New York Times*, January 24, 2015, p. A16.
7 The World Factbook. (2015), https://www.cia.gov/library/publications/the-world-factbook/docs/refmaps.html [Accessed: August 1, 2015].
8 Mihai Avram. (2014), 'Software legal protection: Shaping the EU software patent', *Amsterdam Law Forum*, University of Groningen.
9 'WIPO Arbitration Case Examples', www.wipo.int/amc/en/arbitration/case-example.html [Accessed: October 10, 2009].
10 The World Factbook. (2015), https://www.cia.gov/library/publications/the-world-factbook/docs/refmaps.html [Accessed: August 1, 2015].
11 (2006), 'Senate ratifies treaty on cybercrime', www.smh.com.au/articles/2006/08/05/1154198342696.html [Accessed: August 8, 2006].
12 Czinkota, M., Knight, G., Liesch, P., and Steen, J. (2005), 'Positioning terrorism in management and marketing: Research propositions', *Journal of International Management,* 11(4), pp.581–604.
13 (2015), 'War on terrorism', http://www.gallup.com/poll/5257/War-Terrorism.aspx [Accessed: October, 2015].
14 Nitsch, Volker, and Dieter Schumacher. (2003), 'Tourism and trade', *European Journal of Political Economy*, 20(2), pp. 353–66.
15 Costoiu, A. (2006), 'The reciprocal effect of terrorism and international trade, 1975–2002', University of Illinois at Chicago.

16 Willis, H., Morral, A., Kelly, T., and Medby, J. (2005). *Estimating terrorism risk*. Santa Monica, CA: Rand Center for Terrorism Risk Management Policy, p.xvi.

17 Czinkota, M. (2005). 'International marketing and terrorism preparedness'. Testimony before the House of Representatives Committee on Small Business, Washington, D.C., November 1.

18 Adapted from: Baird Webel. (2014), 'Terrorism risk insurance: Issue analysis and overview of current program', CSR Report R42716. Washington D.C.: Congressional Research Service.

19 Wolfgang Frank, 'Successful partnership for CSR activities in Thailand: The NIKE village development project', http://www.pda.or.th/downloads/csr-thailandfinalrevision-wf0811.pdf [Accessed July 30, 2016].

CASE 4.1   A TORTUOUS ROAD AHEAD FOR PROTON OF MALAYSIA*

It's an unenviable position any company could find itself. Proton's share of the domestic car market in Malaysia fell to 41% in 2005, from 44% in 2004 and about 60% in 2002. Tariffs on foreign-made cars are being slowly lifted under a regional free-trade pact called the ASEAN Free Trade Area (AFTA). The company has been hit by falling sales and has had its worst year in 2006 since its founding in the early 1980s.

Perusahaan Otomobil Nasional Sdn. Bhd. (known much better, simply, as Proton) is one of the two Malaysia's national car manufacturers. Like so much else in modern Malaysia, Proton was the brainchild of ex-Prime Minister Mahathir Mohamad. Proton was founded in 1983 as a joint venture with Japan's Mitsubishi Motors Corp. that ended its connection after nearly 20 years in 2004. Mahathir is now an adviser to the board of the company and still retains an active interest.

MALAYSIA – THE COUNTRY

Malaysia is generally regarded as one of the most successful non-western countries to have achieved a relatively smooth transition to modern economic growth over the last century. It is a country of nearly 25.2 million people and one of the most vibrant economies in South-East Asia. Geographically, it consists of two regions separated by the South China Sea. Politically, it is a federation of 13 States and three federally administered territories. Most of the country's economic and industrial development is concentrated in the western part known as Peninsular Malaysia while the eastern part that consists of the large States of Sabah and Sarawak is comparatively less developed industrially.

Malaysia's multi-ethic society comprises of a majority Malay-Muslim population and a numerically lesser but economically more powerful Chinese population. The third racial segment is made up of the migrant Indians who have negligble presence in the economy. There are tribal groups, Eurasians, and a large pool of expatriate workers besides the three major racial groups. Malaysia has a well-earned reputation as a liberal, progressive, and modern Muslim country.

Trade, internationalization, and globalization are phenomena not new to Malaysia. It has a long history of being an important junction of major world trade routes. The indigenous population has been supplemented by an immigrant labor force mainly from China and India thus making it experience diversity of cultures. Foreign capital has played a critical role throughout its economic development. Malaysia's exports comprise of electronic equipment, petroleum and liquefied natural gas, chemicals, palm oil, timber and wood products, rubber, and textiles. It is among the world's biggest producers of computer disk drives, palm oil, rubber, and timber. Besides, it has a booming tourism industry.

CARMAKING IN MALAYSIA

It's an enigma how a small country could have the temerity to embark upon a large-scale project of manufacturing cars. Most likely, it was an effort to put Malaysia on the path of industrialization firmly as automobile industry is considered a significant engine of industrial development. The history of Malaysian automobile industry goes back to early 1960s, when the Malaysian government developed a policy to promote an integrated automobile industry to strengthen Malaysia's industrial base. The main objectives of the government in promoting an automobile assembly industry were to reduce imports, save foreign exchange, create employment, develop strong forward and backward linkages with the rest of the economy, and transfer industrial technology.

Protective tariffs were announced in early 1966 when all distributors and dealers were required to obtain import licenses. In 1967, the Malaysian government approved the operation of six assembly plants. Initially, the assembly plants were mainly joint venture projects between European automobile manufacturers and local partners who were previously their local distributors. Until the early 1980s, there were 15 assemblers that produced vehicles for European and Japanese manufacturers.

The big push to Malaysian automobile industry was led by the two national car projects, Proton and Perodua. The second national car manufacturer, *Perusahaan Otomobil Kedua Sdn. Bhd.* (Perodua), was established as a joint venture between Malaysian firms and Daihatsu in1993, and Perodua started production of Kancil, a passenger car with a displacement volume of 660cc and modeled after the Daihatsu 'Mira.' While Proton offered larger-capacity cars, Perodua specialized in smaller-capacity, compact, and affordable cars.

Over the years, Malaysia has adopted a strong protectionist policy towards its automobile industry. Hefty tariffs on imported cars and car components have sought to protect the local car manufacturers from foreign competition. This protectionism has served as a double-edged sword. On the positive side, local car manufacturers have prospered, there have been reduced foreign exchange outflows, and higher government revenue from tariffs. There have also been spillover effects of the development of strong components and parts manufacturing, and development of original equipment manufacturers for other car companies. On the negative side, protection to local car manufacturers have made them complacent and inefficient, distortion of markets have taken place, customers have been deprived of high quality cars at affordable prices, and the local car industry is not able to compete internationally.

Statistics show that Malaysia is the largest car market in South-East Asia with more than 400,000 new cars being registered in 2005. (See Table 1) Proton's share of this market is about 40% and that is steadily decreasing over the years.

Often, it is said that the car is a product that evokes varying emotions. It is a house-on-wheels, a companion, a status symbol, offers security and safety, besides being, of course, a means of mobility. For the Malaysians, car making has often

Year	Passenger Cars	Total Vehicles (including commercial and 4X4 vehicles)	
2001	327,447	396,381	**TABLE 1** Number of vehicles registered in Malaysia
2002	359,934	434,954	
2003	320,524	405,745	
2004	380,568	487,605	
2005	416,692	552,316	
Jan – Jun 2006	184,725	248,407	

Source: Adapted from http://www.maa.org.my/info_summary.htm Retrieved October 13, 2006

been seen as a matter of national pride. It hurts terribly when suggestions are made to sell off stakes in the car companies to foreigners. Yet, it is equally distressing that it is no longer possible to follow protectionist policies in a rapidly globalizing world demanding closer integration with the world economy. The choice is difficult indeed. For the typical globalization enthusiast, it is difficult to understand the motives for protectionism. For a person of nationalistic fervor it is not easy to visualize why 'foreign marauders' be allowed to gobble up hard-earned national wealth. There are strong arguments on both sides. As Mahathir Mohamed, the ex-prime-minister credited with setting up Proton, said in a *Business Week* interview: "Korean and Japanese carmakers were protected for 40 or 50 years. Why should we open our own small market after just 20 years?"

FOREIGN CONNECTIONS

It is not as if Malaysia has a hands-off policy towards foreign capital, foreign technology or foreign labor. Proton has had a good record of foreign collaborations over the years. It started operations in alliance with Mitsubishi and sustained it for over 20 years. In February 2006, Proton and Mitsubishi Motors revived their alliance by signing a pact to develop new Proton vehicles by next year.

Proton produced its first car named 'Saga' in 1985 mainly for the domestic market but made an initial export attempt the same year to Bangladesh. In 1989, it started exporting cars to the United Kingdom. Although Proton has diversified export destinations since then, the UK has always been the main absorber of its exports. On its website (http://www.proton.com/about_proton/history/index.php Retrieved October 13, 2006), Proton claims to be exporting to 50 countries in Africa, Asia, Europe, Middle-East, and the Pacific. Export shipments for 2005 were nearly 13500 units. Proton intends to raise exports to 100,000 units by the year 2008 that may seem to be unrealistic looking to its recent export performance.

Dissatisfied with the slow progress of technology transfer from Mitsubishi and the rapid appreciation of yen, Proton established an alliance with Citroen to produce a new model, 'Tiara.' Proton established subsidiaries or related companies to assemble and distribute vehicles in the Philippines and Vietnam. Recently, in September 2006, PSA Peugeot Citroen signed an agreement with Proton to look at forming a strategic alliance in an effort to enter South-East Asia. Earlier, Proton held talks on potential alliances with other car manufacturers, including Rover and Volkswagen, but they did not lead to partnerships. Proton has also been negotiating with Chery Automobile Co. of China on sharing production facilities and developing new vehicle models. There are strong signals that Proton is open to selling equity stake to a foreign partner.

Though the UK and Australia remain major export market for Proton, it is developing the markets in the Middle East and other Muslim countries as well as in the ASEAN countries. Currently, Proton has assembly plants in Iran, China, India (with Hindustan Motors), and a joint venture between its subsidiary, Proton Edar and PT Ningz Multiusaha to assemble and distribute Proton vehicle in Indonesia. This was its first effort to penetrate the regional South-East Asian markets. Proton plans to increase CBU exports to the UK and Australia, as well as CKD assembly in Indonesia, Thailand, the Middle East and Eastern Europe. Proton is also studying the feasibility of CKD operations in China and India.

THE STRATEGIC OPTIONS: ALL MUDDLED UP?

Talking to *Asiaweek* magazine in 2000, Mahathir Mohammed, the then prime minister of Malaysia, said that "it will be very difficult for (Proton) to penetrate the international car market with global car giants exercising mass production," He said, "we do not reject globalization or cooperating with the major players of the industry … but we want to retain (Proton) as ours because it identifies us as a nation on par with other automotive producing nations." It does, but at what cost? Today, Proton can barely utilize just half of its production capacity of 380,000 cars. Its exports are measly at barely 13500 in 2005, half of it to UK. It has a very low brand power outside Malaysia, weak customer loyalty and retention rate besides perceived quality problems in Proton cars. Competition from MNCs in ASEAN area emanates from US giants like Ford, General Motors, and Daimler – Chrysler is already present in neighboring Thailand.

Proton finds itself at crossroads. On the one hand, the government of present Prime Minister Abdullah Badawi has to roll back tariff protections as Malaysia honors its obligations under the AFTA. Tariffs on Southeast Asian-made cars sold in Malaysia were a stiff 50% in 2004 but are 20% in 2006 and will have to fall to just 5% by 2008. On the other hand, its obligations to the ASEAN put Malaysia in jeopardy with regard to 10,000 jobs at Proton, plus 90,000 in the parts and component plants that supply to it.

The supporters of Proton argue that with regional integration such as AFTA, Malaysia's car market is not limited to just its 26-million people but 500 million plus South East Asians. Critics of the company see no future for Proton as an independent company. Quoted in the July 2005 edition of *Business Week*, Graeme

Maxton, Asia analyst for consultancy Autopolis in Hong Kong says "Proton is an anachronism in the automobile industry and it's not going to survive over the long term". As a marginal producer with falling market share even in its home market, he says, Proton lacks the scale it needs to compete against bigger rivals. Strong words, but could turn out to be true!

As the debate goes on, foreign suitor companies are lining up either to buy Proton or to use its facilities to increase their production in the hot Southeast Asian market.

DISCUSSION QUESTIONS

1. Identify the factors for and against the position that Proton needs a foreign equity partner.
2. Suggest measures that Proton could use to increase its sales in export markets.
3. Should Proton give in to the temptation of becoming a part of a larger, global car company such as Volkswagen or Citreon?
4. Should Proton aim at becoming a regional automobile and shelve its dreams of becoming a global company?

NOTE

* Case prepared by Azhar Kazmi, Visiting Professor of Management at King Fahd University of Petroleum & Minerals, Dhahran, Saudi Arabia and formerly Professor of Business Administration at International Islamic University Malaysia, Kuala Lumpur

CHAPTER 5

Integrating Global, Regional, and National Markets

"[G]lobal multinationals have … viewed developing Asia [countries]…as an offshore-production platform. The offshore-efficiency solution is still an attractive option. But what really could be powerful [is] a growing opportunity to tap the region's 3.5 billion consumers."

Stephen Roach, Chairman, Morgan Stanley Asia

LEARNING OBJECTIVES

After Reading This Chapter, You Should Be Able to:

* Be aware of the difference between regional and global trade agreements.
* Understand the difference between various types of regional economic blocs.
* Understand the key issues and concepts associated with emerging markets, especially the BRIC countries.
* Discuss why there is more regional than global trade.
* Make an argument for "fair trade."
* Determine which emerging markets have the most potential and why.

INTRODUCTION

As Rapiscan Systems prepared to bid on a security-equipment contract last year, Vice President of Government Affairs, Peter Kant, thought he deserved an edge over his two competitors because only his company was based in the United States and set to manufacture the equipment domestically. Rapiscan, a manufacturer of baggage- and cargo-screening systems in Hawthorne, Calif., was up against a British-based company and a US company that had paired with a Chinese firm and planned to manufacture its equipment in China. But Chemonics, the prime contractor managing the US Agency for International Development's (USAID) $40 million contract to screen cargo awarded the subcontract to the American-Chinese team. USAID had opted not to include a clause in the contract that would have required the supplier to assemble the equipment in the United States. That decision, and Kant's ensuing disappointment, illustrates the growing debate over "Buy American" regulations as agencies struggle to comply with the complicated, decades-old legislation in a world driven by global supply chains. As agencies and contractors grow increasingly frustrated with the high costs of compliance, industry groups are pushing to liberalize the regulations.

Not a day goes by without an article in the newspaper or a briefing on television about world trade issues. In times of economic crises, there is increased pressure to buy domestic-made products rather than imports. For example, the advertisement in Figure 5.1 is sponsored by those who believe that domestic industry should be protected from foreign competition in order to stimulate the local economy. While most consumers are free to choose between locally made and imported products, in reality, most international commerce involves some sort of government intervention to protect domestic industry.

Governmental protectionist policies include *tariffs* (taxes on imports), *quotas* (limits on the quantity of imports), and *non-tariff trade barriers* such as mandates on the quality or the content of imported goods. It is the latter type of constraints that are most prevalent today. Sales to government agencies in many countries are restricted by "buy local" legislation. The American 1979 Trade Agreements Act requires government agencies (as exemplified by the Rapiscan case previously) to buy products that undergo "substantial transformation," or final assembly, in the United States or one of 30 approved countries that have trade agreements with Washington. However, it is difficult to enforce such legislation in a globalized world.

Even among European Union member states, who have agreed to free trade, and the free movement of labor and capital, there are signs of protectionism. The former British Prime Minister, Gordon Brown, was quoted as saying "British Jobs for British Workers," ostensibly encouraging preference for British employees over other EU citizens. In a non-related incident, the French government was considering subsidizing its struggling automobile industry. Both actions contravene EU policy.

Most economists support trade liberalization in a globalized world. The idea is to get as many nations as possible into multilateral agreements that will increase trade

FIGURE 5.1
"Buy American"
Advertisement
Source: Roger
Simmermaker, *How
Americans Can Buy
American: The Power of
Consumer Patriotism*,
3rd edition, 2015.
Logo reprinted with
permission

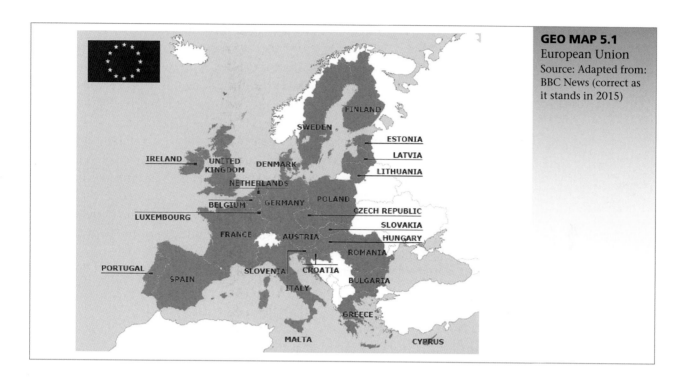

GEO MAP 5.1
European Union
Source: Adapted from:
BBC News (correct as
it stands in 2015)

among them, especially between developed and developing nations. The question is whether agreements to do so can be globalized or not.

This chapter discusses the issue of regional versus global trade agreements. Next, the major types of trade agreements will be explained. Significant growth in domestic markets, as well as in trade, has taken place in emerging markets, especially the so-called *BRIC* (Brazil, Russia, India, and China) countries. The last section of the chapter presents a market potential analysis of the BRICs.

REGIONALISM OR GLOBALISM?

While globalization has led to greater interdependence among economies, regional trade agreements have outpaced global arrangements. In theory, a global trade agreement is an ideal solution in terms of resource allocation, economic welfare, and economic prosperity. Such an agreement would allow many countries to enjoy trade with each other free from most restrictions. The next best solution is the regional trade agreement which lowers trade barriers among members without having to lower barriers for non-members. The difficulties experienced in attempting to achieve multilateral or global trade agreements have led many countries to focus on regional trade arrangements as the primary means to expand international trade. An example of the difficulties inherent in multilateral negotiations was the failure of the Cancun Ministerial Conference (held in Mexico during 2003 under the auspices of the World Trade Organization) to conclude agreement on most of the trade issues on the agenda.

Free trade blocs such as the North American Free Trade Agreement (NAFTA) and customs and monetary unions, like the European Union (EU) resulted in the removal of trade barriers between member countries, while at the same time retaining flexibility over which sectors of industry to liberalize and which issues to negotiate. Trading blocs have resulted in a concentration of trade within regions rather than globally.

The formation of regional blocs also influences market entry. First, preferential trading terms reduce the cost of exporting to member country markets. Locating within a trading bloc provides lower cost access to member country markets than does exporting to non-member countries from outside of the bloc. Second, the costs of serving multiple countries within a trading bloc may differ depending on the base of operations. Strategically locating in one country can lead to greater efficiencies than investing in another country outside of the bloc. Also, it may be easier to harmonize marketing standards on a regional level than globally.

REGIONAL TRADE

The formation of regional economic groups, such as the European Union, has accelerated international trade flows of goods and services. Foreign trade flows are concentrated in developed countries, especially by the *Triad Nations*; China, The United States, and Germany (Figure 5.2). These nations accounted for 56 percent of all world trade in 2012.[1] Moreover, intra-Triad trade (trade only between the three countries), accounts for about 10 percent of world trade. Much of world trade increasingly occurs within regions and between three major economic areas: North America and Mexico, Asia, and Europe.

There is ample evidence that a regional rather than a global strategy prevails among countries and businesses. For example:

1. Triad and regional trade are dominant, e.g. 60 percent of EU members' exports and imports (intra-trade) are to other EU countries.

2. Most multinational corporations pursue regional, not global strategies, e.g. approximately 90 percent of all cars manufactured in Europe are sold in Europe, while 75 percent of all cars manufactured in North America are sold in North America.

While the European Union (28 countries) is the largest exporter and importer of merchandise in the world, China is the largest single merchandise exporting and importing country (2013) followed closely by the United States and Germany. In 2007, Japan was a member of the Triad (in place of China) and the world's second largest economy until 2010. Since then, China's international trade has increased, while that of Japan has decreased. In 2013, Japan's total annual trade was $1.4 trillion, less than half that of China, the United States, and Germany

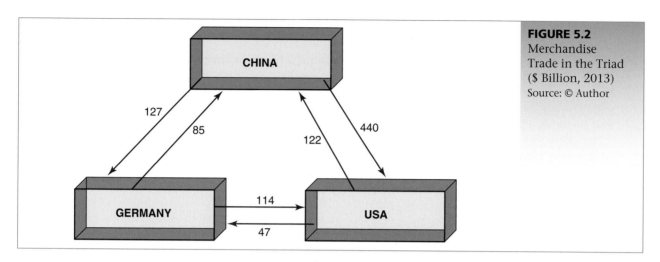

FIGURE 5.2
Merchandise
Trade in the Triad
($ Billion, 2013)
Source: © Author

(all close to $4 trillion, see Table 5.1). Both Germany ($42 billion) and the United States ($318 billion) have merchandise trade deficits with China. In addition, the United States has a trade deficit with Germany ($67 billion). Some of the United States' trade deficit is reduced by its advantage in the trade of services as explained below.

However, in addition to merchandise trade (goods), trade in services should also be considered. Services include banking and other financial transactions, insurance, transportation, tourism, and consulting. If these categories are included in total trade, then the United States is the largest Triad-exporter and importer ($4.94 trillion in 2012), with Germany ($4.43 trillion) and China ($4.40 trillion) tied for second place. The European Union would still be the largest world trader with $5.96 trillion in both merchandise and services.

The rapid increase in China's trade has created opportunities for many countries, but suppliers of textiles and electronic goods now face a major competitor, resulting in increased price competition. Now that quotas have been removed from Chinese textiles there has been a major increase in imports to the United States. Textile mills in the Southeast will, more than likely, shrink in number as a result. Not only American manufactures have been impacted, but those in Asia as well. Garment industries in Japan, Taiwan, and South Korea also face increased competition from China.

Chinese competition also affects other emerging economies such as India. About one-third of the products manufactured by Indian small manufacturing enterprises

	US$ Trillions—2011
1. European Union (27)	4.47
2. China	3.93
3. United States	3.88
4. Germany	3.87
Source: International Trade Statistics, Secretariat, World Trade Organization, 2012	

TABLE 5.1
Who Are the
World's Largest
Merchandise
Exporters and
Importers? (US$
Trillions—2011)

Box 5.1 Country-in-Focus: China Loses Its Allure

The American consumer was the focus of world marketers in the 1950s and 1960s. Now it is the turn of the Chinese. China has become the next consumption superpower and it seems to have surpassed Japan to become the world's second-biggest consumer economy. Its roughly $3.3 trillion in private consumption is about 8 percent of the world total, and it has only just begun.

A massive push to urbanize is also underway, which should produce tens of millions of wealthier citizens seeking retail therapy. McKinsey, a consultancy, forecasts that consumption by urban Chinese households will increase from ¥10 trillion in 2012 to nearly ¥27 trillion in 2022.

According to McKinsey, consumers earning between $16,000–34,000 annually by 2020 will account for 51 percent of the urban population. This segment of 67,000 households or nearly 400 million people will be able to afford family cars and small luxury items. These consumers live in the 100 wealthiest cities in China. The increase in discretionary incomes among this group makes them an important market segment.

Adapted from: The *Economist*, January 25, 2014;

'Meet the Chinese Consumer of 2020', *McKinsey Quarterly*, March 2012.

(SMEs) are also available from China, but at a price lower than the cost of raw materials needed to produce them in India.

On a regional basis, Asia has experienced relatively high growth rates. Asia's share of world GDP is rising, thanks to its economic dynamism. Indeed, the region's economy is now the fastest growing in the world, contributing 43 percent of world growth in 2013. As of 2013, Asia's share of world real GDP exceeded that of Europe, the Americas, and Africa.

The anticipated future growth of Asian markets has made them attractive to potential investors. Executives of transnational corporations (TNCs) ranked developing countries such as China, India, and Indonesia as more attractive for foreign investment than Germany, the United Kingdom, and Japan (Table 5.2). China is considered an attractive location by 45 percent of TNC executive respondents, on a par with the next attractive country, the United States. These results imply that more investment will shift from developed countries that have saturated markets and high production costs to emerging economies, such as Asian countries.

Changes in relative shares of economic growth between regions will be significant, but changes within regions will be no less important. For example, real GDP growth averaged 41.2 percent during 2005–13 in Poland, 13.8 percent in Austria, but only 3.6 percent in Denmark and -4.1 percent in Italy.[2]

REGIONAL ECONOMIC BLOCS

The economic and political forces of globalization have led to the regionalization of societies through the establishment of integrated economies such as the European Union, NAFTA and Mercosur, so-called "single markets," united by harmonized regulatory standards and common levels of social protection. These "single markets"

Rank	Country	Percent Responding*	
1	China	45	**TABLE 5.2**
2	United States	43	TNCs' Top
3	India	30	Prospective Host
4	Indonesia	24	Economies,
5	Brazil	19	2013–15
6	Germany	19	
7	Mexico	18	
8	Thailand	15	
9	United Kingdom	13	
10	Japan	12	

*Percentage of respondents selecting economy as a top destination.
Source: UNCTAD survey. http://unctad.org/en/PublicationsLibrary/webdiaeia2013d9_en.pdf [Accessed: February, 2015]

have provided the framework through which firms, including manufacturers, distributors, and service providers act under a new set of rules: those of the economic region in addition to those of the nation state. These new rules have led to the formation of supranational firms that attempt to globalize marketing operations, on a worldwide or regional basis.

Regional trading blocs such as the EU, NAFTA, and Mercosur were established to liberalize trade between countries and facilitate the flows of goods, services, investment, and communication. A central tenet of these groups is that they have trading and investment policies that are favorable for members. They also have common policies regarding trading arrangements with non-members.

A "single market" is the free movement from one member country to another of people, merchandise, services, and capital. However, the extent to which these "movements" are implemented differs from one regional trading bloc to another. The EU single market remains fragmented by complex and heterogeneous rules at the EU and national levels affecting trade, capital, including foreign direct investment, and labor mobility. For example, an important piece of European Union legislation that was not enacted involved an attempt to enforce a maximum working week across Europe. Moreover, an opinion poll found that a majority of businessmen in Europe think that the cost of EU rules exceeds their benefits. The single market needs more effective basic economic institutions for cross-border activity in areas such as taxation, competition policy, and patent protection. A survey of 28,000 EU citizens found that 94 percent of Europeans who travel outside their home country limit their use of services like Facebook, because of mobile roaming charges.[3]

In order to understand these problems, we begin by examining regional trade agreements.

There are three main forms of cooperative agreements, short of full monetary and political union among members. These are (1) free-trade areas, (2) customs unions, and (3) common markets.

FREE-TRADE AREAS

Free-trade areas (FTAs) are arrangements in which countries give each other preferential treatment in trade by eliminating tariffs and other barriers on goods. Each country continues its normal trade policies with other countries outside of the FTA agreement. An example of a free-trade area is the North American Free Trade Agreement (NAFTA), signed between the United States, Canada and, Mexico in 1994. It resulted in the elimination of customs duties between the three countries on most industrial products traded among them. Free-trade area agreements aim to reduce or eliminate tariffs and non-tariff barriers among member countries. However, each member country may determine the extent of *external tariffs* it wishes to maintain with non-member countries.

United States exports and imports within the NAFTA bloc is another example of the dominance of regional rather than global trade.

The United States had $1.1 trillion in total (two-ways) goods trade with NAFTA countries (Canada and Mexico) during 2013. Merchandise exports totalled $526 billion,[4] while merchandise imports totalled $613 billion. Trade in services with NAFTA (exports and imports) totalled $134 billion in 2012 (latest data available). Services exports were $89 billion, while services imports were $45 billion[5].

Canada is currently the United States' largest goods trading partner and the second largest supplier of goods imports. In 2013, the top export categories were: Vehicles ($51.7 billion), machinery ($45.3 billion), electrical machinery ($26.8 billion), mineral fuel and oil (oil and natural gas) ($24.7 billion), and plastic ($13.0 billion).

The five largest import categories in 2013 were: Mineral fuel and oil (crude and natural gas) ($109.4 billion), vehicles ($55.7 billion), machinery ($19.8 billion), plastic ($10.6 billion), and other goods ($10.2 billion).

Mexico is the United States' third largest supplier of goods imports and the second largest export goods market. US imports from Mexico accounted for 12.4 percent of overall US imports in 2013. The five largest import categories were: Vehicles (cars, trucks and parts) ($59.6 billion), electrical machinery ($57.4 billion), machinery ($42.6 billion), mineral fuel and crude oil ($34.8 billion), and optic and medical instruments ($10.7 billion)[6].

Example of the Mechanisms of a Free-Trade Area

How is the concept of a "free" trade area implemented? Take for example, trade between three countries, two of which are members of an FTA. In the following illustration (Figure 5.3), assume that countries B and C are members of a free-trade area. As a result, there are no customs duties levied on trade between them. Suppose, a manufacturer in country A, a non-member country wishes to export building materials to country B. Country B levies a 15 percent tariff on building materials from non-member countries, which may make country A's products higher priced than local competitors. In order to be more competitive, the manufacturer can export

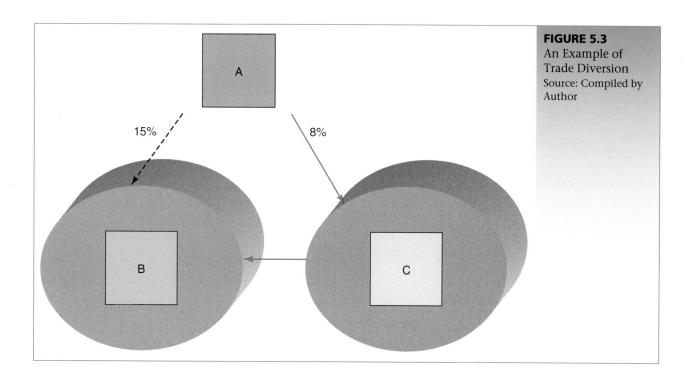

FIGURE 5.3
An Example of Trade Diversion
Source: Compiled by Author

instead to country C, pay the lower 8 percent *external tariff* and then re-export to country B (no tariff between C and B). Today, most countries have domestic content legislation, which requires that products must contain a minimum value added in the country of origin in order to be free of customs duties.

Because the building materials were produced in country A, and not in Country C, they would not enjoy relief from customs duties. Therefore, they would be subject to an additional 7 percent tariff of country B, eliminating any possibility of circumventing customs duties by first exporting to country C.

There are many FTAs, some involving more than two countries, but there are *bilateral agreements* as well, e.g. between the USA and Israel, and the USA and South Korea. The *European Free Trade Area* (Iceland, Liechtenstein, Norway, and Switzerland) includes those countries that did not opt to join the EU since its inception. However, residents in the EFTA countries are more than twice as wealthy as those in the EU. They also enjoy lower inflation, higher employment, healthier budget surpluses, and lower real interest rates. Interestingly, they also export more per capita than EU countries. In 1994 the EU and EFTA established the *European Economic Area* (EEA) thereby creating a European Single Market. While not members of the EU, EFTA countries have free movement of goods, capital, services and people, but without a common monetary and agricultural policy or the same social welfare policies as the EU. Each country is free to negotiate free-trade agreements with other countries. All EFTA countries have a vast network of free-trade and bilateral agreements. Table 5.3 shows those countries with which EFTA has concluded an FTA agreement. Of the countries listed, the United States has bilateral agreements with Israel, Jordan, Mexico, Morocco, South Korea, and

TABLE 5.3 The EFTA Network: EFTA Agreements	**Eastern Europe**	**Balkans**	**Middle East & Africa**	**Americas & Asia**
	Bulgaria Romania	Croatia Macedonia	Israel Morocco Jordan Lebanon Tunisia Turkey Palestinian Authority Southern African Customs Union (Botswana, Lesotho, Namibia, South Africa, Swaziland)	Chile Mexico South Korea Singapore

Source: Adapted from: The World Factbook. (2015), www.ciaworldfactbook.us

Singapore. Mexico has the most bilateral trade agreements, including countries in Latin America, the EU, and EFTA.

CUSTOMS UNIONS

A *customs union* contains the same provisions as a free-trade area with one major addition—a common external tariff. In the building materials example before, countries B and C would have a common external tariff against imports of building materials and other products from non-member countries. In this case, the lower tariff advantage of country B would be eliminated. In the building materials case described previously, the common external tariff of countries B and C would probably fall between the original tariff rates of 8 and 15 percent.

There are a number of customs union trade blocs; examples include the Eurasian Customs Union (Russia, Belarus and Kazakhstan), the East African Community (Kenya, Uganda, Tanzania, Burundi, and Rwanda), and the Southern African Customs Union (South Africa, Botswana, Lesotho, Namibia, and Swaziland).

COMMON MARKETS

The most advanced form of trade bloc is the *common market*. This type of organization combines the provisions of a free-trade area and a customs union with two additional criteria: the free movement of people and capital.[7] The largest of the common markets is the European Union, established as the *European Economic Community* in 1958 with six member countries, increased to 28 members as of 2013. The EU has two additional goals: the establishment of a monetary and political union. A monetary union requires at least a common currency and a central bank. Eleven countries of the EU—Austria, Belgium, Finland, France, Germany, Ireland,

Italy, Luxembourg, the Netherlands, Portugal, and Spain—initially qualified to participate in the monetary union. This required them to adhere to criteria established by the *Maastricht Treaty* regarding price stability, public finance (especially government deficits), interest, and exchange rates. Following this initial agreement, a European Central Bank began functioning in 1998 and a *Euro area* in 1999. Euro notes and coins were introduced in 2002, replacing national ones. Of the EU 28 members, 18 adopted the Euro in addition to six non-EU members: Andorra, Kosovo, Monaco, Montenegro, San Marino, and the Vatican City. Including both users of the Euro and those countries whose currencies are pegged to it, makes the Euro the largest currency area in the world with 506 million people.

A final stage in the integration of countries belonging to a trade bloc is political union. While this stage is included in the *Maastricht Treaty*, it is far from fruition. Political union means relinquishing some if not all national sovereignty to the union, which many countries are unwilling to do, especially Great Britain, Germany, and France. Some forms of political cooperation are possible, such as a common defense and foreign policy as exemplified by membership in NATO. However, formal political union remains a distant goal to be achieved.

A Comparison of the EU and NAFTA

There are a number of bases upon which to compare one of the smallest—in number of members—the NAFTA agreement with the largest member trading group, the EU. However, the NAFTA includes the United States, the largest economy in the world, which brings to the agreement a significant trade volume.

Even though consisting of only three members, the regional GDP of NAFTA is slightly higher than that of the EU (Table 5.4). However, the EU is much more integrated than NAFTA, with an intra-trade volume three times as large and an intra-trade share of 65 percent versus 48 percent among NAFTA members.

HOW "FREE" IS INTRA-EU TRADE?

While internal tariff barriers within the EU have been removed, *non-tariff barriers* still remain, especially in the form of narrow, technical standards that companies

	Intra-Trade Volume	Intra-Trade Share (%)	Regional GDP	Regional GDP Share (%)	**TABLE 5.4** NAFTA and the EU ($ Millions, 2011)
EU	3,886,173	64.7	17,586,699	25.2	
NAFTA	1,101,189	48.3	17,992,982	25.8	

Intra-Trade Volume = Trade volume between member countries.
Intra-Trade Share = Trade within the bloc/total trade volume of member countries.
Regional GDP = Sum of the GDP of members.
Regional GDP Share = GDP of member countries/world GDP.
Source: UN Commodity Trade Database

use to keep their products out of national markets. In an effort to put an end to such barriers, the EU has proposed legislation that would require governments to accept goods approved for sale in another EU country, a principle called *"mutual recognition."* However, the *harmonization* of product standards in the EU and between other countries is far from completed, as the following case illustrates:

> A Dutch food producing company is subject to trade barriers because of a lack of harmonization. For example, there is no European harmonized definition of a sauce, which results in differences in interpretation. A product that in one country is considered a sauce can in another country be described as "vegetables based on solids." Apart from that, different techniques are being used to determine the composition of a product, which creates inconsistencies. Consequently, different import levies are charged in various...countries for the same product.[8]

Of all the common markets in the world, the EU is the largest and most well known in every respect; by the number and size of its members, their economic strength and by the institutions (Parliament and Central Bank) that govern the union. However, there are other trade arrangements and common markets in every region of the world. Below are some examples (Table 5.5). Most do not have a single currency as in the EU (the GCC is planning for a common currency), nor do they actively seek political union, but they have removed barriers to cross country investment and services.

Southern Common Market (Mercosur)

Mercosur is South America's largest trading bloc with a combined GDP of $1.1 trillion. It was established in 1991 by the Treaty of Asunción (Geo Map 5.2) and the Protocol of Ouro Preto which formalized a customs union that provides for the free movement of goods, capital, services, and people among its member states. The bloc's combined market encompasses more than 250 million people and accounts for more than three-quarters of the economic activity on the continent.

Brazil and Argentina have the highest national income and trade of bloc members. Bolivia, Chile, Colombia, Ecuador, and Peru are associate members; they can join free-trade agreements but remain outside the bloc's customs union.

TABLE 5.5 Trade Agreement Examples	Organization	Members
	Association of Southeast Asian Nations (ASEAN)	Brunei, Cambodia, Indonesia, Laos, Malaysia, Myanmar, Philippines, Singapore, Thailand, Vietnam
	East African Community (EAC)	Kenya, Uganda, Tanzania, Burundi, Rwanda
	Gulf Cooperation Council (GCC)	Bahrain, Qatar, Kuwait, Oman, Saudi Arabia, United Arab Emirates
	Southern Common Market (MERCOSUR)	Brazil, Argentina, Paraguay, Uruguay, Venezuela

Source: Adapted from: The World Factbook. (2015), www.ciaworldfactbook.us

GEO MAP 5.2
Asunción, Paraguay
Source: Adapted from:
CIA Maps, The World
Factbook[9]

The **Mercosur Trade Treaty** was signed in Asunción in 1991.

Mercosur tariff policies regulate imports and exports and the bloc can arbitrate trade disputes among its members.[10]

In the future, Mercosur aims to create a continent-wide free-trade area, and the creation of a Mercosur development bank has been suggested. However, there have been tensions among members. For example, the bloc's smaller members, Paraguay and Uruguay, have complained of restricted access to markets in Argentina and Brazil, and have sought to enact bilateral trade deals outside the bloc even though such agreements are not permitted. Talks to secure a trade accord with the EU have stalled, with farm subsidies and tariffs on industrial goods being among the stumbling blocks. Negotiations on a planned US-backed Free Trade Area of the Americas are similarly mired, with some Mercosur leaders rejecting US free-market policies.

East African Community (EAC)

Much smaller than Mercosur, the bloc has a combined population of 120 million people, land area of 1.85 million sq kilometers and a combined gross domestic product of $41 billion. The EAC was formed in July, 2000, with the establishment of an FTA and later a customs union in 2005. They are working to form a common market and a monetary union; and ultimately a political federation of the East African states. The rules of the community and trade issues are handled by a legislative assembly and court of justice.[11]

Association of Southeast Asian Nations (ASEAN)

The ASEAN free trade association was established in 1967 by the five original member countries: Indonesia, Malaysia, Philippines, Singapore, and Thailand; and later joined by Brunei, Vietnam, Laos, Myanmar, and Cambodia. The ASEAN region has a population of about 627 million, and a combined gross domestic product of US$2,409 billion. The bloc's objective is to create a stable, prosperous, and highly competitive economic region in which there is a free flow of goods, services, skilled

GEO MAP 5.3
Association of
Southeast Asian
Nations
Source: Adapted from:
CIA Maps, The World
Factbook[12]

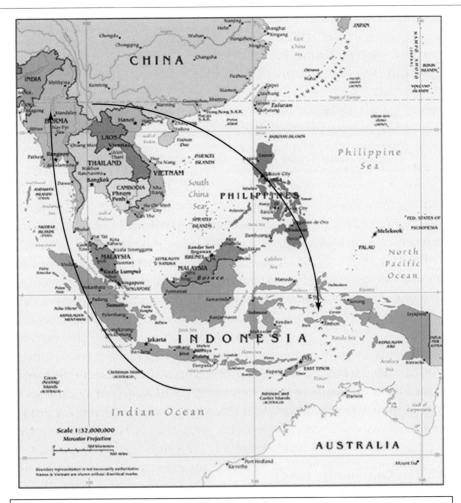

The ASEAN trade members—Indonesia, Malaysia, Philippines, Singapore, Thailand, Brunei, Vietnam, Laos, Myanmar (Burma) and Cambodia.

	Entry Year	Population (Million)	GDP ($Billion)	% GDP Growth (2003–2013)	**TABLE 5.6** Population and GDP of ASEAN Members
Brunei	1984	0	17	1	
Cambodia	1999	15	16	8	
Indonesia	1967	250	868	6	
Laos	1997	7	11	8	
Malaysia	1967	30	312	5	
Myanmar	1997	63	59	9	
Philippines	1967	98	272	5	
Singapore	1967	5	296	6	
Thailand	1967	67	387	4	
Vietnam	1995	92	171	6	

Source: Adapted from: HIS, McKinsey Global Institute Analysis, 2014

labor, investment, and capital. However, there still remains a gap between goals and implementation.[13]

ASEAN's intra-regional trade is considerably lower than other trade blocs, averaging about 25 percent compared to about 60 percent in the EU and 42 percent among the NAFTA countries. The lower regional trade figure for ASEAN is owing in no small part to the disparity in the economic size and growth of member countries as shown in Table 5.6. What is not shown in the table is the fragmentation of member countries exemplified by differences in language, religion, political systems, and personal income levels. The free movement of people has not been implemented, nor does the group have a common tariff with other countries, and has not removed non-tariff barriers to the same extent as the EU and NAFTA agreements. On the bright side is the trend toward technology adaptation as evidenced by the growth of internet and mobile users that is higher than that of Japan, Germany, and the United Kingdom, and the adoption growth of Facebook users greater than that of the United Kingdom, France, Germany, and Italy. In addition, member countries have shown two decades of economic growth greater than many European countries and a low inflation rate (2.8 percent in 2013).

Gulf Cooperation Council (GCC)

The GCC Charter[14] states that the basic objectives are to effect coordination, integration, and inter-connection between member states in all fields, strengthening ties between their peoples, formulating similar regulations in various fields such as economy, finance, trade, customs, tourism, legislation, administration, as well as fostering scientific and technical progress in industry, mining, agriculture, water and animal resources, establishing scientific research centers, setting up joint ventures, and encouraging cooperation of the private sector. In essence, the GCC is both a customs union and a common market, allowing for the free movement of goods, capital, and people among member countries. The GCC members (Geo Map 5.4) have some of the fastest growing economies in the world, mostly due to

GEO MAP 5.4
Gulf Cooperation
Council (GCC)
Source: Adapted from:
CIA Maps, The World
Factbook[15]

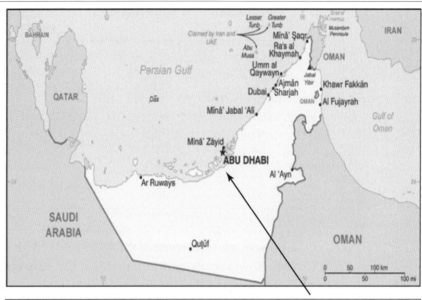

The GCC members include Bahrain, Kuwait, Oman, Qatar,
Saudi Arabia, and the United Arab Emirates.

oil and natural gas revenues along with a building and investment boom financed by decades of accumulated petroleum revenues. The GCC has an economic and technical cooperation agreement with the EU, in the fields of energy, industry, agriculture, fisheries, and science.[16]

FREE VERSUS FAIR TRADE

We have learned that free trade means removing barriers to international commerce among nations. On the other hand, there is a concept known as *Fair Trade*. Fair trade is an approach to international commerce that aims to ensure that producers in developing countries receive a fair price for goods and services, decent working conditions, and a commitment from buyers so that there is reasonable security for the sellers.

There are a number of non-governmental organizations (NGOs) that aim to promote fair trade, including The Fairtrade Foundation (www.fairtrade.org.uk), Oxfam International (www.oxfam.org), Traidcraft (www.traidcraft.org.uk), and the International Fair Trade Association, (IFAT, www.ifat.org). These organizations have defined fair trade as "an alternative approach to conventional international trade. It is a trading partnership which aims at sustainable development for excluded and disadvantaged producers. It seeks to do this by providing better trading conditions, by awareness raising and by campaigning."[17]

There are about 300 Fair Trade Organizations in over 60 countries associated with IFAT, including producers, export marketing companies, importers, retailers, and financial institutions. For example, Organic Partners is a UK-based organization affiliated with the IFAT that is associated with more than 100 producers and suppliers in 40 countries covering over 2,500,000 acres of certified land, specializing in the provision of plant-based raw materials and ingredients to international manufacturers and traders of food, beverages, medicines, and cosmetics. The organization establishes partnerships with farmers and collectors of plants, assisting them in crop production and handling its sale. Organic Partners has developed a profit share structure whereby producers are offered a financial stake in the company based on a share of annual profits. A major contribution to producers is supply chain management, which enables them to obtain "fair" prices for their crops.

Global marketers should be aware of the growing importance of these organizations. Their market share has become significant in some countries: 47 percent of all bananas, 28 percent of the flowers, and 9 percent of the sugar sold in Switzerland are Fair Trade labeled. In the UK, a market with eight times the population of Switzerland, labeled products have achieved a 5 percent market share of tea, a 5.5 percent share of bananas, and a 20 percent share of ground coffee. The annual net retail value of Fair Trade products sold worldwide is estimated from €1.5 to €2.9 billion in 2013, and in Europe approximately €660 million.

EMERGING MARKETS

The term *emerging market* was coined by Antoine W. van Agtmael, then Deputy Director of the Capital Markets Department of the International Finance Corporation of the World Bank. He included all low and middle income countries as emerging. The term's meaning has since been expanded to include more or less all developing countries. Yet, what is a "developing" country? The General Agreement on Tariffs and Trade (GATT) defined developing countries as those having low standards of living, but did not designate how low the living standard should be. The World Trade Organization leaves it up to a country to designate whether it is developed or developing. Others claim that the degree of development

---

Box 5.2   Technology-in-Focus: Emerging Markets

Future technology growth will be driven by emerging markets rather than Europe, North America, or Japan, and consumers in these emerging markets will probably use handheld devices rather than the desktops or laptops that have been our gateways to cyberspace ....

Companies like Nokia …have long been expanding into countries like India and China, where regions are plugging into the world wirelessly because they haven't had the time or cash to run cables…. However, firms will have to fine-tune [their] products for emerging market requirements.

Source: *San Francisco Chronicle.* http://articles.sfgaate.com/2007-08-31/business/1725917_1_emerging-markets-technology-firms
Adapted from: https://www.techinasia.com/nokia-here-crowdsourced-maps-india [Accessed: November 2–13].

should be the money value that people can produce or earn, such as gross national income per capita.[18] More often than not, some measure of national income is the most used indicator of a country's development. However, although measures of national income in emerging markets are lower than that of developed countries, market potential for many products is substantial. Kvint suggests that an *emerging market* country can be defined as a society transitioning from a dictatorship to a free market-oriented economy, with increasing economic freedom, gradual integration within the global marketplace, an expanding middle class, improving standards of living and social stability and tolerance, as well as an increase in cooperation with multilateral institutions.[19] Following this definition, emerging economies include Eastern European countries such as Hungary, Poland, and Romania, the Baltic States, Estonia, Latvia and Lithuania, and Asian countries such as China, Indonesia, and Malaysia.

As *emerging markets*, these countries implement economic reform programs that result in stronger and more responsible performance levels, as well as transparency and efficiency in capital markets. If reforms are successfully implemented, emerging countries are more likely to receive aid from developed countries and from organizations such as the World Bank and the International Monetary Fund.

Referring to the *CAGE* model, there are a number of distances between developed and emerging markets. *Cultural distances* are evident, including wide gaps when it comes to corporate social responsibility and ethical issues. Political risk is also an important consideration when considering investment in emerging markets. *Administrative distances* are most prevalent in the absence of membership of some countries in multilateral groupings such as common markets and the World Trade Organization. Administrative distance also results from institutional weakness and a lack of managerial talent and experience. There is also more government regulation and control over elements of the economy, e.g. such as requiring the use of domestic distributors. *Geographic distances* are both inter-country and intra-country. For example, take the case of distribution in a large country like India (Box 5.3). In rural areas the distribution infrastructure is much more inefficient than in developed areas such as Delhi.

Therefore, supply chain management may be fraught with difficulty and lead to high costs. *Economic distances* are represented by underdeveloped financial institutions, lack of a developed communication and transportation infrastructure and of course, lower incomes and lower domestic investment.

An *emerging market* economy must have to weigh local political and social factors as it attempts to open up its economy to the world. Business people and consumers in *emerging markets* have been accustomed to being protected from the outside world, and can often be distrustful of foreign investment. National pride may also be an issue because citizens may be opposed to having foreign ownership of parts of the local economy. Liberalizing the economy during transition also means that people are exposed to different consumption cultures such as fast food, western movies, and work cultures such as standards and ethics.

Box 5.3   Company-in-Focus: Whirlpool

A quotation by a representative of the Whirlpool Company:

Infrastructure and facilities were the key issues. Being able to deliver a damage-free product in India – you have issues with the roads, issues with the trucks, issues with the loading and unloading the equipment…so damage to a product during transportation was a main issue and also cycle time to market. It took longer to get a product from point A to point B.

Source: Griffith, D. et al. (2005), 'Strategically employing natural channels in an emerging market', *Thunderbird International Business Review*, 47(3), p. 298.

Whirlpool's primary brand names—KitchenAid, Roper, Bauknecht, Inglis, Brastemp, Consul, and its global Whirlpool brand—are marketed and sold through direct sales offices in more than 170 countries worldwide. Sustaining its market position requires Whirlpool to draw from an exceptional foundation of business strategy, technology, and employees every day. With pillars based on innovative design and development, consistent brand management, and proactive customer relationship management, Whirlpool has established the groundwork it needs to support a global house of brands.

Source:http://gilbane.com/case_studies/Whirlpool_case_study.html#ixzz0voKfHBzd [Accessed: November, 2009].

THE BRIC COUNTRIES

One of the fastest growing groups of emerging economies are the so-called BRIC countries. The BRIC countries (Brazil, Russia, India, and China) were first designated as such by the investment firm, Goldman Sachs in 2001, as those that offer high consumer potential and that could overtake the economies of the developed world by 2050. China could become the largest economy in the world by that time, and India the third largest, after the United States. The combined GDP of the BRIC countries could exceed that of the G6 (US, EU, Australia, Japan, India, and China) countries combined. China, especially, is at the forefront of world economic development.

All BRIC countries had experienced real GDP growth until the financial crisis of 2008–09. China had the highest growth, reaching over 10 percent in 2007. India had growth of nearly 10 percent in the same year, followed by Russia (8 percent) and Brazil (6 percent). All of these GDP figures were impressive when compared to developed countries over the same time period.

BRIC countries are not only a major source for manufacturing, but also consumers of basic products like food and clothing, and high technology products as well. Consumer products have to be adapted to local requirements and be priced to make them accessible to a large number of people. As incomes are lower in *emerging markets*, a product that appeals to middle income people in a developed country will have to be positioned to upper-middle income consumers in developing countries or be adapted so that it can be sold at a lower price. Local shopping habits also differ across *BRIC countries*. A McKinsey survey found that clothing shoppers in China have small budgets.

TABLE 5.7 Strengths and Weaknesses of the BRIC Countries	Country	Key Strengths	Key Weaknesses
	Brazil	South America's leading economic power. Brazil is increasing investment in higher education. Abundant natural resources and a diversified economy.	GDP growth and consumer spending power is declining. More investment needed in the infrastructure.
	Russia	Abundant natural resources and a skilled labor force.	The only BRIC country undergoing a population decline reducing the labor market and increasing the number of pensioners.
	India	27 percent of the population will be younger than 15 in 2020; an important future consumer market. Economic growth averaged about 8 percent since 2003. Large population of world-class competitive industries, IT competent workforce. Stable financial institutions and strong legal system.	Limited foreign investment, inadequate infrastructure. Inadequate domestic savings that could fuel investment.
	China	Strong economic growth averaging 10 percent per year. Large population of 1.3 billion can provide growing domestic consumption. Market-oriented reforms continuing (e.g. accession to the WTO).	Weak financial system, growing income gap could lead to social instability. There is a shortage of skilled management. Weak intellectual property laws.

Source: © Author

Table 5.7 summarizes the key strengths and weaknesses of the BRIC countries. One of the major strengths common to all four countries is economic reform. Russia has privatized many industries and businesses, India and Russia have encouraged foreign investment, while Brazil has implemented economic reforms and liberalization measures in its economy. Russia and India possess skilled labor, while Brazil and China are investing in education in order to upgrade human resources, especially skilled managers. On the downside, all BRIC countries must improve their infrastructures in order to achieve economic progress. Bureaucracy is a problem in many emerging countries and the BRIC group is no exception. For example, the time to register a business takes much longer in some emerging economies compared to developed countries like the United States, the UK, and Germany. In Table 5.8, Poland and Belarus are examples. However, the BRIC countries are in line with more developed countries, with the exception of India, which has relatively long waiting times for both ownership registration and contract execution.

Country	Ownership registration		Contract execution		
	Period (days)	Cost (% of property value)	Period (days)	Costs (% of property value)	
Russia	37	0.8	330	20.3	
China	32	3.1	241	25.5	
India	67	13.9	425	43.1	
Brazil	42	2.0	566	16.5	
Portugal	83	7.3	320	17.5	
Poland	204	1.6	1,000	8.7	
Hungary	79	6.8	365	8.1	
Kazakhstan	52	1.8	400	8.5	
Azerbaijan	61	0.5	267	19.8	
Armenia	18	0.9	195	17.8	
Belarus	221	0.2	250	20.77	
UK	21	4.1	288	15.7	
Germany	41	4.2	184	10.5	
Italy	27	1.3	1,390	17.8	
Australia	7	4.3	157	14.4	
U.S.	12	0.5	250	7.5	
DR Cango	106	10.1	909	256.8	

TABLE 5.8
Relative Time to Register Property and to Finalize Real Estate Contracts in Selected Countries

Source: © Author

THE FUTURE POTENTIAL OF EMERGING NATIONS

globalEDGE at the International Business Center of Michigan State University has constructed a market potential index based on a number of accepted economic and market indicators such as market size, potential, growth, and others, as shown in Table 5.9. According to the index, the ten countries with the most potential are China, Hong Kong, Japan, Canada, Singapore, Germany, India, Switzerland, United Kingdom, and South Korea in that order. Of the BRIC countries, Brazil is ranked 20, Russia 15, India 7 and China 1. By looking at the individual indices you can see why a country is ranked as it is. For example, China is ranked first in potential mainly because of its large market and high growth (weighted heavily on the overall index) and moderate country risk. Brazil, on the other hand, is ranked far behind China owing to lower market size, market receptivity, and market consumption capacity.

A study by Goldman Sachs forecasted (Figure 5.4) that by the year 2030 China's GDP will nearly equal that of the United States, still the world's largest economy, but by 2040 China will take the place of the United States as the world's largest economy. Note that by 2050 India's GDP is forecasted to nearly equal that of the United States, while in the same year Brazil and Russia will surpass the GDP of Japan, the United Kingdom, and Germany. Is it possible? Let us see what will happen in 2020 and extrapolate from there.

TABLE 5.9
globalEDGE Market Potential Index

Rank	Country	Overall Score	Market Size	Market Intensity	Market Growth Rate	Market Consumption Capacity	Commercial Infrastructure	Market Receptivity	Economic Freedom	Country Risk
1	China	100	100	4	100	98	56	9	23	80
2	Hong Kong	56	2	100	62	31	96	100	100	95
3	Japan	54	21	77	49	100	81	9	70	90
4	Canada	53	9	80	55	63	89	65	77	90
5	Singapore	50	2	76	76	33	83	89	70	100
6	Germany	48	12	79	48	85	94	18	71	83
7	India	46	37	36	77	57	14	9	47	64
8	Switzerland	41	2	94	52	48		36	78	90
9	United Kingdom	41	8	85	43	69	93	15	72	75
10	South Korea	41		59	67	60		21	63	8
11	France	41	10	72	46	72	94	12	61	75
12	Australia	41	5	75	59	60	96	14	79	83
13	United Arab Emirates	36	2	66	91	37	88	43	43	74
14	Norway	37	3	84	62	49	82	16	68	90
15	Russia	36	19	41	71	51	8	8	28	64
16	Austria	36	2	77	51	51	97	19	70	83
17	Netherlands	36	3	63	40	53	84	40	71	75
18	Belgium	36	3	69	50	44	80	43	67	75
19	Sweden	35	3	67	52	53	90	16	70	90
20	Brazil	34	18	48	62	41	58	6	50	69
21	New Zealand	33	2	67	62	41	88	14	78	83
22	Denmark	33	2	68	39	54	94	18	73	83
23	Ireland	32	1	55	41	42	100	36	73	75

Source: globalEDGE Michigan State University, http://globaledge.msu.edu/mpi

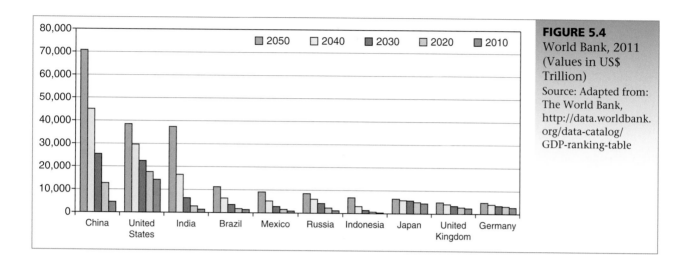

FIGURE 5.4
World Bank, 2011 (Values in US$ Trillion)
Source: Adapted from: The World Bank, http://data.worldbank.org/data-catalog/GDP-ranking-table

SUMMARY

- Intra-regional trade accounts for 10 percent of all world trade. About half of total US trade is with its neighbors, Canada and Mexico. Nearly three-quarters of EU trade is within Europe and half of Asian trade is within Asia. The growth of intra-regional trade is owing to regional trading blocs such as NAFTA and the EU.
- China has become a major economic power. It has more exports and imports than Japan and Germany that are increasing at a higher rate than all developed nations. China is also one of the most attractive countries for investors.
- Most of the world's economic growth is shifting to emerging nations. While not limited to, they are usually represented by the BRIC countries: Brazil, Russia, India, and China. The BRIC countries have experienced rapid economic growth; they have large consumer markets and an abundance of skilled human resources. However, other emerging markets like South Korea, Taiwan and Eastern European countries, such as Poland, Hungary and the Czech Republic are also developing rapidly.

DISCUSSION QUESTIONS

1. Look up export statistics for your State. Are there exports to emerging markets? If so, what is the proportion of exports compared to developed countries?
2. Do you agree that there is little difference between emerging markets and developing countries? Why or why not?
3. You are asked by the owner of a medium-sized firm manufacturing digital alarm clocks. He thinks there is a market for his product in the BRIC countries. How would you advise him on what to look for first?

EXPERIENTIAL EXERCISES

1. Using the CAGE (cultural, administrative, geographic, economic) model, discuss the distances between the four BRIC countries.
2. Using Table 5.9, discuss why the market potential for China is greater than that of India.

KEY TERMS

- Administrative distances
- Association of Southeast Asian Nations
- Bilateral agreements
- BRIC countries
- Cage model
- Common market
- Cultural distances
- Customs union
- East African Community
- Economic distances
- Emerging market
- Euro area
- European economic area
- European Economic Community
- European free trade area
- External tariffs

- Fair trade
- Free trade area
- Free trade blocs
- Geographic distances
- Gulf Cooperation Council
- Harmonization
- Maastricht treaty
- Mercosur
- Mutual recognition
- Non-tariff trade barriers
- Purchasing power parity
- Quotas
- Regional trading blocs
- Single market
- Tariffs
- Triad nations

NOTES

1 Unless otherwise noted, trade data given in this section is from the United States Census Bureau, Foreign Trade Division, Washington, D.C., 2014.
2 EU Commission. (2013), www.ec.europa.eu/trade/policy/countries-and-regions/statistics/index-en.html.
3 European Commission. (2014), http://europa.eu/rapid/press-release_IP-14-152-en.htm [Accessed: March 2014].
4 US International Trade Commission's Interactive Tariff and Trade Web, https://dataweb.usitc.gov
5 International Trade Statistics, WTO; UN Comtrade Database; World Data Bank.
6 International Trade Statistics, WTO; UN Comtrade Database.
7 Ireland and the United Kingdom do not participate in the *Schengen Agreement*, which eliminates internal EU border checks.
8 'It's the internal market, stupid. A company survey on trade barriers in the European Union', Confederation of European Business Associations, 2004, p.13.
9 The World Factbook. (2015), https://www.cia.gov/library/publications/the-world-factbook/docs/refmaps.html [Accessed: August 1, 2015].
10 www.cfr.org.
11 www.customs.eac.int/.

12 The World Factbook. (2015), https://www.cia.gov/library/publications/the-world-factbook/docs/refmaps.html [Accessed: August 1, 2015].

13 www.asean.org/asean/about-asean/overview.

14 See: https://www.gcc-sg.org/eng/indexfc7a.html.

15 The World Factbook. (2015), https://www.cia.gov/library/publications/the-world-factbook/docs/refmaps.html [Accessed: August 1, 2015].

16 www.worldbank.org/en/country/gcc.

17 http://www.fairtrade.net/about-fairtrade.html

18 Cui, F. (2008), 'Who are the developing countries in the WTO?', *The Law and Development Review*, 1(1), p. 144.

19 Kvint, V. (2008), 'Define emerging markets now', *Forbes*, January 28, 2008, http://www.forbes.com/2008/01/28/kvint-developing-countries-oped-cx_kv_0129kvint.html [Accessed: March, 2009].

CASE 5.1 UNDERSTANDING GLOBAL CONSUMER BEHAVIOR IN AESTHETIC SURGERY

Beauty industry is a multibillion dollar business that influences the viability of cosmetics companies, pharmaceuticals, plastic surgeons, department stores, salons, spas, beauty parlors, magazines, and books. A lot of individuals are paying hundreds of dollars to make their appearances younger and more attractive. Motivations differ but the identity reflected in the body itself becomes a saleable commodity in modernity, creating a link among self, body, and consumption. Body becomes saleable because the image of an ideal body is largely displayed through the consumer culture.

One of the most effective ways of enhancing body image is surgical interventions, i.e. aesthetic or cosmetic surgery. Aesthetic surgery remains as a very effective beautification tool, which includes surgical operations on the face (such as rhinoplasty and face lift) and on other parts of the body (such as abdominoplasty, breast reduction, breast augmentation, and liposuction). Major developments in this area have taken place during the World War II, in order to cure the traumatic body dysfunctions of soldiers in particular. Since then, plastic surgery knowledge and technology have advances, accompanied by changing needs and desires on the patient side.

Although it is risky and painful, and requires time, energy, and money, aesthetic surgery has exploded in popularity over the past decade. By definition, this medical branch is perceived as elective and luxurious. Patients are no longer just patients. They are patient-consumers with unique demands and different, and sometimes "unreasonable" expectations. Many doctors are now utilizing advertising to increase demand for their work. If body can be perceived as another consumption item, and patients as patient-consumers, this medical branch becomes an area for global marketing and consumer behavior. The effects of producers (doctors, medical companies, and the media) and consumers (patients of aesthetic surgery) can be discussed on an international basis.

PROMOTION OF A GLOBAL IDEAL IMAGE

How an ideal physical appearance is globally promoted remains to be a topic of hot debate among academic scholars, as well as practitioners. Medicine is such a discipline that a healthy body is defined in numbers. Promoting to achieve those numbers, such as body mass index, ideal muscle weight, or body proportions, consumer culture may encourage people to discipline their bodies in the name of health. The language used in ads for beauty products can be quite technical and scientific, making the claims more believable. Hence the inclusion of physicians as medical authorities contributes to the "medicalization of appearance." Since body now can be quantitatively measured, it becomes easier and more feasible to communicate it globally in the form of statistical averages and medical "facts".

The media, on the other hand, reinforces this view through such healthy and fit images of men and women. One of the most important arguments is that the advertising system establishes, proposes, and promotes an ideal appearance both for men and women. Other than the media itself, fashion, through large-scale mediums such as fashion shows and fashion magazines, and basically fashion models, influences the way people establish a standard about what is (fashionably) beautiful. Film and music represent other areas where consumers in different parts of the world might be exposed to "prevailing" norms of beauty through movie stars, singers, and other celebrities. Beauty pageants are another area of a visual discourse of identity and otherness that serves as a model for the way global and local cultural institutions articulate.

In a globalizing world, therefore, people may establish similar or different, and most of the time, hybrid standards of beauty for themselves. Another cultural ideal, different from their own, may be interpreted as a look that is aesthetically pleasing. This look may become so fashionable across many cultures that it might create a collective mood and thus a preference for a particular style or appearance.

AESTHETIC TOURISM

Aesthetic tourism, i.e., traveling outside one's own country to go through cosmetic surgery, is on the rise. The ease of seeking medical treatment and services overseas contributes to the growing worldwide spending on aesthetic tourism. This rise is supported by the existence of a global market for international hospital chains. Planning for aesthetic tourism trip is similar to planning a vacation using a travel agent. Due to lower costs even with the cost of travel, aesthetic tourism provides an economic benefit. It also offers a social benefit since decisions are relatively autonomous and do not become a community affair. Lastly, it offers a legal benefit because some clinics apply procedures that are illegal in other countries, such as sex change.

Further, these clinics market themselves as romantic gateways, where patients can enjoy having fun in an exotic city. Sometimes the whole package is customized for the individual, including the visa procedures, traveling, being picked up from the airport, having the surgery preceded or followed by a holiday at the destination. It is usually possible to talk to the doctors over the internet, request an approximate price for the total package, and ask for financing options in the host country. International healthcare accreditation of the plastic surgery clinic or the hospital becomes a major concern for patients. Many of the hospitals in developing countries advertise themselves as equivalent to hospitals in the United States and Western Europe, usually by being accredited by the Joint Commission International because it suggests that the hospital has earned sufficient quality and reliability.

GLOBAL CO-CREATION OF A MEDICAL CONSUMPTION EXPERIENCE

With many sources of information about plastic surgery and an increasing number of people going through these operations, plastic surgery patients can now make comments about their appearance problems or deformities, criticize the physician for his/her treatment, and interfere with technical details since medical details – although not necessarily correct- are more readily available. Patients can sometimes "test" the surgeon's knowledge by asking some "Internet-driven" questions. One of the challenges is when the patient wants to see the exact result before the operation. Doctors may try to make sure that the results of the operation may not coincide with what patients imagine; and operation results actually depend on the patient's physical condition and his/her healing characteristics.

Importance of communication between the patient and the doctor is demonstrated especially when the doctor is perceived as a friend rather than a medical doctor. It is generally much less common for a doctor and a patient to become friends in other medical spheres, but since plastic surgeons are seen as experts on beauty, they are also seen as companions along the way towards ideal physical appearance. Trust is established when patients feel that the doctor understands their needs and expectations. Besides medical knowledge and experience, doctor's individual characteristics, such as honesty and friendliness, as well as his/her physical appearance, plays a very important role in building trust.

Similar to doctors, machinery, technology, and software can move around the globe very easily. All kinds of medical knowledge, equipment, pharmaceuticals, and all kinds of tools can be imported and exported with minimum trouble across different countries. Hence "beauty" becomes the universal language for all people and we can talk about a special kind of interdependence among these firms, doctors, and patients all around the world.

DISCUSSION QUESTIONS

1. Can we talk about marketing and consumer behavior in the context of medicine? How? Whether and how is consumer behavior different? What are the marketing tools in a global framework?
2. Who are the global patients-consumers of aesthetic surgery? What are the physical and cultural similarities and differences?
3. How is tourism defined in terms of a global phenomenon in the context of aesthetic surgery? Can we talk about "hotspots" to visit for a physical and spiritual transformation?
4. What are the ethical issues concerning medical marketing? Do you agree, for instance, that aesthetic surgery can and should be marketed just like another product/service?

Sources: Appadurai, Arjun, 1990, "Disjuncture and Difference in the Global Cultural Economy," *Theory, Culture & Society* 7 (2/3): 295–310; Bocock, Robert, 2001, *Consumption*. London: Routledge; Burkett, Levi, 2007, "Medical Tourism: Concerns, Benefits, and the American Legal Perspective," *The Journal of Legal Medicine* 28: 223–245; Featherstone, Mike, 1982, "The Body in Consumer Culture," *Theory, Culture, and Society* 1: 18–33; Howson, Alexandra, 2004, *The Body in Society: An Introduction*, Cambridge: Polity; Parasuraman, A., V. A. Zeithaml, and L. L. Berry, 1985, "A Conceptual Model of Service Quality and Its Implications for Future Research," *Journal of Marketing* 49 (Fall): 41–50.

PART II

Global Marketing Functions and Strategies

CHAPTER 6

Conducting Global Marketing Research

The need for information, the need for sharper, smarter, timelier, quicker information is just increasing.

Sangeeta Gupta, Director of Consumer Insights, Pepsico India

LEARNING OBJECTIVES

After Reading This Chapter, You Should Be Able to:

- Explain why global marketing research is important to multinational firms.
- Understand the differences between marketing research and marketing intelligence.
- Understand the importance of information technology for managerial decision-making.
- Determine how to use a marketing intelligence/information system.
- Explain how firms can anticipate marketing crises.
- Know why some marketing research techniques may not be used in all countries.

Marketing managers at an American company were shocked when they discovered that the brand name of the cooking oil they were marketing in a Latin American country was translated into Spanish as "Jackass Oil." An American company that manufactures heating systems was trying to determine whether its products would be attractive to both industrial and household consumers in Sweden. In order to consider entering the Swedish market, management needed information about the ecological, cultural, technological, economic, political/legal, and competitive environments in Sweden. Specifically, management needed to determine whether its products could be sold as is, or whether they had to be adapted. This is especially relevant when marketing products to both emerging and developed countries. Moreover, other aspects of the marketing mix had to be determined, such as pricing, distribution, and communication strategies. Finally, if there is sufficient demand for the products, what entry mode would be best for the American company? It is the task of marketing research employees to determine, along with management, the sort of information that is needed to help answer questions like the one above. Therefore, the role of global marketing research is primarily to act as an aid to the decision-maker by collecting and analyzing information relevant to solving a given problem.

IMPORTANCE OF GLOBAL MARKETING RESEARCH

In the midst of the global economic meltdown of 2007–09, many marketers had a glum view of the near future; one of the few areas of marketing that retained some of its growth was market research. Global market research revenues reached $32 billion in 2008—an overall growth of 4.5 percent (net 0.4 percent) according to the ESOMAR Global Market Research Report. Five years later in 2013, global market research revenues increased to US$40.3 billion. The North American research market seems to have fully recovered from the economic downturn of recent years and is rewarded with the title of fastest growing region for the first time since 2000. In 2015 it is the USA, which is making up for sluggish performances in some of the world's other large research markets. Growth amounted to 4.4 percent year-to-year and 2.9 percent after correcting for inflation. Performance in Europe was poor, with an absolute growth of 0.4 percent and a decline of 1.4 percent after inflation. More importantly to global marketers, Asia Pacific is the second of two regions that recorded positive growth for the year 2013 with 1.6 percent. Latin America, which was the best performing region in 2012, saw research turnover drop by 0.1 percent, impacted by inflation and declines for the region's largest markets, Brazil and Mexico.[1]

Although many use the terms market research and marketing research interchangeably, market research is considered a part of the larger marketing research field. The American Marketing Association (AMA) defines marketing research as any information used to discover marketing opportunities and problems, give directions to marketing actions, track performance, and contribute to a better marketing process overall.[2] This definition clearly includes market research, which usually studies market sizes and trends, but also encompasses competitive research, price or product research, and other research related to the marketing mix and the customer.

ESOMAR, the global trade organization for the market and opinion research industry, distinguishes market and social research activities from other forms of marketing, such as advertising or selling, by emphasizing that market researchers do not use or disseminate the personal information gathered about research participants for commercial purposes. There are many cultural, methodological, and other considerations for conducting global market and marketing research, as you will learn later in this chapter. It is also important to understand that global marketing research has changed a lot over the course of the last few years.

Traditional and Emerging Market Research

The traditional marketing research industry is defined by the corporate insight functions, their large suppliers, core research tools, such as surveys and focus groups, and a skill set focused on project management, questioning, and statistical analysis. Created in the twentieth century industrial age, the traditional marketing research industry relies very much on an industrialized view of research with data being expensive. The organizing framework of this epoch is the survey, especially the quarterly tracking survey, a product on which many of the larger firms still depend. The traditional marketing research industry has many positive qualities, but also has several significant weaknesses. These include a dependence on self-reported behavior, limited ability to engage subjects in a protracted, cocreative dialogue and a reliance on periodic, as opposed to continuous, reporting. These weaknesses have left the traditional marketing research industry open to significant competition from the wider insights industry.

In contrast, the **emerging marketing research industry** includes new entrants from management consulting, social media, software, and business intelligence that are increasingly providing insight-driven consulting in competition with traditional marketing research. The wider insights industry was created in the information age. It surrounds traditional marketing research with next-generation technologies and firms defined by observation and listening. Examples of these wider insights industry tools include social media analysis, neuromarketing research, insights communities, predictive markets, and mass simulation gaming (see Table 6.1 and further below for individual tools).

When managed correctly, the process of and insights collected through marketing research can yield undeniable results for a company. For example, the European grocer Tesco was able to increase sales of its baby products by 8 percent after monitoring its loyalty card data and combining that with survey research on products that were not popular at some of its stores. Through this research, Tesco found out that young mothers were not buying as many baby products at certain stores because they perceived pharmacies as more trustworthy sources for them. In response, Tesco launched BabyClub, a program that provided expert advice and baby product discounts to that consumer segment. By winning young moms' trust, Tesco was also able to claim a larger share of their wallets.[3]

Another example is the case of LG Electronics. According to the manager of their Insight Marketing Team, the company's success in Western countries is a result of market research undertaken to understand how products fit into people's lives. For example, **cultural differences** between Asian and Western countries determine the design of appliances. In some Asian countries, washing machines are displayed where visitors will see them as a sign of affluence. In the West, appearance is less

	Traditional Marketing Research	Emerging Marketing Research	
Typical Providers	Full-service agencies, sector expertise firms, syndicates	Management consulting, social media, software, data mining	**TABLE 6.1** Traditional Versus Emerging Marketing Research Industry
Representative Examples	Ipsos, GfK, Harris Interactive	McKinsey, BCG, Autonomy, IBM, Comscore, Conversition	
Main Methodology and Tools	Surveys: Custom survey research; tracking surveys; live focus groups	Observation: Data mining; text analytics; model building; insight communities	

Source: Adapted from: Robert Morgan (2011). *The Future of Marketing Research*. In: Kaden, R.J., Linda, G.L., and Price, M. (eds.). *Leading Edge Marketing Research*. Sage: London

GEO MAP 6.1
Tesco
Source: Adapted from:
CIA Maps, The World
Factbook[4]

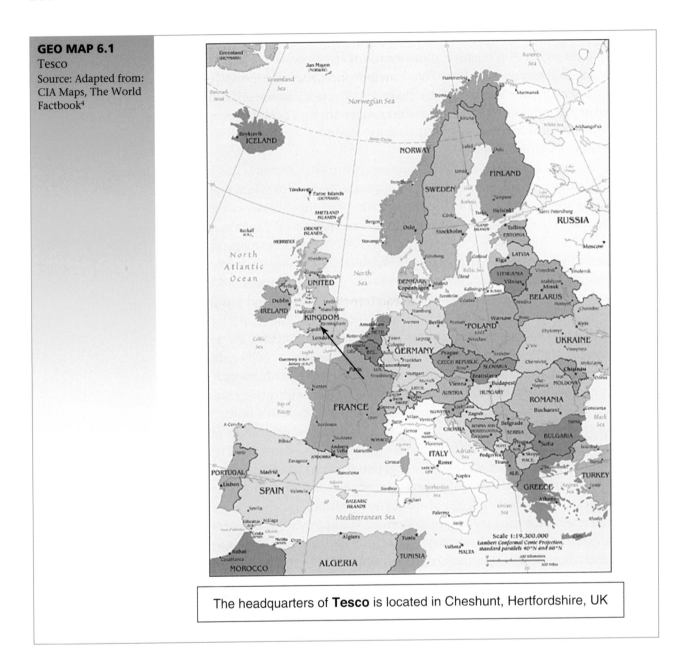

The headquarters of **Tesco** is located in Cheshunt, Hertfordshire, UK

important. This difference led to a line of red wine-colored appliances; in the West a metallic, industrial look is preferred.[5]

SCOPE OF GLOBAL MARKETING RESEARCH

Acquiring marketing insights is critical for marketers who are looking for the best strategies to enter a new market, gain competitive advantage, or increase market share, for example. A simple definition of international marketing research describes it as marketing research performed with the purpose of informing marketing decisions that have to be made in more than one country. The research could be performed in all markets simultaneously or sequentially.[6] Smart companies (and marketers) conduct some form—and many conduct several forms—of global marketing research before they engage in any of the previously mentioned activities. Some of the most important reasons to perform marketing research include:

1. risk management

2. competitive advantage

3. strategic decision-making

4. tactical decision-making

5. performance tracking and reporting.

Listening to customers through various research methodologies and acting on the collected insights is one of the most important distinguishing characteristics of high-performing businesses, across the world. Firms that successfully use marketing research by sharing their findings throughout the organization and aligning them with the organization's priorities tend to have better product innovation, more effective customer communication, and superior return on marketing investment.[7]

Conducting Global Marketing Research

Global marketing research is responsible for gathering, analyzing, and summarizing the information needed to make decisions about potential new markets and marketing opportunities worldwide. On a continuous basis, marketing research is also used to monitor and evaluate marketing performance and recommend changes, if needed. In global marketing, research should inform market entry decisions and any changes marketing managers make to the company's products, pricing, placement, and promotion strategies in order to gain and maintain market share in new markets. Thereby, research could move from description to prescription with increasing degrees of sophistication and relevance for achieving competitive advantages (Figure 6.1).

Types of Research

Market research is conducted in a variety of ways. The most broadly defined techniques are quantitative and qualitative research.

Quantitative Research. Quantitative research relies primarily on the collection and analysis of numerical data, usually gathered via standardized surveys or questionnaires. Quantitative researchers then use statistical analysis methods to draw out insights into a particular area—be it customer behavior, market trends, or pricing discrepancies. Many executives prefer the quantitative research technique because it provides "hard numbers" based on larger audience samples, and thus offers a stronger base for decision-making.

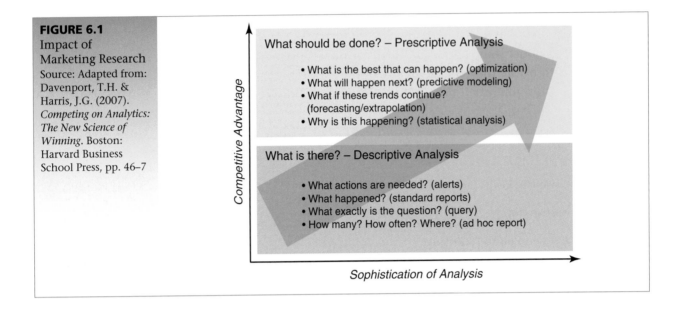

FIGURE 6.1
Impact of
Marketing Research
Source: Adapted from:
Davenport, T.H. &
Harris, J.G. (2007).
*Competing on Analytics:
The New Science of
Winning.* Boston:
Harvard Business
School Press, pp. 46–7

The international shipping company UPS commissioned two surveys for the Chinese market that provided its customers with the information needed to increase their sales (and therefore ship more products) to China and established UPS as a valuable knowledge resource on the Chinese market. The first survey of 1,000 urban, middle-class citizens established what American products are attractive to the Chinese consumers. CDs, DVDs, beauty products, athletic shoes, and washing machines topped the list. The second survey, comprising 1,200 residents of six of the largest cities in China, sought to find out why these products have appeal in the local market. It confirmed the notion that Chinese consumers are about as individualistic as United States consumers when it comes to personal preferences and product choices. UPS made its research findings available to customers who are not yet exporting to China, to customers who don't export at all, and to potential clients. Given the richness of the information provided in the surveys about this high-profile but challenging market, UPS's research received wide coverage across all media.[8]

Of course, quantitative research is useful only when it measures the "right" things. This is why survey design—from deciding what to measure to asking the questions that prompt relevant responses to correctly interpreting the data—is so crucial. The importance of properly designing and conducting quantitative research only grows in international markets, where differences in language, culture, and social norms can render research results completely useless if they were derived from surveys and questionnaires that were not designed with that particular market in mind. This is why some companies focus on the analysis of unstructured data with previously unknown topics to emerge (Box 6.1).

But quantitative research has limitations as well. Quantitative methods presume to have an objective approach to studying research problems, where data is controlled and measured, to address the accumulation of facts, and to determine the

Box 6.1   Company-in-Focus: Attensity Europe GmbH, Real-Time Analytics for Market Research

Attensity Europe GmbH is a leading provider for customer engagement and social analytics. With their technology, Attensity enables companies to turn their customer communication into business value.

Based on natural language processing technologies, Attensity allows companies to understand what customers, business partners or other market-relevant organizations are communicating about products, services, brands, or images. Especially within the area of social activities there is a lot of information, which is helpful for companies enabling them to improve their market position (through better understanding preferences or previously unarticulated demands).

Including social channels opens a complete new opportunity for global market research. By collecting opinions, feedbacks, wishes, and demands from customers, companies obtain an authentic overview about current market situations—in real-time! This helps especially in time-critical situations like global product launches where a fast and detailed feedback about customer experiences is absolutely necessary to reach a high level of customer satisfaction.

In addition, information can be used for detailed analytics, e.g. geographic- or gender-specific feedback could be recognized, country-oriented analytics could be compared, or analysis could be done periodically to recognize emerging trends. For example, Attensity analyzes the feedback about customer service on a yearly basis. The figures below show an example of social media comments about the satisfaction with customer service.

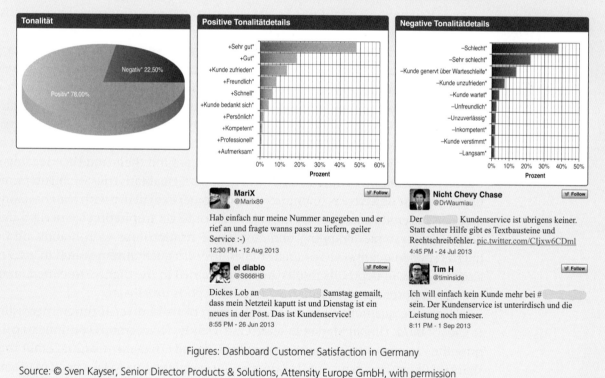

Figures: Dashboard Customer Satisfaction in Germany

Source: © Sven Kayser, Senior Director Products & Solutions, Attensity Europe GmbH, with permission

causes of behavior. As a consequence, the results of quantitative research may be statistically significant but are often humanly insignificant.

Some specific limitations associated with using quantitative methods to study research problems in the social sciences include:[9]

- Quantitative data is more efficient and able to test hypotheses, but may miss contextual detail;

- Uses a static and rigid approach and so employs an inflexible process of discovery;

- The development of standard questions by researchers can lead to "structural bias" and false representation, where the data actually reflects the view of the researcher instead of the participating subject;

- Results provide less detail on behavior, attitudes, and motivation;

- Researcher may collect a much narrower and sometimes superficial data set;

- Results are limited as they provide numerical descriptions rather than detailed narrative and generally provide less elaborate accounts of human perception;

- The research is often carried out in an unnatural, artificial environment so that a level of control can be applied to the exercise. This level of control might not normally be in place in the real world thus yielding "laboratory results" as opposed to "real world results"; and,

- Preset answers will not necessarily reflect how people really feel about a subject and in some cases might just be the closest match to preconceived hypothesis.

Qualitative Research. Unlike quantitative research, qualitative research has a much more subjective, free-form format. Qualitative research techniques usually include face-to-face interviews, focus groups, and observational methods such as ethnography and, increasingly, online focus groups and interviews. These research techniques are designed to bring researchers a better understanding of their customers and their needs and desires. By its very nature, qualitative research relies on the researchers' own interpretations of the world around them and their reading of the meaning behind people's words and actions.[10] Qualitative research is typically used when the objective is to improve the customer experience with the company's products or services, to discover unmet needs, or to get inspiration for new product design, for example. Branding and customers' relationships with brands are frequent topics in qualitative research studies. Because qualitative research focuses on a certain topic in-depth, its results are not presented in the highly structured, numbers-driven format that quantitative research reports usually are.

Today, the qualitative world is on the cusp of rapid diversification. According to the ESOMAR Global Market Research 2013 study, focus groups continue to comprise the vast majority of qualitative research spend (70 percent in 2012), but their share is falling. That same study estimates online qualitative to be 6 percent of total qualitative research spending. Its share is growing.[11]

For instance, Unilever established a global programme of accreditation for qualitative researchers, which was rolled out to the UK in 2012. "We are a big buyer of qualitative research—we spend over £50 million on it annually and use more than 400 agencies—but although we kept asking for them, there were no benchmarks and quality wasn't improving, so we felt the only way to address the problem was to tackle it ourselves," Keith Weed, Chief Marketing Officer, explains. There have been clear benefits, he says. "It has added value to our own research and to the industry as a whole. Individuals are putting their accredited status on their CVs and other clients want to share our list of accredited individuals. However, we don't want to be policing it, so we are now working with other clients and industry leaders to try to outsource it." The Market Research Society is among the industry leaders working with it. Qualitative research is often used in conjunction with quantitative research. This practice is growing in popularity, as marketers attempt to gain an ever more complete and detailed view of their customers and markets.[12]

Table 6.2 provides a comparison between qualitative and quantitative research. *Types of Research Data.* Data is the lifeblood of marketing research. Researchers have two primary methods of obtaining data: collecting original, first-hand responses from research participants in the marketplace, called primary research, or collecting and analyzing existing data from sources such as statistical abstracts, media reports, and previous research studies, called secondary research (Figure 6.2). The majority of quantitative and qualitative research conducted today collects data from direct or primary sources, such as interview respondents and focus group participants. Secondary research (also called desk research) has its place however, because it builds on existing data and is thus a lot cheaper.

	Qualitative Research	Quantitative Research	
Purpose	• Generate research objective • Exploratory	• Specific research questions • Test hypotheses	**TABLE 6.2** Comparing Qualitative and Quantitative Research
Data	• Unstructured, often text-based	• Structured, often numbers-based	
Sample	• Small, non-representative	• Large, representative	
Approach	• Interpretive	• Measurable	
Context	• Context-dependent	• Context-free	
Results	• Individual cases	• Focus on generalizability	
Research Methods	• Focus groups, person (in-depth) interviews, observation, case studies	• Surveys (personal, mail, web), experiment, simulation	

Source: Compiled by Authors

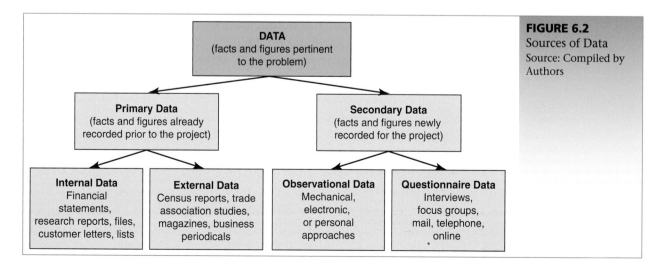

FIGURE 6.2
Sources of Data
Source: Compiled by Authors

DATA
(facts and figures pertinent to the problem)

Primary Data
(facts and figures already recorded prior to the project)

Secondary Data
(facts and figures newly recorded for the project)

Internal Data
Financial statements, research reports, files, customer letters, lists

External Data
Census reports, trade association studies, magazines, business periodicals

Observational Data
Mechanical, electronic, or personal approaches

Questionnaire Data
Interviews, focus groups, mail, telephone, online

When researchers conduct empirical marketing research in multiple countries, the questions of data quality and metrics consistency are two of the most difficult to confront. Yet they are of key importance to ensure that any cross-national market study produces valid results when comparing and contrasting responses to the same issues from different markets. Some studies have found that cultural differences may play a role in how respondents interpret the questions asked[13] or how they perceive the scales offered for formulating their answers.[14] Since these conditions may bias the final analysis of the data, researchers are often urged to assess the consistency of the study's questions, scales, and metrics across markets. But a recent survey found that the process, called measurement invariance assessment, is rarely performed, due to researchers' limited knowledge of it and the perceived complexities of the different measurement invariance methods.[15]

Online Research and "Big Data"

Challenges of Online Research

Increasingly, marketing research of all types is performed online today (see again Box 6.1). Online research encompasses marketing research conducted via online panels, social media channels, online surveys, polls, and other research methods implemented over an Internet connection. Although estimates of how much of total research is performed online range anywhere from 10 to 20 percent, it is clear that online research will only continue to grow as the technologies and methods to perform it will become more and more sophisticated. Lower costs and faster project cycles are two of the most obvious appeals of online research. Easier access, at least in countries with high Internet penetration and increasingly tough conditions for collecting data via traditional methods, also tips the scales in favor of conducting marketing research online.

As with any emerging practice, however, online research still has plenty of issues to work out before it can become an established, mainstream method for conducting marketing research, especially on a global scale. One of the main questions is whether the quality of online research can match that of traditional methods. For issues such as verifying the identity of respondents (to duplication or fraud), using consistent metrics, or crafting questionnaires appropriate for the online environment, researchers are still struggling to come up with quality standards and practices that are widely accepted. Of particular interest to global marketers is the issue of translating online surveys into one or more languages—a practice where shortcuts, such as using machine translation, often lead to highly inaccurate results.[16]

Another big issue is the inherent bias in using only online populations for any kind of research that aims to reveal insights from the general public. Even in countries with deep Internet penetration rates, it is likely that any online-only research sample would remain unbalanced if it excludes the offline population. The bias would be particularly apparent in emerging markets, where Internet connectivity is much lower and the majority of the population has sporadic, if any, access to the Internet (see again Chapter 1).

An ongoing study of global online panels that has collected data from 150 panels across 35 countries highlights the importance of measuring the consistency and validity of sample sources from which respondents are drawn, particularly for multinational marketing research. Using consistent metrics that can be transferred across multiple markets without significant changes to their meaning is also crucial to conducting high-quality global marketing research. Online audience metrics suffer from an almost universal lack of credibility, especially when it comes to international research. A recent survey of marketing researchers in the UK found that, although 96 percent of them agreed that having consistent audience measurements is "extremely important," only 23 percent of them thought that such standards have been established. The research professionals cited inconsistencies in cross-national and regional markets as the biggest issue.[17]

Big Data: The Next Frontier for Online Marketing Research

Despite the challenges of conducting online marketing research, companies have to capture an exploding amount of information about the customers, competitors, and suppliers that require new ways of managing these insights. Today, large pools of data can be captured, communicated, aggregated, stored, and analyzed. **Big data** refers to data sets whose size is beyond the ability of typical database software tools to capture, store, manage, and analyze.[18] As an illustration, imagine: it costs $600 to buy a disk drive that can store all of the world's music; 30bn pieces of content are shared on Facebook every month; 235 terabytes of data was collected by the US Library of Congress by April 2011; there is 40 percent of growth in global data generated per year versus 5 percent growth in global IT spending.[19]

This enormous amount of data is a global phenomenon and can hugely benefit private commerce and national economies if properly managed. For instance, big data is supposed to have an important impact on the future of healthcare. Most healthcare organizations today are using two sets of data: retrospective data, basic event-based information collected from medical records; and real-time clinical data, the information captured and presented at the point of care (imaging, blood pressure, oxygen saturation, heart rate, etc). For example, if a diabetic patient enters the hospital complaining about numbness in their toes, instead of immediately assuming the cause is their diabetes, the clinician could monitor their blood flow and oxygen saturation, and potentially determine if there's something more threatening around the corner, like an aneurism or a stroke. Pioneering technologies have succeeded in putting these two data pieces together in a way that allows clinicians to grasp the relevant information and use it to identify trends that will impact the future of healthcare—otherwise known as **predictive analytics**. And in the future, there is more to come if we talk, for instance, about gene sequencing that could help identify serious illnesses. To put it into perspective, the human body contains nearly 150tr gigabytes of information. That's the equivalent of 75bn fully-loaded

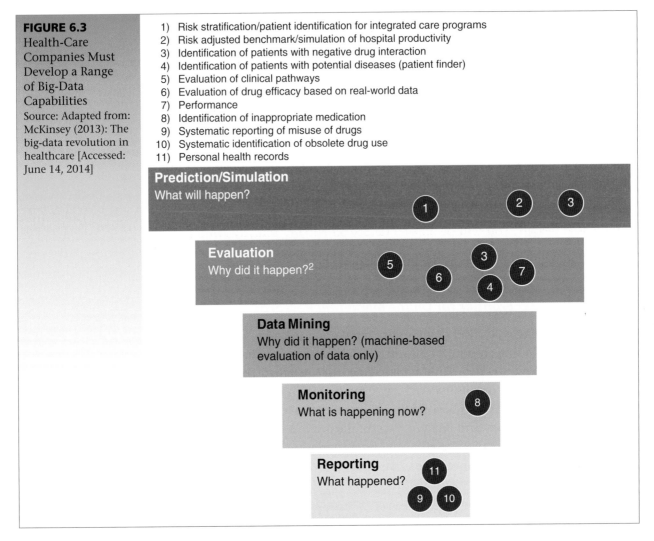

FIGURE 6.3
Health-Care Companies Must Develop a Range of Big-Data Capabilities
Source: Adapted from: McKinsey (2013): The big-data revolution in healthcare [Accessed: June 14, 2014]

1) Risk stratification/patient identification for integrated care programs
2) Risk adjusted benchmark/simulation of hospital productivity
3) Identification of patients with negative drug interaction
4) Identification of patients with potential diseases (patient finder)
5) Evaluation of clinical pathways
6) Evaluation of drug efficacy based on real-world data
7) Performance
8) Identification of inappropriate medication
9) Systematic reporting of misuse of drugs
10) Systematic identification of obsolete drug use
11) Personal health records

Prediction/Simulation
What will happen?

Evaluation
Why did it happen?[2]

Data Mining
Why did it happen? (machine-based evaluation of data only)

Monitoring
What is happening now?

Reporting
What happened?

16GB Apple iPads, which would fill the entire area of Wembley Stadium to the brim 41 times—an unbelievable amount of data to be used.[20] To meet these challenges, health-care companies must develop a variety of capabilities (Figure 6.3).

The research firm Big Data Insight Group summarizes other benefits and challenges of using big data.[21]

1. *Dialogue with consumers:* Consumers today are more demanding than ever and take their time until they decide on product purchases. Big data allows to profile people and facilitates an almost one-on-one, real-time conversation with them. For instance, when a customer enters a shop, the agent can check the profile and learn which products the customer desires and may advise accordingly. Note: profiling has been considered by some people as too intrusive and is not always appreciated.

2. *Redevelop your products:* Analysis of unstructured social media texts allows to see how others see your products (see again Box 6.1). It is possible to identify the

sentiments of customers even in different geographical locations and to adapt or redevelop products according to their desires. Also, big data facilitates testing of prototypes and experimenting with minor changes and their impact on material costs, lead times, and performance.

3. *Perform risk analysis:* The success of your company also depends on environmental factors (see again Chapters 2–4). Predictive analytics, fueled by big data allows you to scan and analyze newspaper reports or social media feeds so that you permanently keep up to speed on the latest developments in your industry and its environment.

4. *Keeping your data safe:* You can also conduct an internal analysis with big data tools (see below). You will be able to detect potentially sensitive information that is not protected in an appropriate manner and make sure it is stored according to regulatory requirements. This involves the whole area of IT safety in your organization.

5. *Customize your website in real time:* Big data analytics allows you to personalize the content or look and feel of your website in real time to suit each consumer entering your website, depending on, for instance, their sex, nationality, or from where they ended up on your site. The best-known example is probably offering tailored recommendations: Amazon's use of real-time, item-based, collaborative filtering (IBCF) to fuel its "Frequently bought together" and "Customers who bought this item also bought" features or LinkedIn suggesting "People you may know" or "Companies you may want to follow." And the approach works: Amazon generates about 20 percent more revenue via this method.

6. *Making our cities smarter:* An increasing number of smart cities are leveraging Big Data tools for the benefit of their citizens and the environment. The city of Oslo in Norway, for instance, reduced street lighting energy consumption by 62 percent with a smart solution. The city of Portland, Oregon, used technology to optimize the timing of its traffic signals and was able to eliminate more than 157,000 metric tonnes of CO_2 emissions in just six years—the equivalent of taking 30,000 passenger vehicles off the roads for an entire year.

To deal with big data, a variety of techniques and tools has been developed that complement traditional marketing research. The challenge of these techniques is that they originate from different research fields, such as statistics, computer science, business studies, psychology, mathematics, economics, etc. Thus, for anybody working in the field, interdisciplinary knowledge becomes paramount. In the following, we present a few of these techniques.

Online Metrics and Tools for Analysis

Web analytics is a new research field that grew out of the increasingly sophisticated uses of the Internet for commerce and marketing. Specifically, web analytics is defined by the Digital Analytics Association as the measurement, collection, analysis, and reporting of Internet data for purposes of understanding and optimizing web usage.[22] Web analytics tools can track a plethora of data associated with visitors' interactions with a company's website (onsite analytics) or with the company's brand elsewhere on the web (offsite analytics)—for example, on social media sites, and third party vendors. The web analytics market remains highly polarized between free tools, such as Google Analytics, WebTrends, StatCounter, Woopra, Nielsen, and Omniture, which was recently acquired by Adobe.

Researchers may use web analytics tools to assess the general performance of a website by tracking visitors' paths through it, the links they clicked on, the length of time spent on specific pages, etc. Others may combine this information with online surveys or traditional research to explore questions such as visitors' satisfaction, and the effectiveness of different marketing offers. By observing and analyzing the application usage over a certain period of time, it is possible to extract users' behavior patterns.

Before using web analytics technologies in countries other than the United States, it is best to first determine their legal status. For example, in 2011, German authorities declared that the use of web analytics tools such as Google Analytics is illegal without the consent of the person being tracked. Restrictions over use may be in place in other countries as well. Despite some of these issues, online research continues to evolve, with new, more advanced trends and emerging forms such as mobile research, and social media research becoming increasingly common.

Data Mining is a set of techniques to extract patterns from large data sets by combining methods from statistics and machine learning with database management (see also below). These techniques include:[23]

- *Association rule learning:* These techniques consist of a variety of algorithms to generate and test possible rules. One application is market basket analysis, in which a retailer can determine which products are frequently bought together and use this information for marketing.

- *Cluster analysis:* A statistical method for classifying objects that splits a diverse group into smaller groups of similar objects, whose characteristics of similarity are not known in advance. An example of cluster analysis is segmenting consumers into self-similar groups for targeted marketing.

- *Classification:* Used to identify the categories in which new data points belong, based on a training set containing data points that have already been classified. One application is the prediction of segment-specific customer behavior (e.g. buying decisions, churn rate, consumption rate) where there is a clear hypothesis or an objective outcome.

- *Regression:* Statistical technique to determine how the value of the dependent variable changes when one or more independent variables are modified. Often used for forecasting or prediction. Examples include forecasting sales volume, for instance.

There is also a variety of methods that is even more specifically tailored for big data, which include Cassandra, Mashup, or Hadoop.

- *Cassandra:* An open source (free) database management system designed to handle huge amounts of data. The system was originally developed at Facebook and is now managed as a project of the Apache Software foundation. Companies that use Cassandra are WalmartLabs, Cisco, and Netflix.

- *Mashup:* An application that uses and combines data presentation or functionality from two or more sources to create new services. These applications are often made available on the Web, and frequently use data accessed through open application programming interfaces or from open data sources. For example, it is possible to combine the addresses and photographs of library branches with a Google map to create a map mashup. The term mashup originally comes from British West Indies slang meaning to be intoxicated, or as a description for something or someone not functioning as intended. In recent English parlance it can refer to music, where people seamlessly combine audio from one song with the vocal track from another—thereby mashing them together to create something new.

Box 6.2 Country-in-Focus: Conducting Research in India

India has become a focal point for global markets, but they are uncertain as to the extent to which social and interactive media can reach target markets. Traditional media is still the best way to reach most Indian consumers. Interactive media is aimed mainly at highly educated young men in the upper income bracket. However, while a minority of Indians use the Internet, those who do are also users of social media. Advertisers that are aiming at India's growing middle class should use an integrated marketing strategy based on interactive and social media as well.

Conducting market research in India can be strikingly different from those undertaken in developing countries. Right from the availability of credible sources of secondary information, to the rate of responses obtained, a researcher is provided with a series of hurdles, before he/she arrives at an inference from the study. For instance, primary research by interacting with reliable experts can give a fair idea on the specific industry. Unfortunately most of the expert conversations with the analyst or the researcher remain as a one-way communication. Industry experts love sharing more information provided that the interaction with the analyst stands as a two-way communication. But the gathering of market intelligence in India has also gone through a paradigm shift since social media became popular. Information gathered by means of surveys is now being assembled using social media tools, which is a brand new concept.

Though India is of great interest to brands, doing research is expensive and difficult. The country has twenty-eight states with different cultural nuances, languages, and consumption habits. Market research has won acceptance in India and an increasing number of companies have made room for it in their budgets.

Sources: Adapted from: Steven Noble, 'Social Technographics in India: While Few Indians Are Online, Most Who Are Use Social Media.' Forrester. Updated October 6, 2010, https://www.forrester.com/Social+Technographics+In+India/fulltext/-/E-res55680 [Accessed: June 10, 2015]; OneDevide Research. (2014). 'Doing Research in India', https://ondeviceresearch.com/blog/tips-for-conducting-market-research-in-india#sthash.kHSdNyua.dpbs [Accessed: 1 July, 2014]; SIS Market Research. (2014), http://www.sismarketresearch.com/global-reach/asia-pacific/market-research-india.html [Accessed: December 28, 2014].

- *Hadoop:* An open source (free) software framework for processing huge data sets on certain kinds of problems on a distributed system. It is designed to scale up from a single server to thousands of machines, with a very high degree of fault tolerance. Rather than relying on high-end hardware, the resiliency of these clusters comes from the software's ability to detect and handle failures at the application layer.[24]

What is important when using these tools is to first identify whether specific cultures appreciate them and actually use the internet in their country (see Box 6.2 for an example in India and Table 6.3 for the application of marketing research methods across countries).

The Role of Social Media in Global Marketing Research

The use of online tools and methodologies goes along with a tremendous increase and an enormous appeal of using social media networks such as Facebook, LinkedIn, and Twitter, or their global competitors such as Viadeo (France), Xing (Germany), or Tianji (China). It is the sheer volume of unfiltered consumer data available to marketing researchers from these networks' hundreds of millions of users that is so attractive. The fact that most of this data is freely available is another advantage, as are its perceived authenticity and the diversity of the online population providing it.

The possibilities for offering valuable services to marketing researchers are not lost on the social media leaders. For example, Facebook provides targeted information about its users and user preferences in order to enable marketers to create better, more relevant ads. LinkedIn has partnered directly with research firms for specific B2B research projects covering topics such as customer satisfaction, market outlook, and brand perceptions. Offering population samples directly to researchers is another service considered by some networks. Currently, the most widely used methods by social media researchers continue to be pop-ups and banner ads for sample sourcing for surveys and text search, sometimes using natural language processing tools for data mining or consumer sentiment research such as brand perception studies[25] (see Box 6.3 for an example of WeChat, an online messaging tool that facilitates information sharing and data analytics).

Many researchers caution, however, that with the advantages of social media research come some pitfalls. In order to meet the basic standards of the marketing research industry, researchers using social media tools should rigorously test their search and source parameters, properly categorize and map the researched content, adjust some of their metrics used for trend identification and, ultimately, summarize all their findings in reports that provide actionable intelligence to executives.[26] The growth of online research technologies has also sparked a vigorous debate over online consumer privacy in many countries. Marketing researchers should stay aware and vigilant about observing the local laws and policies regarding this hot topic. For instance, Facebook has been continuously criticized for violating consumer privacy. The UK *Telegraph* recently reported that the European Union's

> **Box 6.3** Technology-in-Focus: Online Communication and Text Messaging
>
> **WeChat (Chinese: 微信; pinyin: *Wēixìn*; literally: "micro message")**
>
> WeChat was developed by Tencent in China, first released in January 2011. It is the largest standalone messaging app and is expected to bring in 6.8 billion yuan ($1.1 billion) in 2014 and about 40% more in 2015. The app is available on Android, iPhone, BlackBerry, and Windows Phone phones, and there are also Web-based clients but these require the user to have the app installed on a supported mobile phone for authentication.
>
> WeChat provides text messaging, hold-to-talk voice messaging, broadcast (one-to-many) messaging, sharing of photographs and videos, and location sharing. It can exchange contacts with people nearby via Bluetooth, as well as providing various features for contacting people at random if desired (if these are open to it) and integration with social networking services such as those run by Facebook. Photographs may also be embellished with filters and captions, and a machine translation service is available.
>
> Sources: http://qz.com/179007/wechat-is-nothing-like-whatsapp-and-that-makes-it-even-more-valuable/; www.wechat.com; http://stackoverflow.com/questions/19640703/what-is-the-technology-behind-wechat-whatsapp-and-other-messenger-apps [All accessed: August 2, 2014].

Data Protection Working Party, which monitors Internet issues, "wrote a letter to Facebook, saying recent changes that made previously private information publicly viewable by default were 'unacceptable.' … the group said that profile information, and data about the connections between users, should have a default setting in which this information was only shared with 'self-selected' contacts."[27] Facebook has faced mounting criticism from users and industry commentators over recent changes to its privacy policy, especially that some personal information, including names, profile pictures, city, networks, and friend lists, would be made publicly available. Users who did not wish this information to be shared with the wider web would have to "opt out" of the new system by adjusting their privacy settings to make this information private again.

Differences in Conducting Global Marketing Research

Conducting reliable, high-quality global marketing research also means that both clients and vendors (if vendors are used) must understand and agree on the special conditions often imposed on the research methodologies by the particular local culture, social customs, or other contextual factors. For example, United States research clients must realize that international phone interviews may take longer and cost more, due to an obligatory extended introduction and small talk with the interview subjects. Such interview style is required by the social norms in most other countries, where the direct approach used in the United States is considered rather rude. Some other examples of such international differences in conducting global marketing research are shown in Table 6.3. For instance, in the Middle East an interview is often conducted with two participants at once, who may know each other, or may be recruited as strangers. If known to each other, they are sometimes referred to as a friendship pair; this is used especially for children or young respondents (who gain security from the presence of a friend). Another common application is in research concerning decisions made jointly by couples, such as

TABLE 6.3 Preferred Methods of Conducting Global Marketing in Different Countries	**Country/Area**
	China Personal interviews are the preferred method for surveys in China, where the subjects are business executives, doctors, or government officials. Professional and government officials must be shown respect by sending an advance invitation to participate in a survey. While phone interviews may have some use in China, language differences, for example, between Mandarin and Cantonese, or differences in brand name pronunciations, may hamper understanding and skew research findings.
	India Indian consumers are often willing to discuss their shopping preferences and motivations in a personal interview. Observational research at shopping points such as stores and markets is a good way to determine shopping behavior.
	Latin America Most marketing research in Latin America is conducted with respondents in the middle and some upper socioeconomic classes. One cannot generalize about research methods used in the area because of country differences; however, personal interviews are preferred in most countries because of the importance of the social contact between people. Cost differences also dictate the research method used. For example, in Panama it is cheaper to use personal interviewers in homes than to interview the same person on the phone because of very high local phone tariffs.
	Middle East The preferred data collection method in the Middle East is the personal interview. However, the preferred place of interviewing is outside the home. In most Middle East countries, women may be interviewed if accompanied by a male family member, generally in the home. Focus groups, in-depth interviews, paired friendship interviews, and several other qualitative techniques have become widely known as well.
	Source: Compiled by Authors

buying a car or choosing a holiday, or for interviews with mothers and children. If not known to each other, participants may be recruited as having similar behavior and interests, or as a conflict pair. The latter is designed to dramatize differences between, for example loyal users of two different brands.

THE GLOBAL MARKETING RESEARCH PROCESS

The best way to ensure optimal results in any marketing research project is to start with a well-defined plan of action and clear understanding of the steps needed to be taken to accomplish the task. Whether the project concerns a single national market entry or a global competitive analysis, it will require the researchers involved in carrying it out to take a number of smaller steps and make independent decisions along the way. To ensure that all of their actions add up to the desired final product, it is crucial for all parties to understand the purpose and objectives of the research and follow the agreed upon steps in the research process.

The typical marketing research process can be defined in the following six steps (Figure 6.4):

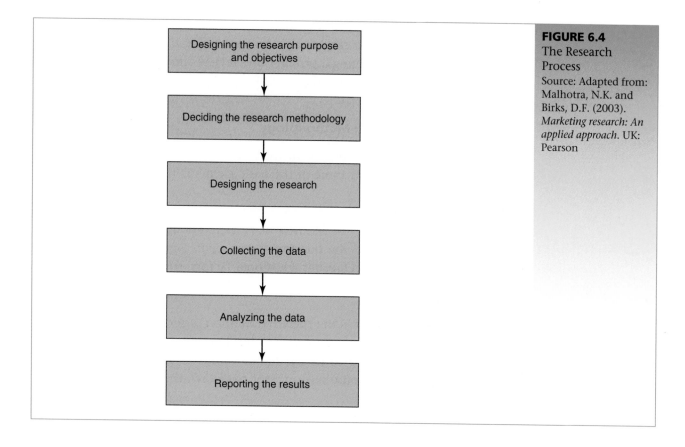

FIGURE 6.4
The Research Process
Source: Adapted from: Malhotra, N.K. and Birks, D.F. (2003). *Marketing research: An applied approach.* UK: Pearson

Defining the Research Purpose and Objectives

Developing a well-defined research purpose and objectives creates a clear target for the research team and makes subsequent decisions—from what sources to use for primary and/or secondary research to composing survey questions and choosing sample sizes—much easier.

The most natural topic of research that comes to mind in global marketing is the identification and evaluation of new markets. Indeed, whether a company is making its first foray into international markets or is an established player in the global scene, it is likely that it will often need new market research.

Despite the common theme, the purpose and the objectives of each research project could be quite different. For example, a small firm may decide to conduct an initial foreign market opportunity analysis, where the purpose is to find out what international markets may be most suitable for their product or services. The objectives then can be defined as assembling profiles of the top ten potential markets with basic information such as population, per capita income levels, sales of specific product categories, trade restrictions, and other relevant indicators, and developing a scoring criterion on which these ten markets can be ranked.

A company with some experience in global markets may be more interested in assessing the competitive landscape in a particular world region. In this case, the purpose of the research could be to identify the main rival firms in the region and their strengths and weaknesses in the market place. Objectives could include performing a SWOT analysis on each competitor, analyzing their marketing strategy and effectiveness, or conducting a product line review aimed at pinpointing gaps in the coverage or underserved market areas.

Determining the Research Methodology

Once the information requirements for the research are established in the initial phase, it is time to decide on some of the basic elements that will constitute this project.

The foremost decision to be made here is how to obtain the information needed. Is it worth conducting primary research or is there enough data available from secondary sources to answer the questions? (see again Figure 6.2). To make this decision, marketers have to consider additional factors, such as the level of data customization desired, data reliability, the costs associated with obtaining it, and the time frame for the project.

Another important factor is the preferred method of project administration: is this project going to be run by the company's headquarters or (in the case of MNCs) is the implementation going to be left to the local offices? Furthermore, is the company going to use in-house resources or outsource the work to a marketing research firm?

The answers to each of these questions hinge not only on the company's internal structure, resources, and culture, but also on the markets' characteristics. The more the researched market is different and unfamiliar to the company, the wiser it is to use market research providers specializing in that market. This strategy may eliminate many potential issues down the road, regarding sampling, translation, data quality, findings interpretation, and others.

Designing the Research

This step of the research process adds more specifics to the project. Now is the time to decide whether qualitative or quantitative data would be more useful (or a combination of both). This decision is best made by referring back to the purpose and objectives of the project and asking whether they can be met by convening focus groups or online panels, by conducting a survey, by using published reports, or a combination of these or other approaches. Other factors that influence the research design have to do with local conditions. If phone interviews seem to be the most suitable technique but local laws restrict phone access to consumers or such market research methods are unfamiliar to consumers in that country, the research design may have to be modified.

Regardless of the technique used, researchers charged with designing the research project should try to avoid being affected by the **self-reference criterion (SRC)**, the often unconscious tendency to assume that people everywhere perceive the world the same way one does and hold similar cultural values or personal attitudes. SRC is most likely to creep up in the process of developing questionnaires for global research projects and in interpreting (wrongly) the answers of survey respondents from other cultures. For instance, cars in the US are designed with larger petrol tanks and with larger size than in some other countries. Assuming that US car-design will automatically be accepted, let's say in Pakistan or Austria, is completely misleading.

Another important element to decide on is sample size. How big a sample is required to collect meaningful data? The answer may depend on the company's requirements for accuracy, level of certainty in the results, and project budget, among other things. Creative Research Systems offers an automatic sample size calculator.[28] You can use it to determine how many people you need to interview in order to get results that reflect the target population as precisely as needed. You can also find the level of precision you have in an existing sample. However, before you use this automatic tool, you should know a little about the target population and the sample you need:[29]

- *Population Size*—How many total people fit your demographic? For instance, if you want to know about mothers living in China, your population size would be the total number of mothers living in China. Don't worry if you are unsure about this number. It is common for the population to be unknown or approximated.

- *Margin of Error (Confidence Interval)*—No sample will be perfect, so you need to decide how much error to allow. The confidence interval determines how much higher or lower than the population mean you are willing to let your sample mean fall. If you've ever seen a political poll on the news, you've seen a confidence interval. It will look something like this: "68 percent of voters said yes to Proposition Z, with a margin of error of +/- 5 percent."

- *Confidence Level*—How confident do you want to be that the actual mean falls within your confidence interval? The most common confidence intervals are 90 percent confident, 95 percent confident, and 99 percent confident.

- *Standard of Deviation*—How much variance do you expect in your responses? Since we haven't actually administered our survey yet, the safe decision is to use .5—this is the most forgiving number and ensures that your sample will be large enough.

Okay, now that we have these values defined, we can calculate our needed sample size. Your confidence level corresponds to a so-called Z-score. This is a constant value needed for this equation. Here are the Z-scores for the most common confidence levels:

- 90 percent – Z-score = 1.645

- 95 percent – Z-score = 1.96

- 99 percent – Z-score = 2.326

Next, plug in your Z-score, Standard of Deviation, and confidence interval into this equation:*

Necessary Sample Size = (Z-score)^2 * StdDev*(1-StdDev) / (margin of error)^2

Here is how the math works assuming you chose a 95 percent confidence level, .5 standard deviation, and a margin of error (confidence interval) of +/− 5 percent.

((1.96)^2 x`5(.5)) / (.05)^2
(3.8416 x .25) / .0025
.9604 / .0025
384.16
385 respondents are needed

Collecting Data

The process of collecting the data also has a number of dimensions that should be well established before the actual collection begins, in order to ensure consistent and valid research results. Protocols for all steps of the process, from obtaining permissions to the types of data sources used and the standards for record keeping, should be clearly understood and followed by all researchers. Ensuring such consistency, whether collecting quantitative or qualitative data, is essential to avoid introducing bias into the process. Researchers use the term *equivalence* to make sure that data is compatible along a variety of dimensions.[30] Craig and Douglas[31] distinguish between the following forms of equivalence:

- *Conceptual equivalence* is "concerned with the interpretation that individuals place on objects, stimuli or behaviour, and whether these exist or are expressed in similar ways in different countries and cultures."[32]

- *Categorical equivalence* "relates to the category in which objects or other stimuli are placed."[33] Categorical equivalence refers to comparability in product category definitions, and in background or socio-demographic classes that exist between countries. For example, beer belongs to the category soft drinks in Southern Europe, whereas beer is considered to be an alcoholic beverage in Northern Europe.

- *Functional equivalence* relates to the question whether the concepts, objects or behaviours studied have the same role or function in all countries included in the analysis. It makes quite a difference whether a bicycle is considered mainly as a means of transport (such as in The Netherlands or India) or as a product for recreational purposes (as in the USA).

- *Translation equivalence* refers to the translation of the research instrument into another language so that it can be understood by respondents in different countries and has the same meaning in each research context.

- *Calibration equivalence* refers to equivalence with regard to units of measurement, for example, monetary units and measures of weight used in questionnaires. Moreover, it refers to the use of colours and shapes in such a way that they are interpreted the same in different countries.

- *Metric equivalence* refers to the specific scale or scoring procedure used for assessment (e.g. celsius vs. fahrenheit).

The researchers' capability to collect data in diverse research environments while maintaining the integrity of the research design is of key importance during this stage of a global research project. Using local staffs that speak the language and can make research respondents feel at ease by interacting with them according to the established cultural and social mores are more likely to maximize responses and collect meaningful, reliable data, while using some of the primary research methods listed in Table 6.4. Professionally trained staffs are also more likely to adhere to the quality and ethical standards established in the marketing research field.

Research Instrument	Description
Interview	Questioning respondents in order to collect information for market research purposes. Interviews may be face-to-face, by phone, fax, or online. They can take place at different locations: in the home, office, street, shopping malls, or at entertainment areas.
Consumer Survey	A survey to determine the demographics of a target audience, why people make certain purchasing decisions, when and where people shop, market potential, and buying habits.
Omnibus Study	A periodic survey conducted on a variety of subjects for more than one client. It allows clients to share the costs of research by pooling questions. All the questions for a given wave are then put to a representative sample, a part of a single questionnaire. Each individual client's questions are of course confidential, and results are processed in such a way as to ensure that each party only sees their own data.
Focus Group	A focus group involves encouraging an invited group of participants to share their thoughts, feelings, attitudes, and ideas on certain subjects.
Observation Study	A research study where data is collected by watching consumer behavior in a shopping situation. The researcher (observer) records the behavior without making contact with the subject being observed.
Questionnaire	A questionnaire is a research instrument consisting of a series of questions and other prompts for the purpose of gathering information from respondents.

TABLE 6.4
Selecting Research Instruments

Source: Compiled by Authors

IN-HOUSE VERSUS OUTSOURCING

A critical decision for a global marketing organization is whether to conduct market research using internal staff and resources or to use outside agencies. Even for firms that have internal market research departments in their affiliates overseas, it may be more efficient to outsource the work to professional market research organizations. A case in point is when the firm plans to conduct regional or worldwide research. In this case, it is critical to ensure that equivalence is maintained in all the research conducted (see earlier). A basic issue in cross-cultural research is the determination of whether the concepts used have similar meaning across the social contexts surveyed. Concepts used in cross-cultural market research predominately come from a particular source culture (e.g. the United States) and were developed in a particular linguistic context (e.g. American English). Conceptual equivalence with target contexts should be assessed before using a United States source or another country source because they may lose some of their meaning in translation and therefore may not be equivalent. A major issue in cross-cultural marketing research is the so called emic versus etic dilemma, which focuses on whether or not the measure is culture bound (emic) or can be used across all cultures (etic). Behavioral-type measures or scales must be examined within each cultural domain to determine if the construct and its measure is relevant in the specific cultural context and that there are equivalent measures. Using local research agents or global agents that have branches in many countries but use local staff who are familiar with the culture will go a long way to ensure that equivalency is maintained. Table 6.5 shows the major global marketing research agencies that have affiliates in many countries. Using such agencies helps to ensure equivalency and the coordination of marketing research projects undertaken in many countries, especially when the research is conducted at the same time frame.

ANALYZING THE DATA

Interpreting the data collected during the previous step and molding it into actionable sets of findings is the main purpose of the data analysis phase. However, the processes used to analyze and interpret qualitative and quantitative data are as different as the two approaches used to collect it.

In qualitative data analysis, researchers usually review recordings of the actual data collection session—for example, from in-depth interviews or focus group sessions—or they may rely on their own notes and recollections from the sessions. Such conditions naturally introduce subjectivity and personal bias into the process and leave much of the final interpretation and analysis of the findings to the skills and experiences of the individual researchers.[34]

Analyzing quantitative data is a much more structured, multi-step process. It begins with a thorough "scrubbing" of the data to ensure that only properly completed, error-free questionnaires are sent for further processing. The processing

Rank Organization 2013		Headquarters	Parent Country	No. of Countries With Subsidiaries / Branch Offices	Global Research Revenues (US$ Millions)	Research-Only Full-Time Employees	**TABLE 6.5** Global Marketing Research Organizations
1	Nielsen Holding N.V.	New York & Netherlands	US	100	6,045.0	36,700	
2	Kantar	London & Fairfield, Conn.	UK	3	3,389.2	22,800	
3	IMS Health Holding Inc.	Danbury, Conn.	US	76	2,544.0	10,000	
4	Ipsos SA	Paris	France	86	2,274.2	15,536	
5	GfK SE	Nuremberg	Germany	74	1,985.2	12,940	
6	Information Resources Inc.	Chicago	US	8	845.1	4,635	
7	Westat Inc.	Rockville, Md.	US	6	582.5	2,044	
8	Dunnhumby Ltd.	London	UK	24	453.7	715	
9	Intage Holding Inc.	Tokyo	Japan	8	435.5	2,527	
10	The NPD Group Inc.	Port Washington, N.Y.	US	14	287.7	1,282	
11	comScore Inc.	Reston, Va.	US	23	286.9	1,166	
12	J.D. Power and Associates	Westlake Village, Calif.	US	8	258.3	738	
13	IBOPE Group	Sao Paulo	Brazil	16	231.1	3,296	
14	ICF International Inc.	Fairfax, Va.	US	6	225.3	908	
15	Video Research Ltd.	Tokyo	Japan	2	204.0	414	
16	Symphony Health Solutions	Horsham, Penn.	US	2	198.7	548	
17	Macromill Inc.	Tokyo	Japan	3	184.7	864	
18	Maritz Research	Fenton, Mo.	US	5	177.6	757	
19	Abt. SRBI Inc.	Cambridge, Mass.	US	41	172.8	1,138	
20	Decision Resources Group	Burlington, Mass.	US		150.3	625	
21	Harris Interactive Inc.	New York	US		139.7	542	
22	ORC International	Princeton, N.J.	US	4	122.0	494	
23	Mediametrie	Paris	France	1	106.1	705	
24	YouGov plc	London	UK	10	101.4	524	
25	Lieberman Research	Los Angeles	US	3	100.3	412	

Source: Adapted from: Marketing News, American Marketing Association (2014)

then may involve running the properly coded and aggregated answers through a number of analytical methods, such as correlation analysis, regression analysis, and other measurement methods designed to establish the relationship between the numbers. Usually, these complex calculations are done by specialized software programs, directed by the researchers. By interpreting the results of the analyses, researchers find the underlying meaning of the data and identify potential trends, hidden tendencies, or other factors that may influence consumer behavior, competitive pressures, or market performance.[35]

For example, a Bank of America study recently found that China outpaced the United States in the production of passenger cars for the first time in 2006. However, on more closer examination, it noted that China includes light vans in its definition of passenger cars, whereas the United States does not. If light vans are not counted, the United States remains ahead in passenger car production, with the difference growing even more significant if light trucks, such as sport utility vehicles (SUVs), are included. Nevertheless, China's growth rate in this industry remains impressive, and increased by 13.9 percent in 2013.[36]

REPORTING THE DATA

Many researchers find nothing more frustrating than to see their final reports—the fruits of their weeks- or months-long research efforts—sitting on an executive's shelf unused. The best way to ensure that research reports are read, understood, and utilized is by making them accessible and relevant to business executives who may not be steeped in research industry jargon or practices.

Following the order and structure of the research objectives in the final report is a reliable strategy to engage executives who are invested in knowing the answers to the questions that prompted the study in the first place. By making a direct connection between the original questions and the study's findings, researchers can make it easy for those not involved in the process to understand the report's logic and conclusions. Researchers who can present these conclusions in an easy-to-follow story format, rather than in a dry, numbers-driven analysis, may generate even greater interest in their reports and create more significant impact in the rest of the organization.

Today's researchers can rely on more than just the written word to educate executives. Multimedia tools such as video or sound recordings can sometimes communicate in minutes what may take hours to read in a report. Such methods of presentation may fit better with executives' own styles of consuming information, and now they can be easily incorporated into presentations or as audiovisual aids to final reports.

Global Marketing Intelligence/Information Systems

"I never dreamed this would happen to us," exclaimed the CEO of a large American pharmaceutical company. The company was unaware that it would be investigated by a Senate subcommittee on health, involving charges that the company mishandled research on two of its best-selling products.

Another example involved Toyota's slow response to safety problems that ultimately led to recalls of 8.5 million vehicles worldwide in 2010. The question is how a Japanese global company like Toyota could have failed to anticipate the problem and not have had a ready-made contingency plan for dealing with it. Some blamed Japan's consensus culture, where the lengthy decision-making processes hinder quick responses.

GEO MAP 6.2
Toyota
Source: Adapted from: CIA Maps, The World Factbook[37]

The headquarters of **Toyota** is located in Toyota, Aichi, Japan

These scenarios show that these companies, like others, did not have an adequate "early warning" capability or intelligence system which could have enabled management to anticipate the crises. Marketing intelligence is not synonymous with marketing research. Marketing research usually focuses on a specific problem or project that has a definite beginning, middle, and end. Marketing intelligence/ information systems involve the continual collection and analysis of marketing information. Moreover, intelligence is evaluated information; i.e. information whose credibility, meaning, and importance has been established, so that the intelligence has application to a present or *potential* marketing situation.

The American Marketing Association (AMA) defines a marketing information system (MIS) as a "set of procedures and methods for the regular, planned collection, analysis, and presentation of information for use in making marketing decisions."[38] In other words, the purpose of the MIS is to not only to aggregate data but also to help change the data into meaningful information and help present it in a manner that facilitates decision-making. A proper MIS should also help integrate marketing information with other pertinent information that may reside elsewhere in the organization—in accounting or operations, for example—since today most organizational functions rely on up-to-the-minute global market information to stay competitive. When viewed in this context, marketing research, which is usually project based, solving one defined issue at a time, becomes a part of the broader marketing intelligence system, which is intended to collect, interpret, and organize marketing information from a variety of sources on an ongoing basis. Some of these sources may include:

- Secondary data analysis

- Human resources

- Executives based abroad, company subsidiaries, and affiliates

- Traveling and building contacts

- Database analysis (internal/external)

- Industry experts

- Formal market research.

Moreover, an MIS should provide not only snapshots of the current state of the markets, but also forecasts that can be used for future or potential marketing initiatives. A model of a marketing intelligence/information system appears as Figure 6.5. The model has five interrelated dimensions: (1) marketing decisions, (2) management functions, (3) marketing environment, (4) information constraints, and (5) system evaluation factors. The first two dimensions of the model are derived from the tasks a marketing manager performs, namely (1) analyzing, (2) organizing, (3) planning, and (4) controlling. These efforts are in four marketing decision areas: (1) product, (2) price, (3) distribution, and (4) promotion. For

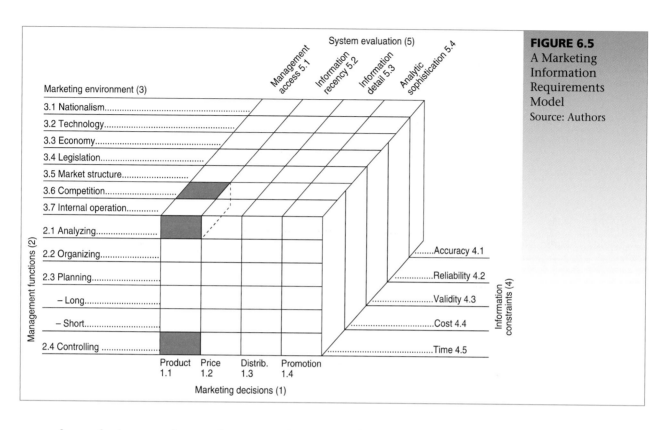

FIGURE 6.5
A Marketing Information Requirements Model
Source: Authors

example, analyzing ongoing product strategies requires knowledge of the marketing environment, dimension being the coordinates 1.1, 2.1, 3.5, again product analysis, but this time involving market structure; market share, market segmentation, and so on. Each cell therefore becomes a page or section in a plan book including all information needed for the marketing decision and managerial function represented by the cell. For any cell, two additional dimensions; for example, time and cost, and intelligence system evaluation. When collecting data, it must be examined for validity and reliability as in dimension 4. Evaluation of the system can be accomplished by applying four criteria: (1) management access, the time interval between a request for information and its receipt, (2) information recency, the time interval between the occurrence of an event and its information storage in the system, (3) information aggregation, the desired detail with which information is stored in the system, and (4) analytic sophistication, the structure of the data in the system, ranging from description of events to statistical evaluation and model building.

One of the factors making the MIS function doable is the democratization of information; it shifted the control over the marketing fate of a product or company from the marketers to the consumers. Today, international marketers have to scan and monitor not only what competitors are doing, but also what kind of information bloggers post about their products, how YouTube videos feature it, and what rating it gets on consumer review sites such as Epinions.com. This explains the increasing popularity of features such as customizable information filters and electronic agents at information portals like Yahoo!, MSN, and Google and the rise of Really Simple Syndication (RSS) tools called "aggregators" or feed readers.

New technological tools (see again the section on online metrics) are also at hand to help marketers. Data management programs, specialized software tools for data mining, text retrieval and classification, patent searching, web page tracking, and Internet monitoring are becoming more and more popular at leading firms in highly competitive industries such as pharmaceuticals, computer technology, telecommunications, defense, and aerospace, among others. They also make it much easier for executives to cover a wider array of media sources, hone in on the most pertinent information for their company, and share that information across the organization.

SUMMARY

The role of global marketing research in formulating marketing strategy takes on increased importance because of the cultural, social, and economic differences between countries. Expanding into new markets requires special expertise to deal with market differences and to coordinate research activities regionally. Companies that operate globally and regionally have to decide whether research should be conducted on a country, regional, or global basis.

In most cases, how research is conducted will depend on the company's global organization of operations. Moreover, global companies have to decide whether marketing research should be done in-house or outsourced to multinational research agencies and local firms who may have a better grasp on survey techniques that are required in a given area or country.

Advances in technology such as the Internet have made significant contributions to global marketing research. Before the advent of the Internet, global (and domestic) marketing research was only affordable to large companies. Today, a substantial amount of international marketing research can be done on a PC within a matter of hours. In addition, data collection devices based on computer technology such as scanners, CATI (computer assisted telephone interviewing), and CAPI (computer assisted personal interviewing) are used frequently in developed countries and are beginning to be used in emerging markets. Of course, multinational corporations still have much more research resources at their disposal, but small and medium-sized firms can download a substantial amount of research at an affordable cost.

There is a growing recognition among global firms that in addition to marketing research, marketing intelligence/information systems are necessary in order to acquire a future-focused perspective on competitors and market structures for long-term planning. They also provide an early warning capability to avoid missed market opportunities or to forecast threats that, if they occur, can be very costly to the firm.

DISCUSSION QUESTIONS

1. How can you determine which data collection method (personal interview, telephone, etc.) would work best in a survey of household consumers in Kenya, Nigeria, Ghana, and South Africa? See Table 6.3.

2. You are requested by the VP Marketing to determine consumer preference for restaurants in New Delhi and New York City. What sources would you use to determine this?

3. Would the imports of consumer goods into a given country be a good indicator of the size of the internal market for those products? Why or why not?

4. What sort of information is critical to the global firm that is not often necessary for a firm operating in the home market only? Detail the sorts of information critical to the global firm.

EXPERIENTIAL EXERCISES

1. Visit www.acnielsen.com and pick one consumer report from the "Trends and Insights" section. Based on the findings reported, recommend a strategy for entering a new geographic market with a specific product category. Justify your recommendations.

2. The mid-sized consumer products company that you work for has decided to expand into China. As the marketing manager, you were tasked with hiring a market research firm to conduct primary research to help you determine which of your product lines you should first offer in this new market. Formulate the research problem that you face and the questions you would like answers to at the end of the research project.

3. Using the Marketing Information Requirements, state which cells should be used to obtain information about the following: a. Suppose that your operations in Country X may be threatened by a change in government. How could you go about determining the probability that this will happen? b. You are informed that your competition in Country Y is in the process of developing a new product that, if successful, can prove to be superior to your product that is currently on the market. How can you obtain information about your competitor's stage of development of this product?

KEY TERMS

- Big data
- Equivalence
- Foreign market opportunity analysis
- International marketing research
- Market research
- Marketing research
- Online research

- Primary research
- Qualitative research
- Quantitative research
- Sample size
- Secondary research
- Self-reference criterion (SRC)

NOTES

1   ESOMAR. (2014). *Global market research report*, http://www.esomar.org/uploads/industry/reports/global-market-research-2014/ESOMAR-GMR2014-Preview.pdf [Accessed: October 1, 2014].

2   American Marketing Association, 'Definition of marketing', https://www.ama.org/AboutAMA/Pages/Definition-of-Marketing.aspx [Accessed: December 12, 2014].

3   Forsyth, J. E., Galante, N. and Guild, T. (2006), 'Capitalizing on customer insights', *The McKinsey Quarterly*, 47(3), pp. 43–53.

4   The World Factbook. (2015), https://www.cia.gov/library/publications/the-world-factbook/docs/refmaps.html [Accessed: August 1, 2015].

5   GfK Asia. (2012), 'Robust demand for washing machines', http://asia-research.net/2012/02/robust-demand-for-washing-machines-propels-major-domestic-appliances-industry-to-achieve-double-digit-growth-in-southeast-asia-in-2011-gfk-asia/ [Accessed: July 15, 2014].

6   Malhotra, N.K. (2014). *Essentials of marketing research*. Harlow: Pearson Education Limited.

7   Holscher, A. and Grogan, A. (2008), 'Breaking the mold', *Research World*, pp. 12–15.

8   Information about UPS surveys is taken from: UPS (2015), China Facts, https://www.pressroom.ups.com/pressroom/ContentDetailsViewer.page?ConceptType=FactSheets&id=1426321550578-587 [Accessed: 8 December, 2015].

9   Babbie, Earl R. (2010). *The practice of social research*. 12th ed. Belmont, CA: Wadsworth Cengage.

10 Rugen, B. (2014). *Qualitative marketing research: An interactive approach*. [Kindle Edition]. DecaBooks.

11 ESOMAR. (2014), op.cit.

12 Sims, J. (2014), 'A man with a purpose', *Research*, 27 October, 2014. http://www.research-live.com/features/a-man-with-purpose/4012445.article. [Accessed: 16 November, 2014].

13 Barner-Rasmussen, W., Ehrnrooth, M., Koveshnikov, A., and Mäkelä, K. (2014), 'Cultural and language skills as resources for boundary spanning within the MNC', *Journal of International Business Studies*, 45(7), pp. 886–905; Harzing, A.W., Reiche B.S., and Pudelko, M. (2012), 'Challenges in international survey research: A review with illustrations and suggested solutions for best practice', *European Journal of International Management*, 7(1), pp. 112–34.

14 Herk, H.H.v., Poortinga, Y.H., and Verhallen, T.M.M. (2004), 'Equivalence of survey data: Relevance for international marketing', *European Journal of Marketing*, 39(3/4), pp. 351–64.

15 Yi, H., Merz, M. A., and Alden, D. L. (2008), 'Diffusion of measurement invariance assessment in cross-national empirical marketing research: Perspectives from the literature and a survey of researchers', *Journal of International Marketing*, 16(2), pp. 64–83.

16 Barner-Rasmussen, W. and Aarnio, C. (2011), 'Shifting the faultlines of language. A quantitative functional-level exploration of language use in MNC subsidiaries', *Journal of World Business,* 46(3), pp. 288–95.

17 (2009, June), 'Online metrics get thumbs down', *Research*, p.6.

18 McKinsey. (2011), 'Big data: The next frontier for innovation, competition, and productivity', www.mckinsey.com [Accessed: May 1, 2014].

19 Kelly, K. (2011). Web 2.0 expo and conference, March 29, 2011. Keynote by Kevin Kelly, Senior Maverick, Wired. Video available at: www.web2expo.com/webexsf2011/public/schedule/proceedings

20 Jones, A. (2014), 'Big data: Enabling the future of healthcare', *The Guardian online*, 4 November, 2014. http://www.theguardian.com/healthcare-network/2014/nov/04/big-data-enabling-future-healthcare [Accessed: 11 November, 2014].

21 Big Data Insight Group. (2012), 'Ten big data benefits', http://datascienceseries.com/stories/ten-practical-big-data-benefits [Accessed: 11 November, 2014].

22 http://www.digitalanalyticsassociation.org [Accessed: October 12, 2015].

23 McKinsey. (2011), op.cit.

24 Watch the video at: http://www-01.ibm.com/software/data/infosphere/hadoop/ [Accessed: July 1, 2014].

25 Poynter, R. (2009, October), 'The rise of observational research', *Research World*, pp. 29–31.

26 Dharmasiri, A. (2014), 'Social media for hiring: Promises and pitfalls', http://www.ft.lk/2014/09/29/social-media-for-hiring-promises-and-pitfalls-2/ [Accessed: July 2, 2014].

27 UK Telegraph. (2010), 'EU criticises Facebook privacy changes. 'Unacceptable' for social networking site to make some profile information public by default, says European Commission', http://www.telegraph.co.uk/technology/facebook/7723320/EU-criticises-Facebook-privacy-changes.html [Accessed: May 14, 2010].

28 Creative Research Systems: http://www.surveysystem.com/sscalc.htm [Accessed: July 1, 2014].

29 Smith, S. (2013), 'Determining sample size: How to ensure you get the correct sample size', *Qualtrics Blog*, http://www.qualtrics.com/blog/determining-sample-size/ [Accessed: July 1, 2014].

30 Herk, H.H.v., Poortinga, Y.H., and Verhallen, T.M.M. (2004), op.cit.

31 Craig, C.S. and Douglas, S.P. (2000). *International marketing research*. 2nd ed. New York, NY: Wiley.

32 Craig, C.S. and Douglas, S.P., op.cit., p. 158.

33 Craig, C.S. and Douglas, S.P., op.cit., p. 159.

34 Akers, H. (2014), 'The disadvantages of qualitative and quantitative research', http://www.ehow.com/info_8321143_disadvantages-qualitative-quantitative-research.html [Accessed: August 5, 2014].

35 Ibid.

36 'China's auto market growth may halve to 7 percent this year: Industry body head', *Reuters*, October 25, 2014. http://www.reuters.com/article/2014/10/25/us-china-autos-idUSKCN0IE04M20141025 [Accessed: November 10, 2014].

37 The World Factbook. (2015), https://www.cia.gov/library/publications/the-world-factbook/docs/refmaps.html [Accessed: August 1, 2015].

38 www.ama.org [Accessed: March 10, 2015].

CASE 6.1 ESTIMATING DEMAND IN EMERGING MARKETS FOR KODAK EXPRESS

David M. Currie and Ilan Alon wrote this case solely to provide material for class discussion. The authors do not intend to illustrate either effective or ineffective handling of a managerial situation. The authors may have disguised certain names and other identifying information to protect confidentiality.

Anna Johnson gazed at the information she had accumulated on various countries and wondered how she could use it to estimate the demand for Kodak Express (KE) outlets. She had learned from the Kodak market research department that demand for KE outlets depended on household income. To support one Kodak Express outlet, one of the following was needed: one million households with annual incomes equal to or exceeding the equivalent of US$15,000, two million households earning the equivalent of between US$10,000 and US$14,999, four million households earning the equivalent of between US$5,000 and US$9,999 or 10 million households with incomes less than the equivalent of US$5,000 (see Exhibit 1). According to the market research department, these averages seemed to apply throughout the world, when international dollars (purchasing power parity adjusted) were used as a benchmark.

Unfortunately, the statistics Johnson was able to find did not tell her the household income in U.S. dollar-equivalents in various countries or how many households in each country fell into a specific income bracket. She would need to complete a series of intermediate calculations to transform the original macroeconomic data to information that was useful for estimating the demand for Kodak Express outlets. Then, on the basis of market demand, Kodak would be able to use this information to decide how to allocate its investments across the various emerging markets.

EXHIBIT 1
Number of Housholds and Income Levels needed to Support One Kodak Express Outlet

Income	# of Households
≥$15,000	1 million
$10,000—$14,999	2 million
$5,000—$9,999	4 million
$0—$4,999	10 million

Source: Company estimates/assumptions.

The purpose of Johnson's calculations was to identify the markets with the most potential. The commitment to open KE outlets in a particular country was a significant investment that needed to have a promising return. Further, determining the markets with the most potential was in line with Kodak's philosophy of "investing where you sell the most."

Johnson sat in front of her computer, attempting to develop a model that would help her to estimate the market demand for KE outlets. She picked up a pencil and paper and began to sketch the process she would follow to use the data at her disposal to determine demand for KE outlets. Once she determined the process, she would prepare a spreadsheet model, plug in the data for a country and see whether the result was reasonable.

KODAK'S GLOBAL STRATEGY

The manufacture and distribution of photography items had been the major focus of Eastman Kodak Corporation since George Eastman commercialized personal cameras using roll film in 1888[1]. The next year, the company became international when it extended distribution of products outside the United States. In 1900, Kodak introduced the first Brownie camera, the company's effort to make photography available to a mass market. By 2002, the company's products were available in more than 150 countries. However, the company was faced with increased competition from two fronts: Japan's Fuji Photo Film Co. produced and marketed many of the same photography products as Kodak, and Kodak had been slow to respond to the emergence of digital photography.[2]

Worldwide revenues for Kodak's products exceeded US$5.5 billion in 2010, a decrease of US$800 million compared with 2009 and a decrease of US$1.6 billion compared with 2008. The decline was partially due to the global economic slowdown, particularly in Europe, Middle East and Africa: revenues from these regions had decreased by more than US$1 billion in the previous two years.[3]

To offset the decline in sales volume in Europe, Middle East and Africa, Kodak's strategy was to expand sales into emerging markets such as India and China. Because of China's enormous population and its citizens' cultural affinity for taking pictures, China was one of the cornerstones of Kodak's emerging market strategy. Even expanding the market to just half of China's population would add the equivalent of another United States or Japan to the world photographic market.[4]

KODAK EXPRESS OUTLETS

Despite Kodak Express outlets being independently owned, they were contractually obliged to buy and display exclusively Kodak products, and they utilized Kodak's store specifications and the company's brand elements. The outlets provided three benefits to Kodak:

1. A front-line retailing presence

2. Wide distribution of Kodak products, services and brand name

3. A strategic asset for Kodak for market development

The company was making an effort to have a more extensive distribution of its Kodak Express outlets throughout the world. Through these outlets, Kodak planned to launch "grass-root marketing development programs."[5]

DATA AVAILABILITY

Johnson focused on four sets of data that were readily available from reliable sources for a variety of countries: population, purchasing power, income distribution and average household size. The first data set, population, seemed straightforward. Any analysis of a country's purchasing habits would begin with consumers, whether on an individual (per capita) basis or a household basis. Population estimates for 2010 are shown in Exhibit 2. More recent statistics were difficult to locate because most countries conducted a census only once every 10 years. Between censuses, all population statistics were estimates.

Determining the dollar-equivalent level of income from one country to another was a more challenging task. Many statistics comparing one country with another merely converted data into U.S. dollars using an average exchange rate for the year. Although this method was useful for some purposes, it was potentially misleading when used for consumption patterns because it ignored the cost of living from one country to another. For example, a family earning RMB65,000 in

EXHIBIT 2 Population Of Selected Countries 2010	Country	Population (in millions)
	United States	310
	Bangladesh	164
	Brazil	193
	Cambodia	14
	China	1,341
	India	1,216
	Indonesia	234
	Laos	6
	Malaysia	28
	Nigeria	156
	Pakistan	167
	Russia	140
	South Africa	50
	Thailand	64
	Vietnam	88

Source: International Monetary Fund, 2010.

China earned the equivalent of approximately US$10,000 using an exchange rate conversion of RMB6.5 RMB per U.S. dollar.[6] But RMB65,000 in China purchased much more than US$10,000 purchased in the United States; thus, the family in China would be considered much better off by Chinese standards, and their consumption patterns might be closer to a family in the United States earning US$48,000.

To account for this difference, economists frequently standardized data for differences in purchasing power, called purchasing power parity (PPP). Johnson was able to find gross domestic product (GDP) per capita in U.S. dollars using PPP for the countries in which she was interested (see Exhibit 3).

A related problem was that GDP was not the same as national income, and Johnson needed to know a household's income. After some research, she discovered that because the difference usually was not significant, economists frequently used GDP as a proxy for national income. Therefore, the GDP per capita for these countries could serve as a substitute for income per capita. That meant that the average person in India earned the equivalent of US$3,339 annually on a PPP basis in 2010.

Income distribution was another important issue because if more people earned low incomes in a country, they wouldn't be able to support as many KE outlets. Johnson needed to determine how many households corresponded to different income levels for any country. Data on income distribution are shown in Exhibit 4. For any country, population was divided into equal portions called quintiles (fifths), and each quintile showed the share of national income accruing to that quintile. For example, in India the bottom 20 per cent of the population accounted

Country	Gross Domestic Product Purchasing Power Parity per Capita (in US$)	
United States	47,284	**EXHIBIT 3**
Bangladesh	1,572	Gross Domestic Product Purchasing Power Parity Per Captia For Selected Countries, 2010
Brazil	11,239	
Cambodia	2,112	
China	7,519	
India	3,339	
Indonesia	4,394	
Laos	2,436	
Malaysia	14,670	
Nigeria	2,422	
Pakistan	2,791	
Russia	15,837	
South Africa	10,498	
Thailand	9,187	
Vietnam	3,134	

Source: International Monetary Fund, 2010.

EXHIBIT 4 Distribution Of Income For Selected Countries — Various Dates (As a Percentage Of Income)

Country

Quintile	United States	Bangladesh	Brazil	Cambodia	China	India	Indonesia	Laos	Malaysia	Nigeria	Pakistan	Russia	South Africa	Thailand	Vietnam
Upper	45.8	40.8	58.7	52	47.8	45.3	45.5	41.4	44.4	48.6	40.5	50.2	62.7	49.4	45.4
Upper Middle	22.4	21.1	19.6	18.9	22	20.4	21.3	21.6	22.8	21.9	21.3	20.7	18.8	21.3	21.6
Middle	15.7	16.1	11.8	12.9	14.7	14.9	14.9	16.2	15.8	14.7	16.3	13.9	9.9	14.1	15.2
Lower Middle	10.7	12.6	6.9	9.7	9.8	11.3	11	12.3	10.8	9.7	12.8	9.6	5.6	9.4	10.8
Lower	5.4	9.4	3	6.5	5.7	8.1	7.4	8.5	6.4	5.1	9.1	5.6	3.1	5.9	7.1

Source: World Bank, World Development Indicators, various dates.

for 8.1 per cent of national income, and the top 20 per cent of the population accounted for 45.3 per cent of national income. Because each quintile represented 20 per cent of the population, about 243 million people (20 per cent of 1,216 million people) earned only 8.1 per cent of the country's total income. At the other extreme, 243.2 million people earned 45.3 per cent of the country's total income. If incomes were distributed evenly in a country, each quintile would account for 20 per cent of the national income (see Exhibit 4).

The average size of a household would help to determine the number of households in a country and, thus, the number of households in each of the quintiles. Data for the average size of household shown as the number of persons per household are shown in Exhibit 5. Dividing the population of a quintile by the number of people per household would yield an estimate for the number of households in the country. Of course, the assumption was that the number of people per household did not change with income. Johnson realized, however, that average household size depended on both cultural and economic factors. In some countries, the custom was for an extended family (parents, children and grandparents) to live in the same household. In most countries, household size varied according to the level of income in the household because families earning higher incomes tended to have fewer children. Household size also varied between urban and rural areas: urban households tended to be smaller. For this analysis, Johnson would need to assume that the average household size applied throughout the country, simply because no reliable statistics were available on the differences between sizes of households for all the countries she wished to examine.

Country	Average Household Size (in persons)	
United States	2.6	**EXHIBIT 5** Average Household Size For Selected Countries, Various Dates
Bangladesh	6.0	
Brazil	3.6	
Cambodia	3.2	
China	3.4	
India	5.3	
Indonesia	3.4	
Laos	5.2	
Malaysia	4.4	
Nigeria	4.9	
Pakistan	7.2	
Russia	2.7	
South Africa	3.7	
Thailand	3.5	
Vietnam	4.4	

Source: Euromonitor International, 2010.

CALCULATING POTENTIAL DEMAND

As Johnson thought more about her task, she realized that she faced a two-step problem. First, she would need to calculate the household income in U.S. dollars for each quintile of the population. Only by doing this step would she then be able to separate households into each of the income brackets. This difference was important because each category was able to support a different number of KE outlets, as Johnson had learned from Kodak's market research department. The second step would be to calculate the potential demand for KE outlets once she knew the number of households in each spending category.

To attain this number, Johnson knew that she would need to complete several interim steps. Using her available data, she could make some initial calculations: she could determine the PPP GDP for the entire population, the population per quintile and the number of households per quintile. Using the population's GDP and each country's income distribution, she could then calculate the income per quintile.

Dividing the income per quintile by the population per quintile, she knew she would derive the individual income per quintile, from which she could easily conclude the household income per quintile. Then, using at the household income per quintile, she would be able to determine how many households fell into each of the categories in Exhibit 1. Knowing how many households fell in each category, she could then determine the potential demand for KE outlets in a specific market. Her goal was to build a model that would enable her to evaluate each of the countries in Exhibit 2. She would test the model using the data for one country. If it worked, the computer would then do most or all of the subsequent calculations. Once the model was complete, Johnson would use it both to predict demand for Kodak Express outlets in selected emerging markets and to make recommendations to Kodak management regarding market entry and resource allocations in these countries.

Finally, Johnson knew that such a significant investment should take not only today's demand into account. To determine the most attractive markets, she would also need to determine whether those markets would still be attractive in the future. Therefore, she decided to also calculate, in addition to the 2010 calculations, each country's demand for the year 2016. She was able to gather projected data on both PPP GDP per capita and populations for 2016 (see Exhibits 6 and 7); however, she was unable to find reliable forecasts for income distribution and average household sizes. She therefore made the naive assumption that these last two variables, income distribution and average household size, would not change significantly.

What is the potential demand for KE outlets in the various emerging markets in 2010? What would be the demand by 2016? Given the assumptions, which markets will be the top candidates for investment?

Country	Population (in millions)
United States	328
Bangladesh	178
Brazil	199
Cambodia	15
China	1,382
India	1,316
Indonesia	253
Laos	7
Malaysia	31
Nigeria	183
Pakistan	183
Russia	137
South Africa	53
Thailand	66
Vietnam	95

Source: International Monetary Fund, 2011.

EXHIBIT 6
Forecasted Population For Selected Countries For 2016

Country	Gross Domestic Product Purchasing Power Parity per Capita (in US$)
United States	57,320
Bangladesh	2,340
Brazil	15,193
Cambodia	3,183
China	13,729
India	5,398
Indonesia	6,556
Laos	3,675
Malaysia	19,541
Nigeria	3,242
Pakistan	3,678
Russia	22,717
South Africa	13,607
Thailand	12,681
Vietnam	4,803

Source: International Monetary Fund, 2011.

EXHIBIT 7
Forecasted Gross Domestic Product Purchasing Power Parity Per Capita For Selected Countries For 2016

NOTES

1. Kodak, "Building the Foundation," http://kodak.com/US/en/corp/kodakHistory/buildingTheFoundation. shtml, accessed January 26, 2004.
2. Daniel Gross, "Photo Finished: Why Eastman Kodak Deserves to Lose Its Dow Jones Industrial Average Membership," Slate, January 6, 2004, http://slate.msn.com/id/2093512/, accessed January 26, 2004.
3. Kodak 2010 Annual Report; www.envisionreports.com/EK/2011/22103MA11E/38495aae46f94783a4829c3 e66124a12/Kodak_AR_10k_Secured_3-28-11.pdf, accessed June 16, 2011.
4. David Swift, "Remarks of David Swift, Chairman & President, Greater China Region, Eastman Kodak Company," Goldman Sachs 21st Century China Conference, September 1999, pp.1-8.
5. Ilan Alon, "Interview: International Franchising with Kodak in China," Thunderbird International Business Review, November/December 2001, pp. 737-754.
6. Exchange rate on April 18, 2011, http://finance.yahoo.com/currency-converter/, accessed June 16, 2011.

CHAPTER 7

Entering Global Markets

"Feet on the Ground, Eyes on the Horizon" This means maintaining a laser-like focus on operating excellence and customer service, while simultaneously looking to the future and making the necessary investments to expand our customer base through-out the world.[1]

Samuel R. Allen, CEO Deere & Company

LEARNING OBJECTIVES

After Reading This Chapter, You Should Be Able To:

- Distinguish between the various options a firm has for establishing presence in foreign markets.
- Compare the risks and the advantages of the export modes, intermediate modes, and hierarchical modes of entry.
- Understand the difference between direct and indirect exports.
- Apply distributor selection process, channel management, and control to export management.
- Explain the characteristics of international licensing, international franchising, and other important contract-based intermediate modes.
- Understand the difference between strategic alliances and joint ventures.
- Explain why joint ventures are prone to failure.
- Compare different hierarchical modes of entry: wholly-owned subsidiaries, subsidiaries, and affiliates.
- Distinguish between *greenfield* and *brownfield* investments.
- Understand the factors that influence foreign market entry decision.
- Understand the dynamics of entry-mode decisions.

INTRODUCTION

This chapter examines the various modes of entry available to small and medium enterprises (SMEs), although much of the material is relevant for larger firms as well. In particular, it discusses export modes, intermediate entry modes (contractual and equity-based), and hierarchical modes.

Entry into foreign markets is very frequently accidental for entrepreneurs. One likely scenario for a company is that its first export order resulted from the company's exposure on the Internet, its presence at a trade fair, or mention of the company's products on a blog. Whether a firm takes deliberate action to enlarge its international market share after the first few successful exports is up to many different factors such as top management's vision for the company and financial resources. Some of the many reasons for going international include the following:

- domestic market characteristics;

- research on new profit sources;

- adding to the firm's competitive edge;

- diversifying and enlarging markets to hedge against economic crises;

- following customers who are going abroad;

- seeking resources in foreign markets.

For example, a large domestic market can make some companies disinterested in expanding internationally owing to the significant growth opportunities at home, whereas a small and saturated domestic market may spur even small companies to seek international expansion sooner.

Other characteristics of the home country that might spur a company to seek international markets include competitive pressure at home, high domestic production costs, and favorable government policies toward exports (tax incentives, trade support programs). Entering foreign markets can also represent a strategic choice for a company that wants to find new sources of profits, diversify to hedge against economic crises, or develop significant competitive advantages. In fact, a company that decides to limit itself to a single domestic market is likely to be much less competitive and successful than its internationalized counterparts. Some companies just "follow" the internationalization of their customers: it is the case of the internationalization of subcontractors who are projected abroad by the internationalization of their supply network,[2] or the example of retailers favoring the internationalization of their suppliers in new markets of entry. Finally, internationalization does not have to be considered only in terms of the internationalization of sales. For example, a study on the internationalization of SMEs in the biotechnology, renewable energy, and ICT industries found that the international behavior of high-tech firms is influenced by a "resource seeking" approach, i.e. by the need to search for, prospect, or "scavenge" for resources, and this approach differs from the "market-seeking" internationalization typical of other industries.[3]

However, business owners today should not think that just because they are well entrenched in their home market, they are immune to the competitive pressures of globalization. It is likely that even if a business does not pursue an international strategy, then international competitors, suppliers, buyers, etc. would eventually pursue it.

This chapter is divided into two sections. The first section is the heart of the chapter, and it analyzes the characteristics, advantages, and disadvantages of the different modes of entry. The second section discusses the factors that motivate the mode of entry decision from the standpoint of the company and the environment in which it operates, and it points out how in some cases, changes in these factors can influence a company's market entry choice.

METHODS OF ENTRY TO INTERNATIONAL MARKETS

Because most entrepreneurial businesses are small to medium in size, their initial choices for international market entry tend to include low- to moderate-risk strategies, such as indirect and direct export (export modes). The firm has low market control, but they benefit from high flexibility because all the activities in the foreign market are externalized. In fact, international operations are performed by another domestic or foreign company (for example, an export company or a foreign distributor). As companies become bigger and more successful internationally, some may decide to deepen their presence and commitment to particular foreign markets by sharing risk and control with a foreign partner (intermediate modes) and enter into contract-based agreements such as international licensing, international franchising, piggyback, contract manufacturing, original equipment manufacturing (OEM), turnkey operations agreements, management contracts, strategic alliances, or equity-based agreements such as joint ventures. They can even afford to take a higher risk abroad (hierarchical modes) by investing in a subsidiary or an affiliate. Alternatively, they can take the wholly-owned subsidiary route by acquiring a foreign company (brownfield investment) or by establishing a new company arm (greenfield investment). Through the hierarchical mode, a company internalizes management of the activities in a foreign market, leading to higher risks and lower flexibility, but also higher market control. Figure 7.1 shows a graphical representation of the aforementioned most common market entry methods, ranked in terms of the increase in investment, risk, and control for the entering firm.

EXPORT MODES

Export is the most common and low-risk method of entering overseas markets, and it is also the one requiring the least financial, marketing and human resources, and time investments. Because of its low commitment requirements, export is the preferred mode of entry for most small and entrepreneurial businesses. It is an especially well-suited method for initial market tests owing to the relative ease of pulling out of a market (high flexibility) if said market turns out to be unprofitable.[4] Exportation has been favored by the diffusion of the Internet. Online channel positively enhances export performance, although research demonstrates that the use of the Internet cannot be considered as an alternative to physical market presence.[5]

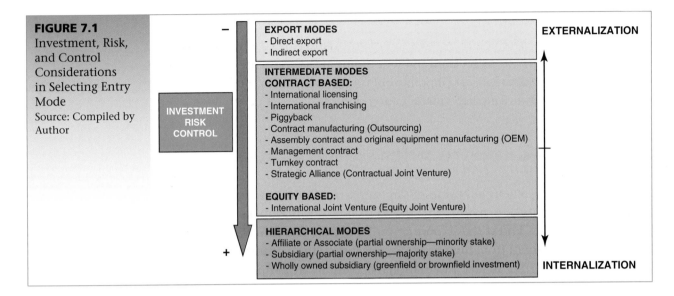

FIGURE 7.1
Investment, Risk,
and Control
Considerations
in Selecting Entry
Mode
Source: Compiled by
Author

Furthermore, export is limited to actual physical products that are produced outside the target country market. By nature, this mode of entry is unsuitable for service companies because they cannot perform/produce their services domestically and then ship them to another country. Therefore, service firms are required to use the intermediate or hierarchical entry modes.

Exported products can be sold abroad by intermediaries who specialize in this activity from the home base—indirect export—or they can be distributed directly through agents and/or wholesalers or retailers in the target country—direct export. An alternative that falls under the direct export method is to export products to a branch or subsidiary of the company, with the assumption that some form of direct investment in the target market has already been made (Figure 7.2).

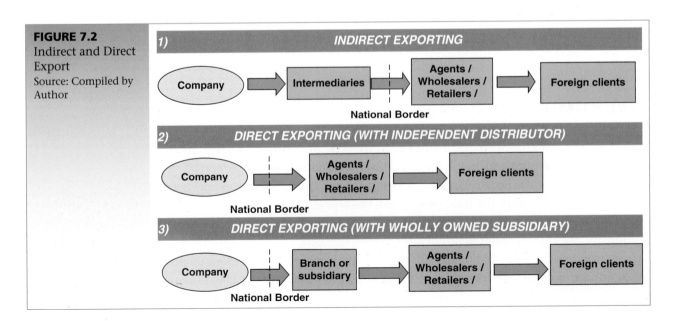

FIGURE 7.2
Indirect and Direct
Export
Source: Compiled by
Author

Indirect Export

Indirect export cannot be defined properly as a form of internationalization because the company sells to an intermediary in the domestic market. The various kinds of intermediaries (Figure 7.3) involved in the process do not help with the implementation of a real strategic and operational presence abroad, but they act as the first step in the internationalization process.

Companies play a passive role in this phase, entrusting the intermediary to use agents or to sell their products to wholesalers, retailers or, as it often happens in business-to-business, directly to the final foreign clients.[6] In some markets, e.g. China, direct export is not always a viable strategy; entering the Chinese market requires presence, control, investments in brand equity, and adaptation of product and communication strategies. All these requirements impede access to the Chinese market without a more direct presence, which the indirect export mode cannot guarantee.

Export Companies

Export companies are commercial companies that undertake export activities of non-competing firms, often belonging to the same industry, or at least the same sector. This mode of entry is often used by companies that have a commercial office but lack an export office. The exporting company essentially operates as an external export office, undertaking the necessary field research and contracting, targeting distribution channels and other sales partners, as well as rolling out promotional activities. All concluded contracts are negotiated on behalf of the producing company, and all estimated prices and orders must be confirmed by it. Hence, the producing company still retains some control in the final markets, but this level of control is still relatively weak, especially when it comes to branding strategies. This is indeed indirect control, managed by the export company, which does not allow on its own to start up a gradual internationalization process.

Buying Offices (Buyers)

Buying offices are typically independent commercial operators representing some abroad-based companies that wish to maintain continuous contact with the sellers operating in the importing countries. They operate as a single physical person or as a representative office, are located in the importing country, and

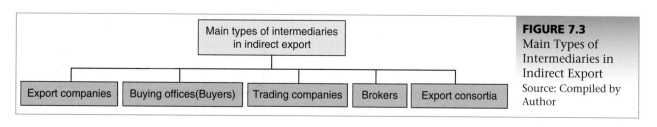

FIGURE 7.3
Main Types of Intermediaries in Indirect Export
Source: Compiled by Author

buy the imported product on behalf of a third company. Eventually, they may support the export activity, suggest adaptation strategies, and offer controlling services and logistical platforms for the products, such as showroom or e-selling. However, these are not long-term relationships because buyers may easily switch exporting companies. Therefore, a long-term strategy is indeed not viable with this entry mode. A further typology of buyers, the so-called big buyer, refers to specialized and big-sized sales operators who establish contracts with abroad-based sellers in order to insert their products in a catalogue sold under their own brand.

Trading Companies

Trading companies are large-sized commercial intermediaries, able to undertake both export and import activities. They may indeed be present in both the domestic and the foreign market. They buy and sell either on their own behalf or on behalf of a third party. In the latter case, they may support the exporting companies with finance, logistics, and managerial and marketing services necessary for the development of the exporting companies' presence abroad. This support may be offered from the outset, beginning with market research, feasibility study, negotiating assistance or, at more advanced stages (e.g. preparation and management of the export process) including contracting and documentation, transportation, logistics management, and storage.

Brokers

A broker connects the exporting company with potential clients abroad, eventually providing consulting support. From the export standpoint, brokers usually operate in the national context, but are not directly involved in the buying and selling process. The broker's main role is indeed to foster commercial relationships between buyers and sellers. Therefore, the broker is an intermediary who does not maintain a continuous relationship with the firm, but is used rather occasionally by the firm to sell the product in the short term.[7]

Export Consortia

Export consortia are voluntary aggregations constituted to organize common activities, e.g. foreign export and global communication. It is possible to classify export consortia as follows:

- **Mono-sectorial or pluri-sectorial.** A mono-sectorial consortium organizes firms within the same sector but with competing products, e.g. the Parmigiano–Reggiano Cheese Consortium. A pluri-sectorial consortium includes firms from different sectors and often undertakes activities that individual members are unable to perform on their own. An example is the Centopercento Italiano

Consortium,[8] composed of 70 different Italian members operating in fashion, luxury leather goods, wine, food, and cosmetics, which defends the quality of products made entirely in Italy.

- Promotion-focused or selling-focused. A promotion-focused consortium offers only supporting services for international activities, e.g. consulting for required documentation, promotional activities, etc. An example is the Italian Wine Alliance Consortium, which has opened an office in Beijing to promote its wine catalogue in the Chinese market. In addition to the above-mentioned activities, a selling consortium undertakes the commercialization of its members' products, either under the consortium's brand or under the manufacturer's individual brand.

Direct Export

In the direct export mode, the commercial organization of the company in question is able to directly manage the selling process in a foreign market. Hence, the company sets up an export office dedicated to the target foreign market. This office is responsible for segmenting a potential market, implementing a communication strategy, and contacting potential customers, final users, retailers, wholesalers (for example distributors, importers, or dealers), or independent agents. A company can also export products to its branch or subsidiary that is in charge of managing the distribution channel in the foreign country. In this case, the company has previously done an investment in the foreign market.

Moreover, in the case of direct export, companies can set up collaborative agreements to jointly manage the export process. Cooperative export is particularly suggested when SMEs have to deal with large intermediaries, which request large quantities and varieties of products, which a single company can hardly satisfy. An example of the cooperative exporting process is shown in Figure 7.4.

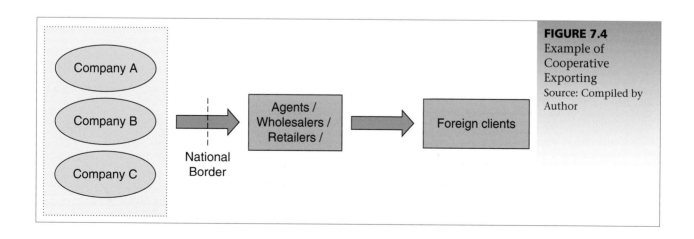

FIGURE 7.4
Example of Cooperative Exporting
Source: Compiled by Author

Direct exporting may be accomplished through the following routes:

- **Negotiating with foreign clients** without any mediation from other domestic entities.

  In this case, the company has direct contact with the foreign market, receives more information and feedback for an eventual product adaptation, directly discusses the contractual terms, and offers an ante and post-sale services. E-commerce and business-to-business are typical examples of direct relations with foreign clients.

- **Implementing own distribution network.**

  This involves organizing a distribution network covering a specific geographic area and target segment. This distribution network may be direct or indirect. In a direct distribution network, the company uses its own sellers, who operate in the foreign country without a fixed structure or through a representative office. In an indirect distribution network, the company entrusts the selling process to an independent agent localized in the foreign market.

- **Relying on intermediaries such as distributors, importers, and dealers.**

  Finally, the company may decide to rely on independent intermediaries operating in the foreign market (Figure 7.5). The choice of the intermediary entrusted with selling in the export market is essential not only for short-term profitability but also for setting up the fundamentals of continuous growth based on the development and strengthening of the producer company's image. The different features of various intermediaries (distributors, importers, and dealers) are described in the Appendix to Chapter 12.

It is possible to point out a few **advantages and disadvantages of the above-mentioned export modes** (Table 7.1). In general, for both direct and indirect export, risk is low, and it is easy to enter or exit a market. In fact, a company faces low operational costs and the investment required is low; thus, it benefits from the resulting high flexibility level. With export, a company can start to gain some information about the foreign market and bypass some restrictions that characterize equity investments (such as joint ventures or foreign subsidiaries). However, the company could lack market control and receive inappropriate feedback from the distributor. Furthermore, the associated export processes, tariffs, and quotas can lead to a significant price escalation, i.e. a significant increase in the price paid by the end consumers[9] and/or a limit on the import quantity. Price escalation can be

FIGURE 7.5
Main Types of
Intermediaries in
Direct Export
Source: Compiled by
Author

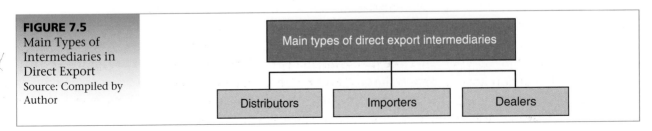

Advantages	TABLE 7.1
Low risk	Advantages and
Easy market entry or exit	Disadvantages of
Low operational costs	Export-Based Modes
Low investment	
Local market knowledge acquisition	
Bypass equity investment-related restrictions	
Disadvantages	
Lack of market control	
Inappropriate feedback from distributor	
Tariffs and quotas	
Transportation costs	
Multiple export intermediaries	
Possible distributor selection and relationship issues	
Source: Compiled by Author	

worsened by high transportation costs and the presence of multiple intermediaries in the export distribution channel.[10] Possible distributor selection and relationship issues are other problems that exporting companies often have to face.

Distributor Selection Process, Channel Management, and Control

As already pointed out, an entrepreneur considering export should research and plan adequately before committing to a distributor. The selection and effective management of distributors is, in fact, extremely critical, especially in countries with a distinctive different business culture, where manufacturers are required to tailor channel governance strategies to fit their distributors' orientations.[11]

When evaluating potential distribution partners, it is important to define contract and relationship development. Distributor selection is a long process, and each phase, from distributor assessment to final review, has to be evaluated carefully. Figure 7.6[12] shows a planning example of a company facing the internationalization process. As pointed out in Figure 7.6, in general the most important attributes to be evaluated during distributor selection are the distribution company's strengths, financial resources, marketing and sales skills, and commitment.

For example, when considering company characteristics and financial resources, it is important to verify the authenticity of the information provided by the potential partner by using reliable sources (for example, companies such as Dun & Bradstreet provide specific products and services for all such information needs) and asking for references from some of its current clients. This is relevant not only from the financial viewpoint but also to verify compatibility between the producer company and the distributors in terms of image, positioning, marketing strategies, and quality and business ethics in general. Furthermore, the existence of facilitating factors such as experience with other exporters and a management culture open to

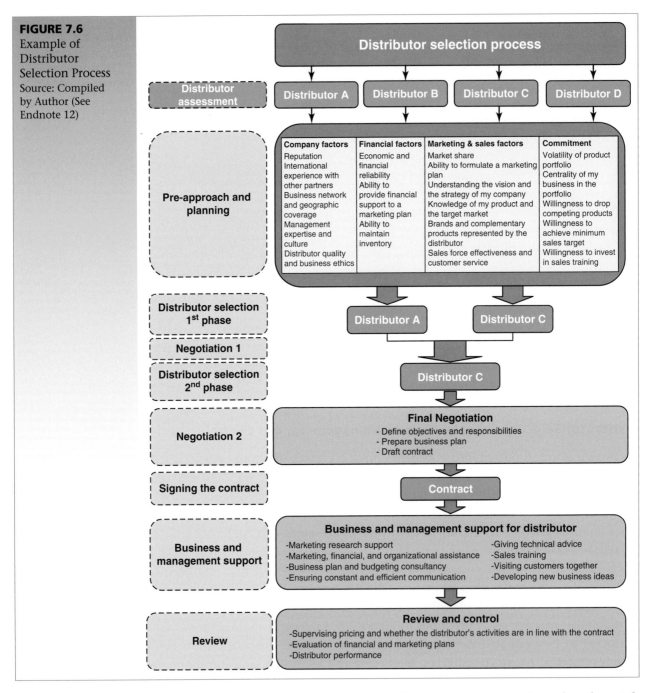

FIGURE 7.6
Example of Distributor Selection Process
Source: Compiled by Author (See Endnote 12)

international collaborations reveals the potential for reducing the cultural, social, and geographic distances between the manufacturer and the foreign distributor.

Marketing and sales factors are particularly relevant when the company must manage not only a product but also a brand image abroad. This is why a manufacturer has to evaluate not only product knowledge and the complementary and competitive products already offered, but also the brands already represented by the foreign channel member. When considering marketing skills, it is very important to evaluate the distributor's market coverage (both the geographical area and market segments) and power within the marketing channel. Marketing skills can be evaluated by checking the distributor's business contacts, capacity to develop promotional activities, selling support, and after-sales services in the local market.

Commitment is extremely relevant when a company wants to develop a long-lasting relationship with a foreign distributor. In fact, the commissions and margins required by the intermediary are not always suitable for maintaining a profitable relationship. The willingness of the distributor to develop a long-term relationship with foreign companies in general can be evaluated examining the volatility of its product portfolio over the past ten years. From the exporting company's standpoint, an indication of the quality of the future relationship can be found in the role (central or marginal) that the distributor assigns to a specific brand and the willingness to drop competing products. Furthermore, an exporting company should evaluate whether the distributor is committed toward achieving a minimum sales target and investing in sales training to support future growth.

It is true that selecting intermediaries is not an easy task because, often, the company has to deal with people from countries that are culturally very different. The selection process is difficult, and it is important to evaluate carefully the costs that the exporting company will incur. The exporting company should not only consider the commissions and margins required by the intermediary, but also all the costs necessary for defining the distribution agreement, supporting promotional expenses, and maintaining the business relationship (for example, travel expenses to visit the distributors). Experience and the use of a method are useful in all of these evaluations for minimizing the risk of failure. An important starting point in the process is a distribution agreement with clear rules covering the following points:

- business and geographical areas
- target segments
- international clients
- products and the use of trademarks
- distribution channels
- advertising and promotion
- pricing and terms of payment
- minimum volumes, orders, and supply conditions
- length and termination of agreement.

Relationship management becomes especially crucial when it is necessary to control product/brand positioning and performance in the foreign market. For this reason, companies are willing to control their distributors by trying to obtain maximum commitment from them, transferring, in lieu, all the knowledge necessary to sell their products. Therefore, it is necessary to guarantee exclusivity whenever possible and to provide information technology, financial, and marketing support. Strengthening the company's liaison with the intermediary generates positive results not only in terms of greater sales but also in terms of higher levels of trust, both of which are fundamental for ensuring a sound relationship and better distribution performance in the long term.[13] This is the case of Diageo's relationship with its distributors worldwide: by using innovative online learning programs, the company is supporting distributors and their sales personnel worldwide. Moreover, Diageo can possibly control the global and individual performance of its international distribution system (Box 7.1 and Geo Map 7.1).

Successful channel management practices should be based on four dimensions:[14]

1. **Performance management**, which identifies those activities that are finalized to improve operating performance through the definition of roles, responsibilities, and measurable performance goals.

2. **Coverage management**, which focuses on channel structure efficiency and its coordination with the target market.

3. **Capability-building programs**, which include all activities that facilitate the channel members' operations. For example, the manufacturer provides marketing and sales support such as promotional material written in the local

---

Box 7.1   Company-in-Focus: Diageo

Growing with International Distributors: The Diageo Experience

Diageo, the world's leading premium alcoholic drinks company, with an outstanding portfolio of brands such as Johnnie Walker, Crown Royal, J&B, Windsor, and many others across spirits, beer, and wine, constantly invests in foreign markets. They recently acquired Mey İçki, the leading spirits company in Turkey; Meta Abo, the second largest brewery in Ethiopia; Ypióca, the leader in the premium cachaça segment in Brazil. In addition, they have invested in Shui Jing Fang, a premium local spirit company in China; Halico, the leading branded spirit company in Vietnam; and in India they have developed a sales promotion agreement with United Spirits Limited, the leading spirits company in the country. Nevertheless, while in some foreign countries Diageo owns and directly controls the market and the distribution channels, in others it operates through third-party distributors. It is especially in the second case that the collaboration with a foreign distributor is crucial. The "Diageo Way of Selling" and the "Platform for Growth" are both examples of programs developed by Diageo not only for their own sales network but also especially to strengthen relationships with its sales people and distribution partners. Training them to become the best sales force in the industry provides mutual benefit to the company and the distributors in terms of increased product category profitability, stronger partnership, and an outstanding education in sales and marketing. As pointed out by Nick Blazquez, President Diageo Africa, Eurasia and Pacific, every month 3500 sales people visit the online learning tool "Diageo Way of Selling" "[…] because it is very valuable, it helps them assess where their capabilities are, identify gaps, work to improve capabilities. Beyond assessing an individual's capability […] we've got tools that allow us to assess the standard of excellence in each market from a total sales perspective." Similarly, the Platform for Growth helps Diageo to assess its distributors and work with them to improve their capabilities.

Sources: http://www.diageo.com/en-us/ourbusiness/aboutus/Pages/our-strategy.aspx; http://www.diageo.com/en-us/ourbusiness/aboutus/pages/default.aspx; http://www.google.com/url?url=http://www.diageo.com/Lists/Resources/Attachments/1596/Building%2520and%2520extending%2520route%2520to%2520consumer_transcript.pdf&rct=j&frm=1&q=&esrc=s&sa=U&ei=cqHyU6TrIqW1iwLhiYCgCQ&ved=0CBQQFjAA&usg=AFQjCNGcOui_6GlHrXsBjzsGtQC4NopB3Q [All accessed: July 10, 2014].

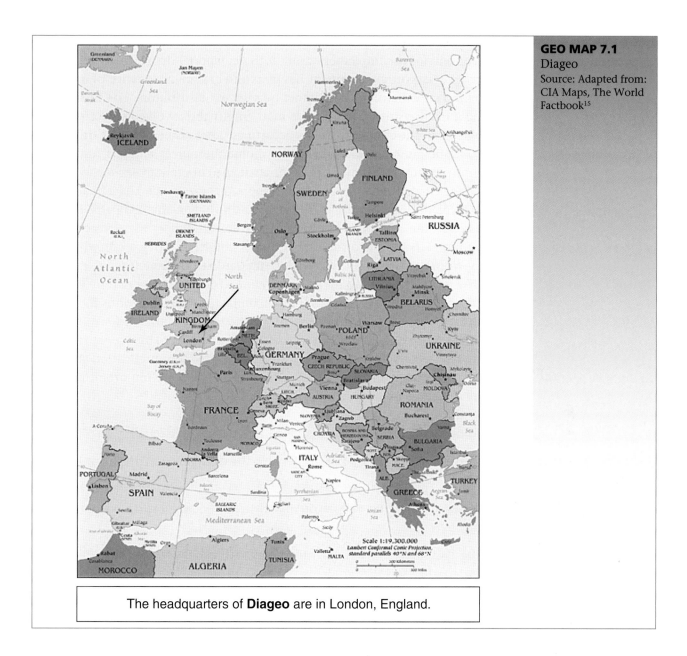

GEO MAP 7.1
Diageo
Source: Adapted from:
CIA Maps, The World
Factbook[15]

The headquarters of **Diageo** are in London, England.

language. In addition, the manufacturer can train the partner's sales personnel, visit clients together, develop business planning, and offer technology support to enhance the efficiency and efficacy of partners' activities.

4. **Motivational programs**: Partners' motivation can be increased not only through monetary benefits (for example, higher commissions) but also by maintaining transparent relationships and providing frequent updates on products, market, and company developments, and inviting partners to visit the company headquarters regularly to share common values that can motivate them to achieve channel goals in foreign markets.[16]

It is important to underline that an efficient internal organizational structure is a prerequisite for the implementation of these channel management programs. In recent years, export management has grown to cover a wide range of activities, including a comprehensive consultancy service for distributors. For this reason, managing a relationship with a middleman entails the involvement of not only the employees in the company's sales department, but also employees in the production, logistics, information technology, human resources, finance, and service departments. Their actions must be coordinated and coherent to ensure good functioning of the channel relationship and to support the export manager's activities.

To monitor the functioning of the relationship when the company manages global clients, the role of centralized key account managers is necessary for providing homogeneous treatment in different countries. They are fundamental, especially, from the viewpoint of ensuring standardized treatment of international clients. The relationship's success and, therefore, its duration are mainly linked to the ability of intermediaries to satisfy the manufacturer's expectations in terms of performance and achievement of the goals defined in the contract.

A central role in the relationship with distributors is played by export customer service as well, which guarantees constant and effective communication and operational activity with distributors and sales people. The most important activities they carry out are as follows:

- providing assistance to export managers and the sales director;

- organizing visits by international clients to the company and preparing business reports;

- placing and managing export orders with all the supporting documents for shipments;

- offering customer service and interfacing with other internal departments, if needed, to solve specific problems.

A difficult aspect of any relationship with an international agent or distributor is performance evaluation. One of the reasons for this stems from the necessary vagueness of the distributorship contract itself. In a dynamic relationship such as the one between manufacturer and distributor, it is impossible to craft an all-encompassing contract that takes into account all possible situations that may arise in the course of the relationship. Therefore, it is difficult to ascertain when the conditions of the contract have not been followed (indicating poor performance). The physical distance separating the manufacturer and the agent, as well as cross-cultural communication that often characterizes such relationships, complicate the evaluation process even further. Thus, two specific methods for controlling distributor relationships have emerged:

1. Control-based: This method gives precedence to costs, and it is control-based. It is exercised by influencing decisions of foreign distributors to

avoid opportunistic behaviors, as well as by obtaining information about their actions.

2. Norm-based: This second method emphasizes the establishment of common values such as trust, commitment, and flexibility, and it is norm-based.

Both of these governance methods have been found to influence the performance of foreign-market agents and distributors. Nevertheless, norm-based governance, where manufacturers showed support and involvement toward their distributors, had double the impact, raising both the distributors' market performance and the manufacturers' satisfaction with the relationship. The positive effect of norm-based governance was even more pronounced in unstable markets with high levels of uncertainty.[17]

However, despite the efforts undertaken by the manufacturer and the intermediary to successfully manage the relationship, distribution agreements are often terminated. A study of the relationship process identified two main triggers for the initiation of legal termination proceedings:

1. proactive terminations

2. reactive terminations.

Proactive terminations occur when internal decisions prompt the manufacturer to want out of the distribution agreement. Examples of such changes include change of ownership, the need to integrate channels for establishing sales subsidiaries in the foreign country, or the decision to form relationships with more appropriate distributors. Reactive termination is initiated when either party finds the other to be uncooperative or opportunistic. Recent legal cases involving distribution agreement termination include, among others, examples of distributors caught selling counterfeit products or giving some dealers more favorable price concessions.[18]

INTERMEDIATE ENTRY MODES

In culturally distant markets with high entry barriers, going with the export-based model may limit the company's long-term growth. With export, control is a critical variable, and because an intermediary always filters the company's direct contact with the foreign market, it is difficult for the company to strengthen and/or expand its own presence.

Companies may rely on a local partner to secure their presence in the foreign market. Ownership and control can be shared between the company and the local partner; the risk is indeed shared between partners. Hence, the partners benefit from their respective strengths, while counterbalancing their individual weaknesses.

This type of agreement may be of the following types:

Contract-based: contract-based modes are ***non-equity agreements,*** such that there is no investment in risky capital. These include the following different alternatives:

- International Licensing

- International Franchising

- Piggyback

- Contract Manufacturing or Outsourcing

- Assembly Contract and OEM—Original Equipment Manufacturing

- Management Contract

- Turnkey Contract

- Strategic Alliances.

Equity-based: In equity-based agreements, an organized entity is set up, with its social capital shared between partners. These agreements are a form of Foreign Direct Investment (FDI), and they include minority joint ventures, 50/50 joint ventures, and majority joint ventures.

The choice between equity and non-equity agreements depends mainly on the firm's objectives in a given foreign market.

INTERMEDIATE MODES WITH CONTRACT-BASED AGREEMENTS

International Licensing

International licensing is the process of transferring the rights of a firm's products to a foreign company for the purpose of producing or selling. For a set royalty fee, the licensor allows the licensee to use its technology, trademarks, patents, characters, and other intellectual property in order to gain presence in the markets covered by the licensee.

Licensing is an attractive mode of entry for many entrepreneurial firms because, like exporting, it involves smaller upfront expenditures and risks. Because most of the costs of developing the licensed products have already been recovered, the royalties received often translate into direct profits for the licensor.[19]

In some cases, the company's core-products are licensed, and the technology directly necessary for producing the product is provided, often at lower costs and, if necessary, the product is adapted to local demands. However, companies do adopt strategies that allow the reduction of potential drawbacks associated with sharing their intellectual property. For example, the technology licensed is often not the most recent. This choice is justified also by the fact that in some countries, especially emerging ones, the most advanced technology available is often not suitable in the broader local technological context, from the production perspective, as well as from the after-sale services or consumer use perspectives.

In other cases, if the innovative technology is required for manufacturing only part of the product, this part is directly assembled in the final product as produced by the licensee, without requiring the licensor to transfer the related knowledge.

The international expansion of famous brands has often been based on the use of licensing contracts. Famous companies such as Benetton use licensing to expand internationally with products often not included in their core business. In the 2008 Olympic Games in China, Benetton (Geo Map 7.2) launched a perfume with Selective Beauty, a Chinese licensee. The licensee suggested that the product

GEO MAP 7.2
Benetton
Source: Adapted from: CIA Maps, The World Factbook[20]

The headquarters of **Benetton** are in Treviso, Italy.

be named *Energy Games Man* and *Energy Games Woman*, using Benetton's well-known brands Energy Man and Energy Woman. Meanwhile, the licensee adapted the product for the Chinese consumer, who prefers rather fruity and delicate perfumes, while disliking strong perfumes. In addition, the licensee used the yellow and red colors of the Chinese flag on the bottle. In this way, thanks to the Chinese partner, Benetton managed to sell its perfume in the Chinese market, while ensuring that it caters to the demands of consumers who have known its brand only for a few years.

Finally, brands are often associated with well-known people or movie characters, who are employed for launching new products or collections in different industries. For example, the character of Harry Potter has been highly profitable thanks to licensing agreements such as the successful one with the Danish company Lego.

Naturally, licensing has its own pros and cons[21] (Table 7.2).

A first advantage is that the licensor gains profit from royalties without requiring any start-up investment and eludes eventual barriers determined by regulations and tariffs. This makes international licensing particularly attractive for small and medium companies that want to grow abroad quickly by obtaining an adequate financial return without incurring high risks. The licensee indeed invests in the business, withstanding most risks when the right to use the brand is signed away or technology is transferred. Another advantage is the possibility to entrust the business to a partner that already knows the features of the local markets and has already set up its own distribution net. This means eventual adaptation of products since their earliest productive phase. Finally, if a fully developed technology is transferred, the company has the opportunity to lengthen the technology's life cycle, as well as the profitability of a product already obsolescent in the domestic market.

TABLE 7.2 International Licensing: Advantages and Disadvantages for Licensor	**Advantages**
	Royalties
	Bypassing regulations and tariffs
	Limited investment in the foreign market
	Fast market access
	Risk is mainly taken by the licensee
	Licensor can gain local market knowledge from the licensee
	Licensor can use the licensee's distribution network
	Licensee can suggest marketing adaptations for the local market
	Licensor can profit from a mature technology
	Disadvantages
	Licensee acquires technological and marketing skills from the licensor and can become a future competitor
	Intellectual property concerns
	Licensee is an independent entrepreneur: risk of limited control over market and revenues for the licensor
	Brand image not homogeneous across countries
	Source: Compiled by Author (See Endnote 22)

In addition to the previously-mentioned advantages, however, there are different risks that the firm should be aware of.[22] First, when the licensing contract is near expiry, the licensee may have obtained the skills and technological capabilities to possibly be a strong competitor to the licensor. Many companies from emerging countries, currently operating successfully in European markets as well, have acquired technological and marketing competitiveness through past licensing contracts with foreign companies. Consequently, guarding own intellectual property rights becomes a critical concern for the licensor.

Another risk is the extent of licensor control. Even if a licensing contract binds the partners to a close collaboration, the foreign partner remains an independent company with strong autonomy, and the licensor's control can be weak. Besides, the collaboration is mainly developed on the distribution and marketing aspects, hence jeopardizing the image positioning of the licensing company and the coherence of its marketing strategies developed in different foreign contexts. There is indeed a strong risk of losing control of the final market or, in any case, of not developing the full potential of its own brand, in terms of profitability or customer value.

Considering the disadvantages, this form of market entry is often appropriate for countries that impose imports barriers such as high tariffs and profit repatriation restrictions, and for mature products with relatively standardized production.[23]

International Franchising

Under international franchising, the company (franchisor) enters a foreign market by giving to a foreign independent company (franchisee) the right to operate its business. In comparison with licensing, international franchising gives the franchisor greater control over the franchisee licensing, the franchisor company's trademarks, products and/or services, and production and/or operation processes. Control is exerted through the franchise fee, which can be expropriated if contracts are not adhered to, and by elaborating contracts that govern the relationship between the franchisor and the franchisees. On the flip side, the franchisor is also required to provide more materials, training, and other forms of support to the franchisee. A well-functioning franchise provides a win-win arrangement for both parties: the franchisor gets to expand into new markets with little or no risk and investment, while the franchisee gets a proven brand, marketing exposure, an established client base, and management expertise to help it succeed. While franchising has been the domain of mostly large, multinational corporations (MNCs) such as McDonald's, Dunkin' Donuts, and Holiday Inn, international franchising is opening unprecedented opportunities for smaller companies to enter new markets and compete successfully, as well as for companies operating in global niches such as Hard Rock Café (Figure 7.7).

Moreover, international franchising can support the production systems of global companies. For example, a strong global franchise system based on contractual agreements with multiple local bottling partners has always been the competitive advantage of Coca-Cola's business (Figure 7.8). With more than 1.8 billion

FIGURE 7.7
Hard Rock Café in Amsterdam (The Netherlands) and Denver (US): More Than 140 Franchising Stores Worldwide
Source: © Author (Both Images)

FIGURE 7.8
World of Coca-Cola in Atlanta (Georgia, US)
Source: © Greta Zaia

servings a day, Coca-Cola is the world's largest beverage company, producing and distributing via local franchisees in more than 200 countries.[24]

Although franchising in most developed countries of North America and Europe has reached a saturation point, many emerging markets are experiencing phenomenal growth in international franchising.[25] To succeed in developing countries, an entrepreneur contemplating this mode of market entry should consider several important environmental factors, such as the rate of economic development and growth of the target country and its market governance policies before starting to look for potential franchisees there.

In China, for example, franchising is an innovative business because it has only been authorized since 2004. Further, until 2007, the franchisor was required to manage at least two stores in China for at least two years before being allowed to set up a distributional net. Today, these norms have been simplified, but Chinese regulations are in constant evolution.[26] Though China has made significant progress in improving the environment for franchising, these continuous changes deter the managements of foreign companies, who are concerned about any changes in their legal rights and about the need to constantly update themselves on said changes.[27]

International franchising can be direct or indirect (Figure 7.9).

In direct franchising, the franchisor is in direct contact with the franchisees in the foreign market. The franchisor may follow the signing of the contract and the management of the franchising network either directly from the domestic market (model A) or through a branch or local subsidiary based in the target foreign market (model B). In the latter case, franchising development is introduced by a direct investment, such as a local branch or a local subsidiary, owned directly by the franchisor. The indirect franchising (model C) is the most popular: the foreign partner invests its own capital and undertakes, along with the franchisor, the responsibility of managing the franchising network. In most cases, the franchisor operates by setting up a strategic alliance (contractual joint venture) or an equity-based joint venture.

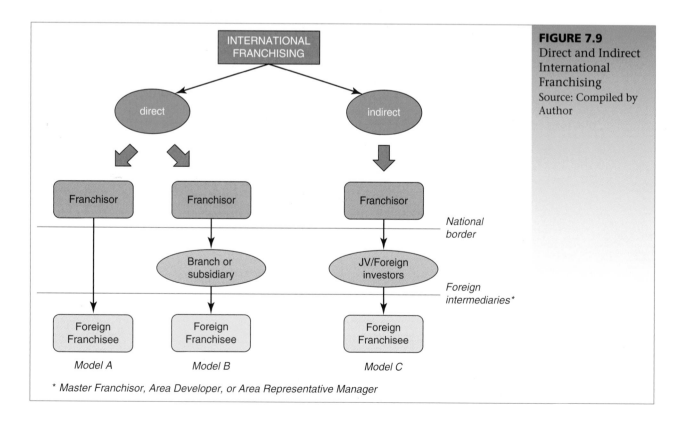

FIGURE 7.9
Direct and Indirect International Franchising
Source: Compiled by Author

As shown in Figure 7.9, in cases where there are numerous franchisees or in situations where the management of the company (regardless of the place in which it operates; from the domestic country, via branch or foreign subsidiary, or indirectly with a joint venture) is particularly complex, third operating parties may be involved, e.g. Master Franchisor, Area Developer, or Area Representative Manager.

Master franchising is a business model in which the company allows a third party (the Master Franchisor) the right to use its know-how with the aim of extending its own business in a specific geographic area by signing franchising contracts with other partners (franchisees) (Figure 7.10). In other words, the Master Franchisor is an intermediary between the company and the affiliated partners, and it acts to foster and ease communication, management, and control. Further, the Master Franchisor directly manages one or more local sales units with the aim of extending its knowledge of the local business.

The area developer agreement gives a third party, the Area Developer (AD), the right to open and develop, in a specific geographic area and under the property of the AD, a certain number of franchising stores (Figure 7.11). This opening must be done within the period specified by the contract, otherwise exclusiveness rights

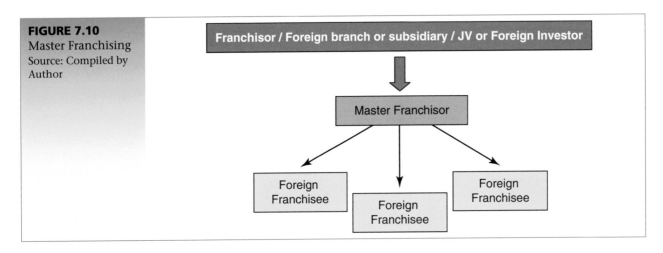

FIGURE 7.10
Master Franchising
Source: Compiled by Author

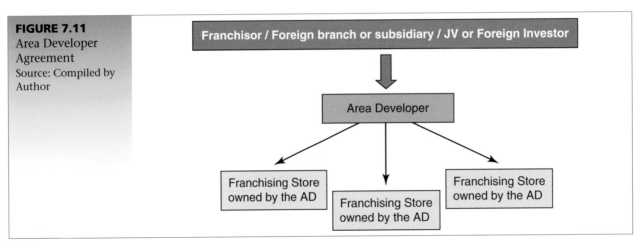

FIGURE 7.11
Area Developer Agreement
Source: Compiled by Author

of franchising in that particular area may be revoked. The AD may further foster network development, but it cannot sign new contracts with independent franchisees, which are managed directly by the franchisor company.

The Area Representative Manager is instead used by companies to offer assistance, services, selection, and training of the stores' staff, as well as to offer supporting services to the franchisees in a specific geographic area. Furthermore, the Area Representative Manager fosters the development of the franchising network, albeit without the option to sign new contracts; this right is again managed by the franchisor company (Figure 7.12).

Internationalizing via franchising has its own advantages, but it presents various challenges as well (Table 7.3).

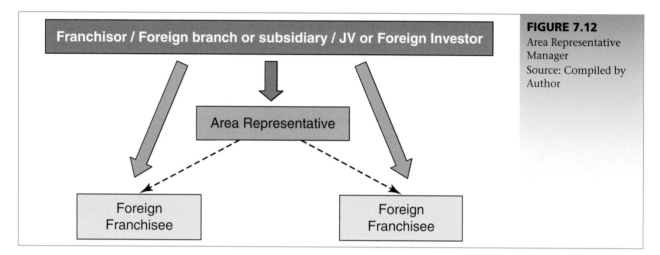

FIGURE 7.12
Area Representative Manager
Source: Compiled by Author

Advantages

Royalties
Relatively quick development of a store chain
Risk is mainly borne by the franchisee
Investment is mainly made by the franchisee
Greater control than the export modes
Rapid increase in brand awareness within the country and in different foreign countries
Franchisor can gain local market knowledge from the franchisee
Franchisee can suggest marketing adaptations for the local market
Economies of scale in production

Disadvantages

In some countries, the legal system is not stable
Identification of a good franchisee is often not easy and time-consuming
Reliability of the relationships with franchisees/potential franchisees
High investments to identify the best adaptation of the franchising format in each foreign country
Limited control over market and revenues

Source: Compiled by Author

TABLE 7.3
International Franchising: Advantages and Disadvantages for Franchisor

The most significant advantage is, beyond royalties, the possibility of developing a widespread network of stores within a relatively short time when compared with the development of mono-brand stores managed directly by the company. Moreover, the franchisor's investment outlay and exposure to risk are limited. Hence, the company may quickly expand the prominence of its brand and, in general, of its own products, while ensuring homogeneous image positioning not only in the domestic but also in international markets, where the franchisor can maintain good control of its brand image, especially when compared with the export modes. Meanwhile, the franchisor may obtain extensive market knowledge and define, if necessary, a strategy tuned to the foreign market, thanks to local partners. These local partners are indeed in the position to satisfy their own local market, while respecting the standards specified in the franchising contract. Finally, the franchisor is able to achieve significant economies of scale by correctly planning production because this directly depends on the number of the franchised stores. The franchisor can indeed determine the quantities that will be purchased by the various franchisees and increase or decrease production accordingly.

Despite these positive aspects, entrepreneurs may be hindered by several problems. As already illustrated, in some foreign markets, such as China, legislation evolves continually. Beyond this, there are other drawbacks to consider. Although it is possible to quickly create a distribution network with franchising, the process of selecting suitable franchisees may be extremely time-consuming. Partner selection is extremely important in international franchising.[28] Especially, in culturally distant countries, it is not easy to contact reliable foreign entrepreneurs, communicate with them easily, and find the right person for management of the company's products and, generally, brands. It is indeed a very lengthy process. Another aspect to consider is valuing the investment correctly. If the franchisor can stipulate contracts with different franchisees investing their own capital, the most apt store format for a given foreign market may not be known at the very beginning. Hence, the franchisor company must first define the format, catalogue, and layout, and evaluate eventual adaptations before entrusting the business to an independent foreign franchisee. Franchising development is often introduced by significant investments in the management of a few DOS (Directly Owned Stores), using which the franchisor may enhance its experience and obtain information on the financial performance of the franchising entity. The franchising entity may indeed be monitored with objective key performance indicators, thus balancing, at least partially, the lack of control over these independent franchisees.

Piggyback

"Piggyback" refers to being carried by someone. This kind of agreement stipulates that the company (rider) gets international by inserting its own products in the product portfolio, and, consequently, in the distribution system of another company (carrier), that sells complementary products in the foreign market.[29]

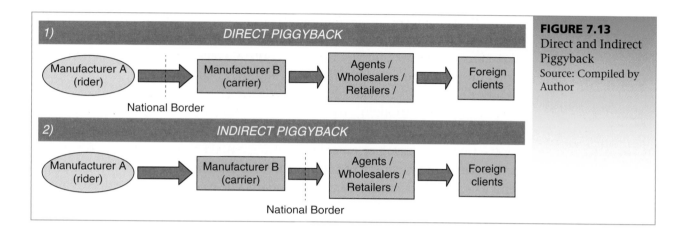

FIGURE 7.13
Direct and Indirect
Piggyback
Source: Compiled by
Author

The carrier may be localized in the export market (direct piggyback) or in the domestic market (indirect piggyback) (Figure 7.13).

As an example of *direct piggyback*, a Spanish company producing women's gloves with a well-known brand has, for instance, signed a piggyback agreement with a French company to sell in the Russian market. The French company exports clothing products to Russia, and it is investing on the development of its own distribution network. There are various advantages for both companies:

- The rider (the Spanish company producing gloves) is entering an already developed foreign distribution network; further, it can ensure coherent image of its own products with the carrier's complementary products, thus enhancing its control on the price positioning and image of its own brand.

- The carrier (the French company producing clothing) extends its own products catalogue by adding to it the rider company's products and, in the process, enhances its own market share in Russia. Further, it is able to extend its own market power within the distribution network; the carrier can now present an extensive and complete catalogue within its own market segment and, consequently, it is more powerful in its negotiations with Russian buyers.

In some cases, *indirect piggyback* may be realized between companies from the same country. For instance, an Italian company producing Parma ham in Italy and selling it in different foreign markets becomes the carrier for another Italian company (rider) producing Parmesan cheese, which is able to penetrate foreign markets through the carrier's catalogue, while maintaining its own brand. In this case, though, the rider does not develop any form of international culture because this is a simple business-to-business sale to a company from its own country.

Piggyback is an interesting choice for small and medium-sized companies operating within high-quality product niches. Even though the limited size of companies is a barrier to a foreign investment, in terms of both financial and human resources, these companies have to control their image and enhance their competitiveness on the international level. This aim is hardly achievable through exporting or through other contract-based modes but is possible by piggybacking. Further, piggyback allows for maintaining distinction and control over the distribution channel in which the product is inserted.

Contract Manufacturing (Outsourcing)

Contract manufacturing or outsourcing has garnered much attention recently for its economic and business benefits, as well as for its controversial but inherent trend to move production jobs across borders. The growing popularity of contract manufacturing is ascribed to the large savings it can generate in the financial and human resources areas of a business.

The arrangement of using cheaper overseas labor for the production of finished goods or parts by following an established production process is called contract manufacturing or outsourcing. Companies using this mode of entry benefit not only from lowering their production costs, but also by gaining entry to a new market with small amounts of capital and no ownership hassles. The company outsourcing production (contractor) maintains control over the marketing and distribution channels, but faces relevant risks from the standpoints of quality and productive context.[30] In fact, one of the drawbacks of using outsourcing methods is the loss of control over the manufacturing process and the working conditions in the facilities, which can potentially lead to lower quality of goods and/or human rights abuses and, consequently, result in bad publicity and financial damages to the company's brand. Nike and several other high-profile American firms have served as unintentional examples of this undesirable scenario.[31] A key element of such a contract is indeed the choice of the supplier, which must offer not only quality, on-time supply, and financial solidity, but work as well with exclusive supplying such that competitors do not benefit from the know-how transferred previously to the supplier.[32] In recent years, multiple firms from emerging markets such as China and India have helped SMEs lower their costs by sourcing products, manufacturing, and services abroad. While India is reported to be the leading recipient of outsourcing contracts, SME outsourcing is not limited to developing countries.

Assembly Contract and OEM (Original Equipment Manufacturing)

In the assembly contract format, the company sends abroad product components for transformation or assembly. The finished products are sent back for selling.

In the original equipment manufacturing (OEM) format, the company buys the "original product" from a foreign partner to then finish and resell it as its own, hence appearing as the official producer in the market. Babei Group Co., a large Chinese producer operating in the Hangzhou silk district, has various OEM contracts with Italian clothing producers, who buy the products of the Chinese company and brand them as their own. The Chinese company benefits not only from increased production, but also from the chance to work with large international companies, and learning by collaborating.

Management contract

A mode of entry into new markets that is most widely used in the hotel and airline industries is management contract. Under a management contract, a company in one country can utilize the expertise, technology, or specialized services of a company from another country to run its business for a set time and fee or percentage of sales.

For example, many owners of hotel buildings contract with well-known hotel management firms such as the Ritz-Carlton Hotel Company, LLC, Accor, Mariott, and Hilton to develop and manage their own properties. While the management company is responsible for day-to-day operations, it cannot decide on ownership, financial, strategic, or policy issues pertaining to the business. Such an arrangement is suitable for companies that are interested in earning extra revenues abroad without getting entangled in long-term financial or legal obligations in the foreign market.

For instance Parkson Corporation, one of the most important Malaysian fashion/design retailers, has grown in the Chinese market by setting up a management contract with a Chinese retailer. Parkson started managing the stores by replacing the previous trademark with its own brand and presenting itself in the Chinese market with a catalogue comprising modern, medium- to high quality, local and global products. Following this approach, the company has gained a distribution network of 46 stores spread across 30 cities in China.[33]

As determined by management contract, the proprietor of the outlet (or outlet chain) entrusts its management to a foreign company with extensive commercial and managerial experience, tested technology, and adequate human resources. The aim is to maximize revenues and profits from the activity. Practically, the foreign company manages the productive/commercial activity set up and financed by the local investor previously. Hence, the main advantage to the foreign company is that its capabilities and brand are put into practice without it having to incur massive investment in the form of start-up capital, as well as not having to deal with administrative matters such as permits and authorization. However, the foreign company has no guarantee of existing in the long-term, since the owners may, at the end of the contract, choose to retain the management of the business.[34]

On expiry, a management contract may be renewed, but the foreign company managing the business may indeed avail its option to buy back the business entity. The risk of such an investment is inferior since the foreign company, after a few years of management contract, would have had the chance to evaluate the business' profitability and eventual growth opportunities. If the business entity is well managed, the local partner may consider taking over the management directly, but such an event is rare.[35]

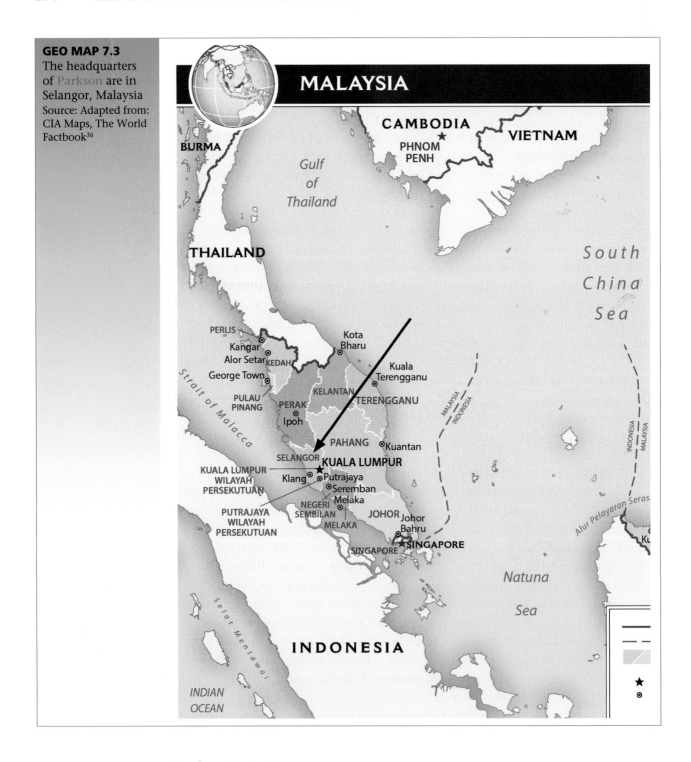

GEO MAP 7.3
The headquarters of Parkson are in Selangor, Malaysia
Source: Adapted from: CIA Maps, The World Factbook[36]

Turnkey Contract

Another contractual entry mode to a new market is participation in a turnkey project. Turnkey operations typically involve the design, construction, and equipment of a large facility, and, often, the initial personnel training, by a foreign company (exporter), which then turns over the key to the ready-to-run facility to the purchaser (importer).

Often the domain of the largest specialized construction and manufacturing companies, turnkey operations projects are usually contracted out by governments for enormous developments such as dams, oil refineries, airports, energy plants, etc. Nevertheless, opportunities exist for the participation of smaller entrepreneurial firms as subcontractors.[37]

Turnkey projects can be self-engineered versus construction to specification. In the first case, the importer sets the performance requirements, while the exporter defines the equipment and plant design. In the second case, the importer sets all the specifications, and the exporter constructs accordingly. Obviously, in the first case the risk of performance failure rests with the exporter, while in the second situation, the importer bears the risk.[38]

Because of their extraordinary size and scope, many such projects require long-term commitments in terms of personnel, financial reserves, supplies, and other resources. Before a small company decides to participate in turnkey operations, it should carefully examine whether it is ready to absorb the long-term currency exchange fluctuations; extended drain on its resources; and other high political, economic, and financial risks that are likely to crop up in such complex undertakings.

Strategic Alliances (Contractual Joint Ventures)

As part of the larger category of international business alliances, a strategic alliance is a formal, contractual relationship between two or more firms that share resources to pursue a common goal. In short, these are non-equity agreements in which partners to the alliance share some strategic assets such as technology, trademarks, or other assets to create synergies or gain access to resources that one or both firms do not possess. For these reasons, strategic alliances are also defined as contractual joint ventures. They can reach the same goals of an equity joint venture[39] but differently from equity joint ventures, a strategic alliance or contractual joint venture does not create a new company. An example of a strategic alliance in the ICT industry, between Fujitsu and Cisco, is reported in Box 7.2.

What makes an alliance "strategic"? According to the Director of Operations of Global Alliances at Hewlett Packard Company in California, five criteria determine whether an alliance is strategic:[40]

1. It is critical to a core business goal or objective.

2. It is critical to the achievement of a competitive advantage.

3. It is necessary to preempt competition.

4. It can be vital for future strategic options of the company.

5. It can help manage risks that threaten strategic objectives.

> **Box 7.2   Technology-in-Focus: Fujitsu and Cisco**
>
> **Fujitsu and Cisco Expand Strategic Alliance to Deliver Unified Communications Solutions in Japan**
>
> Fujitsu and Cisco have expanded their strategic alliance to deliver Unified Communications Services (UCS) in the Japanese market. This expansion of Fujitsu and Cisco's strategic alliance combines Cisco's industry-leading advanced unified communications technology and proven global experience with Fujitsu's Information and Communications Technology (ICT) product development capabilities. UCS is a new cloud-based service that delivers a communications system environment over the Internet from Fujitsu's datacenters, thus reducing operational burdens for customers and improving the efficiency of customers' business processes by accelerating decision-making. The solution allows customers to use servers that manage contact status such as being online, in a meeting, or absent; furthermore, it improves IP telephony and enables efficient and smooth office communications by integrating customers' landlines, mobile terminals, video/web conferencing equipment, e-mail, and voicemail facilities. The service is based on Cisco products and incorporates Fujitsu's product development and service delivery know-how.
>
> Based in Tokyo, Fujitsu is the world's fourth-largest IT services provider and no. 1 in Japan; it is among the world's top five server providers. Founded in 1935, Fujitsu has approximately 162,000 employees supporting customers in about 100 countries. Its turnover in FY2014 was $46 billion. The company combines a worldwide corps of systems and services experts with highly reliable computing and communications products and advanced microelectronics to deliver added value to customers.
>
> Headquartered in San José (CA), Cisco was founded in 1984. Cisco delivers intelligent networks and technology architectures built on integrated products, services, and software platforms. Currently, Cisco employs about 75,000 people, and it generated revenues of $48.6 billion in FY2013.
>
> Sources: Adapted from: Cisco at a Glance, https://drive.google.com/file/d/0B8CFjUqFSnkGcTVtLWcxMWFFeVE/preview?pli=1, [Accessed: August 8, 2014]; Fujitsu at a Glance, http://www.fujitsu.com/global/about/corporate/info/index.html, [Accessed: August 8, 2014]; 'Fujitsu unveils unified communications service', October 18, 2010, http://dcseurope.info/news_full.php?id=15954#axzz3AkwGoFXO [Accessed: July 16, 2014]; Cisco press release, April 19, 2009.

Despite the risk factors associated with strategic alliances, this mode of entry into foreign markets has its **advantages**. For example, strategic alliances have the potential to lower transaction costs, hedge against strategic uncertainties, acquire needed resources, allow firms to evade international entry barriers, protect a firm's home market from international competition, broaden a firm's product line, enter new product markets, and enhance resource usage efficiency. Firms utilizing strategic alliances could enhance their firm-specific resources (physical assets, intangible property, patents and trademarks, human resources, and complementary resources), technical capabilities (R&D, manufacturing, marketing, sales, and market knowledge), and managerial competencies (management skills and abilities, and value-added activities).

The advantages gained by using international strategic alliances depend on the type of industry and the way in which an alliance is structured. For example, some researchers contend that firms in a mature industry are more likely to benefit from strategic alliances, whereas others propose that technology-based alliances tend to benefit high-tech industries more than traditional industries.

Strategic alliances can face many difficulties related to managing a business jointly. Many different frameworks have been developed for the proper formation and execution of an international business alliance, including conducting SWOT, goal compatibility, and value-added analyses of the participating firms, and/or examining their market power, efficiency, and competencies. Nevertheless, similar to international joint ventures, which will be introduced in the following paragraph, the most vital issues for a successful international strategic business alliance are selecting the right partner, developing trust, and developing the appropriate contractual framework.

INTERMEDIATE MODES—EQUITY-BASED AGREEMENTS

International Joint Ventures

International joint ventures (IJVs) have been one of the most popular methods for entering international markets. Equity-based IJVs are a form of foreign direct investment (FDI) when two or more companies agree to share ownership of a third commercial entity and collaborate in the production of its goods or services to pursue a common goal. Differently from strategic alliances (contractual JVs), where the operations in the foreign market are based on a contract, in international equity JVs two or more parent companies (Company A and B) create a third new company (Company C, "the child") in the foreign market of entry (Figure 7.14). The result for the company that enters a foreign

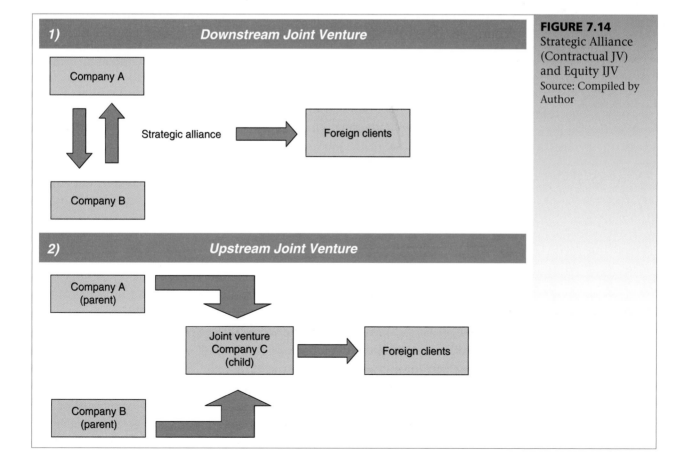

FIGURE 7.14
Strategic Alliance (Contractual JV) and Equity IJV
Source: Compiled by Author

market can be a minority joint venture (less than 50 percent of the shares), a 50/50 joint venture, or a majority joint venture (more than 50 percent of the shares).

IJVs are attractive to businesses because of their shared risk, shared knowledge and expertise, and the potential for synergy and competitive advantage in the global marketplace. International joint ventures are formed for different reasons, such as to continue the expansion of an existing business, introduce the company's products to new markets, introduce foreign products to the company's existing markets, and branch out into new business. For entrepreneurs, joint ventures are a fitting way of entering into new markets, sometimes with limited international business experience, and for entering some specific countries where a local partner with an in-depth knowledge of the market and distribution is needed.

IJVs can also take many different forms:

- Two or more companies from the same country form an alliance to enter another country.

- An overseas company joins a local company to enter the local company's domestic market.

- Firms from two or more countries band together in a JV formed in a third country.

- A foreign private business and a government agree to join forces to pursue mutual interests.

- A foreign private firm enters into a JV with a government-owned firm to enter into a third national market.

As pointed out below, a JV can be described considering the sectors of operation of the partner companies and the activities of the value chain involved in the equity agreement.

Vertical or Horizontal JV

In a vertical JV, firms from different sectors cooperate. For example, Generali China Insurance Co., Ltd is a Chinese JV company between China National Petroleum Corporation (CNPC) and the Italian insurance company Generali Group.

In a horizontal JV, firms are from the same sector. For example, the JV between China's second largest grocery retailer by value CRE (China Resources Enterprise), which owns 80 percent, and the UK's grocery retailer Tesco, with 20 percent, has the common goal to enlarge their retail presence in China, both in traditional and online retail.[41]

Downstream and Upstream JV

A downstream JV occurs when two or more partners form a company (the JV) to produce a final or intermediate product, or to integrate wholesale and retail activities. An upstream JV is formed when two or more partners establish the JV to manage upstream activities. In Figure 7.15, two cases showing a downstream and an upstream JV have been exemplified.

An example of a downstream JV is the one between Shell (45 percent), Yanchang Petroleum Group Corporation (46 percent) and Shaanxi Tianli Investment (9 percent). The Anglo-Dutch and the Chinese companies, both operating in the energy and petrochemical industry, and the Chinese investment company, have launched a retail JV with the aim to jointly build and operate gas stations in China. The success of the JV has paved the way for the formation of a new JV between the petrochemical companies for expanding their retail activities in other provinces of China.[42]

LNG Canada is an example of an upstream JV among four companies: Shell Canada Energy (now holding 50 percent), PetroChina Corporation (20 percent),

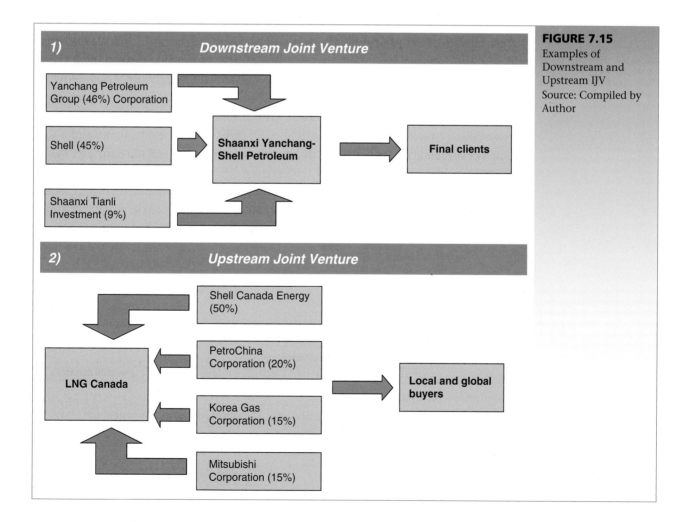

FIGURE 7.15
Examples of Downstream and Upstream IJV
Source: Compiled by Author

Korea Gas Corporation—KOGAS (15 percent), and Mitsubishi Corporation (15 percent). The new JV is located in British Columbia and aims to develop a proposed liquefied natural gas (LNG) export project and enter into commercial agreements and contracts with local and global potential suppliers and contractors, especially in growing economies across the Pacific, which are always in need of stable energy sources. The proposed project includes the design, construction, and operation of a gas liquefaction plant and LNG storage and export facilities. The four companies share complementary resources of technical depth, financial strength, and market access.[43]

X model and Y model JV

A JV can be developed with an X model or a Y model. The two models differ in terms of the integration of activities in the value chains of the parent companies when forming the new company.

Take the example of a German company entering the Indian market via a JV agreement with an Indian company. The German and the Indian companies form an X joint venture (Figure 7.16) when they contribute with complementary resources: typically, the German company focuses on technology, management design, and production, while the Indian company has more in-depth expertise with the local market and, hence, higher capabilities in terms of marketing, sales, distribution, as well as an already-developed distribution network, thus allowing fast market access.

In the second typology (Y joint venture), the German and Indian firms contribute equally to the management of the JV, fully investing resources and capabilities developed previously in the different businesses of the supply chain (Figure 7.17).

Generally, the success of a JV depends significantly on the management of the pre-contract phases and on the attentive evaluation of the partnership's strategic components. The phases that must be followed precisely are listed below:[44]

- aim formulation

- cost-benefit analysis

- evaluation and partner choice

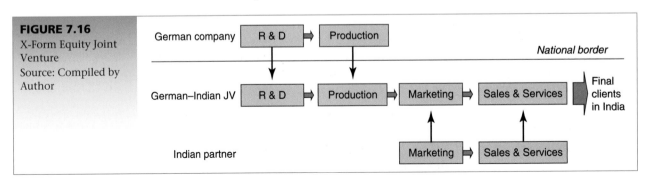

FIGURE 7.16
X-Form Equity Joint Venture
Source: Compiled by Author

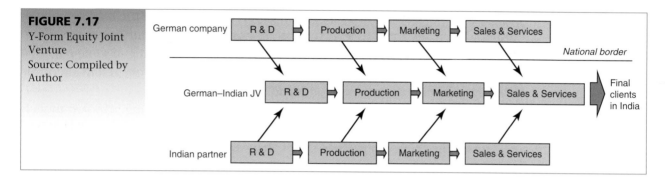

FIGURE 7.17
Y-Form Equity Joint
Venture
Source: Compiled by
Author

- business plan development

- JV agreement and contract

- performance evaluation.

The **aims linked to the formation of a JV** may be various. As already shown, there may be complementary capabilities in terms of production and technology, distribution, brand, and post-sales service, all depending on the company's sector and competencies. The creation of a JV may also have the aim to associate, through a local partner, with high-quality suppliers, obtain better prices and better guarantees for a continuous relationship, solve cultural problems that a foreign company may not only find difficult to face but is often not even able to fully comprehend. Entering a JV by involving the local partner in setting up a shared society may further give the foreign company advantageous access to sectors with high entry barriers for potential foreign entrants and, in general, speed up procedures, thus allowing for faster entry.

In a **cost-benefit analysis**, though, these advantages have to be evaluated carefully. However, many points require consideration, and not all of these points are easily assessable. Which are the real synergies obtainable from the two or more partners? What is the managerial as well as financial commitment? Is there, especially from the foreign partner, the willingness to invest in and expand the partnership? What are the risks? What are the problems pertaining to control? The negative experience of some companies teaches us that it is necessary to consider these and other features even when choosing and evaluating the partner. Further, in the **partner evaluation** process, the same variable may be negative as well as positive. For instance, the position of power that a potential foreign partner enjoys, especially with local institutions, is considered as a key factor for a successful international JV. With a powerful local partner, the foreign company indeed has greater negotiating power with suppliers, as well as a preferred lane for authorizations and certifications.[45] But the same variable may be viewed as a negative factor: the foreign company may not be able to deal successfully in the case of a conflict with a powerful local partner.

Attentive and in-depth planning throughout the development of a detailed **business plan** is critical for running a successful JV, especially in emerging markets, where transparency is limited and managerial competencies of the local companies are not taken for granted, as is the case in mature markets. Further, especially in drafting the business plan, the company may not fully comprehend some potential gaps of the future partner; which if do not lead to an immediate rescission of the plan, may provide the company with additional information useful for defining the agreement and the joint-venture contract. For the latter, using standard models proposed by local authorities is not recommended because these contracts attempt to protect the domestic partner rather than discuss qualitative aspects. It is then preferred to write within the contractual laws of a country an ad hoc contract that considers peculiarities of the company and of its products.

The last phase, performance evaluation, is one of the most critical.[46] More often, supervision-related difficulties and scarce transparency make it more difficult for foreign companies to exercise control of the objectives reached within the JV. In other cases, when the objectives of the JV are complex and only partially based on short-term profitability, success and failure are difficult to distinguish. However, there are situations in which failure is evident, and exit may be difficult, especially for the foreign company.

Insuring Against JV Failure

A number of studies[47] have shown that about half of all JVs fail. An extreme view is that JVs last for only five to seven years, only a little longer than the average career of a National Football League running back![48] What are the reasons for the high rate of JV failure and what can be done to prevent it? Here are a number of causes and suggested remedies:[49]

- *Bad ideas*. In the classic JV situation, companies form a JV because neither of them has adequate resources to undertake the venture on its own. Increasingly, JVs are motivated less by resource sharing than by risk sharing. Unfortunately, "risky" is often a code word for not worthwhile or commercially viable. If a project is not worth undertaking alone, it may not be worth undertaking at all.

- *Insufficient planning*. One of the most prevalent reasons for a failed JV is the lack of sufficient planning. JV "plans" consisting of nothing more than a statement of each party's intended contributions to the JV and their respective share of profits seldom work. The parties have nothing based on which to shape their expectations or govern their disputes. Parties to the JV should agree to a comprehensive written plan including the form of the JV, each party's contribution, logistical issues (who will be doing what and where), governance and ownership of jointly developed assets, dispute resolution, and the terms for winding up the JV if needed.

- *Inadequate capitalization*. JVs are typically allocated a fixed amount of capital based on the estimated funds necessary to accomplish the JV's goals. It is critical that any plan provide for not only the current capital needs, but also future or excess requirements.

- *Lack of leadership.* Too often, JV partners insist on sharing the leadership role. The parties should agree from the beginning as to who will have day-to-day operational control of the project (or different parts of the project). Agreement should only be required in cases of fundamental decisions, for example, a sale or disposition of the JV or its assets, incurrence of debt, or admission of a new partner. Even in those situations, the governing document should provide a method for dispute resolution in the event of a stalemate.

- *Lack of commitment.* Many companies enter into JVs looking for a quick profit. When that profit is not realized, or is not realized as quickly as expected, they lose interest.

- *Cultural and ideological differences.* In evaluating JV partners, companies should perform the same compatibility and integration analyses as they would do for an acquisition, including a thorough evaluation of corporate culture, management style, personnel and employee benefits, and IT systems. In international JVs, where the partners originate from two or more countries, cultural differences may impede a good working relationship much more than differences in corporate culture. Opposites may attract each other, but unless a way is found to blend the differences, the JV would likely be unstable.

To summarize, the most general issue with such an arrangement is maintaining the delicate balance between the partners' goals and objectives, management requirements, contributions, organizational and national cultures, and the myriad other factors that make some collaborations successful and others not. Many failed JVs can be attributed to the so called Prisoner's Dilemma. It is a situation in which both partners have a chance to benefit from collaboration. However, due to the lack of trust, both parties end up competing with each other and get lower benefit as a result.

HIERARCHICAL MODES

Hierarchical entry modes are equity-based. They are a form of foreign direct investment (FDI) in which a company assumes direct ownership of facilities in a foreign market. Hierarchical entry modes are the riskiest, but they are the most suitable choice for companies endeavoring to grow in the market while maintaining a high degree of control over operations and gaining deeper knowledge of the clients and the competitive environment.

In the simplest form, a company can invest in a foreign market by creating a representative office or a branch. A representative office is an office usually established to support marketing and service activities for the company's exports in countries where it is unviable to open a branch or a subsidiary (for example, because the market potential is limited) or it is too risky to do so (for example, because of political and legal reasons). This office only "represents" the parent company in the foreign market by supporting the local distribution network and maintaining constant relationships with the local economic and institutional entities. As a consequence, the representative office cannot buy and sell goods or services. On the other hand, a branch can carry out a much broader range of activities such as selling goods and signing contracts. A branch should not be confused with a sales subsidiary. In fact, the branch is not a separate legal entity of the parent corporation. The sales subsidiary, however, is a society with its own juridical personality separate from the parent company, and it may operate as an importer as well as manage the distribution and sales activity for the parent company in the foreign country (Figure 7.18). A subsidiary can be constituted as any type of separate legal entity (the most common forms are corporations and limited liability companies) based on the laws of the foreign country of entry, with its own income, liabilities, and local taxation. When the subsidiary performs production activity in the foreign country, it is called a sales and production subsidiary (Figure 7.19).

According to the degree of ownership of the parent company in another company abroad, these entities are classified as follows:

- wholly-owned subsidiary: If the parent company owns 100 percent of the subsidiary;

- subsidiary: If the share of the parent company is higher than 50 percent (majority stake);

- associate or affiliate: These two terms are generally used synonymously when the share of the parent company is lower than 50 percent (minority stake).

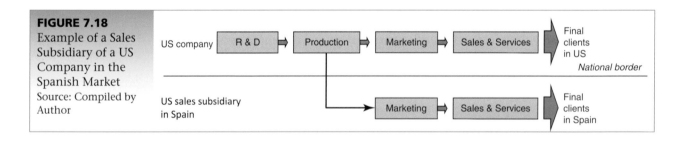

FIGURE 7.18
Example of a Sales Subsidiary of a US Company in the Spanish Market
Source: Compiled by Author

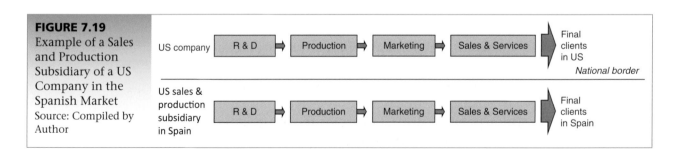

FIGURE 7.19
Example of a Sales and Production Subsidiary of a US Company in the Spanish Market
Source: Compiled by Author

Wholly-owned subsidiaries in foreign markets can be developed through the following routes:

- new establishment (greenfield investment)
- merger or acquisition (brownfield investment).

If choosing a greenfield investment, the company has the advantage of building a new ad hoc entity reflecting both the market and internal organizational needs and goals. Further, by establishing a completely new company in the foreign market, new jobs are created and new technology is introduced. However, the introduction of a new company takes more time and leads to greater competition in the market. Greenfield investments are frequent not only to build a new manufacturing company but also to enhance retailing activities: examples are the directly owned stores (DOS) developed by many companies when their brand equity is strongly contingent on the shopping experience. This choice is particularly suggested when the distribution infrastructure in the foreign market is weak and the company has to create its own sales and shopping environment. This is the case with most luxury companies.

A brownfield investment consists of buying an existing foreign company. This operation generally requires a shorter period, but the process of finding the best company to acquire can be time-intensive. Further, the company needs to consider also the additional time (and costs) required for integrating the new entity within its organization, which means integrating its technology, production processes, informatics systems, and organizational culture as well.

From the competitive standpoint a brownfield investment is less aggressive because there is simply a change in the ownership of a local company. The main disadvantage is that in contrast with the establishment of a new company (greenfield investment), there is no job creation.

While both of these scenarios allow companies to exercise the maximum control over their operations and to decisively enter the target country's markets, they also expose the company to the highest level of political, environmental, legal, and financial risks.

FACTORS THAT INFLUENCE MODE OF ENTRY DECISION PROCESS

Based on the characteristics of the different entry modes pointed out in the previous paragraphs, selection of the most suitable mode of entry for the company is influenced by a number of factors that may often pull the decision-makers in opposite directions.

To enable the discussion of all the different factors involved in the entry mode decision process, we categorize them into two major groups: internal and external.

Internal Factors

The internal factors have to do with the firm's resources, overall strategy, management mindset, time commitment and, very importantly, types of products or services considered for international markets. For most entrepreneurial firms, the key issues discussed during this initial stage of the decision process revolve around the following aspects:

Financial resources: Different modes of entry require different levels of investment. The following questions are typically considered in this regard: How much can we spend on international market expansion? Should we borrow funds or use accumulated financial assets? Are the potential rewards of this initiative worth the financial risks of a direct investment? How much can we invest? How many years can we afford to wait to reach the break-even point?

Human resources: Different modes of entry require different levels of involvement, capabilities, and human resource expertise, and the company can decide to directly manage foreign activities or rely on foreign partners (internalization versus externalization).[50] As pointed out in a recently proposed model, important antecedents that influence companies' internationalization patterns are the mindset, experience, and entrepreneurial orientation of its managers (for example, risk taking and proactiveness).[51] Another important variable is the managerial perception of ownership risk (such as expropriation), operating risk (exchange, price controls, etc.), and transfer risk. If the perceived risk is high, the company will probably opt for exporting or for an intermediate mode instead of bearing the risk of a more direct investment.[52]

There are other aspects to be considered, such as: How many employees are working in the export department? Should we hire new staff or use existing personnel to lead the expansion effort? Do we have managers with international expertise? Can we run a negotiation in the foreign market of entry? Do we need to expatriate some managers? What would be the compensation for the new positions abroad? And so on. For example, a company with few export managers or with limited international experience should probably rely to a greater extent on foreign distributors or foreign partners.

Type of product and/or service: If we locate the production abroad, what are the concerns about intellectual property rights (IPR)? Is the brand equity high? Is our asset specificity high? For example, a company concerned about its IPR, its high brand equity, and asset specificity will probably choose an entry mode that guarantees a higher degree of control.

Time horizons: How much time can we dedicate to the international expansion effort? Are we willing to accommodate longer receivables cycles, etc? Hierarchical modes, for example, require a long-term strategy. Indirect export can be used for occasional export activity.

Risk tolerance: Are we prepared to absorb the higher risks inherent in dealing with currency exchange rates, unfamiliar political, legal and market environments, economic cycles, etc? If not, a company would be better off by opting for an export mode over an intermediate or a hierarchical mode.

In general, considering internal factors, an analysis of the company value chain can provide significant insights into the decision of whether an export method fits better than an intermediate mode or a hierarchical mode. In fact, the choice of market entry method can differ significantly for small and large companies, depending on their capitalization, R&D, production capacity, and marketing resources, among other issues.

External Factors

Factors that affect a company's choice to enter a foreign market, but are independent of management's decisions are called external factors.

Market: Its size, growth, marketing infrastructure, distribution system, etc. For example, the company can decide to invest more and afford higher risk if the market potential is high. Many companies in the luxury industry invest in directly owned stores (DOS) because there is no suitable marketing infrastructure in the foreign market for selling their products. Furthermore, it is important to consider what is required to make our product ready for the target market in terms of adaptation. For example, can we get all the information about market needs and incorporate these requirements in the company's product or do we need a foreign partner? A research carried out on a sample of 150 foreign entries by Dutch firms found that firms pursuing higher levels of marketing adaptation assign more value to the marketing adaptation advantages of acquisitions (brownfields) over those of greenfields, especially if there are risks associated with implementing the planned adaptation. The preference for acquisitions is stronger for firms that are establishing relatively larger subsidiaries, have less experience with the industry entered, or are entering less developed countries.[53]

Consumer factors: Characteristics of local consumers are important and need due consideration. For example, it has been demonstrated that in a high-animosity host country, consumers prefer foreign products launched through an acquisition JV to those that are imports or derivatives of full acquisition. Also, consumers in such countries prefer the JV that adopts a local brand or local–foreign co-branding over one that adopts a foreign–local co-branding. In contrast, in low-animosity host countries, purchase intentions were not at all influenced by the entry mode and branding strategies.[54]

Competitive environment: Porter five forces analysis can provide significant insights about rivalry among firms, potential entrants (economies of scale, entry barriers), substitute products and services, and bargaining power of suppliers and clients. The mode of entry has to support the company in dealing with local competition.

Production conditions: This encompasses everything from the cost, quality, and quantity of local materials and labor to transportation, communications, energy supply, and other similar economic infrastructure components. The company needs to decide whether to export or produce locally. If the size of the foreign market is larger than the minimum efficient scale of production, the company can find it advantageous to localize production abroad. Similarly, a company can decide to localize production abroad because shipping costs and export tariffs are very high.[55]

Environmental conditions: This broad category includes most political, economic, geographic, cultural, and social factors. For example, in some cases, the government imposes the mode of entry on foreign entrants, as has been the case of JVs in China and Brazil for many years. In other cases, localization is required because of high local content requirements. In addition, physical and psychic distances should be considered. The farther and more dissimilar the foreign target market, the greater is the need for the company to rely on a local partner. Nevertheless, it is also important to underline that in the past years, improvements in communication and information technologies have reduced the impact of both types of distance on internationalization patterns.[56]

DYNAMICS OF MARKET ENTRY

Market entry is not static, and entry modes may have to be restructured as environmental conditions change. These conditions include economic factors, competition, market structure, consumer characteristics, and government regulations. India provides an interesting example of these changes, and it is illustrative of other emerging markets (see Box 7.3).

Another aspect to be pointed out is that the choice of the entry mode is not always sequential, as hypothesized in the Uppsala model (see Chapter 8). In the Uppsala model, firms gradually progress through a series of stages based on experiential learning and commitment of resources; lower in exporting decisions, medium in intermediate modes, and higher in equity-based modes. On the contrary, in some cases, the dynamics of the industry and the competitive system, as well as the characteristics of the product, the target market, or the macroenvironment, can require or suggest a different approach, such as developing a JV agreement from the outset or opting for a wholly-owned subsidiary with high investments and risks. For example, in the case of China, some companies prefer to enter the Chinese market by exporting. Only after having better understood the market characteristics and dynamics do companies switch to more committed and engaging modes of entry. Others choose instead to invest and risk more since the very beginning via a JV or wholly-owned subsidiaries in order to retain greater control over their foreign businesses.[57] In this latter case, some companies believe that they can manage the enormous present and future opportunities offered by the Chinese market only by establishing a strong market presence since the very beginning, through an equity investment. In many cases, the company may choose more than one entry mode given the complexity of the market and the multiplicity of targets. For instance, particularly, when considering large markets such as China or India, some companies in some provinces sell through distributors in specialized stores (export mode), while in other provinces they have invested in directly owned mono-brand stores (hierarchical mode). This, in turn, has opened

---

Box 7.3 Country-in-Focus: India

The Evolution of the Mode of Entry in the Indian Market

Many international companies in India have structures different from those at the time they entered the market. For example, in 1977, the Indian government passed a law that required foreign companies to dilute their equity stake in subsidiaries to 40 percent if they wanted to continue operating in the country. This regulation required wholly-owned foreign subsidiaries to share ownership with Indian nationals or cease operations, which Coca-Cola and IBM did. However, the law was changed in 1996, allowing 100 percent voting control even though the home corporation owned only 51 percent of the equity shares.

Several multinational companies and brands have changed their operating modes in India over time. VF Corporation, an American company headquartered in North Carolina, whose brands include Nautica, Wrangler, and Lee, entered India in the 1980s by licensing its brand to Dupont Sportswear. Since then, it has launched a variety of brands in different product categories with a number of Indian partners over a period of 20 years. It finally formed a JV called VF Arvind Brands Pvt. Ltd. (India).

Another example of a company that has evolved its presence is Benetton, which first entered India through a licensee (Dalmia). Benetton then transitioned in 1991 into a 50–50 JV, and finally in 2004, it took over the Indian business completely. However, it adopted the franchising route in 2006 for its premium fashion brand, Sisley, appointing Trent (a Tata Group company) as the national retail franchise owner of the Westside stores.

Each of these changes in strategy has cost the brands time, management effort, money, and, occasionally, market share. In many cases, the original entry mode was restructured because of changing market conditions, including the growth of modern retailing in India and increased consumer buying power. Those companies that anticipated these changes had the advantage of making strategic adjustments to their mode of operation and thus gain an edge over competition. This is another example of why environmental scanning is so important to global marketing planning.

Sources: Thakurta, P.G. (2003), 'How Coke Arm-Twisted the Indian Government', http://www.indiaresource.org/campaigns/coke/2003/howcokearm.html; International brands: India entry strategies, http://www.udel.edu/fiber/issue4/world/internationalbrands.html; Devangshu Dutta and Tarang Gautam Saxena. (2009), International brands: India entry strategies, http://thirdeyesight.in/blog/2009/05/09/international-brands-india-entry-strategies/ [All accessed: June 14, 2014].

---

the possibility of developing a franchising chain (intermediate contractual entry mode), necessary to expand the distribution network and strengthen brand identity. In some cases, it is even possible to talk about hybrid entry modes, including JVs associated with distribution contracts, own-property stores, or franchising managed by subsidiaries.

Recent studies have focused on the accelerated time frame in which small and medium-sized firms move from domestic to internationalized operations, leading academics to question the stage model for the internationalization process. The rapid internationalization of these companies, defined as born global firms, follow two major dimensions: geographic scope, as reflected by the number, spread, and diversity of targeted foreign markets; and the extent of foreign operations committing different value chain activities to global markets.[58] These companies are distinguished by strong international motivation, innovation propensity, risk attitude, market orientation, and proactiveness that significantly favor their early internationalization.[59] These findings further underscore the importance of internal evaluation before moving into international business.

SUMMARY

- We have examined the various alternative entry strategies a firm can take during its internationalization. It should be emphasized that when a firm enters more than one market at a time, it may choose different entry modes for each market. Such a strategy is most often used for two reasons: to enter several markets at the same time or to leverage the advantages of one entry mode before transitioning to another. As global communications, travel, and trade have become increasingly easier and more widespread, many companies have found it possible and even beneficial to use more than one entry mode simultaneously.
- Because most entrepreneurial businesses are small to medium in size, their initial choices for international market entry tend to include low- to moderate-risk strategies, such as indirect and direct export (export modes). The firm has low market control, but they benefit from high flexibility because all the activities in the foreign market are externalized. In fact, international operations are performed by another domestic or foreign company (for example, an export company or a foreign distributor).
- As companies become bigger and more successful internationally, some may decide to deepen their presence and commitment to particular foreign markets by sharing risk and control with a foreign partner (intermediate modes) and enter into contract-based agreements such as international licensing, international franchising, piggyback, contract manufacturing, original equipment manufacturing (OEM), turnkey operations agreements, management contracts, strategic alliances, or equity-based agreements such as joint ventures.
- They can even afford to take a higher risk abroad (hierarchical modes) by investing in a subsidiary or an affiliate. Alternatively, they can take the wholly-owned subsidiary route by acquiring a foreign company (brownfield investment) or by establishing a new company arm (greenfield investment). Through the hierarchical mode, a company internalizes management of the activities in a foreign market, leading to higher risks and lower flexibility, but also higher market control.
- A more stable and economically and politically secure country would be more inviting to an equity mode of entry, whereas a country with political or social turmoil and frequent economic crises would be suitable for non-equity modes of entry.

DISCUSSION QUESTIONS

1. What in your opinion are the most difficult challenges facing SMEs deciding to enter foreign markets?
2. In your opinion, are there any differences facing SMEs and larger firms when dealing with an entry mode decision?
3. Joint ventures in emerging countries have higher failure rates than in more developed countries. Why do you think this is so?

EXPERIENTIAL EXERCISES

1. You are going to advise a small to medium-sized service firm considering expanding to the UK. None of its managers have any international business experience. How would you go about determining their readiness to consider such a move?

2. Search United States Department of Commerce sources to determine which market entry strategy has been used most frequently over the last decade by American firms in emerging countries. Explain the reasons for this trend.

KEY TERMS

- Affiliate
- Assembly contract
- Associate
- Brokers
- Brownfield investment
- Buying offices
- Contract manufacturing
- Contractual joint venture
- Direct exporting
- Distributors
- Downstream joint venture
- Export companies
- Export consortia
- Export modes
- Greenfield investment
- Hierarchical modes
- Importers
- Indirect exporting
- Intermediate modes
- International franchising
- International joint venture
- International licensing
- Management contract
- OEM
- Outsourcing
- Piggyback
- Strategic alliance
- Subsidiary
- Trading companies
- Turnkey contract
- Upstream joint venture
- Wholly-owned subsidiary

NOTES

1 'Chairman's message: Deere achieves record results as drive to expand global customer base moves ahead', http://www.deere.com/en_US/docs/Corporate/investor_relations/pdf/financialdata/reports/2014/2013chairm ansmessage.pdf, p. 6 [Accessed: June 12, 2014].

2 Balboni, B., Bortoluzzi, G., and Vianelli, D. (2014), 'The impact of relational capabilities on the internationalization process of industrial subcontractors', *Transformations in Business & Economics*, 13(2), pp. 21–40.

3 Hewerdine, L.J., Rumyantseva M., and Welch, C. (2014), 'Resource scavenging: Another dimension of the internationalisation pattern of high-tech SMEs', *International Marketing Review*, 31(3), pp. 237–58.

4 Deresky, H. (2011). *International management: Managing across borders and cultures*. International Edition. Upper Saddle River, NJ: Pearson.

5 Sinkovics, N., Sinkovics, R. R., and Ruey-Jer 'Bryan' Jean. (2013), 'The internet as an alternative path to internationalization?' *International Marketing Review*, 30(2), pp. 130–55.

6 Mühlbacher, H., Leihs, H. and Dahringer, L. (2006). *International marketing: A global perspective*. London: Thomson Learning.

7 Hollensen, S. (2013). *Global marketing: A decision oriented approach*. 6th ed. Harlow, England: Prentice Hall.

8 Translates to: *one hundred percent Italian* consortium.

9 The concept of price escalation will be described in Chapter 11 (Setting Global Prices).

10 Short and long distribution channels will be analyzed in Chapter 12 (Global Placement and Distribution Channels).

11 Dong, M., Tse, D., and Hung, K. (2010), 'Effective distributor governance in emerging markets: The salience of distributor role, relationship stages, and market uncertainty', *Journal of International Marketing*, 18(3), pp. 1–17.

12 Varis, J., Kuivalainen, O., and Saarenketo, S. (2005), 'Partner selection for international marketing and distribution in corporate new ventures', *Journal of International Entrepreneurship*, 3(1), pp. 19–36; Cavusgil, S. T., Yeoh, P., and Mitri, M. (1995), 'Selecting foreign distributors: An expert systems approach', *Industrial Marketing Management*, 24(4), pp. 297–304; Hollensen, S. (2013). *Global marketing: A decision oriented approach*. 6th ed. Harlow, England: Prentice Hall.

13 Obadia, C. (2008), 'Cross-border interfirm cooperation: The influence of the performance context', *International Marketing Review*, 25(6), pp. 634–50.

14 Bellin, H. (2006), 'Best practice channel management: The channel management framework', *Journal of Marketing Channels*, 14(1–2), pp. 117–27.

15 The World Factbook. (2015), https://www.cia.gov/library/publications/the-world-factbook/docs/refmaps.html [Accessed: August 1, 2015].

16 Kashyap, V. and Sivadas, E. (2012), 'An exploratory examination of shared values in channel relationships', *Journal of Business Research*, 65(5), pp. 586–93.

17 Gencturk, E. F. and Aulakh, P. S. (2007), 'Norms- and control-based governance of international manufacturer-distributor relational exchanges', *Journal of International Marketing*, 15(1), pp. 92–126; Zhang, C., Griffith, D. A., and Cavusgil, S. T. (2006), 'The litigated dissolution of international distribution relationships: a process framework and propositions', *Journal of International Marketing*, 14(2), pp. 85–115.

18 Zhang, C., Griffith, D. A., and Cavusgil, S. T. (2006), 'The litigated dissolution of international distribution relationships: A process framework and propositions', *Journal of International Marketing*, 14(2), pp. 85–115.

19 Griffin, R. W. and Pustay, M.W. (2009). *International business*. 6th ed. Upper Saddle River, NJ: Pearson Education.

20 The World Factbook. (2015), https://www.cia.gov/library/publications/the-world-factbook/docs/refmaps.html [Accessed: August 1, 2015].

21 Cateora, P., Graham, J., and Gilly, M. (2012). *International marketing*. 16th ed. New York: McGraw-Hill/Irwin; Hollensen, S. (2013). *Global marketing: A decision oriented approach*. 6th ed. Harlow, England: Prentice Hall; Hill, J.S. (2009). *International business: Managing globalization*. Los Angeles: Sage.

22 Somaya, D., Kim, Y., and Vonortas, N.S. (2011), 'Exclusivity in licensing alliances: Using hostages to support technology commercialization', *Strategic Management Journal*, 32(2), pp. 159–86; Hollensen, S. (2013). *Global marketing: A decision oriented approach*. 6th ed. Harlow, England: Prentice Hall.

23 Deresky, H. (2011). *International management: Managing across borders and cultures*. International Edition. Upper Saddle River, NJ: Pearson.

24 The Coca-Cola Company. (2013), 'The Coca-Cola Company commences implementation of 21st century beverage partnership model in the United States', April 16, 2013, http://www.coca-colacompany.com/press-center/press-releases/the-coca-cola-company-commences-implementation-of-21st-century-beverage-partnership-model-in-the-united-states [Accessed: October 2, 2015].

25 Alon, I. (2012). *Global franchising operations management: Cases in international and emerging markets operations*. NJ: FT Press; Alon, I. and Welsh, D., (eds.) (2001). *International franchising in emerging markets: China, India and other Asian countries*. Chicago, IL: CCH Inc. Publishing.

26 Invest in China. (2007), 'Regulations on administering commercial franchises', http://www.fdi.gov.

cn/1800000121_39_3485_0_7.html [Accessed: October 2, 2015]; Ministry of Commerce. (2007), 'Administrative measures for archiving commercial franchises', April 30, 2007, http://tradeinservices. mofcom.gov.cn/en/b/2007-04-30/9548.shtml [Accessed: October 2, 2015]; Ministry of Commerce. (2007), 'Administrative measures for the information disclosure of commercial franchise', http://www.lawinfochina. com/display.aspx?lib=law&id=6040&CGid= [Accessed: October 2, 2015].

27 Wang, Z.J., Zhu, M., and Terry, A. (2008), 'The development of franchising in China', *Journal of Marketing Channels*, 15(2–3), pp. 167–84.

28 Merrilees, B. (2014), 'International franchising: Evolution of theory and practice', *Journal of Marketing Channels*, 21(3), pp. 133–42.

29 Albaum, G., Duerr, E., and Strandskov, J. (2005). *International marketing and export management*. 5th ed. Upper Saddle River, NJ: Prentice Hall.

30 Keegan, W.J. and Green, M. (2012). *Global marketing*. 7th ed. Upper Saddle River, NJ: Prentice Hall.

31 Nisen M. (2013), 'How Nike solved its sweatshop problem', *Business Insider*, May 9, 2013, http://www. businessinsider.com/how-nike-solved-its-sweatshop-problem-2013-5?IR=T [Accessed: September 28, 2015].

32 Mühlbacher, H., Leihs, H., and Dahringer, L. (2006). *International marketing: A global perspective*. London: Thomson Learning.

33 Thomas White International. (2011), 'Retail sector in China: The next big thing?', http://www.thomaswhite. com/pdf/bric-spotlight-report-china-retail-june-11.pdf [Accessed: October 2, 2015]; Deloitte. (2009), 'China's consumer market: What next?',www.deloitte.com.mx/csgmx/docs/china_consumer_market_ whatsnext.pdf [Accessed: March, 2012].

34 Hill, J.S. (2009). *International business: Managing globalization*. Los Angeles: Sage.

35 Caroli, M. (2012). *Gestione delle imprese internazionali*. Milano: McGraw-Hill.

36 The World Factbook. (2015), https://www.cia.gov/library/publications/the-world-factbook/docs/refmaps.html [Accessed: August 1, 2015].

37 Daniels, J. D. and Radebaugh, L. H. (2007). *International business: Environments and operations*. 11th ed. Upper Saddle River, NJ: Prentice Hall.

38 Beamish, P.W., Morrison, A.J., Inkpen, A.C., and Rosenzweig, P.M. (2003). *International management: Text and cases*. 5th ed. New York: McGraw-Hill.

39 In fact, similarly to equity joint ventures, they can be horizontal or vertical as well as upstream or/and downstream. See equity joint ventures in the next paragraphs for more details.

40 Wakeam, J. (2003), 'The five factors of a strategic alliance', *Ivey Business Journal*, May–June, 67(5), pp. 1–4.

41 Crabbe, M. (2014), 'Tesco gains approval for joint venture with China resources enterprises in China', June 3, 2014, http://www.mintel.com/blog/retail-market-news/tesco-gains-approval-for-joint-venture-with-china-resources-enterprises-in-china [Accessed: July 12, 2014].

42 'Shell, Shaanxi Yanchan Petroleum to jointly 100 gas stations', *Xinhua Economic News*, October 13, 2009, http://www.downstreamtoday.com/News/ArticlePrint.aspx?aid=18650&AspxAutoDetectCookieSupport=1 [Accessed: July 2, 2014]; 'Shell and Yanchang Petroleum launch a retail joint venture in Guangdong', *Shell. com*, May 27, 2014, http://www.shell.com.cn/en/aboutshell/media-centre/news-and-media-releases/2014/ retail-joint-venture.html [Accessed: July 2, 2016].

43 'Companies behind LNG Canada formalize joint venture; Milestone for proposed project', *Bloomberg.com*, April 30, 2014, http://lngcanada.ca/media-items/companies-behind-lng-canada-formalize-joint-venture-milestone-for-proposed-project [Accessed: July 30, 2016].

44 Vianelli, D., de Luca, P., and Pegan, G. (2012). *Modalità d'entrata e scelte distributive del made in Italy in Cina*. Milano: Franco Angeli.

45 Amtmann, M. (2006). *International joint ventures in China*. Saarbrucken: VDM Verlag Dr.Muller E.K. und Lizenzgeber.

46 Child, J. (2007) Performance in international joint ventures in China: Critical factors. In: Clegg, S., Wang, K., and Berrel, M. (eds.). *Business networks and strategic alliances in China*. Cheltenham, UK: Edward Elgar Publishing Limited.

47 Turowski, D. (2005), 'The decline and fall of joint ventures: How JVs became unpopular and why that could change', *Journal of Applied Corporate Finance*, 17(2), pp. 82–6; Bamford, J., Ernst, D., and

Fubini, D. (2004), 'Launching a world-class joint venture', *Harvard Business Review*, February, 82(2), pp. 90–100.

48 MacMillan, T. (2006), *CIBC Mellon: A joint venture success story*, Speech to the Financial Services Institute, http://www.academia.edu/11540389/A_Joint_Venture_Success_Story_CIBC_Mellon_A_Joint_Venture_Success_Story [Accessed: July 30, 2016].

49 Spranger, D. (2004), 'Why joint ventures fail', http://www.saul.com/sites/default/files/1134_pdf_29.pdf [Accessed: July 4, 2014].

50 See the choice between internalization versus externalization discussed in the beginning of the chapter.

51 Kuivalainen, O., Sundqvist, S., Saarenketo, S., and McNaughton, R. (2012), 'Internationalization patterns of small and medium-sized enterprises', *International Marketing Review,* 29(5), pp. 448–65.

52 Koch, A.J. (2001), 'Factors influencing market and entry mode selection: Developing MEMS model', *Marketing Intelligence and Planning*, 19(5), pp. 351–61.

53 Slangen, A. L. and Dikova, D. (2014), 'Planned marketing adaptation and multinationals' choices between acquisitions and greenfields', *Journal of International Marketing*, 22(2), pp. 68–88.

54 Cher-Min, F., Chun-Ling, L., and Yunzhou, D. (2014), 'Consumer animosity, country of origin, and foreign entry-mode choice: A cross-country investigation', *Journal of International Marketing*, 22(1), pp. 62–76.

55 Gupta, A.K and Govindarajan, V. (2000), 'Managing global expansion: a conceptual framework', *Business Horizons*, March–April, 43(2), pp. 45–54.

56 Håkanson, L. (2014), 'The role of psychic distance in international trade: A longitudinal analysis', *International Marketing Review*, 31(3), pp. 210–36.

57 Vianelli, D., de Luca, P., and Pegan, G. (2012). *Modalità d'entrata e scelte distributive del made in Italy in Cina*. Milano: Franco Angeli.

58 Hashai, N. (2011), 'Sequencing the expansion of geographic scope and foreign operations by 'born global' firms', *Journal of International Business Studies*, 42(8), pp. 995–1015.

59 Gabrielsson, M., Gabrielsson, P., and Dimitratos, P. (2014), 'International entrepreneurial culture and growth of international new ventures', *Management International Review (MIR)*, 54(4), pp. 445–71; Deresky, H. (2011). *International management: Managing across borders and cultures.* International Edition. Upper Saddle River, NJ: Pearson.

CASE 7.1 HUAWEI ENTERS THE UNITED STATES[1]

Huawei Technologies Corporation had a company vision to become not only a global technology leader, but also an international giant, competing with such telecommunication equipment firms as Cisco Systems. To make this a reality, Huawei needed to increase its presence in one of the largest markets for telecommunications equipment products and services, the United States. Ren Zhengfei, CEO of Huawei, led Huawei in its transformation from a company focused on the domestic Chinese market into an international competitor involved in partnerships with all the major European operators, with the majority of its sales coming from international contracts. Huawei had established four R&D centers in the United States by 2001 and formed the joint venture H3C with American electronics manufacturer 3Com in 2003.[2] However, Huawei was running into resistance in the U.S. market, and its presence in the market was small compared to its relative international success. The U.S. Committee on Foreign Investment in the United States (CFIUS)[3] had blocked deals involving Huawei on the grounds that Huawei had possible ties to the Chinese government, and the strategic nature of the telecommunications industry made such deals potential threats to national safety and security.[4]

In May 2010, Huawei bought assets of the American server technology company, 3Leaf, but did not file the acquisition with CFIUS until November of that year.[5] In February 2011, CFIUS recommended that Huawei voluntarily deconstruct its purchase of 3Leaf assets. This would cause Huawei to incur some financial costs for canceling the deal, but more importantly, Huawei executives felt it was a major blow to their reputation as a trustworthy international company. Huawei had been in the process of transforming into an international company for over a decade but was running into a ceiling in the U.S. market. Questions arose as to whether they could ignore the recommendation by CFIUS or whether there was something that they could do as a company to gain approval from the U.S. authorities. Huawei executives needed to decide how to respond to the recommendation by CFIUS and the possible outcomes for the future of their company.

HUAWEI FROM 1987 TO 2000

In less than two decades, the privately held company grew from an importer of basic telecommunications equipment into a telecommunications giant, supplying equipment and services to millions of people across the globe and applying for a total of 10,650 patents under the Patent Cooperation Treaty (PCT) by 2011.[6]

Zhengfei founded Huawei in the city of Shenzhen after the Engineering Corps of the People's Liberation Army, in which he was a deputy director, was disbanded in 1987.[7] He used RMB21,000[8] (equal to $4,400 at that time) of his own money to begin importing basic telecommunications equipment from Hong Kong and sell it to vendors in China[9]. When that business became saturated with competitors, Huawei began to develop and manufacture its own equipment. Choosing to design and manufacture products without a relationship or joint venture with a foreign multinational partner was unique for a homegrown Chinese company. Huawei's first focus was on the rapidly expanding domestic market, where telephone subscriptions grew 15.5 times from 1992 to 2000 and mobile phone subscriptions grew 500 times over the same time period.[10] There is little doubt that during this time, Zhengfei's *guanxi*[11] network, which likely reached deep into the Chinese military and Chinese Communist Party hierarchy, was an invaluable asset to the company for winning large state contracts and obtaining cheap financial support from state-owned banks.[12] However, Zhengfei was a particularly reclusive CEO, never granting interviews or making public appearances, which did not help Huawei when rumors about ties to the military and the Party started to spread in later years.

In early 2000, sensing an imminent end to sustained growth in China, Huawei's vision evolved as it focused on becoming an international competitor. Huawei's internationalization strategy was very successful, first winning international contracts from neighbouring Asian countries, and then moving into developing markets in the African and Latin American regions. Huawei's main advantage was its ability to provide quality equipment and service for about 30 per cent less than its global competitors. This advantage was largely due to the abundance of Chinese engineers, who could be paid much less than their foreign counterparts. Huawei recognized this comparative advantage early on and made R&D a cornerstone of its marketing strategy, with a standard company policy to invest no less than 10 per cent of annual revenue in R&D (see Exhibit 1 for financial highlights).[13]

EXHIBIT 1 Huawei Five-Year Financial Highlights	**CNY Million**	**2011**	**2010**	**2009**	**2008**	**2007**
	Revenue: China	65,565	62,143	59,038	–	–
	Revenue: Overseas	138,364	120,405	90,021	–	–
	Total Revenue	203,929	182,548	149,059	123,080	92,155
	Operating Margin	9.1%	16.8%	15.2%	13.9%	10.1%
	Total Assets	193,283	178,984	148,968	119,286	89,562

Source: "Huawei Annual Report 2011," www.huawei.com/en/about-huawei/corporate-info/annual-report/annual-report-2011/index.htm, accessed February 20, 2013.

THE TELECOMMUNICATIONS INDUSTRY FROM 1960 TO 2000

The telecommunications industry is one of the most important industries to emerge over the last four decades, as it accounts for a major share of the global economic growth and technological innovation. Globalization has also played a major role in the rapidly evolving make-up of the industry. In the 1960s and 1970s, the telecommunications industry had few equipment suppliers. Most suppliers specialized in a single product category and supply chains were decentralized, serving regional markets with regional subsidiary suppliers.[14] But in the 1980s, digital technology changed the industry. Product lines became much more diverse, and global organizations started to form with integrated, centralized supply chains that increased production volume and decreased unit costs. By the 1990s, network equipment suppliers evolved into providers of entirely integrated telecommunication systems. The market for global networking products went from $15 billion in 1995 to $50 billion in 2000. Although the dot-com bubble would result in a cooling down of the telecom industry, it did not prevent the emergence of new technology that would continue to drive the industry.

Foreign multinational telecom firms had been in China since the 1980s. Most foreign multinationals had to form joint ventures with local Chinese companies in order to enter the potentially massive Chinese market. Foreign multinational telecom firms not only added to the growth of China's telecommunications infrastructure during this time, but also contributed to the growth of domestic manufacturers. The presence of foreign multinational firms greatly accelerated the evolution of domestic telecom manufacturers, from positions far behind industry competitors in the early 1980s into positions where they were domestically competitive in the switch industry by the early 1990s; by the late 1990s, they were in positions as major domestic players, beginning to go abroad in a wide variety of product categories. In 2001, the leading firms in the global telecom equipment industry were Ericson, Nortel, Nokia, Lucent, Cisco, Siemens, Motorola and Alcatel[15] (see Exhibit 2). In 2011, the leading firms in the global telecom equipment industry were Ericsson, Huawei, Alcatel-Lucent, Nokia Siemens Networks, ZTE, Cisco and Motorola[16] (see Exhibit 3).

The landscape and the players in the telecom industry changed quite dramatically between 2000 and 2011, which led to a new set of issues for telecom industry players to manage. Prices became more competitive as accessibility to cheaper R&D skill became more available. The market for telecommunications equipment shifted toward major investments into the construction of wireless networks, with major profits being made in software and services.[17] Consumers demanded high-quality products and services as well as leading-edge technology, which opened up new markets and room for expansion. The growing perception of cyber-security and the possible threats to information systems challenged the reputations of individual companies, as well as the industry as a whole, because of the interdependence of global supply chains.

EXHIBIT 2 Top Telecommunication Equipment Manufacturers – 2001	Company	2000 Revenue (Billions US$)	1999 Revenue (Billions US$)	Growth (%) Based on Revenue
	Ericson	31.3	25.7	21.5
	Nortel	30.3	21.3	42.2
	Nokia	27.2	20.1	35.4
	Lucent	25.8	33.8	−23.5
	Cisco	23.9	15.0	59.3
	Siemens	22.8	20.0	14.5
	Motorola	22.8	19.7	15.3
	Alcatel	21.6	17.1	26.6

Source: Gartner Dataquest, February 2001.

EXHIBIT 3 Top Telecommunication Equipment Manufacturers – 2011	Company	2011 Revenue (Billions US$)	Growth Based on Revenue	2011 Operating Profit (Billions US$)
	Ericsson	203.3	12%	11.2
	Huawei	32.8	11.5%	12.3
	Alcatel-Lucent SA	19.9	−2.1%	1.4
	Nokia Siemens	13.6	10.6%	3.7
	ZTE	13.9	23.4%	0.15
	Cisco Systems	43.2	7.9%	6.5
	Motorola Solutions	8.2	7.2%	1.15

Source: Ericsson Annual Report 2011, Huawei Annual Report 2011, Alcatel-Lucent SA, Nokia Siemens, ZTE, Cisco Systems, Motorola Solutions.

Both the Chinese and U.S. governments indicated that the telecommunications sector played a critical role in national and security interests. Some members of the media were critical of the fact that the Communist Party of China "ensured that 'national champions' dominate through a combination of market protectionism, cheap loans, tax and subsidy programs, and diplomatic support in the case of off-shore markets."[18] Other members of the media criticized the U.S. telecom industry as being a "good old boys" network that catered to incumbent relationships and kept new players out.[19] International trade followers described the issue of telecommunications in foreign and international trade policy as "the mother of all cases" because of the huge commercial and strategic value of the industry (see Exhibit 4 and Exhibit 5).[20]

CFIUS

The Committee on Foreign Investment in the United States is an inter-agency committee composed of the heads of the Department of Commerce, the Department of Homeland Security, the Department of Justice, the Department of Defense and five

Country or Area	Value (million US$)	Growth (%) 2010 to 2011	World Share %	Cum.
World	506,103.3	13.3	100.0	–
China	162,171.4	21.5	32.0	32.0
China, Hong Kong SAR	64,056.3	12.6	12.7	44.7
USA	38,248.6	14.5	7.6	52.3
Republic of Korea	35,388.6	0.3	7.0	59.2
Mexico	18,515.2	–10.7	3.7	62.9
Germany	18,403.8	13.5	3.6	66.5

Source: UN Comtrade.

EXHIBIT 4
Top Telecommunication Equipment Exporting Countries Or Areas In 2011

Country or Area	Value (million US$)	Growth (%) 2010 to 2011	World Share %	Cum.
World	557,900.0	13.3	100.0	–
USA	93,097.5	7.6	16.7	16.7
China, Hong Kong SAR	58,408.0	19.2	10.5	27.2
China	42,897.3	25.1	7.9	35.0
Japan	26,332.1	23.6	4.7	39.7
Mexico	25,401.2	–1.4	4.6	44.3
Germany	24,727.8	21.1	4.4	48.7

Source: UN Comtrade.

EXHIBIT 5
Top Telecommunication Equipment Importing Countries Or Areas In 2011

other departments and offices.[21] The committee is authorized to review transactions that could result in control of a U.S. company involved in interstate commerce by a foreign entity or foreign persons. This is not limited to transactions involving majority shares, but any transactions that result in controlling power of any sort. The process involves a voluntary filing by a U.S. company that is looking to sell equity or to be acquired. The filing includes a description of business lines, which includes clear and detailed accounts of each company's products and services, and a description of the transaction, which includes clear descriptions of all entities involved and the nature and structure of the transaction. CFIUS also suggests submitting organizational charts showing the control and ownership interests of the foreign persons who are party to the transaction, as well as information related to the foreign persons and their parents.

Each notice of transaction is reviewed, and further investigation may occur based on the buyer's country of origin and the industry in which the purchase is involved, such as the banking, transportation, infrastructure or technology industries (see Exhibit 6 and Exhibit 7 for transaction details).

Ninety-three notices of transactions were filed with CFIUS in 2010, of which CFIUS conducted subsequent investigations with respect to 35.[22] Twelve of the notices were withdrawn (see Exhibit 8). In five of these cases, the parties filed

EXHIBIT 6 Cfius Transaction Notices By Sector And Year, 2008 To 2010 Add In-Text Referrence	Year	Manufacturing	Finance, Information and Services	Mining, Utilities and Construction	Wholesale and Retail Trade	Total
	2008	72 (46%)	42 (27%)	25 (16%)	16 (10%)	155
	2009	21 (32%)	22 (34%)	19 (29%)	3 (5%)	65
	2010	36 (39%)	35 (38%)	13 (14%)	9 (10%)	93
	TOTAL	129 (41%)	99 (32%)	57 (18%)	28 (9%)	313

Source: 2011 CFIUS Annual Report to Congress.

EXHIBIT 7 Cfius Transaction Notices: Top Intra-Sector Manufacturing, 2008 To 2010	Manufacturing	Number of Transactions	% of Total Manufacturing
	Computer and Electronic Products	62	48%
	Transportation Equipment	21	16%
	Machinery	15	12%
	Primary Metal	8	6%
	Chemical	7	5%

Source: 2011 CFIUS Annual Report to Congress.

EXHIBIT 8 Cfius Transactions, Withdrawals And Presidential Decisions, 2008 To 2010	Year	# of Notices	Notices Withdrawn During Review	#of Investigations	Notices Withdrawn During Investigation	Presidential Decisions
	2008	155	18	23	5	0
	2009	65	5	25	2	0
	2010	93	6	35	6	0
	TOTAL	313	29	83	13	0

Source: 2011 CFIUS Annual Report.

a new notice. In five other cases, the parties abandoned their transactions. In two cases, the parties withdrew and re-filed in 2011. If a transaction occurs without a notice being filed to CFIUS, the committee can intervene at any time and undo the deal.

HUAWEI IN INTERNATIONAL MARKETS

By 2005, Huawei had captured 30 per cent of China's domestic market,[23] had international contracts exceeding domestic sales and was employing 30,000 people worldwide.[24] Huawei brought in world-class management consultants from IBM, PriceWaterhouseCooper, Intel and Microsoft to bring the company up to modern and efficient global management standards. The company expanded into developed

European markets, first winning contracts from budget-constrained operators, but eventually winning contracts from a number of major operators. By the end of 2007, Huawei had a partnership with all the top European operators, such as France Telecom, Vodafone and the BT Group.

Huawei formed a joint venture, H3C, with the American electronics manufacturer 3Com in 2003, but it still had little presence in the United States market relative to its international success. *H3C* would raise the profile of Huawei in the U.S. market, and 3Com found the joint venture successful enough to buy out Huawei's 51 per cent share in 2006.[25] However, when Huawei teamed up with Bain Capital to purchase 3Com in 2008, security concerns at CFIUS about the acquisition led to the termination of the deal. A Bain Capital press release stated that they were informed that CFIUS intended to take action to prohibit the sale if the deal was to continue. The U.S. Department of Defense had used 3Com products for cyber security intrusion detection, which was a major red flag for U.S. policy makers.[26] The reclusiveness of Ren Zhengfei, who had never released more than a 200-word biography or granted an interview, as well as the lack of transparent corporate governance or transparent company ownership and the lack of a single non-Chinese member in the "inner-management sanctum," made it very hard to see the inner-workings of Huawei.[27] However, *Xinhua News*, the vehicle of the Communist Party of China, described the problems as the struggle of a highly competitive, non-Western company with the "rising protectionist sentiments in the United States," which were possibly planted by the hometown favorite, Cisco Systems.[28]

In 2010, Huawei had $22 billion in sales and was becoming one of the world's top three sellers of telecom equipment.[29] Huawei partnered with a newly formed consulting company, Amerilink Telecom Corp., which could have been a way for Huawei to win business from Sprint. Amerilink was located in Sprint's hometown and was composed of a former vice-chairman of the U.S. Joint Chiefs of Staff and former Sprint executives. However, Huawei and fellow Chinese telecom supplier ZTE were excluded from the $5 billion contract to build a 4G network for Sprint Nextel Corporation. Several U.S. senators had sent letters to the Obama administration expressing their concerns about Huawei potentially gaining access to and undermining the critical U.S. telecom infrastructure. The U.S. Commerce Secretary, Gary Locke, also personally called Sprint's CEO, Dan Hesse, to discuss concerns about awarding the contract to a Chinese firm. Both Huawei and ZTE submitted bids that were lower than those of the other competitors.[30]

A LESSON

In the summer of 2011, Huawei was the world-leading ICT provider, providing services to one-third of the world's population with operations in 140 countries.[31] Huawei was popularly labeled as China's most successful privately held company and one of China's "national champions." However, the overly private nature for which the company had become known and its popularly assigned title as a Chinese National Champion seemed to be impediments to further expansion of its global business, particularly in the U.S. market.[32]

In February 2011, CFIUS recommended that Huawei voluntarily deconstruct its purchase of assets in the American computer company, 3Leaf Systems. Huawei had not immediately disclosed the purchase to CFIUS in the spring of 2010, which some cite as the cause of the deal's failure. Teng Bingsheng, a Cheung Kong Graduate School of Business (CKGSB) professor of strategy, saw the ordeal as a lesson for Huawei, courtesy of the U.S. Government; if Huawei wanted to operate in the U.S. market, it had to play by the rules and respect the authorities.[33] *Xinhua News* saw this as the U.S. government again interfering with its "valued fair market system" by preventing beneficial business that would bring much-needed jobs, investment and spending to a slowing U.S. economy.[34] *Xinhua News* also noted the "very dangerous market-distorting policy precedent" the U.S. government was setting and the possible consequential dangers to U.S. companies operating overseas. Other than the lost financial costs of canceling the deal with 3Leaf, Huawei executives felt that abandoning the 3Leaf purchase was a major blow to their reputation and brand image.[35] Huawei could follow CFIUS's recommendation to withdraw its purchase agreement with 3Leaf or Huawei could decline CFIUS's recommendation and force their application to be decided by President Barack Obama, which at the time was an unprecedented action.[36] Zengfei and his executives needed to determine how they would lead their company in order to ameliorate their current troubles in the U.S. market.

NOTES

1 This case has been written on the basis of published sources only. Consequently, the interpretation and perspectives presented in this case are not necessarily those of Huawei Technologies Corporation or any of its employees.

2 Leila Abboud, "Chinese Telco Gear Makers Aim to Leap U.S. Barriers," 2011, www.reuters.com/article/2011/02/16/us-mobilefair-chinagear-idUSTRE71F19S20110216, accessed February 2, 2013.

3 CFIUS is an inter-agency U.S. government panel that reviews acquisitions and mergers of U.S. entities by foreign companies for possible national security implications.

4 Steven R. Weisman, "Sale of 3Com to Huawei Is Derailed by U.S. Security Concerns," The New York Times, February 2008, www.nytimes.com/2008/02/21/business/worldbusiness/21iht-3com.1.10258216.html?pagewanted=all&_r=0, accessed February 15, 2013.

5 "Huawei Backs Away from 3Leaf Acquisition," Reuters, February 2011, www.reuters.com/article/2011/02/19/us-huawei-3leaf-idUSTRE71I38920110219, accessed January 29, 2013.

6 "Research and Development," www.huawei.com/en/about-huawei/corporate-info/research-development/index.htm, accessed March 5, 2013.

7 Mike Rogers and Dutch Reppersberger, "Investigative Report on the U.S. National Security Issues Posed by Chinese Telecommunications Companies Huawei and ZTE," House of Representatives: Permanent Select Committee on Intelligence (HPSCI), p. 32.

8 All currencies are in US$ unless otherwise stated.

9 "The Long March of the Invisible Mr. Ren," The Economist, June 2011, www.economist.com/node/18771640, accessed February 23, 2013.

10 Victor Zhang, "Huawei Technologies UK CEO Speaks on Internationalization and Innovation by Chinese Multinational Companies," February 2013, www.tmd-oxford.org/content/huawei-technologies-uk-ceo-speaks-internationalisation-and-innovation-chinese-multinational, accessed February 27, 2013.

11 Guanxi is an informal network of trust-based relationships grown from family, school and work ties.

12 Ali F. Farhoomand, "Huawei: Cisco's Chinese Challenger," Asia Case Research Centre, 2006.

13 Ibid.

14 Ibid.

15 P. Fan, "Catching up Through Developing Innovation Capability: Evidence from China's Telecom-Equipment Industry," Department of Urban Studies and Planning, MIT, November 2004.

16 "Cisco, Alcatel-Lucent, Juniper Gain Carrier IP Edge Router/Switch Share in Q1; N. America up 27%," Infonetics Research, May 2012, www.infonetics.com/pr/2012/1Q12-Service-Provider-Routers-Switches-Market-Highlights.asp, accessed March 5, 2013.

17 "The Long March of the Invisible Mr. Ren," The Economist, June 2011, www.economist.com/node/18771640, accessed February 23, 2013.

18 John Lee, "The Other Side of Huawei," Business Spectator, March 30, 2012, www.theworld.org/2013/02/chinas-telecommunications-giant-huawei-under-scrutiny/, accessed February 20, 2013.

19 Mary Kay Magistad, "China's Telecommunication Giant Huawei under Scrutiny," The World, February 2013, www.theworld.org/2013/02/chinas-telecommunications-giant-huawei-under-scrutiny/, accessed February 20, 2013.

20 Joshua Chaffin, "EU Faces up to China over 'Mother of All Cases,'" Financial Times, 2012, www.ft.com/intl/cms/s/e4edbcca-6bab-11e2-8c62-00144feab49a, accessed February 20, 2013.

21 "Resource Center," U.S Department of the Treasury, www.treasury.gov/resource-center/international/Pages/Committee-on-Foreign-Investment-in-US.aspx, accessed February 26, 2013.

22 "Annual Report to Congress for CY 2011" U.S. Department of the Treasury, www.treasury.gov/resource-center/international/foreign-investment/Pages/cfius-reports.aspx, accessed February 26, 2013.

23 Winter Nie, "How Chinese Companies Test Global Waters: The Huawei Success Story," International Institute for Management Development, 2010, www.imd.org/research/challenges/TC067-10.cfm, accessed June 13, 2013.

24 "Milestones," www.huawei.com/en/about-huawei/corporate-info/milestone/index.htm, accessed February 27, 2013.

25 Ibid.

26 Steven R. Weisman, "Sale of 3Com to Huawei is Derailed by U.S. Security Concerns," The New York Times, February 2008, www.nytimes.com/2008/02/21/business/worldbusiness/21iht-3com.1.10258216.html?pagewanted=all&_r=0, accessed February 15, 2013.

27 "The Long March of the Invisible Mr. Ren," The Economist, June 2011, www.economist.com/node/18771640, accessed February 23, 2013.

28 "Huawei Down, Not Out, in Acquisition Bid on U.S. Firm," Xinhuanet, February 2008, http://news.xinhuanet.com/english/2008-02/22/content_7647378.htm, accessed February 22, 2012.

29 Paul Ziobro, "Huawei Enlists an Ex-Sprint Team," The Wall Street Journal, August 2010, http://online.wsj.com/article/SB10001424052748703846604575447803097958776.html, accessed February 23, 2013.

30 Joann Lublin and Shayndi Riace, "Security Fears Kill Chinese Bid in U.S.," The Wall Street Journal, November 2010, http://online.wsj.com/article/SB10001424052748704353504575596611547810220.html, accessed February 15, 2013.

31 Victor Zhang, "Huawei Technologies UK CEO Speaks on Internationalisation and Innovation by Chinese Multinational Companies," February 7, 2013, www.tmd-oxford.org/content/huawei-technologies-uk-ceo-speaks-internationalisation-and-innovation-chinese-multinational, accessed February 27, 2013.

32 M. Zeng and P. Williamson, "The Hidden Dragons," Harvard Business Review, October 2003, http://hbr.org/2003/10/the-hidden-dragons/ar/1, accessed June 13, 2013.

33 "Huawei and 3Leaf: What Went Wrong?" March 2011, http://knowledge.ckgsb.edu.cn/2011/03/04/technology/huawei-and-3leaf-what-went-wrong-chinese-telecoms-set-sights-on-strategic-foreign-assets/, accessed February 22, 2013.

34 Wang Zongkai, "News Analysis: Chinese Tech Firms Hurt by U.S. Political Illusions," Xinhua News 2012, http://news.xinhuanet.com/english/indepth/2012-10/09/c_131895231.htm, accessed February 23, 2013.

35 Ken Hu, "Huawei Open Letter," Chairman of Huawei Technologies USA, 2010, http://online.wsj.com/public/resources/documents/Huawei20110205.pdf, accessed February 22, 2013.

36 "Huawei Waits for White House Review Before Selling Unit," February 2011, www.bbc.co.uk/news/business-12461553, accessed January 29, 2013.

CHAPTER 8

International Market Planning

When Estée Lauder opened a store selling M.A.C. makeup in Lagos, Nigeria, in February, it didn't have much company. While the country is Africa's largest oil producer, 68 percent of Nigerians live on $1.25 or less a day, according to the World Bank. Yet going where rivals aren't is standard operating procedure for the 29-year-old cosmetics line. M.A.C. has long courted various ethnic groups, including black Americans, and Estée Lauder sees the brand as the key to unlocking growth in emerging markets.[1]

LEARNING OBJECTIVES

After Reading This Chapter, You Should Be Able to:

- Understand what motivates a firm to expand abroad rather than in its domestic market.
- Identify the drivers of international market expansion.
- Understand measures of competitiveness.
- Understand the fundamentals of internationalization theories.
- Apply theories of internationalization to case studies of business firms.
- Know more about "born global firms" and why they are different from traditional players.
- Realize that there are many indicators that can be used to evaluate market attractiveness.

INTERNATIONALIZATION

Since 2009, Estée Lauder, the US cosmetics giant, has widened its presence in sub-Saharan Africa, entering new markets and expanding its product portfolio. In the last five years, the company has made forays into Nigeria, Kenya, Ghana, and Côte d'Ivoire. After decades of doing business in South Africa and its neighbouring countries, in 2014, the company operates in a total of 14 markets on the continent. In Kenya for instance, Estée Lauder first launched a range of products in 2011. In October 2014, it partnered with a local entrepreneur to open in Nairobi the first cosmetics outlet in East Africa. Estée Lauder is focusing on cities with the biggest growth potential, and has identified key locations such as Lagos, Abuja and Port

Harcourt in Nigeria, as well as the capitals of Ghana, Kenya, Tanzania, Mozambique and Angola. "It is a fantastic opportunity to be able to launch new brands in new markets, to build those brands and to bring new consumers into those brands. Across the globe there aren't that many markets that are left to launch," says Sue Fox, managing director for Estée Lauder in the sub-Saharan region.[2]

Estée Lauder's sales in the US slowed after the recession as consumers traded down to less pricey brands such as Revlon and Procter & Gamble's CoverGirl. While Estée Lauder's US sales have recovered in the past two years, the cosmetics company is increasingly focused abroad, where it generated 63 percent of its revenue in fiscal 2012. Of M.A.C.'s 529 free-standing stores, 380 are outside the US. Estée Lauder, which doesn't break out M.A.C. sales, had revenue of $9.71 billion in fiscal 2012.

In 2014, Estée Lauder, as well as rival Avon, has grappled with a tough market in North America. However, sales rose 11 percent in the Americas, including the US, and 15 percent in Europe, the Middle East and Africa. Shoppers in the company's core markets reacted enthusiastically to new cosmetics offerings from its leading brands, including Clinique, M.A.C., and Smashbox. Skincare sales, the largest contributor to revenue, rose 14 percent to $1.21bn. Make-up sales climbed 12 percent to $1.06bn, while fragrance sales grew 13 percent to $309.3m. "We achieved record results across many metrics, including sales, operating margin, earnings per share and operating cash flow in fiscal 2014," said Chief Executive, Fabrizio Freda, adding that the company's online, freestanding store and travel retail channels had boosted overall growth. Mr Freda also pointed to strong growth and increased penetration in emerging markets including Mexico, central Europe, Turkey, and South Africa.[3]

The objective of the firm has been to significantly increase its presence in international markets, especially entering those emerging markets with a huge market growth. Internationalization occurs when a firm makes a strategic decision to enter foreign markets and adapts its operations to international environments by committing both tangible and intangible assets, experiential knowledge, learning, and human resources to this effort. But management must realize that foreign or international markets are more competitive than domestic markets owing to the complexity of consumer demands across different countries and because of intensive rivalry from both domestic and international firms.

On the one hand, international markets provide firms like Estée Lauder with an opportunity for expansion and profitability, but on the other hand, represent a tough environment. Looking at Figure 8.1, one of the major challenges in the above example is how Western products can be sold in Africa and how an adequate advertising strategy looks that takes into account differences in skin colour, composition, cosmetics preferences, as well as income and user behavior. These and further issues make up the psychic distance between African and European countries. The origin of the "psychic distance" (PD) concept can be traced back to research conducted by Beckerman (1956)[4] and has since been a prominent concept in both global marketing and management. In most general terms,

FIGURE 8.1
Estée Lauder
Cosmetics
Source: © Authors

it relates to "the sum of factors preventing the flow of information from and to the market" (Johanson &Vahlne, 1977).[5] That is, differences between markets may impede the collection of information, the selection of adequate marketing strategies, and the choice of product variants being sold in a foreign market. In addition, management's choice of which markets to enter, the mode of entry, and timing are of critical importance.

This chapter deals with the alternatives open to the firm and the motivation for internal (domestic) versus external (foreign) expansion. It deals with the factors that favor market entry into one country and potentially impede entry into another. One of the very first decisions management must take is whether to concentrate on the domestic market, to expand abroad, or both. Suppose that it is decided to expand abroad. The next step is to locate specific market opportunities. Once promising markets are located, then an expansion strategy must incorporate issues such as competition analysis, market entry timing, and market targeting. In this chapter, we will present the tools, methods, and theories for preparing these questions. We will link them to business case examples to illustrate how theory and practice interlink. In chapter seven, market entry modes have been discussed and chapter nine investigates the details of market entry screening where it must be decided to enter one market (concentration) or several markets over a short period of time (diversification). To start with, an excellent framework for understanding expansion alternatives is a model developed by Ansoff (1965).

THE ANSOFF EXPANSION MODEL

It is axiomatic that in order to be competitive and profitable, firms must expand their operations. According to Ansoff, they can do this in four ways: market penetration, market development, product development, and diversification. The following matrix (Figure 8.2) illustrates these possibilities. Note that commercial risk increases as the firm introduces new products and/or penetrates new markets.

Present Markets/Present Products—Market Penetration

Firms choosing this strategy attempt to gain higher market share in existing markets using existing products. More resources are dedicated to marketing effort through adjusting the marketing mix, such as more aggressive advertising and sales promotion. Penetration can also be accomplished by offering price discounts and a better relationship with customers. Of the four growth strategies, market penetration has the lowest risk. For example, many Chinese companies can still benefit from the huge Chinese market before they venture into international markets. The example of China Resources Snow Brewery Ltd. (CR Snow) is a good example. CR Snow is a brewing company headquartered in Beijing, China. It is a joint venture between China Resources Enterprise and the UK-based multinational SABMiller making the largest brewing company in China, with a market share of around 21 percent, and

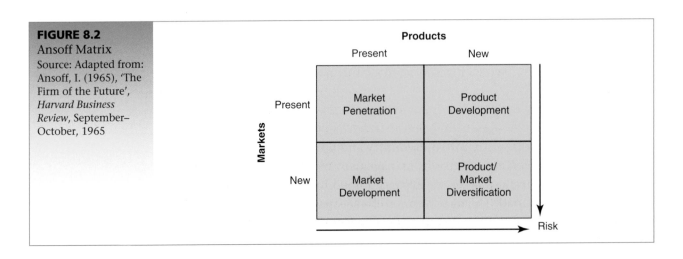

FIGURE 8.2
Ansoff Matrix
Source: Adapted from: Ansoff, I. (1965), 'The Firm of the Future', *Harvard Business Review*, September–October, 1965

a total of 10.3 billion liters of beer sold in China in 2013. In a recently published report by Euromonitor, figures indicate that the world's biggest beer market in terms of volume sales, China, will overtake the United States in terms of value sale by 2017. "As the legal drinking age population is expected to grow faster in China than in the USA over 2013–18 in absolute terms, brewers will be capturing prospective demand that has been dormant for years," said Amin Alkhatib, a drinks analyst at Euromonitor. Given the sheer number of inhabitants and prospective beer drinkers, market penetration seems to be a very good strategy for the company even though other market options become increasingly interesting for CR Snow.[6]

Present Markets/New Products—Product Development

This strategy entails offering new products to current markets. It requires developing or acquiring new products or line expansion. A good example of this strategy is the German company, Mont Blanc, best known for its fountain pens. However, once you purchase one of their pens or sets, you are set for life. Only a few collectors will purchase additional pens or pencils. In order to expand sales among existing customers, Mont Blanc expanded into accessories, such as wallets and cuff links. However, this strategy is not an easy one because these products need to be accepted by consumers and should not be too far away from the branding of the original product because this is what has created the product image in the past.

New Markets/Present Products—Market Development

New markets may be solely domestic or both domestic and global. Dressbarn, one of the largest retail women's clothing chains (about 1,500 stores in 48 states and the District of Columbia) operated initially in the eastern part of the United States from its founding in 1962, but purchased the Maurices chain in 2005 to expand to the Midwest and western United States. They do not have stores outside the United States, but most of their clothing is contract-manufactured in Asia, the Middle East, and Africa.

On the other hand, Tesco, the UK's largest food retailer, has diversified globally. After a gradual expansion into Ireland and an unsuccessful expansion into France in the 1990s, Tesco began a rapid expansion in the late 1990s into emerging markets focusing on Eastern Europe and Southeast Asia. These areas have relatively undeveloped grocery retail markets, but ones that are changing rapidly giving Tesco major opportunities. Tesco PLC operates over 7,599 stores (including franchising) in the UK, Ireland, Hungary, Poland, the Czech Republic, Slovakia, Turkey, and Asia. Tesco's operations include convenience (Tesco Express), small urban stores (Tesco Metro), hypermarkets (Tesco Extra), financial services, and a telecom business. Tesco is also a leader in online grocery sales through its online store at www.tesco.com.

New Markets/New Products—Product/Market Diversification

With the increasing interest in emerging markets, companies have begun to target the specific needs of the emerging consumer. This strategy may not only result in new products for developed markets, but may also benefit developed countries these innovations can be transferred back to. For companies, this implies no longer taking a known product and removing features to make it cheaper. Instead, companies now begin with their experience and knowledge of their customers in distant markets and use information to conceive, design and make a new, locally appropriate product from the ground up. This alternative product development cycle is a natural evolutionary step for most companies trying to thrive in emerging markets. Among Nokia's cell phone models in India, for example, are models that have flashlights (because of electrical blackouts) and multiple "phonebooks" (because bottom-of-the-pyramid consumers often share a phone among several owners). And McDonald's menus in India feature items with familiar Indian spices.[7]

Internationalization and the Ansoff Matrix

Internationalization has been defined as the process of adapting a firm's operations (strategy, structure, resources) to international environments. Therefore, only a market development strategy—entering foreign markets—would fit this definition. However, most of the firms described previously have expanded their operations both domestically and internationally by adopting most, if not all, of Ansoff's suggested strategies. Looking at the matrix again (Figure 8.2), this time using the Tesco Company as an example, we see that they have adopted all four strategies at one time or another.

Tesco has increased its market share both domestically and internationally by using all elements of the marketing mix, including line extension and differentiation (e.g. financial services to existing customers and consumer electronics to both current and new customers). It has also expanded internationally (new markets). What are some of drivers that have motivated the above and other companies to internationalize their operations?

MOTIVATION TO INTERNATIONALIZE

The idea or urge to internationalize may be internal or external to the firm. It may occur internally by the realization of management that there is more potential for growth overseas than in the domestic market. Or the motivation can be an external source, resulting from an unsolicited contact from a potential buyer overseas who heard something about the company's products by word of mouth or a news write-up on the Internet. The unsolicited trigger to follow up and investigate markets abroad is a reactive motive. It is similar to motivation fostered by the occurrence of a domestic event not under the control of the firm such as a recession at home.

On the other hand, there are proactive motives to internationalization such as the desire of management to become global players.[8] Some authors distinguish between internal and external motives.[9] According to Mwiti et al. (2013),[10] the internal motives can be considered all factors related to the influences from within the enterprise, while external factors are those stemming from the company's external environment, whether domestic or foreign.

Proactive Motives

Generally speaking, proactive motives stem from management's beliefs that internationalization improves the current position of the firm. For instance, four main intentions drive Chinese companies to go abroad: (1) securing natural resources, (2) gaining access to new markets, (3) buying strategic assets, and (4) improving domestic and overseas efficiency.[11] Tan and Ai (2010)[12] differentiate further between motives of state-owned enterprises (SOEs) and non-state-owned enterprises, as can be seen in Table 8.1 below.

With regards to internationalizing to Europe, many surveys and studies show that the most important reason for Chinese companies is the "market-seeking" motive,[13] which means either to secure or expand already existing market share. To date, Europe is the first consumer market overseas for China, explaining the importance of the services industry.[14]

The second important motive driving Chinese companies in Europe is the search for strategic assets, e.g. technologies, brand names, management capabilities, etc. in order to raise competitiveness. They either obtain these assets through cumulative experience or collaborations, such as joint ventures or partnerships, or through the acquisition of distressed firms or non-core subdivisions (see also the Linkage-Learning-Leverage approach later in this chapter). For instance, two of China's four largest acquisitions were in the resource sector. State-owned China National Petroleum Corporation purchased 100 percent of PetroKazakhstan in August 2005. And Sinopec, a member of the state-owned China Petrochemical Corporation, bought a 96.9 percent stake in the Russian oil company, Udmurtneft, in June 2006. China's resource-seeking acquisitions have been distributed all over the world, with Canada, Australia, and Russia leading target countries.[15]

The third motive is the "efficiency-seeking" intention, which is quite recent since it is an issue usually related to multinationals from developed countries. The

SOEs	Non-SOEs	**TABLE 8.1**
Natural resource seeking	Strategic asset seeking	Differences in the Outward Direct Investment Motives of Chinese SOEs and Non-SOEs
Increasing international competitiveness	Access to new markets	
Maintaining domestic leading position	Seeking technologies	
	Diversification	
	Seeking efficiency	
Source: Adapted from: Tan and Ai, 2010[16]		

main objective is cost reduction, especially labor costs. Indeed, Chinese labor costs have steadily risen during the last few years, even though there is still a considerable gap with Western labor costs. Thus, efficiency seekers are usually firms that are already established abroad but look to rationalize their operations by gaining economies of scale and scope through common governance and knowledge sharing.

The remaining motive of securing natural resources is not playing a major role in Europe. Large investments in natural resources are mainly flowing to developing resource-endowed countries, such as in Africa. Not surprisingly Africa has become a very interesting investment target for many Chinese firms (Box 8.1).

A major **external motive** or initiator is the change agent. These may be resident buyers for foreign companies such as department store chains. They seek out products for sale in the chain and initiate contact with the domestic supplier. They may suggest how to modify the product for sale in the foreign market. Another sort of change agent is the so-called **roving export manager (ROV)** employed by the

---

Box 8.1   Country-in-Focus: Africa and China

Africa as an Increasingly Interesting Target Market for China

Bagamayo, Tanzania was the capital of the colony of German East Africa from 1888 to 1891, when the administrative seat was moved to Dar es Salaam because the shore in Bagamayo was too shallow for a real seaport. Since then, time seems to have stood still. But soon nothing will be as it once was in Bagamayo because now the new rulers of the world, the Chinese, are coming.

China was making a low-interest loan of $10 billion (€7.4 billion) available for the construction of a modern container terminal 15 kilometers (9 miles) south of the city, and also planned to fund the establishment of a special economic zone in the hinterlands behind the port.

It wasn't easy to gain a foothold in Tanzania, Huang, an engineer, says, "but we Chinese are not afraid of taking risks. We see Africa with different eyes than the West, not as a rotten continent, but as an economic region with enormous potential." Huang's privately-owned company has had a hand in constructing many buildings. Most recently, it built the Crystal Tower in downtown Dar es Salaam. "We invest and create jobs. It's a win-win situation for both sides," he says.

China, Asia's economic superpower, is hungry for natural resources, energy, food, and markets for its products. Africa can offer all of these things: about 40 percent of global reserves of natural resources, 60 percent of uncultivated agricultural land, a billion people with rising purchasing power and a potential army of low-wage workers.

Also, to be more relevant in the twenty-first Century, Africa must develop its human capital and have access to new technology. China has provided both. It has offered training to many African professionals under its commitment to train Africa's emergent workforce. Machinery, electronic equipment, and high-tech products have been exported to Africa. Above all, China has built more factories to process African raw materials in Africa rather than just extracting low value-added African commodities for processing in China. Africa also gains from favorable loans offered by Chinese banks. This comes along with a combination of grants as well as concessional and commercial rate loans. Because of Africa's poor credit ratings, they must pay huge risk premium to access commercial capital. On the other hand, Chinese concessional loans are subsidized through aid budget thus permitting lower interest rates than those available through commercial lending houses.

Sources: Grill, B. (2013), 'Billions from Beijing: Africans divided over Chinese presence', *Spiegel Online*, 29 November, 2013, http://www.spiegel.de/international/world/chinese-investment-in-africa-boosts-economies-but-worries-many-a-934826.html   [Accessed: March 13, 2013]; Ayodele, T. and Sotola, O. (2014). China in Africa: An Evaluation of Chinese Investment. IPPA Working Paper Series (2014).

Israel Export Institute. These agents are retired export managers who have amassed significant experience and knowledge in a variety of industries. They act as the representative of SMEs who wish to internationalize but lack the knowledge and skills for doing so. The ROV negotiates on behalf of the local firm, concludes the sale, and arranges for the exportation of the goods. He is compensated partly by the Institute and by the firm.

Trade agreements are also motives for internationalization. An agreement that serves to reduce trade barriers will certainly encourage domestic firms to take advantage of lower tariffs in order to export. Similarly, the removal of barriers such as banking and investment regulations in host countries may motivate these institutions to establish branches or affiliates abroad. Also, higher prices abroad may be a strong incentive to export.

Reactive Motives

Reactive motivated firms view internationalization as a necessary response to unfavorable conditions in their current markets. Such conditions may be increased competitive pressures, excess capacity given domestic market conditions, or a declining domestic market. Ersson and Tryggvason (2007)[17] found that a major internationalization motive of Nordic banks was a saturated home market. In addition, management can react to negative changes within the firm by choosing internationalization as a method for improving or overcoming internal problems. However, their motives in these examples may be more tactical than strategic, or short-term rather than long-term.

Much of the literature reflects reactive motives as negative, while proactive ones are positive. There is some evidence to show that firms that engage in proactive planning are more successful than those that do not (reactive).[18] Small firms with limited resources and lack of international experience are more prone to reactive expansion. However, even larger companies may be reactive in the beginning stages of internationalization, but become proactive later. A case in point is the Chinese sportswear company Li Ning, which has very gradually increased their international sales and intends to challenge big global players like Adidas or Nike (Table 8.2), though mainly in China for the time being. That is, it adopted an inward-internationalization, whereby it competes against the major players in its home market. Outward internationalization started in 2001, when Li Ning established the first retail store in Spain. However, the real start of internationalization can be connected to the Olympic Games in Beijing 2008. Shortly afterwards, the company established a multiplicity of stores outside China, located in Singapore, Indonesia, Brunei, and Malaysia. In 2010, Li Ning established a large design center in Nike's hometown Portland.

Over the last years, Li Ning has gradually increased its efforts to internationalize and to become present on a global scale. However, regarding revenues, Li Ning is internationally still very limited as only 1 percent is generated outside of China. The company has seen explosive growth in shoe sales in the past several years.

TABLE 8.2 A Comparison Between Different International Sportswear Companies and Their Internationalization Strategies		Li-Ning	Adidas	Nike
	Foundation Date	1990	1949	1971
	Employees (2013)	3,592	50,728	48,000
	Revenues (2013) in US$	948.9 million	15.88 billion	25.3 billion
	First Internationalization	2001: Spain	1950: First exports to Switzerland, Scandinavia, and Canada	1972: Canada; 1974: Australia
	Internationalization Motive	Creation of trends and enhancement of the brand	Ensure future growth	Cost-effective production
	Source: Compiled by Authors			

Li Ning's major shoe lines include the "Flying Armor" series of basketball shoes and "Flying Feather" running shoes.

THEORIES OF INTERNATIONALIZATION AND MARKET ENTRY

In this section, we want to explain the conditions under which it is more efficient for a firm to create an internal, domestic market or to enter foreign ones. In addition to the theoretical discussion in Chapter 3, where we focused on country-related issues, we investigate now what explains a firm's internationalization behavior.

The criteria for determining whether to expand in an internal, rather than a foreign market, are based on the transaction costs of information, opportunism, and asset specificity. Generally speaking, the cost of information acquisition in foreign markets is far more expensive than acquiring information in internal markets. Control over agents abroad may be more difficult resulting in opportunistic behavior (agents operating in their own interest rather than that of the principal, or where one party to an agreement tries to better his/her position at the expense of the other). Examples of opportunistic behavior include not reporting all sales, disregarding codes of conduct required by headquarters, and outright fraud. Also, a firm with technological or marketing know-how advantages is better able to protect them in its home market. If transaction costs of operating abroad are higher they cause market failure and serve as a barrier to internationalizing the firm.

Nevertheless, firms do internationalize in spite of higher transaction costs. They do this by internalizing firm specific advantages, such as technological know-how, by using entry modes such as direct investment rather than licensing the know-how to an agent, which carries the risk of losing it. Internalization theorists suggest that foreign direct investment occurs when the benefits of internalization outweigh its costs.

Other explanations take into account that emerging market firms often follow internationalization patterns, which are very different from those of developed market firms. For instance, they try to collaborate, build linkages with global competitors with the objective to catch up and improve their latecomer position. Very often, they also need to engage in dual strategies, that is they strive for capability building and capability exploitation at the same time and adopt different trajectories of doing business in other emerging markets and in highly developed markets. Especially, younger firms seem to ignore many of the principles suggested by internationalization theories. This is why we also introduce insights from international entrepreneurship and born globals literature, which explain the internationalization of firms that go international shortly after foundation. Table 8.3 provides an overview of the different approaches, which we are going to explain with more details and concrete examples in what follows.

Theoretical Perspective	Main Author(s)/ Year	Focus
OLI Model	Dunning (1981, 1988, 2006)	• Inside-out oriented asset exploitation. Modified OLI-paradigm with inward investment and more collaborative linkages.
Incremental Process Theory (Uppsala Model)	Johanson & Vahlne (1977, 2009, 2013)	• Inside-out orientation built on substantial home advantage as an antecedent to internationalization, sequential market entry. • Later focus on relationships, which connects to network approach.
Network Approach	Johanson & Mattson (1988)	• Internationalization occurs within the network by making use of existing information and resource exchanges.
Transaction Cost Analysis	Hirsch (1976)	• Internationalization is linked to the costs that occur in dealing with specific entry-mode options.
Linkage-Learning-Leverage Model	Mathews (2006)	• Outside-in orientation with latecomer firms using overseas investments and global linkages to leverage their existing cost advantages, and learn about new sources of competitive advantage.
International New Venture Theory	Oviatt & McDougall (1994); Jones & Coviello (2005)	• Internationalization starts right after foundation by ignoring psychic and cultural distance.

TABLE 8.3
Summary of Theoretical Perspectives to Explain Emerging Market Firms' Internationalization Processes

Source: Compiled by Authors

Dunning's Eclectic OLI-Model

John Dunning (1981)[19] posited that entry-mode decisions are based on three conditions or advantages: Ownership (who is going to produce abroad), Location (where to produce), and Internalization (why to produce rather than license someone else to produce for you using your assets and know-how). Foreign direct investment (FDI) will be the preferred mode when three conditions are fulfilled:

1. The firm must have net ownership advantages over competing firms. These advantages must be sufficient to offset the additional costs of operating in a foreign environment.

2. It must be more profitable for the firm possessing these unique assets to use them itself rather than transfer the rights to others.

3. It must be advantageous for the firm to exploit its unique assets through production outside its home country rather than by exporting.

FDI is possible when a firm has some monopolistic advantage over local firms. This advantage can be in the form of assets (the firm's size, which gives it economies of scale, an advantage of common governance over a number of operations abroad) and skills (the marketing of differentiated products, managerial experience). The monopolistic advantage must be greater than the costs of establishing and operating a foreign subsidiary. Taken together, these are the ownership advantages of the model.

Locational advantages stem from the attractiveness of a given country. A firm interested in investing abroad chooses the most favorable location where it can control financial risk and achieve sufficient returns. In this case it is the country that possesses specific advantages in the form of raw materials, low production costs, good infrastructure, and the like. Location advantage may also be a function of spatial market failure where trade barriers make imports prohibitive or very expensive to local consumers.

Internalization advantages accrue when the firm can overcome risk and uncertainty through the choice of a hierarchical mode of organization where subsidiary organizations are subordinate to headquarters. Such an organization structure results in the integration of different activities of the chain in different countries. It can also protect property rights and ensure quality control of the production process. However, the higher the costs of governing a hierarchical organization, the more likely management will prefer a shared equity form such as a joint venture. Transaction costs can be reduced by finding a local partner in the foreign market who is familiar with the territory and the company's products. Such a partnership can result in faster penetration of the market, while at the same time managing risk and uncertainty.

For instance, when VW entered the Mexican market, this marked an important step in the internationalization process the company had already begun in

Brazil and South Africa in the 1950s. Mexico was another emerging automotive nation where one focus of government industrialization policy involved establishing a national automotive industry. Volkswagen already began exporting to Mexico in 1954, establishing an import company for the purpose called "Volkswagen Mexicana S.A." which set about obtaining import quotas and contracting companies to assemble CKD (completely knocked-down) Beetle kits. However, government import restrictions meant that annual sales initially failed to move out of the three digit range, and structures were unstable. In 1958, responsibility for the Mexico operations was transferred to "Volkswagen Interamericana S.A." which was in charge of exports to other Central and South American countries.

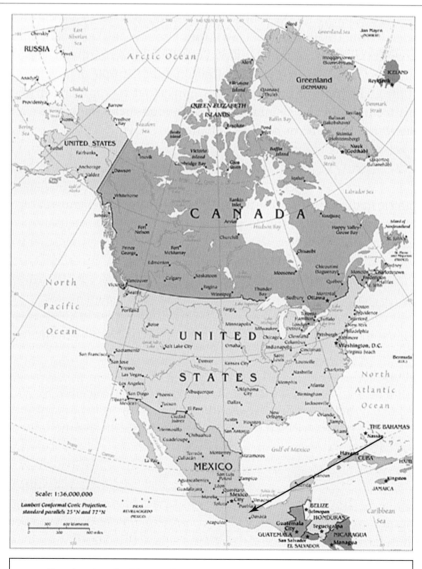

GEO MAP 8.1
VW
Source: Adapted from: CIA Maps, The World Factbook[20]

Production facilities of **VW** are located in Puebla, Mexico.

In order to comply with the government's requirements and consolidate the market position now held by Volkswagen in Mexico, it was essential for the company to build its own production plant (Geo Map 8.1 for production facilities in Puebla, Mexico). Placing their faith in the growth potential of the market, the first step involved the acquisition of Promexa S.A. by Volkswagenwerk AG effective January 1, 1964, and this was followed by the founding of an import, production and sales company called "Volkswagen de México, S.A." (VWdM) on January 15, 1964.[21] In 2013, yet another new factory was built in the Mexican state of Guanajuato, in the city of Silao. According to Martin Winterkorn, CEO of VW, "The Silao factory is the Volkswagen Group's 100th plant and therefore represents one of the largest and most international production networks in the automotive industry [. . .] With this new plant we are driving our ambitious major North American offensive forward. Over the next three years the Volkswagen Group will be investing more than $5 billion in North America alone. Silao is thus also a strong symbol of our uninterrupted growth trajectory and the Group's continuing internationalization."[22]

This short story of VW's internationalization is an example of how the company followed the OLI-criteria: it possesses huge managerial and production know-how; it benefits from financial advantages in the foreign location; and it can control business activities through its own subsidiaries.

Critique

In the eclectic framework, location advantages are treated independently from ownership advantages. However, the decision of where to expand internationally is not

---

Box 8.2   People-in-Focus: John Dunning

Professor Dunning was awarded honorary doctorates from the University of Uppsala in Sweden, the Autonomous University of Madrid, and the University of Antwerp. He was also honorary Professor of International Business at the University of International Business and Economics at Beijing. He was past president of the International Trade and Finance Association, and of the Academy of International Business. A book edited by Peter Buckley and Mark Casson was published in his honor in 1992, and, a second book was published in 2003 embracing his work at Rutgers University. A volume edited by John Cantwell and Rajneesh Narula entitled *International Business and the Eclectic Paradigm* was devoted to his theoretical contributions to international business. In August 2002, Professor Dunning was honored as Distinguished Scholar in International Management at the Academy of Management's annual meeting at Denver. In December 2004 he was presented with a Lifetime Achievement Award at the annual meeting of the European Academy of International Business in Ljubljana, Slovenia.

Dunning died on January 29, 2009. In the same year, the *Journal of International Business Studies*, the most prestigious academic journal in international business, commented, "John Dunning is widely recognized as the father of the field of international business" and "Today, John's influence is demonstrated by a citation count on Google Scholar of over 30,000, many times that of any other scholar in the field of international business."

Sources: http://aib.msu.edu/fellow/21/John-H-Dunning [Accessed: March 25, 2013]; http://www.theguardian.com/education/2009/mar/10/higher-education [Accessed: March 25, 2013]; Dunning, J. (2008). *Seasons of a Scholar: Some Personal Reflections of an International Business Economist*, Edward Elgar, Cheltenham, UK and Northampton, MA.

independent of ownership advantages or of the route by which these advantages will be used. In other words, there is a constant interplay between O, L, and I.[23]

Further, the model is mainly valid for Western firms but may not be able to explain the reality of emerging market firms (EMFs), which tend to internationalize even if they do not necessarily have unique ownership advantages based on superior technology, competitive products, or management know-how. There have been several modifications to the OLI theory to account for this, including the argument that EMFs do possess ownership advantages, albeit of a different kind.[24] These ownership advantages include customer knowledge, operating experience in volatile environments, and ultra-low-cost production; which all give them advantage in coping with institutional voids and accelerating rapidly in other less developed countries. In terms of investment, OLI arguments purport full control modes (see Chapter 7), which may not be easy to realize abroad and EMFs may prefer exporting, licensing, or franchising to benefit from internationalization. Relational modes of collaboration rather than full contractual engagements provide more flexibility and seem more appropriate to EMFs' learning objectives. However, one of the myths is the fact that especially Chinese firms invest in distant countries to engage in strategic asset seeking, primarily to exploit these assets at home before they venture out again (see again Box 8.1).

The Incremental Process or Uppsala Model

The Uppsala model was developed by Swedish researchers from Uppsala University to explain the sequential steps in the direction of increased foreign dedication.[25] According to the Uppsala model, firms first enter into markets that are psychically close to their home base and later enter more distant markets as their experiential knowledge increases. The concept of psychic distance is defined as factors preventing or disturbing the flows of information between firm and market. Examples of such factors are differences in language, culture, political systems, level of education, level of industrial development, etc. (see again the introductory case example).[26] A basic assumption of the model is that "the lack of knowledge is an important obstacle to the development of international operations."[27] The absence of market-specific knowledge is presumed to have forced the Swedish manufacturing firms, which formed the original sample of the model, to develop their international operations in incremental steps to reduce the market uncertainty.

Johanson and Weidersheim-Paul (1975)[28] further found four different stages of entering international markets (see Figure 8.3). Basically, firms remained domestic unless some internal or external driver motivated them to expand, such as an unsolicited export order. Over time, firms gradually progress through a series of stages based on experiential learning and commitment of resources. Each stage represents a higher degree of international market commitment and geographic diversification as shown in Figure 8.3. In the first stage there are only sporadic exports, mostly from unsolicited orders. Regular exporting is accomplished in the

FIGURE 8.3
An Incremental
Approach to the
Internationalization
of the Firm
Sources: Adapted
from: Forsgren, M.,
and Johanson, J.
(1975). *Internationell
företagsekonomi
(International business
economics).* Stockholm:
Norstedts; Dervilée,
F., Rieche, M., and
Zieske, A. (2004).
*Internationalization
and foreign market
entry choice: An
alternative approach
to the Kristianstad
30 Model.* [MBA
thesis]. Högskolan:
Kristianstad

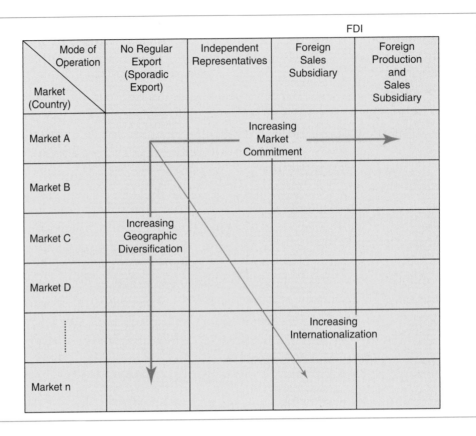

second stage, via contracts with established, independent distributors and sales representatives abroad. In the third stage, a foreign sales subsidiary is organized. Finally, in the fourth stage, a manufacturing subsidiary is established. Following this stage approach, Swedish firms would first enter low psychic distant markets such as Finland and Denmark and then later more distant ones through higher market commitment.

It seems like a couple of major international, mostly large, firms have followed the incremental approach. For instance, traditional ventures, such as the French retailer Carrefour or the Swiss hearing healthcare solutions producer, Sonova (formerly Phonak), started internationalization at a later age and benefitted most from home-consolidated knowledge and experience that is positively related to internationalization. Similarly, Argentinean candy producer, Arcor, a leading industrial group in Latin America, waited 25 years before it went international. Today, it is the world's first candy manufacturer and the main exporter of confectionery of Argentina, Brazil, Chile, and Peru. The company was founded in 1951 in the city of Arroyito, Córdoba (Argentina), with the aim of offering quality products to consumers all over the world. Arcor's products are manufactured in 39 industrial plants located in Argentina, Brazil, Chile, Mexico, and Peru, and its products are commercialized in more than 120 countries of the world. As Geo Map 8.2 illustrates, the company internationalized very incrementally and mainly expanded within Latin America before it went to the US and to Europe.

Arcor's Internationalization Trajectory

Founded 1951 in Argentina

1976: Paraguay
1979: Uruguay
1981: Brazil
1989: Chile
1990: Bolivia
1993: Miami, US
1996: Peru
1998: Chile, Ecuador
1999: Brazil
2000: Chile, Colombia, Mexico
2001: Canada
2002: Barcelona, Spain
2006: Venezuela, South Africa
2007: Chile, Brazil, China

GEO MAP 8.2
Arcor
Source: Adapted from:
CIA Maps, The World
Factbook[29]

Arcor's headquarters is located in
Buenos Aires, Argentina.

Critique

There are a number of criticisms of the stage models. Why can't firms leapfrog stages? Acquisition of knowledge is faster than indicated by the stage model. Knowledge may be acquired by hiring experienced international managers, by attending seminars sponsored by export institutes and from consulting organizations. Another explanation may be that since the exposition of such models, the world has become flat and integrated, facilitated by rapid dissemination of information. Another criticism of the model is that it is uni-directional; it does not consider the possibilities of changing strategies at a given stage, e.g. divestment or choosing a cooperative mode such as a strategic alliance. Especially born global firms show a totally different internationalization behavior which opposes the insights of the Uppsala model. However, some of the advantages of a stage approach are that companies find the time to digest new experiences, minimize risks, and transfer learning experiences to similar environments. From a marketing perspective, it may take longer to build global brand awareness. If companies sell products with a short life cycle, incremental market entry may not be the optimum solution because the time available for return on investment is short and entering foreign markets in an accelerated way may be preferable.

Later developments of the theory have taken some of these aspects into account, for instance, by emphasizing the importance of network relations, the role of uncertainty, and a more dynamic perspective by emphasizing opportunity development capabilities, internationalization capabilities, and relational capabilities that all support the manner and extent of a firm's venturing abroad.[30]

The Network Approach

One more often used and cited part of the theoretical framework of internationalization processes is the work by Mattson & Hertz (1998),[31] who discuss the occurrence and importance of having international networks (Figure 8.4). Network participants are governed by exchange relationships rather than through the market. Because many small companies do not have infinite resources, network collaborations are seen as an important internationalization strategy. An industrial network normally includes different players involved in production, distribution, and usage of services and products (Johanson & Mattson, 1988).[32] Financial networks are important for SMEs since these companies normally need to finance their expansion with external capital. In some cases it might be easier to find financing in the country of expansion instead of on the home market. This has

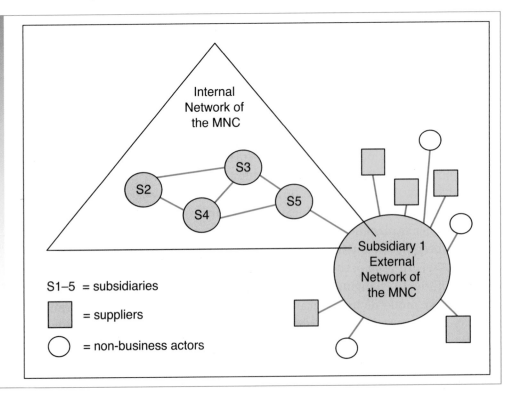

FIGURE 8.4
Illustration of a Multinational Firm's Network
Source: Compiled by Authors

Internal Network of the MNC

S3
S2
S4
S5

Subsidiary 1 External Network of the MNC

S1–5 = subsidiaries

■ = suppliers

○ = non-business actors

to do with the fact that some venture capitalists prefer to invest in their own home region, where they have a better understanding of the market.

All different forms of networks have in common that they require complex strategies to ensure their viability and success.[33] Companies need to simultaneously engage with corporate, international, and network strategies.

Table 8.4 shows some of the differences between network and market-based relationships. In a network, knowledge is shared, not only by wholly-owned subsidiaries (e.g. best practices), but also with suppliers. For example, buyers and suppliers may be connected via computer to each other's inventory system, which will automatically inform global suppliers, who are partners in the network, when to ship goods to their related customers. Therefore, both subsidiaries and suppliers are interdependent. Finally, the network model is more prevalent in Scandinavian countries than in the United States and the UK. Note that this partly stems from the fact that the Scandinavian countries have more collective cultures on Hofstede's scale, while the United States and the UK are more individualistic.

During the internationalization process a company can form new networks in three ways: by creating new relations to networks in the country of expansion that were previously unknown to the company, by creating new relations to actors in networks that were previously known to the company, or by using existing contacts in order to connect to new networks.[34]

Indeed, Johanson and Mattson[35] have argued that the stage and network theories complement each other. We would agree that today the theories complement each other, since organizational learning takes place within multinational corporations and this intangible, firm-specific advantage is common to both theories.

Figure 8.4 illustrates a network configuration of a multinational corporation. The network is made up of the MNC's corporate headquarters along with five subsidiaries in, let us assume, different countries. The figure details the network of Subsidiary S1 with its headquarters, other subsidiaries in the network, and interdependent agents. In addition, it shows that each subsidiary is networked with headquarters and with one or more of the additional subsidiaries. MNC subsidiaries are not only part of the network, they also develop relations with network actors, such as suppliers, distributors and regulatory agencies, and competitors. Firms interact and build relations with local network actors in order to exchange resources, including goods,

Network	Market	
Shared Knowledge	Knowledge Serves Competitive Advantage	**TABLE 8.4** Network Versus Market-Based Relationships
Interdependent	Independent	
Consent	Contracts	
Trust	Price	
Learning	Power	
Partners	Customers	
Scandinavia	UK, US, Australia	
Source: © Authors		

services, knowledge, and information. By building network relations, subsidiary management learns how to function in the local environment.

A central point in network theory is that different processes within a company cannot be explained without analyzing the networks that a company is directly or indirectly a part of. The roles of networks have attracted a lot of attention in the last decades. It is often said that having a good network is one of the keys for success. For instance, Chongqing is China's third largest centre for motor vehicle production and the largest for motorcycles. Leading makers of cars and motorbikes includes China's fourth biggest automaker; Chang'an Automotive Corp, as well as Lifan Hongda Enterprise, and the Ford Motor Company, with the US car giant having three plants in Chongqing (Geo Map 8.3). Thus, being located in the city provides access to a huge network of companies.

Transaction Cost Approach

The decision of whether or not to internationalize the firm is also based on transaction costs. A transaction cost is a cost of making an economic exchange. All forms of market entry incur transaction costs. Basically, there are three sorts of costs:

1. *Search and information costs.* Market research, research to find suitable distributors or partners abroad.

2. *Bargaining costs.* Once a potential distributor or partner is located, bargaining on the terms of an agreement follows. The bargaining process incurs costs, such as legal and consultant fees, travel expenses, and telephone and other communication expenses.

GEO MAP 8.3
Chang'an
Automotive
Source: Adapted from:
CIA Maps, The World
Factbook[36]

The headquarters of **Chang'an Automotive** is located in Chongqing, China

3. *Monitoring (governance) costs*. Once an agreement has been concluded, it has to be enforced to make sure that both sides are living up to the terms of the contract. In the case of suspected breach of contract, these costs can be substantial when arbitration or legal action has to be taken.

We can discern at least three scenarios of transaction costs by mode of entry. Production at home for export involves local manufacturing costs, search and bargaining costs for distributors, and governance costs. Licensing includes search and bargaining costs for a licensee, governance costs, and the risk of dissemination. Dissemination risk occurs when control over an asset such as a brand name, a patent, and knowledge is low. The loss of such assets carries a cost to the firm that can be considerable. A classic case occurred with the American firm, Radio Corporation of America (now known as the RCA Corporation, owned by Thomson SA, France). In 1939 RCA unveiled its electronic TV system at the World's Fair in Flushing Meadows, New York. The company began manufacturing TV sets for sale in the United States after World War II. In 1953, its color TV system became the standard (NTSC) approved by the government. Sets were marketed to the public in 1955. Later, the company sold its proprietary knowledge to Japanese companies, who succeeded in taking over the American market.

Production abroad involves manufacturing costs in the foreign country, possible bargaining costs, if the subsidiary is not wholly-owned, and some governance costs. According to transaction cost theory, a firm will tend to export or license when transaction costs are low, or shift production abroad when transaction costs are high. Hirsch (1976)[37] viewed exporting and foreign direct investment (FDI) as alternative strategies for market entry. Producing at home for export bears costs of (1) domestic production costs, Pd, (2) export marketing costs, Md, and (3) domestic governance costs, Cd. Producing abroad incurs costs of (1) foreign production, Pf, (2) local marketing, Mf, and (3) foreign governance, Cf. The difference between export marketing and domestic marketing costs (M) is defined as:

M = Mf – Md

The difference between foreign and domestic governance costs (C) is defined as:

C = Cf – Cd

The decision to export or produce abroad (FDI) is determined as:

If Pd < Pf + M + C, then export
If Pd ≥ Pf + M + C, then FDI

Critique

Transaction cost theory assumes that exporting and production are substitutes. In reality there are many examples where a firm both manufactures abroad *and* exports from its home market, as well. Of Honda's total car sales in the American market, about 84 percent is manufactured in the United States, while the remainder is exported from Japan. There are similar examples of other car manufacturers producing abroad and exporting from their home market such as Toyota and Volkswagen.

A firm may invest abroad in order to gain raw materials or know-how that are not available at home. This behavior is not explained by transaction costs. Another criticism of the theory is that it is difficult to measure transaction costs, especially in advance of choosing an entry mode.

Small and medium enterprises (SMEs) tend to reflexively rely on non-equity modes of entry (exporting, licensing, see Chapter 7) because they would rather preserve capital and avoid high risks when moving into international markets. However, research suggests[38] that using transaction cost analysis to select an international mode of entry—a method usually associated with large corporations—can actually improve their chances of selecting the most efficient method for their specific organization. The authors of the study recommend that SMEs evaluate three specific transaction cost criteria:

1. Level of investment required for each asset. If no particular asset requires a large investment, non-equity modes such as licensing or franchising may be suitable for market entry. If such entry requires a high level of specific-asset investment, equity modes of entry, such as IJVs or fully-owned subsidiaries, may be more appropriate.

2. Environmental factors of the target country. A more stable and economically and politically secure country would be more inviting to an equity mode of entry, whereas a country with political or social turmoil and frequent economic crises would be suitable for non-equity modes of entry.

3. Status of internal control systems and processes. A business that is built on strong internal culture and regulations would be more comfortable upholding them in their new markets by entering through equity modes. On the other hand, a more open and flexible firm may be comfortable with relying on the controls of partners such as exporting agents or licensees.

SME decision-makers can rely on transaction cost theory to make more informed decisions about the most appropriate mode of entry for their company. Decisions made using this method seem to lead to a better performance abroad, according to this study. Whether a firm uses transaction cost analysis or any other accepted method to evaluate its international market strategy, the choice of entry mode should be carefully considered and planned to ensure smoother, more profitable operations abroad.

Linkage-Learning-Leverage Model

With the increasing attention given to Asian multinationals and their different way of internationalization, i.e. accelerated and ignoring psychic distance constraints, researchers have developed an interest to think about different theories to explain this behavior. The term "Dragon Multinationals" was coined for these firms and researchers like John Mathews (2006)[39] noted that these firms became leaders in their respective industries by overcoming the difficulties they face on the world market and instead turning their inefficiencies into competitive advantages. In contrast to the previous group of theories, they introduced a "Linkage-Learning-Leverage" (LLL) Model, which emphasizes that linking to foreign partners and building corporate capabilities by exploring external assets may greatly improve a firm's market position at home.

Linkage refers to how the newcomers and latecomers focus on the advantage that can be developed abroad, while temporarily neglecting their own disadvantages. Firms use joint ventures and partnerships to internationalize new knowledge, which is a lot quicker than building their own subsidiaries in the foreign country. Learning may involve both cost-based efficiency improvement and operations, as well as learning about technologies, brands, marketing, and management issues, which is most often the predominant objective. Leverage, finally, means that knowledge acquired abroad can be transferred back home and used to improve competitiveness in the local market.

For instance, many Chinese brands have yet to make global impact. Lenovo and Haier are the best known outside of the country, but neither is in the same league as the likes of IBM, Dell , HP, and General Electric. Nor have China's automakers been able to establish outside of China brands to the value of Volvo, GM's Hummer, whose acquisition by Sichuan Tengzhong is awaiting Beijing's sign-off, or MG Rover, the last domestically owned mass-production car manufacturer in the UK, which wound up in 2005 in the hands of Nanjing Automobile Group, now merged with Shanghai Automotive Industry Corp. In many cases, acquisition is not the only route to technology, and brands like China's automakers have long pursued the "linkage, learning, and leverage" model of development, by conducting joint ventures with foreign manufacturers seeking access to the Chinese market; SAIC

FIGURE 8.5
Chinese Carmakers
Trying to Catch Up
Source: © Author

with GM (now jointly heading for the Indian market, too) and FAW with Toyota, for example. News that Ford Motor has agreed to terms with Zhejiang Geely for the Chinese carmaker to acquire its Volvo Cars division is the latest example of the next wave of Chinese foreign investment. Manufacturers—mostly privately owned, not state enterprises—are increasingly looking for brands and technology to use as the foundation of a new generation of innovative and branded Chinese products for both domestic and global markets.[40]

The LLL model is also close to theories in the field of international entrepreneurship or international new ventures[41] (see below), which study the internationalization process of firms that go international at an early age and seek superior international business performance by entering foreign markets at an accelerated speed, bypassing the domestic market. Here, internationalization success is predicated on the ability to treat global competition as an opportunity to move into more profitable industry segments and adopt strategies that turn EMFs' latecomer status into a source of competitive advantage.

Critique

Depending on the financial and economic power of EMFs, linkages that imply loose forms of collaboration may no longer be the preferred option to obtain knowledge and increase technological quality. For instance, recent figures of Chinese acquisitions abroad, especially of non-state-owned companies, seem to illustrate that full ownership could be a desired choice, indicating long-term commitment and transfer of more tacit components of competitive advantage. For instance in 2014 alone, 188 overseas purchases worth $21 billion have been undertaken by non-state-owned Chinese firms, just $2 billion less than their bigger government counterparts, according to Dealogic data. Four years ago, state purchases, such as the $7.1 billion acquisition of Repsol Brasil SA by China Petrochemical Corp., contributed to a $24 billion gap.[42]

International New Venture Theory

Due to environmental changes and the limited explanatory potential of the incremental process theory of internationalization, Johanson & Mattson (1988)[43] have pointed out that some firms might follow a different pattern of internationalization than suggested by the stage models. Other authors have emphasized a new phenomenon of small and medium enterprises that are becoming international soon after being founded.[44] This idea gave the impetus for the concepts of "born globals" and "international new ventures" with the latter providing the name for the theory.[45] This new stream of research started from the definition of international new ventures as "a business organization that, from inception, seeks to derive significant competitive advantage from the use of resources and the sale of output in multiple countries"[46] or "born globals," defined as firms that have reached at least 25 percent of foreign sales within three years after establishment.[47]

In recent years, many born global firms have entered the global landscape. With their dynamic and fast-growing type of international organization, their youth, small size, limited resources, and entrepreneurial orientation, they clearly differ from large multinationals. As they do not have the hierarchical structures established, which we often find in larger organizations, they exhibit more flexibility and can thus more easily adapt to changes. This adaptability explains why they are usually successful at expanding globally within the first three years of their existence. To do so, they depend strongly on technology, their innovative strategies and products, and their network of foreign distributors. Most importantly for marketers, these firms possess a strong international marketing orientation and competency that allows them to focus intensely on the needs of customers in each new market and deliver high-quality, unique products.

The rapid growth of such born global firms all over the world is a testament to a new, evolutionary trend in the global business arena where company size, age, and national origin are no longer the determinants of success internationally.

Critique

The theory of international new ventures mostly relates to early and rapid internationalization processes. However, internationalizing at an earlier stage involves more risk-taking than the well-established internationalization processes of older firms. This may be due to the fact that new ventures choose to pursue international opportunities aggressively in order to capture capabilities on a global-scale. The

---

Box 8.3   Company-in-Focus: Seaflex AB

Born Global Firm

Seaflex AB, a Swedish company of 10 employees, was founded in 1999. The company sells an environmentally-friendly elastic mooring system that secures pontoons and buoys or floating docks without damaging the sensitive ecosystem on the seabed.

Like most inventions, the Seaflex mooring system came about by chance. In the 1960s, Bertil Brandt, a Swedish innovator active within the mining industry, invented a highly durable compound rubber. In 1968, Brandt visited a fishing harbour in Cannes where he witnessed the chaos that occurred when fishing boats berthed. This inspired the idea for a simple and secure rubber mooring arrangement with specially manufactured rubber straps. Realising the potential of his invention, Brandt continued to develop a secure anchoring system on his return to Sweden. Bertil's son, Lars, now continues the family business as the president of Seaflex.

The company is mainly dependent on foreign sales with a domestic market share of around only 2 percent. Over eight years, Seaflex has increased its sales by around 30 percent each year and doubled its staff. CEO, Lars Brandt, stated in an interview: 'During those first years, I tried to find international customers because Sweden is so small and I think if you have a product that everyone else can use, it is a missed opportunity to sell it only on the domestic market ... the whole world is our market!'

Sources: Lars Brandt, CEO of Seaflex, taken from the interview conducted by Ullah and Mir, 2012. Ullah, T. R. And Mir, R. (2012), 'The 'go-global' notion of entrepreneurs from non-metropolitan regions – Evidence from SMEs located in north region of Sweden', [Master's Thesis], Umeå School of Business and Economics, Umeå; http://www.seaflex.net/index.php?option=com_content&view=article&id=43&Itemid=15 [Accessed: September 14, 2015].

approach presents a unique challenge to incrementalism and stage theory. If internationalization were possible only by knowledge accumulation and experience, then new ventures could not be international and successful from inception. Older firms with the necessary resources and skills that enable investments in learning, and thus effective adaptation, were clearly in a superior position. Yet those established firms are often subject to structural inertia that prevents or limits their ability to grow quickly abroad. In this vein, internationalizing at an earlier stage may have advantages as compared to an established company whose ability to learn and develop its operations may be limited.

In order to solve the dilemma posed by the inconclusive performance results of both incremental and new venture theory, researchers have suggested that internationalization should not only be considered from a content but also through a process lens.[48] This includes the rates and patterns by which firms organize their internationalization processes and incorporates the notion of time. We will focus on these internationalization patterns in the next section.

PATTERNS AND MEASURES OF INTERNATIONALIZATION

Previous theories of internationalization provided varying explanations of how firms internationalize. With regards to two major proponents, the following patterns can be differentiated (Table 8.5).

Specifically, internationalization processes can be distinguished according to the time elapsed until a firm starts international activities, i.e. internationalization age and further to the speed of internationalization (the number of foreign market entries irrespective of entry-mode choice). Differences in these two parameters suggest new ways of accounting for different internationalization processes that are likely to entail performance differentials. By combining those two dimensions, it is possible to

TABLE 8.5 Different Internationalization Patterns	**Incremental Internationalization**	**New Venture Internationalization**
	Major Driving Forces: Control, uncertainty avoidance, risk reduction. Internationalization is a process built upon knowledge accumulation and experience.	**Major Driving Force:** Discovery and innovation: Accelerated internationalization in new and unknown territories is based on the development of hitherto non-existing capabilities.
	Theoretical Model: Uppsala (Johanson & Vahlne, 1977, 1990)	**Theoretical Model:** The New Venture theory (Oviatt & McDougall, 1994)
	Process: Path dependent and incremental stages of internationalization. Slow and regular process with a limited number of targeted countries. Increasing commitment to foreign markets.	**Process:** Speed, irregularity, geographic dispersion. Focus on the role of entrepreneurs. Risk-taking posture and international experiences encourage rapid internationalization at a young age.

Source: Adapted from: Verdier, S., Prange, C., Atamer, T., and Monin, P. (2010), 'Internationalization performance revisited – The impact of age and speed on sales growth', *Management International,* 15(1), pp. 19–31

		Internationalization Speed		TABLE 8.6
		Slow	Fast	A Matrix with Internationalization Patterns and Examples from Retailing
Internationalization Age	Young	Case 1—Aldi (7 years old, 0.84 % internationalization speed)	Case 2—International New Venture Theory Metro (5 years old, 1.16 % internationalization speed)	
	Mature	Case 3—The Uppsala Model Tesco (74 years old, 0.34 % internationalization speed)	Case 4—Casino (87 years old, 4.33 % internationalization speed)	

Source: Adapted from: Verdier, S., Prange, C., Atamer, T., and Monin, P. (2010), 'Internationalization performance revisited – The impact of age and speed on sales growth', *Management International*, 15(1), pp. 19–31

establish a 2*2 matrix that may enrich theoretical development (Table 8.6) and help managers to maximize the success of their internationalization trajectory.

In the following, we provide some examples from the grocery retailing industry, and then explore the performance differentials across internationalization patterns. Research[49] shows that some retail firms begin their internationalization right from inception and others very late in their history. For instance the German company METRO started its first international outlet in the Netherlands in 1968, four years after its foundation. The Portuguese retailer CONTINENTE MODELO did the same in Brazil in 1989. On the opposite end, another Portuguese retailer, JERÓNIMO MARTINS, created as early as 1792, and one of the first retailers in the world, started its internationalization very late in 1995 in Poland and in 1997 in Brazil. WAL-MART expanded abroad to Mexico only after 30 years of operations in the US.

Speed is considered a time-based measure representing how fast a firm develops outlets abroad, i.e. changes in the ratio of foreign entities to total entities. The larger the change over a seven-year period, the higher is the expansion speed. Slow internationalizers are firms that choose a gradual process with a low increase in the ratio of foreign stores to total stores during our period of observation. Fast internationalizers register a high increase in this ratio.

- ALDI was created in 1960 and started its internationalization in 1967. In 2004, it was implanted in 14 countries. However, from 1998 to 2004, the ratio of its foreign stores to total stores increased only by 0.84 percent. This ratio is low considering that ALDI entered four countries during this period: Luxembourg (1997), Ireland (1999), Australia (2001), and Spain (2002).

- METRO was created in 1964 and operated its first international establishment in the Netherlands in 1968. It is implanted in 26 countries and during the period of observation, its ratio of foreign stores to total stores increased by 1.16 percent.

- TESCO started its internationalization at the age of 74 years and its speed is about 0.34 percent during this period, while its number of countries increases from 7 to 13. This means that TESCO experiments carefully in these new countries.

- CASINO increases its foreign presence at a rate of 4.33 percent during the period. It increases its number of countries by 18 in 7 years.

Interestingly, the two industry leaders, namely CARREFOUR and WAL-MART, have followed completely different internationalization processes, and do not support the two dominant theoretical approaches. CARREFOUR started its internationalization at a young age, and though the number of countries of implantation increased, its foreign stores ratio decreased during this period. Until 2004, CARREFOUR entered 38 countries and only exited two. On the contrary, WAL-MART started its internationalization process rather late at 31 years of age. However, its increase in foreign stores ratio reached almost 3 percent with only half the number of Carrefour's countries.

In terms of performance consequences, different internationalization patterns also yield different results. Young internationalizers that pursue a slow internationalization process enjoy higher international sales growth rates as compared to young internationalizers that pursue a fast internationalization process. But mature internationalizers that pursue a fast internationalization process reach higher performance results than mature internationalizers that pursue a slow internationalization process. For instance, CARREFOUR and EDEKA both followed a slow internationalization process, but started their first international expansion at different ages. CARREFOUR began its internationalization at a younger age and enjoyed an international growth of 17.74 percent. In turn, EDEKA started its international expansion at 84 years of age and experienced an international sales growth rate of 1.06 percent. Among fast internationalizers, METRO and WAL-MART are two well-known firms. METRO internationalized early (5 years old) and enjoyed a 7.99 percent international sales growth. WAL-MART internationalized at a much older age (30 years old), yet experienced an international sales growth of 38.8 percent. As a consequence, slower internationalization may be advisable for young companies, while older companies need to try to increase flexibility by increasing market entry speed.[50]

Apart from internationalization age and speed, patterns of internationalization can further be distinguished according to rhythmic/non-rhythmic and regular versus irregular expansion patterns. Researchers[51] argue that the profits from internationalization are also influenced by the regularity of process, or the rhythm at which new international activities take place. Results show that firms with a constant, rhythmic pace are better able to benefit from foreign expansion than firms that expand in an irregular, ad hoc fashion.

MEASURES OF INTERNATIONALIZATION AND COMPETITIVENESS

So far, we have talked about internationalization performance or success without being precise about what we want to measure. Thus, in this section we will introduce a few of the customary measures for the degree of internationalization, performance measures of internationalization success, and some general measures of competitiveness.

Internationalization Performance

Many authors have developed indices of internationalization and most distinguish between two conceptualizations. One is built on the dichotomy between foreign versus home activities and assesses the degree of internationalization by the amount of foreign sales to total sales (FSTS), and foreign assets to total assets (FATA), independently of whether those foreign activities take place in one single country or in many of them. The other approach focuses on the extent to which those activities are geographically spread among many countries.[52] The two measures of FSTS and FATA remain the most often used to document the weighted corporate strategy in which the relative number of subsidiaries is taken into account in terms of their contribution to overall sales and assets.

Profit Versus Growth

While it has been argued that growth and survival are closely interlinked,[53] from a resource allocation point of view, they are clearly distinct and paradoxical. Growth typically involves huge investments whereas profit-oriented survival strategies imply that investments into new market creation will be limited. The latter is the case when firms prefer to penetrate existing markets and/or expand only into a small number of foreign markets to avoid uncertainty and decrease operational risks stemming from multiple market entry. Thus, striving for differential performance outcomes requires the deployment of different capabilities and marketing strategies.

CONCENTRATION RATIOS

The two most common measures of market concentration are the Herfindahl–Hirschman Index and the CR4 and the CR8, which means the market share of the four and the eight largest firms. These two are known as the traditional structural measures of market concentration (based on market shares).[54]

Herfindahl–Hirschman Index (HHI)

The HHI is a commonly accepted measure of market concentration. It is calculated by squaring the market share of each firm competing in a market, and then summing the resulting numbers. The HHI number can range from close to zero to 10,000. The HHI is expressed as:

$$HHI = s1^2 + s2^2 + s3^2 + \ldots + sn^2 \text{ (where sn is the market share of the ith firm).}$$

The closer a market is to being a monopoly, the higher the market's concentration (and the lower its competition). If, for example, there was only one firm in an industry, that firm would have 100 percent market share, and the HHI would equal 10,000 (100^2), indicating a monopoly. Or, if there were thousands of firms competing, each would have nearly 0 percent market share, and the HHI would be close to zero, indicating nearly perfect competition.[55]

C-Ratio

The concentration ratio is the percentage of market share held by the largest firms (m) in an industry and can be expressed as CRm.

The concentration ratio can be expressed as:

$$CR_m = s1 + s2 + s3 + \ldots \ldots + s_m$$

where s = market share of the ith firm.[56]

If the CR4 were close to zero, this value would indicate an extremely competitive industry since the four largest firms would not have any significant market share. In general, if the CR4 measure is less than about 40 (indicating that the four largest firms own less than 40 percent of the market), then the industry is considered to be very competitive, with a number of other firms competing, but none owning a very large chunk of the market. To the other extreme, if the CR1 measure is more than about 90, that one firm that controls more than 90 percent of the market is effectively a monopoly.

While useful, the concentration ratio presents an incomplete picture of the concentration of firms in an industry because by definition it does not use the market shares of all the firms in the industry.

SUMMARY

- The decision to expand a firm is necessary for its survival. Firms can expand domestically or internationally. Choosing an initial entry mode was already discussed in Chapter 7. This initial mode is critical because it locks the firm into a particular strategy in the short run. However, as the firm internationalizes, it may change its mode of operation as it expands into additional markets.
- Choosing the internationalization option must be done for the right reasons. Once the management of a firm decides to internationalize, it must determine the best route to do so. A first step is given by the Ansoff matrix, which helps to explore different options.
- Different theories of internationalization emphasize how firms can proceed, e.g. by adopting an incremental stage-wise process or by concentrating on asset exploration.
- However, a new and emerging breed of firms has entered the global landscape of business activities, which expands abroad shortly after foundation and seems to bypass

all the considerations of incremental stage-wise international expansion. These firms exhibit huge flexibility and often enter many markets simultaneously.

- Differences in firms' internationalization age, speed, rhythm, and direction of market entry can have a significant impact on internationalization performance. Research shows, that variation, e.g. between slow and accelerated internationalization can have a beneficial effect.
- Several indicators can be checked to identify market concentration, e.g. the Herfindahl–Hirschman Index or the C-ratio.

DISCUSSION QUESTIONS

1. Why does the LLL Model explain emerging market firms' internationalization behavior so well?
2. Can the Uppsala Model explain the actions of large MNCs?
3. How can a manager make use of the eclectic decision framework?
4. What are the advantages of a born global firm as opposed to a large multinational company?
5. How can you use the HHI Index to determine market entry?

EXPERIENTIAL EXERCISES

1. Interview a top executive of a small or medium-sized firm in your area that has international operations. Did they follow an accelerated international process as identified in this chapter? Yes? If no, why not?
2. Choose another firm that has international operations in more than three countries and describe the rhythm, scope, and direction of their internationalization process.

KEY TERMS

- Ansoff matrix
- Born-globals
- Efficiency seekers
- Herfindahl–Hirschman Index (HHI)
- International networks
- Internationalization
- Latecomer strategy
- Market seeking firms

- Dunning's OLI model
- Proactive motives
- Psychic distance
- Reactive motives
- Resource seeking companies
- Strategic resource seekers
- Transaction cost
- Uppsala IP model

NOTES

1 Coleman-Lochner, L. (2013), 'With M.A.C., Estée Lauder enters emerging markets', *Bloomberg Business Week,* http://www.businessweek.com/articles/2013-03-21/with-m-dot-a-dot-c-dot-est-e-lauder-enters-emerging-markets [Accessed: November 15, 2014].

2 Mulup, D. (2014), 'Estée Lauder scents opportunity in sub-Saharan Africa', December 8, 2014, http://www.howwemadeitinafrica.com/estee-lauder-scents-opportunity-in-sub-saharan-africa/45407/ [Accessed: December 28, 2014].

3 Paton, E. (2014), 'Estée Lauder gloss provided by emerging markets', https://next.ft.com/content/6c82c506-2486-11e4-be8e-00144feabdc0 [Accessed: July 30, 2016].

4 Beckerman, W. (1956), 'Distance and the pattern of intra-European trade', *The Review of Economics and Statistics*, 28(1), pp. 31–40.

5 Johanson, J. and Vahlne, J. (1977), 'The internationalization process of the firm: A model of knowledge development and increasing foreign market commitment', *Journal of International Business Studies*, 8(1), pp. 22–4.

6 Aitken, T. (2014), '5 biggest beer brands in China by volume', *CEO World Magazine,* January 28, 2014, http://ceoworld.biz/2014/07/28/5-biggest-beer-brands-china-volume [Accessed: January 26, 2015].

7 Mundim, A., Sharma, M., Arora, P., and McManus, R. (2012), 'Emerging market product development and innovation. The new competitive reality', *Accenture*, https://www.scribd.com/document/242681576/Accenture-Emerging-Markets-Product-Development-and-Innovation [Accessed: July 30, 2016].

8 Czinkota, M. R. and Ronkainen, I. A. (2012). *International marketing*. 10th ed. Mason, OH: South-Western Cengage Learning.

9 Korsakiene, R. and Tvaronaviciene, M. (2012), 'The internationalization of SMEs: An integrative approach', *Journal of Business Economics & Management*, 13(2), pp. 294–307.

10 Mwiti, E., Ofafa, G. A., and Mkim, A. J. (2013), 'Determinants of initial export market participation: An empirical study on the internal-proactive and internal-reactive factors among micro and small enterprises in the commercial craft sector in Kenya', *International Journal of Business and Social Science*, 4, pp. 64–88.

11 Hanemann, T. and Rosen, D.H. (2012), 'China invests in Europe – patterns, impacts and policy implications', *Rhodium Group*, http://rhg.com/wp-content/uploads/2012/06/RHG_ChinaInvestsInEurope_June2012.pdf [Accessed: May 22, 2014].

12 Tan, H. and Ai, Q. (2010). China's outward mergers and acquisitions in the 21st century: Motivations, progress and the role of the Chinese government. In: Finkelstein, S. and Cooper, C. L. (eds.). *Advances in mergers and acquisitions*. Bradford, UK: Emerald Group Publishing Ltd.

13 Milelli, C. and Sindzingre, A. (2013), 'Chinese outward foreign direct investment in developed and developing countries: Converging characteristics?' *Paris: EconomiX, Université Paris Ouest*. Available: http://economix.fr/docs/35/SindzingreMilelli-ChinaFDI-WP_EcoX_2013-34.pdf [Accessed May 13, 2014].

14 Ibid. See also: Steven, I.J. (2014). *Sociocultural post-merger integration management of Chinese enterprises in Europe*. [Unpublished Master's Thesis] EM Lyon.

15 Alon,T., Hale, G., and Santos, J. (2010), 'What is China's capital seeking in a global environment?' *Economic Letter*, March 22, 2010, http://www.frbsf.org/economic-research/publications/economic-letter/2010/march/china-capital-seeking-global-environment/ [Accessed: January 5, 2014].

16 Tan, H. and Ai, Q.(2010), China's outward mergers and acquisitions in the 21st century: Motivations, progress and the role of the Chinese government. In: Cary L. Cooper, Sydney Finkelstein (eds.) *Advances in mergers and acquisitions (Volume 9)*. Bradford, UK: Emerald Group Publishing Limited, pp. 25–50.

17 Ersson, M. and Tryggvason, J. (2007). *Internationalization of two Nordic banks*. [Master's Thesis, unpublished]. Luleå University of Technology.

18 van Gelder, J., Reinout, E., de Vries, M. F., and Goutbeek, J. (2007), 'Differences in psychological strategies

of failed and operational business owners in the Fiji Islands', *Journal of Small Business Management,* 45(3), pp. 388–400.

19   Dunning, J. (1981). *International production and the multinational enterprise.* London: George Allen & Unwin; Dunning, J. (1988), 'The eclectic paradigm of international production: A restatement and some possible extensions', *Journal of International Business Studies,* 19(1), pp. 1–31.

20   The World Factbook. (2015), https://www.cia.gov/library/publications/the-world-factbook/docs/refmaps.html [Accessed: August 1, 2015].

21   Website Volkswagen. http://www.volkswagenag.com/content/vwcorp/info_center/en/themes/2014/01/ Volkswagen_de_Mexico/50_years_of_Volkswagen_de_Mexico.html [Accessed: January 12, 2015].

22   Nedella, A. (2013), 'Volkswagen opens 100th plant in Mexico', http://www.autoevolution.com/news/ volkswagen-opens-100th-plant-in-mexico-54067.html [Accessed: January 12, 2015].

23   Cantwell, J. and Narula, R. (2001), 'The eclectic paradigm in the global economy', *International Journal of the Economics of Business,* 8(2), pp. 155–72; Dunning, J. (2001), 'The eclectic (OLI) paradigm of international production: Past, present and future', *International Journal of the Economics of Business,* 8(2), pp. 173–90.

24   Ramamurti, R. (2012), 'What is really different about emerging market multinationals?', *Global Strategy Journal,* 2(1), pp. 41–7.

25   Johanson, J. and Vahlne, L. (1977), 'The internationalization process of the firm—a model of knowledge development and increasing foreign market commitments', *Journal of International Business Studies,* (Spring/ Summer), 8(1), pp. 3–32; Johanson, J. and Vahlne, J-E. (1990), 'The mechanism of internationalization', *International Marketing Review,* 7(4), pp. 11–24 ; Johanson, J. and Wiedersheim-Paul, F. (1975), 'The internationalization of the firm – Four Swedish cases', *Journal of Management Studies,* 12(3), pp. 305–22.

26   Johanson, J. and Wiedersheim-Paul, F. (1975), op.cit. For more recent discussions of psychic distance see: Ambos, B. and Håkanson, L. (2014), 'The concept of distance in international management research', *Journal of International Management,* 20(1), pp. 1–7, and the articles in this special issue.

27   Johanson, J. and Vahlne, L. (1977), op. cit., p. 23.

28   Johanson, J. and Wiedersheim-Paul, F. (1975), op cit.

29   The World Factbook. (2015), https://www.cia.gov/library/publications/the-world-factbook/docs/refmaps.html [Accessed: August 1, 2015].

30   Vahlne, J-E. and Johanson, J. (2013), 'The Uppsala model on evolution of the multinational business enterprise – from internalization to coordination of networks', *International Marketing Review,* 30(3), pp. 189–210; Johanson, J. and Vahlne, J-E. (2009), 'The Uppsala internationalization process model revisited: From liability of foreignness to liability of outsidership', *Journal of International Business Studies,* 40(9), pp. 1411–31.

31   Mattson, L. and Hertz, S. (1998), 'Domino effects in international networks', *Journal of Business-to-Business Marketing,* 5(3), pp. 3–32.

32   Johanson, J. and Mattson, L. (1988). Internationalization in industrial systems—a network approach. In: N. Hood (ed.). *Strategies for global competition.* London: Croom Helm.

33   Neamtu, A.C. and Neamtu, L. (2014), 'Strategic approaches for the business networks', *Procedia – Social and Behavioral Sciences,* 109, pp. 35–9.

34   Johanson, J. and Mattson, L. (1988), op. cit.

35   Johanson, J. and Mattson, L. (1988), op. cit.

36   The World Factbook. (2015), https://www.cia.gov/library/publications/the-world-factbook/docs/refmaps.html [Accessed: August 1, 2015].

37   Hirsch, Z. (1976), 'An international trade and investment theory of the firm', *Oxford Economic Papers, New Series,* 29(2), pp. 258–70.

38   Brouthers, K. D. and Nakos, G. (2004), 'SME entry mode choice and performance: A transaction cost perspective', *Entrepreneurship: Theory and Practice,* 3(3), pp. 229–47.

39   Mathews, J. A. (2006), 'Dragon Multinationals: New players in 21st century globalization', *Asian Pacific Journal of Management,* 23(1), pp. 5–27.

40   Maidman, P. (2009), 'The next wave from China', *Forbes,* http://www.forbes.com/2009/12/23/volvo-geely- ford-business-autos-china.html [Accessed: December 30, 2014].

41 Jones, M.V. and Coviello, N.E. (2005), 'Internationalisation: Conceptualising an entrepreneurial process of behaviour in time', *Journal of International Business Studies,* 36(3), pp. 284–303.

42 Lee, Y. (2014), 'Chinese overseas buying increasingly shifts to private from state', *The Wall Street Journal*, September 21, 2014, http://www.wsj.com/articles/chinese-overseas-buying-increasingly-shifts-to-private-from-state-1411335001 [Accessed: January 5, 2015].

43 Johanson, J. and Mattson, L. (1988), op. cit.

44 Rennie, M. W. (1993), 'Born global', *McKinsey Quarterly*, 4(4), pp. 45–52; Oviatt, B. M. and McDougall, P. P. (2005), 'Defining international entrepreneurship and modelling the speed of internationalization', *Entrepreneurship Theory and Practice*, 29(5), pp. 537–53.

45 McDougall, P.P., Shane, S., and Oviatt, B.M. (1994), 'Explaining the formation of international new ventures: The limits of theories from international business research', *Journal of Business Venturing*, 9(6), pp. 469–87.

46 Oviatt, B. M. and McDougall, P. P. (1994), 'Toward a theory of International New Ventures', *Journal of International Business Studies*, 25(1), pp. 45–64.

47 Madsen, T.K., Rasmussen, E., and Servais, P. (2000), 'Differences and similarities between born globals and other types of exporters', *Advances in International Marketing*, 10, pp. 247–56; Coviello, N. (2015), 'Re-thinking research on born globals', *Journal of International Business Studies*', 46(1), pp. 17–26.

48 Vermeulen, F. and Barkema, H. (2002), 'Pace, rhythm, and scope: Process dependence in building a profitable multinational corporation', *Strategic Management Journal*, 23(7), pp. 637–53.

49 Verdier, S., Prange, C., Atamer, T., and Monin, P. (2010), 'Internationalization performance revisited – The impact of age and speed on sales growth', *Management International*, 15(1), pp. 19–31.

50 Verdier et al. (2010), op. cit.

51 Vermeulen, F. and Barkema, H. (2002), op. cit.

52 Ietto-Gillies, G. (1998), 'Different conceptual frameworks for the assessment of the degree of internationalization: An empirical analysis of the various indices for the top 100 transnational corporations', *Transnational Corporations*, 7(1), pp. 17–39.

53 Steffens, P., Davidsson, P., and Fitzsimmons, J. (2009), 'Performance configurations over time: Implications for growth- and profit-oriented strategies', *Entrepreneurship, Theory & Practice*, 33(1), pp.125–48.

54 London economics in association with global energy decisions. *Structure and Performance of Six European Wholesale Electricity Markets in 2003, 2004, and 2005*, presented to DG Comp, February 26, 2007, p. 52 and p. 8.

55 Investopedia. 'Herfindahl-Hirschman Index – HHI', http://www.investopedia.com/terms/h/hhi.asp [Accessed: February 6, 2015].

56 'Industry Concentration', http://www.quickmba.com/econ/micro/indcon.shtml.

CASE 8.1 HUMMUS BAR: DIPPING INTO INTERNATIONAL MARKETS

Ilan Alon, Yusaf Akbar and Jennifer Dugosh and wrote this case solely to provide material for class discussion. The authors do not intend to illustrate either effective or ineffective handling of a managerial situation. The authors may have disguised certain names and other identifying information to protect confidentiality.

This publication may not be transmitted, photocopied, digitized or otherwise reproduced in any form or by any means without the permission of the copyright holder. Reproduction of this material is not covered under authorization by any reproduction rights organization. To order copies or request permission to reproduce materials, contact Ivey Publishing, Ivey Business School, Western University, London, Ontario, Canada, N6G 0N1; (t) 519.661.3208; (e) cases@ivey.ca; www.iveycases.com.

Copyright © 2013, Richard Ivey School of Business Foundation   *Version: 2013-06-12*

Hummus, meaning "chickpea" in Arabic, had unclear origins. Some historians suggested that ancient Egyptians were the first to mash chickpeas and mix them with vinegar. The earliest known recipe of a modern hummus-like food dated to the 13th century. Much debate surrounded the nationality of the dish, particularly between the Lebanese and the Israelis. This controversy was dubbed "The Hummus Wars" and had been ongoing for many years. Despite the debate, hummus was gaining popularity around the globe.[1] Uri Gotlibovich, founder and chief executive officer (CEO) of Hummus Bar, pondered the company's position in the international marketplace and considered its growth opportunities. It was 2012. Gotlibovich understood that expanding internationally required prioritizing the markets but struggled to identify and select the most promising markets. Was international expansion the way to go, or should he consider pursuing his concept through domestic growth? Gotlibovich also wanted to ensure that the company executed the most appropriate entry strategy. He wanted to recruit and involve additional investors, both to spread risk and to enhance the brand through diversified skill sets. As he finished his lunch, Gotlibovich pulled out his cellphone and selected his business partner's number.

GOTLIBOVICH'S STORY

Gotlibovich was born in 1973, in Hod Hashharon, a city in the Central District of Israel; however, he had spent most of his early life in Raanana, Israel. In 1994, at age 19, he started his first business venture in Raanana as the second franchisee for a store concept called Happening. Happening was an Israeli pop shop that sold balloons, greeting cards and games. A year later, Gotlibovich opened a second shop in Petach Tikva, Israel. The franchising model, which involved taking 3 per cent of turnover, meant that profitability margins were low. To combat these margins, Gotlibovich integrated backward with the purchase of one of the franchise's key suppliers. This supplier provided Happening with beanbags, one of the store's bestsellers. With this purchase, Gotlibovich became a supplier for the Happening outlets and for other shops in the beanbag market. In 2000, recognizing the potential of the beanbags, Gotlibovich sold his Happening shops.

Two years later, Gotlibovich realized another opportunity in the computer and software support industries. He and partners opened a business called PC Doctor, which offered support, sales and network development for companies and individuals. Part of the business model involved selling or leasing hardware. This venture also turned out to be profitable. By 2003, however, Gotlibovich had to sell all his businesses due to medical issues.

Unexpectedly, a friend of Gotlibovich's encouraged him to travel to Hungary for a visit. There, Gotlibovich was invited to join another business venture, a high-technology company selling entertainment systems to hospitals. Gotlibovich agreed, investing $300,000,[2] all of which he eventually lost due to an unsuccessful business model. At the time, Gotlibovich was faced with a huge decision: should he return to Israel or start a new business venture in Hungary?

After deciding to stay in Hungary, Gotlibovich opened a hummus bar because Budapest had no such restaurant. He assumed that the many Israelis who lived in Budapest loved the cuisine, and he could count on them as a market for the hummus bar. He and a partner invested $20,000 equally to kick-start the business. Gotlibovich knew nothing about the culinary industry or the hummus business, but had a good feeling about the venture. To start, Gotlibovich and only one other employee worked 14-hour days.

THE HUMMUS BAR CONCEPT

Gotlibovich's first Hummus Bar location was a small location, close to many bars and clubs frequented by young people in Budapest's up and coming seventh district. The original idea was for a small, cozy vegan restaurant that made good food and offered good service. Surprisingly, this commitment to service was unusual for a typical restaurant in Hungary. Service quality in restaurants in Hungary was a problem across numerous dimensions: efficiency, friendliness, consistency, to name a few. For example, one of McDonald's restaurants located in the downtown area of Budapest introduced a stopwatch policy — guaranteed service time of five minutes or less during the slowest time of the day. The location could not, however, meet the guarantee, and it quickly abandoned the policy.

Initially, Hummus Bar's food was not very appetizing due to Gotlibovich's lack of culinary experience. Luckily, a neighbouring entrepreneur knew how to prepare delicious dishes. Despite initial success, the new partnership soon became strained. Gotlibovich bought him out and brought in another partner, named Aviad.

It took about six months before the restaurant attracted enough customers to earn a profit. Clearly, the Hummus Bar concept had potential. In 2007, Gotlibovich opened a second restaurant, this time in the fifth district near the Hungarian Parliament. Gotlibovich asked his partner to co-invest; however, Aviad declined because of his recent engagement. Unlike the first location, this second restaurant was very successful from the start. Within two months, it generated positive cash flow.

Gotlibovich's focus soon turned to creating a chain of Hummus Bar restaurants. A direct implication of this focus was the establishment of a central kitchen to maximize consistency. Coincidentally, Gotlibovich lived in the fifth district. On the ground floor of his building was an Indian restaurant that was vacating. Gotlibovich rented the location for his central kitchen. The third Hummus Bar was opened in 2008 with an investment of roughly $215,000.

Gotlibovich approached Aviad again, proposing that he invest in the chain. He offered 25 per cent of the business for €180,000, approximately $257,000. This time, Aviad agreed and again became a partner. The year that followed was difficult, due to street renovations that significantly slowed foot traffic to the restaurant; however, the business quickly picked up following the overhaul. Based on the growing success of the business, Gotlibovich and Aviad opened a fourth restaurant in 2010 near one of Budapest's biggest universities.

By the end of 2011, Gotlibovich had opened a fifth restaurant in the 13th district with a new partner and former customer, Pavel Mintz. Mintz invested approximately $57,000 for 30 per cent of the fifth outlet. Mintz had moved to Hungary to study in 2006. He became friends with Gotlibovich through being a regular customer of Hummus Bar. After graduation, Mintz had married a Hungarian woman and decided to stay, making an investment in the business a reasonable decision. Following the rapid success of Hummus Bar in Budapest, Gotlibovich's concentration turned to international expansion, particularly in Europe (see Exhibit 1).

THE EMERGENCE OF A FRANCHISE MODEL

Hummus Bar's growth had been financed by direct ownership through partnerships. In 2010, Gotlibovich considered the idea of a franchise model. A franchise contract was first drafted in late 2010, before the sixth restaurant was opened, when Gotlibovich was approached by the general manager of a hotel in the 9th district that was part of the Leonardo Hotels chain. The hotelier wanted to use the copyrighted Hummus Bar name (see Exhibit 2). Gotlibovich agreed to let the hotel use the name and created the Hummus Bistro at the Leonardo Hotel — a restaurant that combined traditional hotel foods with Hummus Bar recipes. The "bistro" model required the hotel to buy food from Gotlibovich. Hummus Bar earned a percentage of restaurant turnover but charged no franchise fee. Additionally, employees of the Hummus Bistro at the Leonardo Hotel were required to wear the same clothes as the staff of the Hummus Bar restaurants.

In April 2012, the first "real" franchise contract was signed with Amir Degani, an Iranian entrepreneur who opened a Hummus Bar restaurant in Budapest's 11th district. The franchise fee for this contract was Ft3 million, equivalent to €10,000, or roughly $14,000, with Degani being obliged to buy ingredients, and pay 2 per

EXHIBIT 1 Hummus Bar's Marketing Policies	**Product**	The Hummus Bars were divided into four types of restaurants: two were vegetarian, one was full service (including lafa — a flat bread served with the entrees and meat options), three were limited service (without the lafa) and one was a bistro licence, offering a Hummus Bar's full menu combined with hotel foods and services. In addition to the variety of food, some products, such as T-shirts, were offered at all the restaurants
	Price	The average customer spent €5.00.
	Placement	Gotlibovich avoided opening restaurants near the many Turkish fast-food outlets in Budapest and on Budapest's main ring road, which circled the centre of the city.
	Promotion	Hummus Bar relied heavily on social media for market research and promotional efforts. The company had 10,000 subscribers to Facebook. Of these, 27 per cent were male between the ages of 20 and 35. Most subscribers were Hungarians, but some were international. Tourists wrote many reviews on the Facebook page. To supplement social media and to help promote the brand, Gotlibovich sold T-shirts with the store's slogan, "Hummus is sexy."
	Target Market	Gotlibovich sought out middle- and upper-income customers and consumers seeking alternatives to Italian, American and Hungarian cuisine.
	Personnel	Hummus Bar's wait staff were paid a low fixed salary of €1.60 per hour and pooled their tips. Each staff member took home approximately €10 to 15 in tips per shift. All staff received a labour contract with a 30-day notice provision. Hummus bar provided uniforms. No formal training was offered for wait staff; they were expected to learn on the job. Training was, however, in the company's future plans.

Source: Company files.

EXHIBIT 2 Basic Elements of Hummus Bar's Franchise Agreement	1. The restaurant must bear the name "Hummus Bar" and the company rents the location for the franchisee; 2. The franchisee must buy all the products from the company — nothing outside the standard menu could be sold without permission; 3. Due to the Hungarian legal system, a contract must be signed and notarized because immediate execution of all contract clauses is considered easier with a unilateral declaration; 4. The franchisee must pay two (2) per cent of total revenues for corporate marketing costs (websites, Facebook, etc.); 5. The franchise must bear all expenses of fitting out the restaurant (typical expenses amounting to €50,000); 6. The franchisee must provide a deposit of €5,000 and; 7. The franchisee must pay a franchise fee of €10,000. The franchise duration is equal to the length of the rental contract that is typically ten (10) years in duration. If Gotlibovich decides to sell the chain, the franchisor is required to pay the equivalent of two (2) years food cost from Hummus bar (this was also equal to the price of buying out the franchise rights).

Source: Company files.

cent of revenues for marketing and a management fees. In August 2012, a seventh shop was scheduled to be opened. Mintz took 24 per cent ownership in this restaurant, for just over $37,000. By August 2012, Hummus Bar had seven restaurants and a joint-venture bistro in Budapest.

COMPETITION

Hummus Bar was in an excellent competitive position in Budapest. The only direct competition was a small chain called Hummus Point, whose founders, Boaz and Merav Kening, were regulars at Hummus Bar. When the West End Shopping Mall in central Budapest approached Gotlibovich to open a Hummus Bar in its food court, the Kenings approached Gotlibovich for a partnership. In 2008, both parties made an agreement to open in the West End Shopping Mall. Omer Dar was appointed manager and registered owner; however, the partnership did not work out and was eventually dissolved.

Based on company research, Gotlibovich and Mintz identified the following 11 cities as having the highest potential for Hummus Bar:

- Bratislava, Slovakia

- Ljubljana, Slovenia

- Warsaw, Poland

- Prague, Czech Republic

- Zagreb, Croatia

- Belgrade, Serbia

- Debrecen, Hungary

- Athens, Greece

- Sofia, Bulgaria

- Istanbul, Turkey

- Berlin, Germany

THE FUTURE OF THE BAR

To successfully internationalize, Gotlibovich and Mintz knew it would be vital to evaluate certain factors in each potential market. They identified eleven factors to help them make the international selection decision (see Exhibit 3):

1. Gross domestic product (GDP) per capita (country level)

2. Median monthly disposable income of residents (city level)

3. Unemployment rate (country level)

4. Population (city level)

5. Urbanization rate (country level)

	Factor	Level	Unit of Measure (if applicable)	Bratislava, Slovakia	Ljubljana, Slovakia	Warsaw, Poland	Prague, crech Republic
EXHIBIT 3 Hummus Bar's Factors In Its Marketing Selection Decision	GDP per capita	Country	US dollars ($)	$ 23,300	$ 28,800	$ 20,200	$ 27,100
	Median monthly disposable income (after taxes)	City	US dollars ($)	$1,137.13	$ 1,268.69	$1,088.25	$ 1,161.13
	Unemployment rate	Country		12.80%	12.30%	12.60%	8.60%
	Population	City	# of people	5,397,036	280,607	1,708,491	1,268,796
	Urbanization rate	Country	% of population	0.1%	0.2%	–0.1%	0.3%
	Prevalence of diningout	City	#of Subway locations in city	6	0	25	6
	Ease of doing business rank	Country	Rank out of 183 coutries (1 – 185)	46	35	55	65
	Corruption index score	Country	0 – 10; 0 = Highly corrupt, 10 = Clean	4.0	5.9	5.5	4.4
	Meat consumption per capita	Country	Average pounds per person	130.4	185	168.8	188.6
	Expenditure of vegetarian foods per person	City	US dollars ($) spent per person (total dollars spent/ population)	$ 8.06	$ 56.84	$ 55.99	$ 53.48
	Expenditure of vegetarian foods per Year	Country	US dollars (mil.)	43.5	15.95	95.65	67.85

Note: GDP = gross domestic product

Sources: (1) CIA World Factbook, https://www.cia.gov/library/publications/the-world-factbook/, accessed February 18, 2013.
(2) Numbeo, "Cost of Living," www.numbeo.com/cost-of-living/, accessed February 18, 2013.
(3) Subway, "Store Locator," www.subway.com/storelocator/default.aspx, accessed February 18, 2013.
(4) Chartsbin, "Meat Consumption per Capita," http://chartsbin.com/view/bhy, accessed February 18, 2013.
(5) Philip Parker, The 2009 Report on Vegetarian Foods: World Market Segmentation by City, Insead, Icon Group International, San Diego CA, USA, 2009
(6) The World Bank, Doing Business 2012: Doing Business in a More Transparent World, www.doingbusiness.org/reports/global-reports/doing-business-2012, accessed February 18, 2013.
(7) Transparency International, "Corruption Perceptions Index 2012," www.transparency.org/cpi2012/results, accessed February 18, 2013.

Zagreb, Croatia	Belgrade, Soerbia	Debrecen, Hungary	Athens, Greece	Sofia, Bulgaria	Istanbul, Turkey	Berlin, Germany
$18,000	$ 10,400	$ 19,600	$ 26,300	$ 13,800	$ 14,400	$ 38,100
$882.28	$ 557.81	$ 593.40	$1,070.24	$ 547.20	$ 1,129.94	$2,781.70
19.00%	25.90%	11.20%	24.40%	9.90%	9.00%	6.50%
790,017	1,659,440	208,016	3,089,698	1,296,615	13,624,240	3,501,872
0.4%	0.6%	0.3%	0.6%	-0.3%	1.7%	0.0%
0	0	1	0	19	9	29
84	86	54	78	66	71	20
4.0	3.3	4.6	3.4	3.3	4.2	8.0
110.5	181.5	176.7	167	99.9	53.8	193.7
$ 30.32	–	$ 34.66	$ 27.52	$ 15.98	$ 11.46	$ 98.89
23.95	–	7.21	85.02	20.72	156.19	346.29

6. Prevalence of dining out (city level)

7. Percentage/number of vegetarians (city level)

8. Meat consumption per capita (country level)

9. Expenditure of vegetarian foods per person (city level)

10. Ease-of-doing-business rank (country level)

11. Corruption index score (country level)

International expansion led to some uncertainty, especially when researching at the city level. This uncertainty was due to the difficulty of finding information at the city level. Gotlibovich and Mintz had identified cities for entry, not countries. Ideally, they would want to collect city-level information, which would make the information set more accurate; however, city-level information was not possible for many of the factors selected.

Hummus Bar's great success led to numerous questions. On a strategic level, Gotlibovich and Mintz recognized that Budapest offered limited growth opportunities. Should they consider other cities in Hungary, or should they internationalize the Hummus Bar concept by expanding into select European cities? Maybe a combination of both would be the best option. What criteria should Hummus Bar use to select countries and locations for expansion? What kind of entry mode should they execute — master franchising, area franchising, direct franchising, licensing or something else? Evidence from the Budapest outlets suggested that meat dishes were more popular and profitable. Should Hummus Bar focus on a meat-based menu for its franchises or stay closer to one of the core values of Hummus Bar, which was healthy eating? Did the decision to include meat on the menu vary by market? As Hummus Bar expanded, Gotlibovich and Mintz saw a greater need for higher investments in branding. How should they develop the strategy and what channels should they consider?

Many more questions surfaced as Gotlibovich paced the restaurant. After the phone rang twice on Gotlibovich's end, Mintz answered.

Mintz:	Hello?
Gotlibovich:	Mintz . . . I'd like to get a move on the expansion plans we've been discussing. When can we talk?
Mintz:	Glad to hear it. I will be in the office this afternoon. . . .

NOTES

1. Ari Ariel, "The Hummus Wars," Gastronomica: The Journal of Food and Culture, Vol. 12, 2012, pp. 34–42.

2. All currency amounts are shown in U.S. dollars unless otherwise noted.

CHAPTER 9

Segmenting, Targeting, and Positioning for Global Markets

"Everything in marketing should start with a consumer insight."

Nuno Teles, Chief Marketing Officer of Heineken USA[1]

LEARNING OBJECTIVES

After Reading This Chapter, You Should Be Able to:

- Develop an international market selection process.
- Segment global markets through macro- and micro-segmentation.
- Evaluate market attractiveness and competitive strength.
- Apply different methods to define market size.
- Apply the criteria for targeting markets.
- Understand the difference between concentration and diversification.
- Understand the difference between concentrated, differentiated, and undifferentiated strategies.
- Show how to gain competitive advantage through positioning.

INTRODUCTION

Segmentation, targeting, and positioning are some of the most fundamental concepts in marketing strategy and practice today. Simply put, marketers have to identify the best criteria for segmenting the market and profiling the different segments (Segmentation), to evaluate segment attractiveness and competitive position for a specific product and brand, in order to select target segments (Targeting), and to develop positioning for different target segments (Positioning), communicating them in appealing ways in order to convince target segments to buy company's products instead of competitors' ones. After implementing the STP process, the company can develop marketing mix decisions for each segment.

In global markets, the STP process is more complex because it includes both the selection of target countries (macro-segmentation, prioritization, and targeting of countries with the highest strategic value) and the identification of target consumers within the countries (micro-segmentation and targeting of micro-segments).

Segmentation, in some cases, allows marketers to simplify their decision-making process by using the same set of guidelines for segments that exist across different national markets. For example, if a company is able to identify in foreign markets the same segments recognized in the domestic market, it will be easier to standardize the marketing mix strategy, saving operational costs for the company.[2] On the other hand, segmentation can also identify target market groups across the world that differ from the standard parameters and require a completely new marketing approach.

The continuous fragmentation of both audiences and marketing channels in global markets creates a number of additional challenges for marketers. As new technologies allow consumers to communicate their interests and preferences to marketers, and congregate (especially online) with people who share those interests and preferences, they have in essence created an infinite number of customer segments that demand relevant, customized communications from the brands that are trying to reach them. The goal for a company becomes not only to identify and engage the right customer segments, but also to preserve the true identity of the brand while answering the need to position it in very customized, segment-specific communications.

It is also worth noting that while Web 2.0 technologies, for example, have brought a new level of complexity to the segmentation, targeting, and positioning efforts of global marketers, it has also given them unprecedented access to their customers. The amount of information from online panels, cookies, search engine statistics, blog comments, and the myriad of other consumer behavior tracking tools have provided a veritable treasure trove to marketers, who can now find everything from the browsing habits and preferred shopping methods of their customers, to their opinion of specific brands and products, to name a few examples. What's more, marketers can get instant feedback on how their campaigns resonate with their target segments. Armed with all this instantaneous and detailed knowledge about their customers, marketers should be able to correctly identify their target markets and communicate with them effectively.

GLOBAL MARKET SEGMENTATION AND INTERNATIONAL MARKET SELECTION

Segmentation is defined by the American Marketing Association as "The process of subdividing a market into distinct subsets of customers that behave in the same way or have similar needs. Each subset may conceivably be chosen as a market target to be reached with a distinct marketing strategy."[3]

At least five are the criteria for a good segmentation. For the company, each segment must be:

1. Homogeneous within the segment: to guarantee a similar response to marketing mix variables.

2. Heterogeneous between segments: different enough to warrant changes in the marketing mix for different segments.

3. Measurable: it is possible to calculate market potential.

4. Substantial: large enough to be profitable.

5. Operational: the segmenting dimensions should allow the identification of customers and the formulation of effective marketing mix decisions.[4]

Only segments that have all of the above dimensions can help marketers design appropriate marketing campaigns that address real customer needs, reach customers through effective channels of communication, and have a measurable financial impact on sales. It is important to underline that the segmentation analysis can be general, but each company has to do its own evaluation: in fact, for example, a segment can be considered by a large company not large enough to be profitable; vice versa for a small company it can be sufficiently profitable.

Global segmentation is more complex:

- First of all there is the necessity to segment and identify target countries (macro-segmentation and prioritization).

- Secondly, it is important to go in-depth when analyzing segments in each country or across a group of countries (micro-segmentation).

As pointed out in Figure 9.1, starting from a list of countries (for example, 15 countries identified by the company), the segmentation based on macro-economic variables (macro-segmentation) allows to carry out a first screening of the countries (8 countries, in the example). A second screening should be done after analyzing the attractiveness of the specific market and the competitive position of the company. This step is important to identify the top countries (4 countries, in the example) where the company can decide to invest. This decision will be taken after an in-depth segmentation analysis in each selected country.

The above process will be now described more in detail, presenting the general models that can be used for an effective segmentation and selection of target countries and segments. Getting market segmentation right is not an easy or quick process in any market. In global markets, where segments, especially in developing countries, may shift with each social, political, or economic change, the task of identifying the right segments is even harder. Despite the many challenges inherent in market segmentation analysis and implementation, however, when done well, the practice can give a company a substantial competitive advantage.

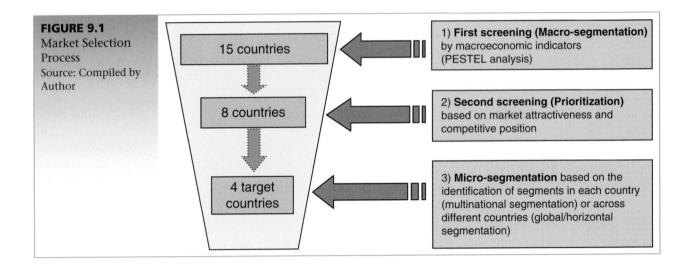

FIGURE 9.1
Market Selection
Process
Source: Compiled by
Author

15 countries

8 countries

4 target
countries

1) **First screening (Macro-segmentation)**
by macroeconomic indicators
(PESTEL analysis)

2) **Second screening (Prioritization)**
based on market attractiveness and
competitive position

3) **Micro-segmentation** based on the
identification of segments in each country
(multinational segmentation) or across
different countries (global/horizontal
segmentation)

MACRO-SEGMENTATION: FIRST SCREENING

With macro-segmentation a company can carry out a first screening based on
macroeconomic factors. This approach uses some PESTEL analysis variables
(Chapter 2), such as GNP size, GNP growth, GNP per capita, population size, family
size, etc. to group countries into market segments.

For example, considering its business of operation, a company may decide to
use income and population size as variables for macro-segmentation. Variables are
categorized as illustrated in Figure 9.2 (per capita income less or more than $10,000
and population size less or more than 50 million) and the macro-segmentation
leads to the identification of four clusters. The output of the first screening can be
the decision of the company to market its product only in countries where population size is over 50 million and per capita income is above $10,000 (Cluster 4).
Such an approach enables a company to make a first segmentation and targeting without carrying out an in-depth analysis of each country, that could be
expensive and time-consuming. Nevertheless, this analysis is not able to identify
which countries of the selected target may represent a priority opportunity. For this
reason, it is necessary to develop a second screening based on market attractiveness
and competitive position.

PRIORITIZATION: SECOND SCREENING

The purpose of the second screening is to select those markets that have the best
potential for expansion in foreign markets. Each firm must decide for itself which
criteria are relevant to its performance and consequently evaluate, in each screened
country, factors such as market size and growth, product match, intensity of competition, required capabilities and resources, entry barriers, etc. For this purpose, it

	15 countries to be screened

Per capita income	Population size	
	< 50 million	≥ 50 million
< $10,000	**Cluster 1:** Country G Country B	**Cluster 2:** Country C Country N
≥ $10,000	**Cluster 3:** Country D Country I Country O	**Cluster 4:** Country A Country E Country F Country H Country L Country M Country P Country Q

FIGURE 9.2
First Screening: An Example of Macro-Segmentation
Source: Compiled by Author

is possible to use directional policy matrices or other models useful to prioritize countries screened in the macro-segmentation.

Second Screening Based on the McKinsey/General Electric Matrix

The McKinsey/General Electric matrix is the most appropriate for prioritizing and successfully selecting countries for market entry (Figure 9.3). In fact, it can be used in the screening stage of market entry, replacing strategic business units (SBUs) with countries that become the objects of analysis. The McKinsey/General Electric matrix is preferred to the Boston Consulting Group (BCG) matrix because, in the target potential markets, the company has no market share and that is the only parameter used in the BCG matrix to calculate competitive position. In the McKinsey/General Electric matrix applied to the selection process, market/country attractiveness and competitive strength replaces market growth and relative market share that are instead used as unique indicators in the BCG matrix.

Indicators of market/country attractiveness include market size and growth, barriers to entry, political risk, cultural distance, competitive intensity, industry profitability, distribution structure, and other market specific indicators of attractiveness. Competitive position or business strength may be measured by brand awareness/image, other firm-specific assets, cost structure compared to competition, international experience, and other company/market specific indicators of competitive position. In Table 9.1 and Figure 9.3 the McKinsey/General Electric matrix is applied to prioritize the eight countries screened in the macro-segmentation. Each indicator of attractiveness and competitive position has been rated and weighted, resulting in a final score that is reported in the matrix.

TABLE 9.1
An Example of Prioritization of Countries on Market Attractiveness and Competitive Position

Market Attractiveness	Weight	Country A		Country E		Country F		Country ...	
		Rating (1-5)	Score	Rating (1-5)	Score	Rating (1-5)	Score	Rating (1-5)	Score
Growth rate	0.20	5	1	3	0.6	2	0.4	...	...
Industry profitability	0.15	4	0.6	3	0.45	3	0.45	...	...
Intensity of competition	0.10	3	0.3	3	0.3	2	0.2	...	...
Market size	0.15	4	0.6	3	0.45	2	0.3	...	...
Political risk	0.20	5	1	4	0.8	2	0.4	...	...
Entry and exit barriers	0.10	2	0.2	2	0.2	2	0.2	...	...
Government regulation	0.10	3	0.3	4	0.4	2	0.2	...	...
Total	**1.00**		**4**		**3.2**		**2.15**	...	...

Competitive Position	Weight	Country A		Country E		Country F		Country ...	
		Rating (1-5)	Score	Rating (1-5)	Score	Rating (1-5)	Score	Rating (1-5)	Score
Marketing capacity	0.20	4	0.8	4	0.8	3	0.6	...	...
Product match	0.15	4	0.6	4	0.6	2	0.3	...	...
Brand recognition	0.25	5	1.25	5	1.25	3	0.75	...	...
Quality relative to competitors	0.15	5	0.75	5	0.75	4	0.6	...	...
Managers' experience with the country	0.05	3	0.15	2	0.1	2	0.1	...	...
Access to distribution channels	0.10	4	0.4	3	0.3	2	0.2	...	...
Profit margin relative to competitors	0.10	3	0.3	4	0.4	3	0.3	...	...
Total	**1.00**		**4.25**		**4.2**		**2.85**	...	...

Rating: 1 = very poor; 5 = very good;
Score: rating × weight
Source: Compiled by Author

In Figure 9.3, Countries A and H have the highest strategic value because the market attractiveness and the company's competitive/business strength is greatest. They certainly would be the first choice for entry. Countries E and P follow, with an average attractiveness but with a strong competitive position. Countries F, Q, and L

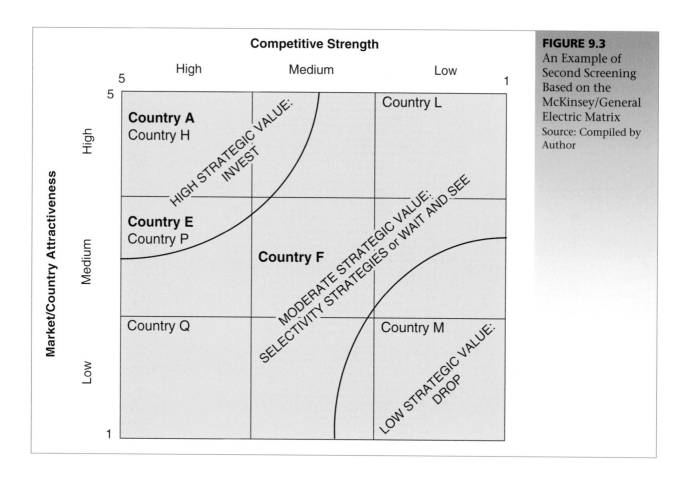

FIGURE 9.3
An Example of
Second Screening
Based on the
McKinsey/General
Electric Matrix
Source: Compiled by
Author

have a moderate strategic value either because they have a moderate competitive position and market attractiveness, or because their attractiveness or competitive position is weak. When this happens, a company can decide to wait and see future trends or, alternatively, develop a selectivity strategy, for example focusing only on some strategic business units that seem to offer more opportunities. Finally, countries with a low strategic value, such as Country M, should be dropped because the opportunities are now inexistent.

Second Screening Based on Portfolio Analysis

The McKinsey/General Electric matrix is not the only method that can be used to prioritize countries identified through the macro-segmentation. Companies can use different models that can be useful to support their decisions. For example, they can decide to make a portfolio analysis in each potential country of entry; evaluating the market attractiveness and competitive position for each strategic business unit (SBU), leading to an overall evaluation of the available opportunities.

As pointed out in Table 9.2, first of all this analysis can help to identify countries where it is worth investing. For example, the screened countries of the macro-segmentation (Cluster 4 in Figure 9.2) have been analyzed considering each SBU

TABLE 9.2
An Example of Second Screening Based on Portfolio Analysis

	Country A	Country E	Country F	Country H	Country L	Country M	Country P	Country Q
SBU 1	H	H	M	H	M	L	H	H
SBU 2	M	L	M	L	L	L	H	L
SBU 3	H	M	H	H	M	M	H	L
SBU 4	H	H	M	H	M	L	M	M
SBU 5	M	H	L	M	L	M	H	H
SBU 6	H	H	H	H	H	L	H	M
Overall evaluation by country	INVEST	INVEST	Selectivity or Wait & See	INVEST	Selectivity or Wait & See	Drop	INVEST	Selectivity or Wait & See

H = high potential; M = moderate potential; L = low potential
Source: Compiled by Author

of operation of the company. Each of them is more or less attractive, considering both the attractiveness of the specific market and the competitive strength of the company. For Countries A, E, H, and P there are four SBUs with high potential for the company. For this reason, it is worth investing. In other countries, the suggestion is to invest only in SBUs with high potential or decide to wait and see how the market or the competitive position of the company evolves. Obviously, if the evaluation is low for almost all the SBUs (such as Country M), the decision to drop is inevitable. However this matrix is also useful for a second type of analysis. In fact, companies can identify if it is possible to develop a global presence in different countries. For example, SBU 6 clearly points out the existence of high potential for the company in most of the countries, showing the possibility to develop a global presence.

Methods for Estimating Market Potential

As pointed out in the analysis of market attractiveness, market size is one of the most important factors to be considered. Nevertheless in a global context its evaluation is often critical because most of the time companies lack information about foreign markets and data is not always reliable. For this reason, different methods can be suggested to calculate market size. Using more than one method can be useful to increase the reliability of the estimation.

Traditional Method

This method is based on the analysis of consumer demand and can be calculated as:

Total population × % of potential clients × frequency of use × average unit sales per client

For example, let's consider a country with a population of 5 million people, of which about 15 percent can be the target for the product: if they buy the product about 8 times a year and they spend $40 on average every time; the estimated market size is $240 million.

$$5,000,000 \times 15\% \times 8 \text{ times/year} \times \$40 = \$240,000,000$$

The main limit of this method is that it is not always easy to find out information about the percentage of potential clients, the frequency of use and/or the average expenditure.

Method by Analogy

In this method, a company estimates the market potential of a country considering another country similar in terms of consumer behavior, which is considered a benchmark for the calculation of the market value. In other terms, the market potential is estimated by analogy between the analyzed country and the country taken into consideration as a benchmark.

For example, let's consider the calculation of market potential for premium sport footwear in Country A. The company is already present in Country Y, which is considered a benchmark because of similar consumer behavior. In Country Y the sport footwear spending is about 40 percent of footwear. Using the data in Table 9.3, it is possible to calculate the market potential of Country A.

Competitors' Based Methods

In some cases, especially if there are few competitors and the market's concentration is high, a company can estimate the actual market size deriving the information from the analysis of competitors. In this case the market size can be obtained by:

	Country A (Market Analysis)	Country Y (Benchmark)
(a) Total population (mn)	50	12
(b) Average disposable income ($)	4,000	2,500
a x b = Total disposable income (bn $)	200	30
(c) Footwear market size (bn $)	---	5
(d) Footwear market potential (X) (bn $): 200:30=X:5	33.33	---
(e) Sport footwear market size (40% of c) (bn $)	---	2
(f) Sport footwear market potential (40% of d) (bn $)	13.33	
Premium sport footwear market size (8% of e) (bn $)		0.16
Premium sport footwear market potential (8% of f) (bn $)	**1.06**	

TABLE 9.3
An Example of Calculation of Market Potential by Analogy

Source: Compiled by Author

a) summing up the sales of all the competitors

b) identifying one competitor and its market share. For example, if a competitor has sales for $5 mn and it is known that its market share is about 10 percent, the total market size will be approximately $50 mn.

The first method can be difficult to apply because it is not easy to identify all the competitors. The second method is easier, because a company can get information talking with distributors, retailers, etc. Sometimes public companies can have market share and sales information which can be used to extrapolate market size.

Method Based on Import/Export Information

This method is suggested by Hollensen (2013)[5] and it is based on production, import, and export figures. The main limit of this method is that it can be used only if the product has an identifiable customs position. The total market volume for a specific product can be calculated as follows:

Local production + import – export +/– changes in stock size

MICRO-SEGMENTATION

After the macro-segmentation and the identification of the countries with the highest opportunities (prioritization), a company has to start taking into consideration consumer differences within each country and among the country markets that are clustered together. In fact, the macro-segmentation approach incorporates some of the most basic segmentation methods, but their simplicity often underlies their limitations. For example, a wireless communication provider that wanted to launch new mobile-payment services in Africa, started with an analysis of countries with the highest GDP per capita. But they soon realized that official data was not able to provide a reliable picture of the distribution of the actual purchasing power, and they had to investigate more to understand the internal dynamics in each selected country.[6] For this reason, it is important to go to the third step previously pointed out in Figure 9.1.

Micro-segmentation is based on product and/or demand characteristics (Figure 9.4). Each country is subdivided into different groups based on product characteristics (the example is related to the segmentation of the special steel market in distinct segments), on characteristics of individuals (Business to Consumer segmentation), of companies (Business to Business segmentation), or of channels of distribution, characterized by distinct characteristics, preferences, needs, and behaviors.

The key to good segmentation is selecting useful dimensions by which to identify each customer segment. For example, a segment can include individuals with the same psychographic characteristics and looking for the same benefits. Or companies located in the same region (geographic segmentation) and characterized

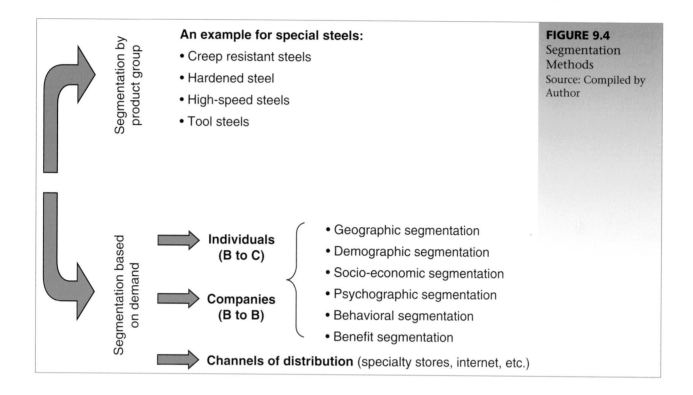

FIGURE 9.4
Segmentation
Methods
Source: Compiled by
Author

by the same size (demographic segmentation based on turnover). In Table 9.4 the most important segmentation variables have been identified.

Each group of individuals (consumers) or companies has to be similar enough in relation to some dimensions of segmentation (geographical, demographical, psychographic, etc.) to allow selling a product with the same marketing mix. However different groups might require different marketing mixes.

A company operating internationally can decide to make a segmentation country by country (multinational segmentation) or across multiple countries (global or horizontal segmentation).

Multinational Segmentation

In the case of multinational segmentation, a company identifies different segments in each country and consequently develops a targeting strategy country by country. Considering the four countries screened after the macro-segmentation and the prioritization (countries A, E, H, and P) (Figure 9.3 and Table 9.2), a multinational segmentation can be described as in Figure 9.5.

In each country the company's managers have two alternatives.

They can use similar segmentation variables (for example income level) and identify similar segments: as is the case of Country A and H. Nevertheless, even if the segmentation variables can be the same, the categorization of the variable can be different. For example, in both the countries the low income segment is considered to be individuals with less than $5,000 per year (Segment C, the same in both

TABLE 9.4 Main Segmentation Variables in Global Marketing	Geographic Variables	Demographic Variables	Socio-Economic Variables	Psychographic Variables	Behavioral Variables	Benefit Sought
	Region Country City Rural vs Urban areas County Climate	Age Gender Nationality Race and ethnic origin	Income/turnover (B to B) Family/company (B to B) size and life cycle Family life cycle Occupation/ industry (B to B) Education Religion Social class Population density	Lifestyles Personality Interests Values Attitudes Opinions	Shopping habits Product use Usage situation Frequency of use Loyalty	Product features Price Experience Status

Source: Compiled by Author

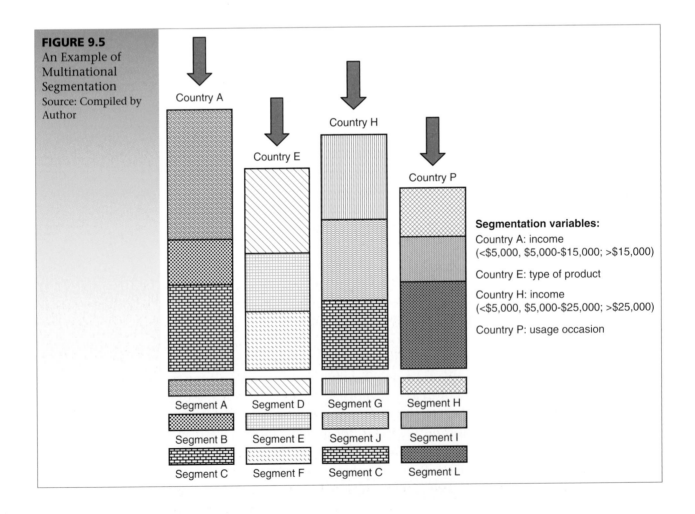

FIGURE 9.5
An Example of Multinational Segmentation
Source: Compiled by Author

Segmentation variables:

Country A: income
(<$5,000, $5,000-$15,000; >$15,000)

Country E: type of product

Country H: income
(<$5,000, $5,000-$25,000; >$25,000)

Country P: usage occasion

countries). Then in Country A the average income has been categorized between $5,000 and $15,000 per year and the medium-high income more than $15,000. In country H the average income has been identified between $5,000 and $25,000 per year and the medium-high income is more than $25,000. For this reason, segments B and J, and A and G are different and not always comparable. It is important to underline that in some cases, even if the categorization of variables is different, the resulting segments can be comparable. For example, in one country the low income is considered to be "less than $5,000," in another country it is "less than $1,000." In this case, the segment is identified with a different income category but the result in terms of behavior, needs, etc. is the same. For this reason, if it is necessary to guarantee comparability, it is important to pay attention to the choice of the dimensions of segmentation. For example, instead of considering absolute values of income distribution, it is better to identify different segments using the distribution of income in quintiles, that identifies the 20 percent of the population with the highest income (top quintile), the 10 percent with the lowest (bottom quintile), etc.

In other cases, segmentation variables can be completely different. In country E the local managers can apply, for example, a product-based segmentation, and in country P they can chose a segmentation method based on usage occasion. Given this situation, it is clear that if the company decides to use segmentation variables and/or categories that are country specific, each country is targeted with a different marketing mix (favoring adaptation). This approach is typical of multinational companies characterized by a high level of decentralization of the decision process. Local subsidiaries are very independent, the coordination of activities between them is very limited, and the marketing strategy is not coordinated between different countries.

Global Segmentation

Differently from multinational segmentation, global segmentation aims to identify segments that are similar in distinct countries. In this way, thanks to the high degree of similarity, the different country segments can be grouped in homogeneous horizontal segments that can be targeted with a standardized global marketing strategy (Figure 9.6).

The best segmentation methods that can be used to identify horizontal segments are the psychographic segmentation (mainly based on lifestyle and personality) and the benefit segmentation. For example a company can group consumers of different countries that look for the same benefits when they buy their products. However, it is important to consider that within any given culture, consumer behavior can be influenced by symbolic and functional benefits and the nature of this combination of benefits is often mediated by the cultural context.[7] Similarly, consumers with a similar lifestyle can be grouped and considered homogeneous in different countries.

Other methods of segmentation can be misleading. For example, demographic variables can identify consumers that only apparently are homogeneous.

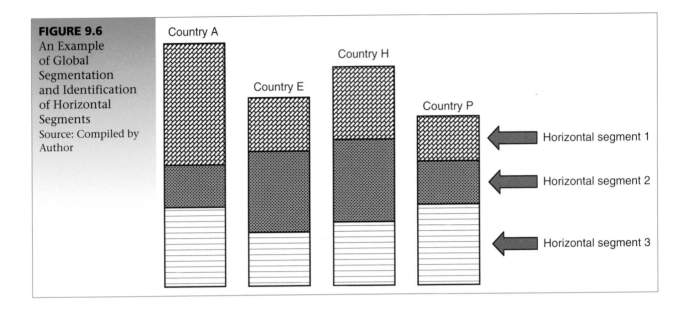

FIGURE 9.6
An Example of Global Segmentation and Identification of Horizontal Segments
Source: Compiled by Author

Consider the case of age. A twenty year old person can be very different in the US (already living alone and working and/or attending a college far from his/her family), in Italy (most of the time still living with the family), or in emerging countries (already independent with his/her own family, children, etc.): the variable of segmentation is the same but the needs and lifestyle of consumers are probably very different and cannot be considered an homogeneous segment. However it is important to underline that the variables used for international market segmentation also depends on the product category. For example, recent research[8] found that in the European and Asian countries considered in the analysis, age dominates the behavior associated with consumer electronics. Similarly, in almost all the analyzed countries the most robust predictor of the consumption of luxury goods was gender: in fact the female consumers segment offers the highest opportunities.

One of the most long-lived and authoritative systems that segment people on the basis of personality traits is VALS, owned and operated by Strategic Business Insights (SBI), an SRI International spin-out. (VALS was originally known as the Values and Lifestyles program).[9]

The basic tenet of VALS is that people express their personalities through their behaviors. VALS specifically defines consumer segments on the basis of those personality traits that affect behavior in the marketplace. While its beginnings can be traced to the late 1970s, the VALS model was redefined in 1989 to allow it to predict consumer behavior on the basis of enduring personality traits rather than social values that change over time. The current VALS system for the US consumer marketplace contains eight segments:

1. Innovators are successful, sophisticated, take-charge people with high self

esteem. Image is important to innovators; not as evidence of status or power but as an expression of their taste, independence, and personality.

2. Thinkers are motivated by ideals. They are mature, satisfied, comfortable, and reflective. They tend to be well-educated and actively seek out information in the decision-making process. They favor durability, functionality, and value in products.

3. Believers are strongly traditional and respect rules and authority. Because they are fundamentally conservative, they are slow to change and technology adverse. They choose products they are familiar with; established well-known brands.

4. Achievers have goal-oriented lifestyles that center on family and career. They avoid situations that encourage a high degree of stimulation or change. They prefer premium products that demonstrate success to their peers.

5. Strivers are trendy and fun loving. They have little discretionary income and tend to have narrow interests. They favor stylish products that emulate the purchases of people with greater material wealth.

6. Experiencers appreciate the unconventional. They are active and impulsive, seeking stimulation from the new, the offbeat, and the risky. They spend a comparatively high proportion of their income on fashion, socializing, and entertainment.

7. Makers value practicality and self-sufficiency. They choose hands-on constructive activities like building a deck or outdoor grill and spend leisure time with family and close friends. In product selection, they prefer value over luxury and usability over style.

8. Survivors lead narrowly-focused lives. Because they have the fewest resources, they purchase fewer products than other groups and therefore do not exhibit a strong primary consumer motivation. While the past often seems fuller to them than the future (i.e. when their spouse was living or when the kids were at home), they are not necessarily sad or hopeless about the present but are accepting of life's smaller pleasures. They are concerned about safety and security, so they tend to be brand loyal and buy discounted merchandise.

VALS systems have also been developed for other countries, such as China, the Dominican Republic, Japan, Nigeria, the United Kingdom, and Venezuela. SBI's research shows that similar psychological traits drive similar kinds of consumer behavior no matter what culture you are in, but the expression of the trait varies by culture. For example, every culture has consumers who are motivated to buy goods based on the status the good confers to them. However, the specific status symbols vary by country and culture. For example, the Japanese VALS model classifies consumers into ten consumer segments ranging from a high to a low degree of innovation strength. The segment having the highest degree of innovation strength is classified as "integrators." They are highly educated and modern, highly social, high up on the income scale, read and travel frequently, and follow the latest trends. Traditional innovators and adapters follow religious customs and are socially conservative. These beliefs color their purchasing behavior that favors familiar products. Self-innovators and adapters are positioned relatively high on the innovative strength scale. As the term implies, these consumers regard self-expression as an ideal. Self-expression can be realized through consumption of products that broadcast self-image, such as fashion clothing, or that provide personal experiences. Ryoshiki ("social intelligence") innovators are middle-aged and career-oriented, and adapters are concerned about both personal advancement and family and social status. High pragmatics are withdrawn, while low pragmatics are uncommitted to life-styles and prefer inexpensive products. Sustainers or realists are resistant to change and have minimal education and income. They are lowest on the innovation scale and are past-oriented.

In the last years, as pointed out in Box 9.1, with the increasing role of technology, global segmentation analysis based on technology adoption has been introduced, in order to differentiate marketing decisions in relation to the characteristics of different market and country segments.

In conclusion, developing a global segmentation means to identify global segments that are focused on cross-cultural commonalties rather than differences between consumers, allowing the implementation of a global marketing strategy. Globalization and global markets have had a polarizing effect on segmentation. On one hand, as globalization brings the world closer, certain segments of similar consumers are becoming easier to identify across the world. Think of the tech gadget fans that line up outside Apple stores in many countries around the world, for the launch of the Apple's new products, for example (Figure 9.7).

On the other hand, as more global markets are becoming accessible, marketers find it increasingly difficult to contend with the variety of segments spurred by the difference in cultures, social habits, regional and national preferences, and other factors. To this point, it is clear that the identification of a global segment leads to the choice of a global target that can be reached with a global standardized marketing mix, as it will be pointed out in the following chapters.[10] Nevertheless it is also important to point out that many differences within the horizontal segment still exist. For this reason, the global marketing mix strategy will be developed first taking into consideration the characteristics of the country-segment that has the highest sales potential in the horizontal segment. This global strategy developed for the most important country of the segment, will be extended to the other countries of the horizontal segment, introducing some adaptations only if localizing the strategy to fit local needs results to be favorable in terms of cost-benefit analysis. For example, the fashion European brand, Dirk Bikkembergs (Figure 9.8), has identified the global segment of the "modern man." In the vision of the Belgian designer, guided by the principle of

Box 9.1   Technology-in-Focus: Consumer Segments and Technology Adoption

Nowadays technology is not only influencing product decisions, but is actually involving areas such as retailing and promotional strategies. Hence understanding consumers' segments in relation to new technology adoption becomes extremely important for many companies in various industries of activity. Nielsen (Geo Map 9.1), for example, has developed a proprietary model, Nielsen Technodoption, that measures the willingness of a household to adopt new technology early in its life cycle. This model has led to the identification of four segments, from High Tech to No Tech, where consumers are distinguished from technology trendsetters, willing to try every new technology, to an opposite situation where consumers do not experiment with new technology and also reveal a refusal to adopt well established technology. These segments are combined with the Nielsen Lifestage classification (ConneXions©), where some segments are highly tech-oriented, differently from other segments where technology is not central in their daily life. For example, consumers acquiring the latest communications and entertainment technology, equipping their homes with wireless computer networks, plasma TV screens, Slingboxes and home theater systems, belong to the segment defined by Nielsen as Technovators. Most of them are adults, executives, and white-collar telecommuters, whose employers provide them with BlackBerries, cell phones, and laptops.

Also, GFK is investing in analysis of consumer behavior in relation to new technology. The aim is to optimize marketing strategies and communication to different target markets, improving consumer experiences in different buying contexts. Nevertheless, segmentation analysis has to be adapted to different market contexts. For example, a recent analysis by Accenture on Digital Consumers points out how 80 percent of Indian consumers living in urban areas intend to buy a smartphone in the next 12 months, against a percentage of 45 percent in the US. Similar differences can be found with tablets; 65 percent of Indian consumers plan to buy a tablet, against 33 percent of consumers in the US.

Sources: Accenture Digital Consumer Tech Survey (2014), 'Racing toward a complete digital lifestyle: Digital consumers crave more', https://www.accenture.com/ma-en/~/media/Accenture/Conversion-Assets/DotCom/Documents/Global/PDF/Technology_1/Accenture-Digital-Consumer-Tech-Survey-2014.pdf; Nielsen ConneXions Lifestage Group. (2014), https://segmentationsolutions.nielsen.com/mybestsegments/Default.jsp?ID=9010&menuOption=learnmore&pageName=ConneXions%2BLifestage%2BGroups&segSystem=CLA.CNE; Nielsen Technodoption, https://segmentationsolutions.nielsen.com/mybestsegments/Default.jsp?ID=9020&menuOption=learnmore&pageName=Nielsen%2BTechnodoption&segSystem=CLA.CNE; http://www.gfk.com/insights/ [All accessed: July 30, 2016].

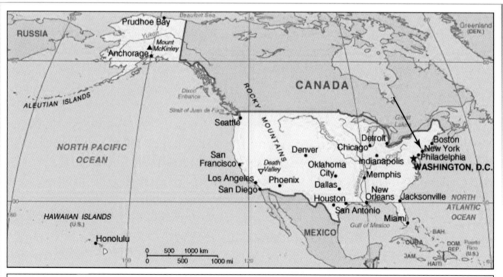

GEO MAP 9.1
Nielsen
Source: Adapted from: CIA Maps, The World Factbook[11]

The headquarters of **Nielsen** are in New York, USA.

FIGURE 9.7
The Apple Store in Place de l'Opéra in Paris
Source: © Author

FIGURE 9.8
An Outdoor Advertising of the Fashion Brand Dirk Bikkemberg in Milan
Source: © Author

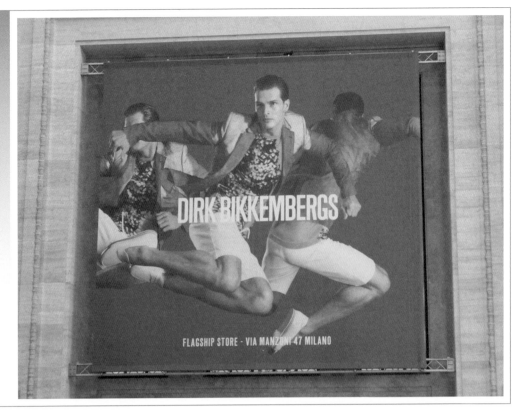

"Mens Sana in Corpore Sano" (Healthy Mind in Healthy Body), the modern man is "strong, healthy and virile."[12] This global principle, based on the union of fashion and sport, which is considered the language of a positive and genuine way of life, allows standardization of the brand perception, but does not exclude local product adaptation when entering new regions such as the Asiatic market.

In Figure 9.4, it has been pointed out how the same segmentation dimensions (demographic, psychographic, etc.) can be applied both to the Business to Consumer and the Business to Business market strategy. However, several major differences become apparent when one compares the segmentation process in the consumer marketplace and the business-to-business environment. The most apparent one is the size of the markets. While consumer marketers often have to contend with a market that reaches in the many thousands and even millions of individual consumers, the business-to-business marketplace for a company rarely exceeds several hundreds of companies and only a few very large firms can claim a business client base of many thousands. However, when purchasing capacity is considered, the scenario is reversed. Business purchasing volume far outstrips individual consumer purchasing, especially when compared on a single transaction basis.[13] Another differentiating point is the dynamics of the actual purchasing process. From motivation to selection to execution, business purchasing is a distinctly more complex affair, given the number of people, factors, and systems involved, than the steps involved in an individual consumer's purchasing decision and ultimate action.

TARGETING

Once all viable segments have been identified in the targeted markets, the process of selecting the most promising segments—those with the highest potential to generate sales and profits for the company—and deciding how to address their needs begins.

Criteria for Targeting

Just as in the second screening of prioritization, the criteria used for selecting the best potential target segments are extremely important. Some of the basic and most widely used targeting criteria are:

- market size—the larger the segment, the more sustainable and profitable it is likely to be;

- growth rate—the faster a segment is growing, the more sales it is likely to generate;

- competitive position—the less competitive offerings are available for the target segment, the more likely the company is to gain large market share;

- market accessibility—the more cost-effectively and quickly a segment can be reached, the more attractive it will be;

- customer fit—the more compatible the segment is with the company's brand and resources, the more likely it is that sales will follow.

The question of customer fit—whether the pursuit of a particular segment is compatible with the company's overall goals and established sources of competitive advantage—is illustrated with the example below of a small soft drinks producer that was able to challenge the global conglomerates thanks to a good targeting strategy.

Although Pepsi and Coca-Cola are firmly entrenched in the Latin American market, a small Peruvian competitor, Kola Real, was not afraid to take them on. At the time of Kola Real's entry, the two soft drink giants had nearly 100 percent of the Peruvian cola market. This would appear to be a difficult position to challenge, but because Kola Real used a no-frills, minimal advertising, and low price strategy that was appealing to its target segments, it was able to quickly capture almost 20 percent of the Peruvian market and successfully carve out a place for itself in Ecuador, Venezuela, and Mexico. Today Kola Real has become an important brand of AJE Group (Geo Box 9.2) that is one of the largest multinational beverage companies, with presence in more than 20 countries in Latin America, Asia, and Africa.[14]

GEO MAP 9.2
AJE Group
Source: Adapted from:
CIA Maps, The World
Factbook[15]

The headquarters of **AJE Group** are in Lima, Peru.

Often, several criteria are used simultaneously to develop a detailed analysis of the most attractive segments. For example, China is an attractive market based on its huge market size and fast-growing middle class, especially in large metropolitan areas. However, in general it is important to consider the specific product category to evaluate the variables that are relevant for the targeting strategy, as pointed out in Box 9.2 for the toy market.

How are these global companies targeting their new markets? There are two main questions that allow the identification of the target market strategy. The first one is: should the company opt for concentration or diversification? And the second one follows: should the company develop an undifferentiated, concentrated, or differentiated approach?

Concentration Versus Diversification

Expansion into markets abroad requires management to decide between two main strategies: concentration or diversification. Both strategies require different levels of marketing effort and resources.

Box 9.2   Country-in-Focus: Targeting Kids in the Global Toy Market

Companies selling toys to the global kids market have to face different markets potential that significantly influence their marketing strategy and their long term objectives.

In terms of population, India is by far the country with the highest opportunities, with a segment of 0–14 year olds counting approximately 370 million. In India the most attractive sub-segment is the 0–4 year olds. However, the Indian market is far from profitable because the per child spend is the lowest in the Asia-Pacific region—about $4.1. Of this, only 30% (US$1.3) comes from legitimate sales, while the rest is made up of illegal sales. Due to low incomes and a 70% rural population, targeting this country requires high attention to the price point. It is not a case that the highest share of imported toys in the Indian market comes from China. Nevertheless, an increasing attention to quality is expected to determine a growing interest towards high-quality products and, as a consequence, well-known branded toys, with the most popular product categories being electronic toys, soft animals, and hard toys.

China is the market with second largest child population and a traditional toys and games spend per child of about US$40. Even if, with these values, it is still difficult for parents to be able to afford expensive toys, the CAGR (Constant Average Growth Rate) in traditional toys and games over 2012–17 will be one of the highest worldwide, higher than 10%.

The above data contrasts with the analysis of the kid target in the US and Europe. In the US, for example, the per capita spend is at US$321. And in Europe the aging of society and the low birth rate is opening new challenges for toy manufacturers, putting a focus on new target groups such as adults.

Sources: Porter, R. (2014), 'Toy manufacturers seek to bridge the gap between toys, with both developed and emerging markets offering good potential', *Euromonitor International*, 3 Feb, 2014; World of Toys, Toy Market Europe, Spielwarenmesse eG, http://www.world-of-toys.org/india/toy-market-india/?L=1, [Accessed: January 4, 2015]; BS Reporter. (2013), 'Indian toy industry hit hard by imports', August 19, 2013, http://www.business-standard.com/article/sme/indian-toy-industry-hit-hard-by-imports-says-study-113081901059_1.html [Accessed: January 5, 2015]; World of Toys, India's market potential, Spielwarenmesse eG, http://www.world-of-toys.org/india/toy-market-india/?L=1, [Accessed: January 4, 2015]; Rana, P. (2014), 'How to tap the full potential of toys and games in India', *Euromonitor International*, 4 November, 2014.

A concentration strategy involves focusing marketing effort and resources on one or a few key markets in the short run and gradual expansion into other markets in the long run. For example, considering the countries selected after the first and second screening, and combining with information gathered with the micro-segmentation, a company can decide to target country A, and only later on to target country E, followed by countries H and P.

A diversification strategy, on the other hand, requires investing marketing effort and resources into a larger number of markets in the short run. In our example, the four countries will be targeted simultaneously.

In both cases, the amount of resources required depends on the entry mode. For example, fewer resources are required for exporting than for direct investment in subsidiaries. Given a fixed amount of resources, the amount assigned to each market in a diversification strategy would be less than for concentration. Therefore, for SMEs, which are often characterized by small amounts of resources, an export concentration strategy would be preferable in order to reduce the risk of low effectiveness in the countries of entry. Concentrating marketing effort and resources in one or a few markets should gain larger market share and, subsequently, higher profits. However, if competition is intense, then small firms should avoid direct competition with larger firms. In this case, it would be preferable to have small market shares in a larger number of markets. Therefore firm size and market factors (such as competition) are variables that influence expansion strategies. In addition, there are market factors such as growth rates and sales stability in each market and the need for standardization or adaptation of products and advertising messages. For example, if sales are not stable and/or the market growth is limited, it is risky to concentrate only in one country and it is better to diversify. Vice versa, if entering in a foreign market requires adaptation of the product or the advertising (that means, as will be pointed out in the following chapters, higher costs), the company will probably opt for concentrating all its efforts in one country and only later expanding in other markets.

The costs of penetrating a market are among the most important considerations in choosing an expansion strategy. One of the tools available, the sales response function, is a calculation that relates the value of investment (x) in marketing effort to the revenue (y) generated (or profit, units sold, etc.). Figure 9.9 shows that the sales curve can be S-shaped or concave, and demonstrates the different functions of both curves.

Expanding into one market and investing at point "A" will yield a return of "C" sales if the curve is S-shaped, and a return of "E" sales if the curve is concave. However, an additional marketing investment in the same market of "F" will yield sales of "J" if the curve is S-shaped, but only "H" if the curve is concave. Therefore, if the market is characterized by an S-shaped curve, it would pay to select a concentration strategy and invest more resources. In fact, a limited investment would lead to limited sales because in the first stage, market entry is based on building brand awareness and demand. Afterwards, further investment in

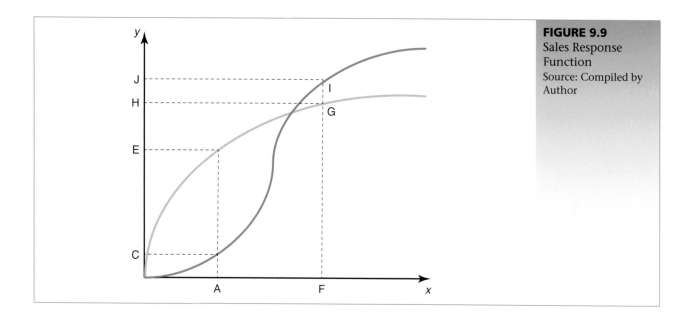

FIGURE 9.9
Sales Response
Function
Source: Compiled by
Author

marketing effort results in growing market share and marginal revenue, much like the growth stage in the product life cycle. This is based on studies that show that high market shares are associated with higher profitability. Vice versa, a market with a concave curve immediately responds to a limited investment. Then further investment in one or a few markets would result in low or no marginal revenue, hence making preferable a diversification approach to get the maximum sales from different markets since the beginning. Additional factors that point to a diversification strategy (and opposite for a concentration strategy) are low growth rates and sales stability (e.g. seasonality, that suggest to sell simultaneously in different markets in order to improve sales stability), short competitive lead time (which makes it important to enter markets quickly), high spillover effects between countries (e.g. the use of the same patents), little need to adapt products and promotion, and little gain from distribution economies of scale. In reality, these factors are not dichotomous (either high or low), but somewhat in between.

Undifferentiated, Concentrated, and Differentiated Approach

Are they simply transferring their existing products to Russia or are they developing new or modified products in order to reach specific segments within this market? The strategies used to target attractive global markets can vary, but their difference can always be traced back to the age-old question in global marketing of standardization versus adaptation, that will be analyzed in depth in chapters 10 to 13 dedicated to the marketing mix analysis. The three most common market selection approaches used in targeting are the undifferentiated approach, the differentiated approach and the concentrated approach.

Undifferentiated Approach

Also called mass marketing or standardized marketing, at the center of the undifferentiated approach to target marketing is the assumption that customer segments across the world will accept the same product or service regardless of their cultural, behavioral, or socio-economic differences. In other words, when using an undifferentiated approach, a company is basing its marketing on the common needs of its customers, instead of on the differences.

Very few brands have managed to be successful on a global scale by using a standardized, global strategy. It is easier if they have the same positioning worldwide (for example, Disney), if they focus on a single product category (such as Intel), or if the company name is the brand name and all marketing dollars are concentrated on that one brand (as is the case of GE and IBM).[16]

For some products, especially commodities such as gasoline or sugar, or for brands that dominate the global business-to-business market, such as Boeing and Airbus, this standardized marketing approach is more viable. However, even in the most commoditized markets, the undifferentiated marketing strategy is beginning to fade away as competition intensifies around the world. Some studies have found empirical evidence that standardized marketing in similar target markets may have a significant positive effect on the performance of a brand over time. However, this positive effect is often distorted by the simultaneous tendency to centralize decision-making when undifferentiated strategy is pursued.[17]

Differentiated Approach

In contrast to undifferentiated marketing, the differentiated approach aims to adapt the product and the marketing mix to each target market segment. Most global brands today use a version of this approach to stay competitive and expand their appeal to more market segments through products and advertising designed specifically for their needs and tastes. An example is the beauty industry. Despite the commonalities that can be found at a global level, companies have to opt for adapted strategies. In fact, within the global segment of women characterized by the same needs, in mature developed markets, sales growth is driven through developing presence in specific niches based on age, gender, and ethnicity, with a price ranging from low to high. In emerging markets, facing an increasing level of competition, it is becoming important to customise product benefits to suit regional preferences, offer brands at accessible pricing points, and develop appropriate packaging sizes.[18]

Concentrated Approach

Sometimes called niche targeting, the concentrated approach is used when a company focuses intensely on one segment of the market and designs its marketing efforts with that segment in mind. Think of the company that targets skateboarders across the world or the services firm that focuses on attracting government contracts only. Focusing on a single segment can have its benefits, such as decreased competition and (if successful) dominant market share. However, when executives end up "putting all of their eggs in one basket," the risk of losing all is also a possibility. If skateboarding declines in popularity, for example, or global economic crisis forces governments to decrease spending, the companies servicing those markets exclusively are likely to suffer. The same happens also when political instability or a war forces companies to exit the only market of export: there is no way to compensate with sales in other countries. Take the case of Coca-Cola and the sportswear maker Adidas. Both companies have been hit by the escalating standoff between Russia and the West. A lot of western products have been banned from the Russian market, significantly affecting market shares of western companies. For Adidas, Russia is the third biggest market, and not only did the German company have to drastically scale back store openings in the country, but they are now also suffering from a general low profitability due to boycotting of their products. Luckily both these companies have a wide portfolio of countries, which can compensate this negative trend in Russia.[19]

Customized Approach

With the advent of the Internet age, online sales and communication channels, and social media networks, a new approach to marketing has been gaining success and popularity. Called the customized or micromarketing approach, it entails an even deeper segmentation of the target market and the creation of even more nuanced and specialized products and marketing campaigns aimed at very specific sub-segments of consumers. The "I ♥ New York" campaign is an example. As Thomas Ranese, the CMO at the New York office of the government agency responsible for attracting tourists to New York State, notes, "In marketing today, you're trying to find the market of one." To do that, his agency relaunched the famous "I ♥ New York" campaign. In contrast to previous years, about half of the campaign budget has been spent on the Internet for customizable brochures and videos, as well as for search engine marketing and targeted banner ads. In addition, the geographic reach of the campaign has been much more targeted, with specific messaging and designs for the audiences in nearby states and Canadian provinces only. With these investments, the "I ♥ New York" Facebook page is adding about 70,000 fans per week, from all over the world, allowing the development of a new relationship and engagement that without the new technology a few years ago would have been impossible.[20]

Such a tailored approach to marketing to individuals with very specific needs and near very specific places has been available to marketers only in most recent years. The online environment has played a key role in the growth of the marketing customization trend, particularly since sophisticated data analysis programs have made it easy to track and report return on marketing investment (ROMI) for online campaigns.

While micromarketing can become expensive, advancements such as mobile marketing, embedded global positioning systems (GPS), behavioral tracking on the Internet (via cookies), and digital printing for direct mail continue to make it easier and more cost-effective to implement for smaller and smaller target segments of the market.

POSITIONING

Positioning is a process that is, for the most part, out of the hands of marketers, since it represents "the way consumers, users, buyers, and others view competitive brands or types of products."[21] In fact, positioning is something that happens mainly in the mind of the consumer, who, by comparing similar brands and products, creates a sort of mental map of how each of them relates to his or her individual needs and wants. Thus, as marketers devise their positioning strategies (planned positioning), the goal is to influence the position their brands have in the minds of consumers (perceived positioning).

Successful positioning should result in strong, long-term emotional ties to the brand for the consumer. Such connection can only be built by consistently sending marketing messages that resonate on a personal level with the consumer and following through with products and services that deliver on the promises made.

The promise is implemented through the marketing mix and the perceived promise represents the positioning in the mind of consumers. The critical point of this process in global marketing strategies is how consumers perceive the brand: in different countries there are different competitors, different needs and buying behavior, different motivations, culture, and attitudes. Furthermore, the control of the channel of distribution can be weak, and the distribution strategies and tactics can be implemented by intermediaries in the wrong way; similarly, price sensibility can be different and communication requires adaptation. Will the company be able to transform the planned positioning in the consumer perceived positioning? This is one of the big challenges that marketing managers have to face every day. For example, Xiaomi Mi Note smartphone, recently launched by Xiaomi Technology Co., Ltd, is trying to position itself as an innovative product, and the company has all the characteristics of an innovator in the industry, but unfortunately its brand image fails to shed its continuing image as an Apple and/or Samsung follower.[22]

In order to succeed, it becomes extremely important to define a correct positioning strategy that underlines the connection between the brand, its target, the product type (important for the identification of direct competitors), the point of difference, the benefits, the brand personality, and, in summary, the unique selling proposition (USP) that identifies in practice what makes the brand different from the others (Figure 9.10).

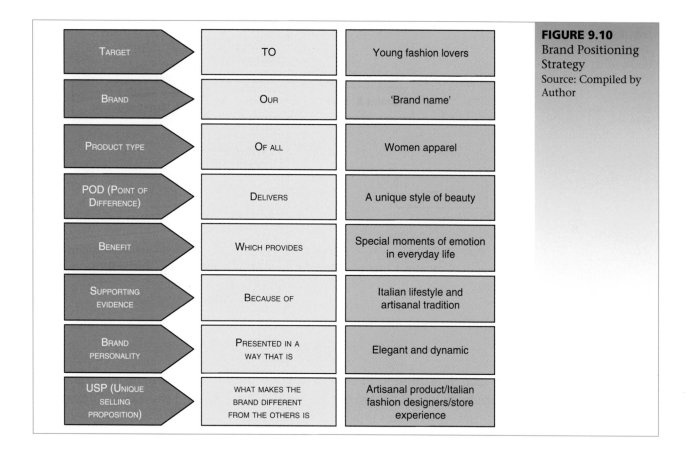

FIGURE 9.10
Brand Positioning
Strategy
Source: Compiled by
Author

The main challenges in the development of a brand positioning strategy are:

- Evaluating if the positioning strategy can be standardized in different countries or it has to be adapted: for example, can the point of difference or the supporting evidence be the same?

- Communicating the chosen position.

- Developing a marketing mix that is able to support the chosen strategy. As we will see in the following chapters, in global markets this is far from easy, and it will probably require an adaptation of the product, pricing, distribution, or promotion.

Another factor to be considered is that positioning has to be analyzed and managed at product and brand level. Positioning at product level reflects how a product category is perceived by consumers. This perception can be different across countries: for example, the role of food, perfumes, fashion, etc. Hence the positioning of the brand has to also take into consideration the perception at product level. Positioning at brand level is often conceptualized with a positioning map, also called a perceptual map. As pointed out in Figure 9.11, brands are positioned

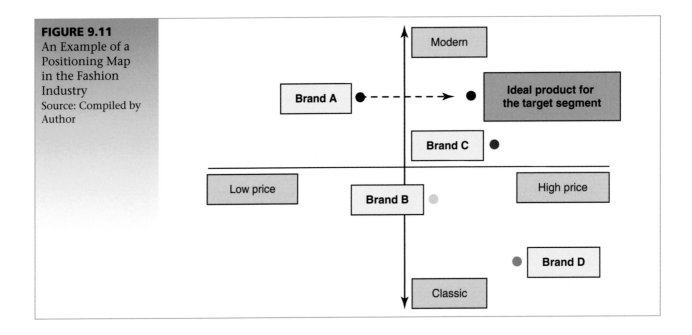

in the map in relation to positioning bases (in the example, price and style). The map clearly points out the position occupied by the brand (for example, Brand A) and by competitive brands in the mind of consumers. In different countries, due for example to cultural differences, consumers' perception can be different, and also competitive brands can vary. In the map it is also possible to identify what the position of the ideal brand is for the target segment. Brand A is quite far from the ideal product, and to be successful the company has to plan a repositioning strategy in order to move closer. Repositioning strategies can be very expensive, especially if carried out at a global level.

Finally, as pointed out in Figure 9.11, positioning requires the identification and communication of the POD (point of difference) that will be operationalized through the USP (unique selling proposition). The POD can be based on one or more of the following different criteria:

- Benefit, attribute or price: the "Everyday Low Price" by Walmart is an example, as well as companies focusing on performance, high quality, or design.

- Usage situation: After Eight mints are positioned as a dessert for *after dinner* (but not only).

- Product use: Studio 6, by the French hotel group Accor, is communicated as a *Long stay hotel ("extend your stay, not your budget")*.

- Users: HSBC, one of the largest banking and financial services institutions in the world, underlines its focus on a *global business clientele*.

- Against competitors: this positioning is based on pointing out the differences against some direct competitors, typically with comparative advertising. Examples are Pepsi versus Coke and Nike versus Adidas.

- **Product class**: Weight Watchers is a global brand associated with *weight loss food*.

- **Company's image**: this criteria is based on the company's characteristics. For example, Danieli, an Italian company that ranks among the three largest worldwide suppliers of plants and equipment to the metals industry, is positioned on the concept of *innovation*. This concept wants to indicate *"innovation in action,"* thanks to the remarkable number of innovative process technologies successfully developed and applied by the company.

Guinness, the popular and distinctive Irish stout nowadays owned by Diageo, uses a virtual community to position and reinforce its marketing to a devout fan base that spans the globe. From selling product-related items in their Internet store, to their 1759 Society for "true Guinness Draught lovers," to the collectors community site, and the free downloadable screensavers, different segments of Guinness drinkers are consistently reminded of what the product is all about while forging emotional connections with it and with other Guinness drinkers. Thanks to the web, Guinness has found a way to connect with drinkers around the world and encourage its members to stay in touch with the company, with fellow consumers, and with the brand, dramatically increasing its "real estate" in the consumers' minds, and remaining consistent in its positioning across the globe. The cohesion around the brand has been reinforced by the recent advertising campaign that is conveying an impactful and unique message promoting qualities like dedication, loyalty, and friendship: global values that can be recognized despite cultural differences. Guinness wants to communicate that beer-drinkers can be both strong and sensitive. The commercial shows a game of wheelchair basketball followed by a pint of Guinness. Actually only one of the basketball players is a wheelchair user: the others are his friends who are playing wheelchair basketball to have fun all together, without distinctions.[23]

Can such positioning consistency work on a global basis for most brands? Much depends on whether the brand can appeal to universal human needs and desires or whether it is suitable for more limited audiences with specific lifestyles, cultural preferences, or particular tastes. Certain positioning themes, such as quality, price, or performance can transition easily from local to global scale and back. Think of Nestlé's "Good Food, Good Life," Walmart's "Everyday Low Prices," or Nike's "Just Do It" positioning statements—they represent broad and broadly appealing sentiments to which people from around the world can relate. This can also be the case for small companies targeting global segments, such as the Italian high-end furnishing company Moroso (Box 9.3). Nevertheless, cultural preferences or traditions also can have a lasting effect on the global positioning strategy for a brand, however. Hence some brands reposition their products based on the benefits considered most appealing to the local market.

Box 9.3 Company-in-Focus: Moroso

Positioning Based on Fashion and Design in the High-End Furnishing Market

Moroso is a small company located in the North East of Italy, which produces luxury sofa and seating. Since 1952 the Moroso family, headed today by the second generation with Roberto, the CEO, and Patrizia, the Art Director, has been working in close collaboration with some of the world's most talented designers and architects. The company operates in the global residential and contract markets. In the residential market they target both the segments of indoor and outdoor sofa and seating. In the contract market the main segments are restaurants, waiting hall, shops, hotels, theatres, and the naval industry. The point of difference (POD), around which the global standardized positioning of the company is based, is brand creativity and innovation, consisting of concretizing creative ideas through new products and processes (Figure 9.12). The identity of the company represents the supporting evidence of this successful global positioning. In fact their high-end furnishings, made entirely in Italy, are realized by carefully selecting every single element that contributes to them, in order to obtain a perfect and recognizable product, which is distinguished by high quality and certified materials. The design is a unique synthesis of architecture, art, and fashion, where the quality is the result of a perfect blending of artisan craftsmanship and industrial processing. The recognized value of Moroso products worldwide has made possible long-term collaborations with the major institutions and event organizers in the world of contemporary arts, such as the Guggenheim Bilbao, Centre Pompidou, Palais de Tokyo, La Biennale di Venezia, Art Basel, and many others.

It is thanks to its focus on the global values of art, design, and family values, deep-rooted in a territory of traditions made in Italy, that Moroso can be considered as an example of a small company able to develop a successful positioning on a global luxury niche.

Sources: Company's slides [Obtained: December 8, 2014]; Company's internet site http://www.moroso.it [Accessed: January 22, 2015].

FIGURE 9.12
Victoria & Albert (2000): An Example of Moroso Famous Creations
Source: © Reprinted with Permission

SUMMARY

- Through market segmentation, the similarities and differences of potential buying customers can be identified and grouped.
- In a global context, marketers can use macro-segmentation based on a country's or a region's demographic and economic statistics, or a micro-segmentation method based on individuals' or companies' geographic, demographic, socio-economic, psychographic, and behavioral patterns to define market segments.
- The first screening in market analysis and selection is based on macro-segmentation that allows to group countries into market segments. The purpose of the second screening is to identify markets that have the best potential for the company: this screening can be done with directional policy matrices (McKinsey/General Electric matrix) and/or with portfolio analysis.
- Market size is one of the most important factors to be considered in the analysis of market attractiveness. Different methods are available for calculating market potential and the use of more than one method can increase the reliability of the estimation.
- Micro-segmentation is carried out after the macro-segmentation and the identification of countries with the highest opportunities (prioritization). A company operating internationally can decide to make a micro-segmentation country by country (multinational segmentation) or across multiple countries (global or horizontal segmentation).
- To target the appropriate consumer segments, marketers must evaluate and compare them on the basis of market size, growth potential, market accessibility, competitive position, and compatibility.
- In selecting the right market targeting strategy, marketers must decide to opt for concentration or diversification. Secondly, if the company wants to use an undifferentiated, differentiated, concentrated, or customized approach. Each requires a different degree of standardization or adaptation of the product and the marketing mix for each segment.
- Positioning occurs in the mind of the consumer, who, by comparing similar brands and products, creates a mental map of how each of them relates to his or her individual needs and wants. Marketers strive to influence the position their brands have in the minds of consumers in relation to competitor brands.

DISCUSSION QUESTIONS

1. Explain the difference between segmenting, targeting, and positioning.
2. Illustrate how Fiat is targeting its cars in the United States.
3. China is characterized by regional differences. Describe how retailers in China market to these differences.

EXPERIENTIAL EXERCISES

1. Visit the World Bank's World Development Indicators (WDI) site, accessible from www.worldbank.org. Learn more about the different categories of indicators used and make a list of the ones that can be particularly helpful to marketers looking to enter new international markets with products related to the consumer-side of the telecommunications industry.

2. List your favorite clothing brands and try to guess the targeting and positioning strategies used by the company that made it appealing to you. Would you do anything differently if you were the marketing executive in charge of that brand?

KEY TERMS

- Business-to-business segmentation
- Business-to-consumer segmentation
- Concentrated strategy
- Concentration
- Customization
- Differentiated strategy
- Diversification
- Macro-segmentation
- Market potential
- McKinsey–General Electric matrix
- Micro-segmentation
- Perceptual map
- Prioritization
- Segmentation
- Positioning
- Targeting
- Undifferentiated strategy
- Unique selling proposition
- VALS

NOTES

1 Elliott, T. (2014), 'Heineken hopes star power will do the trick', *The New York Times*, July 16, 2014, http://www.nytimes.com/2014/07/17/business/media/heineken-hopes-star-power-will-do-the-trick.html?_r=1 [Accessed: January 2, 2015].

2 The standardization/adaptation of the marketing mix will be analyzed in-depth in Chapters 10, 11, 12, and 13.

3 American Marketing Association Dictionary. 'Market segmentation definition', https://www.ama.org/resources/Pages/Dictionary.aspx?dLetter=M#market+segmentation [Accessed: December 16, 2014].

4 Perreault, Jr., W.D., Cannon, J.P., and McCarthy, E.J. (2015). *Essentials of marketing: A marketing strategy planning approach.* NY: McGraw-Hill/Irwin.

5 Hollensen, S. (2013). *Global marketing: A decision oriented approach.* 6th ed. Harlow, England: Prentice Hall, p. 269.

6 Valdeviesa de Uster, M., Vander Ark, J., and Weldon, W. (2012), 'Act like a local: How to sell in emerging markets', *Chief Marketing & Sales Officer Forum*, adapted from http://www.mckinseyonmarketingandsales.com/act-like-a-local-how-to-sell-in-emerging-markets [Accessed: January 3, 2015].

7 Cannon, H.M. and Yaprak, A. (2011), 'A dynamic framework for understanding cross-national segmentation', *International Marketing Review*, 28 (3), pp. 229–43.

8 Cleveland, M., Papadopoulos, N., and Laroche, M. (2011), 'Identity, demographics, and consumer behaviors', *International Marketing Review*, 28(3), pp. 244–66.

9 SRI Consulting Business Intelligence (SRIC-BI), 'The VALS™ Survey', http://staff.ycp.edu/~mblake/SRIC-BI%20%20VALS%20Survey.htm Accessed: January 7, 2015]; Strategic Business Insights. (2015), 'About VALS™', http://www.strategicbusinessinsights.com/vals/ [Accessed: January 7, 2015]; Strategic Business Insights. (2015), 'US Framework and VALS™ Types', http://www.strategicbusinessinsights.com/vals/ustypes.shtml#types [Accessed: January 7, 2015].

10 The standardization/adaptation debate will be deeply analyzed in Chapters 10, 11, 12, 13.

11 The World Factbook. (2015), https://www.cia.gov/library/publications/the-world-factbook/docs/refmaps.html [Accessed: August 1, 2015].

12 Company's website. (2015), 'Dirk Bikkembergs, fashion designer', http://www.bikkembergs.com/BrandHeritage [Accessed: October 4, 2015].

13 Hague, P. and Harrison, M. 'Market segmentation in B2B markets', *B2B International, Ltd*, http://www.b2binternational.com/publications/b2b-segmentation-research/ [Accessed: January 3, 2015].

14 AJE. 'A worldwide company', http://www.ajegroup.com/about-aje/map/ [Accessed: January 4, 2015]; Luhnow, D. and Terhune, C. (2003), 'Latin pop: A low-budget cola shakes up markets south of the border', *Wall Street Journal*, October 27.

15 The World Factbook. (2015), https://www.cia.gov/library/publications/the-world-factbook/docs/refmaps.html [Accessed: August 1, 2015].

16 Quelch, J. (2007), 'How to build a global brand', *Harvard Business Review*, October 16, 2007, http://discussionleader.hbsp.com/quelch/2007/10/how_to_build_a_global_brand.html [Accessed: January 12, 2015].

17 Ozsomer, A. and Prussia, G. E. (2000), 'Competing perspectives in international marketing strategy: Contingency and process models', *Journal of International Marketing*, 8(1), pp. 27–50.

18 Euromonitor International. (2014), 'Customization and increasing segmentation spell growth in beauty', October, http://www.euromonitor.com/customisation-and-increasing-segmentation-spell-growth-in-beauty/report [Accessed: January 12, 2015].

19 Kollewe, J. (2014), 'Russia tensions with west over Ukraine hit Coca-Cola bottler and Adidas', *The Guardian*, August 7, 2014, http://www.theguardian.com/business/2014/aug/07/russia-import-ban-coca-cola-bottler [Accessed: January 8, 2015].

20 I love New York Staff. (2012), 'I love New York tops 1 million milestone on Facebook', May 15, 2012, http://www.iloveny.com/thebeat/post/2012/15/I-LOVE-NEW-YORK-Tops-1-Million-Milestone-on-Facebook/4942/ [Accessed:January 11, 2015]; Elliott, S. (2008), 'Calling on tourists to come for New York City, but stay for the state', *The New York Times*, May 6, 2008, www.nytimes.com/2008/05/06/business/media/06adco.html [Accessed: January 11, 2015].

21 American Marketing Association Dictionary, 'Product positioning definition', https://www.ama.org/resources/Pages/Dictionary.aspx?dLetter=P#product+positioning [Accessed: January 20, 2015].

22 Loo Wee Teck. (2015), 'XiaoMi Note product launch – still obsessed with Apple', *Euromonitor International*, January, 2015, www.euromonitor.com [Accessed: January 11, 2015].

23 Schoultz, M. (2016), 'Guinness marketing campaign makes storytelling a big difference maker', *Digital Spark Marketing*, http://digitalsparkmarketing.com/creative-marketingmarketing-strategy-creative-marketingguinness-marketing-campaign/ [Accessed: July 30, 2016]; Flavián, C. and Guinalíu, M. (2005), 'The influence of virtual communities on distribution strategies in the Internet', *International Journal of Retail & Distribution Management*, 33(6/7), pp. 405–25.

CASE 9.1   HONG KONG DISNEYLAND: CHINESE TOURISTS' BEHAVIOR AND DISNEYLAND'S INTERNATIONALIZATION STRATEGY

Mainland China has been making unprecedented economic growth in the previous three decades, and one of the major contributors is its tourism industry. The mainland Chinese tourists are a major force in world tourism. Considering its proximity to mainland China, the Hong Kong Special Administrative Region (HKSAR) has all the benefits to gain from the increasing demand by mainland Chinese for traveling abroad and for shopping. To enhance Hong Kong as a first choice for mainland Chinese tourists, the Hong Kong government successfully sealed a joint venture with Walt Disney Company for the establishment of a Hong Kong Disneyland Park. However, the Hong Kong government also gave Ocean Park, its local theme park, all the needed support to rejuvenate itself in the wake of impending competition from Disneyland, and to give a boost to attract more tourists to Hong Kong.

Hong Kong Disneyland Park, owned and managed by Hong Kong International Theme Parks, is an incorporated company jointly owned by The Walt Disney Company and the Hong Kong Government. Located on reclaimed land in Penny's Bay, Lantau Island, it opened for visitors on September 12, 2005, after protracted negotiations and construction hassles. The Walt Disney Company dealt with a lot of cultural backlash and therefore had to incorporate Chinese culture, customs, and traditions into the design and construction of the resort, including following the principles of Feng Shui. The park was designed to handle 34,000 visitors per day. The park attracted 5.2 million visitors in its first year of opening, compared to its expectations of 5.6 million. In the second year, the visitors fell by 20 percent to four million, and in the third year increased by 8 percent to 4.5 million visitors. Since the opening of Hong Kong Disneyland in 2005, the theme park has attracted 15 million guests.

Hong Kong Disneyland Park's competitor, Ocean Park, was Hong Kong's only homegrown theme park, which opened in 1977. It was Asia's largest marine-based theme park and claims to be the only Asian park accredited by the American Zoo and Aquarium Association. It features a giant panda exhibit, a butterfly garden, a shark tank, and a three-story aquarium, as well as numerous rides. It has an area of 870,000 square meters and currently has over 40 rides and attractions. With the opening of Hong Kong Disneyland Park, Ocean Park expected a 25 percent decrease in visitors.

DISNEY THEME PARKS AND RESORTS

The Walt Disney Company is a brainchild of Mr. Walt Disney, after whose name the theme park and its related entertainment businesses were named. The first Disneyland in Anaheim, California, opened its doors for the first time in 1955. Since then the company has become an icon of children's entertainment and more. Six years after opening the first Disneyland theme park in Anaheim, the Walt Disney Company opened its second theme park in Florida in 1971. Its first foray into foreign land was with the development of Tokyo Disneyland in 1983. Tokyo Disneyland turned out to be a huge success with mostly Japanese visitors. In fact, it is one of the world's most popular theme parks. However, because of the licensing agreement, the royalties stipulated in the agreement limited the Walt Disney Company's earnings. In Europe, Euro Disney opened in 1992, and was the second Disney theme park built outside the United States It performed very badly due to a combination of factors, including cultural disparity between the United States and Europe; high interest rates; low tourist spending as a result of the European recession; and a strong franc currency. In late 1994, it required a huge restructuring effort to get Euro Disney back on track. Its lenders agreed to suspend interest payments on debts for 24 months and to delay payment of principal for three years. From 1992 to 1998, the Walt Disney Company agreed to forgo management fees and sold its equity to raise funds. Its recovery was also backed by a US$500 million investment from a Saudi Arabian prince. A last ditch effort was made to attract more European visitors by renaming the park as Disneyland Paris, which connotes magic and romance.

HONG KONG DISNEYLAND

The sheer size and continued strong economic performance of the Mainland China market lured the Walt Disney Company. Other locations vying for a Disney park were Shanghai, Zhuhai, and Singapore. Shanghai was a very interesting option for Disney since it was one of the most progressive and strategically located cities in China. However, its inferior infrastructure, lack of a Western legal system, lack of easily convertible currency, and less accessibility to the rest of Asia, among other reasons, made it less attractive than Hong Kong. Zhuhai fared poorly compared with both Hong Kong and Shanghai considering its less-developed infrastructure and lower GDP. Although Singapore has the basic conditions to make it a feasible location for the third Disney outside the United States, its location did not help it achieve the Walt Disney Company's ultimate goal of clinching a foothold on the China market (Chan and Wang, 2000). Negotiations with the Hong Kong government ended up with a joint venture agreement between the Hong Kong government and The Walt Disney Company in a 57 percent to 43 percent equity structure (Hong Kong Government, 1999). Hong Kong Disneyland was supposed to serve as springboard for The Walt Disney Company's future operations in Mainland China. The Hong Kong government, on the other hand, saw it as a means of revitalizing its sagging tourism industry and of signaling to the international business community that Hong Kong is still the place to be.

In addition to its financial woes, Hong Kong Disneyland was also beset with an unhappy workforce clamoring for equal treatment to their counterparts abroad. This is in stark contrast to the success that Ocean Park experienced in the process of its reinvention. Ocean Park aspired to be the world leader in providing excellent guest experiences in a theme park environment connecting people with nature. Ocean Park's mission to connect people with nature through conversation, entertainment, and education is what truly differentiates them within the market. It believes that its cutting edge is this "edutainment" experience, which enables visitors to get up close and understand how animals behave in the wild. As a bridge to the natural world, the park awakens respect for the beauty of animal and marine life and, in the process, also an awareness of the importance of conservation. As a result of the commitment to this ethos, Ocean Park's popularity grew ever stronger. Essentially a homegrown park with a local heart, Ocean Park has reached global markets through innovative products that ignite and inspire its guests' imaginations. Its recent ranking in 2006 by Forbes.com as one of the world's 10 most popular theme parks was a proud moment for both Ocean Park and Hong Kong, reinforcing the quality of Ocean Park and its ability to compete at the global level while remaining relevant to the local needs. Most people may view Hong Kong Disneyland as the only competitor to Ocean Park. However, the latter sees theme parks all over the world—particularly marine parks—as competition.

FACTORS LEADING TO HONG KONG DISNEYLAND'S WOES

Cultural Adaptation

Although Hong Kong Disneyland tried its best to understand the culture of its market, the company failed to culturally adapt the theme park in prelaunch stages. The Mainland Chinese market was very unfamiliar with the Disney characters. Those in their middle age did not grow up watching American television shows or movies. The younger generation, who were born after China's opening up in 1978, were brought up with Japanese cartoons rather than American heroes. Japanese pop culture exerted a lot of influence on the younger generation. In short, Mickey Mouse and Donald Duck were foreign products to the Chinese market. Thus, when the Mainland Chinese tourists visited Hong Kong Disneyland, they did not easily connect with the characters in the park. They were unfamiliar with the product. Even though Hong Kong Disney-land tried to address this by introducing the Disney characters even before it officially opened, and even introduced a short program at the entrance of the park to introduce the Disney stories to those unfamiliar with them, these efforts seemed insufficient to attract the Mainland Chinese to the park. Hong Kong Disneyland perhaps assumed, given its global brand and despite lessons in Paris, that unlike Western tourists—for whom vacations are very experiential—the Chinese enjoy focusing on what they can buy, eat, and bring home. Furthermore, taking pictures and bringing them back home to show friends and relatives of their trip abroad seem to be more important to Chinese tourists than the experience of being in the place itself. For example, when Chinese go to the beach, many of them do not actually swim in the water. Being there and seeing the place would be enough. Actually swimming in the sea and sunbathing are not necessary. In fact, many Chinese avoid the sun since they want to keep their skin fair. For them there is a saying: "The whiteness of your face can cover its ugliness."

CHINESE TOURIST BEHAVIOR

For Western tourists, going abroad for vacation is a good time to relax and experience the foreign culture. However, for the tourists from Mainland China, going to Hong Kong means a shopping experience, and so they choose the cheaper alternative to Hong Kong Disneyland, which is Ocean Park. In fact, for many local tourists, Ocean Park provides a perceived better experience at a lower price. Thus Hong Kong Disneyland might have anticipated this local demand by reducing entry costs or going for innovative pricing so as to increase the footfalls in the theme park first and to generate revenue subsequently. Hong Kong Disneyland could not successfully handle the pressures of local demand in terms of the need to travel for shopping and the price-sensitive nature of Chinese shoppers and tourists. In apparent management hubris, Hong Kong Disneyland believed that Chinese tourists would lap and hug the Disney brand (case writers' assessment) because of its global appeal, without realizing that they were culturally more closely connected with Ocean Park and its theme.

In general, the Chinese people also put a premium on education, and look at it as a means of social mobility to provide them with financial security. Thus a typical Chinese family would make sure that their children will go to the best universities in the country and even abroad. The educational slant provided by Ocean Park would seem to have a stronger pulling power than the fantasy experience Hong Kong Disneyland provides. Hong Kong Disneyland again failed to look at or overlooked this local cultural nuance.

RELATIONSHIP WITH TRAVEL AGENTS

Unlike Western tourists, Mainland Chinese tourists depend a lot on travel agents for their trips abroad. The travel agents are gatekeepers of information and they exert great influence on the decisions made by mainland tourists. Hong Kong Disneyland failed to spot this practice and did not heed too much attention to building a relationship with the travel agents. Meanwhile Ocean Park, being a pioneer in the region, gave a lot of concessions to the travel agents, who then promoted visits to Ocean Park over Hong Kong Disneyland.

Some Afterthoughts

In hindsight, The Walt Disney Company's decision to develop its third Disneyland park outside the United States seems to have been a big lesson for the company.

As The Walt Disney Company's intention was to gauge the mainland Chinese market through its operation in Hong Kong, it may find its experience a record of its success, though it may be an apparent failure. This experience has taught Walt Disney to carefully watch its step when the time comes for it to enter Mainland China. The success of Ocean Park affirms the importance of a visionary leadership in an organization, exemplified in the case of Ocean Park by its tandem of entrepreneurial talent in Mr. Zeman and technical expertise in Mr. Mehrmann.

On the other hand, Hong Kong Disneyland failed despite its global competitive advantages because it failed to meet the pressures of local demands. Multinational Corporations or MNCs with strong corporate controls and powerful global brands often fail to adapt to local markets, either because they are worried that brands would be diluted locally through adaptation, or because of a simpler case of oversight in understanding or implementing consumer insights. This also resulted in several instances of negative publicity. The Hong Kong Disneyland case possibly suggests validates beyond doubt that for businesses to internationalize, pressures from brand extension and localization need to be successfully balanced; success in one cannot compensate for the other.

DISCUSSION QUESTIONS

1. What led to the eventual woes experienced by Hong Kong Disneyland in its first year of operation? How should Hong Kong Disneyland rectify its market situation?
2. To what extent could Hong Kong Disneyland adapt its product to Chinese consumers without diluting its image?
3. How should Hong Kong Disneyland address competition?

SOURCES

Anonymous. (2003). Ocean Park. *Hong Kong Chamber of Commerce*, Member's Profile, Ocean Park.

Chan & Wang. (2000). Hong Kong Disneyland (A): The Walt Disney perspective. *Asia Case Research Center*, University of Hong Kong.

Crawford, B. (2006, July 31). Mr. Enthusiasm. *South China Morning Post*.

Doz, Y. (1976). *National policies and multinational management*. Unpublished doctoral dissertation. Boston: Harvard Business School.

Emmons, N. (2002). Hong Kong Disneyland on time, on budget. *Amusement Business*, 114(13), 6.

Fan, M. (2006). Disney culture shock. *Washington Post*. Retrieved from www.thestandard .com.hk/news_detail.asp?pp_cat=20&art_id=32372&sid=10991562&con_type=1& d_str=20061122&sear_year=2006.

Hong Kong Disneyland (Accessed from http://en.wikipedia.org/wiki/Hong_Kong_ Disneyland (accessed on July 9, 2009).

Hong Kong Government. (1999). Background information on Hong Kong Disneyland. Press release.

Hong Kong Institute of Marketing. (2004). Lan Kwai Fong—Over two decades of success. Retrieved from www.hkim.org.hk/event_20041211.html. http://www.chamber.org.hk/info/member_a_week/member_ profile.asp?id+32&P=3&KW=&search_p (accessed 24 March 2003).

Lau, J. (2005, March 21). HK theme park plans revamp to compete with Disneyland. *Financial Times*, p. 6.

Leung, W. (2005). Wong under fire as Disney escapes action in FEHD case. *The Standard*. Retrieved from www.thestandard.com.hk/news_detail.asp?pp_cat=11&art_ id=25410&sid=5401592&con_type=1&d_str =20051110&sear_year=2005.

Liu, E., & Wong, E. (1999, November 10). Information note—Disneyland Paris: Some basic facts. *Legislative Council Secretariat*.

Miller, P. M. (2007, January/February). Disneyland in Hong Kong. *The China Business Review*, 34(1), 31–33.

Murphy, J. (2006, May 19). Morale Crisis Shakes HK's House of Mouse. *Media*, 1. Ocean Park Corporation. (2003). Annual report.

Pierson, D. (2007, June 30). Hong Kong theme park outsmarts the mouse. *Times*.

Prahalad, C. K. (1975). The strategic process in a multinational corporation. Unpublished doctoral dissertation, Harvard Business School. ___ , & Doz, Y.L. (1987). The multinational mission: Balancing local demands and global vision. New York: The Free Press.

Reckard E. (1999, December 19). Disney discovering it's a small world after all. Los *Angeles Times*.

Reuters. (2006, September 9). Disneyland struggles to make magic in Hong Kong.

Roberts, G. (2004, February 27). HK park gears for battle with Disney. *Media*, 8.

Roth, K., & Morrison, A. J. (1990). Empirical analysis of the integration-responsiveness framework in global industries. *Journal of International Business Studies*, 21(4), 541–564.

Whaley, F. (2001, May). Move over Mickey. *Asian Business*, 37(5), 28.

Yim, B. (2007). Ocean Park: In the face of competition from Hong Kong Disneyland. *Poon Kam Kai Series*. Asia Case Research Center, Hong Kong University.

Yim, C. K. (2004). Hong Kong Disneyland: Where is the magic. *Poon Kam Kai Series*. Asia Case Research Center, University of Hong Kong.

PART III

The Four Ps of Global Marketing

CHAPTER 10

Developing Global Products
and Brands

"Our brands are well established and positioned in a distinctive and complementary manner and, based on long-term structural changes of population and 21st century consumer trends, they are full of organic growth potential."[1]

François-Henri Pinault, President and CEO, Kering Group

LEARNING OBJECTIVES

After Reading This Chapter, You Should Be Able to:

- Define global products and services.
- Understand what is meant by "international product life cycle."
- Discuss the standardization versus adaptation alternative.
- Describe product features and perception in a global context.
- Discuss why many differences in product attributes are found in emerging markets.
- Explain the key approaches to branding decisions in global markets.
- Identify and discuss the main international product strategies.

INTRODUCTION

Once the target markets and the international entry modes have been chosen, the company's first and most critical decisions to face are those relative to product management in foreign markets. This applies both to products and services. As a matter of fact, it is important to note that while most people think of a tangible object when they hear the word "product," services such as insurance and financial advice, or experiences such as vacations or shows, are also included in this definition.

Some of the variables that a company has to take into consideration in order to reduce the risk of failure in a foreign market are differences in product use and expected benefits; product and brand perception; and preferences in style, color, and design, just to name a few.

It is not enough to think that if a product is successful in one market, it will necessarily be as successful in other markets. A company that is introducing a product to a target country often has to wonder if it should **modify it to make it more appealing to that market.** For example, multinational companies producing culinary products, beverages, and dairy and confectionery products, adapt their products to address the needs of lower-income consumers in underdeveloped countries. Not only do they use different formats (for example single serving portions to make the unit price affordable) but they also fortify the food with micronutrients that help to address the deficiencies (iron, zinc, iodine, and vitamin A) significantly diffused among lower-income consumers. For example, in Central and West Africa Nestlé sells iodine-enriched Maggi products (bouillons, seasonings, and noodles) developed using iodized salt.[2]

Costa Cruises, the Italian brand of Carnival Corporation, the world's number one cruise operator, is very successful nowadays in the American market. What is the reason for success? Design, elegance, style, and... first of all... Italian food... seven, eight, 15 days of world-famous Italian cuisine? Well, not exactly, because one of the main reasons why American clients were not satisfied with the first editions of Costa Cruises was in fact the food, which was not in line with their expectations. Costa was serving real Italian dishes, while the American clients were used to and liked the recipes of Italian restaurants in the United States—two ways of cooking that have grown apart. The company had to take this into consideration and adapt the recipes to create a successful product and service.

In many cases, for example when a company is targeting a completely new segment in the foreign market, **adaptations are not enough to be successful abroad: the company has to develop a completely different marketing approach.** Such is the case of the gourmet coffee company Starbucks, which is certainly betting on the Chinese market, that has become its second largest market (Figure 10.1).

With an initial presence largely in major international cities such as Beijing, Shanghai, and Guangzhou, the company is now expanding to among hundreds of second-tier cities across China, targeting consumers with growing purchasing power. Faced with the fact that the majority of China's population drinks tea as a taste preference and centuries-old tradition, Starbucks' coffee products and culture are not things the Chinese flock to naturally. Therefore, the company has targeted the young, brand- and status-conscious professional class, open to Western culture and products—and has begun introducing them to coffee and the coffeehouse culture's intricacies. From stocking its stores with educational brochures to holding frequent tasting sessions and passing out free samples, Starbucks is on a mission to change Chinese tastes from tea to coffee. Nevertheless, the company has also adapted in order to fit better with Asian preferences. It has changed its stores to offer more food and seating and has altered its product offerings to include black sesame green-tea cake roll and Chinese moon cakes during the mid-autumn festival. Also the core products have been adapted: facing the problem of a coffee that is often described as "too bitter" to enjoy, Starbucks' R&D center in Shanghai has responded by developing popular fruity drinks such as Strawberry Soy Frappuccino and the Refresha line of juice beverages.[3]

FIGURE 10.1
Starbucks in China
Source: © Author

Companies can be forced to modify the product not only to fit consumer needs but also because there are significant differences in competition. For example, product adaptation is required to get closer to the market when local competitors are very strong. In China the local company Baidu provides the Internet with Chinese characteristics, offering a web page that looks like Google's. But the competitive advantage of Baidu has been the capacity to fit with country's peculiarities better than Google does.[4]

This chapter discusses product decisions in international marketing strategy. The goal is to underline the importance of the more complex variables that need to be taken into consideration before offering a product in a foreign country. We don't pretend to be comprehensive, also because every product or service has its very distinctive characteristics in relation to its classification based on the category it belongs to (industrial versus consumer, durable versus non-durable, convenience/preference/shopping/specialty, etc.). Furthermore, in each country, consumer characteristics and behavior can vary, the situations and the way in which they use a product change over time, and competition can be different. As a result, marketing strategies need to be re-evaluated. The company may need to redefine a product that represents the key of its success in global markets.

LOOKING FOR NEW GROWTH OPPORTUNITIES: THE PRODUCT LIFE CYCLE ACROSS COUNTRIES

The course a product's sales and profits takes over its lifetime, from its introduction to its final withdrawal from the market, is described by the product life cycle (PLC) which is divided into five different stages (Figure 10.2).

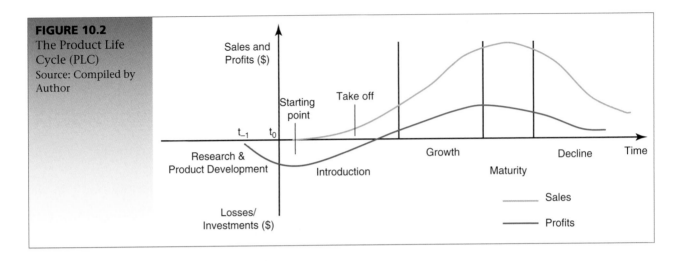

FIGURE 10.2
The Product Life Cycle (PLC)
Source: Compiled by Author

The **research and product development** stage occurs when the company identifies and develops a new product idea, with high research and development costs. If marketing research demonstrates that the idea could be successful, the product is launched in the market.

In the **introduction phase**, sales pick up very slowly and the company may incur a loss if it does not manage to compensate for high product development costs with new sales. The potential consumers aren't aware of the product benefits yet, because it is targeted for an emerging potential need. Demand is limited and is mainly led by the country's innovative segment. The product offered is still in its early stages and marketing communication is mainly informative. In this phase, given the limited availability of information related to product benefits, the company can easily influence the consumer's cognitive system and therefore the purchase decision process.

The third stage is the **growth phase**, characterized by a swift increase in sales. Now it is time for the company to begin to offer a wider selection to stimulate demand for the specific brand.

The **maturity phase** is defined by a demand slowdown that settles on a steady growth rate, usually equivalent to the GDP growth rate or population growth. The product is well-known, price competition is high, and marketing communication has shifted from an information to a persuasion tool, more often playing on the product's emotional characteristics.

The last stage is the **decline phase**, where a structural decrease in demand occurs and consequently a decrease in sales and profits.

The PLC can significantly vary across different countries. We can find differences in:

- the shape of the PLC curve

- the product phase in the life cycle.

In relation to the shape of the PLC curve, there are three **differences in the diffusion process of innovation among various countries:**[5]

- the starting point

- the take-off point

- the rate at which acceptance occurs (depicted by the slope of the diffusion pattern after take-off).

As indicated in Figure 10.2, the **time frame from when a new product is introduced** into the market (time 0), to the **time of adoption** of a specific product by "innovating" consumers (**starting point**), can vary in length depending on the degree of receptiveness in the target foreign market.

Also, the time frame between the starting point and the **take-off point**, or rather between when the new product is adopted and then grows steadily in the market, can vary depending on the number of "innovators" in the segment or country analyzed.

Finally, the **increase of the adoption rate after the take-off point** is mainly due to the interpersonal communication development (word-of-mouth) among the members of the foreign target segment, which can vary from country to country.

Even the **life cycle phase that the product goes through can be different** in a given country. As pointed out in Figure 10.3, a specific product, at a certain time t_x, can be in the decline stage in the domestic market, in the maturity stage for country X and in the introduction stage for country Y. Managing the PLC across different countries can guarantee to the company the maintenance of a constant level of profits.

For example, in Western countries, disposable diapers are a commodity (maturity phase). However, it's not the same in the Chinese nursery market, where the culture is different: disposable diapers were only introduced a few years ago and even if recently there has been rapid growth, today many mothers still use open pants called kaidangku (Figure 10.4).

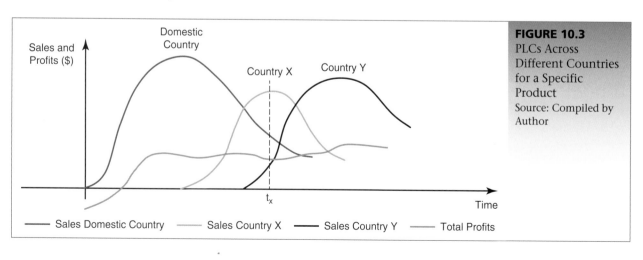

FIGURE 10.3
PLCs Across Different Countries for a Specific Product
Source: Compiled by Author

FIGURE 10.4
A Chinese Child
with Kaidangku
Source: © Author

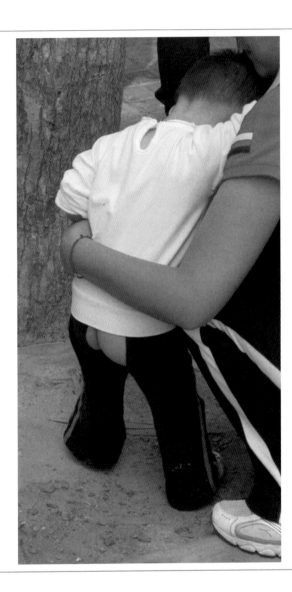

The PLC model can be defined from different perspectives. For example it can be related to the whole **product category** or to a specific **brand**. In all cases, in order to identify the phase occupied by a product/brand in the PLC, it is necessary to analyze the market demand. The existence of **wide disparities in the demand for a product or brand from one market to the next** can be a good indication of the possible potential for that product in the low-saturation-level market. Ready meals (a product category) and Nivea (a brand) are two representative examples. Ready meals is a product category that was first introduced in the US market and only later, as a result of life-style changes (working women, singles, fast food, no time to cook), to European countries and to new emerging economies. Today Europe is in the maturity phase while other countries are growing. For example in 2013 in Russia ready meals increased by 3 percent in volume and 11 percent in value: a higher income, the development of modern retailing, and new life-styles with more

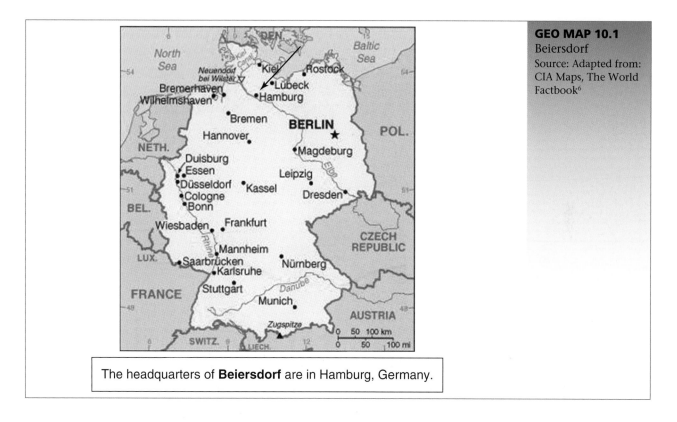

GEO MAP 10.1
Beiersdorf
Source: Adapted from:
CIA Maps, The World
Factbook[6]

The headquarters of **Beiersdorf** are in Hamburg, Germany.

and more Russians spending less time on cooking and increasingly opting for ready meals, are the main drivers that are influencing the growth of the product category, which is expected to perform positively in the following years with a constant 2 percent average growth rate in constant value terms till 2018.[7]

In the case of the Nivea brand, the biggest skin and beauty care brand worldwide, the German company Beiersdorf is focusing, in addition to Western Europe, on regions with above-average growth rates and low per capita sales, such as Asia, South America, and Eastern Europe, where Beiersdorf's substantial growth potential emerges. Target countries where sales are still limited can represent a good market opportunity. For example, in 2013 Beiersdorf (Geo Map 10.1) recorded growth of more than 19 percent in the Africa/Asia/Australia segment. Nivea provides an example of a successful brand that occupies the mature phase of the PLC in Western Europe and the introductory or growth phase in emerging markets.[8]

The potential **difference in the product or brand life cycle** obviously **requires differentiation in the company's marketing choices**. In the case of illy Coffee (Figure 10.5), a household brand for premium Italian coffee marketed in more than 140 markets worldwide, the concept of illy espresso coffee is presented differently in each country depending on the life cycle phase the product is going through. Where the espresso and the illy brand are in the introduction phase, it is necessary to explain and provide information on the product characteristics. In countries like Italy, where espresso is in its maturity phase, the marketing message is not about the product but about life-style and emotions.

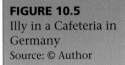
FIGURE 10.5
Illy in a Cafeteria in
Germany
Source: © Author

It is important, however, when defining marketing strategies, to always evaluate the **product knowledge level** that consumers have achieved. We could be talking about a product unknown to the majority of consumers, known only generically, or known to the majority of consumers but with limited commercialization, for example because of insufficient disposable income in the country. Various choices can be made in the growth phase and, subsequently, in the maturity phase. A global company, for example, begins by offering a differentiated product assorment addressing the various demand segments that it identifies on a transnation level, with potential adaptations to the specific characteristics of each country. Th company's offer, in fact, may be made more attractive through the adaptation some of the product's characteristics to consumers' needs. In the decline stag companies usually choose a standardized product strategy, because they cann sustain high costs in a contracting market.

THE STANDARDIZATION VERSUS ADAPTATION DILEMMA

The choice between standardization and adaptation of marketing strategies and policies that define the positioning of the company's product or brand in international markets has always played a central role in the business literature. This choice, in fact, is often held responsible for the effectiveness and the efficiency of marketing campaigns or for the company's chances to successfully enter a market. A simplified approach to the standardization and adaptation dilemma points out five alternatives:

1. The **domestic product is exported abroad without modifications**: in this case a company standardizes the domestic product to enter foreign markets.

2. The **domestic product is exported abroad with some adaptations**.

3. A **global standardized product is created to target a transnational segment** across different foreign markets.

4. A **global standardized product is created to target a transnational segment** across different foreign markets, **but some adaptations are required** to meet local country differences.

5. A **new product** is created to target a foreign market. For example, Piccolini Barilla, a small-sized pasta, was first introduced in France, and it was created by Barilla for some foreign markets that did not appreciate the big format typical of the Italian market.

The debate in favor of or against standardization in international markets began in the 1960s. The first studies dealt with communication strategy.[9] Then, with Buzzel (1968)[10] and Bartels (1968),[11] attention shifted to marketing strategy analysis. Multiple factors influence the standardization–adaptation decision. The phenomenon is in fact very complex, because it has to simultaneously take into consideration the relationship among **market, industry, and company factors**.[12] It affects not only product decisions, but also price decisions (Chapter 11), distribution (Chapter 12) and advertising decisions (Chapter 13). The logic behind a standardization strategy assumes the existence of a global or regional market and calls for the development of similar marketing activities across national boundaries. The adaptation school, on the other hand, suggests opting for a differentiated strategy that allows for adapting to the specific material, social, cultural, and symbolic characteristics of foreign markets and to competition. Therefore relevant cost savings using a standardization strategy often outweigh the disadvantages of not being perfectly adapted to the consumers' requirements. On the other hand, with adaptation a company can increase customer satisfaction by tailoring products to the specific needs to consumers.

Standardization and adaptation are two extremes of a continuum, inside of which it is possible to identify an infinite number of alternative options. In the case of adaptation, costs of manufacturing are high and decrease when a company moves toward full standardization. However, in the case of standardization, customer satisfaction risks being low because the company doesn't meet local needs, therefore resulting in lost sales in the foreign market. With adaptation, consumer satisfaction is high and the company can increase sales in the foreign market: the aim of the company is to reach a perfect equilibrium between the two alternatives, gaining both the benefits of adaptation and standardization.

To evaluate the ideal combination of standardization and adaptation, we have to take into consideration when standardization is favorable and when adaptation is favorable.

Environmental Factors

Differences in the environment are perhaps the first factors that have to be taken into consideration when evaluating standardization or adaptation. As already pointed out in Chapter 2, elements such as the physical characteristics of the country, socioeconomic and demographic differences, religion, political aspects, language, and culture can significantly influence marketing decisions. An example is represented by Nutella, the chocolate cream manufactured by the Italian company Ferrero, famous everywhere for its taste and appreciated in many countries all over the world. In the case of Nutella, adaptation is required. In some countries the hot climate has imposed upon the production of a cream chocolate that has to be resistant to high temperatures to avoid the alteration of ingredients. Furthermore, due to different food cultures, the taste of Nutella is not the same everywhere. For example, in Italy it's richer with nuts, while in Germany the taste of chocolate is dominant.

Cost Reduction

A standardized international marketing program strategy favors cost reduction thanks to the accomplishment of economies of scale in R&D, production, marketing, and managerial and organizational processes.[13] Cost reduction can be determined not only by economies of scale but also by the product's concept engineering, and the technical and productive efficiency obtainable from the cumulative experiences deriving from mass production. Moreover, the company can exert greater contractual power both with suppliers (lower supply costs) and with customers (lower distribution costs). Lower production costs allow the company to achieve greater competitiveness in price determination than the competition in order to obtain higher margins that can be reinvested to effectively promote the product in foreign countries.

Global Image

A homogeneous strategy also contributes to the strengthening of the corporate image and the brand on an international level. The company communicates one message that is recognizable all over the world. Such a message not only takes its form from the product's tangible characteristics or its advertising, pricing, and distribution policies, but also in the post-sale assistance and consumer warranty policies. The creation of a global image is particularly favorable when the company's offer fits with the emergence of global customer segments. Brands like Nike, Coca-Cola, McDonald's, Lego, and Sony are just a few examples of products and brands targeted to transnational segments characterized by a high level of homogeneity.

Easier Planning and Control

The development of a standardized approach can also benefit the company with greater control over the development and implementation of strategies and marketing mix policies. A company that commercializes products with a standardized positioning and marketing strategy can implement control procedures and performance comparisons between different countries more easily than companies that adapt their positioning in international markets.

Diffusion of Innovation

A successful exploitation of new innovative products cannot rely only on domestic markets and companies increasingly look to foreign markets to realize their full potential.[14] If standardization is applied, development costs can quickly be reabsorbed thanks to the minimal adaptations of the product's commercialization and promotion on an international level. The possibility to obtain a quick return on investment with standardization, therefore, favors the spread of product innovations. In fact, delays in the international new product rollout due to the necessity of adaptation can have a negative impact on new product performance. Nevertheless in recent years, through design innovation, MNCs can accommodate the heterogeneity of different national markets without a high impact on costs, by building functional versatility into products, thanks to modularity and programmability in product design.[15]

Motivation of Local Managers

Adaptation can be advantageous for the company as an innovation stimulus in the different countries of operations. Managers of local subsidiaries are in fact less motivated if they only have to implement guidelines provided by the headquarters. When the role of managers of local branches is limited to product commercialization, they end up gradually losing motivation to contribute to improving products because creativity and innovation are discouraged. On the other hand, opting for adaptation can create stronger staff commitment, thus favoring a continuous search for the solutions that can strengthen the competitive potential of the company abroad.[16]

Benefits for Local Consumers

Various researchers have underlined how nowadays customized rather than standardized marketing activities have a positive impact on the company's performance. The consistent negative impact of product standardization on international performance strongly indicates that adapted products are more attractive to consumers and more competitive in foreign markets.[17] As a matter of fact, consumers often tend to refuse to purchase standardized products, preferring instead a product that values their traditions, uses, and customs. The logic of adaptation to demand is an essential requirement to increase the company's competitive potential in those countries where customers have differentiated needs, values, tastes and culture in general.[18]

The example of Gibson Guitar Corporation in the Japanese market highlights this critical variable that positively influences the adaptation choice for the product. The company, headquartered in Nashville, TN, is known worldwide for producing classic models in every major style of fretted instrument, including acoustic and electric guitars, mandolins, and banjos. Gibson makes a range of guitar models that are available only in Japan—its largest international market. The Tak Matsumoto limited edition Les Paul model, for example, is sold exclusively there and is offered in special shades such as canary yellow and sunburst. The company's Japanese image conveys coolness and authenticity and inspires reverence that is not matched in its domestic market. Its fans are predominantly Japan's baby boomers, who witnessed music legends such as Jimi Hendrix, play Gibson guitars in the 1970s and are now able to indulge their nostalgia by collecting this quintessentially American and quintessentially rock 'n' roll instrument. The acquisition in 2013 of the 52.6 percent of the Japanese company TEAC, which has now become a member of the Gibson family, points out the increasing attention of Gibson in the Japanese market. TEAC manufactures and distributes high-grade audio video electronics, consumer electronics, computer data recording and storage devices, computer peripherals, professional recording equipment, and disc publishing products. Its acquisition will support Gibson's Pro Audio Division and will improve Gibson's global commercialization competences.[19]

Legal Issues and Differences in Technical Standards

A standardized product strategy cannot be adopted when individual country requirements are different in terms of technology, standards, and approval procedures. In all these cases managers have to make a significant effort to customize the product in order to satisfy local differences.[20] In other cases, like in the telecommunications, office equipment, or consumer electronics sectors, customers do not buy a product but rather select a system. From the company's point of view, this implies an offer that consists of locally differentiated, more flexible systems. The video game industry is a good example. The three different video game systems that dominate the world today—Microsoft's Xbox, Sony's Playstation, and Nintendo's Wii—require different standards for video games that can be played on their consoles. In addition, different United States, European, and Japanese video signal standards also prevent a game that plays on one brand's console in the United States from playing in the same brand's video game system sold in Germany, for example. As a consequence, video game companies are forced to design products that comply with every single type of technical requirement in each regional market.

Costs of Distribution, Coordination, and Customer Services

Standardization obtained with centralized production, operating on a global scale, involves production cost reduction. On the other hand, there are consistent increases in shipping costs, global demand coordination costs, and customer service costs that can be overcome with adaptation and also offer localization advantages.[21]

Global Versus Local Competition

If the company is confronted with global competition, the rules of the game tend to be similar on an international level, favoring standardization. On the other hand, if the company has to compete with very strong localized brands defending their competitive (and often only) territory, adaptation is necessary in order to meet local consumer needs. This is accomplished by working closely with local intermediaries and offering personalized services. In some countries the only way to compete with local brands is to buy a local competitor's brand.

Global Versus Local Customers

When the company's target is based on global clientele that often have purchasing functions centralized on a global basis, standardization is necessary because consumers in every country demand products and services of similar quality. This is valid not only in relation to the product but, for example, also for pricing policies. In fact, if there are significant price differences, a global retailer can easily buy in the country where the prices are cheaper and sell in the others.

The identification of the best solution comes from careful examination of all the costs and benefits for the company. The company must focus on the goals it wants to pursue in foreign markets and on the material and non-material resources it wants to assign to the internationalization process. Nowadays we can see from experience that the optimal solution in terms of performance comes from a careful equilibrium between standardization and adaptation.[22] This requires the centralization of some activities and decentralization of others, and the coordination of marketing activities on an international level in order to:

- Replicate the solutions that have been successful in some countries by sharing information and allowing for adaptation of marketing strategies and policies if necessary.

- Integrate marketing activities developed by managers of different countries (or clusters of countries) through a company's communication network that creates transnational synergies that maximize the benefits of both standardization and adaptation models.

The impact of an adaptation strategy on organizational decisions is not insignificant. When choosing adaptation a company usually creates local units in each national market that completes all the steps in the supply chain, whereas when choosing standardization, a company tries to group the development and production processes.

In order to create the sought-after balance between standardization and adaptation, product decisions can only be made after the target market has been analyzed. Some fundamental questions can be raised at this point. What is the use for the product? What are the expected benefits? What are the style, design, packaging, and service preferences? Which are the best product and branding strategies and policies? What is the role of management orientation?

PRODUCT USE

Differences in product use can influence the company's marketing strategies and policies because they are closely tied to consumer behavior. To speak of product use in a foreign market means to consider:

- the use function

- the use situation

- the use conditions

- the product utilization level.

Let's consider, for example, the product's use function. Rich Chinese families often have two kitchens in their houses; one "to be shown" to friends and guests and one "for cooking." For the first one they buy luxury kitchen cabinet brands with European design, while for the second one they buy locally made and less expensive furniture. Whirlpool managers discovered that it is not wise to sell top-load washing machines in India because many families used them for stirring curd and making buttermilk: compared to electronic stirrers, they are cheaper and more suitable.[23] Vicks VapoRub is another example: this cough and cold over-the-counter medicine is still used to fight mosquitoes in some countries.[24]

The analysis of the use situation is also particularly critical because it can frequently vary according to the foreign market considered. Use situation means considering all the factors that identify a "time" (for example, for breakfast, for lunch, or for dinner) and/or a "place" (at a party, at school, or at home) that have a proven and systematic effect on the consumer's behavior. A different use situation can modify, for example, the importance consumers give to the product's characteristics, the price perception, and the number and the type of brands taken into consideration in the purchase process. For example, it is frequent for Italians to drink espresso standing up at the cafeteria, they pay about one euro, they stay five minutes, and then they leave. In other countries, consumers prefer to sit at a table and order espresso, staying longer in the cafeteria, and accepting to pay more for the service.

Also, product use conditions often have different characteristics depending on the country. When Coca-Cola tried to introduce its two-liter bottle in Spain, it was not successful due to local storage conditions: in fact, few Spaniards have refrigerator doors large enough to accommodate the large two-liter bottle.[25] Use conditions can even influence the product's technology, imposing modifications on a technical–functional level. Let's take the example of mobile phones: more than half of Africa's 1.1 billion people own a mobile phone, but the access to electricity is still limited, particularly in non-urban areas, and key features are long battery life and energy-frugal applications.[26]

The utilization level is another variable that needs to be taken into consideration in order to define the characteristics of the product and of the marketing mix. The use of a laundry dryer in Mediterranean countries, for example, is very limited in comparison with countries like the United States. This is due to various reasons other than climate. On one hand, there is the idea that it's healthier to let the laundry dry naturally outside; on the other hand, there is fear that laundry can get ruined in the dryer because of high temperatures and fast spinning (American cotton clothes are also thicker and stronger then European ones). The dryer is therefore a niche product in Europe; there are few models available at a higher price in comparison to the American standard.

PRODUCT PERCEPTION AND EXPECTED BENEFITS

The culture and environment of the consumer can greatly influence consumer needs, and consequently product perception and expectations. If the expected benefits change, the importance given by consumers to the product's different attributes will also vary, thus influencing the company's choices in terms of product decisions.[27]

Much research has studied product perception, its expected benefits, and the evaluation system of product characteristics on an international scale. Industrial products typically satisfy specific needs that most of the time are quite homogeneous among countries, hence standardization is prevalent. Vice versa consumer goods point out that in many cases adaptation is required. In the United States, Heineken is continuously adapting product characteristics to the market's expected benefits (Geo Map 10.2). The Dutch brewer knew that it had to get the taste of its new Premium Light lager just right in order to make inroads with American consumers, who prefer pale and less flavorful beer than Heineken's traditional offerings. After 20 trial versions and a successful marketing campaign that highlighted the new, attractive bottle design of Heineken Premium Light, the company launched the new product. But after an initial success, with US consumers becoming tired of the taste of light brands considered too watery and not providing a rewarding enough experience, Heineken has recently changed the flavor profile of Heineken Premium Light by adding Cascade hops, one of the most popular craft beer styles, with hops found in brews such as Sierra Nevada Pale Ale and Anchor Steam Liberty Ale. A humorous campaign with Neil Patrick Harris that includes television, online commercials, and a special website (besttastinglight.com), has been developed to promote the adaptation of the product.

In some instances, the company must meet the consumer's specific requirements and must develop products with highly innovative characteristics that are specifically targeted for the consumers of that country. For example, German skin and beauty care company, Beiersdorf, is continuing to expand the distribution in the Asiatic market of its Nivea whitening products fitting the needs of people in Asia that favor a pale, white complexion.[28] While in the United States and Europe people buy sunless self-tanners to give a healthy image to their skin, for both Asiatic men and women, sunburned skin is associated with people of a lower class working outdoor under the sun.

On top of the expected benefits, the importance given to product characteristics can also vary, depending on the country. Consumers attribute different importance to product characteristics: for example, when buying appliances, in some countries design is very important, in others it plays a minor role. More often, differences in the evaluation of product characteristics depend on the way in which the product is perceived across cultures. Such is the case with passengers' transport modes. In the US to reach a distant place consumers consider the airplane or the car. In Europe consumers mainly consider airline services or trains, with a preference for the latter. For example, in France, airline companies compete with TGV, high-speed trains with all the comforts and, differently from the airplanes, taking the passengers downtown without the need to reach the airport early in advance. As a consequence, the buying process of US versus European consumers is different, and airline companies have to face a different competitive

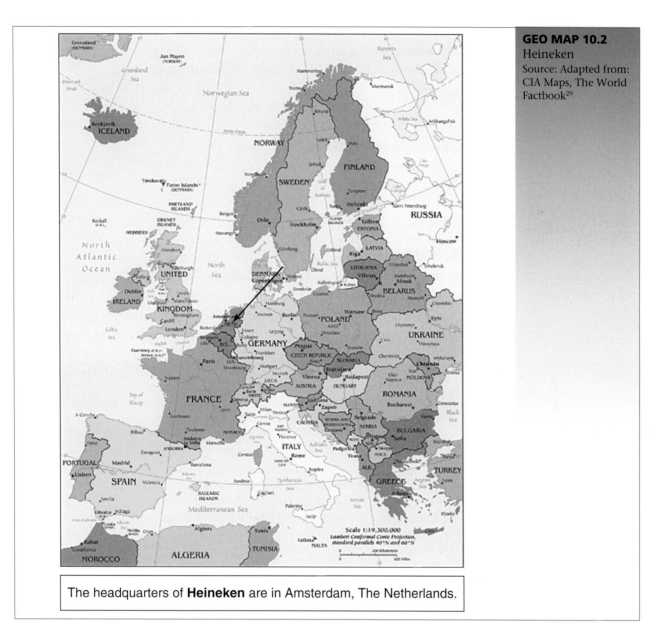

GEO MAP 10.2
Heineken
Source: Adapted from:
CIA Maps, The World
Factbook[29]

The headquarters of **Heineken** are in Amsterdam, The Netherlands.

environment adapting not only the characteristics of the product but also the marketing mix.

PRODUCT ATTRIBUTES

One of the main issues defining the international product offer is to determine which product attributes can be standardized and which have to be adapted. Physical characteristics, color, shape, style, design, packaging, country of origin, branding, and service attributes are all elements of the total product offer which need to be examined accurately before entering a foreign market. Some of these elements—for example, color or style—can be a physical characteristic and convey a symbolic meaning at the same time.

Product attributes that have to be analyzed include the following:

- regulations and standards

- physical characteristics

- style and design, color, and product quality

- packaging

- branding

- country of origin

- service attributes.

Especially when considering emerging markets such as Africa, China, or India, the challenge for a company is to take into consideration not only differences between countries but also diversities within a specific country itself. As shown in Box 10.1, Africa, as a country, is so heterogeneous in culture and values that

---

Box 10.1   Country-in-Focus: Africa

When International Marketing Struggles with In-Nation Diversity: The Case of Africa and Its Passion for Sports

According to the World Bank 2015 Doing Business report, ten of the world's 15 worst places to do business are in Africa. Despite the difficulties plaguing the region, many global companies find it interesting to penetrate these countries, adapting their marketing decisions to local needs. But what are "local needs"? The answer is not simple when one realizes that Africa is not a single place, and that not even a single African country is homogeneous for marketers. Take the example of Nigeria. The religion, which can influence consumer behavior, is Christianity in the south and Islam in the north, while Traditional religion is transversal in the two areas. The result is that, for example, beer and other alcoholic beverages are sold everywhere in the south, but they are forbidden in the north. Another element of in-country diversity is language, which represents a vehicle of culture: with 374 ethnic languages and groups in Nigeria alone, it becomes very complex to promote a product using the same brand, packaging, advertising, etc. In both cases, product and promotion adaptation is required, affecting marketing performance of global and multinational companies.

   But there is another face of Africa, where fragmentation is overcome by their sport culture. As pointed out by Hassen Adams, executive chairman of Grand Parade Investments and its subsidiary, Burger King, talking about their recent investment in the South African Football Association (SAFA), "We believe that success on the football field can be the catalyst for uniting the whole of Africa and we look forward to this being the start of a campaign to bring World Cup success to Africa and more particularly South Africa." In a country of cultural diversity, football is a common culture, and brands who want to speak to the African consumers as a whole can use the common language of the passion for sports.

Sources: World Bank Group. (2015), 'Doing business 2015. Going beyond efficiency', http://www.doingbusiness.org/~/media/GIAWB/ Doing%20Business/Documents/Annual-Reports/English/DB15-Full-Report.pdf [Accessed: April 2, 2015]; South African Football Association. (2014), 'Investing in the future of SA football', March 20, 2014, http://www.safa.net/index.php?page=articles&id=2128 [Accessed: March 30, 2014]; Ekerete, P. P. (2001), 'The effect of culture on marketing strategies of multinational firms: A survey of selected multi-national corporations in Nigeria', *African Study Monographs*, 22(2), pp. 93–101; Kamcilla Pilly And Sapa. (2010), 'Show Dem Bafana Show Dem!', *Iol Sport*, http://www.iol.co.za/sport/show-dem-bafana-show-dem-1.2310#.Vhu77vntmko [Accessed: October 11, 2015]; Manqele, S'bu. (2009), 'Tapping Africa's passion for sports', *Communication World*, March/April, 26(2), p. 36.

identifying commonalities in African culture becomes very complex for a marketer willing to introduce a product to the country: the coexistence of many different subcultures significantly influences the adaptation of marketing activities.

REGULATIONS AND STANDARDS

We have already pointed out how a standardized product strategy cannot be adopted when individual country regulations are different in terms of technology, standards, and approval procedures. The **process of standards harmonization**, carried out, for example, with the ISO standard (International Organization for Standardization) or on a European level with the objective of supporting the creation of a global market,[30] will reduce the need to modify the product characteristics depending on the country, thus favoring economies of scale in the production process.

Country laws and standards for various products have always strongly influenced company policies, sometimes imposing radical modifications on the product and its marketing in general. For example, in most cases the environmental laws introduced to support environment protection, are different depending on the country of entry. Furthermore, the increasing number of local standards is often the result of the reduction of tariff barriers. In fact, many countries have introduced new regulations and standards to create an entry barrier. Companies that want to enter a market in a given country must fulfill specific requirements concerning quality, safety, size, and ingredients composition. In some cases such requirements can act as a barrier when they are used in order to prevent or hinder international trade and protect the local economy.[31] European Union countries are interested in international harmonization of product standards to encourage internal trade through the elimination of technical barriers, increase market access, and promote and disseminate technologies.

Product changes that need to be made in order to adapt to another country's laws can in fact strongly affect product cost, therefore making it not very competitive when exported abroad. There are still significant variations in different business sectors on an international level. For example, different countries are still using different types of broadcast TV systems. The NTSC system was originally developed in the United States by the National Television Standards Committee and is generally used in the majority of 60 Hz based countries. A modified version of NTSC is known as PAL (Phase Alternate Lines) and is mainly used by countries based on 50 Hz systems. Moreover, the French designed a system of their own, SECAM (Sequential Couleur Avec Memoire), primarily to protect their domestic manufacturing companies.

The definition of different standards is often also linked to competitive targets. An example can be the software joint venture, SoftAtHome, between three leading French telecommunications technology groups—France Télécom, Sagem Communications, and Thomson—created with the goal of competing against Microsoft. SoftAtHome is an operator-backed software company delivering the best of connectivity, Pay TV and digital services to the home, improving communications between Internet set-top boxes, televisions, phones, and other electronic devices. Its ambition is to create the industry standard and license the software to telecom operators around the world. The company is taking aim at the Microsoft standard, which has made a big push in Internet Protocol-based television over the past years and licensed its Mediaroom software to operators like AT&T, BT Group, Deutsche Telekom, and Bell Canada. Nowadays SoftAtHome solutions, also thanks to the presence of sales team not only in France but also in Belgium and UAE, are already deployed on over 20 million Home Gateways and Set Top Boxes throughout the world in multiple broadband and broadcast deployments.[32]

PHYSICAL CHARACTERISTICS

Mandatory adaptations are often less frequent in comparison to physical adaptations that are required to meet differences in consumer behavior and national marketing environments.[33] As already pointed out previously, the differences in local product usage, consumer preferences, needs, and so forth impose adaptations among countries. For example, the food market is far from standardized. Take the case of Asian countries. Japan is one of the most innovative countries when it comes to soft drinks. Ito En (Geo Map 10.3), for example, is a Japanese multinational beverage company producing, among others, a new and successful vegetable-based drink with no added sugar or salt that contains 25 different vegetables: carrots, celery, moroheiya, broccoli, kale, tomatoes, sweet potato, red bell peppers, green beans, kidney beans, pumpkin, lettuce, green bell peppers, asparagus, Chinese cabbage, sweet potato stalk and leaf, green peas, mustard spinach, angelica, parsley, cress, cabbage, radish, spinach, and Japanese wild chervil. *Ichinichibun no Yasai* (a day's worth of vegetables) contains the nutritional equivalent of 350 grams of vegetables, the daily amount recommended by the Ministry of Health, Labour and Welfare of Japan.[34] How could it be successful in regions such as the United States and Europe, where the high vegetable content is not as appreciated as in other countries?

Similarly, in the United Arab Emirates dairy market, there is an increasing interest in camel's milk products (cheese, flavored drinks, cappuccinos, and ice cream). Camel milk is said to have an improved nutritional profile over cow's milk: lower in fat than cow's, four times higher in vitamin C, ten times as much iron as cow's milk, tolerated by lactose-intolerant, high in lactoferrin, i.e. with anti-inflammatory and antibacterial properties, and it contains insulin that can help regulate some types of diabetes. The UAE has recently been authorized by the European Union to export camel milk to the region, but these characteristics will probably not be enough in order to market this product successfully in other countries.[35]

Adaptation of physical characteristics is not an exception even with products that are already considered global and that are commercialized all over the world. Nestlé, for example, markets more than 200 blends of NESCAFÉ to cater to the differences in tastes in different markets. For example, in the Philippines, NESCAFÉ

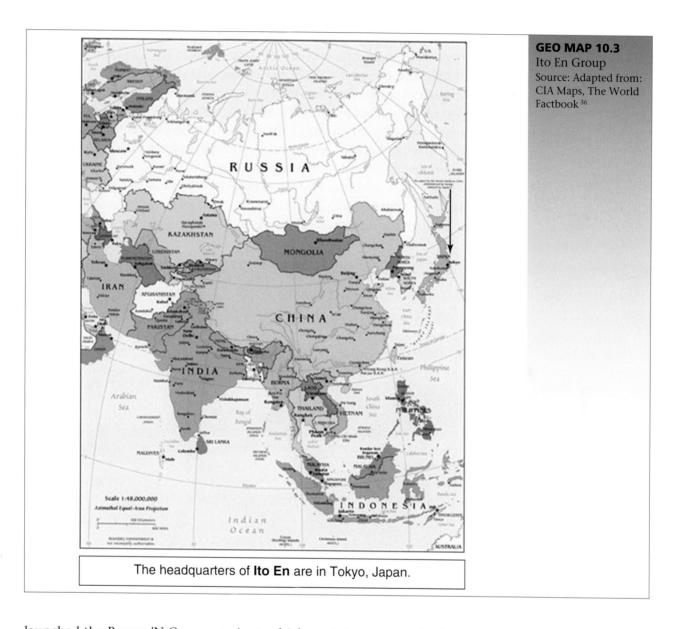

GEO MAP 10.3
Ito En Group
Source: Adapted from:
CIA Maps, The World
Factbook[36]

The headquarters of **Ito En** are in Tokyo, Japan.

launched the Brown 'N Creamy variant, which contains muscovado (brown sugar) to meet the local country tastes. Vietnamese love a strong and bold taste, which is offered by NESCAFÉ CAFÉ VIET. In Mexico, the blend Café de Olla is a unique coffee mix with cinnamon and piloncillo (panela), while South Africans prefer the aroma of NESCAFÉ RICOFFY which is made from coffee beans, chicory, and glucose.[37]

STYLE AND DESIGN, COLOR AND PRODUCT QUALITY

In international marketing, product design, style, color, dimensions, and quality variations occur frequently. Design often holds an essential role because it allows the creation of a link between technological and market innovation. Managers are required not only to be creative, but also to take advantage of creativity in order to meet market demands. Many products are purchased because of their unique design and style; think about Danish furniture or Italian fashion, for example.

However, design preferences can vary considerably from country to country. Obviously, every product is a case in itself when planning its design, as illustrated in the case of Nokia (Box 10.2). The challenge for the company is how to successfully adapt a product to local needs and technology requirements while at the same time minimizing developmental costs.

Design differences are often necessary in order to reduce the product's final price so that it becomes affordable to the final consumer. As already pointed out in Chapter 1, in emerging markets there can be changes from the traditional 4Ps

---

Box 10.2   Technology-in-Focus: Nokia's Design Research Is Facing a Technology Challenge in Emerging Markets

Nokia is continually expanding its services in emerging markets such as China, Africa, Brazil, India, and Indonesia. It is well known that in emerging markets companies cannot just offer "updated" or cheaper versions of current products or services; vice versa there is a need to create new products, services, and business models based on local customer needs. For example, Africa's cellular and smartphone market is one of the fastest growing in the world because mobile technology can be very useful to the local population. In rural Togo, for example, information on agricultural market prices in the capital are checked in real time by local farmers. Nokia is one of the most active companies in emerging markets. For example, Nokia Life Tools is an SMS based information service which allows consumers access to agricultural information, education, and entertainment services without the use of GPRS (General Packet Radio Service) or Internet connectivity.

In launching new products to emerging markets, one of the key issues is design, which has to take into consideration local technology while satisfying specific needs and tastes. Nokia operates through a group of psychologists, industrial designers, materials experts, and anthropologists, analyzing local needs that can inspire innovative products for which technology and design are the key issues, and they are strongly connected. For example, in rural areas, mobile phones are shared among villages or families. For these areas, Nokia designs models which have shared use as the top priority. Since the mobile phone is used by many people, they have physical features that guarantee higher robustness, such as a seamless keypad to protect them from dust and special grip areas to make them easier to hold in hot conditions. They have a shared address book so that each member of a family or village can save their own contacts and numbers separately from others. They also provide a call tracker that allows people to preset a time or cost limit on each call, which allows for lending the mobile phone while maintaining the control of the cost of the telephone call. Nokia has recently introduced three new devices using the Android operating platform: the Nokia X, Nokia X+ and Nokia XL smartphones. These innovative products aim to bring Internet and cloud services combined with Nokia's industrial design, high quality, and an attractive user interface. And the price, with a range between $125–$150, has been set to capture the fast-growing affordable smartphone market in emerging countries.

Sources: Barton A. (2014), 'Nokia X affordable smartphones target emerging markets', *Developing Telecoms Ltd.*, March 17, 2014, http://www.developingtelecoms.com/tech/apps-services-devices/166-devices/5203-nokia-x-affordable-smartphones-target-emerging-markets.html [Accessed: February 2, 2015]; Torkkeli, M. (2009), 'The future of innovation', http://thefutureofinnovation.org/contributions/view/580/the_future_of_innovation_in_emerging_marketsm [Accessed: February 4, 2015]; Lakshman, N. (2007), 'Nokia's global design sense', *Business Week*, August 10, 2007, www.businessweek.com/innovate/content/aug2007/id20070810_686743.htm; (2007), 'Nokia's design research for everyone', *Business Week*, March 14, 2007, www.businessweek.com/innovate/content/mar2007/id20070314_689707.htm [Accessed: February 4, 2015]; Africa Recovery. (2010), 'Africa takes on the digital divide', www.un.org/ecosocdev/geninfo/afrec/vol17no3/173tech.htm [Accessed: May 30, 2010]; 'Nokia in 2009', http://phx.corporate-ir.net/External.File?item=UGFyZW50SUQ9NDE1NDZ 8Q2hpbGRJRD0tMXxUeXBlPTM=&t=1 [Accessed: June 13, 2014].

to the 4As, where affordability is one of the 4As. In emerging markets Apple introduced a solid and rigid, yet plastic iPhone 5C, allowing the implementation of a high-low strategy on pricing which is likely to give Apple more volume. With this adaptation in product design, the iPhone price goes for 16GB priced at $99 with contract and 32GB at $199.[38]

Another very critical element is color, which may be interpreted differently by consumers in various countries. There are numerous examples of the symbolic content of colors: in the United States, Europe, Australia and New Zealand, red is considered to be aggressive, energetic, and represents danger, while in the Côte d'Ivoire, dark red is associated with death; the color white, that in many countries is perceived as pure, clean and simple, in some Far East countries is the symbol of mourning, as already pointed out in Chapter 3.[39]

Also quality is a dimension of the product which has to be carefully considered. The same product quality can be considered high in one country, medium, or low in another one. This has significant implications for international marketing strategy formulation, product and service development, distribution, pricing, and communications. The case of white goods sold by an Italian company in France is a good example. In Italy, the Italian brand was positioned in the middle-upper-level market. In France, because it was "made in Italy," it was perceived to be low quality. Therefore, Italian producers would have had to offer their product at a price from 10 to 30 percent lower than French competition; instead German-made household appliances that were perceived to be of high quality could be sold at a price at least 20 percent higher than French products. The development of a marketing plan consistent with product positioning that required a low price was the only possible strategy to succeed in the French market, but this approach could not easily be accepted by Italian managers.

Quality perception becomes even more critical for services, where it was found that national culture influences the evaluation of service quality.[40] Research carried out in the hospitality industry in the Czech Republic and Slovenia pointed out that in hotel quality perception and service experience, respondents from Czech Republic were found to generally rely more on tangible elements, followed by responsiveness. On the other side, the most influential elements in forming Slovenian quality judgment were responsiveness and reliability, followed by tangibles. Another research study carried out in the banking sector of three different countries—the United States, India, and the Philippines—underlined systematic differences between developed and developing countries based on service quality dimensions, pointing out how a common marketing strategy for these two kinds of countries may not be appropriate. For example, in developing countries, quality perception depends on core service aspects, such as competitive interest rates and extended banking hours. On the other hand, in developed countries, a bank should put more emphasis on augmented services, such as credit card services or Internet banking, that are more intangible. Also, service delivery expectations and evaluations are very different. In developing countries, customers tend to have higher tolerance levels for ineffective services and lower quality expectations. In developed countries, service defects may lead to loss of customer patronage. Technology level, "breakthrough" service, timely response, a pursuit of continuous improvement, and a proactive effort are crucial to be able to establish reliability and responsiveness. It is important to specify how the quality concept is strongly linked to perceived product characteristics. Therefore, marketing mix variables assume a meaningful role, and not only those tied to the product (for example, packaging, brand, or country-of origin): the company's price and distribution policies also play prominent roles.

PACKAGING

The role of packaging is of primary importance to product innovation. Packaging is central to both how products are used, how they communicate benefits to consumers, how they are able to create a sensory appeal.[41]

Packaging represents a form of protection, but at the same time it is a relevant and essential marketing and communication vehicle. It determines differentiation on the supermarket shelf. Furthermore, it is able to convey a product's ethical and sustainability position.

There are four elements to packaging analysis:

1. labeling

2. packaging style and design

3. packaging dimensions

4. functional characteristics.

Each of these elements must be carefully analyzed in order to evaluate not only whether the packaging is in line with the norms of the foreign country, but above all whether it conveys the meaning and the company's product values to the final consumer, and whether these are in line with the company's positioning choices. In spite of the advantages obtainable with standardized packaging (for example, lower production and distribution costs), companies rarely succeed in standardizing their products' packaging on an international level.

In general, labeling needs to be modified according to the country in which the product is sold; the language is different, and in the great majority of cases, laws and regulations impose specific informative and descriptive content. In some countries, the label must be bilingual. For example, in Canada, the product identity must be shown in English and French, which are the official languages of the country.[42] In Uruguay, the law requires that the manufacturer has at least 80 percent of cigarettes' packaging covered in photos of decaying teeth, premature babies, and medical warnings in general.[43] In the United States, the label for imported wine has to be adapted adding the name of the importer and the government warnings.

Packaging can play an important promotional role as well. It is important therefore to consider how the package looks. The wrong choice of color, style, design, or size runs the risk of creating a distorted consumer perception of the product. For example, research has pointed out how Chinese children generally prefer figurative shapes more than US children, and for this reason designers need to consider adaptation of package design across countries, also developing country-specific packaging.[44]

Often it is the law that regulates; for example, environmental laws in some countries can impose the use of reusable glass bottles or recyclable plastic bottles.[45] Other times it is the consumer that imposes significant modifications. The reasons can be connected to symbolic aspects characterizing the country's culture. In some East Asian countries, such as China, Japan, Korea, and Taiwan, some consumer products are sold in three-packs instead of the usual four-packs, because number four is considered to be unlucky. The reason is that the word for the number "four" (四 [sì]) sounds similar to the word for "death" (死亡 [sǐwáng]).[46]

Or different product usage in different cultures can influence its characteristics. When analyzing the options for a global market strategy development for The Hershey Company, the largest North American manufacturer of quality chocolate and sugar confectionery products, it has been pointed out that in countries like China, where chocolate is still primarily used for gift giving, Hershey's traditional brown and silver paper packaging could not be successful. The current perception of Hershey's chocolate is in fact that of a snack. By changing the use function, the appearance should be more luxurious, refined, or sophisticated. Obviously, in a market dominated by Nestlé, Ferrero and Dove, which represent 70 percent of the market share in value for imported chocolate, modifications of the package have to be proposed with an enlarged product portfolio including new products with taste tailored to Chinese consumers. It is the case of Hershey's three flagship products in China: Ice Breakers (refreshing candies), Deluxe Kisses, and Kisses Deluxe gift packages called "Hand-to-Mouth platforms."[47]

The education level and the country's economic development are also factors that need to be taken into consideration. In some countries where education is limited, packaging should help to inform the final client giving clear information about the product. Furthermore, the use of bottles and cans in standard size is preferred since in this way consumers can compare prices and they are not confused when evaluating a wide variety of products. Finally, if the income is low the product is sometimes sold without packaging or it is single packaged, in some cases also with a reduced size. Heineken in Africa and Middle East has introduced new packaging formats to broaden consumption occasions, adding smaller pack-sizes in order to make the brands more affordable and attractive to consumers.[48] Packaging is also influenced by transportation conditions and channel length. With a long channel, or with complex transportation conditions, packaging must guarantee a higher protection level and allow a much longer shelf life. These considerations are also valid for those countries where climatic characteristics influence the products' preservation techniques.

In all these cases, when packaging modifications incur higher costs, a company could decide to increase the product's final price. On the other hand, especially in countries where purchasing power is limited, it is more likely that the company will decide to leave its price policies unchanged, instead reducing production costs through the introduction of a much simpler product to the foreign market.

BRANDING

A brand identifies the manufacturer or seller of a product or service. It can be built through the development of a name, phrase, design, symbols, or a combination of these.[49] The role of branding in international marketing strategy is underlined by the vast literature on the subject and by the increasing awareness of the centrality of brands in the global context.[50] In general, branding is even more important when the emotional dimension prevails in the product positioning strategy.

Brand development managers have to make challenging decisions that become more critical and complex when facing global markets. The most important are the following:

- brand strategy

- brand name and logo selection.

Brand positioning (already introduced in Chapter 9) and the communication of the brand will be analyzed in Chapter 13.

Brand Strategy: Global or Local Brands?

Brands have acquired such an important position that they are considered an essential part of the company's intangible knowledge assets contributing added-value. In some cases, the brand value of a company is greater than its revenue. For example, based on Interbrand's brand ranking and companies' yearly reports,[51] the number one brand, Apple, in 2013 presented a brand value of $118.8 billion compared to $37.5 billion revenue. The brand value of Coca-Cola was $81.5 billion compared to revenue of $46.8 billion. While in the opposite direction, Toyota's brand value was $42.3 billion, and its revenue was $234.6 billion.

Those companies that have managed to obtain a strong brand value are more prone to exploit this advantage through global branding. This way, in fact, they manage to more easily defend their product position in the market offering the potential for higher profit margins, increasing customer loyalty, amplifying channel power and guarding against competitive attacks.[52] Furthermore, recent research has pointed out that consumers evaluated global (versus non-global) brands more positively, regardless of brand ownership (local versus foreign).[53] The main advantage of a global branding approach is the possibility to standardize other marketing activities, particularly communication, that are feasible because of the brand's uniqueness. However, the global branding strategy doesn't limit the possibility to "localize" the brand. For example, the global brand The North Face, sold by the technical advanced outdoor products manufacturer, part of the American VF Corporation, has recently introduced in China the "Asian fit" to better fit the size of Asians, and this adaptation will be written on the product label.[54]

On the other hand, we can identify other motivations that could induce a company to develop different local brands in the countries or geographic areas where it markets its product. In fact a local brand can be the only way to be able to fit local needs, especially in all those cases when a company has to compete against strong and dynamic local competitors. The choice of a local brand, moreover, introduces other advantages. In the first place, it eliminates the risk of acquiring negative connotations. Potential mistakes made in a country could in fact have repercussions in the other countries in which the enterprise operates with the same brand.

In addition, it can be difficult for a company to guarantee uniform product quality on an international level, especially if it is not centralized. In this case, local brands should be considered. Otherwise the risk is that consumers will be confused by the existence of products of different quality under the same brand.

Finally, a local brand becomes an international brand when it is exported in other countries. In conclusion, the utilization of multiple local brands promotes the development of customized marketing that creates a strong appeal in individual markets. On the other hand, adoption of a single global brand allows for a standardization strategy. In practice, market leadership is obtained through the development of a portfolio of products characterized by both global and local brands that allow the maximization of market share in every target segment. The case of the Belgium brewing company Anheuser-Busch InBev is a representative example (Table 10.1). In almost all countries worldwide, the company is present with global brands (brands launched to global markets since the time they were born), international brands (brands born in one country and then exported worldwide) and local brands.

As in every national context, there are different sponsors behind brands. Options that can be identified include the following:

- Manufacturer's own brand: it occurs when a brand is owned by a producer of a product or service. Dove, San Pellegrino, and Bulgari are some examples (Figure 10.6).

- Private brand: the brand owner is the retailer. H&M, Carrefour, Zara, Amazon. com, and Toys 'R' Us are all examples of retail brands. From the manufacturer's perspective, in many countries it is possible to export a product through modern distribution producing only for a local or global retailer.

- Co-branding or ingredient branding: the established brand names of two different companies are used on the same product. It becomes ingredient branding when one of the two brands is an ingredient or component of the final product. An example of co-branding is Martini Gold, the alcoholic drink developed by

TABLE 10.1 Anheuser-Busch InBev Product Portfolio: Global, International, and Local Brands in North America and Europe	Region		Market Position	Global Brands	International Brands	Local Brands
	North America	USA	1	Budweiser, Stella Artois	Beck's, Hoegaarden, Leffe	Bass, Brahma, Bud Light, Busch, Michelob, Natural light
		Canada	1	Budweiser, Corona, Stella Artois	Beck's, Hoegaarden, Leffe	Alexander Keith's, Bass, Bud Light, Kokanee, Labatt, Lucky, Lakeport, Oland
	Europe	Belgium	1	Budweiser, Stella Artois	Beck's, Hoegaarden, Leffe	Belle-Vue, Jupiler, Vieux Temps
		Germany	2		Beck's, Hoegaarden, Leffe	Diebels, Franziskaner, Haake-Beck, Hasseröder, Löwenbräu, Spaten, Gilde
		UK	1	Budweiser, Corona, Stella Artois	Beck's, Hoegaarden, Leffe	Bass, Boddingtons, Brahma, Whitbread, Mackeson
		Russia	2	Budweiser, Stella Artois	Beck's, Hoegaarden, Leffe	Bagbier, Brahma, Klinskoye, Löwenbräu, Sibirskaya Korona, T, Tolstiak

Source: Adapted from: http://www.abinbev.com/content/dam/universaltemplate/abinbev/pdf/media/press-kit/AB_InBev_AR_OurTopTenMarkets.pdf [Accessed: January 29, 2015]

Martini and Dolce & Gabbana. On the other side, the Dell computer with an "Intel core" is an example of ingredient branding, because the Intel processor is a component of the laptop.

- **Licensed brand**: it occurs when a company uses a brand name offered by the brand owner for an agreed fee or royalty. An example is the brand Benetton and Sisley. The production and distribution of the brands were licensed by the international fashion group Benetton, to the Allison Group, leading company in the production of optical frames and sunglasses.[55]

Brand Name and Logo Selection

The brand name and logo are an integral part of the company's product. Their relevance is significant because they are part of the communication strategy created for target clientele. Therefore they cannot be randomly chosen, as often happened in the past; instead, the choice has to be carefully evaluated in order to avoid mistakes, either symbolic or legal, that sometimes can be irreparable.[56]

FIGURE 10.6
Bulgari in
an Outdoor
Advertising:
An Example of
Manufacturer's
Brand
Source: © Author

For example, Volkswagen has pushed a global naming strategy for decades, and at times has come up with controversial names as a result. There was the Bora, which is also a strong wind that blows north to northeast across the Adriatic Sea. After complaints from dealers that the name Bora sounded like "boring," VW eventually renamed the car the Jetta (as in jet stream) in the United States.[57]

The main questions a company needs to answer when defining its brand and logo for selling abroad are:

- Can we use the same brand name in all our potential foreign markets?

- Can we standardize our logo on an international level?

There are various choices that can be made in reference to the brand name and logo.

- **Entering the market with the original brand name.** For imported products with a strong image, this strategy can be successful. Consider, for example, fashion labels. Luxury brands, such as Chanel, Louis Vuitton (Figure 10.7), Versace, Salvatore Ferragamo, Bulgari, and Dolce & Gabbana, are among

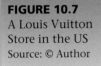

the numerous examples of luxury brands that enter foreign markets with the same brand name. Sometimes they are pronounced differently, however they are kept homogeneous because they represent status symbols on an international level.

- **Opting for a translated brand.** The Coca-Cola case represents a brand example that has been phonetically translated in various local languages. In different countries, Coca-Cola appears as Coca-Cola, Coke, and other translations, but it is always recognizable as the Coca-Cola brand. The translation, on the other hand, is not always necessary. In Italy, foreign brands like Nike, Levi's, Adidas, or Colgate, to name a few, are pronounced differently, but this doesn't have a negative impact on the product image; therefore changing the brand name would be completely useless. In other instances, when the brand name has a different meaning, translation can become necessary in order to relay a homogeneous meaning to the final consumer. Think about Danone low-calorie products: Vitalinea (Ireland), Vitasnella (Italy), Taillefine (France), Light & Fit (US), and Silhouette (Canada) are all translations of the brand name conveying the same meaning for the same product category of low-fat yogurt.

- **Using a completely different brand name.** This strategy is often used by multinationals that enter a foreign market by acquiring local brands. These companies, in order to standardize their brand image in the various countries, often link different brand names with a homogeneous logo that makes it possible to recognize the product on a global level. The Unilever ice cream brand has different names but they are all united by the famous heart-shaped logo (Table 10.2).

Brand Name	Country
Algida	Serbia, Greece, Italy, Poland, Slovak Republic, Turkey, Hungary, Czech Republic, Romania
Bresler	Chile, Bolivia
Eskimo	Croatia, Austria, Slovenia
Frigo	Spain
Frisko	Denmark
GB Glace	Finland, Sweden
Good Humor	United States
Holanda	Mexico
Kibon	Brazil
Kwality Wall's	India, China
Langnese	Germany
Pierrot Lusso	Switzerland
Miko	France
Ola	Belgium, South Africa, Netherlands
Olá	Portugal
Pinguino	Ecuador, Colombia
Selecta	Philippines
Streets	Australia, New Zealand
Tio Rico	Venezuela
Wall's	Ireland, UK

TABLE 10.2
Heartbrand Ice Creams by Unilever: A Unique Logo for Different Brand Names

Source: Author's Elaboration on Unilever Country Sites

COUNTRY OF ORIGIN AND PLACE BRANDING

Country of origin, or made-in effect, represents the extension of the perception of a specific country to its products or brands, because consumers react differently depending on the country where the product has been manufactured. In general, the attitude toward the made-in label is linked to the perception of the representative products for that country and to its historical, socioeconomic, political, and cultural characteristics. In other instances, instead, attitudes are linked more specifically to the general perception on the quality of the products manufactured in that country. Since the 1970s, numerous studies have investigated the effect that perception of the made-in country has on the consumer evaluation process.[58] It has been demonstrated that consumers use stereotypical country-related product associations as a summary cue to evaluate similar products from a country. However it is important to distinguish the influence on product evaluations of country-related effect from country-related product associations. Recent research pointed out that it is always important to improve positive country-related product associations first, before investing in building nation equity through nation image advertising.[59] This is what most countries have been trying and are still trying to do, both to overcome negative perceptions that can undermine their products, and therefore their economy, and meanwhile to reinforce the image of the nation of origin. They deliberately work on changing a negative image into a positive, or, at least a neutral one. In the same way, they invest on strengthening a positive country identity. This phenomena is called **place branding**: a nation is like a brand whose winning characteristics can be communicated with the aim to build a strong national image and reputation. **Similarly to a brand, the value of a nation can be measured evaluating its strengths and weaknesses.** An interesting method applied to measure brand value of a place is the Anholt-GfK Nation Brands Index[SM] (NBI), which is based on six dimensions:[60]

1. **Exports**: image of products and services from each country is taken into consideration, as well as the extent to which consumers proactively seek or avoid products from a specific country.

2. **Governance**: it reflects the public opinion about national government competency and fairness. In addition, nation's perceived commitment to global issues such as peace and security, justice, poverty, and the environment is measured.

3. **Culture and heritage**: this dimension of the index measures global perceptions of each nation's heritage and appreciation for its contemporary culture (i.e. music, art, literature, sport, etc.).

4. **People**: nation's branding is also based on the population's reputation for competence, openness and friendliness, and other qualities such as tolerance.

5. **Tourism**: is measured considering the level of interest in visiting a country and the attractions available (for example, natural attractions) or created (such as a museum) to attract tourists.

6. **Investment and immigration**: this important dimension reflects the capacity of a nation to attract people to live, work, or study in each country and the perception of a country's quality of life and business environment.

In the latest release of the Anholt-GfK Nation Brand Index[SM], the top ten countries were, in order of value, the United States, Germany, UK, France, Canada, Japan, Italy, Switzerland, Australia, and Sweden.[61] But other countries are trying to invest to strengthen their awareness and improve their brand equity. Famous marketing and communication campaigns such as "Incredible India," point out how emerging markets are also aware of the importance to create a nation brand.

An important aspect of country-of-origin analysis is the **ethnocentrism** phenomenon, originally defined as "the beliefs held by consumers about the appropriateness, indeed morality, of purchasing foreign made products."[62] If the foreign target consumers are highly ethnocentric, they will prefer local products and they can be reluctant to buy foreign products even if they have been exposed to the massive globalization phenomena. Ethnocentrism includes affective, cognitive, and behavioral components[63] and can create a barrier to the penetration of foreign products, because even if they are superior in quality, design, or other characteristics, local consumers do not buy them just because they are imported. An example of a brand that is trying to enhance the value of Made in China is Shanghai Tang.

Especially in recent years, animosity is also a sentiment that has to be considered. Consumer animosity is the attitude of antipathy related to previous or ongoing economic, political, and military events with a country, and it has a direct and negative effect on consumers' purchase behavior towards the products of that country.[64] An example of animosity is the antipathy of China against Japan.

The product nationality perception can be influenced, among others, by the following elements:

- the positioning of national products versus imported or global products;

- the product country of origin fit: for example, fashion evokes France or Italy, jeans the United States, espresso and pasta is linked with Italy;

- the country of manufacturing;

- the country of brand;

- the country of design;

- the country of origin of the company.

All of these dimensions of the made-in concept define the product image, and the company has to build the marketing mix around it. This is not an easy task. Very often, in a globalization context, we find hybrid products, which are products with more than one country of origin, as pointed out in the example in Figure 10.8 where a US company owns an Italian brand that is manufactured in China.

For example, the brand Gucci (Figure 10.9) has Italy as a country of manufacturing and country of brand, France as the country of origin of the company (Gucci is part of the Kering Group), and a product country of origin fit that, for fashion products, can be Italy or France.

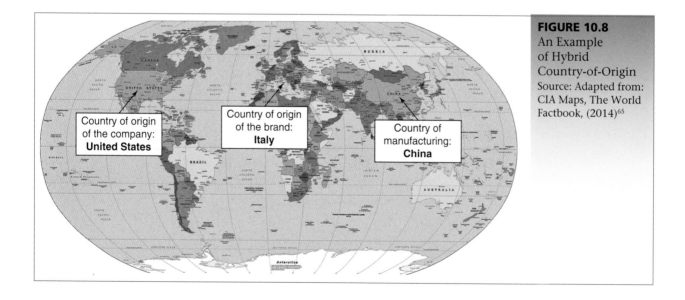

FIGURE 10.8
An Example of Hybrid Country-of-Origin
Source: Adapted from: CIA Maps, The World Factbook, (2014)[65]

FIGURE 10.9
Gucci in an
Outdoor
Advertising in
Rome
Source: © Author

In some cases, the company must be able to define the best marketing decisions that will allow compensating for a **negative made-in image**. In the majority of cases, products manufactured in a foreign country have perceived risk, especially if the company's image is not globally established. The ideal tools to have in order to be able to win over consumer reticence about a foreign product and to strengthen the brand image include detailed information about the product given by independent manufacturers or external labs tests, warranties, partnerships with prestigious distributors. The positioning needs to be able to underline these aspects about the product in order to neutralize negative perceptions. This usually implies the development of different choices from the ones adopted in the country of origin. For example, a potential negative country-of-origin effect can be reduced or nullified if there is a shift of the consumer attention from the manufacturer to the distributor. For this reason, when a company makes an agreement with a foreign distributor, it has to be chosen carefully, because the point of sale is one of the factors that greatly influences the consumer choice, especially for specific types of products.

In other cases, companies have decided to **invest in the strength of their made-in**. For example, Canada Goose, a Canadian company famous for the manufacturing of extreme weather outerwear, such as parkas, coats, jackets, pants, gloves, etc., has always considered its local made-in as a source of competitive advantage. With the slogan "Proudly Made In Canada Since 1957" the company states: "We've kept 100 percent of our production at home in Canada because we are committed to outstanding craftsmanship. [...] But there's a more important reason than that. Cold weather is part of our national identity, [...]. We're proud to have Canadians rely on us for protection in unspeakably cold conditions. We stay in Canada because that's who we are."[66]

But let's take, for example, the Barilla company. Barilla is the best-known brand of pasta worldwide, selling in most of the countries of the world, from the United States to China. Who should have been able to sell pasta in a foreign market better than an Italian company? Well, the internationalization of the premium segment hasn't been so obvious and easy, and the reason, surprisingly, is the perception of "made in Italy" that came with the product (Box 10.3).

Box 10.3 Company-in-Focus: Pasta Barilla

When we think about pasta, it's natural to think that Italian pasta would "sell itself." "Made in Italy" has always been a winning strategy. But when Barilla, the world's number one pasta, started going international in the 1970s, it soon realized that the concept had already been used by other companies in other countries where pasta, although an Italian specialty, was loved and eaten in big quantities.

Panzani had already launched its pasta in France, letting people believe he was Italian. Panzani became a leader in the market using communication that mixed Don Camillo, an Italian-French character, with the smile and good appetite of the actor and singer Fernandel, who was famous in the sixties.

In Spain, the leading pasta brand was Gallo, an Italian name again, perceived as Italian, and on top of that, the word "Gallo" means rooster in both languages, and the rooster in Spain is a symbol of national pride. In Germany, the market leader was Birkel, a German company that consumers appreciated for product quality.

Therefore, in this context, can we believe that the use of the "made in Italy" label alone to represent the high quality of Barilla could be enough to be successful in the global food industry? Can the consolidated image of Italian cuisine in Europe with macaroni, bread, pasta, chefs with long mustaches, moms with big smiles, and the background of the Naples bay, match with the high positioning at which Barilla was entering the market? No, it wasn't possible. If Barilla wanted to be perceived as a premium product, it had to match the perception of its pasta with a different "made in Italy" association. The marketing choice was to link the Barilla brand with the "made in Italy" of the luxury, fashion, and jewelry industries. Slogans like *"Das ist Fusilli, ein Stück aus meiner Lieblingskollektion"* in Germany and *"La collection préférée des italiens"* in France, presented Pasta Barilla as a "collection of jewels." This choice was proven to be successful, underlying, once again, how product management in a foreign market always needs to come to terms with different cultures and multifaceted and complex competitive contexts.

Source: Adapted from: Gonizzi, G. (2003). *125 anni di pubblicità e comunicazione*. Milano: Amilcare Pizzi.

SERVICE ATTRIBUTES

Service attributes can be of **significant importance for the evaluation of product quality.** This consideration can be valid not only in relation to the company's image and the product image in the eyes of the final consumer (business to consumer) but also for companies that work in the business-to-business segment. Services include **installation, after-sales services, warranties, repair and maintenance, spare parts, returns, instruction manuals,** and so forth. Brand equity can be significantly improved with the presence of a proper after-sale service.[67] It is not infrequent that companies outsource labor-intensive customer relationship management activities like after-sales service to countries like India and the Philippines:[68] this is something that has to be carefully evaluated in order to guarantee the quality of the post-sale relation.

The guarantee of an after-sale service can be essential not only if the product ends up being faulty after it is bought, but also before the sale in order to **reduce potential customer reticence toward a foreign product,** especially when the product evaluation is difficult, incomplete, or if there is a negative made-in image. Sometimes consumers prefer to buy a local product or a locally-made global product just because they have a perception of a better warranty. One of the main problems recently faced by the car manufacturer Fiat in India is the woeful perception of their after-sales service and the perception that Fiat cars had expensive parts. To address these problems, Fiat has asked all their dealers to store adequate stock of all key "fast-moving" spares. Furthermore, the company has built one of Asia's largest parts warehouses in India, with the aim to reach "any corner of India" within three working days.[69]

Warranty standardization is not always possible. Some countries lack a consumer culture and customers do not behave as a company would have expected. For example, services offering "fast product delivery or free" as well as "satisfied or 100 percent money back," cannot work in countries where consumers frequently act with opportunistic behaviors. If a company operates in the business-to-business sector, the evaluation of services offered to customers is more complex and needs to be considered together with the level of standardization and the type of warranties offered in the country of origin and abroad. The manufacturer itself doesn't have specific advantages in offering a standardized service. In fact in some cases services are adapted to fit local differences: for example, climatic differences, economic or political reasons, technological characteristics of the country, etc.

On the other side, **client companies prefer a standardized post-sale assistance and warranty policy** on an international level. The main reasons are the following:

- If the client company has different subsidiaries, they would end up using the same product but they would benefit from different types of warranties and post-sale services depending on the location.

- If the product is purchased by a subsidiary in a country and then moves to another subsidiary abroad, the lack of service standardization risks making the product assistance service confusing and difficult.

As a consequence, it is very important to justify cross-countries differences in service warranty, avoiding the risk of undermining the company's reputation and reliability. Nevertheless it is important to note, especially for the business-to-consumer market, that post-sales service is not relevant in all countries. In some countries, the concept of ordinary and extraordinary maintenance is totally unknown, or there is lack of specialized labor available to offer the service. For this reason, especially in countries where post-sales service is weak, it is important to reduce the risk of breakage and improve product reliability reducing the need for assistance.

PRODUCT STRATEGIES IN INTERNATIONAL MARKETS

Potential differences in consumer characteristics and competition in company strategies determine whether a company can replicate its marketing strategy on an international level or must opt for adaptation. Sometimes the company can disregard these choices when it launches a new product that is created from the start for a global target.

From a strategic point of view, even if it is true that the adaptation/standardization issue concerns all of the marketing mix variables, it is important to underline how the most critical decisions are those relative to the product and its communication. As pointed out by and Keegan and Green (2013),[70] the company is faced with five strategic alternatives:

Strategy 1: product–communication extension (dual extension)
Strategy 2: product extension–communication adaptation
Strategy 3: product adaptation–communication extension
Strategy 4: product–communication adaptation (dual adaptation)
Strategy 5: product invention.

Dual extension occurs when a company is selling the same product with the same communication strategy across different countries. This strategy is usually easier to carry out for industrial rather than consumer products. The latter are too often linked with local culture characteristics to allow a total product and communication extension. Some marketers have learned the hard way that a dual extension approach does not work in every market. For example, the Wal-Mart every-day-low-price strategy was not successful in Japan, where the company had to deal with the Japanese perception of good value and Japanese seem to put more weight on quality within a certain price range.[71]

Product extension–communication adaptation is a strategy that can be pursued by those companies that, when offering a product with homogeneous features, are faced with consumers who perceive the product's quality and value differently, or who are using it for a different purpose and are looking for different benefits to satisfy different needs. This is the case of De'Longhi. De'Longhi is an Italian group world leader in the portable heating, air-conditioning, and air-treatment appliances market. Its goal is to achieve European leadership in cooking, ironing, and floor care appliances. With group revenues of 1,632.6 million €[72] and about 75 percent of group sales coming from international markets, the company has grown a lot during the last few years, especially thanks to the communication adaptation that took into consideration consumers' product perception and expected benefits. In fact their product is the same in Europe and the United States, but the communication is different. In Italy the communication is strongly based on emotional benefits. In the rest of Europe, the product value of De'Longhi is linked mainly to technical and aesthetic characteristics, and attention to detail. In the United States, the most important characteristic is that the product must be easy to use.

The **product adaptation–communication extension** strategy targets a market that can be similar in the communication approach but needs product adaptation to meet the needs, customs, and characteristics of the local context. Take, for example, the McDonald's strategy. Its burgers are sold all around the world with modifications and additional items to fit local food culture. However, its communication emphasizing its family-friendly brand has been well received in virtually every country. As in the case of McDonald's, most of the time communication extension is not implemented in its purest form. In fact, McDonald's pro-family values underlie its global marketing campaigns, but they are often positioned in varying contexts across countries. For example, in the United States the context may be convenience; in India they want to represent Indian family values and culture and at the same time they want to be perceived as comfortable and easy.[73]

Product and communication adaptation is a mandatory choice for companies that need to enter markets that are totally different, both in the offer that satisfies their needs, and in the communication that conveys the message efficiently to the target client. For example, Whirlpool in India is a leading company and the brand growth is mainly driven by innovation, design, performance, and quality. All the products and innovations brought to market are based on well-researched insights and consumer studies in the Indian market. For example, in washing machines, they have introduced the possibility to remove 15 different types of stains.[74] Adaptation of advertising is part of the localization of the marketing strategy. The recent "Ice Ice baby Whirlpool Refrigerator Old Indian doordarshan" ad is an example of this.[75]

The product and/or communication adaptation represents a choice that in some cases will not be enough for growth in a foreign market. In emerging markets it is often necessary to enter in a totally different way to satisfy needs that are not present in other parts of the world. Therefore, the new product conceptualization (**product invention**) is often linked to satisfy existing needs with products accessibly priced to mass markets. Colgate-Palmolive is an example. The company realized that Indian villagers were cleaning their teeth with charcoal, brick dust, and similarly abrasive substances. For this reason they decided to replace its toothpaste with "toothpowder."[76] But also in industrialized countries, where products are in the maturity phase of their life cycles and where competition doesn't easily leave room for growth, the development of a company is often based on the launch of new products.

MANAGEMENT ORIENTATION

In many cases, management orientation (ethnocentric or global oriented) is an aspect that can make the difference in the choice between standardization or adaptation. Take the example of Lenovo; the first Chinese quasi-private enterprise founded in 1984. Today, thanks to the acquisition of IBM's personal computer business in 2005, Lenovo is the fourth largest PC company in the world, number one in China, ahead of foreign competitors like HP and Dell and domestic rivals like Founder and Tongfang. Lenovo is a perfect example of a global/local company, with no fixed headquarters, leadership meetings in Paris one month and Cambodia the next, marketing decisions made in Bangalore (India) and design work done in Beijing (China), Raleigh (North Carolina), and Yamato (Japan). The name Lenovo comes from the words legend and novo, i.e. the Latin word for "new." It does not sound Chinese: as pointed out by Brion Tingler, Lenovo's director of global media relations, "we don't go anywhere with the idea that we are a Chinese company, but more that we are a global company."[77] With this global culture, managers are aware of the cost advantages of standardization, but are also open to adaptation, understanding the local needs especially of faster-growing but also low-income markets such as India, Russia, Brazil, and Turkey on which the company is focusing, especially after the acquisition of the cellphone maker Motorola. Six different nationalities are represented within the top ten people of the management team. However, it is not the case that the people that run the markets where Lenovo operates are actually from those markets: Brazilians run Brazil, Europeans run Europe, etc.[78]

Alternatively, other companies can reveal a completely different culture. Such was the case of an Italian company producing a rather famous brand of underwear and swimwear. The company was strongly involved in exporting, but the entrepreneur always refused to make any kind of product adaptation to meet local needs: for example, in Germany, distributors and retailers were asking for women's swimwear in sizes from one to six, not only for classic bikinis but also for sexy ones. For the latter, the entrepreneur never agreed to produce all of the sizes, arguing that it was not coherent with the Italian style where "aggressive" models tend to be offered only in sizes one to three.

The company recently failed and was acquired by an international fashion group that maintained the brand but changed the company's culture, eliminating any ethnocentric thinking and teaching managers that there can be some commonalities across countries but that the reality is the "differences," especially when considering fast-growing emerging markets that are the future for Western companies.

SUMMARY

- The product is the most important element of a marketing program. Global marketers face the challenge of formulating a coherent global product strategy for their companies.
- Product strategy requires an evaluation of the basic needs and conditions of use in the company's existing and proposed markets.
- When defining the marketing strategy, a company should take into consideration the stages of the product life cycle across countries.
- The market potential for products is determined by many factors such as product saturation levels, national income levels, technology standards, and cultural conditions.
- Marketers should be able to identify the optimal level of standardization or adaptation of their products according to the countries they serve, in order to define the opportunities for each product in different markets.
- Marketers must consider four factors when designing products for global markets: product use, product perception and expected benefits, adaptation or standardization of product attributes, and management orientation.
- Five strategic positioning alternatives are open to companies pursuing global market expansion for their products: product–communications extension; product extension–communications adaptation; product adaptation–communications extension; dual adaptation; and product invention. Choosing a strategy for global market expansion should be based on analysis of the factors that would make the product most profitable in each market.

DISCUSSION QUESTIONS

1. How can you define a global product or service? Discuss and give some examples of local products and global products.
2. List and briefly describe the main product features. Considering a product that is representative of your country and is marketed abroad, define the stage of the product life cycle in your country and in other countries and discuss the standardization/adaptation alternative. Which features are standardized? Which are adapted?
3. What are the most important branding decisions managers have to take in international markets?
4. How can a company manage a negative country-of-origin perception? What are the opportunities associated with a positive country of origin? Discuss some examples of negative and positive countries of origin in your country.
5. What are the advantages and disadvantages of different product expansion strategies?

EXPERIENTIAL EXERCISES

- Listen to the NPR story "Video Game Pioneer Kutaragi Leaves Sony," about Sony's Playstation 3 and its struggles against rivals such as Microsoft's Xbox 360 and Nintendo's Wii (www.npr.org/templates/story/story.php?storyId=9884088).
- Based on the comments of the young gamers, what, besides the high price, were Sony's biggest misses in launching this product?
- Do you believe that Sony can recover after its initial stumble in the US market? If so, what steps do you recommend that it takes?
- Select a product from your daily life that is very useful, but costs over US$100. Recommend design, production, and functionality changes that would not reduce its usefulness but would make it more affordable and practical in poorer countries. Develop a marketing strategy for this product in one third-world target market of your choice.

KEY TERMS

- Adaptation
- Brand name
- Brand positioning
- Brand value
- Branding
- Color
- Country of origin
- Decline phase
- Design
- Expected benefits
- Global branding
- Growth phase
- Interpersonal communication
- Introduction phase
- Labeling
- Local brands
- Logo
- Made-in effect
- Maturity phase
- Packaging
- Product attributes
- Product life cycle (PLC)
- Product perception
- Product use
- Quality
- Regulations
- Research and product development stage
- Service attributes
- Standardization
- Standards
- Take-off point
- Word-of-mouth

NOTES

1 Kering. (2013), 'Activity Report 2013: Interview with the Chairman', http://www.kering.com/sites/default/files/document/kering_ra-2013-gb.pdf [Accessed: March 1, 2015], p.5.

2 Payaud, M. (2014), 'Marketing strategies at the bottom of the pyramid: Examples from Nestlé, Danone, and Procter & Gamble', *Global Business & Organizational Excellence*, 33(2), pp. 51–63.

3 Beattie, A.C. (2012), 'Can Starbucks make China love Joe? As chains pop up daily, biggest marketing challenge will be cultivating a coffee culture', *Advertising Age*, November 5, 2012, http://adage.com/china/

article/china-news/can-starbucks-make-china-love-coffee/238101/ [Accessed: January 3, 2015]; Adamy, J. (2006), 'Different brew: Eyeing a billion tea drinkers, Starbucks pours it on in China; Its big challenge: Creating a new taste for coffee, and charging top prices; Wooing the "little emperors."', *The Wall Street Journal*, November 29, 2006, A1, retrieved from ProQuest on February 2, 2015.

4 Schumpeter. (2011), 'Bamboo innovation. Beware of judging China's innovation engine by the standards of Silicon Valley', May 5, 2011, *economist*.com, http://www.economist.com/node/18648264 [Accessed: January 25, 2015].

5 Kumar, V. (2014), 'Understanding cultural differences in innovation: A conceptual framework and future research directions', *Journal of International Marketing*, 22(3), pp.1–29; Vianelli, D. and Valta, E. (2014), 'Transcultural marketing and product life cycles in international markets. In: *Effective Marketing in Contemporary Globalism*. Hershey PA: IGI Global, pp. 377–92; Parthasarathy, M., Jun, S., and Mittelstaedt, R. A. (1997), 'Multiple diffusion and multicultural aggregate social system', *International Marketing Review*, 14(4), pp. 233–47.

6 The World Factbook. (2015), https://www.cia.gov/library/publications/the-world-factbook/docs/refmaps.html [Accessed: August 1, 2015].

7 Euromonitor International. (2014), 'Ready meals in Russia', February 21, 2014, http://www.euromonitor. com/ready-meals-in-russia/report [Accessed: April 16, 2015]; Datamonitor. (2009), 'Global ready meals', www.datamonitor.com [Accessed: January 12, 2012]; Mescam, S. (2008), 'Innovation and NPD in ready meals', *Business Insights Ltd.*, 51.

8 Beiersdorf. (2014). 'Annual Report 2013', http://www.beiersdorf.com/investors/financial-reports/annual-reports [Accessed: January 28, 2015]; Reuters. (2013). 'UPDATE 2-Emerging markets lift Nivea-maker Beiersdorf's sales', January 24, 2014, http://www.reuters.com/article/2013/01/24/beiersdorf-results-idUSL6N0AT2J120130124 [Accessed: January 27, 2015].

9 Roostal, I. (1963, October), 'Standardization of advertising for Western Europe', *Journal of Marketing*, 27, pp.15–20; Ryans, J. K., Jr. (1969, March/April) 'Is it too soon to put a tiger in every tank?', *Columbia Journal of World Business*, 4(2), pp. 69–75.

10 Buzzel, R.D. (1968), 'Can you standardize multinational marketing?', *Harvard Business Review*, (November/ December), 46, pp.102–13.

11 Bartels, R. (1968, July), 'Are domestic and international markets dissimilar?', *Journal of Marketing*, 32, pp. 56–61.

12 Powers, T. L. and Loyca, J. J. (2007) 'Market, industry, and company influences on global product standardization', *International Marketing Review*, 24(6), pp.678–94. Chung, H. (2007) 'International marketing standardization strategies analysis: A cross-national investigation', *Asia Pacific Journal of Marketing and Logistics*, 19(2), pp.145–67.

13 Tan, Q. and Sousa, C. M. P. (2013), 'International marketing standardization', *Management International Review*, 53(5), pp.711–39. Waheeduzzaman, A. N. M. and Dube, L. F. (2004) 'Trends and development in standardization adaptation research', *Journal of Global Marketing*, 17(4), pp.23–52.

14 Griffith, D.A., Lee, H.S., Yeo, C.S., and Calantone, R. (2014), 'Marketing process adaptation', *International Marketing Review*, 31(3), pp. 308–34.

15 Lehrer, M. and Behnam, M. (2009), 'Modularity vs programmability in design of international products: Beyond the standardization-adaptation tradeoff?', *European Management Journal*, 27(4), p.281; Chryssochoidis, G. M. and Wong, V. (2000), 'Customization of product technology and international new product success: Mediating effects of new product development and rollout timeliness', *Journal of Product Innovation Management*, 17(4), pp.268–85.

16 Lages, L. F. and Montgomery, D. B. (2004), 'Export performance as an antecedent of export commitment and marketing strategy adaptation: Evidence from small and medium-sized exporters', *European Journal of Marketing*, 38(9/10), pp. 1186–214.

17 Tan, Q. and Sousa, C. M. P. (2013), 'International marketing standardization', *Management International Review*, 53(5), pp.711–39; Waheeduzzaman, A. N. M. and Dube, L. F. (2004), 'Trends and development in standardization adaptation research', *Journal of Global Marketing*, 17(4), pp. 23–52.

18 Usunier, J-C. and Sbizzera, S. (2013), 'Comparative thick description', *International Marketing Review*, 30(1), pp. 42–55.

19 Gibson. (2013), 'Gibson guitar announces agreement to make strategic investment in TEAC', *Reuters*, Saturday, March 30, http://archive.gibson.com/absolutenm/templates/FeatureTemplatePressRelease.aspx?articleid=1366&zoneid=6 [Accessed: July 30, 2016]; Kageyama, Y. (2006), 'The Japanese dream: Japan market warmly welcomes Gibson Guitars', *Marketing News*, September 15, 2006, p. 48, https://archive.ama.org/archive/ResourceLibrary/MarketingNews/documents/22265058.pdf [Accessed: October 11, 2015].

20 Bruce, M., Daly, L., and Kahn, K. (2007), 'Delineating design factors that influence the global product launch process', *Journal of Product Innovation Management,* September, 2007, 24(5), pp. 456–70; Chryssochoidis, G. M. and Wong, V. (2000), 'Customization of product technology and international new product success: Mediating effects of new product development and rollout timeliness', *Journal of Product Innovation Management*, 17(4), pp. 268–85.

21 Hsu, C., and Li, H. (2009), 'An integrated plant capacity and production planning model for high-tech manufacturing firms with economies of scale', *International Journal of Production Economics,* 118(2), pp. 486–500.

22 Tan, Q. and Sousa, C. M. P. (2013), 'International marketing standardization', *Management International Review*, 53(5), pp. 711–39; Waheeduzzaman, A. N. M. and Dube, L. F. (2004), 'Trends and development in standardization adaptation research', *Journal of Global Marketing*, 17(4), pp. 23–52.

23 'Washing machine: New application', www.1000ventures.com/business_guide/new_product_devt_design_observing-people.html [Accessed: January 29, 2015].

24 SkinVERSE. (2015), 'Vicks VapoRub repels mosquitoes', March 15, 2015, http://skinverse.com/vicks-vaporub-repels-mosquitoes/ [Accessed: October 11, 2015].

25 Bennet, A. G. (2010). *The big book of marketing*. New York: McGraw-Hill.

26 Wall, M. (2014), 'Africa's mobile boom powers innovation economy', *BBC News*, http://www.bbc.com/news/business-28061813 [Accessed: March 2, 2015].

27 Perreault Jr., W.D., Cannon, J.P., and McCarthy, E.J. (2015). *Essentials of marketing: A marketing strategy planning approach*. New York: McGraw-Hill/Irwin.

28 (2014), 'Different skin, different needs', http://www.nivea.co.uk/about-us/beiersdorf/NIVEAHistory#!stories/different-skin-different-needs [Accessed: March 3, 2015].

29 The World Factbook. (2015), https://www.cia.gov/library/publications/the-world-factbook/docs/refmaps.html [Accessed: August 1, 2015].

30 The European standards bodies CEN (European Committee for Standardization), ETSI (European Telecommunications Standards Institute), and CENELEC (European Committee for Electrotechnical Standardization) are the most important organizations in terms of standards unification; they are based in Brussels, Belgium.

31 Valdani, E. and Bertoli, G. (2014). *Marketing internazionale*. Milano: Egea.

32 (2014), 'SoftAtHome Universal Cast Dongle wins this year Broadband Infovision Award for Best Customer Experience Innovation', October 23, 2014, http://www.softathome.com/releases/display/84 [Accessed: March 3, 2015]; Wendlandt, A. (2008), 'France Telecom software JV aims to rival Microsoft', http://www.reuters.com/article/2008/02/20/francetelecom-jv-idUSL2019156020080220 [Accessed: February 26, 2015].

33 Usunier, J. and Lee, J. A. (2013). *Marketing across cultures*. 6th ed. Harlow, England: Prentice Hall, Pearson Education Ltd.

34 www.itoen.co.jp and http://www.itoen.co.jp/eng/products/our_products/index.html [Accessed: November 26, 2014].

35 Walsh, P. (2013), 'Camel milk in Abu Dhabi', June 18, 2013, http://www.marktforschung.de/studien-shop/marktdaten/emerging-food-and-drinks-markets-growth-opportunities-in-brazil-russia-india-china-and-the-uae-581/ [Accessed: July 30, 2016]; Van de Weyer, C. (2007), 'Emerging food and drinks markets: Growth

opportunities in Brazil, Russia, India, China and the UAE', http://store.business-insights.com/Product/emerging_food_and_drinks_markets?productid=BI00012-013 [Accessed: February 15, 2015].

36 The World Factbook. (2015), https://www.cia.gov/library/publications/the-world-factbook/docs/refmaps.html [Accessed: August 1, 2015].

37 Jamivaro. (2015), 'Coffe culture', https://javimaro.wordpress.com/tag/abc/page/9/ [Accessed: July 30, 2016]; Salvatore, D. (2006), 'Globalization, international competitiveness, and European regions', *General Assembly of the Assembly of European Regions (AER)*, Palma de Mallorca. www.aer.eu/fileadmin/user_upload/GoverningBodies/GeneralAssembly/Events/AG2006/speeches/Dominick-Salvatore.doc [Accessed: February 1, 2015].

38 Dignan, L. (2013), 'Apple launches iPhone 5C: Color, costs aimed at emerging markets', September 10, 2013, http://www.zdnet.com/apple-launches-iphone-5c-color-costs-aimed-at-emerging-markets-7000020491/ [Accessed: February 3, 2015].

39 Gunelius, S. (2014), 'International color meanings and blog design: Color psychology differences across the globe', http://weblogs.about.com/od/blogdesign/tp/International-Color-Meanings-And-Blog-Design.htm [Accessed: February 3, 2015].

40 Dedić, G. and Pavlović, D. (2011), 'A tale of two nations – empirical examination of influence of national culture on perceived service quality', *International Journal of Management Cases*, 13(3), pp. 92–104; Malhotra, N. K., Ulgado, F.M., Agarwal, J., Shainesh, G., and Wu, L. (2005), 'Dimensions of service quality in developed and developing economies: Multi-country cross-cultural comparisons', *International Marketing Review*, 22(3), pp. 256–78.

41 Punchard, B. (2014), 'Packaging design: 10 of the most innovative examples of packaging globally', April 8, 2014, http://www.mintel.com/blog/innovation-market-news/packaging-design-10-of-the-most-innovative-examples-of-packaging-globally [Accessed February 3, 2015].

42 Competition Bureau. (1999), 'Guide to the Consumer Packaging and Labelling Act and Regulations', http://www.competitionbureau.gc.ca/eic/site/cb-bc.nsf/eng/01248.html [Accessed: January 22, 2015].

43 NPR. (2014), 'Philip Morris sues Uruguay over graphic cigarette packaging', September 15, 2014, http://www.npr.org/blogs/goatsandsoda/2014/09/15/345540221/philip-morris-sues-uruguay-over-graphic-cigarette-packaging [Accessed: February 3, 2015].

44 Zhang, D. (2014), 'A cross-cultural exploration of children's preferences of package design: The U.S. and China', *Journal of International Consumer Marketing*, 26(5), pp. 391–404.

45 Lascu, D.N. (2013). *International marketing*. 4th ed. Saint Paul, MN: Textbook Media Press.

46 (2011), 'Why the number four is considered unlucky in some east Asian cultures', http://www.todayifoundout.com/index.php/2011/01/why-the-number-four-is-considered-unlucky-in-some-east-asian-cultures/ [Accessed: December 4, 2014].

47 Marketing China. (2013), 'Hershey's, shark in Chinese chocolate market?', http://marketingtochina.com/hersheys-shark-in-chinese-chocolate-market/ [Accessed: February 5, 2015]; Frost, R. (2007), 'Hershey's chocolate dips into foreign markets', www.brandchannel.com/print_page.asp?ar_id=397&section=main [Accessed July 3, 2011].

48 Toulantas, G. and Hiemstra, S. (2014), 'World television – Heineken what's brewing seminar', June 19, 2014, http://www.theheinekencompany.com/~/media/Websites/TheHEINEKENCompany/Downloads/PDF/Investors/Heineken%20NV%202014%20Whats%20Brewing%20Seminar%20Africa%20Middle%20East%20Transcript.ashx [Accessed: October 13, 2015].

49 Kerin, R.A., Hartley, S.W., and Rudelius, W. (2015). *Marketing*. 12th ed. New York: McGraw-Hill Education.

50 Ozsomer, A., Batra, R., Chattopadhyay, A., and ter Hofstede, F. (2012), 'A global brand management roadmap', *International Journal of Research in Marketing*, 29(1), pp. 1–4.

51 Interbrand. (2014). 'Best Global Brands 2014', http://www.bestglobalbrands.com/2014/ranking/ [Accessed: February 12, 2015]; Apple Press Info. (2015), 'iPhone sales grow 26% to establish new September quarter record', Apple Reports Fourth Quarter Results, http://www.apple.com/pr/library/2013/10/28Apple-Reports-Fourth-Quarter-Results.html [Accessed: February 2, 2015]; The Coca Cola Company. (2014), 'The Coca-Cola Company reports full-year and fourth quarter 2013 results', February 18, 2014, http://www.coca-

colacompany.com/press-center/press-releases/the-coca-cola-company-reports-full-year-and-fourth-quarter-2013-results [Accessed: February 2, 2015].

52 Steenkamp, J-B. (2014), 'How global brands create firm value: The 4V model', *International Marketing Review*, 31(1), pp. 5–29.

53 Winit, W., Gregory, G., Cleveland, M., and Verlegh, P. (2014), 'Global vs local brands: How home country bias and price differences impact brand evaluations', *International Marketing Review*, 31(2), pp. 102–28.

54 Donald, A. (2014), 'Why The North Face made Chinese customers run the gantlet', *Advertising Age*, February 5, 2014, http://adage.com/article/global-news/north-face-s-strategy-china/291160/ [Accessed: February 4, 2015].

55 VM. (2014), 'Allison renews Benetton license', October 16, 2014, http://www.visionmonday.com/latest-news/article/allison-renews-benetton-license/ [Accessed: February 4, 2015].

56 Fromowitz, M. (2013), 'Cultural blunders: Brands gone wrong', October 7, 2013, http://www.campaignasia.com/BlogEntry/359532,Cultural+blunders+Brands+gone+wrong.aspx [Accessed: February 4, 2015].

57 (2008), 'One world, one car, one name', March 12, 2008, http://www.businessweek.com/stories/2008-03-12/one-world-one-car-one-name [Accessed: February 4, 2015].

58 Chattalas, M., Kramer, T., and Takada, H. (2008), 'The impact of national stereotypes on the country of origin effect: A conceptual framework', *International Marketing Review*, 25(1), pp. 54–74.

59 Chen, C.Y., Mathur, P., and Maheswaran, D. (2014), 'The effects of country-related affect on product evaluations', *Journal of Consumer Research*, 41(4), December, pp. 1033–46.

60 GFK. 'Place Branding Research', https://www.scribd.com/document/267843403/GfK-Place-Branding-pdf [Accessed: July 30, 2016].

61 GFK. (2013), 'Nation Brand Index 2015', http://nation-brands.gfk.com/ [Accessed July 30, 2016].

62 Shimp, T. A. and Sharma, S. (1987), 'Consumer ethnocentrism: Construction and validation of the CETSCALE', *Journal of Marketing Research*, 24(3), p. 280.

63 Sharma P. (2014), 'Consumer ethnocentrism: Reconceptualization and cross-cultural validation', *Journal of International Business Studies*, 46(2), pp. 1–9.

64 Fong, C.-M., Lee, C.-L., and Yunzhou, D. (2014), 'Consumer animosity, country of origin, and foreign entry-mode choice: A cross-country investigation', *Journal of International Marketing*, 22(1), pp. 62–76.

65 https://www.cia.gov/library/publications/the-world-factbook/docs/refmaps.html [Accessed: February 1, 2015].

66 Canada Goose. (2015), 'Our history', http://www.canada-goose.com/canada-goose---our-story/our-story-canada-goose-about-us.html [Accessed: February 5, 2015]; Shaw, H. (2012), 'Canada Goose's made-in-Canada marketing strategy translates into success', May 18, 2012, http://business.financialpost.com/2012/05/18/canada-gooses-made-in-canada-marketing-strategy-translates-into-success/ [Accessed February 6, 2015].

67 Perreault, Jr. W.D., Cannon, J.P., and McCarthy, E.J. (2015). *Essentials of marketing: A marketing strategy planning approach*. NY: McGraw-Hill/Irwin.

68 Steenkamp, J.-B. (2014), 'How global brands create firm value: The 4V model', *International Marketing Review*, 31(1), pp. 5–29.

69 Mitra, K. (2014), 'Fiat India hopes to gain lost ground in 2014', February 8, 2014, *The Pioneer*, http://www.dailypioneer.com/columnists/business/fiat-india-hopes-to-gain-lost-ground-in-2014.html [Accessed February 6, 2015].

70 Keegan, W. J. and Green, M. C. (2013). *Global marketing*. 7th ed. Upper Saddle River, NJ: Pearson International Edition.

71 Lee, J. (2012), 'Why has WalMart failed in Korea, Japan and Germany? And, why is it successful in China?', *Asia Business Insight*, http://asianconsumerinsights.blogspot.it/2012/08/why-has-walmart-failed-in-korea-japan.html [Accessed February 6, 2015].

72 Fiscal Year 2013.

73 Goorha Kashyup, P. (2010), 'Brand Yatra: A McDonald's in every neighbourhood... well almost', May 10,

2010, *Exchange4Media.com*, http://www.exchange4media.com/brandspeak/brandspeak_FS.asp?section_id=42&news_id=38093&tag=3723 [Accessed February 6, 2015].

74 Tiwari, A.K. (2012), 'Whirlpool will launch products for premium India', March 28, 2012, *DNA*, http://www.dnaindia.com/money/interview-whirlpool-will-launch-products-for-premium-india-1668219 [Accessed February 6, 2015].

75 https://www.youtube.com/watch?v=a6sslvO5zeQ

76 Mundim, A., Mitali, S., Arora, P. and McManus R. (2012) 'Emerging-markets product development and innovation: The new competitive reality, *Accenture*, retrieved from https://www.scribd.com/document/242681576/Accenture-Emerging-Markets-Product-Development-and-Innovation [Accessed: July 30, 2016].

77 Rhally, C. (2014), 'Don't say you're a Chinese company: How Lenovo grew as a global brand', April 15, 2014, *World Economic Forum Davos 2014*, http://projourno.org/2014/04/dont-say-youre-a-chinese-company-how-lenovo-grew-as-a-global-brand/ [Accessed: January 13, 2015].

78 Rhally, C. (2014), 'Don't say you're a Chinese company: How Lenovo grew as a global brand', April 15, 2014, *World Economic Forum Davos 2014*, http://projourno.org/2014/04/dont-say-youre-a-chinese-company-how-lenovo-grew-as-a-global-brand/ [Accessed: January 13, 2015]; Buckman, R. (2008), 'Not East or West', *Forbes*, 182(13), pp. 50–2.

CASE 10.1   THE BRAND CALLED YOU: MARKETING YOURSELF FOR SUCCESS GLOBALLY

INTRODUCTION

Your personal marketing plan is your guide to your business. It organizes your thoughts as to why you are in business. It defines your customers and competitors. It points out your strengths and weaknesses. It details what your plans are for the future. It is an important part of your overall business plan.[1]

The natural outgrowth of the planning process is a personal marketing plan—a detailed description of resources and actions an individual needs to achieve his or her stated marketing objectives. A marketing plan is an important part of an entrepreneur's overall business plan.

"Of all the Charlie Browns in the world, you're the Charlie Browniest."

— Charles M. Schulz, Peanuts

In preparing your personal marketing plan, keep in mind what you are going to market about yourself, to whom, and why. This is your map for planning and measuring your performance, so include as many hard facts as possible, as well as measurable goals and timelines. The plan should be concise, factual, and easy to read.

Marketing plans vary in length and format; however, most contain the following components:

Mission Statement: Summarizes your purpose, vision, and overall goals. The mission statement provides the foundation upon which further planning is based.

Personal Goals: Describes what your personal focus and goal settings are on the basis of favored field of expertise in the short and long term.

Branding "Yourself": Describes strategies for informing potential customers about goods and services that are offered, and describes strategies for winning repeat business.

Situation Analysis: Now that you've defined your brand, the next step is your situation analysis. For this, you will need to come up with the relevant background information required to create your plan.

Planning: Describes how the individual will go about producing his or her service in the most efficient, cost-effective manner possible.

Implementation: Discusses the action you want to take to achieve your objective with its intended impact and other pre-set standards.

Control: Now it's time to re-evaluate, regroup, and grow further through introspection.

Planning Contingencies: The final step. Planning for foreseeable deviations from the plan and setting up a backup strategy.

Exercise Chart

STRATEGIC MARKETING PROCESS	DESCRIPTION

Mission Statement:			**My Reason for Being:**
I. Peronsal Goals	Focus and Goal Setting	My Top Three Industries:	**Industries:**
	Specific **M**easureable **A**chieve **R**ealistic **T**ime	My Top Three Job Profiles:	**Short Term:**
			Long Term:
		My Top Three Companies:	**Short Term:**
			Long Term:
II. Branding YoUrself	Brand Name		**Name, Nickname, Symbol, Title, etc.**
	Core Competencies		**Areas of Expertise:**
	Points of Difference		**Personality:**
			Education & Experience:
			Other:
	Points of Parity		**Necessary Competitive Qualities:**

STRATEGIC MARKETING PROCESS	DESCRIPTION

	SWOT Analysis	Location of Factor	Kind of Factor	
			Favorable	Unfavorable
III. Situation Analysis		Internal: Me Personality Job Experience Motivation Family Other:_____	**My Strengths:**	**My Weaknesses:**
		External: My Competitive Environment (PESTEL Analysis) Political Economic Social Technical Environment Legal Other:_____	**Opportunities for Me:**	**Threats Affecting Me:**

IV. Planning Phase	Product Strategy	**Formal Education/Courses:**
		Job Experiences/Projects:
	(Actions to Improve My "Marketability")	**Extracurricular/Volunteer Activities:**
		Obstacles to Overcome:
	Pricing Strategy	**Income:**
	Promotional Strategy	**Contact Strategy:**
	Placing Strategy	**Desired Location:**

STRATEGIC MARKETING PROCESS	DESCRIPTION		

	Objective	Action	Intended Impact	Deadline
V. Implementation Phase	**Goal:**	a. b. c. d. e.	a. b. c. d. e.	a. b. c. d. e.

	Evaluation	**What Did and Didn't Work:**
VI. Control Phase		
	Control	**How to Modify Strategy:**
VII. Planning Contingencies	Contingency Plan	**My Backup Approach:**

NOTES

1. Kotler, Philip, and Keller, Kevin L. Marketing Management. 13th ed. Upper Saddle River, NJ: Pearson Education.

CHAPTER 11

Setting Global Prices

"We will develop a budget car in the price class between €6,000 and €7,000.[1] More than three million cars a year can be sold in this segment in China alone, as well as a million in India. Africa is also a very promising market."

Volkswagen CEO, Martin Winterkorn[2]

LEARNING OBJECTIVES

After Reading This Chapter, You Should Be Able to:

- Understand the centrality of pricing in the international marketing mix.
- Identify the main competitive, consumer, product, distribution, and country factors influencing pricing decisions.
- Understand how to define objectives, strategies, and pricing policies.
- Distinguish between cost- versus market-based pricing approaches.
- Learn how to manage new product pricing.
- Discuss the standardization versus adaptation alternatives.
- Recognize pricing strategy prototypes.
- Understand how to manage transfer pricing.
- Describe terms and methods of payment.
- Understand the concept of countertrade.

A CHALLENGING DECISION

When considering pricing strategies and policies, there are complex decisions that the company has to make. Price is a key driver of consumer purchase behavior, and in international markets a company has to face the hard task of setting a price which has to be coherent with brand equity and meanwhile consistent across different countries. But there are countless factors that need to be taken into consideration. Many of them depend not only on internal company variables such as corporate strategy or product cost, but also on external factors such as the characteristics of the target market, global and local competitors, and a country's economic and legislative structure. A manufacturer's pricing policy is also influenced by the relative pricing power of intermediaries in the channel of distribution, and has to satisfy the requests of big international retailers expecting to pay a similar price for the same product across countries. For these reasons, pricing should be approached by companies in a structured way. A research study[3] based on a sample of managers—from CEOs and CFOs to heads of business units and professionals in marketing, pricing, and finance functions—pointed out that regardless of their industry, companies with top managers with higher skills in pricing, had more success in achieving a better price for their product than their competitors. With the aim to achieve pricing power, it becomes clear that deep research into customer needs, willingness to pay, and perception of value, is becoming more and more a powerful weapon for companies to overcome price pressure by retailers and become more profitable.

Price, together with other marketing mix variables, must reflect the value that the consumer is willing to pay for the company's product, taking into consideration competitive products as well. For example, a recent analysis by McKinsey points out how with green products companies can pursue sustainability in a way that creates value, improving revenues through price premiums by marketing sustainability attributes.[4]

On the other hand, consumers are increasingly looking for high quality, low price goods, and companies gain a key advantage if they have the ability to build high quality inexpensively. To develop the Wal-Mart everyday-low-price promise, the company had to restructure the supply chains; the Chinese company Huawei did the same for telecommunications technology.[5] Prices have to be competitive because many customers look for cheaper deals not only in traditional retailing but also through the Internet.

Price is a tangible value of an offer created through product, distribution, and communication decisions. Therefore, pricing decisions are intrinsically tied to other marketing mix variables, such as product innovation and brand value. Nintendo, for example, is a brand that seems to be losing its consumer appeal. The launch of the Wii console, with its physically active and convincing interface and DS range, sparked consumers' interest. Nintendo differentiated itself from competitors through its "enjoyment of gaming" theme and repositioned its brand to attract new consumers, not only in the teenage male segment but anybody who enjoys playing. Wii's sales grew beyond expectations. In the launch phase, lines forming outside stores were not uncommon, and consoles were selling on eBay for twice the retail price.[6] Today Nintendo is facing a price drop.[7] The competition of smartphones and tablets, and new business models like free-to-play have emerged: CEO, Satoru Iwata, is planning some product innovations to relaunch the brand and face the transition era of the traditional console industry.[8]

In a global context, the price that a product can gain in the market often determines its development. In low-income countries, price must be in line with purchasing power. A company must first evaluate the price that the consumer is willing to pay for the product. Only then will it be possible to define the most suitable product features and distribution and communication policies.

Take P&G, for example: in 2013 their Gillette brand's market share for razors and blades in India has grown to 49.1 percent, up from 37.3 in 2007. The company recently introduced Gillette Guard, a low-cost razor designed for emerging markets like India. A group of P&G managers spent 3,000 hours with more than 1,000 Indian consumers at their homes, in stores, and in small group discussions, to identify the needs of local men which frequently have to shave without water, without a mirror, and in the dark of the morning. The new Guard razor has one blade instead of the two to five blades of the US model, to put the emphasis on safety rather than closeness. The handle is textured to allow for easy gripping: in fact, one insight from observing shavers was that Indians grip the razors in many different ways. A hole at the handle's base makes it easier to hang up, and a small comb by the blade was added since Indians' hair growth tends to be thicker. To be price competitive in the Indian market and produce the razor at the right target price, P&G analyzed all the smallest details. The number of components in the razor was cut down from the 25 components needed for a regular Gillette's three-blade razor, to only four. The razor's handle was even made hollow so it would be lighter and cheaper to make. The cost of the new razor was about one third of what it costs to make the Gillette's low-price Indian razor before Guard. As reported by a P&G associate director for product engineering, "I can remember talking about changes to this product that were worth a thousandth, or two thousandths of a cent." The Guard is today sold for 15 rupees (about 34 cents), and each razor blade costs 5 rupees (about 12 cents).[9]

Another example is that Microsoft, despite the popularity of its Windows operative system and Office Suites, is facing many problems in the Chinese market. Microsoft started working with governments in emerging countries to price software in a way that is relevant to those markets. The choice to make its products affordable, particularly to companies in the Pacific Rim, was fully justified, because consumers have low purchasing power.[10] Today Microsoft is earning in China (approx. 1,354 billion people)[11] less revenue than in the Netherlands (approx. 16.7 million people).[12] What are the main reasons of this underperformance? The first issue is piracy: despite the lower prices, few people in emerging markets buy legitimate copies. The second is the Chinese government trying to limit the dominance of foreign companies and encouraging local technology firms to become viable competitors. The third reason is that, in contrast to other developed countries where about only 25 percent of the PCs are so-called "naked," (meaning without a pre-installed Windows operating system), in Asia this percentage is up to 60 percent, favoring the diffusion of piracy especially among price-sensitive consumers.[13]

This chapter explores the main issues that need to be faced when making pricing decisions in international markets. After analyzing the numerous influencing factors, we will discuss pricing strategies and policies. Finally we will focus on some specific problems that need to be managed by the global company, such as price escalation, transfer prices, terms of payment, and countertrade.

FACTORS INFLUENCING PRICING DECISIONS

There are several factors influencing international pricing decisions that can be categorized into **five groups**:

1. competitive factors

2. consumer and cultural factors

3. product factors

4. distribution channel factors

5. country factors.

Also, company factors are important elements to consider, especially at a strategic level. Their role will therefore be underlined when considering international pricing strategies and objectives.

Competitive Factors

The **structure and intensity of competition varies significantly from country to country** and therefore affects pricing strategy. In the beauty and personal care market in Turkey, for example, multinationals such as P&G, Avon, L'Oreal and Unilever have a strong power due to the huge investments in advertising and promotion. However they have to face the **competition of leading local companies**, for example Evyap (Geo Map 11.1) and Kopaş Kozmetik Pazarlama, whose competitive advantage is based on a significant price advantage over the multinationals.[14]

In India, the competitive landscape is different if we consider different regions within the country. While Hindustan Unilever is the leading company in urban areas, domestic manufacturers have a strong regional presence in areas where the consumers are highly price sensitive, especially due to their **competitive and affordable price that favor market penetration**.[15] This is a situation that is also facing Coca-Cola in China, where the company is the leader in big cities, but finds it difficult to develop a strong penetration in the populated rural areas of the country (Box 11.1).

The **intensity of competition** is sometimes so high that many companies find it difficult to price competitively. The bike department of some supermarkets in China is a clear example of how competitors can find it hard to differentiate from each other (Figure 11.1).

However, it is important to emphasize how the power to determine a given price is strongly linked to the value that the company is able to create around its offer through different marketing mix variables. Companies that have been able to create **differentiation relative to competition** are the ones that are less subjected to price pressures.

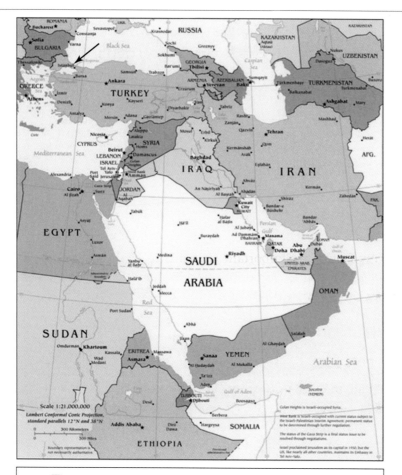

GEO MAP 11.1
Evyap
Source: Adapted from:
CIA Maps, The World
Factbook[16]

The headquarters of **Evyap** are in Istanbul, Turkey.

Box 11.1   Company-in-Focus: Coca-Cola and Wahaha

Competition Heats Up When Targeting China

China's rural market was considered a neglected market for years, because it was vast in terms of population, but too small in terms of purchasing power, and too costly in terms of distribution and logistics. This led foreign giants like Coke to target only major cities, such as Shanghai and Bejing, where the consumption and the target segments are very similar to western markets. In these locations, marketing strategies can be focused on the creation of brand awareness with the use of social media, innovative packaging, etc. For example, in the first quarter of 2014, China's sparkling beverage volume was up 10%, partially driven by the company's Share a Coke campaign launched in June and replacing the Coca-Cola logo with first-names in the company's iconic white script. In addition, Coca-Cola has introduced the 'lyric bottle': lyrics and short clips from some of China's most famous and best loved songs can be downloaded with a QR code on Coca-Cola packaging and shared in social media. But China is not only big metropolitan and international cities: the rural areas are growing tremendously. Today one of the major competitors of Coca-Cola in China is Hangzhou Wahaha Group (Figure 1.1).

The Chinese company launched a soft drink named Future Cola, mainly to target rural areas. Its competitive advantage is the flavor, adapted to the taste of Chinese consumers, the packaging, initially copied from Coca-Cola, the brand image, based on "The Chinese People's Own Cola" and especially the price, that is significantly lower thanks to the establishment of localized production in rural areas. Today Wahaha has a distribution system deeply rooted in China's rural areas, with about 6,000 wholesalers and approximately 20,000 distributors. The company was able to set an affordable price for the right composite bundle of product characteristics, allowing penetration in areas where billions of consumers, at the bottom of the world income pyramid, are willing to buy products that are already consumed by medium and high income consumers.

Sources: Mourdoukoutas, P. (2013), 'Coca-Cola's real overseas problem–How to pap into neglected markets', July 16, 2013, http://www.forbes.com/sites/panosmourdoukoutas/2013/07/16/coca-colas-real-overseas-problem-how-to-tap-into-neglected-markets/; Sharf, S. (2014), 'Coca-Cola profits slip as too few 'Share A Coke'', July 22, 2014, http://www.forbes.com/sites/saman-thasharf/2014/07/22/coca-cola-profits-slip-as-too-few-share-a-coke/; Campaign Brief Asia. (2014), 'Isobar launches latest summer campaign 'lyric bottles' for Coca-Cola in China', June 4, 2014, http://www.campaignbrief.com/asia/2014/06/isobar-launches-latest-summer.html [All accessed: January 2, 2015].

FIGURE 11.1
Bike Department in a Chinese Supermarket in Shanghai
Source: © Author

Consumer and Cultural Factors

Globalization has not yet resulted in convergence of consumer perception. In fact, factors linked to the consumer and its culture that can influence price policies are very complex. From the company's point of view, product unit price represents a clearly defined numeric value; however, from the consumer point of view, the concept of perceived price comes into play. For this reason, it is important to analyze consumers in relation to:

- the perception of price: monetary, non-monetary price, and retail price ending;

- price and perception of quality;

- the role of the Internet in price evaluation.

Perception of Price

It is important to distinguish between two dimensions regarding the perceived price: monetary and non-monetary. Monetary price represents the idea that a consumer has regarding a product's price, for example, expensive or cheap. This idea often depends on the consumer's past experience, on the information he or she has had access to, and competitive offerings.[17]

Non-monetary price represents the sacrifice that a consumer must face when purchasing a product: taking into consideration, for example, the time necessary for the purchase, the effort necessary to learn how to use it, and the risks involved.[18]

Also, in this case, perception of the non-monetary price will tend to vary significantly from country to country; for example, in cultures that can be defined as "time saving" rather than cultures where time economy is not important. Or it can depend on the importance the consumer attributes to the product, and therefore to the effort that he or she is willing to expend in order to be able to acquire it. The final price perception, therefore, will depend on a careful evaluation of costs (monetary and non-monetary) and benefits (tied to the obtainable advantages linked with the purchase of a product or service). Finally, the perceived functional and other product benefits will be balanced against costs of acquisition, internal costs (learning to use new product, lost time, disposal of previous product, etc.), and purchase risks (financial, social, and physical).[19]

Consumer and cultural factors can also influence price-ending practices. A study in low context (Western countries) and high context cultures (non-Western countries) suggests that the perception of retail prices ending in 0.5 (even ending) and 9 (odd ending) is not homogeneous. Non-Western cultures seem to be less deceived by the cheapness or gain that an odd ending price wants to convey. In some cases they feel that someone is attempting to "fool" them.[20]

Price and the Perception of Quality

There are many studies demonstrating how cultural factors influence the relationship between price and the perception of quality.[21] However, generalization of findings is difficult because this relationship has to be analyzed for different product categories and brand strategies. In general, for luxury products, characterized by factors such as uniqueness, high quality, and rarity, it is frequent to find a Veblen effect: a higher rather than a lower price can determine an increase in demand for a product.[22] In Box 11.2 the perception of luxury products by Japanese and Chinese consumers clearly points out the dynamics between price and quality

Box 11.2   Country-in-Focus: Japan and China

Price-Quality Perception Differences in Japan and China: The Future for Luxury Products

Japan. Clear needs and desires and high expectations for products for which they are willing to pay premium prices: this is the picture of Japanese consumers, which can be classified among the highest product-quality seekers in the world. Japan is the second largest luxury goods market in the world and luxury brands will continue to invest in this market. Fendi, for example, is investing in the renovation of its existing stores and in a new flagship store in Tokyo, and its example is followed by many other luxury brands planning to expand their store openings in the country. In fact Japanese consumers view information other than price (e.g. brand, packaging, advertising) to assess product quality and make a decision. Even the Wal-Mart "Everyday Low Prices" philosophy doesn't seem to attract many Japanese consumers, because they often associate low price with low quality; i.e. yasu-karou, warukarou, or "cheap price, cheap product." Some companies are quick to understand this. Procter & Gamble sought the best available materials for product formulations and packaging. In order to become the country's largest fast food chain, McDonald's opened its first store in Tokyo's Ginza district, which is identified with luxury brand name goods. And Levi's are sold at very high prices because they are perceived as the designer's elite brand product and representative of the American life-style. Nevertheless, there is also another segment of young people displaying alternative consumer behavior. On the one hand, they prefer very low-priced products for everyday use. On the other hand, they are still willing to pay premium prices for select quality products—especially those from Europe—to achieve self-satisfaction and social status. The outcome is that products that fall in the middle of the price range (for example, local designer products) generate limited profits.

China. This country is evolving and facing contradictory behaviors. Many consumers are price sensitive and money savers. In most cases, affordable prices are necessary if a company wants to penetrate the market. This explains why P&G needed three years before it was able to become profitable in China, why, L'Oreal took nine years, and why the world's most popular chicken restaurant chain, KFC, spent ten years improving its business model and successfully running restaurants in 450 Chinese cities. Nevertheless, Chinese consumers also report significantly high prestige sensitivity. The younger generations and the new Chinese middle classes are especially attracted by Western and luxury brands which represent a way to show they have made it. The number of luxury consumers in China count more than 50 million and they are constantly increasing. If it is true that they frequently end up buying pirated versions and creating enormous anti-counterfeiting control problems, it is also a matter of fact that the luxury market is constantly growing. This growth is interesting also for some Chinese companies that are increasingly attracted to the premium segment. Take the example of Shanghai Tang, a Chinese brand in the fashion market that promotes high-quality innovative design and high prices yet does not hide its "made in China" label, but rather emphasizes its "proud to be Chinese" image. The perceived value of the brand is demonstrated by the fact that the company was bought by the Compagnie Financière Richemont SA, known all over the world for its Cartier brand. This led to growth not only in China but also internationally, with stores in cities such as London, Miami, and Dubai.

Sources: Euromonitor International. (2015), 'Luxury goods in Japan', January, 2015, http://www.euromonitor.com/luxury-goods-in-japan/report [Accessed: March 12, 2015]; Kotabe, M. and Jiang, C. (2006, March/April), 'Three dimensional: The markets of Japan, Korea, and China are far from homogeneous', *Marketing Management*, 15(2), pp. 39–43; Meng, J. and Altobello Nasco, S. (2009), 'Cross-cultural equivalence of price perceptions across American, Chinese, and Japanese consumers', *Journal of Product & Brand Management*, 18(7), pp. 506–516; Analysis of Japanese consumers. (2010), 'Intelligent bridges', www.intelbridges.com/japaneseconsumer.html [Accessed: February 3, 2015]; www.shanghaitang.com; The Economist. (2014), 'China's addiction to luxury goods', April 29, 2014, http://www.economist.com/blogs/economist-explains/2014/04/economist-explains-17 [Accessed: March 1, 2015]; The Economist. (2014), 'Disillusioned hedonist shoppers', February 11, 2014, http://www.economist.com/blogs/schumpeter/2014/02/luxury-goods-market [Accessed: March 3, 2015].

that in recent years have led Western luxury brands to increasingly invest in these attractive markets.

For other products, the relation between price and quality is influenced by the perception of local and global brands. For example, a recent analysis carried out in Thailand for different product categories, points out that Thai consumers consider juice and airline local brands as superior and preferable to their foreign-owned counterparts; vice versa Thai-owned jeans and coffee shop brands are perceived inferior and less desirable to the foreign-owned alternatives. In this second case, if there is no price difference consumers maintain their foreign preferences. However, if the prices of foreign alternatives are relatively higher, high-ethnocentric consumers more quickly switch their buying intentions to the local alternatives.[23]

The consumer culture should also be considered in terms of buying behavior distinguishing consumers of one country or region from those ones of other countries. For example, in Western markets, for many products consumers expect a good quality even if the product price is low. The approach to pricing is similar in Mexico, where shoppers are cautious and price sensitive, and they appreciate outlets offering promotions all year long. It is not the same in Guatemala, where limited-time offers are particularly popular. This is one of the main reasons for the slow development of Wal-Mart Every Day Low Price (EDLP) recently introduced in Guatemala: consumers are more used to one-off, time-limited discounts. Hence, even if consumers' perceptions are gradually changing, it is still hard to convince them that quality can be high even if the price is low.[24]

It is also important to consider that the relation between low income consumers and affordable prices should not be generalized. For example, Coca-Cola entered the Philippines with a soft drink called "Sakto," the Filipino word for "exactly," at a very low price of 5 Philippine Pesos (US$0.12). The target was made up of consumers, such as students, who had very little pocket change and wanted "the exact amount of Coke at the exact price." But the product was often ridiculed by some Filipino consumers, considering Satko as "exactly" what poor people could afford. The result was that students, who were considered by Coca-Cola one of the most important targets, viewed the product as a statement of poverty and used to avoid purchasing Satko amongst friends.[25]

Internet and Price Evaluation

The growing use of the Internet has definitely given a push toward consumer rationality. In fact, on a global scale, the Internet is helping shoppers throughout the world to compare prices of similar products. Sites such as NexTag.com, which has German, French, Italian, Spanish, Japanese, and British versions, as well as its United States site, not only allow consumers to compare prices for everything from diapers to online education degrees, but also offer tools such as historic price charts, product reviews, vendor ratings, and more. These sites are also particularly used in emerging markets, as they emerge from the success of Tencent, the largest and most used Chinese Internet service portal. The mission of Tencent, founded in 1998, and today counting more than 180 million active users, is to provide value-added Internet mobile and telecom services and online advertising, through its leading internet platforms QQ (QQ Instant Messenger), WeChat, QQ.com, QQ

Games, Qzone, 3g.QQ.com, SoSo, PaiPai, and Tenpay. Users can share opinions, compare prices, buy products, and communicate with one another.[26]

In more and more industries all over the world the use of internet is expected to intensify in the next years. Internet will be used not only to make a rational decision but also, thanks to mobile devices, it will be used to compare prices of products in different stores. As a consequence, especially in the future, internet will allow not only price comparison between brands but also between retail prices for the same brand, allowing consumers to compare the price of the desired products whenever they want.

Product Factors

An important variable to consider in pricing decisions is the stage of the product life cycle (PLC) that exists in different countries. As discussed in Chapter 10, each stage needs different management of marketing mix policies, including price choices in each country. For example, the price will be higher in countries where the product is in the introductory phase, and lower in countries where the product category is in its maturity stage.

Another aspect that needs to be taken into consideration is the company's ability to convey to consumers the real quality of the product, a goal that is not always easy to implement if the company operates in industries where competition relies mostly on the price variable rather than on differentiation strategies. It is in these circumstances that it often becomes important to support price with appropriate communication leveraging on product or company attributes that can be recognized on an international level, with the objective of transferring the product value to the target client. GranitiFiandre, for example, is a leading Italian company in the business-to-business luxury ceramic tiles industry. It distinguishes itself by premium price positioning. The company conveys the perception of its products' value in an international context through the image of some of its customers who have used GranitiFiandre tiles for their luxury stores or their company sites. Among these are Ferrari, Armani, Benetton, Givenchy, and Porsche, all companies whose brand and reputation are well known by potential international clients. The company has been able to develop a high-quality perception coherent with a high price. Value creation is the focus of their communication, which describes tiles as the perfect combination of performance and aesthetics.

When determining the final price of a product in international marketing, expenses for adapting, manufacturing, and selling a product, as well as export-related costs and a profit margin, are all essential elements for the product's final price definition. Product costs to be taken into account are:

- variable costs (raw materials, labor, energy, etc.)

- marketing expenses (marketing research, communication, etc.)

- finance and bank charges

- export-related charges (translation, labeling, country-of-origin marking, packaging adaptation, documentation, insurance, tariffs, shipping costs, etc.).

Most of the time product costs are higher when targeting low income countries where the company often has to invest in adapting the product, meeting local requirements, translating labels in different languages, etc. The paradox is that in these countries especially the final price should be lower because of the low purchasing power of the population.

Distribution Channel Factors

Companies operating in a global context have to coordinate prices across countries, taking into consideration that the final price paid by consumers is the result of a process of value creation that involves intermediaries such as distributors, importers, retailers, etc. The company set a price to the first intermediary (sell-in price), then all the intermediaries involved in the export channel charge a margin, resulting in a final price paid by the final clients (sell-out price). It is not difficult to understand that control of pricing decisions in the distribution channel is particularly critical in international marketing, especially if the exporter has little control of the intermediaries' behavior.

The length of the distribution channel (i.e. the number of intermediaries), together with export charges such as insurance, shipping, export documentation, and tariffs, can determine a relevant increase of the final export price if compared to the domestic price. This phenomenon, known as price escalation, can be seen in Table 11.1, where two export scenarios are compared to a typical domestic situation.

In the first case (Italy), only the retailer is present in the channel, allowing the company to charge a higher manufacturer's margin (70 percent instead of 50 percent). In the second case (the United States), the distribution channel has been lengthened with a foreign importer. The third scenario adds a wholesaler. Even if both the United States and Russia's manufacturing margin is lower, the escalation is significant 40.34 percent and 82.35 percent, respectively.

In order to avoid the risk that the final price ends up being out of the market, the company must implement some alternatives that would allow avoiding or limiting price escalation.[27]

The first alternative would be to reduce the length of the distribution channel. Such as the case of Nokia. After assessing India's notoriously fragmented retail marketplace, management decided to bypass retailers and distributors altogether and began selling its phones directly to consumers via its own fleet of specially marked and equipped vans.[28] Alternatively, it is possible to lower the producer's net price eliminating, for example, expensive features or shifting production of the product or of some of its components to low-cost countries. Finally, it is evident that the possibility of limiting price escalation will strongly depend on the company's power to control final

TABLE 11.1 Export Price Escalation: An Example for Coffee in the Retail Channel		Italy	USA	Russia
		Domestic Channel With Retailer (*Manufacturer Margin: +70%*)	Foreign Channel With Importer and Retailer (*Manufacturer Margin: +50%*)	Foreign Channel With Importer, Wholesaler, and Retailer (*Manufacturer Margin: +50%*)
	Manufacturer's Cost	5.00	5.00	5.00
	Manufacturer's Margin (%)	+70%	+50%	+50%
	Manufacturer's Margin ($)	3.5	2.5	2.5
	= Manufacturer's Price	8.50	7.50	7.50
	+ Insurance, Shipping Cost, Export Documentation (2%)	–	0.15	0.15
	= Landed Cost	–	7.65	7.65
	+ Tariff (20%)	–	1.53	1.53
	= Importer's Cost	–	9.18	9.18
	+ Importer's Margin (30% on Cost)	–	2.75	2.75
	= Wholesaler's Cost	–	–	11.93
	+ Wholesaler's Margin (30% on Cost)	–	–	3.58
	= Retailer's Cost	8.50	11.93	15.51
	+ Retailer's Margin (40% on Cost)	3.40	4.77	6.20
	= Consumer's cost (=Retailer's Price)	11.90	16.70	21.70
	Price Escalation over Domestic		+40.34%	+82.35%

Source: Compiled by Author

prices, also imposing lower margins on channel members of each target country.

Country Factors

Socioeconomic and political country characteristics are among the elements that can influence a company's pricing strategies and policies. These factors are not controllable by the company, so it must adapt to them when selling its products to a specific country. Per capita income, for example, is an important factor to consider in emerging economies where many global companies want to penetrate not only to a minority of relatively rich consumers, but also to target the mass market.

Some companies opt for a low price strategy. In India, many leading food chains target lower- to middle-income customers with heavily value-focused menus. Domino's was among the first to launch a Pizza Mania line, priced at Rs44 (US$0.70), supported by an advertising campaign promoting the idea that even young people in their first job can afford Domino's. KFC and McDonald's did the same with super low-priced menus aimed at students and other young people, and Pizza Hut is offering the lowest price of any pizza player with 5-inch pizzas at a starting price of Rs29 (US$0.47). To maintain margins and stay competitive, all these companies obviously have to lower their operational costs.[29]

Many premium brand owners adopted the strategy of introducing second brands or product lines to access the low-priced markets of Eastern Europe, Middle East Africa, and Asia. In these cases, care must be taken not to cannibalize sales of existing brands or cheapen the brand's image. Examples of tiered pricing can be found in the pharmaceutical industry, where drug prices can vary in order to penetrate low and middle income markets.[30]

The main country factors which have to be considered in pricing decisions are:

- currency;
- inflation;
- government regulations, tariffs, and taxes.

Currency Considerations

One of the key elements in international trade is the currency used for invoicing. Exchange rate risk could be transferred to buyers if they agree to pay using the exporter's currency. However, in many transactions there is no choice, as trade conventions are standard. For example, crude oil trading is done in United States dollars only.

Quite often, small or medium-sized companies refuse to pay for imports in any currency other than their own. This behavior is often related to excessive exchange rate volatility and the associated risk.

Financial and currency crises are frequent, typically in emerging countries. Exchange rates, such as the $/€ or yen/$, are flexible and not easily predictable, even in the short run. Changes in exchange rates alter the firm's ability to compete, therefore affecting international pricing strategies.

A weakening of a domestic currency can stimulate exports and also create new market opportunities. As the dollar began to weaken in the early 2000s, a small United States boat sail manufacturer saw it as an opportunity to enter the competitive European market with its new-found price advantage. Hampered by 14 percent tariffs, Neil Pryde Sails International had not been able to compete in this large market. However, with the dollar losing nearly 25 percent of its value against the euro, the company's products became about 10 percent cheaper than those of their European rivals, allowing it to nearly double its sales in that region.[31]

Purchasing power parity theory can shed some light on long run exchange rate movements. The theory states that the very same good or basket of tradable goods should sell for the same price in different countries when measured in a common currency, taking into account transaction costs as well. The Economist's Big Mac Index represents a practical example (Table 11.2).

TABLE 11.2 The Economist's Big Mac Index: Some Examples	Big Mac Prices		Implied PPP of the Dollar	Actual Exchange Rate	Under (–) / Over (+) Valuation Against Dollar (%)
	In Local Currency	In $			
USA	$4.80	4.80			
India	Rupee 105.00	1.75	21.90	60.09	–63.6
Norway	Kroner 48.0	7.76	10.01	6.19	+61.8

Note: PPP = Purchasing Power Parity

Source: Adapted from: (2014), 'The big mac index', *The Economist*, July 24, 2014, http://www.economist.com/content/big-mac-index [Accessed: March 4, 2015]

The basket consists of a similar product produced in 57 countries: a McDonald's Big Mac. According to Table 11.2, Indian producers enjoy a comparative advantage, as they can sell the Big Mac for 105.00 Rupee or $1.75, according to the actual exchange rate of 60.09 (105.00R/60.09 = 1.75$), while the price in America is $4.80. In case of PPP (i.e. same price of Big Mac in the United States), the Rupee should have been changed at 21.90 (105.00 Rupee / 4.80$); that is, 63.6 percent less when compared to the actual exchange rate (21.90–60.09)/60.09). Indian exports to the United States would change both local prices, via demand, supply and forex, appreciating the Rupee versus the US dollar. Actually, the local price in India entails an undervaluation of the Rupee by 63.6 percent and equivalently an overvaluation of the US dollar.[32]

Inflation and Price Decisions

Inflation should be taken into account when pricing. The challenge is to manage different inflation rates in multiple countries while maintaining a price position. If inflation is high in the production country, a company may not be able to adjust prices as necessary in order to cover rising costs. The company may be forced to absorb the added costs resulting in a decrease of margins. Nevertheless, in these cases the alternative is the decision between maintaining a competitive presence in a foreign market and waiting for a recovery of the economic cycle, or abandoning the market, with a high cost and risk of not being able to enter again in the future. On the other hand, if inflation is high in the customer's country, a price increase may be necessary, taking into consideration customer reaction, government controls, and operative costs related to price changes such as updating price tags, and reprogramming cash registers. In price negotiations, the company must also cover the risk of payment delay if the customer is located in an inflationary market, because the real price paid would be lower.[33]

Government Regulations, Tariffs, and Taxes

Government regulations, tariffs, taxes, quotas, and various non-tariff barriers are further elements a company has to take into consideration. It is rather common to have to deal with government intervention introduced to maintain trade balances, develop domestic industries, and defend local employment and national security. For example, some countries introduce the above barriers to ensure that local production is not at a disadvantage relative to imports from other foreign countries. Some interference in the market can also be due to political reasons.

Government regulations are frequent in many industries. For example, the National Pharmaceutical Pricing Authority (NPPA) in India has recently imposed price controls on 652 "active ingredients" used to treat diseases ranging from diabetes to HIV/AIDS. The goal is to improve access to healthcare for the 70 percent of the population living on less than US$2 a day. With price reductions ranging from 25 to almost 50 percent, many global companies such as GlaxoSmithKline (Geo Map 11.2) and Eli Lilly, leading suppliers in the country, are facing a dramatic reduction of profit margins that might cause supply shortages with a reduction

GEO MAP 11.2
GlaxoSmithKline
Source: Adapted from: CIA Maps, The World Factbook[34]

The headquarters of **GlaxoSmithKline** are in London, England.

of exports into India. Meanwhile, this reduction can also have a negative effect on local companies that may decide to reduce R&D if their margins are affected. Last but not least, the risk is to improve the imports of low price drugs from other countries, determining a concern over quality in the Indian pharmaceutical market.[35]

The government can also influence pricing positions introducing subsidies to reduce local prices to increase domestic companies' local or global competitiveness. For example, after the Chinese government increased its energy subsidies to the steel industry, the country's local production and exports rose significantly. In some cases, exports of government subsidized products are considered a form of dumping in the importing country.[36] Nevertheless, government subsidies can also force a company to make strategic product modifications in order to be price competitive. For example, both Ford in Europe and General Motor's Saab division quickly converted some of their cars destined for the Swedish market to use the modified E85 fuel, which is made of 85 percent ethanol and 15 percent gasoline, because Sweden began subsidizing ethanol fuel.[37] Subsidies are diffused in some industries, for example in the energy sector. Nevertheless, due to austerity and budget deficits during the economic crisis, some countries are, for example, cutting the annual petrol subsidies, with a lot of local protests and pressures: such is the case of Indonesia and Malaysia, with petrol price and energy bills going up by 44 percent and 15 percent respectively.[38]

Tariffs and taxes are other instruments of local protection, used to increase the domestic price of an imported product. The Mercosur area, for example, introduced a taxation system on imports so high as to make it almost compulsory for many companies that wanted to operate in Latin America to opt for foreign direct investment. And despite efforts on an international level to develop fair agreements that encourage free commerce guaranteeing competition, there have been many attempts to evade them. A clear example is the new "green tax" introduced in China in the automobile industry. With the aim to encourage foreign car manufacturers to use more local suppliers and reduce imports, China has imposed a special 25 percent tariff on imported car parts, in addition to the usual 25 percent tariff requested for imported new cars. The tariff was eliminated by the WTO, but less than a month later China introduced a new 40 percent tax on sales of cars exceeding an engine capacity of 4.1 liters. The official scope was to reduce fuel consumption and pollution, but it seems not to be a coincidence that this characteristic is typical of foreign cars.[39] In fact, around three quarters of the overall Chinese market is controlled by foreign carmakers and their local partners: imported cars of companies such as Volkswagen's luxury division, Audi, BMW, and Mercedes are twice as expensive in China than in overseas markets (Figure 11.2). The companies argue that most of the price differences result from import duties and taxes in China, but the China Automobile Dealers Association (CADA) is collecting the information for a government agency to investigate if foreign carmakers are actually making exorbitant profits selling imported luxury cars in China.[40]

FIGURE 11.2
Foreign Car Brands
in China
Source: © Author

Objectives, Strategies, and Pricing Policies

In planning international pricing strategies, differences between countries and company objectives have to be taken into consideration. Price decisions will therefore be influenced by variables such as short- versus long-term internationalization objectives, entry modes, competitive strategies, and profit and cost factors.

A company's ability to efficiently choose and pursue specific strategies that are considered more suitable to its objectives will strongly depend on the possibility to control the final product price. The export pricing control level is correlated with internal organizational factors, such as:[41]

- the degree of centralization

- company size and experience

- channel dependence

- manufacturer asset specificity.

Centralized decision-making in international pricing leads to higher control of final prices and of their coordination across different countries. More experienced firms understand the complexity of foreign operations and prefer to internalize and centralize pricing decisions. Larger firms have the human and financial resources necessary to support foreign distributors, monitor prices, and acquire the information necessary to control prices in export channels. Channel dependence is another relevant variable affecting price control, because if the company significantly depends on intermediaries that have the power to determine their profit margins, the control on the final price becomes very problematic. Finally, asset specificity in the export country (i.e. specialized investments supporting the distribution function in a specific foreign market) increases the degree of pricing control. In fact, dedicated investments increase distributor dependency on the manufacturer, enabling it to reduce opportunistic behaviors and impose authority in order to exercise a high degree of control in price setting.

Becoming a profitable exporter does not depend on one particular pricing strategy but on a **combination of the strategies**. What is important is the existence of a **rational and consistent strategy that fits the company's goals** as it expands in foreign markets. In fact, the proliferation of prices and pricing strategies across channels, geographies, and brands, can cause problems. In some cases, consumer packaged goods companies are forced to deal with millions of price points every year. Clearly, achieving profitable pricing in all of these instances is a challenge even for the most disciplined companies.[42] However, technology is today supporting pricing decisions, for example thanks to the possibility of using technology platforms to analyze big data (Box 11.3).

Box 11.3   Technology-in-Focus: Using Big Data to Make Pricing Decisions

Big data identify any collection of data sets that are too large for the processing capacity of conventional database systems. However, new technologies related to big data applications can offer many opportunities of exploiting this large amount of data with the goal of driving a company's business and becoming the backbone of value creation. Pricing is one component of value creation and companies can significantly benefit from the analysis of the large amount of data available from consumer interactions, public and proprietary sources, retailers, web communities, etc. Top big data analytic platforms such as SAP, Oracle, Teradata, 1010data, and many others, can make possible the shift from time-consuming, manual practices for setting prices, to high-technology platforms that allow large companies to get granular and manage the complexity of pricing variables, constantly changing for thousands of products. Granular data means data written in every invoice, and segmented by product, by customer, by packaging. A big data analytic platform provides price guidance at the level of individual deals, decision-escalation points, incentives, performance scoring in different countries and for different customer segments.

The first companies to use big data for testing factors that drive performance have been Web-based companies, such as Amazon.com, eBay, and Google, as well as financial institutions, which could analyze an enormous amount of data from their customer database. Companies such as Ford Motor, PepsiCo, and Southwest Airlines are doing the same; analyzing consumer postings about them on social networks such as Facebook and Twitter, to evaluate the immediate impact of their marketing campaigns and to understand consumer sentiments about their brands.

It is estimated that up to 30 percent of the thousands of pricing decisions companies make every year fail to deliver the best price, resulting in lost revenue. This is even more complex when operations are carried out in foreign markets. Harnessing big data to find the best price at the product level, not the category level, could benefit the company with higher margins and less failures.

Sources: Baker, W., Kiewell, D. and Winkler. (2014), 'Using big data to make better pricing decisions', June, 2014, *McKinsey Quarterly*, http://www.mckinsey.com/insights/marketing_sales/using_big_data_to_make_better_pricing_decisions [Accessed: March 12, 2015]; Dunbill, E. (2014), 'Defining big data', *Forbes*, http://www.forbes.com/sites/edddumbill/2014/05/07/defining-big-data/, [Accessed: May 2, 2015]; Bughin, J., Chui, M., and Manyika J. (2010), 'Clouds, big data, and smart assets: Ten tech-enabled business trends to watch', *McKinsey Quarterly*, http://www.mckinsey.com/insights/high_tech_telecoms_internet/clouds_big_data_and_smart_assets_ten_tech-enabled_business_trends_to_watch [Accessed: January 23, 2015]; Henshen, D. (2014), '16 top big data analytics platforms', January 30, 2014, *Information Week*, http://www.informationweek.com/big-data/big-data-analytics/16-top-big-data-analytics-platforms/d/d-id/1113609?image_number=2 [Accessed: January 23, 2015].

There are a number of **strategic alternatives or approaches to setting interna-tional prices:**

- cost versus market-based approach;

- new product pricing: skimming versus penetration pricing;

- standardization versus adaptation approach;

- centralized versus decentralized approach;

- preparedness for internationalization and industry globalization: pricing strat-egy prototypes.

COST- VERSUS MARKET-BASED APPROACH

Cost-Based Method

The cost-based method focuses on setting prices by fixing a profit margin over established product costs and thus ensures a more stable, predictable profit. This method has a serious weakness because it ignores demand and competition in foreign markets. In fact, it is based on the equation:

$$cost + margin = price.$$

The cost-based method includes **three alternative options:**[43]

- full-cost pricing

- incremental-cost pricing

- profit-contribution pricing.

Full-cost pricing represents the sum of total unit costs attributed to a product (direct production costs, direct marketing costs, allocated production, and other overheads) plus a profit margin. It is very easy to determine, and it guarantees that each sales transaction is profitable. However, indirect costs are arbitrarily allocated. Furthermore, ignoring demand and competition, it does not consider the price influence on sales volume. As a consequence, it fails to take into consideration the effect of price on production volume and therefore on total unit costs. Finally, if the determined price is not competitive, profit margins may be cut, with the result of obtaining a less-than-full-cost price.

Incremental-cost pricing distinguishes between variable costs and fixed costs. Based on this distinction, this approach takes into consideration production and marketing costs that the company must face when exporting. Incremental produc-tion and marketing costs plus a profit margin will determine the final price. Take into consideration a German company selling sport apparel in the US. When the company entered the US, they had to pay to translate the catalogue in English, adapt the product labels and packaging, etc. All of these costs had to be considered. But if they successively decide to enter the Canadian market, they can use the same catalogues and packaging, and they can determine the final price considering only the incremental costs of adapting the labels and the packaging with the integration of the French language that is required in Canada. Through this method, a company defines a floor price that cannot be lowered or it will result in a loss.

Profit-contribution pricing takes into consideration demand elasticity. The demand curve shape and demand elasticity abroad can significantly differ from the domestic market due to different preferences, buyer behaviors, and competition. A company must determine how total sales revenue will fluctuate in relation to price changes. Profit contribution represents the difference between incremental revenues and incremental cost of exporting in a foreign target market. The best price occurs when the highest profit contribution is generated (Table 11.3). In the example, the best price is €6,60, corresponding to the highest profit contribution.

Market-Based Method

The market-based method requires a much more dynamic approach that takes into consideration not only costs but also competitors' prices and how much consumers are willing to pay. Hence this method is based on the equation:

$$affordable\ unit\ price - margin = target\ cost.$$

Using the above, a company can calculate the maximum target cost backwards, starting from the affordable unit price (determined considering competition and consumers) and then determining a suitable profit margin. For example, a Belgian manufacturer selling beer found that the affordable unit price for Polish consumers was €3 per bottle. Considering not only the profit margin for the Belgian company but also the margins due to the importer and the retailer, the manufacturer's target costs should have been €1 per bottle. If the costs (production, distribution, etc.) for the company were higher than €1 per bottle, the Polish market would have been unprofitable. If they are lower than €1, the Belgian company can also have an extra profit margin.

TABLE 11.3 Profit Contribution Pricing: An Example of a French Company Exporting Wine in the German Market	Price (€/Liter)	Estimated Sales Volume (Liters)	Incremental Revenue (000 €)	Incremental Cost (000 €)	Profit Contribution (000 €)
	8,00	0	0	0	0
	7,50	220.000	1650,00	990,00	660,00
	6,60	380.000	2508,00	1635,00	**873,00**
	6,25	400.000	2500,00	1700,00	800,00
	Source: Compiled by Author				

Given the competitive environment in global markets, the latter approach is much more appropriate for exporting firms,[44] especially in countries where it is the market and competition that drive the company in its price decisions.

NEW PRODUCT PRICING: SKIMMING VERSUS PENETRATION PRICING

A skimming strategy is based on the concept that a company can charge some consumer segments higher prices for a product. Starting from the high end of the market, which represents the "cream" (i.e. consumers who are willing to pay more), price is successively lowered to reach all other segments, achieving maximum profitability from different target consumers. This strategy results in high margins, but there are numerous risks. High prices should be justified by distinctive product features, while competitors should not be aggressive. Furthermore, the company has to take the risk of creating a market easily conquered by other competitive products. Finally, if price is lower in the domestic market, there is always the possibility of favoring parallel imports.[45] An example of a company using a skimming pricing is Apple. The average cost of a new iPhone is $609, compared with $249 for smartphones globally. The Apple Watch has a starting price of $349. The company has the possibility to implement a skimming strategy for some main reasons. First of all thanks to the technological and design appeal that differentiates its products from competitive products. For example, the Apple Watch is a triumph of design and technology: its tiny device contains sensors that measure the user's pulse to help in fitness activities, and people can communicate by sending their heartbeat as a new sort of expressive message to other watch-wearers. Secondly, Apple has been able to target a "luxury global niche" of loyal consumers that are willing to buy the new products despite the high introductory price. Finally, Apple consumers use software and services that locks into the firm's platform for life. Obviously, the risk of this strategy is high because rivals like Samsung, Huawei, Lenovo, and LG, with their cheaper phones, and Google's Android operating system, which runs on 71 percent of the world's smartphones, can erode the segment of Apple's loyal consumers.[46]

On the other hand, penetration pricing sets a low price for the new product in order to enter a foreign market, and often tends to base its communication campaign on this same strategy. Penetration pricing allows the company to quickly penetrate the market and obtain a significant market share, hence gaining market awareness and economies of scale related to production and distribution. This strategy is efficient when consumers are price sensitive, enabling the company to gain a competitive advantage against competition. The attractiveness of a penetration price must be evaluated not only as a strategy to gain market share, but also how it affects the company's overall global business strategy. For example, there are 886 million active mobile subscriptions in India, i.e. a cellular penetration rate of 70 percent. However, India has only 243 million Internet users and this is offering a big opportunity to smartphone producers that can penetrate the market with low-cost products. This is what local competitors are doing, continuing to gain market share at the expense of both Samsung and Apple. In fact, the Indian mobile brands Micromax, Karbonn, and Spice, are collaborating with Google, that is pushing smartphones that cost as little as 6,399 rupees (about $105). But the cheapest price goes to the new phones from Mozilla that recently introduced Firefox smartphones costing as little as 1,999 rupees.[47]

STANDARDIZATION VERSUS ADAPTATION OF PRICING POLICIES

When entering foreign markets, a company can set the same price in different markets or adapt pricing policies to local market conditions.

Price standardization implies the same price positioning strategy across different markets. Factors that are potentially important in influencing the price standardization level are the economic and legal environment, distribution infrastructure, customer characteristics and behavior, and product life cycle stage.[48] Basically, a standardization strategy is possible when the company operates in global sectors. It often becomes necessary when the company sells to global retailers. The retailers expect the product to be delivered at the same price in each country. If this does not happen, they would concentrate their purchases in the country where the product is offered at the lowest price. For example, a multinational company discovered that one of its most important brands of deodorant had a price difference between Switzerland and Portugal of 80 percent, and that European retailers could very conveniently buy the product in Portugal and sell it in other countries. The company immediately reacted, reducing the price gap to a maximum of 20 percent. This difference doesn't enable opportunistic behavior, because the price advantage for the retailer is eliminated by higher transportation costs. In general, it is necessary to negotiate a global-pricing contract between the supplier and the customer.

Price adaptation occurs when a company is compelled to adopt a different price positioning strategy, owing to heterogeneities in consumers' preferences, product perception, the intensity of competition, and country-of-origin effect. Global giants such as IBM and Coca-Cola have been adamant about maintaining consistent pricing for their distributors across the world. However, they and many other large companies have modified their strategy in low-income but emerging markets such as India and China, much to the dismay of their distributors in developed countries.[49]

Adaptation can be evaluated not only in relation to the final listed price, but also in reference to the entire transaction. Managing transaction pricing means determining which discounts, allowances, payment terms, bonuses, etc., should be applied to single transactions. To this end, the behavior of companies can be different, as described as follows.

Some companies opt for one fixed discount scale based on the overall quantity ordered by the client/distributor (for example, a 3 percent discount if the client buys more than a certain quantity). Following this approach can be easy to apply and transparent with clients/distributor, because they all benefit from the same discounts if they reach the goals. The main problem is that, considering the foreign markets targeted by a company, big clients/distributors are favored because they easily get the discounts. On the other hand, in countries where market potential is still small and for this reason it would be more important to strengthen the investment, small distributors can find it difficult to grow.

To overcome the limits of a fixed discount, some international companies apply a pay per performance approach. With this method, where the main goal is to improve the performance of clients/distributors, the discount depends on different variables. For example, it can vary from 0 to 4 percent in relation to:

- 0.5 percent—total sales in the country/geographical area
- 1.0 percent—sales growth
- 0.5 percent—market share
- 0.5 percent—number of clients
- 0.5 percent—percent of key clients
- 0.5 percent—in-store activities developed by the client/distributor
- 0.5 percent—assortment growth.

Since the goal of the discount is to improve the performance of clients/distributors, the transaction price will be different (adaptation) not only country by country, but also among clients/distributors operating in different geographical areas within the same country.

Price Dumping

When adaptation requires exporting at lower prices than those quoted in the importer's country, dumping may occur. Dumping is defined as selling products in a foreign country (importing country) below the price of that product in the domestic market (exporting country), with the objective of obtaining relevant market shares in the foreign country. Dumping can also be used to get rid of excess of inventory, but it leads to the same result of undermining competition.[50] However, dumping is controlled by many laws developed both at national (to hedge local companies against dumping) and international levels. This legislation is designed to counter unfair price competition but it can also be used as a barrier to trade (non-tariff barrier). Since the creation of the WTO in 1995, anti-dumping activities have been reduced. Nevertheless anti-dumping investigations are still numerous, with China being the biggest target.[51]

Parallel Imports or Gray Markets

Parallel imports (sometimes referred to as gray—or grey—market goods) occur when products, purchased in low price markets, are diverted to other markets without the authorization of the manufacturer or the brand owner. These products are priced lower than goods sold by authorized distributors in the target market. The goods have been manufactured by, or for, or under license from the brand owner (they are not counterfeit goods), but they may have been formulated or packaged for a particular geographical area where, for example:

- the competitive situation requires a lower price;

- the target consumers have a limited purchasing power, which is typical of low-income countries.

The price can be lower also because the exchange rate makes the product cheaper, the taxes are lower, or because the wholesalers had been able to benefit from big discounts in buying higher quantities. In fact, in many cases, parallel imports come from authorized wholesalers which start to sell the products to other countries without any authorization, to get more profits or to get rid of excess inventory.[52] An example of parallel import can be found in the export of wine from Hong Kong to Mainland China: a case of Château Lafite bought in Hong Kong and undeclared on arrival in China enables a saving of as much as 3,000 yuan, corresponding to about $500.[53] It is not difficult to understand why wholesalers try to buy in the low-priced Hong Kong market to sell in the rest of China.

If a company wants to minimize the risk of parallel imports, some guidelines can be followed:[54]

- First of all, a standardized pricing strategy, reducing price disparities across markets, is actually preferable. If the price differential is low, opportunities for opportunistic behaviors are less.

- A second strategy to avoid parallel imports is to clearly communicate that the product is different and for this reason it fits with one market but it can be less attractive or it doesn't work for another market. For example, DVD players are region-locked and they only play DVDs encoded to their region or without any region code. Therefore, wholesalers cannot buy low priced DVDs, for example, in the US market, and sell them in Europe.

- Finally, after-sales services can be planned and managed in order to avoid parallel imports. In fact, a consumer can buy a car in the parallel import market but the risk can be high because if the product guarantee is not international, it will not be valid for his/her own country.

CENTRALIZATION VERSUS DECENTRALIZATION

Centralized versus decentralized decision-making in international pricing is a rather critical issue in a company's strategies, especially in the case of multinational companies (MNCs). The conditions that can push MNCs toward a centralized pricing choice or toward decentralized pricing are numerous. Reasons that favor centralization can be summarized as follows.[55]

- Increasing globalization requires standardized prices in different markets, or there would be a risk of the development of parallel imports that are difficult to control. This is also true in regards to the globalization of retailers, who can develop an opportunistic behavior of buying the product in another country where the price is lower.

- Internationalization of competition and homogenization of competitive structure requires globally coordinated competitive strategies.

- Price decisions are often closely related to production volume planning, production capacity, economies of scale, etc. Hence, centrally directed prices facilitate the forecast of worldwide annual revenues, and this activity is performed at the corporate level.

- Finally, price positioning is a relevant component of brand image. Global positioning requires price homogeneity, which is coordinated better centrally by the company headquarters.

Similarly, there are many reasons that can lead a company to prefer a decentralization strategy:[56]

- Local prices are a necessity if the company has to target different price segments in different countries or if the competitive structure is different. In some cases, especially if the company is a price follower, the company has to set local prices to react to price changes of competitive leading products.

- Decentralization is necessary when there are significant differences in end-user characteristics (typically a lower income), in price sensitivity, and in consumer preferences.

- Flexibility in local price setting is often required when specific factors such as added taxes, product adaptation costs, differences in transportation costs, and local economic and financial conditions (e.g. interest rates and inflation) cause situations that induce a company to diverge from the standard corporate guidelines.

- Decentralization in price setting can also be related to different retail power, which forces local managers to reduce selling prices. On the other hand, terms and conditions diverging across different countries can also impose price decentralization.

What clearly emerges is how some of these factors are strictly linked to the alternative choice between standardization and adaptation. Similarly, the final decision is a balanced approach between centralization and decentralization.

PRICING STRATEGY PROTOTYPES

Some researchers have suggested that companies' pricing strategies are influenced by the industry in which they operate and by the firms' own level of experience when selling internationally, and thus can be sorted into **four general pricing prototypes:**[57]

1. local price follower

2. global price follower

3. multi-local price setter

4. global price leader.

As identified by the authors of the research, a multi-domestic industry where the exporter shows low preparedness for internationalization identifies a "local price follower." The exporter has little knowledge of foreign market conditions. Information is received from local agents and distributors; this information, which can sometimes be altered to pursue personal interests, often lacks local insight and market knowledge. This induces the exporter to be local cost-oriented and competitor-based, which results in setting different prices for each of its foreign markets.

The "global price follower" has limited internationalization experience but operates in a more globalized industry characterized by standardized prices across different countries, mainly set by global price leaders. They are sometimes able to target special niches where they can set higher prices associated with better quality. Nevertheless, they are under constant pressure by local distributors and by pricing strategies of competitive global brands.

The third typology is the "multi-local price setter." International experience allows these firms to control and receive adequate feedback from their distributors, adapting price strategies to local requirements and to each country's market conditions. They are often price leaders and implement this multi-local approach by leaving pricing decision-making to the autonomy of local subsidiary managers. Nevertheless, the latter are often induced to align their prices across different subsidiaries in order to avoid gray market imports.

The "global price leader" can be considered among the major "chess players" within its industry at a global level.[58] They often target and dominate a transnational segment where prices are rather homogeneous. Their price level tends to be higher, often resulting in a lower market penetration compared to multi-local competitors who are more adapted to the needs of domestic consumers and distributors.

TRANSFER PRICING

Transfer pricing is the price set and paid for products shipped between units of the same organization. The unit can be a division, a foreign subsidiary, or a joint venture. Not only will these prices determine duties and taxes that are relevant for customs and tax authorities, but they will also affect the profitability of the divisions involved in intra-corporate exchange. The latter is particularly critical when the foreign unit is an intermediary, whose financial performance strongly depends on transfer price levels.

Different methods can be used to determine transfer price:

- cost-plus pricing;

- market-based transfer price;

- negotiated transfer prices;

- arm's-length transfer pricing.

The cost-plus pricing method uses product costs as a base for determining final price.

The market-based transfer price is based on the market price of goods, services, or know-how internally transferred. Hence it would be the local market price minus the margin to be obtained by the subsidiary to cover its costs.[59]

The negotiated transfer price applies when market prices frequently change.[60] In these cases a constant internal price becomes a necessity between subsidiaries.

The arm's-length transfer price is based on the results of a hypothetical negotiation with an independent business partner. The limitations of applying this method are numerous. Not only is data extremely hard to obtain, but there can also be significant difficulties in identifying the right market price in the open market, since most of the time there are no substitutes or the quality of similar products and services is different. In addition, suppliers' cost structures can be significantly different, determining a non-comparability of the alternative offers. Actually, for products flowing from the parent company to its foreign subsidiaries, transfer prices are determined at a higher level than arm's-length prices when the company finds it beneficial to maximize profit in the domestic market. Reasons can include the following:[61]

- corporate income tax is higher in the foreign country than in the parent country;

- a significant political risk of nationalization exists or expropriation of high profit foreign firms;

- the foreign country is characterized by political instability and/or a high inflation rate;

- the desire of the parent company is to mask foreign profitability, keeping competitors out of the market.

TERMS AND METHODS OF PAYMENT

Payment methods regulate commercial relations between all parties directly or indirectly involved in the exchange of goods and services. Parties such as the exporter, the importer, and importer and exporter banks, can be directly involved. On the other hand, third parties such as other banks or professional traders involved in the financial arrangement can, at the same time, be indirectly involved in the transaction.

Payment methods are characterized by different risk levels. For this reason, it is always advisable to insure export orders against non-payment. The following are the available payment methods, starting from the most secure:[62]

Advance payment—The payment, which can be done with a bank transfer, is cleared before the goods are shipped. This method is typical in the case of high-risk countries or low reliability of the customer. It is also preferred by small and medium enterprises which cannot be exposed for a long-term period. To avoid possible alterations in the communication of payment, it is usually preferable to create a direct link between the seller's and the buyer's banks.

Letters of credit—This method can be considered a guarantee more than a method of payment. In fact, it is an undertaking by a bank to make a payment to the supplier (seller), against the presentation of documents that certify the transaction. Its main advantage is providing security to the exporter, because if the payment occurs regularly, the letter will not be activated. Vice versa, the exporter will send the documents to the bank, which will then proceed with the payment. Also, an importer may open a letter of credit in order to ensure that the exporter or seller has correctly performed the requirements of the sales contract. However, the main disadvantage of the letter of credit is related to the additional costs resulting from bank charges.

Documentary collection—This is a process developed to facilitate import and export operations. After shipping the goods to the customer, the exporter sends the related shipping documents (necessary for the buyer to obtain the goods and clear them through customs) to its bank, which will conclude the payment and satisfy all the related requested payments of the exporter. The bank can send the shipping documents to the buyer after receiving the payment ("documents against payments") or after receiving the acceptance of a bill of exchange issued by the seller ("documents against acceptance").

Open account—This method of payment is highly risky because the goods are shipped before payment; therefore, it is recommended only when none of the above methods are suitable or when there is a complete trust between the exporter and the importer. In an open account, the credit will be paid at a future date, and the terms can be 30 or 60 days or more. It is recommended to check the buyer's credit reliability because of the high risk level.

COUNTERTRADE

Countertrade is an umbrella term that encompasses the trading or exchange of goods or services without using currency. A variety of trading practices are included, from the simple exchange of goods for goods at an agreed value (barter) to more complex export transactions. An example of a countertrade agreement is the one signed between Lockheed Martin (US) and the Norwegian government requiring the company to contract with Norwegian companies for goods and services in exchange for Norway's purchase of jet planes.[63]

According to the London Countertrade Roundtable (LCR), countertrade practices can vary according to local regulations and requirements, to the nature of the goods to be exported, and to the current priorities of the parties involved in the deal.[64]

From a marketing point of view, the main advantages given by countertrade are:

- The potential to capitalize excess capacity and transforming unproductive assets in profitable deals, helping domestic industries to find new foreign markets.

- The capacity to stimulate trade between markets that are unable to pay for imports; for example, because of lack of commercial credit or having a non-convertible currency.

There are many forms of countertrade. Nevertheless, as pointed out by the London Countertrade Roundtable, deals frequently involve several countertrade arrangements instead of fitting into only one specific category.

SUMMARY

- Price is one of the more challenging decisions of a global marketing program. Defining a correct global pricing strategy is fundamental to long-term success.
- Price must reflect the value that the consumer is willing to pay for the company's product.
- Factors influencing international pricing decisions can be categorized into competitive factors, consumer factors, country factors, product factors and distribution channels, and company factors.
- There are several strategic alternatives or approaches to be considered when setting international prices: cost- versus market-based approach; new product pricing; standardization versus adaptation; centralized versus decentralized approach; alternative pricing strategy prototypes.

- The price set and paid for products shipped between units of the same organization is defined as transfer pricing and can be determined using different methods.
- Countertrade refers to the trading or exchange of goods or services without using currency. This can range from simple goods exchanges (barter) to more complex export transactions.

DISCUSSION QUESTIONS

1. What are the factors influencing international pricing decisions? Take the example of a foreign brand that is marketed in your country: what local factors have to be taken into consideration when defining pricing decisions?
2. When you compare prices using the Internet, in what way do you use this information in your buying process?
3. Compare two similar products with a different price positioning (for example, two brands of jeans or motorcycles): what are the factors that affect value creation?
4. What are the advantages and disadvantages of using a cost- versus a market-based approach?
5. When a company launches a new product abroad, what are the opportunities and risks of a skimming versus a penetration pricing policy?
6. In which sectors is gray marketing more frequent? Why? Give some examples.

EXPERIENTIAL EXERCISES

1. How is Mattel managing Barbie's prices in a sensitive price market like China? Listen to the NPR story "Mattel hopes Shanghai is a Barbie world" (http://www.npr.org/templates/story/story.php?storyId=101479810) and describe the marketing strategies that support the upper-end price. In your opinion, how can they compete against cheap copies? After two years, the Barbie flagship store closed in March 2011 (http://www.bbc.co.uk/news/business-12670950). Can you identify the main mistakes of the company?
2. Select a product from your country and develop a pricing strategy in one emerging market of your choice. Identify which factors (competitive, consumer, country, product, and distribution channels) are influencing your international pricing decisions.

KEY TERMS

- Cost-based method
- Countertrade
- Currency
- Dumping
- Full-cost pricing
- Gray marketing
- Incremental cost pricing
- Inflation
- Market-based method
- Monetary price

- Non-monetary price
- Parallel imports
- Payment methods
- Penetration pricing
- Price adaptation
- Price escalation

- Price standardization
- Pricing decisions
- Pricing prototypes
- Profit-contribution pricing
- Skimming strategy
- Transfer pricing

NOTES

1   $7,970 to $9,300, on August 21, 2014.

2   Kröger, S.T. (2013), 'Interview with Volkswagen CEO: 'European auto crisis is an endurance test'', Spiegel Online International, February 13, 2013, http://www.spiegel.de/international/business/interview-with-volkswagen-ceo-martin-winterkorn-a-882918.html [Accessed: March 4, 2015].

3   Hinterhuber, A. and Liozu, S. (2012). 'Is it time to rethink your pricing strategy?', *Mit Sloan Management Review*, June 19, 2012, http://sloanreview.mit.edu/article/is-it-time-to-rethink-your-pricing-strategy/ [Accessed: March 3, 2015].

4   Bonini, S. and Swartz, S. (2014), 'Profits with purpose: How organizing for sustainability can benefit the bottom line', McKinsey on Sustainability & Resource Productivity, July, 2014, McKinsey & Company, http://www.mckinsey.com/search.aspx?q=profits+with+purpose%3A+how+organizing [Accessed: October 13, 2015], pp. 5–15.

5   Heck, S. and Rogers, M. (2014), 'The human factor: Amassing troops for the 'resource revolution'', McKinsey on Sustainability & Resource Productivity, July, McKinsey & Company, http://www.mckinsey.com/search.aspx?q=amassing+troops [Accessed: October 13, 2015], pp. 16–22.

6   Interbrand. (2007), 'Best global brands 2007', http://gtmarket.ru/files/research/Interbrand-globalbrands-2007.pdf [Accessed: October 12, 2015].

7   Fleming, R. (2013), 'Nintendo drops the Wii U price, and 3D from the 3DS', *Digital Trends*, August 28, 2013, http://www.digitaltrends.com/gaming/nintendo-drops-the-wii-u-price-and-3d-from-the-3ds/ [Accessed: October 13, 2015].

8   Interbrand. (2007), 'Best global brands 2007', http://gtmarket.ru/files/research/Interbrand-globalbrands-2007.pdf [Accessed: October 12, 2015].

9   Anderson, M. (2013), 'Cheap razor made after P&G watches Indians shave', October 3, 2013, http://bigstory.ap.org/article/going-homes-make-product-people [Accessed: March 11, 2015].

10 Evers, J. (2004), 'Microsoft rethinks unified pricing strategy company pondering different price points', http://www.infoworld.com/article/2666708/applications/microsoft-rethinks-unified-pricing-strategy.html [Accessed:October 13, 2015].

11 World Population Statistics. (2015), 'China population 2015', http://worldpopulationreview.com/countries/china-population/ [Accessed: October 12, 2015].

12 World Population Statistics. (2015), 'Netherland population 2015', http://worldpopulationreview.com/countries/netherlands-population/ [Accessed: October 12, 2015].

13 Wagstaff, J. and Shih, G. (2014) 'Naked PCs' lay bare Microsoft's emerging markets problem', August 10, 2014, *Reuters Edition*, http://www.reuters.com/article/2014/08/10/microsoft-emergingmarkets-idUSL4N0QE5BF20140810 [Accessed: February 23, 2015].

14 Euromonitor International. (2014), 'Beauty and personal care in Turkey, industry overview', May 30, 2014, www.euromonitor.com [Accessed March 1, 2015].

15 Euromonitor International. (2014), 'Beauty and personal care in India, industry overview', July 24, 2014, www.euromonitor.com [Accessed: March 1, 2015].

16 The World Factbook. (2015), https://www.cia.gov/library/publications/the-world-factbook/docs/refmaps.html [Accessed: August 1, 2015].

17 Monroe, K. B. (1990). *Pricing. Making profitable decisions*. London: McGraw-Hill; Grewal, D. and Levy, M. (2014). *Marketing*. New York: McGraw-Hill.

18 Perreault, W.Jr. et al. (2014). *Basic marketing*. New York: McGraw-Hill; De Chernatony, L., Harris, F., and Dall'Olmo, R. F. (2000), 'Added value: Its nature, roles and sustainability', *European Journal of Marketing*, 34(1/2), pp. 39–56; Gronroos, C. (1997), 'Value driven relational marketing: From products to resources and competencies', *Journal of Marketing Management*, 13, pp. 407–19; Zeithaml, V. A. (1988), 'Consumer perception of price, quality and value: A means end model and synthesis of evidence', *Journal of Marketing*, 52(3), pp. 2–22.

19 Blythe, J. (2012). *Essential of marketing*. Harlow, Essex: Pearson.

20 Nguyen, A., Heeler, R. M., and Taran, Z. (2007), 'High-low context cultures and price-ending practices', *Journal of Product & Brand Management*, 16(3), pp. 206–14.

21 Usunier, J. and Lee, J. A. (2013). Marketing across cultures. 6th ed. Harlow, England: Prentice Hall, Pearson Education Ltd.

22 Keller, K.L. (2013). *Strategic brand management: Building, measuring, and managing brand equity*. Upper Saddle River, NJ: Prentice Hall.

23 Winit, W., Gregory, G., Cleveland, M., and Verlegh, P. (2014), 'Global vs local brands: How home country bias and price differences impact brand evaluations', *International Marketing Review*, 31(2), pp. 102–28.

24 Euromonitor International. (2012). 'Convenience and low prices: The appeal of modern grocery retailing in Latin America', www.euromonitor.com [Accessed: February 26, 2015].

25 Feliciano, J. (2013), 'Smaller packaging increases access, raises value in emerging Asian markets', *Euromonitor*, October, 2013, www.euromonitor.com [Accessed: February 26, 2015].

26 http://www.tencent.com/en-us/at/abouttencent.shtml

27 Gillespie, K., Jeannet, J-P., and Hennessey, D. (2010). *Global marketing*. 3rd ed. Mason, OH: South Western Educational Publishing; Cavusgil, T. S. (1988), 'Unravelling the mystique of export pricing', *Business Horizons*, 31(3), pp. 54–63.

28 Ewing, J. (2007), 'First mover in mobile: How Nokia is selling cell phones to the developing world', *Business Week*, May 4, 2007, http://www.bloomberg.com/bw/stories/2007-05-04/first-mover-in-mobilebusinessweek-business-news-stock-market-and-financial-advice [Accessed: January 3, 2015].

29 Friend, E. (2014), 'Domino's keys to success in India: Local menu, local pricing, and local outlet strategy', *Euromonitor International*, January 10, 2014, www.euromonitor.com [Accessed: February 28, 2015].

30 HIS. (2014), 'A critical pricing strategy for optimizing sales in emerging markets', http://www.ihs.com/info/0614/tiered-pricing-strategies.aspx [Accessed: February 25, 2015].

31 Wahlgren, E. (2003), 'Trade winds. Inc', November, 2003, www.inc.com/magazine/20031101/casestudy.html [Accessed: February 26, 2015].

32 (2014), 'The big mac index', *The Economist*, July 24, 2014, http://www.economist.com/content/big-mac-index [Accessed: February 15, 2015].

33 Lascu, D.N. (2013). *International marketing*. 4th ed. Saint Paul, MN: Textbook Media Press; Mühlbacher, H., Leihs, H., and Dahringer, L. (2006). *International marketing: A global perspective*. London: Thomson Learning.

34 The World Factbook. (2015), https://www.cia.gov/library/publications/the-world-factbook/docs/refmaps.html [Accessed: August 1, 2015].

35 Economist. (2014), 'Pricing pressures mount', July 28, 2014, http://www.eiu.com/industry/article/1022100686/pricing-pressures-mount/2014-07-28 [Accessed: March 3, 2015].

36 Dumping takes place when products are sold in other countries' markets below cost or below domestic prices, with the objective of obtaining relevant market shares in the foreign countries.

37 Edmondson, G. (2007), 'Europe looks beyond ethanol', *Business Week*, April 27, 2007, www.businessweek.com/print/globalbiz/content/apr2007/gb20070427_164153.htm [Accessed: February 11, 2015].

38 Economist. (2014), 'Fuelling controversy', January 11, 2014, http://www.economist.com/news/finance-and-economics/21593484-economic-case-scrapping-fossil-fuel-subsidies-getting-stronger-fuelling [Accessed: February 15, 2015].

39 Economist. (2008), 'Taking another road', August 21, 2008, www.economist.com/node/11967001 [Accessed: March 2, 2015].

40 Economist. (2013), 'China cars: Carmakers under scrutiny in China amid price-fixing fears', August 14, 2013, http://www.eiu.com/industry/article/420838226/china-cars-carmakers-under-scrutiny-in-china-amid-pricefixing-fears/2013-08-15 [Accessed: March 2, 2015].

41 Myers, M. B., Cavusgil, T. S., and Diamantopoulos, A. (2002), 'Antecedents and actions of export pricing strategy', *European Journal of Marketing*, 36(1–2), pp. 159–88; Cavusgil, T. S. (1996), 'Pricing for global markets', *Columbia Journal of World Business*, 31(4), pp. 67–78.

42 Myers, M. B., Cavusgil, T. S., and Diamantopoulos, A. (2002), 'Antecedents and actions of export pricing strategy', *European Journal of Marketing*, 36(1–2), pp. 159–88; Cavusgil, T. S. (1996), 'Pricing for global markets', *Columbia Journal of World Business*, 31(4), pp. 67–78; Bright, J. K., Kiewell, D., and Kincheloe, A. H. (2006), 'Pricing in a proliferating world', *The McKinsey Quarterly* [web exclusive], www.mckinseyquarterly.com/article_page.aspx?ar=1841 [Accessed: March 5, 2015].

43 Root, F. R. (2008). *Entry strategies for international markets*. San Francisco, CA: Jossey-Bass.

44 Cavusgil, S. T., Chan, K., and Zhang, C. (2003), 'Strategic orientations in export pricing: A clustering approach to create firm taxonomies', *Journal of International Marketing*, 11(1), pp. 47–72.

45 Parallel imports (also known as grey or gray markets) occur when channel members located in low price markets, not authorized by the manufacturer, resell its products to market areas for significantly higher prices.

46 Economist. (2014), 'Watched, the future of Apple', September 10, 2014, http://www.economist.com/news/business-and-finance/21616765-apple-becoming-very-different-company-and-not-just-because-its-newly-unveiled?fsrc=email_to_a_friend [Accessed: March 3, 2015].

47 Einhorn, B. (2014), 'Cheap phones from Google and Mozilla add to Samsung's India problems', *Business Week*, September 15, 2014, http://www.businessweek.com/articles/2014-09-15/googles-cheap-phones-mean-more-india-trouble-for-samsung [Accessed: March 9, 2015].

48 Theodosiou, M. and Katsikeas, C. S. (2001), 'Factors influencing the degree of international pricing strategy standardization of multinational corporations', *Journal of International Marketing*, 9(3), pp. 1–18.

49 Feliciano, J. (2013), 'Smaller packaging increases access, raises value in emerging Asian markets', *Euromonitor*, October, 2013, www.euromonitor.com [Accessed: February 22, 2015]; (2002), 'The price is wrong', *The Economist*, May 23, 2002, www.economist.com/node/1143622 [Accessed: February 25, 2015].

50 Mühlbacher, H., Leihs, H., and Dahringer, L. (2006). *International marketing: A global perspective*. London: Thomson Learning; Lascu, D.N. (2013). *International marketing*. 4th ed. Saint Paul, MN: Textbook Media Press.

51 World Trade Organization. (2014), 'Technical information on anti-dumping', http://www.wto.org/english/tratop_e/adp_e/adp_info_e.htm [Accessed: March 1, 2015].

52 International Trademark Association. (2014), 'What are parallel imports?', http://www.inta.org/Advocacy/Pages/ParallelImportsGrayMarket.aspx [Accessed: March 12, 2015]; Lascu, D.N. (2013). *International marketing*. 4th ed. Saint Paul, MN: Textbook Media Press; Muhlbacher, H., Leihs, H., and Dahringer, L. (2006). *International marketing: A global perspective*. 3rd ed. London: Thomson Learning.

53 Economist. (2013), 'Hong Kong's parallel trade: Days of wine and milk powder', August 16, 2013, http://www.economist.com/blogs/analects/2013/08/hong-kongs-parallel-trade [Accessed: March 10, 2015].

54 Myers, M. B., Cavusgil, T. S., and Diamantopoulos, A. (2002), 'Antecedents and actions of export pricing strategy', *European Journal of Marketing*, 36(1–2), pp. 159–88; Lascu, D.N. (2013). *International marketing*. 4th ed. Saint Paul, MN: Textbook Media Press.

55 Cavusgil, T. S. (1996), 'Pricing for global markets', *Columbia Journal of World Business*, 31(4), pp. 67–78; Bertoli, G. and Valdani, E. (2014). *Mercati internazionali e marketing*. Milano: Egea; Hollensen S. (2013). *Global marketing: A decision oriented approach*. 6th ed. Harlow, England: Prentice Hall.

56 Cavusgil, T. S. (1996), 'Pricing for global markets', *Columbia Journal of World Business*, 31(4), pp. 67–78; Bertoli, G. and Valdani, E. (2010). *Mercati internazionali e marketing*. Milano: Egea; Hollensen, S. (2013). *Global Marketing: A decision oriented approach*. 6th ed. Harlow, England: Prentice Hall.

57 Solberg, C. A., Stöttinger, B., and Yaprak, A. (2006), 'A taxonomy of the pricing practices of exporting firms: Evidence from Austria, Norway, and the United States', *Journal of International Marketing*, 14(1), pp. 23–48.

58 Solberg, C. A. (1997), 'A framework for analysis of strategy development in globalizing markets', *Journal of International Marketing*, 5(1), pp. 9–30.

59 Muhlbacher, H., Leihs, H., and Dahringer, L. (2006). *International marketing: A global perspective*. 3rd ed. London: Thomson Learning.

60 Keegan, W. J. and Green, M. C. (2008). *Global marketing*. 5th ed. Upper Saddle River, NJ: Pearson International Edition.

61 Bradley, F. (2004). *International marketing strategy*. 5th ed. Essex, UK: Pearson Education Limited.

62 Johnson, T. E. and Bade, D. L. (2010). *Export import procedures and documentations*. New York: Amacom; (2014), 'International Terms of Payment', http://www.foreign-trade.com/reference/payment.cfm.

63 Economist. (2012), 'Norway, regulatory/market assessment', January 4, 2012, http://country.eiu.com/article. aspx?articleid=1978712982&Country=Norway&topic=Finance&subtopic=Market+assessment&subsubtopic =Regulatory/market+assessment [Accessed: March 11, 2015].

64 London Countertrade Roundtable. (2011), www.londoncountertrade.org/index.html [Accessed: March 11, 2015].

CHAPTER 12

Global Placement and Distribution Channels

"At VF, we think of ourselves as brand builders, not retailers. It may sound like a subtle distinction. But it makes a big difference in driving our decisions and investments. We work with our portfolio of brands to optimize their growth, while we connect with consumers—in stores and online—to build relationships based on mutual trust and loyalty."

Mike Gannaway, Vice President—VF Direct / Customer Teams[1]

LEARNING OBJECTIVES

After Reading This Chapter, You Should Be Able to:

- Understand the role of distribution in the international marketing mix.
- Identify the main internal and external factors influencing distribution decisions.
- Understand how to manage global placement and international distribution channels.
- Evaluate different types of channel intermediaries.
- Recognize the existence of differences in the retailing system of different countries.
- Analyze the internationalization of retailers.
- Describe the main activities related to physical distribution.

THE POWER OF DISTRIBUTION

Distribution can be very powerful in the development of market penetration worldwide. In fact, after defining the appropriate entry mode for a company targeting a foreign market, the dimensions to be determined are, on the one hand, the definition of distribution channels with all its members: organizations, agents, wholesalers, retailers, etc., who move the product to the final consumer. On the other hand is the organization of physical distribution, which involves logistics activities such as transportation, packaging, inventory, and storage of the product to be exported to another country. Designing and managing efficient international distribution networks should concentrate on giving the final customers product information and accessibility, maintaining profitable distribution, partner relationships, and strengthening the company's global marketing strategy. But the **challenging issues** are: what kind of influencing factors, such as differences in the macroenvironment, the competitive structure, or the distribution system, have to be taken into consideration when designing a distribution network internationally? Which managerial factors are relevant in channel and logistics decisions? What is the involvement level of retailers in the internationalization process? All these issues will be presented and discussed in this chapter, and the importance of distribution decisions in the company's international marketing strategy will be emphasized.

FACTORS INFLUENCING INTERNATIONAL DISTRIBUTION DECISIONS

After defining the entry strategy into a foreign market, a company has to **evaluate the most suitable channels** in terms of structure, management, and control. Several internal and external factors have to be taken into account when a company is planning to build and develop its intended position in the global market. Among the **internal factors** are:

- the international marketing strategy of a company, with a given entry mode strategy and the degree of control that the company aims to reach;

- the distribution strategy, mainly influenced by the objectives of market penetration, the competitive structure, and the financial strength of the company;

- the product complexity;

- the size and development of the company's marketing and sales functions (export department).

On the other hand, **external factors** include:

- the characteristics of the distribution system;

- local regulations;

- the stage of the product's life cycle;

- consumer purchasing and shopping habits;

- market size and density of population;

- the competitive climate.

INTERNAL FACTORS

Company Entry Mode

One of the main elements to take into consideration when making distribution decisions in foreign markets is the company entry mode (Chapter 7) and the degree of control that the company aims to obtain in the foreign market. As a matter of fact, the choice of less risky modes of entry, which do not allow complete control of the foreign marketing strategy (for example, indirect export), often force the company to delegate its distribution choices to a foreign partner, who is autonomously responsible for the product distribution in the country. Intermediate entry modes, strategic alliances, franchising agreements, joint ventures, or greenfield investments allow the company to develop direct or short distribution channels that allow constant monitoring of sales activities abroad.

Distribution Strategy

Another important element is the determination of distribution strategy: does the company want to develop an intensive, selective, or exclusive strategy?

An **intensive distribution strategy** occurs when producers use as many outlets as possible. For example, the France-based Michelin Group is strengthening its presence worldwide with an intensive distribution strategy, integrating its networks not only through acquisitions but also with franchising, aiming to increase its worldwide network of franchising dealers from 2,000 to 5,000 sales outlets by 2017.[2] Moreover, an intensive strategy is common when considering fast-moving goods manufactured by large multinational companies that aim to penetrate their brands to all segments of the population. This goal is far from easy, especially in emerging markets, requiring the development of innovative distribution models. For example Vodafone is targeting about 600,000 villages in rural India, 92 percent of them with fewer than 10,000 residents, thanks to the development of a two-tier distribution model. The main distributors, responsible for a specific area, can directly serve either retailers or, for smaller villages, they can select local retailers to act as associate distributors and serve remote villages for a modest mark up. Today there are about 8,500 associate distributors and the model is profitable both for the company, the main distributors, and the associate distributors. In a very cost effective way, Vodafone is able to intensively cover rural India, with a sales network of 23,000 channel sales people.[3]

Companies such as the Italian Valentino Group, use a **selective distribution strategy**. A selective strategy is based on using fewer but selective intermediaries. In fact, Valentino distributes its high quality products not only through its own stores (exclusive approach) but also penetrates some countries by selecting the finest apparel stores in the main cities. In Figure 12.1, for example, Valentino is distributed in the United States through the luxury specialty department stores of Neimann Marcus.

FIGURE 12.1
Valentino in
Neimann Marcus
US Department
Stores
Source: © Author

Finally, in the case of **exclusive distribution strategy**, the producer gives a limited number of retailers the right to sell its products in their specific territories. In exchange the retailer is generally requested not to sell competitive products. An example of a company using an exclusive strategy is Inditex, the Spanish group famous worldwide for brands like Zara, Pull & Bear, Massimo Dutti, Bershka, Stradivarius, Oysho, Zara Home, and Uterqüe. With a retail network of 6,340 stores in many countries worldwide, the company usually penetrates foreign countries through store chains where only the company's brand is sold. These stores are managed directly by companies in which Inditex holds all or the majority of the share capital (87 percent of the stores), with the exception of certain countries, mainly in the Asia–Pacific area, where the retail selling activity is performed through franchises (13 percent of the stores).[4]

The choice of intensive, selective, or exclusive distribution will depend on the company's market penetration objectives, the competitive structure, and its financial strength. For example, high penetration objectives necessarily require an intensive strategy that cannot be pursued unless strong financial investment is forthcoming.

Product Complexity

Product complexity is another element that needs to be taken into consideration. Given different levels of product complexity, exporters should differentiate their relationship with intermediaries, because complex products require extensive information exchange and interaction in order to solve functional problems related, for example, to product delivery, installation, and after-sales service.[5] Sales people need to be trained and, in some cases, complexity is so high that even top management can be directly involved.

Organization of the Export Department

Finally, one last important element that influences companies' distribution choices is constituted by the characteristics of the export department's internal organization. Organization is defined by the number of managers employed in the department, their international professional background, marketing skills, and their operating budget. Companies that have a very simplified export department are not able to directly manage diverse foreign markets, and as a result, they will tend to opt for indirect distribution choices using local intermediaries and delegating all distribution activities to them despite lower control over the target market.

EXTERNAL FACTORS

Differences in the Distribution System, Logistics, and Transportation Infrastructure

Some external factors play a relevant role in international distribution decisions. A company must often come to terms with differences in the distribution system, logistics, and transportation infrastructure that will influence not only distribution decisions but also their own product and price decisions. For example, the inefficiency of logistics and of transport infrastructure makes it necessary for the company to use local intermediaries that are able to manage any problems that may occur. At the same time, using numerous intermediaries means lower control over the final market and may cause price escalation (Chapter 11) that can make the product unsellable. Similarly, differences in distribution systems require, for example, the use of alternative channels in which both the company and its sales network have no experience.

Take, for example, the beer industry. In some countries such as Germany, Russia, and India distribution is dominated by the off-trade channel (supermarkets, hypermarkets, and specialty retailers), while in countries such as Brazil and Singapore it is the on-trade channel[6] that prevails. The differences that we have just underlined can be determined by various factors such as local regulations, the stage of the product life cycle, shopping habits, market size, and the competitive environment.

Local Regulations

Local regulations are one of the most frequent reasons for differences in the distribution system. For example, a recent study on retail globalization in Southeast Asia underlines that countries (such as Malaysia, Thailand, Vietnam and Indonesia) are exposed to the same international influences that should lead to homogeneity in terms of retail trade policies. Actually these countries are highly diversified in their social, political and economic contexts, determining significant differences in retail policies and regulations.[7]

In China, due to legislative changes, companies such as Mary Kay, Amway, and Avon were no longer permitted to engage in the use of direct marketing. After losing 50 percent of their sales, these companies had to adapt to new regulations which impose on their sales people to go through extensive training and pass an exam administered by local authorities in order to obtain a business license. The law is also very detailed in requiring the direct sellers to wear a badge at all times that sales are being conducted, and fixes the commissions of an individual direct seller at 30 percent of his/her sales (that includes bonuses, commissions, and any other benefit). Nevertheless, differently from Taiwan and Hong Kong, the Chinese law considers multi-level marketing (Chuanxiao) illegal, reporting that any commission payouts of more than one level may be met with legal action.[8]

Stage of the Product Life Cycle

Differences in distribution systems can also be linked to the stage of the product life cycle (Chapter 10). In the introductory stage, market penetration and market coverage are very low; in the growth stage, selective distribution is recommended, while in the maturity stage, intensive distribution is usually required. Hence, companies operating in different countries have to implement different distribution strategies if they are facing different stages of the product life cycle.

Purchasing and Shopping Habits

Other dimensions that need to be considered are consumer purchasing and shopping habits as well as outlet preferences. These represent behaviors that are deeply rooted in the country's culture and are difficult to change. Due to weak response to international investments, Wal-Mart recently closed 29 stores in China and 26 in Brazil. Similarly, in India the agreement with a local distribution partner was abrogated. The main problem faced by Wal-Mart worldwide is the difficulty in understanding local customers and shopping customs in every country served. For example, while in the United States big stores are a symbol of low prices, in China they are considered to be expensive. Secondly, the price advantages offered by Wal-Mart via bulk purchasing, is not appreciated by Chinese and Indian consumers that see sales in bulk as less fresh, and consequently prefer to buy fresher food in smaller stores and in small quantities.[9] Another example is Thailand, where differences in culture and consumer behavior require an adaptation of strategies by international retailers. For instance, in Thai culture time has a low importance, few consumers shop online, they prefer fresh food, and their desire for status limits the diffusion of private labels in the country.[10]

Market Size and Density of Population

Additional external factors that are worth considering are market size and density of population, connected also to the distribution of consumers across the country.

The distribution strategy Procter & Gamble developed to target rural China demonstrates how the company's success, in relation to competition, has been determined by its ability to develop distribution strategies that target a huge market with a rural population spread over a vast area (Box 12.1).

Box 12.1 Company-in-Focus: Procter & Gamble in China

With headquarters located in Guangzhou, Procter & Gamble (P&G) has eleven factories in China, and multiple branches located in Guangzhou, Beijing, Shanghai, Chengdu, Tianjin, Dongguan, and Nanping, as well as a technical center in Beijing developed to gain market insight. In addition to key success factors such as affordability, lower costs, and product adaptation, P&G recognized early on that it needed a robust and flexible distribution network to move into the fast-developing consumer products market of rural China. In addition to conducting thorough market research on consumer tastes and preferences deep within China's interior, P&G is giving a great deal of time and attention to building a large network of distributors that can reach even the most remote villages. Its current distributors cover half a million shops in most towns and cities, and many are now entering ever-smaller populated areas where mom-and-pop stores are the main retail centers. From vans branded with P&G's most popular lines, such as Tide, Safeguard, and Pantene shampoo, these distributors deliver products as well as colorful posters, signage, and other sales props that help establish the company's identity and communication in the local market. But P&G is going a step further: it signed an agreement with China's Ministry of Commerce to update existing stores, build new ones, and teach the local workforce in nearly 10,000 villages how to sell consumer products. These investments are not only part of its distribution strategy, but also of a commitment of contributing to the local community: the over RMB8 million donated in May 2013 by Procter & Gamble for the reconstruction of the city after the devastating Ya'an, Sichuan earthquake, is only one of the many examples of high corporate social responsibility.

With a market share of 13 percent, China is the second largest market for P&G, following the United States. These actions will further boost P&G's presence in rural China, put the company in direct competition with regional and national Chinese enterprises often characterized by lower costs and better market knowledge, and also make it harder for rivals such as Unilever to compete. The Anglo-Dutch company, which lost market share to P&G due to a lack of clear distribution strategy, is now working to catch up. "We have made some errors and that has made us into a wiser company," says Frank Braeken, Unilever's chairman for greater China.

Sources: Euromonitor International. (2014), 'Procter & Gamble (Guangzhou) Ltd in beauty and personal care (China)', 21 May, www.euromonitor.com [Accessed: January 22, 2015]; Roberts, D. (2007), 'Scrambling to bring Crest to the masses in China', *Business Week*, June 25, 2007, http://www.bloomberg.com/bw/stories/2007-06-24/scrambling-to-bring-crest-to-the-masses-in-china [Accessed: October 16, 2015]; Penhirin, J. (2004), 'Understanding the Chinese consumer', *The McKinsey Quarterly* [Special Edition], pp. 46–57. http://mkqpreview2.qdweb.net/PDFDownload.aspx?ar=1468 [Accessed: August 23, 2010]; China Retail News. (2010), 'New president for P&G', *China Retail News*, March 25, 2010, www.chinaretailnews.com/2010/03/25/3467-new-president-for-pg-greater-china/ [Accessed: February 12, 2015].

Competitive Climate

Distribution strategies can also be influenced by choices made by competitors, which have paved the way for sales strategies in the country using specific channels. Moreover, competitors may have exclusive contracts with local retailers or wholesalers, creating entry barriers that tend to bar the company from some key channels. In other instances, competitors own their sales channels, allowing them to stay very close to the local market. Voluntary chain stores developed by Shiseido in Japan and, more recently, in China, that has become the key driver of growth, represent a tool that provides high-quality counseling and services tailored to each consumer's request, and constantly meets customer needs for skincare and makeup. In line with the premium positioning of the brand, direct control of the distribution channel allows Shiseido to train its employees to fully acquire high service skills with high-level techniques and the spirit of *omotenashi* (hospitality; i.e. "enriching people's spirits through interactions between customers and products") in order to respond to customer needs.[11]

MANAGING INTERNATIONAL DISTRIBUTION CHANNELS

From a company's perspective, managing a distribution channel requires many decisions based on the evaluation of the advantages and disadvantages of different options:

1. direct versus indirect channels;

2. conventional distribution channels versus vertical marketing systems (VMS);

3. selection among different types of intermediaries (agents, wholesalers, and retailers) identifying which ones are considered more suitable;

The above decisions can be strongly influenced by many factors such as the country's economic development, the efficiency of intermediaries, and the local government distribution policies.

Direct and Indirect Distribution Channels

In a direct distribution channel, the manufacturer sells directly to the final customer through the Internet, directly operated stores, etc. A channel is indirect when one or more intermediaries (i.e. agent, wholesaler, retailer) are involved in the transaction creating different levels of sales. While direct and indirect strategies are quite different, it is not unusual that both are used in a given country.

Figure 12.2 describes the options pointed out above. Options 1 to 3 represent examples of direct channels, while options 4 to 8 are examples of indirect channels.

The structure of the distribution channel can be described considering its length and its width. The length of a distribution channel is determined by the number of levels and types of intermediaries which perform some work to bring the product to the final user. For example, in Figure 12.2, channel number 8 is longer than channel number 4 because more types of intermediaries are involved in the transaction. In some long channels, there can also be different levels of the same type of intermediary; for example, there can be a principal wholesaler, an intermediate wholesaler, and an ultimate wholesaler. The width of the channel can be evaluated for each type of channel member, and it is defined by the number of intermediaries of the same typology operating in the channel. For example, the width of

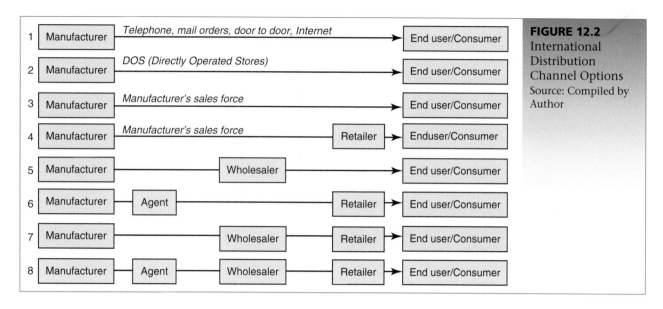

FIGURE 12.2 International Distribution Channel Options
Source: Compiled by Author

the channel is high when retailing is very fragmented (take the example of Coca-Cola, sold in an enormous number of retailers all over the world), and is low in the case of concentration: for example, Rolex collections of watches are sold in a select number of stores.

Direct Channels

Until a few years ago, besides the company sales force, there were only direct channels for door-to-door sales, mail orders, or telephone selling. Today, the direct marketing channel has been developed through the growth of Internet selling (option 1). Online worldwide sales still account for only about 5 percent, but in recent years their growth has been incredibly fast. Leading countries for Internet sales are the United States, followed by China, the UK, Japan, Germany, and France.[12] With global Internet users expected to go beyond the four billion consumer mark by 2023,[13] it is easy to understand why many companies perceive the Internet not only as a communication tool but also as a sales generator. Similarly, with the growing importance of the shopping experience in increasing consumer involvement, and the necessity to create brand value and differentiation against competitors, direct channels based on Directly Operated Stores are also acquiring significant importance (option 2). This distribution model is frequently used by fashion and luxury brands that also need to maintain brand value and image through the creation of a shopping experience.

For example, brands such as Armani and Ermenegildo Zegna first entered China opening their fully owned stores in luxurious hotels.[14] Today they have also developed DOS in the form of flagship stores in the major cities where they can offer consumers the entire "experience" conveyed by their brand. If a company has a limited number of customers, it can serve the market directly through a specialized internal sales force or through a global key account organization that works in close contact with these clients (option 3). In general, a direct channel is recommended when **technical products and services** are provided to the consumer or the industrial target only by an internal qualified staff. A direct control channel is typically used for **industrial goods**, where the scenario is that of a business-to-business transaction between the manufacturer, through its sales force, and a company that uses the product in its production process. If the **product is complex**, it has to be presented and explained directly by the company to its clients. In some cases, with important clients, a high-level manager conducts the negotiation. An important aspect to consider is the required **level of service**; if it is high, the company has to work in direct contact with its clients, and must react directly and promptly to their requests and provide all the necessary technical skills to solve the problems that may emerge after the sale.

Similarly, if the company is a retailer, it tends to control its purchasing activity backward through agents that are internal to the company, called **purchasing offices**. International retailers usually localize purchasing offices in the main countries of interest.

Indirect Channels

In the case of indirect marketing channels, **the relation between the manufacturer and the final consumer is filtered by intermediaries**—agents, wholesalers, and retailers— who perform different functions such as holding inventories, financing, selling and promoting, and managing after-sales services.[15]

The **channel can be short or long**, depending on the number of intermediaries used by the company. When the company has many foreign clients, the role of these intermediaries is fundamental to reduce the number of exchanges, to overcome cultural barriers, and to simplify the selling process. On the other hand, using indirect channels carries the risk of losing control of the physical flow of products, the ability to determine pricing policy at every stage of the channel, inventory payment, and promotion policy.

Conventional Versus Vertical Marketing Systems

Channel organization is another important issue that considers using **conventional distribution channels** versus **vertical marketing systems (VMS)**.

In a **conventional distribution channel**, intermediaries are independent and act as if they are running a separate business: the manufacturer is in charge of manufacturing and selling, the wholesaler develops the wholesaling activities, and the retailer manages the store.

In a **vertical marketing system**, intermediaries are linked in a unique integrated system that favors cooperation and synergies. A manufacturer can control both the wholesaling (the process of sorting, assembling, and warehousing goods) and retailing activity (for example, managing direct stores). The same can be done by a wholesaler, which can manufacture its own goods and perform retail activities or by a retailer that can perform both manufacturing and wholesaling activities. Integration can also be limited to just a few of the functions.

In all of these cases, control can be developed as a corporate, contractual, or administrative VMS. In a corporate VMS, the control is determined through the ownership of the company (an example is DOS—Directly Operated Stores). In a contractual VMS, control is realized through contracts with independent firms at different levels of production and distribution (this is the case in franchising, for example). Finally, when considering an administrative VMS, production and distribution can also be coordinated and controlled through the size and power of one of the parties.

A vertical system is usually required in situations where it is necessary to manage a complex product both in the sale and after-sale phases. There are also cases in which a company cannot find reliable distribution partners or where the channel partners operate with very high mark-ups that make the manufacturer's final price uncompetitive.

In both of these situations, a manufacturer can be interested in increasing the control of its sales process by integrating distribution activities. Consequently, if the size of the foreign market justifies the investment, many manufacturers often create sales branches and offices that perform the wholesale function, since they sell the parent manufacturer's products directly to retailers and industrial users.[16]

Furthermore, when the retailing format available in the foreign country is not suitable for its goods, a company can opt for forward integration through owned stores (Directly Operated Stores) or franchising. It is a known fact that the owners of luxury brands open their own stores, especially in markets where they see the potential for growth and where they want to maintain an image of quality and exclusivity.

Multichannel Strategies

Depending on the characteristics of the foreign market, companies usually combine multiple channels (direct and indirect, with different types of intermediaries), often proposing differentiated offers or brands, and choosing the more suitable channel organization (conventional or vertical).

The Italian company Ferrero, known worldwide for brands such as Nutella and Kinder, uses a mixed distribution model in China to position its products both in modern and more local retailers. Its sales force is made up of about 200 employees that directly interact with drugstores and with the most important international retailers such as Auchan, Metro, Carrefour, and Wal-Mart, guaranteeing the presence of the Ferrero products in more than 20,000 stores (option 4 in Figure 12.2). Alternatively, relationships are developed with local retailers through local wholesalers (option 7 in Figure 12.2).[17]

FIGURE 12.3
L'Oréal Advertising
in Venice
Source: © Author

TABLE 12.1	**Distribution Channels**	**Brands**
Distribution Channels for L'Oréal Brands	• Hairdressing salons	L'Oréal Professionnel, Kérastase, Redken, Matrix, Mizani, Pureology, Shu Uemura Art of Hair, Essie, Carita, Decléor
	• Mass retailing channels: hypermarkets, supermarkets, drugstores and traditional stores	L'Oréal Paris, Garnier, Maybelline New York, SoftSheen Carson, Essie
	• Cosmetic stores, travel retail, department stores, own-brand boutiques and dedicated e-commerce websites	Lancôme, Biotherm, Helena Rubinstein, Diesel, Giorgio Armani Beauty, Yves Saint Laurent Beauté, Kiehl's, Guy Laroche, Ralph Lauren, Cacharel, Shu Uemura, Clarisonic, Victor&Rolf, Paloma Picasso, Yue Sai, Maison Martin Margiela, Urban Decay
	• Pharmacies, drugstores, medi spas	Vichy, La Roche-Posay, SkinCeuticals, Sanoflore, Roger&Gallet
	• Directly Operated Stores (DOS)	The Body Shop

Sources: Adapted from: http://www.loreal.com/group/our-activities.aspx and http://www.loreal.com/brands/consumer-products-division.aspx [Accessed: January 17, 2015]

L'Oréal is a French cosmetics industry giant with 28 international brands in 130 countries and five continents worldwide (Fig. 12.3). L'Oreal is one of the few cosmetics groups using a wide variety of distribution channels (Table 12.1): hairdressing salons with professional products, mass retailing channels with consumer products, cosmetic and own brand boutiques, travel retail, department stores and dedicated e-commerce websites with luxury products, and healthcare outlets with active cosmetics. L'Oréal also uses a vertical marketing system exemplified by the acquisition of the natural and socially engaged beauty retailer, The Body Shop.

One of the main issues in a multichannel strategy is the coordination necessary in order to convey the same message to the final consumer, that wants to access his/her brand anywhere at any time and opt to use more than one channel to complete the transaction. The Allstate Corporation, operating in the United States and Canadian insurance industries with a distribution network of approximately 12,000 exclusive agencies and financial representatives, is an example of successful coordination that has also been achieved thanks to technology (Box 12.2).

Box 12.2   Technology-in-Focus: Multichannel Coordination Requires IT Investments

The Allstate Corporation Case

Being a multichannel company is not a guarantee of success if integration is not pursued. In order to reach integration, technology is the essential starting point. Allstate Corporation undoubtedly understands that investments in business process management and data management can be the key success factors for implementing multichannel projects characterized by a strong integration.

The Allstate Corporation is the largest publicly held personal lines insurer in the United States. Founded in 1931, it became a publicly traded company in 1993. Today the company has $123.5 billion in total assets and total revenues of $34.5 billion. Its product portfolio is made up of some major lines of insurance, including private passenger auto, homeowners insurance, life insurance, retirement and investment products, voluntary accidents and health insurance products, business and consumer household insurance. All of these product lines are offered through a multichannel distribution network based on Allstate agencies, allstate.com, 1-800 Allstate, independent agencies, financial institutions, and broker-dealers.

The main consumer advantage is the possibility to benefit from a distribution network that is not only extremely varied but also strongly integrated. Allstate agents are connected with customer call centers and the Internet. This implies that a consumer can use the Internet but also has the ability to conduct the transaction through traditional routes such as the agent or via phone. For example, a potential customer can obtain estimates on auto policies in about two minutes, and the company immediately displays on its website the name of an agent who can be contacted at any time. Technology allows the customer to start the transaction on the Internet and to conclude it with an agent, but eliminates the need to redo the entire transaction; they simply continue where they previously stopped and then conclude the process.

Multichannel integration also represents an advantage for the agents, who can quickly and easily quote, follow up, and track new sales, pursuing their sales objectives more efficiently than in the past. Nevertheless, multichannel distribution also imposes integrated communication: in fact, it becomes crucial for the company to ensure that all channels are all emitting the same service and message, conveying brand and information consistently and enhancing a coherent positioning strategy.

Allstate Insurance Corp. started this project of channel integration in 2000, and since then sales have significantly improved. The company has also acquired Esurance, one of the first auto insurance websites, to expand its presence on the Web. Technology, integration, and continuous investments in enhancing distribution channels: these are the main ingredients of a successful relationship between the company and the clients. As a manager of distribution, marketing, and process solutions at Northbrook, Ill.-based Allstate Insurance Corp. says: "We want to provide a superior customer experience, and being multichannel is essential."

Sources: http://www.allstate.com/about.aspx, http://www.allstate.com/about/product-overview.aspx, http://www.insurancenetwork-ing.com/news/allstate_esurance_aut_insurance_direc_sales_merger-27951-1.html, https://www.esurance.com/about/company, [Accessed: January 18, 2015]; Burns, C. (2008), 'Channels work together toward the same goal (cover story)', *Insurance Networking News*, 12(1), pp. 1–9, Business Source Premier, EBSCOhost [Accessed: October 17, 2015]; Viscusi, S. (2009), 'Allstate agents improve sales and marketing capabilities with Leads360 and Quote Burst', *Tmcnet.com*, June 4, 2009, http://outbound-call-center.tmcnet.com/topics/outbound-call-center/articles/57392-allstate-agents-improve-sales-marketing-capabilities-with-leads360.htm   [Accessed: October 16, 2015].

TYPES OF CHANNEL INTERMEDIARIES

Basically, three groups of channel intermediaries can be identified: agents, wholesalers, and retailers. **Agents** operate in the name of the company but they do not take title to the goods they sell. **Wholesalers** take title to the goods and sell them to customers buying for reselling or for business use. **Retailers** manage the final link between the provider and the consumer. Each and every one of these intermediaries often has different characteristics, depending on the developed strategy; for example, some wholesalers are integrated forward, and they also manage retailing activities. Similarly, some retailers can be integrated backward and carry out activities that are typical of the wholesaler. Within the single categories of agents, wholesalers, and retailers, different types of intermediaries can be identified and will be presented in the following paragraphs.

From an operational point of view, these actors are generally highly reliant on the services offered and on the industry in which they operate, often resulting in a mixture of the types of intermediaries and contracts used by a company in different foreign markets.

Agents and Wholesalers

Agents sell supplier-owned products primarily to retailers and other wholesalers, but do not take title to goods or act in the name of the company they represent (called the "principal"). They offer a limited service and usually work for a commission or fee. Agents are generally used for products such as textiles, clothing, and footwear.

Wholesalers sell goods supplied by other firms to retailers or directly to industrial, commercial, and other end users serving a specific geographic area. They are distinguished from other types of intermediaries in that they take title to the goods they sell. Functions performed by wholesalers are numerous, from sorting, assembling, and warehousing goods to providing services such as packaging and labeling, contacting new clients, negotiating, and selling.

When analyzing the activity carried out by this type of intermediary, it is possible to distinguish between "full service wholesalers," offering a full line of services to the company, and "limited service wholesalers," providing a limited number of services. Depending on their relationship with the supplier or customers, or the distribution method employed, wholesalers assume different trade designations. The most important typologies of agents and wholesalers in an international context (the most common being the importer or the distributor) are described in the Appendix at the end of this chapter. It is important to understand that these are not always universal definitions but rather tend to vary depending on the sector.

Especially in underdeveloped country markets, wholesalers play a fundamental role in bridging the gap between demand and supply. Scattered markets throughout the countryside, where consumers have a limited income and local retailers can buy a very limited volume of many different products, can be reached by wholesalers who are able to handle a large variety of low-priced products.[18]

While the wholesaler role remains critical in providing value-added services, nevertheless, their structure can differ significantly country by country, mainly due to the economic development of the market. An important aspect to consider is the power concentration of wholesaling activities. In some countries, power is concentrated in the hands of a few companies that operate on a nationwide basis and benefit from significant economies of scale in purchasing. If wholesalers have a global presence, they can also distribute their products in global markets. Their strength influences foreign companies that wish to enter the country, since the possibility of distributing the product is almost completely in their hands. To have an idea of the power of wholesalers, we can consider the revenues of some of the world's largest distributors, such as the Swiss company Glencore International AG, operating in the wholesale of metals and metal ores, with more than two hundred billion dollars.

However, power is not always this concentrated. Many companies operating in global niches know that there can be small and specialized wholesalers with the exclusive right to import a product in their own country. In this case, it is not the size but their specialization that determine their power and control of the market.

The degree of vertical integration also influences the power of a foreign wholesaler. Take for example the Chinese holding group China Resources Enterprise Limited. The group, primarily operating in Mainland China and Hong Kong, is both integrated backward into research and development and the manufacturing of beer and foodstuffs, and forward through wholesaling, retailing, logistics and international trade.[19]

Retailers

Retailers are intermediaries that sell directly to the final consumer. Among the different activities carried out by retailers are: ordering, storing, creating assortments, presenting goods in the most attractive way, packaging, financing, and providing after-sales services. Besides the store-based retailers, many bricks and mortar retailers (also called bricks & clicks) are expanding into global markets using both traditional stores and online sales.[20] In addition, internet retailers are growing worldwide, improving the accessibility of products and brands both in mature and emerging markets. Nowadays, retailers have a lot of opportunities to build their differentiation using up-to-date technology. For example, targeted messages can be sent in-store thanks to smartphones via GPS technology; retailers' apps can enhance the buying process with information, coupons, in-store navigation. Online sales can be facilitated by innovative services such as the Virtual Fitting Room, a solution that provides the fitting room experience, showing the shoppers exactly what a garment will look like on them.[21] All of these improvements have consistently improved the consumer shopping experience and engagement, both in-store and online.

There can be vast differences in the retailing format between countries due to local shopping habits, life-style, economic progress, and local regulation.[22] Emerging markets present grocery retail formats ranging from predominantly traditional (cooperatives, independent grocers, free markets, and food specialists) to predominantly modern trade (hypermarkets, supermarkets, discounters, department stores, and convenience stores). For example, predominantly traditional markets are India (with 98 percent of traditional outlets), Indonesia (85 percent), the Philippines (78 percent), and Argentina (68 percent). Countries that can be considered in transition (50–60 percent of all grocery sales from traditional outlets) are Venezuela, Thailand, Turkey, and Brazil. Finally, there are countries such as Russia, China, South Africa, and Mexico where more than 50 percent of the grocery sales come from modern outlets.[23] Sometimes differences in the retailing format have been determined by local legislation. For example, some countries (such as India) have been closed to foreign retailers in part to protect the millions of small, family-run stores.

However, even when considering developed markets such as Europe, it is impressive how the retailing formats for groceries are so differentiated. For example, in France, about 47.2 percent of the retailing formats are represented by hypermarkets and superstores (32.1 percent and 15.1 percent, respectively), followed by supermarkets and neighborhood stores (about 40 percent), and only about 11 percent of other formats (such as discount stores). The situation is completely different in other countries. For example, in Germany only 21.7 percent is represented by hypermarkets and superstores, about 30 percent of supermarkets and neighborhood stores, while discount stores cover more than 30 percent of the retailing formats for grocery goods.[24]

It is also important to remember that differences in retailing formats not only exist between countries, but also within the countries. For example, in China, big

FIGURE 12.4
Examples of Traditional and Modern Retailing Formats in China
Source: © Author

modern retailers or experiential specialty stores run by Chinese or western companies, are in contrast with the reality of small traditional mom-and-pop stores located in rural areas or in neighborhoods (Figure 12.4). The latter are small, with no self-service shelving, few product categories and brands, most of the time situated directly on the border of the pavement, with a stock room on the second floor and a place on the third floor where the shopkeeper and his family live and sleep.[25]

Manufacturers have a number of options to sell their products to the final consumer. First of all, they can consider the variety of independent retail intermediaries that can be used in a foreign market and choose those that are best for their products. In some cases, manufacturers have taken advantage of strong partnerships with some global retailers that heavily invest in their foreign development. For example, Unilever expands in international markets through the continuous internationalization process of global retailers like Carrefour, Wal-Mart, Ahold, and Tesco, with whom it has developed strong partnerships.

The choice of an independent retailer already present in the market doesn't eliminate the option of introducing innovations that can favor product sales, as happened for Beiersdorf, the German group selling brands such as Nivea, La Prairie, Juvena, and Eucerin. The company, with €6,141 million sales, is not only trying to innovate products but is also focusing on retail formats. In its traditional distribution of outlets, supermarkets, and drugstores, the company launched the Blue Wall, an area that features only Nivea products grouped together, all characterized by the common blue color of all Nivea packaging. Closeness to consumers is also reached with Nivea Haus, first opened in Hamburg but today present in cities like Dubai, and with Nivea Temporary Shop, opened in some European cities such as Milan and Rome.[26] This strategy is also frequently followed by food brands. In Figure 12.5 it is possible to see how the French brand of biscuits LU has created a distinctive aisle in a Chinese supermarket, to differentiate itself from competitive products.

FIGURE 12.5
LU Biscuit Brand
in a Chinese
Supermarket
Source: © Author

Manufacturers can also organize their presence inside large stores with the form of a leased concession, typical of department stores such as Harrods, Saks Fifth Avenue, and Nordstrom. Traditionally, department stores dedicate a space to a brand, creating a "boutique" where the department store operates the shop, its staffing, merchandising and display. With a leased concession, the "boutique" located in a larger store is operated by the brand, in return for paying a lease and/ or a percentage of their sales.[27]

Nevertheless, in some cases manufacturers have to develop wholly-owned stores (DOS—Directly Operated Stores) or franchising networks that are more suitable to promote and sell their brands. For example, Bulgari's retail network consists of exclusive Bulgari stores, mainly directly owned or in franchising, travel retail, and wholesale stores. Bulgari also distributes through independent watch retailers and through the finest select perfumeries and department stores.

In other cases, the choice of a famous retailer is the strategy to launch a new brand. For example, the tennis player, Maria Sharapova, first launched her Sugarpova brand of premium candies through the famous Henri Bendel store in New York. Today the Sugarpova candies are sold in over 30 countries, such as Japan (at Plaza Ginza stores in Tokyo), in the UK (in Selfridge stores in London and Oxford), and in Singapore (in Robinsons Jem stores).[28]

INTERNET RETAILING

In the global retailing industry, the Internet category, generating about 5 percent of global value, has to be included in this discussion because its growth in recent years has been amazing. As pointed out by Euromonitor International,[29] the United States is definitely the largest market, but also countries like China are rapidly catching up, and e-commerce also represents an opportunity for other emerging markets. Apparel and footwear, consumer electronics, digital entertainment, and food and beauty products are by far the most important categories. Consumers' shopping behavior is also different when comparing developed and emerging markets. For example, in mature markets internet retailing is mainly preferred because of price and flexibility, while in emerging markets, brand variety is the most important reason. Nevertheless, in these markets e-commerce has to face the problem of consumers' low trust in online payment security.

One of the companies that has undoubtedly paved the way for Internet selling is Amazon, followed by three other big players; Tmall, (which is part of the Chinese Alibaba group and has 45 percent of Internet retailing in China), eBay, and Apple. While booksellers were stuck in the old model of selling books in brick-and-mortar stores, Amazon was busy building its market share by using the Internet for marketing and enlarging its customer base. The low-cost Internet operations allowed Amazon to offer substantial price discounts and larger selections. More importantly, Amazon's online model provided it with the ability to offer two differentiating services that became critical to its early success: customized recommendations based on tracking a customer's browsing and buying patterns, and product peer-reviews that gave it a sense of community. Amazon has been successful in replicating this model in several international markets, reaching a global market share of 12 percent. But its growth is also due to diversification, introducing new services such as Amazon Prime, Fire TV, Amazon Fresh, Amazon Smile, and many others.[30]

INTERNATIONALIZATION OF RETAILING

Internationalization of the retailing industry is a growing phenomenon that involves big retailers as well as small ones. The prerequisite to manage the development of an international network is the creation of a store brand value recognized by foreign consumers. But the model of value creation is not the same for all retailers. Take the examples of Wal-Mart, H&M, and Dior. Wal-Mart is targeted to mass consumers and offers a wide assortment of "value for money" products of different brands in a store environment that conveys, with its design and atmosphere, the Wal-Mart brand image around the world. H&M has a different approach, which is focused on its store brand built around the philosophy of bringing fashion and quality to consumers at the best price: the shopping experience enhances this philosophy, which is conveyed to consumers through more than 2,200 stores around the world, from Sweden to Italy and from South Korea to China (Geo Map 12.1).

In contrast to H&M, Dior is a producer first and a retailer second, and this characteristic determines a different approach to the retailing model. The brand

GEO MAP 12.1
H&M
Source: Adapted from:
CIA Maps, The World
Factbook[31]

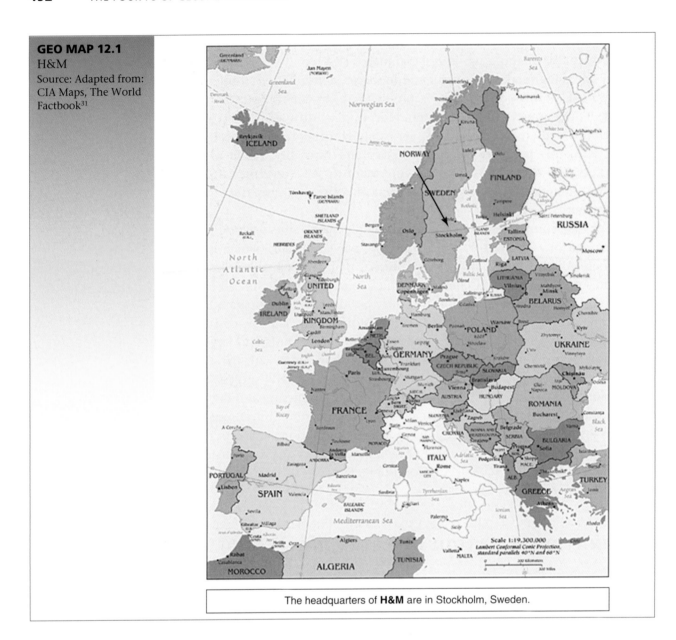

The headquarters of **H&M** are in Stockholm, Sweden.

is sold all over the world through independent retailers, franchisees, and directly owned stores. But the store is built around the manufacturing brand, not vice versa (Figure 12.6).

Similarly to manufacturing companies, retailers have to identify the best mode to enter a foreign market. There are basically five options:[32]

Investment with a Minority Control

The retailer is usually in its initial stages of internationalization and has limited knowledge of the local environment and low expertise. Acquiring a minority stake of an established retailing business is an investment that can give the retailer

FIGURE 12.6
A Dior Boutique in China
Source: © Author

the possibility to improve its understanding without risk. In fact, even if with a minority investment the retailer has no control over store management, it can be the best choice to start the internationalization process without a high involvement of resources and minimizing the entry risk.

Directly Operated Stores (DOS)—Greenfield Investment

The retailer chooses to open one or more stores in important locations, fashion capitals or, in general, capital cities, creating store brand awareness in the most attractive markets. Thanks to the direct control, opening a DOS gives the retailer the possibility to develop a deep knowledge of the market, implementing some format and/or assortment adaptation, and laying the foundations for a wider expansion in the host markets.

Franchising

The retailer signs franchise agreements with local business partners, providing the store brand and the format, marketing support, and training. International fashion brands typically develop franchising agreements after the opening of some DOS, with the goal of improving the diffusion of their brands in the foreign markets, especially in key provincial cities. An example is the expansion of Gap Inc., the American leading international specialty retailer with six brands—Gap, Banana Republic, Old Navy, Piperlime, Athleta and INTERMIX.[33] Nowadays Gap Inc. operates with about 3,700 stores in 90 countries worldwide. In India and China, Gap is present with franchising operated stores. In India franchising is developed through a partnership with Arvind Lifestyle Brands Limited, which belongs to one of the largest textile companies in India.[34]

Joint Venture

Retailers can enter a foreign market through a joint venture with a local partner. Usually the foreign retailer has the brand name and manages important activities such as product assortment and store management, but the foreign partner can give a fundamental contribution in terms of local relations and operations. An example is the retail joint venture signed in Brazil by Carrefour with the distribution group Grupo Pão de Açúcar.[35]

Acquisitions—Brownfield Investments

Retailers can buy a local retail chain gaining immediate access to the foreign market. This entry mode is only an option for companies that already have both international experience and in-depth market knowledge. The main advantage of this option is the availability of an already established store network, with infrastructure and resources, nevertheless the retailer is often asked to invest and improve the existing infrastructure in order to align the retail chain to the company image and organizational culture.

Country and firm level factors can significantly influence retailers' internationalization.[36]

One of the main decisions that international retailers must face is related to standardization/adaptation issues. On the one hand the growing globalization of consumer goods is seen as one of the variables that will gradually encourage standardization. On the other hand, the analysis of local markets clearly points out that format adaptation (i.e. the adaptation of the style, design, layout, and assortment of the store) is an almost necessary choice.[37] The need to adapt to national cultures is strongly perceived by global retailers who are far from standardizing not only their retailing format but also their local offer in terms of assortment, promotion, and selling techniques. In general, it is important to analyze whether consumer perceptions of core attributes of the retailing format differ between countries[38] and how a retailer can adapt to these variations. Take Carrefour, for example. One of the reasons for its success internationally is attributed to its ability to adapt to local reality, to understand its needs and purchasing behaviors, and adapt both format and assortment (Figure 12.7).

Global retailers face a highly competitive environment in their internationalization process. Domestic competition is strong even in many emerging countries where local retailers are speeding their expansion plans improving their merchandising, products, and know-how, in order to strengthen their presence before the arrival of foreign retailers. This often requires global retailers to develop local strategic alliances. In India, for example, the British-based retailer Tesco has recently signed a joint-venture agreement with Tata Group's Trent Hypermarket retailer. The two retailers will operate a dozen of stores under the brands "Star Bazaar" and "Star Daily," offering both grocery and non-grocery products.[39] These alliances are often developed to overcome the many obstacles of entering foreign

FIGURE 12.7
Local Assortment in
a Carrefour Store in
China
Source: © Author

markets. In India, for example, with more than 12 million shop owners representing 97 percent of all retail sales, the opposition to liberalization of the retail sector is very high. Despite the central government of New Delhi now allowing the opening of foreign supermarkets, individual states can still refuse direct investments of foreign retailers, representing a barrier to the growth of modern distribution.[40]

Entering foreign markets is not easy. Retailers have to **invest time and resources to identify differences in the host countries,** and adapt to these differences crafting their strategies and their operative decisions. A recent study[41] has pointed out that the degree of international retailer involvement, defined as the number of geographic regions in which a retailer operates, is negatively related to retailer performance. Nevertheless, it was found that retailers perform better when they establish operations in countries that are more distant culturally, economically, and politically. This paradox can be explained by the fact that when a foreign country is similar, there is the risk of underestimating some important differences, resulting in low performance. Vice versa, the awareness of the existence of significant differences motivates the retailer to dedicate more resources on understanding the foreign market and consequently adapting the format, the assortment, and other important aspects that can favor higher performance.

PHYSICAL DISTRIBUTION

The prime objective of **physical distribution** is to manage the movement of finished products from the company to its customers. Efficiency and service quality are guaranteed by an effective coordination of **logistics activities** that include handling, transport, inventory, labeling, and storage. All of these activities are mainly formalized by export documents such as the commercial invoice, the consular invoice, the certificate of origin, transport and banking documents, government documents, and many others.

It is not uncommon, in some countries, that companies encounter a lot of difficulty in obtaining the requested documents from the government; in some cases bureaucratic obstacles become strong entry barriers that foreign companies can only overcome through alliances with local partners that support physical distribution activities.

Transport decisions are also a big issue. Where there are poor transportation and logistics standards, foreign companies have to face inefficiencies that can significantly affect their costs (Figure 12.8).

As an example, Box 12.3 shows the case of China and India, emerging markets where transportation and logistics remain difficult not only in the countryside but also in fast-growing cities. A recent analysis of the Chinese logistics and distribution industry estimates that total company spending (including rail, road, inland water, air, and warehousing storage) amounts to nearly 18 percent of China's GDP. Compare that figure to the United States, where logistics spending makes up only 8.5 percent of GDP.[42] It is important to underline how the growing presence of foreign companies can bring improvement of physical distribution management. For example, fast-food chains like McDonald's and KFC have set up cold chain systems that service 1,964 and 5,850 outlets respectively throughout China.[43]

The need to improve physical distribution efficiency is strongly felt in most of the companies that operate on an international level. On the one hand, cost control has become more critical; on the other hand, there is an increasing need to distribute products quickly to customers and to guarantee high quality service

FIGURE 12.8
Transportation of
Goods in Beijing
Source: © Francesco
Venier

Box 12.3   Country-in-Focus: China and India

With the world's largest network of toll roads, high-speed trains, and six of the ten busiest container ports, logistics management in China is highly fragmented, and a lot could be done to improve the efficiency and the quality of the physical distribution system. The cost of logistics is high and the government recognizes the need to build a much more extensive transport infrastructure. Furthermore, if compared to other emerging and developed markets, China is very weak in terms of the number of airports with paved runways: 452 airports, a small number if compared to Brazil, with 713 airports, and the United States, with 5,194. And in forty-four Chinese cities with more than one million people, buses are the only transportation system.

Today, for example, once shippers have delivered a load to a retailer, trucks are often empty on the return trip. In addition, current regulations influence long-haul freight, causing delays and increasing costs. For instance, some drivers avoid toll roads to cut expenses. Consequently the use of non-toll roads, poorly maintained and indirectly routed, lengthens transportation time and increases indirect costs and the likelihood of delays. Also, the lack of nationwide connectivity in transportation significantly affects material movement flows, costs, and throughput capacity. When a truck reaches provincial borders, it must often unload and reload its cargo into a new truck with the appropriate provincial license plates. This can determine an increase of material handling costs and may lead to product damage. City restrictions to alleviate traffic jams can also complicate distribution. During certain times of the day, distribution companies have to choose between the use of smaller cars and vans or, vice versa, pay high taxes for truck circulation.

The situation is not so different in India, where a lot has to be done to improve infrastructure; for example, with no warehousing or refrigerated trucking from the farm to the shelf, today 40 percent of the farmer's fruits and vegetables go to waste. India's cold chain logistics cannot be fixed unless large-scale investments are made, and the New Delhi government decision of opening to foreign direct investment in the retail industry, is still strongly opposed by millions of middlemen. However the government plans of investing one trillion dollars in ports, roads, rail system, and power plants in the five years to March 2017, will hopefully contribute to determine an improvement of the logistics infrastructures.

Sources: Euromonitor International. (2014), 'India: Country profile', 24 October, 2014, www.euromonitor.com [Accessed: February 21, 2015]; Boumphrey, S. (2014), 'Dealing with the infrastructure deficit in emerging markets', 9 September, 2014, http://blog.euromonitor.com/2014/09/dealing-with-the-infrastructure-deficit-in-emerging-markets.html [Accessed: March 12, 2015]; Orr, G. (2013), 'What's in store for China in 2013?' *McKinsey Quarterly*, January, 2013, http://www.mckinsey.com/insights/economic_studies/whats_in_store_for_china_in_2013 [Accessed: March 12, 2015]; Feuling, B. A. (2008), 'China supply chain development', September/October, 2008, http://chinabusinessreview.com [Accessed: March 11, 2015]; Schept, K. (2008), 'Retailing in India: Challenges and opportunities', *Chain Store Age*, 84(7), pp. 23–25, Business Source Premier, EBSCOhost [Accessed: October 17, 2015]; Kazmin, A. and Leahy, J. (2010). 'Grocery debate', *Financial Times*, 5 July, 2010, p. 19; Feuling, B. and Nath, S. (2010), 'Developing China sales and distribution capabilities', *China Business Review*, 37(4), pp. 12–15, Business Source Premier, EBSCOhost [Accessed: October 17, 2015].

and sustainability in moving millions of products from factories to the points of sale every day. Such is the case of Unilever, which has established a logistics network integrating transportation with global and regional distribution hubs, with the aim of improving operational efficiency and reducing environmental impact significantly.[44]

There are **companies that have turned logistics into a corporate philosophy.** One of these is undoubtedly the Spanish Group Inditex (Geo Map 12.2), whose most famous brand is Zara, which believes that logistics is at the service of the store and has always considered the efficiency of physical distribution as one of the key factors for success. Inditex's business model considers the control of the supply chain throughout the various stages of design, manufacture, and retailing

GEO MAP 12.2
Inditex
Source: Adapted from:
CIA Maps, The World
Factbook[45]

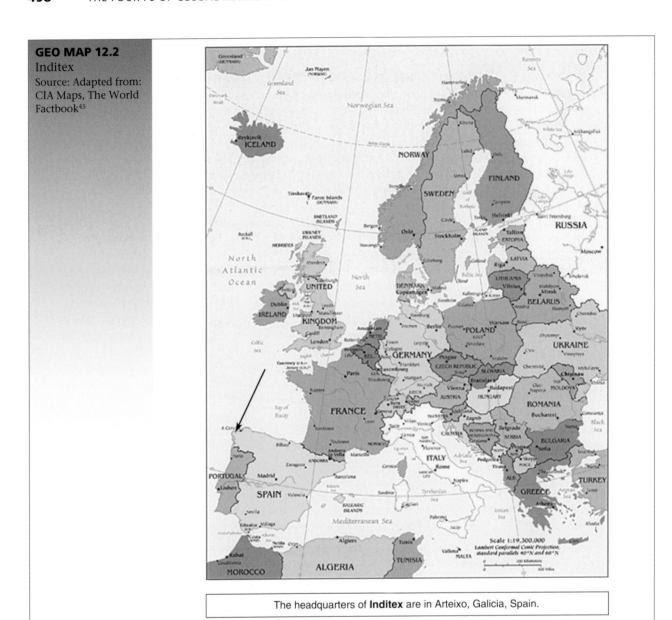

The headquarters of **Inditex** are in Arteixo, Galicia, Spain.

a priority. The distribution centers of the various commercial formats operate through a centralized logistics system, storing and distributing inventory to the group's stores worldwide.[46]

Also in the business to business sector there are companies where the logistics system is a key element of competitive advantage. Flora Holland is a Dutch company selling plant and flowers all over the world. With an annual turnover of about €4.5 billion and over 3,500 employees, the company sells 12.8 billion items a year, to its 2,400 customers. The necessity to bring fresh flowers and plants to clients' in different countries, has required the development of sophisticated logistics processes that enable the delivery of products as soon as the auction is over,

FIGURE 12.9
Flora Holland:
Flowers and
Plants Ready to Be
Delivered After the
Auctions
Source: © Author

and which guarantees the quality, availability, and distribution of all logistics supplies at all locations (Figure 12.9).[47]

SUMMARY

- When a company is planning to build and develop its intended position in the global market, the most suitable distribution channels in terms of structure, management, and control have to be defined.
- Several internal and external factors have to be taken into account when defining distribution in foreign markets. Among the internal factors are the international marketing strategy of a specific company, the size and development of its marketing and sales functions, the financial strength, and the complexity of its products. On the other hand, external factors include the characteristics of the distribution system, local regulations, the phase of the product's life cycle, consumer shopping habits, and the competitive climate.
- The distribution channel structure is strongly influenced by the country's economic development, which creates a need for more efficient channels.
- Managing a distribution channel requires many decisions based on the evaluation of the advantages and disadvantages of different options: direct versus indirect channels; conventional distribution channels versus vertical marketing systems (VMS).
- When entering foreign markets, a company has to choose among different types of intermediaries (agents, wholesalers, and retailers), identifying which are considered most suitable. Different typologies of agents and wholesalers can be identified in an international context.
- In the global retailing industry the growth of internet retailing has been amazing, both in mature and in emerging markets.

- There can be vast differences in the retailing format between countries due to local shopping habits, life-style, economic progress, and local regulation.
- A growing phenomenon is the internationalization of the retailing industry. Similarly to manufacturing companies, retailers have different modes of entering a foreign market.
- Decisions related to physical distribution are also a big issue; where there are poor transportation and logistics standards, foreign companies have to face inefficiencies that can significantly affect their costs.

DISCUSSION QUESTIONS

1. What are the external factors influencing international distribution decisions?
2. Take the example of a foreign brand that is marketed in your country: compared to other countries, which local factors have to be taken into consideration when defining distribution decisions?
3. What are the advantages and disadvantages of direct versus indirect distribution channels? Discuss and give some examples of brands using one of the two channels or both.
4. How can companies be successful developing a vertical marketing system (VMS)? What are the main risks? Discuss some examples of global companies successfully implementing VMS (for example, Inditex Group–Zara, or McDonald's).
5. Discuss the problem of coordination of brand image in multichannel strategies.
6. Discuss advantages and disadvantages of using an agent to enter foreign markets.
7. Discuss advantages and disadvantages of using a wholesaler to enter foreign markets.
8. Compare two different global retailers operating in your country and describe their competitive advantages.

EXPERIENTIAL EXERCISES

1. As a marketer for a large United States-based clothing company targeting the youth segment, you have the task of developing the online channel marketing strategy for the firm's entry into the European Union market. Your main competitors are Zara, H&M, and Mango, which have already developed online stores. In the course of your research, you have also found the following information:
   - 78 percent of Europeans shop online and buy an average of 10 items with a total value of €750 in a six-month period.
   - The product categories with the highest conversion rates (consumers who research a product online and go on to buy it online) in Europe are event tickets (75 percent), travel tickets (72 percent), books (71 percent), and clothes (70 percent).
   - Online shoppers in the United Kingdom and Scandinavian countries are the most active.
   - Shoppers from the Netherlands, Germany, and France use the Internet to do the most comparison shopping.
   - Auction sites are most popular in Germany and the UK.[48]

Given these considerations, make a competitive analysis and propose a channel strategy that includes product, pricing, promotion, and distribution suggestions that will make your brand relevant and attractive to European consumers.

KEY TERMS

- Agents
- Channel structure
- Control
- Conventional distribution channels
- Direct channels
- Distribution system
- Exclusive distribution strategy
- Indirect channels

- Intensive distribution strategy
- Logistics activities
- Physical distribution
- Retailers
- Selective distribution strategy
- Shopping habits
- Vertical marketing systems (VMS)
- Wholesalers

APPENDIX

Agents and Wholesalers in an International Context

Typologies of agents in an international context

Representatives

Representatives operate in a specific geographic area on behalf of the principal, without taking physical possession of the product. They develop relationships with new customers or maintain contacts with old ones. In exchange for a commission, they arrange sales but cannot sign contracts and must pass all legal documents to the principal that will take the credit, market, or exchange risk. If the contract is approved, the principal will arrange for shipping and handling. Representatives represent either buyers or sellers on a more permanent basis than brokers do.

Manufacturers' Agents

Manufacturers' agents are hired by small manufacturers who cannot afford the cost of developing their own sales network, but they are also used by large manufacturers to enter new countries where the limited market potential and high risk do not suggest the use of full-time salespeople. They are located in the clothing, furniture, and electrical goods industries and usually represent two or more manufacturers of complementary lines. The written agreement that regulates the relationship usually covers pricing, territories, order handling, delivery services, warranties, and commission rates.

Selling Agents

Selling agents are hired by manufacturers that are not interested in the selling function or that feel unqualified. They serve as a sales department and have the contractual authority to sell a manufacturer's entire output. As a consequence, even if they do not take title to goods, they have a key role in setting prices and general terms and conditions of sales.

Purchasing Agents

Purchasing agents make purchases for buyers. They usually establish a long-term relationship, offering numerous services such as receiving, inspecting, storing, and delivering the merchandise to buyers. Purchasing agents also represent a precious information source for the buyers in relation to the best goods and prices available in the market.

Brokers and Factors

Brokers and factors are independent individuals or organizations that facilitate buying and selling, assisting in negotiation and legally binding the principal to a sale contract without taking any risk themselves. In exchange for the service offered, they receive a commission on the selling price. Both brokers and factors usually do not develop a long-term relationship, and the contract is not expected to be exclusive. They are usually specialized by product line or customer type (food brokers, insurance brokers, etc.). Factors perform all normal brokerage functions plus financing.

This is the reason why factors are frequently banks that may finance goods and cover the credit risk.

Wholesale Merchants

Wholesale merchants can be classified by the number of product lines they carry. *General merchandise wholesalers* carry several merchandise lines; i.e. a wide variety of non-perishable items such as hardware, electrical supplies, and furniture. *Single-line* (or *general-line*) *wholesalers* carry only one or two lines (only food, or only a specific type of industrial tools, for example) but in greater depth than general merchandise wholesalers. As a consequence, they generally serve single-line and limited-line stores. When they sell industrial products, they usually cover a wide geographic area and offer a more specialized service.

Specialty wholesalers carry a very narrow range of products and in only one part of the line (for example, biological food or children's food). For this reason they are able to offer more information on their target market and more specialized services than other wholesalers.

Distributors

Distributors sell primarily to wholesalers, retailers, or final consumers. They usually stock the products up to one year or more. They have a formalized and long-lasting relationship with the manufacturer, with exclusive selling rights for a specified geographic area. This close collaboration allows the manufacturer to exercise higher control over the final price, promotional activities, inventory, and service policies than when it sells its products through a merchant wholesaler.

In the business-to-consumer market, distributors sell large volumes of goods to retailers such as supermarkets or hypermarkets. They can also sell to merchant wholesalers that serve a specific retail channel. In the business-to-business sector, industrial distributors handle large quantities of standardized items such as standard industrial components, or building materials, to be sold to manufacturers.

Distributors negotiate their margin with the supplier, represented by the difference between the buying and selling prices of the products they carry, minus their costs. Margins can vary significantly country to country, and they mainly depend on different factors such as the level of service offered by the distributor, the intensity of competition, sales volume, and purchasing power.

Commission Merchants

Commission merchants are wholesalers that are mostly used in agriculture. For farmers who do not want to perform sales activity and do not belong to producers' cooperatives, commission merchants take commodities to a central market, sell it for the best price, and remit the revenues to farmers after deducting commission and expenses.

Dealers

Dealers execute trades for their company's own account and provide the manufacturer (the principal) with a great deal of market information. Furthermore, besides having the same type of continuing relationship with suppliers that distributors have, they also carry out the same functions as retailers, since they sell the principal's products directly to final customers. Dealers frequently have exclusive selling rights for the manufacturer's products in a specified area. Sometimes the control of the manufacturer over the relationship is strengthened by holding an equity share in the dealer's business.

Importers

Importers provide the same services as distributors but they may be either wholesalers or retailers and, generally, they do not have exclusive territorial rights. The principal has limited control over them, because they may sell the products of many suppliers, sometimes even for competing product lines. Similarly to distributors, they negotiate their margin with the supplier, with significant differences between countries depending on the level of service and local competition.

Cash-and-Carry Wholesalers

Cash-and-carry wholesalers are limited service wholesalers. They supply those retailers that are too small to be served profitably by merchant wholesalers. In recent years their target has been significantly extended to the *horeca* segment (hotels, restaurants, etc). Customers must pay cash, but they can benefit from lower prices; in fact, these wholesalers can operate at lower costs because retailers or customers take over many wholesaling functions. For this reason, cash-and-carry operators are especially common in less-developed nations.

Truck Jobbers

Truck jobbers provide almost the same functions as full-service wholesalers; their characteristic is that they stock perishable products in their own trucks and may be able to deliver an order door to door within hours, operating 24 hours a day every day.

Drop Shippers

Drop shippers are limited service wholesalers because they sell goods, but they do not actually handle, stock, or deliver them, so their operating costs are lower. More specifically, they get orders from buyers that can be other wholesalers, retailers, or business users in general. They take title to the products they sell, but they ask the producer to ship the order directly to the customers. This system can be advantageous to avoid handling bulky products, reducing costs and the risk of damage.

Producers' Cooperatives

Producers' cooperatives are diffused in agricultural markets where many small producers join together creating a cooperative which operates like a full-service wholesaler. Profits are shared between the members who are at the same time members and customers of the cooperative. Some of these cooperatives are successful in creating well-known brands, affording marketing costs that they wouldn't have been able to afford had they acted alone.

Rack Jobber

Rack jobbers are wholesalers specialized in non-food products such as stationery, books, and magazines. They sell through grocery stores and supermarkets, displaying their products on their own wire racks, fixing prices, and so forth. This allows retailers the freedom of not having to reorder and guarantees the maintenance of displays of small quantities of many different kinds of non-food items. For their service, rack jobbers are usually paid cash for what is sold or delivered.

Mail-Order Wholesalers

Mail-order wholesalers sell their products to small industrial customers or retailers through catalogs that include complete lines of specific products. Items such as jewelry, computer accessories and supplies, sporting goods, and general merchandise lines are the most diffused for this type of wholesaling. For example, LTD Commodities is a business-to-business supplier of apparel, home and garden accessories, jewelry, electronics, luggage, toys, etc., selling its products through catalogs and the Internet and shipping only to business addresses.

Sources: Kotler, P., Armstrong, G. (2013). *Principles of marketing* (15th Global ed.). Essex, England: Pearson Education Ltd.; Sciarelli, S. and Vona, R. (2009). *Management della distribuzione*, Milan: McGraw-Hill Companies; Mühlbacher, H., Leihs, H., & Dahringer, L. (2006). *International marketing: A global perspective*. London: Cengage Learning.

NOTES

1 VF. (2013). *Annual Report.* http://reporting.vfc.com/2013/consumer/index.html [Accessed: February 1, 2015].

2 The Michelin Group. (2015), 'The four strategic pillars – Growing to serve our customers', http://www.michelin.com/eng/michelin-group/strategy/4-strategic-pillars [Accessed: October 16, 2015].

3 Baumgartner, T., Hatami, H., and Vander Ark, J. (2012), *Sales growth: Five proven strategies from the world's sales leaders*, Hoboken, New Jersey: John Wiley & Sons; Valdeviesa de Uster, M., Vander Ark, J., and Weldon, W. (2012), 'Act like a local: How to sell in emerging markets', *Chief Marketing & Sales Officer Forum*, http://www.mckinseyonmarketingandsales.com/act-like-a-local-how-to-sell-in-emerging-markets [Accessed: July 30, 2016].

4 Inditex. (2013). *Annual Report.* http://www.inditex.com/documents/10279/18789/Inditex_Group_Annual_Report_2013.pdf/88b623b8-b6b0-4d38-b45e-45822932ff72 [Accessed: February 12, 2015].

5 Solberg, C. A. (2008), 'Product complexity and cultural distance effects on managing international distributor relationships: A contingency approach', *Journal of International Marketing*, 16(3), pp. 57–83.

6 On-trade channel is also known as the Horeca channel (hotel/restaurant/café).

7 Brillo, B.B.C. (2014), 'Shifting economic regimes for retail in the Philippines: External impetus amidst the workings of domestic politics', *The International Review of Retail, Distribution and Consumer Research*, 24(5), pp. 516–30.

8 Warren, S. (2014), 'MLM laws in China', February 3, 2014, http://w-wlaw.com/mlm-laws-in-china/ [Accessed: February 11, 2015]; Ambler, T., Witzel, M., and Xi, C. (2008). *Doing business in China*. 3rd ed. New York: Routledge.

9 Loeb, W. (2014), 'Walmart's international challenge: Trying to understand local shoppers', *Forbes*, March 26, 2014, http://www.forbes.com/sites/walterloeb/2014/03/26/walmarts-international-challenge-trying-to-understand-local-shoppers/ [Accessed: February 20, 2015].

10 Shannon, R. (2014), 'The expansion of modern trade food retailing in Thailand', *The International Review of Retail, Distribution and Consumer Research*, 24(5), pp. 531–43.

11 Euromonitor International. (2014), 'Shiseido Co Ltd in beauty and personal care (world), global company profile', June 19, 2014, http://www.euromonitor.com/shiseido-co-ltd-in-beauty-and-personal-care/report [Accessed: March 1, 2015]; (2014), 'Shiseido annual report', http://www.shiseidogroup.com/ir/library/annual/pdf/2014/anu00001.pdf [Accessed: March 3, 2015].

12 Euromonitor International. (2014), 'Internet vs store-based shopping: the global move towards omnichannel retailing strategy briefing', August 28, 2014, www.euromonitor.com, [Accessed: February 15, 2015].

13 Euromonitor International. (2014), 'Digital life and consumers', December 22, 2014, www.euromonitor.com [Accessed: February 15, 2015].

14 Bonetti, F. (2014), 'Italian luxury fashion brands in China: A retail perspective', *The International Review of Retail, Distribution and Consumer Research*, 24(4), pp. 453–77.

15 A description of the types of intermediary that international companies can use is provided in the Appendix of this chapter.

16 Sales branches set up by manufacturers in foreign countries are not considered wholesalers. However, since in practice they perform a wholesale activity, they are usually classified as wholesalers by national statistical offices. The difference between sales offices and sales branches is that sales offices do not carry inventory. See Chapter 8 for a discussion of entry strategies.

17 Ranfagni, S. and Guercini, S. (2014), 'Guanxi and distribution in China: The case of Ferrero Group', *The International Review of Retail, Distribution and Consumer Research*, 24(3), pp. 294–310.

18 Samli, A. C. and El-Ansary, A. I. (2007), 'The role of wholesalers in developing countries', *International Review of Retail, Distribution and Consumer Research*, 17(4), pp. 353–8.

19 China Resources Enterprise Limited. (2013), 'Financial and operational review 2013 first quarter', May 16, 2013, http://www.cre.com.hk/home/investorrel/announcements/2013/201410/P020141022565842995709.pdf [Accessed: January 18, 2015].

20 Molla-Descals, A., Frasquet, M., Ruiz-Molina, M., and Navarro-Sanchez, E. (2014), 'Determinants of website traffic: The case of European fashion apparel retailers', *The International Review of Retail, Distribution and Consumer Research*, 24(4), pp. 411–30.

21 'Fits.me virtual fitting room', http://fits.me [Accessed: July 30, 2016].

22 An example is the case of Southeast Asia, described in a recent study by Coe and Bok: Coe, N.M. and Bok, R. (2014), 'Retail transitions in Southeast Asia', *The International Review of Retail, Distribution and Consumer Research*, 24(5), pp. 479–99.

23 Diaz, A., Magni, M., and Poh, F. (2012), 'From oxcart to Wal-Mart: Four keys to reaching emerging-market consumers', *McKinsey Quarterly*, http://www.mckinsey.com/industries/retail/our-insights/from-oxcart-to-wal-mart-four-keys-to-reaching-emerging-market-consumers [Accessed: July 30, 2016].

24 Tackett, K. (2014), 'European grocery retailing', May, 2014, http://www.planetretail.net/presentations/ApexBrasilPresentation.pdf [Accessed: January 12, 2015].

25 Mandhachitara, R. (2014), 'Old traps for new players: Western direct retailing investment in emerging Asian markets', *International Review of Management and Marketing*, 4(2), pp. 150–9.

26 Nivea Haus. http://www.beiersdorf.com/newsroom/topic-collection/nivea-haus [Accessed: October 18, 2015].

27 Chiu, S. (2014), 'North American trends: Concessions within department stores', *Retail Insider*, http://www.
retail-insider.com/retail-insider/2014/3/trend-in-luxury-retailing-concessions-within-department-stores
[Accessed: February 21, 2015].

28 http://www.net-a-porter.com/magazine/261/10 [Accessed: January 18, 2015]; http://www.sugarpova.com/
[Accessed: January 18, 2015].

29 Euromonitor International. (2014), 'Internet vs store-based shopping: The global move towards omnichannel
retailing', August, 2014, www.euromonitor.com [Accessed: February 20, 2015].

30 Amazon. (2013). *Annual Report.* http://phx.corporate-ir.net/phoenix.zhtml?c=97664&p=irol-reportsannual
[Accessed: January 13, 2015]; Euromonitor International. (2014), 'Internet vs store-based shopping: The
global move towards omnichannel retailing', August, 2014, www.euromonitor.com [Accessed: February 15,
2015]; Flavián, C. and Guinalíu, M. (2005), 'The influence of virtual communities on distribution strategies in
the Internet', *International Journal of Retail & Distribution Management*, 33(6), pp. 405–25.

31 The World Factbook. (2015), https://www.cia.gov/library/publications/the-world-factbook/docs/refmaps.html
[Accessed: August 1, 2015].

32 An in-depth analysis of entry modes is carried out in Chapter 8.

33 Gap Inc. 'History', http://www.gapinc.com/content/gapinc/html/aboutus/ourstory.html [Accessed: January
25, 2015].

34 Trefis Team. (2014), 'Gap beats on profits, raises outlook, gets aggressive on Asian expansion', *Forbes,*
http://www.forbes.com/sites/greatspeculations/2014/08/25/gap-beats-on-profits-raises-outlook-gets-
aggressive-on-asian-expansion/ [Accessed: March 1, 2015].

35 Dennis, N. (2011), 'Carrefour up on Brazil retail joint venture', *Financial Times*, http://www.ft.com/cms/
s/0/15481b1a-a167-11e0-baa8-00144feabdc0.html [Accessed: March 1, 2015].

36 Chan, P., Finnegan, C., and Sternquist, B. (2011), 'Country and firm level factors in international retail
expansion', *European Journal of Marketing*, 45(6), pp. 1005–22.

37 Diaz, A., Magni, M., and Poh, F. (2012), 'From oxcart to Wal-Mart: Four keys to reaching emerging-market
consumers', *McKinsey Quarterly*, http://www.mckinsey.com/industries/retail/our-insights/from-oxcart-to-wal-
mart-four-keys-to-reaching-emerging-market-consumers [Accessed: July 30, 2016].

38 Swoboda, B., Berg, B., and Dabija, D. (2014), 'International transfer and perception of retail formats',
International Marketing Review, 31(2), pp. 155–80.

39 Shankar, S. (2014), 'Tesco confirms joint venture with Tata Trent for $140 million; will operate in Indian
retail market worth $500 billion', *International Business Times*, http://www.ibtimes.com/tesco-confirms-
joint-venture-tata-trent-140-million-will-operate-indian-retail-market-worth-500 [Accessed: March 3,
2015].

40 Euromonitor International. (2014), 'India: Country profile', October 24, 2014, www.euromonitor.com
[Accessed: February 14, 2015].

41 Dimitrova, B.V., Rosenbloom, B., and Larsen Andras, T. (2014), 'Does the degree of retailer international
involvement affect retailer performance?', *The International Review of Retail, Distribution and Consumer
Research*, 24(3), pp. 243–77.

42 Xinhua, english.news.cn. (2013), 'Logistics costs remain high in China: Report', http://news.xinhuanet.com/
english/china/2013-02/08/c_132159928.htm [Accessed: January 2, 2015]; Joc.com. (2013), 'Logistics costs
stay at 8.5 percent of US GDP', June 19, 2013, http://www.joc.com/economy-watch/us-economy-news/
logistics-costs-stay-85-percent-us-gdp_20130619.html [Accessed: January 2, 2015].

43 China Daily. (2014), 'Top ten fast food chains in China', July 28,2014, http://www.chinadaily.com.cn/
bizchina/2014-07/28/content_17932826_6.htm [Accessed: February 12, 2015].

44 Unilever Transport & Distribution. http://www.unilever.com/sustainable-living-2014/reducing-environmental-
impact/greenhouse-gases/transport-and-distribution/ [Accessed: January 20, 2015].

45 The World Factbook. (2015), https://www.cia.gov/library/publications/the-world-factbook/docs/refmaps.html
[Accessed: August 1, 2015].

46 Inditex. (2013). *Annual report.* http://www.inditex.com/documents/10279/18789/Inditex_Group_Annual_
Report_2013.pdf/88b623b8-b6b0-4d38-b45e-45822932ff72 [Accessed: February 16, 2015].

47 https://www.floraholland.com/en/buying/logistics-and-facilities/ [Accessed: February 28, 2015]; 'Flora

Holland Facts and Figures', https://www.floraholland.com/en/about-floraholland/who-we-are-what-we-do/facts-and-figures/ [Accessed: February 28, 2015].

48 Harwood, S. (2007), 'Brits and Scandinavians top web shoppers', *Revolution,* 27, March, 2007, http://revo-online.com/ [Accessed: August 10, 2010].

CASE 12.1   FHM—ADAPTING TO MAKE AN INTERNATIONAL PUBLISHING BRAND

By Conor Carroll, University of Limerick

In the early 90's a new phenomenon emerged in publishing, which captured the cultural zeitgeist of the time – *"the lads' magazine"*. Magazines such as Loaded, FHM, and Maxim emerged, causing a sensation in publishing and the popular media. Now young men were buying these monthly magazines in droves, which were very different from traditional *"Top Shelf"* magazines. Previously men's magazines were seen only as pornographic magazines or those focused on the car industry. These new publications captured huge readership figures through their mix of sexy covergirls, lads' advice, fashion, sport, fitness, interviews, reviews and sheer irreverence. This revolutionary format at the time, has now been mimicked by countless clones, and has become formulaic. Loaded started the publishing revolution by creating the genre in 1994, using the tagline *"for men who should know better"*. This UK publishing sensation, a previously untapped market, is now turning into an international success story. The format is now conquering foreign markets with the same formula.

FHM magazine, which stands for "For Him Magazine", has become an international success story. It is owned by British publisher EMAP, which has a used, a variety of entry techniques to launch the brand in over 27 editions, including countries such as USA, China, Spain, Turkey, and Greece. In an effort to transform FHM into becoming an international brand, EMAP utilised different entry techniques such full ownership, joint ventures, and licenses with other international publishers. The company first launched an international edition in Singapore, through a licensing arrangement, in 1997. Based on this initial success, FHM Turkey (License), FHM Australia (Full Ownership), FHM US (Full Ownership), FHM South Africa (Joint Venture), and so on were rolled out in their internationalisation strategy. EMAP was able to utilise its editorial content, making adaptations based on cultural needs. Through this leveraging of original content, it was also able to gain access to its global advertisers' client list such as Seiko, Nokia, Sony, Reebok, Smirnoff amongst others. The image below illustrates the subtle differences in colour and language used in a variety of international editions, yet the cover model remains the same.

As can be seen below, an initial editorial story would be conceived in the UK parent magazine, and then rolled out in other geographic markets, making suitable adjustments in the language and visuals used, which are in line with the national culture, and psyche of their international edition. Colours and language have an embedded meaning within certain cultures, and require adaptations to make them culturally acceptable.

These magazines are even garnering success in very religious countries such as Turkey and Indonesia. These editions and even their very successful UK and US editions have to be very careful with cultural norms and try not to invoke the wrath of conservative watchdogs. The initial success of these magazines was partly

EXHIBIT 12.1

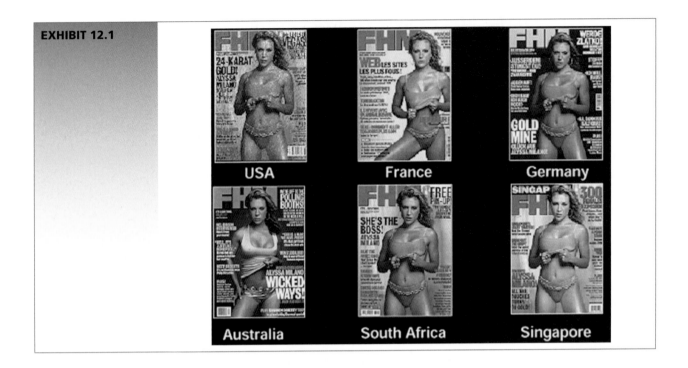

EXHIBIT 12.2

due to them achieving intensive distribution with retailers, stocking their titles on lower shelves and gaining access to prominent displays. Now the UK's leading retailer, Tesco is changing their merchandising policy towards these magazines, by placing them on higher stand positions, and covering some of the content so that only the magazine mastheads are in view. The retailer argues that they are family supermarket, and that some of their customers have complained of the outrageous and sexually explicit content. Others view this as a form of quasi censorship, where the mammoth retailer is using its power to dictate cultural norms, determining what is morally acceptable within society. All of the major men's titles have been issued with this policy change. The supermarket will however still stock the titles as long as sales are strong. In the United States where Wal-Mart practically controls retailing, the supermarket has even de-listed some men's monthly magazines due to clashes over editorial content, which were seen as too risqué with the American heartland.

CHAPTER 13

Launching Global Communication and Advertising

If communication is to change behavior it must be grounded in the desire and interests of the receivers.

Aristotle

LEARNING OBJECTIVES

After Reading This Chapter, You Should Be Able to:

- Explain what constitutes a global promotional strategy and what marketing activities are included in it.
- Discuss some of the challenges and opportunities marketers face on a global scale when developing their communication mix.
- Define the differences between global and localized marketing communications.
- Understand how culture influences advertising preferences.
- Provide examples of regulatory issues that advertising executives may encounter around the world and explain why they are needed.
- Know about the practical issues when designing a communications campaign.

A REGIONAL BRAND GOES INTERNATIONAL

France is believed to be the capital of perfume and some people even think it was the French who invented it. But as a symbol of civilization, perfume has had a history almost as long as the human race. Some 4000 years ago, the Mesopotamians began using incense, the first form of perfume. In ancient times, scents and perfumes were quite popular among the ancient Greeks and Romans to hide unpleasant body smells. Later in the eleventh and twelfth century, through trade with the Islamic world and with the returning crusaders, perfume was brought to Europe. And thanks to the popularity of perfumed gloves in the mid-seventeenth century, the use of perfume grew steadily in France.

After more than 300 years' development, French firms now belong to the top leading players in the perfume market. In addition, the French luxury giant LVMH and Clarins are both listed within the world top-10 perfumes and cosmetics group list of 2009.[1] And, of course, everybody knows about the great French names in the global perfume industry, such as Chanel, Christian Dior, and Yves Saint Laurent. What has mainly gone unrecognized is the emergence and development of **Group L'Occitane International S.A.** (Figure 13.1), which specializes in manufacturing and distributing perfume, cosmetics, and well-being products. It has succeeded in building a strong brand identity, while conserving its underlying regional roots and the natural origin of its products.[2]

L'Occitane's story began in Provence, a region in the southeast of France. Drawing inspiration from his childhood in Provence, Olivier Baussan purchased a steam distiller to produce pure rosemary essential oil, with the purpose of recreating the tradition of his region. At first, he sold this essential oil to local villagers and his products quickly became popular in the local market. In 1976, he chose the brand name **L'Occitane** to refer to the ancient province that once covered the south of France, northeastern Spain, and northern Italy. In 1978, the first boutique and factory was opened. In 1996, L'Occitane was renamed **L'Occitane en Provence** and the first boutiques were opened in Hong Kong and New York. In 2010, L'Occitane en Provence, raised $US708 million on the Hong Kong Stock Exchange, and became the first French company to go public in Hong Kong. According to its presentation of annual results for the year ended March 31, 2014, it achieved net sales in Japan (€177.7 million), the USA (€133.3 million), Hong Kong (€110.7 million), China (€79.9 million), and France (€87.1 million), which

FIGURE 13.1
L'Occitane en Provence
Source: © Authors

are the most important markets.[3] Total net sales globally amounted to €1,054.9 million.

In recent years, the demand for natural- and organic-based products has been growing worldwide and in 2005, L'Occitane Trading (Shanghai) Co. Limited was established and this subsidiary opened the first L'Occitane boutique in mainland China, in Beijing. Since then, L'Occitane has continued its expansion and brand building activities in this dynamic market. **Until 2014, L'Occitane maintained 1295 of its own retail stores of which 136 were in China.** These shops are located in 38 cities, most of which are amongst the top 50 richest cities (in terms of GDP) in China. Sales in China amounted to €79.9 million in 2014, an increase of 19.9 percent. Marketing expenses worldwide increased by 6.1 percent, or €6.5 million, to €113.9 million in 2014.[4] This increase was attributable to:

- a brand mix effect, with the development of new brands, accounting for 0.1 points;

- investments in digital media for 0.3 points notably in Japan, the USA, France, and the UK;

- investments in mailings and customer relationship management ("CRM") particularly in France, the USA, and the UK, for 0.2 points; and

- investments in samples, windows, other communication tools, and other effects for 0.1 points.

The lowered investment in traditional media allowed to partly help balance the increased efforts in marketing expenses by 0.2 points. So how did L'Occitane manage its communications strategy in China to achieve these results?

Brand Name—L'Occitane en Provence

For non-francophone people, the word "L'Occitane" is very difficult to pronounce. In a video called "How to say L'Occitane," which can be found on most L'Occitane websites (www.loccitane.com), people from all over the world pronounce this name in various funny ways with different accents. What is interesting is that, although some people did not know how to say it correctly, they were pretty sure this was a French name because of the typical French way of spelling. For those who were not so familiar with Latin languages, it was still easy to recognize the link between the brand and France by seeing "en Provence." Actually, there are many brand names like this, for instance, L'Oréal Paris, Maybelline New York and Lancel Paris. These well-designed brand names create strong links between the brand and its origin. This is what we mean when we refer to the **country-of-origin (COO) effect.**[5] The symbolic value of the brand allures Chinese consumers to import products. To make full use of the favorable images that French origin may bring about, L'Occitane claims on its official Chinese website that "all of L'Occitane's products are developed and produced in Manosque, Provence."[6] For L'Occitane, "Made in France" is fully deserved, as its origin country, its production country, and the main sourcing country are the same, i.e. France.

As many people in China are not sensitive to the Western alphabet, foreign brands always enter the Chinese market with a tailored Chinese name. These names are usually translated into Chinese characters by trying to match the pronunciation, which is called "transliteration," and each selected character has a suitable meaning. Although L'Occitane in China keeps its French name in many occasions, it also has a Chinese name, which is usually used for communication. L'Occitane in Chinese is

"欧舒丹"

and is pronounced as "Ou Shu Dan," which means Europe, pleasure, and a magical medicine in Chinese myth, which keeps people forever young and healthy. This Chinese name communicates to consumers the brand's European origin, its sensuality and its effectiveness.

Communication Through Packaging

After hundreds of years of development, packaging is not just used for containing or protecting the products, more importantly it elevates the products' commercial value by serving as an important marketing tool to communicate product information, brand concept, and company value to its audiences. For L'Occitane, as the Provence/France origin is one of its selling points, we can find clues about COO in the packaging design.

- **Primary packaging:** As part of its commitment to minimize environmental impact, L'Occitane uses environmentally friendly material and tries to reduce primary packaging. The pure, simple, and traditional design of L'Occitane packaging may not be directly associated with France's luxury image, however, its vintage style labels, typical paper wrappers of Savon de Marseille, and linen perfumed sachets keep reminding consumers of the Provencal legend about L'Occitane. To make the French origin more obvious to consumers, "Made in France" is written on the front side of each pack. At the same time, L'Occitane keeps the original French packaging in the Chinese market, combined with a Chinese sticker showing the translation of key information. Even though most people do not understand French, the original packaging makes its French story more credible.

- **Gift packs:** Besides primary packaging, L'Occitane gift packs are also aiming to communicate the brand's concept. The green keynote indicates its nature ingredient, and the typical Provencal landscape with blue sky, green tree and lavender field in the picture is clearly associated with its origin, where the tradition and inspiration came from.

Place Communications

In mainland China, L'Occitane has built its one hundred and twenty-seven boutiques within the past seven years, in twenty out of the twenty-two provinces and in all four directly controlled municipalities.

Boutique Location: According to L'Occitane's website, until now, L'Occitane is present in thirty-eight different cities in China, mainly located in developed areas around the southeast coast. Thirty-one of these cities can be found in the Top-50 city list ranked by GDP for the first quarter of 2012. To match its premium positioning as well as the French luxury image, L'Occitane only opens its boutiques in the most prosperous commercial centres in each of these cities, and usually next to other luxury or premium brands.

Online Promotions

Official website: L'Occitane has local versions of websites for 48 countries or regions. Through its website for mainland China, local consumers can shop online and find presentations of products, as well as stories behind the products, information about the location of boutiques, after-sales services, etc.

One of the key messages the company wants to transfer to clients is nature and beauty. For example, while using the portal of its Chinese website, angelicas are used with drops of water in the light-blue sky as the background.

Offline Promotion

Like many other brands, L'Occitane does not limit its promotion to using the Internet. Its brand story was and is being narrated through numerous offline channels in different ways. For example, the promotion or animation in boutiques, the presentation of brands and products in fashion and beauty magazines, face-to-face conferences, or activities with clients are all examples for this. The company communicates directly with specific clients. For instance, in 2009, L'Occitane organized a series of events named "Go into top 500" with the female fashion and beauty magazine "Today's style, OGGI." Through these events, L'Occitane aims to communicate directly with the female employees of the world's top 500 companies in China.

The print media-like magazine is also one of the channels used by L'Occitane for brand promotion. Since 2005, the year of entry into mainland China, the company has advertised its products and brands in fashion and beauty magazines, such as Cosmopolitan, Elle, Vogue, Modern Weekly, etc.

The use of multiple channels and communication instruments by L'Occitane is just one example of how companies today need to think about integrated marketing communications.

GLOBAL INTEGRATED MARKETING COMMUNICATIONS

With many changes in the world related to globalization, digitization, and complexity, it seems that traditional approaches of marketing communication have exhausted themselves and traditional tools are becoming less effective. Namely the consumers are determining the needs they want fulfilled now. Consequently, a rational marketing and communication approach must be demand rather than supply-oriented. That is why integrated marketing communications (IMC) have become more urgent and powerful nowadays. As defined by the American Association of Advertising Agencies, integrated marketing communications "... recognizes the value of a comprehensive plan that evaluates the strategic roles of a variety of communication disciplines advertising, public relations, personal selling, and sales promotion and combines them to provide clarity, consistency, and maximum communication impact."[7]

The latest thinking on the IMC approach recognizes that the various elements of a company's communication strategy must be not only carefully coordinated, but that their impact as a whole on the market should also be considered. Figure 13.2 provides an overview of the elements of marketing communications, several of which can be used both online and offline, as well as nationally and internationally. Some other activities are also part of the promotional mix but are harder to categorize, such as sponsorship, product placement, events, and others.

International advertising refers to advertising conducted in foreign markets. International advertising traditionally has required different strategies than domestic advertising, because of the differences in culture, economic systems, government regulations, and consumer needs.[8]

International advertising can be exercised in channels like newspapers, magazines, journals, television, radio, cinema, or the Internet. In addition, companies are shifting their spending from traditional media to Facebook, blogs, and their own websites; they are experimenting with advertising on tablet computers, with location-based services on telephones, and real-time information about products

Advertising	Public Relations	Sales Promotion	Direct Marketing	Personal Selling
• Newspapers	• Annual reports	• Rebates and	• Direct mail	• Sales
• Magazines	• House magazines	price discounts	• Database	presentations
• Journals	• Press relations	• Catalogues and	marketing	• Sales force
• Television	• Events	brochures	• Internet	management
• Radio	• Lobbying	• Samples,	marketing	• Trade fairs
• Cinema	• Sponsorship	coupons, gifts	• Mobile	• Exhibitions
• Outdoor		• Competitions	marketing	
• Internet			(SMS, MMS)	
			• Viral marketing	
			• Advertising	
			games	

FIGURE 13.2
Individual Elements in Integrated Marketing Communications
Source: Compiled by Authors

and companies. For most of its existence, marketing communications simply meant marketers repeating their brand's message through advertisements, jingles, billboards, and other "one-way" mass communications. With the arrival of the Internet, customers build their own blogs, wikis, videos, etc., and share their views and their brand experiences with other consumers and with the brands themselves. Marketers are learning the importance of these one-on-one, personalized communications and are incorporating them into their communication plans more and more often. Different types of advertising include primary demand stimulation, selective demand stimulation, direct response advertising, delayed response advertising, corporate advertising.

International public relations "is a strategic communication process that builds mutually beneficial relationships between organizations and their publics"[9] involving international actors. As a management function, public relations also encompasses the following:

- Anticipating, analyzing, and interpreting public opinion, attitudes and issues that might impact, for good or ill, the operations and plans of the organization.

- Counseling management at all levels in the organization with regard to policy decisions, courses of action, and communication, taking into account their public ramifications and the organization's social or citizenship responsibilities.

- Researching, conducting, and evaluating, on a continuing basis, programs of action and communication to achieve the informed public understanding necessary to the success of an organization's aims. These may include marketing, financial, fund raising, employee, community or government relations, and other programs.

- Planning and implementing the organization's efforts to influence or change public policy. Setting objectives, planning, budgeting, recruiting and training staff, developing facilities—in short, managing the resources needed to perform all of the above.[10]

Although public relations has been studied as a social science and formalized only in the twentieth century, evidence of its practice can be traced back to ancient civilizations in Egypt, Babylon, China, Greece, and Rome, to name but a few. In medieval India, sutradhars, or traveling storytellers, spread rulers' messages, serving a common public relations function. The Egyptian leader Hatshepsut, the first female pharaoh, might not have been able to hire a public relations agency to help improve her image, but she was surrounded by advisors who guided her using public relations techniques.

Despite the increasing application of public relations, there is little consistency among practitioners across the world. In Asia, public relations professionals commonly see their work as tantamount to sales and marketing, in Latin America event planning might be viewed as public relations, and in the United States it is often called a strategic management function. The gap between these forms of public relations is evident in the lack of a truly international public relations theory that addresses disparate nations, varying economic and sociopolitical systems, and different cultures.[11]

International sales promotion refers to any paid consumer or trade communication program of limited duration that adds tangible value to a product or brand, involving international players. Typically there is a distinction between price versus non-price promotions and consumer versus trade promotions.

Non-price promotions may take the form of free samples, premiums, "buy one, get one free" offers, sweepstakes, and contests. **Consumer sales promotions** may be designed to make consumers aware of a new product, to stimulate nonusers to sample an existing product, or to increase overall consumer demand. **Trade sales promotions** are designed to increase product availability in distribution channels. At many companies, expenditures for sales promotion activities have surpassed expenditures for media advertising. At any level of expenditure, however, sales promotion is only one of several marketing communication tools. Sales promotion plans and programs should be integrated and coordinated with those for advertising, public relations, and personal selling.

In countries with low levels of economic development, low incomes limit the range of promotional tools available. In such countries, free samples and demonstrations are more likely to be used than coupons or on-pack premiums. Market maturity can also be different from country to country: consumer sampling and coupons are appropriate in growing markets, but mature markets might require trade allowances or loyalty programs. In addition, local perceptions of a particular promotional tool or program can vary. Japanese consumers, for example, are reluctant to use coupons at the checkout counter. A particular premium can be seen as a waste of money. Statistics on the use of coupons in the USA reveal the following insights:[12]

- 79.8 percent of consumers regularly shopped with coupons in 2012, compared to 63.6 percent during pre-recession 2007.

- The average value of a coupon in 2012 was $1.53 overall, a penny less than in 2010 and 2011.

- 46 percent of shoppers cited lack of coupons for products they buy as the reason personal coupon usage dropped between 2011 and 2012.

- 39 percent of smartphone owners use their devices to redeem mobile coupons in-store, compared to just 10 percent of tablet users.

- The number of mobile coupon users has jumped 10 percent since 2010.

- Approximately 25 million Americans use mobile coupon apps each month.

- Nearly two-thirds of consumers use coupons for more than half their shopping trips.

Recently, mobile coupons have generated significant interest and development in mobile marketing.[13] Mobile coupons are electronic tickets transmitted to mobile phones. They can include text, pictures, audio, and even video. Consumers receive and store mobile coupons on their mobile phones until they decide to redeem the coupons for a financial discount or rebate when purchasing a product or service. Around three-quarters of the world's inhabitants now have access to a mobile phone and the number of mobile subscriptions worldwide has increased to 6 billion.[14] With the rapid growth in the prevalence of mobile phones, the delivery of coupons has expanded beyond traditional newspaper flyers and street distribution to mobile coupons. This change has led to consumers not having to passively acquire coupons from newspapers, magazines, or products, because they can download the coupons offered by stores according to their needs. Online couponing requires that localized online access is available (Box 13.1).

International direct marketing refers to any communication with a consumer or business recipient that is designed to generate a response in the form of an order, a request for further information, and/or a visit to a store or other place of business. Companies use direct mail, telemarketing, television, print, and other media to generate responses and build databases filled with purchase histories and other information about customers. By contrast, mass marketing communications are typically aimed at broad segments of consumers with certain demographic, psychographic, or behavioral characteristics in common.

Direct marketing is the most efficient way of gaining new customers and retaining existing ones in international markets. Direct marketing allows a company to align communication concepts with the needs of specific target groups, and to address target audiences using personalized and individual messages. It also means a company can deploy its financial resources precisely where they are

---

Box 13.1   Technology-in-Focus: Adapting B2B Sales Promotions to Local Tastes

Sales promotions and communications are an important part of the global promotional mix and as such they require their own set of considerations, especially when it comes to online business-to-business marketing. In a recent report, Forrester Research analysts discussed the importance of localizing promotional sales communications, particularly for technology B2B buyers. They identified the following three important considerations for designing B2B communications for the global markets:

Find out who the key decision-makers are in each market and what the main business concerns are for them. It is likely that each participant in the decision-making process will have different priorities. It is important to address as many of these top issues as possible in your localized sales communications.

Familiarize yourself with the preferred ways in which business executives collect information during the decision-making process and make your sales communications available through those channels. For example, Forrester's research found that 73 percent of American executives rely on information from industry, vendor, or trade websites during their decision-making process, while only 52 percent of French executives do.

Ensure that localized online access is available not only for information, but also for features such as free trials and demonstrations, payment options, etc.

Source: Adapted from: Jennifer Bélissent, 'Expanding globally, marketing locally', [Teleconference presentation slides 15–17], Forrester Research, March 25, 2009.

needed and stay informed about customers' current position, since direct marketing enables it to measure the success of the measures it has put in place. The response it receives gives valuable information about the needs and behavior of target audiences, allowing it to optimize the services it offers and send audience messages that speak to customers on an even more personal level. A recent study by McKinsey[15] illustrates that emails remain a very significant means of reaching customers in the US; they are even more effective than social media. This is because 91 percent of all US consumers still use emails daily, and the rate at which emails prompt purchases is not only estimated to be at least three times that of social media, but the average order value is also 17 percent higher. But this also implies serious challenges for a marketing organization because creating and sending out thousands of direct marketing emails a day is very different from sending a mass email blast.

Companies can also use many other types of direct marketing campaigns. The key is finding one that best suits one's type of business. The first step in executing a direct marketing campaign is finding quality leads. The best example for direct marketing is probably Amazon which interacts directly with customers on its websites to help them discover and buy almost anything and everything on the Internet, with only a few clicks of the mouse button. Or similarly Dell, where consumers can order directly, and Dell quickly and efficiently delivers the new computers to their homes or offices.

International personal sales involves the building of relationships through communication for the purposes of creating a sales transaction. Personal selling is an interpersonal process whereby a seller tries to uncover and satisfy a buyer's needs in a mutually, long-term beneficial manner suitable for both parties.[16] Thus, personal selling is an interpersonal, two-way communication between a buyer and seller whereby the seller employs persuasive communication regarding goods and/or services. Communication is the most basic activity for the sales representative during personal selling exchanges.

Personal selling is a social situation involving two persons in a communication dyad. Success depends on how well both parties achieve a common understanding enabling mutual goal fulfillment through social interaction. But interaction in an international environment can be hampered by many factors:

- **Political risk:** Unstable or corrupt governments can completely change the rules for the sales team. For example, Colombia offers great market potential and its government projects an image of openness. However, many companies have found the unspoken rules of business to be inordinately burdensome. In a country ruled by a dictatorship, the target audience and accompanying message of the sales effort tend to be far narrower and restricted because government planners mandate how business will be conducted.

- **Regulatory hurdles:** Governments sometimes set up quota systems or impose tariffs that affect entering foreign sales forces. In part, governments consider such actions to be an easy source of revenue, but, even more importantly, policymakers want to ensure that sales teams from local firms retain a competitive edge in terms of what they can offer and at what price. Regulations can also take the form of rules that restrict certain types of sales activities. In 1998, for example, the Chinese government banned door-to-door selling, effectively blocking Avon's business model. Avon responded by establishing a network of store representatives; today, China is Avon's fastest growing global market. CEO Andrea Jung expects that, within just a few years, China will be adding $1 billion a year to Avon's bottom line.[17]

- **Currency fluctuations:** There have been many instances where a company's sales effort has been derailed not by ineffectiveness or lack of market opportunity but by fluctuating currency values. In the mid-1980s, for example, Caterpillar's global market share declined when the dollar's strength allowed Komatsu to woo US customers away. Then, while Caterpillar's management team was preoccupied with domestic issues, competitors chipped away at the firm's position in global markets.

- **Language issues:** Doing sales in different countries does not only require knowledge of either the local language or of English as the international business language (EIB), but necessitates insights into customs, body behavior, linguistics, and cultures. For instance, some countries prefer emotional language whereas others tend to be rather rational.

Integrated Marketing Communications and Consequences for Managers

Integrated marketing communications combines different media to improve the results of marketing campaigns. Using direct marketing to follow up an advertising campaign and linking the direct marketing piece to a dedicated website page is an example of integrated marketing communication. Each element of the campaign reinforces the others and moves prospects toward a purchasing decision. Consistency of the message is one of the most important elements of integrated marketing communication. The copy style and content should be consistent across all media. When prospects read an advertisement, visit a website, pick up a leaflet, or take a call from a telemarketing specialist, they should perceive the same product descriptions and benefit statements in each communication.

What does all of this mean for global marketers? Communicating the essence of a brand on a global scale has never been easy. Creating a coherent, effective, and efficient global campaign in today's increasingly connected and digital world presents new challenges, such as selecting appropriate tools, suitable media channels, deciding between online- and offline communications, etc. The following points illustrate some of the major challenges:[18]

- A number of new channels with global reach have opened up for marketers with satellite and Internet networks, multimedia mobile phones, and popular social networking tools such as Facebook, YouTube, Myspace, Flickr, blogs, and others. This has not meant that traditional channels such as TV or print adds are no longer viable in certain markets, however, only that global promotion campaigns would have to incorporate all of the above and be planned accordingly.

- Digital technologies have nearly erased the distinction between global and local communications (but there are still some important differences, for instance, in terms of culture and language use, see below). Today, a promotional video posted on YouTube can "go viral" and be accessible to 20 million viewers in more than 20 countries every month, regardless of what audience it was intended for originally. This certainly offers more reach for each marketing dollar, but it also increases the chances for misinterpretation across cultures and languages.

- Communications about a brand can be started by a consumer as well as by companies. This is forcing marketers to relinquish some of the control over their campaigns, pick up new skills such as reputation management, and aim for the type of authentic and open communications that are valued by today's consumers.

- Audience tracking, sales conversion rates, and other measurements available through digital marketing campaigns have raised the bar of accountability for marketers, who are required now more than ever to provide clear return on investment (ROI) metrics for their campaigns.

Taken collectively, there are a couple of differences between classic communications and integrated marketing communications.[19] Table 13.1 highlights the changing nature of communications and the changing attitude of the consumer. IMC are much more personalized, customer-oriented, relationship-based, and interactive. The main drivers for IMC are a loss of faith in mass media advertising, media cost inflation, need for more impact, need for more cost-effectiveness and efficiency, media and audience fragmentation, and a move toward integrating the customer into the creation of messages (see also the last section of this chapter).

Classic Communications	Integrated Communications	**TABLE 13.1** Classic Versus Integrated Marketing Communications
Mass communications	Selective communications	
Monologue	Dialogue	
Information is sent	Information is requested	
Information provision	Information—self service	
Sender takes initiative	Receiver takes initiative	
Effective through repetition	Effective through relevance	
Offensive	Defensive	
Transaction-oriented	Relationship-oriented	

Source: Adapted from: Van Raaij, W.F. (1998). 'Integration of communication: Starting from the sender or the receiver?' *Effectiveness in Communications Management*, pp. 169–84, Deventer: Samson.

GLOBALIZED VERSUS LOCALIZED COMMUNICATION

Along with increasing globalization, many multinational firms are facing the question of standardizing or localizing (adapting) their communications campaigns. If we think of global companies and global standardized communications, McDonald's and Coca-Cola are probably the first that come to our minds. This is mainly because we think of them as global brands. In academic literature, the term "global brand" was largely unknown until the 1980s even though global brands have existed in one form or another for a very long time. As already pointed out in Chapter 10, global branding is an important topic among researchers today.

From a practical perspective, Interbrand identified the top brands leading the global brand list in 2013 (Table 13.2).[20] There are several criteria for inclusion in Interbrand's annual Best Global Brands report. The brand must be truly global and needs to have successfully transcended geographic and cultural boundaries. It must have expanded across the established economic centers of the world, and be establishing a presence in the major markets of the future. In measurable terms, this requires that: at least 30 percent of revenues must come from outside the brand's home region; it must have a presence in at least three major continents, as well as broad geographic coverage in emerging markets; there must be sufficient publicly available data on the brand's financial performance; economic profit must be expected to be positive over the longer term, delivering a return above the brand's operating and financing costs; the brand must have a public profile and awareness above and beyond its own marketplace.

While we all perceive these brands as more or less global, we cannot automatically say that all companies adopt a 100 percent global approach. They differ with regard to globalizing individual functions like sales, marketing, human resources and even with respect to the brand, we can distinguish between brands that are more local and those that are more global. This choice strongly impacts on the

TABLE 13.2 Top Global Brands in the World (2013)	**No. in the World**	**Company**	**Brand Value in US$ Million**
	1	Apple	98,314
	2	Google	93,291
	3	Coca-Cola	79,213
	4	IBM	78,808
	5	Microsoft	59,546
	6	GE	46,947
	7	McDonald's	41,992
	8	Samsung	39,610
	9	Intel	37,257
	10	Toyota	35,346

Source: Adapted from: Interbrand (2013), http://interbrand.com/best-brands/best-global-brands/2013/ranking/ [Accessed: December 16, 2014].

characteristics of the communication strategy. In fact Interbrand suggests some dimensions that can be critical for the success of a global brand, where communication plays an important role: recognition, consistency, emotion, uniqueness, relevance, and management.[21]

- **Recognition** is typical of leading brands and is based on a strong awareness that enables rapid penetration into new markets. An example is the BMW car, which is the symbol of "performance" in engineering and design and identifies the owner as a "successful in career" person.

- **Consistency** is reached when a brand is able to deliver a consistent customer experience worldwide, creating a visual, verbal, auditory, and tactile identity across borders, often due to a global marketing investment. McDonald's is an example (Figure 13.3). Not only does it have a global message, but at the same time it appropriately modifies its approaches, in-store appearance, and the menu to satisfy local consumers.

- The **emotional dimension** is strongly connected with human values and aspirations, and must have a common appeal despite cultural differences. An example is Nike, which was able to target the mass market worldwide around the passion for different sports.

FIGURE 13.3
McDonald's: An Example of a Global Brand
Source: © Author

- Great global brands need to express their **uniqueness** not only through product features, but also through communication. Apple has created its brand uniqueness worldwide around the concept of innovation, becoming the symbol of technology solutions that can be used in everyday life.

- **Relevance** is reached when a global brand demonstrates that it is able to respect local needs, desires, decision criteria, and tastes across all geographies, communicating a "global" advantage. An example is the HSBC Group, the "world's local bank," which pursues local adaptation while fulfilling a global mission (Geo Map 13.1).

- Finally, global brand success is not possible without **management commitment**, which is always involved in ensuring that the corporate culture will put the brand at the center of every activity.

GEO MAP 13.1
HSBC
Source: Adapted from: CIA Maps, The World Factbook[22]

The headquarters of **HSBC** is located in London, UK.

Global brand positioning is also hard to implement because of the markets' progressive fragmentation. This has become a critical factor, especially for companies that operate on a transnational level because, as mentioned in Chapter 9, they face the necessity of identifying significant horizontal segments at a regional or global level. Companies can offer their product in a standardized way, but at the same time have to keep in mind the symbolic differences associated with the product by consumers of the different countries. This is why the brand is important, because it reflects the uniqueness of the product image and therefore allows coordination of the company's positioning choices in the identified transnational segments, respecting at the same time the differences from country to country in relation to the product, distribution, and communication. These differences, if sometimes minimal, play a determinant role in local consumer choice processes, and at the same time constitute an element of differentiation from local competition. The example of the Ritu Kumar designer wear brand—a leading Indian designer brand, which sells in markets like the United States, the UK, and the Middle East, highlights a transnational segment of contemporary women willing to wear authentic Indian style. Ritu Kumar managed to develop unique product positioning even though it had to take the differences between the various countries into consideration when implementing the marketing mix.

Finally, a global brand's positive and strong image can allow companies not only to achieve the goals mentioned above, but also to overcome potential negative attitudes toward a foreign product, or, on the other hand, to highlight the positive elements of the country to which the product is associated, as we have seen in the L'Occitane case and in Chapter 10.

A brand's image plays a fundamental role not only for products that have a strong emotional dimension, but also in the opposite case, for high-technology products. In these cases, the consumer overcomes difficulties connected with the inability to adequately evaluate complex product characteristics and trusts only the brand. In fact, the brand can convey the perception of functional and performance characteristics that for high-technology products can constitute a beneficial competitive element against competition. Samsung is an example of this. Thanks to its focus on "accelerating discoveries and possibilities" by investing in R&D, both in terms of design and technology, Samsung has been able to strengthen its brand image launching new products such as the Samsung OLED TV: panels consisting of thousands of organic LED pixels that independently display richer and brighter images compared to current LED TVs, color richness, floating canvas with a curved design and the multi view option that allows two people to simultaneously watch different full-screen programs in Full HD and stereo sound. With a global communication and a launching price of about $10,000, Samsung OLED TV is a niche product, but important in extending the perception of a high performance manufacturer to all of its models.[23]

Research conducted by Research International Observer (RIO) suggests that it makes sense to globalize some brands and localize others, depending on these four key factors:[24]

1. *Type of brand.* The RIO study discovered four types of global brands that display specific characteristics:

   - **Prestige brands** (Chanel, BMW, Gucci, Mercedes) also possess a powerful attraction based, however, on much more specific myths associated with the country-of-origin, company founder, or the emblematic technology developed by the particular company. Think of Swiss precision embodied in a watch and Italian design defined by a Ferrari car. Prestige brands represent the desire for status and high aspirations and they, too, actively refuse to localize in order to maintain their inherent exclusivity.

   - **Master brands** (Nike, Sony, Coca-Cola, Nokia) have come to be associated with universal ideals and narratives, such as independence, connection, friendship, quality, individualism, etc. Thus, these brands have built a powerful appeal that often transcends their national origins to become truly global. They must remain so and resist localization for strategic reasons.

   - **Super brands** (Procter & Gamble, Colgate-Palmolive, Dove, Philips) are category-specific and are more known for their dependability than for their mythology, as master brands are. They often localize their offerings and constantly innovate to remain relevant in their markets.

   - **Glocal brands** (Nestlé, Danone, Jollibee) are distributed worldwide but "hide" their origin to blend into the local culture and market. They rely on building a familiarity and comfort level with their consumers and aim for the greatest degree of localization. Often found in categories such as food products, these brands may become aspirational in developing countries, as consumer societies begin to emerge there.

2. *Nature of the category.* The higher the display value of a category, or the aspirational positioning of a brand within it, the less likely it is for that brand to localize. As mentioned above, food, household, cleaning, and personal care products, which have low display value, are the most localized.

3. *Level of aspiration.* Although Toyota is a brand in a high display value category, it intentionally positions itself in the low end of the spectrum to blend in with the local culture and values. Conversely, Nike is known for sponsoring local events, such as a marathon in Budapest, Hungary, but it signals the high aspirational value it carries with the high profile spokespeople it associates with, like Michael Jordan and Tiger Woods.

4. *Nature of the local culture.* A culture's orientation toward brands may be defined by degrees of individualism or collectivism and of local or global focus, but those

values may not always correspond to the traditional definitions assigned to these terms in Chapters 3 and 4. For example, Japan, which is defined as a highly collectivistic society in Hofstede's framework, rates as highly individualistic when it comes to brands. Japan, together with Germany, Belgium, Italy, and Sweden, among others, represents the Global Individualists category. The Cultural Individualists countries, including France, the United States, the UK, Austria, Russia, and Spain, among others, require more localized products that still reflect their individual tastes and values. The global–local axis also divides Cultural Sensitives from Global Sensitives. Both of these categories are represented by collectivist markets, but the former (China, Turkey, India, Indonesia, Hungary) expect global brands to respect and adjust to local culture, while the latter (Brazil, Korea, Kenya, Chile, Colombia) are more open to global brands and require only some degree of localization. However, Global Sensitives are conscious of a brand's origin, as well as the country in which individual products are manufactured.

Based on these four key factors, the authors of the study have designed a road map (Figure 13.4) that guides marketing managers in their decision process of whether to pursue a local or a more standardized strategy in their global communications plans. It is important to note that, since brands do not remain static in their perceived stature or character, marketers need to periodically adjust their approach to achieve the desired positioning in a particular market. As brands have already been discussed, the rest of this chapter will focus on other instruments, among which advertising is the most prominent.

GLOBAL ADVERTISING STRATEGY

Overall, global advertising remains among the most important instruments of integrated marketing communications with worldwide spending of US$519 billion in

Brand Type	Prestige	Master	Super	Glocal
Nature of the category	Luxury examples: Rolex, Ferrari, Louis Vuitton, Mercedes, Gucci	Fashion examples: Pierre Cardin, Benetton, Donna Karan, Lacoste	Household Services, Personal Care Examples: Colgate-Palmolive, Unilever household care, Procter & Gamble beauty products	Food retail: Nestlé, Danone, McDonald's, Jollibee (Philippines), Kentucky Fried Chicken
Level of aspiration	High	High-medium	Medium-low	Low
Nature of the local culture	Global	Global	Local	Local

Extent of localization required

FIGURE 13.4
Localization Road Map
Source: Compiled by Authors

are more easily standardized than campaigns for food or personal care products, for example. The former aim to appeal to their customers' ambitions and desire for exclusivity—more universal feelings—while the latter have the goal of becoming part of the cultural landscape in every market and the personal routine of consumers.

Life Fitness, a maker of high-performance fitness equipment, has been rather successful in launching a new standardized global campaign that aims to broaden the appeal of its products to include not only their traditional hard-core fitness enthusiasts, but also regular gym-goers and practitioners of healthy lifestyles. The company, which derives 45 percent of its sales internationally, recognized the growing interest among consumers worldwide in achieving overall health and well-being and designed its new ads with a focus on the everyday benefits of fitness for all people. Its earlier ad campaigns had emphasized the machines' technical features and performance by showing muscular, bodybuilder types. Now the new tag line, "What We Live For," is reinforced with images and messaging that show healthy, fit people enjoying activities such as mountain biking, hiking, surfing, and other common pastimes. Ninety percent of the new marketing campaign is distributed to the gyms and other fitness facilities around the world which comprise the vast majority of Life Fitness's clients. The company still needed to tweak its globally standardized message and imagery, however, to take into consideration local cultural mores. Thus, its ad featuring a bikini-clad snorkeler was removed from the lineup for Dubai, whereas its ads for Italy and Spain required an extra helping of sex appeal to match local tastes.[32]

However, many challenges to the successful implementation of standardized advertising remain. Besides the different cultural tastes for images, another of those challenges is the effectiveness of the message. As Marieke de Mooij (2005) notes, people across the world may be willing to buy standardized products, but they're likely buying them for completely different reasons—for some that pair of Levi's jeans may symbolize status or American life-style affiliation, while for others it is simply everyday clothing. "If buying motives for standardized products vary by country or area, how can a standardized advertising campaign be equally effective in all countries?"[33]

ADAPTED ADVERTISING

As the name suggests, adapted (or localized) advertising communications reflect each market's cultural and social conditions. The goal of adapted advertising is to increase recognition and acceptance of the advertised brand and product. The theory is that presenting a brand in the context of local cultural values and tastes will allow more people to identify with the brand, creating higher affinity for that brand and, ultimately, more sales.

Sometimes, localization is necessary because the environmental (e.g. legal or economic) context is dramatically different. For instance, in 2014, the US eased decades of trade and financial restrictions on Cuba, opening up the country to US telecommunications, construction, and financial services in a slew of changes announced by the US Departments of Commerce and Treasury. The new rules let US citizens that fall into 12 categories, such as educational travelers, visit Cuba without applying for a specific license. And they can spend what they want (per diem spending limits are lifted), use US credit and debit cards, and bring back $400 in goods, including $100 in alcohol and tobacco products.[34] However, the consequences for companies in general and for their marketing and advertising strategies in particular are less than clear. Most likely, advertising will have to adapt due to a variety of constraining factors (Box 13.2).

Very often, localized advertising is necessary because of **differences in language and culture**. For instance, a few years ago a famous hair products company launched a curling iron called Mist Stick. The product was a success, and like all successful products, they tried to expand the market for it. One of the new markets would be Germany, but they didn't take into account that in German "mist" means manure. Strangely enough, people didn't eagerly run to the store shelves to try out this new hair treatment. Another interesting case is that of a famous fast food chain whose specialty is fried chicken. It's slogan is "Finger Lickin' Good!" but when it expanded its franchise to far-off China, this was translated as "eat your fingers off." Another example relates to the particularity of Arabic (as with many other languages) that is written from right to left. When dealing with more graphic pieces, this entails the inversion of the entire graphic layout. Unfortunately a well-known

---

Box 13.2   Country-in-Focus: Advertising in Cuba

A New Eldorado for Marketing Communications?

On December 17, 2014, the President of the United States and various members of his administration announced sweeping changes in the 50-plus year economic embargo against Cuba. Diplomatic relations were normalized, increasing travel started, and the ability to use US debit and credit cards increased commerce. This scenario makes one feel like ginning up advertisements for the Cuban market. But the "buzz" has yet to come and there are still a number of major hurdles in the way of full-scale trade:

The administration must issue new regulations. These will come from the Office of Foreign Assets Control (OFAC), part of the US Treasury. Not only must OFAC draft the regulations, but they must then be approved by the Department of State, the National Security Council, and the Office of Management and Budget.

Next, there is the problem of the Helms–Burton Act. This 1996 act (Pub.L. 104–114, 110 Stat. 785, 22 U.S.C. §§ 6021–6091) codified the Cuban Assets Control Regulations (31 C.F.R. Part 515) into law. So, there is considerable doubt as to the ability of the President, without Congress' changing the law, to make more than cosmetic alterations to the present embargo, not to mention other major conditions the law placed on normalizing relations.

The large—and valuable—number of claims filed by US persons against Cuba for land and property expropriated during the Castro-led revolution need to be resolved. The US Foreign Claims Settlement Commission has adjudicated these claims for submission, in the normal course, to the Cuban government for payment. This tender may not be met with a smile and an abrazo by the Cubans.

This brings us to the last major hurdle—the Cuban Government, is still run by the Castro brothers. What makes us think they are going to throw open the doors to US commerce and capitalism? Let's recall that it was, in part, US domination that helped create the revolution.

Sources: Wilson, E. and Bigart, E. (2014). 'Advertising in Cuba? Not yet says uncle Sam', http://www.allaboutadvertisinglaw.com [Accessed: January 10, 2015]; Fisher, D. (2014), 'Cuba opening could reopen fight over billions in seized property', *Forbes*, http://www.forbes.com/sites/danielfisher/2014/12/18/cuba-opening-could-mean-mother-of-all-property-disputes/ [Accessed: January 5, 2015].

US drug company appears not to have taken this into account when they launched their product in the United Arab Emirates, including an image with two drawings depicting before and after taking the drug. But in translating the campaign, they only changed the orientation of the text and not of the images, so in the Arabic version, the relation between text and images was inverted: prior to taking the drug you were perfectly healthy and after taking it you would become ill. There were similar cases with laundry detergent ads, in which the clothing would be all dirty after being washed with the detergent.[35]

Marketing consumer services, as opposed to marketing products, globally, also tends to be more effective when advertising is localized. Because services are experienced personally by the client, it is easy to see why conforming to local cultural considerations, language, and social norms would be more important to service providers.

The appeal of standardized marketing and advertising on a global scale is by now well understood: it offers savings, consistency, control, stronger brand recognition, and the ability to leverage products and know-how across multiple markets. However, there are only a few brands that have been able to fully benefit from these advantages (see Table 13.2 again for some of the most globalized brands). Although extensive research has been done regarding the benefits and barriers of standardization, the results are complex and no general conclusions have been reached.[36] One of the biggest reasons is that there is no clear definition of standardization, and companies today combine both standardization and adaptation/localization. For instance, Apple is using a very strong standardization approach in their product portfolio; iPhone and iPod are launching in different countries all around the world. However, when it comes to its TV advertising in China, Apple uses both the US version as well as different versions produced in China. This combined strategy has the advantage of attracting different consumer segments. However, it also makes it very hard to test the efficacy in either standardization or localization. Because whatever the business outcome is, it is not possible to establish a correlation with either of those approaches.

When it comes to localizing advertising strategies, indeed many companies opt for a mixed approach. One of the solutions is to apply pattern advertising, where the basic approach of the global advertising strategy is standardized but then adapted to local markets when needed. For instance, Vodafone uses the same global approach when it comes to layout, dominant visuals, brand signature, and slogan. However, photos and body copy are localized not simply translated which increases the ability to leverage products and know-how across multiple markets (Figure 13.6).

LEGAL CONSTRAINTS

When planning a global marketing strategy, marketers have to consider the myriad standards, regulations, and laws that govern the advertising industry in the different countries and regional jurisdictions. The regulatory bodies that monitor

FIGURE 13.6
Pattern Advertising:
Vodafone in Spain
and Germany
Source: © Authors

and control advertising have been established, among other things, to respond to public complaints, to ensure that claims made by advertisers are accurate, and to ensure that the products advertised are legal. This oversight is particularly pertinent for certain categories of products such as pharmaceuticals, alcohol, tobacco, and gambling, where consumer protection is important.

The Consumer Protection from Unfair Trading Regulations 2008 (the CPRs) implemented the EU Unfair Commercial Practices Directive to introduce a general prohibition against unfair commercial practices, specific prohibitions against misleading and aggressive practices and a blacklist of 31 practices that will be deemed unfair in all circumstances. While regulations differ across continents, basic rules are very similar.[37]

Misleading actions and omissions are unfair commercial practices. In each case, the action or omission must cause or be likely to cause the average consumer to make a different decision. A misleading action contains false information or in some way deceives (or is likely to deceive) the average customer. Examples include:

- providing misleading information about the main characteristics, availability or origin of a product, or false information about the trader himself (e.g. qualifications or awards);

- marketing a product in such a way that creates confusion with a competitor's products (e.g. by using a similar brand name or logo); and

- agreeing to be bound by a code of practice that contains a firm commitment (e.g. that its members will only use wood from sustainable sources), displaying the code logo, but breaching that commitment.

Misleading omissions are made when a trader omits or hides material information, provides it in an unclear, unintelligible, ambiguous or untimely manner, or fails to make it clear he has a commercial intent. What is material will depend on the circumstances, but it is generally defined as information the average consumer needs to make an informed decision.

Limitations of space or time and whether the trader has taken other steps to convey the information (such as stating "terms and conditions apply" and where they can be found) will be taken into account as part of the context. When a trader makes an "invitation to purchase" (e.g. by including an order form in a press advertisement, or a page on a website enabling consumers to place an order) the regulations specify the material information that must be included unless that information is apparent from the context. In addition to pyramid promotion schemes, bogus sales, and "doorstepping" consumers at home, the blacklist includes:

- "Bait advertising"—advertising products at a specified price without disclosing that the trader has reasonable grounds to believe he may not be able to supply them or their equivalent at that price for a reasonable period or in reasonable quantities.

- "Bait and switch"—inviting consumers to buy one product but then trying to persuade them to buy a different one—e.g. by refusing to show them the original item, or to take orders or make delivery arrangements, or by showing a defective sample.

- Falsely stating a product will only be available (or available on certain terms) for a very limited time to persuade the consumer to make an immediate decision.

- Using "advertorials" (editorial comment to promote a product) without making it clear that the trader has paid for the promotion.

- Passing on materially inaccurate market information to persuade the consumer to buy on less favourable terms than normal market conditions.

- Claiming to offer a competition or prize promotion without awarding the prizes described or a reasonable equivalent.

- Describing a product as "free," "without charge," or similar, if the consumer has to pay anything other than the unavoidable cost of responding, collecting, or paying for delivery of the item.

- Making persistent and unwanted solicitations by telephone, fax, email, or similar, except in circumstances and to the extent justified to enforce a contractual obligation (e.g. legitimate debt collection).

- Requiring a consumer claiming on an insurance policy to produce irrelevant documents, or deliberately failing to respond to correspondence to dissuade the consumer from pursuing his contractual rights.

- Including in an advertisement a direct encouragement to children to buy advertised products or persuade their parents or other adults to buy advertised products for them.

Certain countries, like China, react to specific problems associated with advertising. For instance, China as the world's biggest tobacco producer, has a dire smoking problem. One out of every three cigarettes consumed worldwide is smoked in China, according to the World Health Organization (WHO). Nearly a third of the population smokes. And tobacco kills one million people in China every year. China is attacking the problem with an anti-smoking draft law submitted to the State Council that would fine people up to $80 for smoking in public places. The proposal would also ban all tobacco ads, promotions and sponsorships, including in schools. However, there are questions about how fiercely the tobacco industry will fight to water down the proposal.[38]

As legal issues involving advertising and communications have become so complex over the years, several law firms have specialized in providing tailored services. For instance, in Germany, it is illegal to use any comparative terminology; you can be sued by a competitor if you do. Belgium and Luxembourg explicitly ban comparative advertising, whereas it is clearly authorized in the United Kingdom, Ireland, Spain, and Portugal. Comparative advertising is heavily regulated in Asia as well. A variety of restrictions on advertising of specific products exist around the world. Advertising of pharmaceuticals is restricted in many countries. Advertising on television is strictly controlled in many countries. China is relaxing some regulations while strengthening others. Some country laws against accessibility to broadcast media seem to be softening. Australia ended a ban on cable television spots, and Malaysia is considering changing the rules to allow foreign commercials to air on newly legalized satellite signals. Companies that rely on television infomercials and television shopping are restricted by the limitations placed on the length and number of television commercials permitted when their programs are classified as advertisements. Internet services are especially vulnerable as EU member states decide which area of regulation should apply to these services. Barriers to pan-European services will arise if some member states opt to apply television-broadcasting rules to the Internet while other countries apply print-media advertising rules. Some countries have special taxes that apply to advertising, which might restrict creative freedom in media selection. Box 13.3 describes the services of a specialized law firm that works for the largest advertisers in the US.

Box 13.3   Company-in-Focus: Venable LLP

The Need for Specialized Advertising Law Firms

Venable is a specialized law firm with more than 600 attorneys in nine offices in the US; it helps to advance its clients' business objectives at home and abroad. The firm is ranked 71st in the 2014 Am Law 100 survey. It was founded in Baltimore in 1900.

Today, the company represents 10 of the top 20 largest national advertisers. Venable was ranked in 92 national and regional categories and was named Law Firm of the Year for Advertising Law. Chambers USA presented its Award for Excellence to Venable's Advertising, Marketing, and New Media practices in 2010 and 2011. Specialized services have included:

Providing advertising counsel to a leading national retailer. This engagement has included handling several Federal Trade Commission (FTC) matters involving pricing issues, green claims, comparative performance claims, and textile act issues.

Supplying comprehensive regulatory compliance counseling to one of the largest food companies in the United States. This includes guidance on claim substantiation, advertising to children, food marketing and packaging, sweepstakes and promotions, coupons and rebates, social media marketing, and privacy/data security matters.

Performing a comprehensive assessment and update of a Fortune 500 diversified financial service company's regulatory database to ensure that all future advertising and marketing practices were compliant with federal and state regulations and the condition of a Consumer Financial Protection Bureau consent order.

Advising a leading consumer electronics company on the global launch of its latest mobile handset. This engagement included compliance advice for online and offline marketing in the United States, as well as coordination of local counsel in jurisdictions around the world.

In a world where new avenues of advertising and promotion seem to spring up overnight, Venerable offers advice in social media, sweepstakes, green marketing, gift cards, affiliate marketing product placement, or traditional television advertising. It is an unfortunate reality that one advertising problem can give rise to a host of others. A self-regulatory proceeding can lead to class action litigation or a class action can spawn multiple inquiries by State Attorneys General in the USA.

Sources: http://www.venable.com/advertising-and-marketing/; http://www.venable.com/NEP/pressreleases/NewsDetail. aspx?news=3e4c9045-1745-49ab-a299-34a9e621dfa1; http://investing.businessweek.com/research/stocks/private/snapshot. asp?privcapld=2158476; http://www.allaboutadvertisinglaw.com [All accessed: 15 December, 2014].

CULTURE, SYMBOLS, AND TRADITIONS IN ADVERTISING

Apart from legal issues, one of the biggest challenges in global advertising involves cultural issues (see again Chapter 3). Culture plays a central role in how people perceive and react to advertising. Much research over the years has confirmed that the more likable advertising is, the more likely it is to be effective. One recent study was designed to see what attributes exactly make commercials likable in Asian countries and how they differ from the attributes in American and European markets, particularly for Generation X consumers. The study found that Asians most liked ads that evoked "entertaining" qualities most, followed by "warmth," "soft sell," "strong/distinctive/sexy," "relevant to me," "trendy/ modernity/stylish," and "status appeal." The results were remarkably close to the findings in the other two world regions, where "entertaining," "warmth," and "relevant to me" were also considered most likable qualities for ads. However, several other attributes were deemed distinctly Asian, including "soft sell," "strong/distinctive/sexy," "trendy/ modernity/stylish," and "status appeal."[39] The role of cultural differences in advertising styles have long been the topic of research for Marieke de Mooij, whose summary of country-specific advertising styles is shown in Table 13.3.

Cultural awareness should be applied in every aspect of marketing: in selling, label-printing, advertising, and promotion of products. It covers language, the lifestyle, and the behavioral patterns of the people in the country of interest. Of course the company should print in the local language, but that's not where the language barrier ends. For instance, IBM announces on its website that cultural sensitivity is important when creating Web content to avoid using words and images that might be offensive to various cultures around the world. Some information and graphics might cause minor offense, while others could have major consequences. Content that should be avoided are national flags, maps which depict national borders, which can lead to misunderstandings. There is also a fundamental rule to keep in mind while designing international icons: icons are not universal. Pictures and symbols create powerful and different associations in each culture and context.[40]

Country	Advertising Style
China	Emotional, emphasis on quality, tradition, status, respect
France	Symbolism, sensuality, humor
Germany	Logic, testimonials, tradition, value for money, authority
Italy	Emotional, lifestyle, use of celebrities, theatrical
Japan	Indirect appeals, soft-sell, entertainment, symbolism
Spain	Indirect appeals, idealistic, pleasant
The Netherlands	Entertainment, realistic, modesty
United Kingdom	Presentational, humor, subtle, testimonials, show class differences
United States	Lecture, direct appeals, hard-sell, argumentative

TABLE 13.3
Country-Specific Advertising Styles

Source: Adapted from: de Mooij, M. (1997/2010). *Global marketing and advertising: Understanding cultural paradoxes.* 3rd ed. (2010). Thousand Oaks, CA: Sage. pp. 272–83

Religious traditions can also cause a source of irritation when not properly respected. For instance, a sandwich-shop chain, Pret A Manger, said that it had withdrawn a brand of tomato-flavoured crisps called "Virgin Mary" after receiving protests from Catholics. In a message to the complainers, the company said "we are extremely sorry that the crisp name we had selected has offended you…[the CEO] has taken your advice and decided to remove all of the crisps from our shops…we will be donating all the unsold crisps to homeless charities that we support across the country."[41]

Perhaps it's surprising that the worlds of faith and advertising don't clash even more frequently. At a deep level, both activities are competing for the same space in people's conscious and subconscious minds. Pope Francis has taken issue with many aspects of capitalist culture, where "priority is given to the outward, the immediate, the visible, the quick, the superficial and the provisional" in the name of "unbridled consumerism."[42] But paradoxically enough, the papacy, especially in the early years of John Paul II and perhaps now again under the current pontiff, is itself a global brand which relies on modern technology to transmit arresting and abiding images around the world. For believers in any religion, perhaps the most challenging thing about modern advertisements is the way they proclaim a global community—based on common enthusiasm for a consumer product—of the kind that in centuries past was mostly constituted by faith. An ad for an American steakhouse chain mixed the religious music of Bach with the slogan "if steaks were a religion, this would be its cathedral," and the message resonated, because we unconsciously acknowledge that for many people, steaks and their preparation (especially outdoors) are indeed a sort of sacred rite, an ultimate reference point.[43]

On other occasions, religious traditions are used explicitly to attract a target group that does not even belong to the religious adherers. For instance, Malaysia is a multicultural and multiconfessional country. As of the 2010 Population and Housing Census, 61.3 percent of the population practices Islam; 19.8 percent Buddhism; 9.2 percent Christianity; 6.3 percent Hinduism; and 1.3 percent traditional Chinese religions. The remainder is accounted for by other faiths, including Animism, Folk religion, Sikhism and other belief systems.[44] Even though Christianity is under-represented in the country, large shopping malls like Suria KLCC and others customarily use Christmas trees to attract shoppers and create "adequate feelings."

THE GLOBAL ADVERTISING AGENCY

The accelerated rise in ad spending is being influenced in part by growing revenues from leading Internet media companies, particularly those that are capitalizing on mobile revenues. eMarketer projects advertising revenues for a handful of the top US digital ad-selling companies, which collectively will represent 18.2 percent of total media ad spending in 2016—led by Google and Facebook.

Google alone already accounts for more than 10 percent of all advertising spending in the US, and in 2016, Google and Facebook together will take a 15.0 percent share of the $200.00 billion total media advertising market. Mobile ads on Facebook will total 68.0 percent of its US ad revenues this year, up from 46.7 percent last year, eMarketer estimates, and while Google's ad revenues in the US won't flip to majority-mobile until 2016, they're shifting quickly. This year, Google's US mobile revenues will comprise only 36.8 percent of its overall ad revenues, but by 2016, the medium will account for 65.8 percent.[45]

In the challenging global market, many companies rely on the help of global advertising agencies to find a competitive edge in marketing. The degree to which an agency is integrated into the marketing function of a company can vary, depending on the size of the company, its strategic marketing focus and leadership, its industry or its markets, to name a few factors. For most MNCs, however, relationships with one or more advertising agencies or networks are important and often scrutinized aspects of their global marketing strategy. In a recent study, 1,850 Chief Marketing Officers (CMOs) were asked to weigh in on advertising agencies and rank them according to their preferences.[46] Table 13.5 shows the results.

Some large global advertisers prefer to hire local ad agencies for each market they enter, others may opt to retain their home market agency, and yet others may hire a large agency with offices around the world or align themselves with one of the worldwide networks such as Leo Burnett Worldwide, Y&R, or McCann Erickson. Many of these agencies form the WPP Group, the largest multinational ad agency, headquartered in Ireland. WPP has 146,000 employees in 2,400 offices operating in 107 countries. Next in size is the Omnicom Group. As mentioned earlier, many MNCs maintain relationships with different agencies to match the goals and objectives for specific campaigns.

For example, Visa selected the independent, London-based Wieden+Kennedy agency for its World Cup soccer sponsorship, while maintaining California-based TBWA/Chiat/Day as its agency on record for the Visa brand (Geo Map 13.2).[47]

Company	2012	2013	2014	2015	2016
Google	9.1	10	10.6	11.1	11.3
Facebook	1.3	1.9	2.7	3.2	3.7
Yahoo	1.5	1.5	1.5	1.5	1.5
Microsoft	1.1	1.3	1.4	1.7	2
AOL	0.6	0.6	0.6	0.7	0.7
Amazon	0.3	0.4	0.5	0.6	0.7
IAC	0.6	0.6	0.5	0.5	0.5
Twitter	0.1	0.3	0.4	0.6	0.5
Total Digital	22.3	25.2	28.2	30.9	33.2

TABLE 13.4
Net US Digital Ad Revenue Share, by Company, 2012–16 (% of Total Media Ad Spending)

Source: Adapted from: eMarketer, June 2014, emarketer.com [Accessed: November 5, 2014]

TABLE 13.5 Preferred Advertising Agencies as Rated by CMOs	Company	Selected By...	Selected Clients
	Wieden+Kennedy	66%	Old Spice, Coke, Nike
	Droga5	36%	UNICEF, American Express, Unilever, Google
	Grey	34%	Direct TV, Febreze
	BBDO	30 %	Wells Fargo, Bayer/Merck, Emirates, Melitta
	Ogilvy & Mather	24%	Procter & Gamble, Pfizer, VW
	The Martin Agency	16%	Exxon Mobile, Nespresso, Wal-Mart
	Leo Burnett	14%	Fiat, Samsung, GM, Coca-Cola, Altria
	CP+B	12%	Coke Zero, Microsoft, Milka, MetLife
	Goodby Silverstein & Partners	9%	Adobe, Cisco, eBay, Fritos, Seagate
	Publicis	6 %	HP, Garnier, AXA, Procter & Gamble, T-Mobile, Citi

Source: Adbrands. (2014), http://www.adbrands.net/fr/publicisww_fr.htm /

GEO MAP 13.2
Visa
Source: Adapted from: CIA Maps, The World Factbook[48]

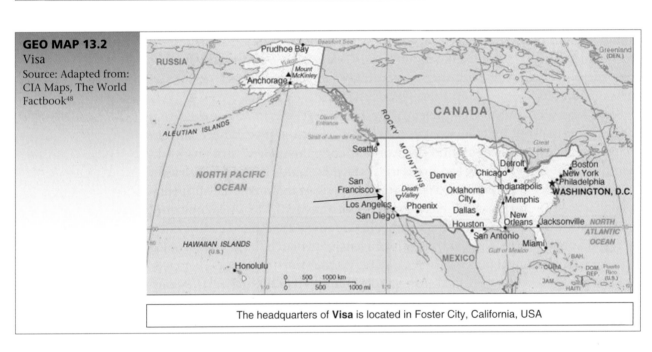

The headquarters of **Visa** is located in Foster City, California, USA

There are many reasons why companies choose advertising agencies for their global marketing needs. Some of them are:

- **Cost-effectiveness.** As companies expand internationally, it may become financially unproductive to enlarge the internal marketing and creative services units to meet all international marketing needs. By selecting an agency with the right market reach, a company can save resources and centralize decision-making at the same time. Additionally, agencies can deliver media-buying savings based on preferred relationships with media outlets.

- **Market knowledge.** In choosing a global agency with offices around the world or a number of local agencies in their target markets, a company is presumably buying the expertise that will make its advertising campaigns effective for local audiences.

- **Superior creative work.** Ad agencies specialize in the development of original, polished creative materials designed by talented and experienced professionals. Such creative focus and expertise is hard to build up or maintain internally for most companies.

- **Specialized services.** Some agencies develop signature competencies like media planning and buying or digital marketing. In addition, they usually offer a number of other specialized services such as crisis communications, market research, or other support services that are often sought by companies with limited internal resources.

Most companies consider additional factors, such as strategic marketing alignment, agency reputation and size, or industry specialization as they review their agency relationships. Often, changes within the company, at the agency, or both could prompt a change in direction. Coca-Cola had its own agency, Edge Creative, for most of the 1990s, but switched strategies in 2000, appointing Interpublic as its global ad agency while still using the services of outside agencies such as WPP's Red Cell Berlin Cameron and UK's Mother. More changes came in 2005, when the company handed its Classic Coke account for North America to yet another agency, Wieden+Kennedy.[49] Similarly, as Toyota prepared to introduce Lexus, its luxury brand, in Japan (the company's home country) in 2005, it selected Dentsu, Japan's advertising giant, and several other Japanese agencies to handle the advertising for the launch, in addition to its own in-house ad firm.[50] For a list of the most common reasons why companies select and switch agencies, and for the agencies' perspective on the same issue, see Table 13.6.

It is indisputable that the relationship between an agency and its client is important to the firm's business. It can impact changes in its strategic marketing direction, deliver a successful image makeover, and have a direct effect on sales, for example. When the Korean conglomerate LG Electronics decided to appoint the London-based, Bartle Bogle Hegarty (BBH), for the strategic and creative development of its worldwide marketing communications, its global brand marketing executive cited the company's desire to develop "one single powerful LG brand."[51] IKEA's agency, Mediaedge:cia, noticed that the furniture retailer's image was suffering in Poland and that growth was stagnating. The agency designed an unconventional campaign that prompted the Polish market to jump 22 percent in visitor growth, becoming the leader for all of Ikea's worldwide stores in that category. The campaign also increased traffic to the IKEA Poland website by 45 percent.[52]

As evident from these examples, client-agency partnerships can take on many forms and dynamics. But few basic factors remain at the core of any successful partnership between a client and its agency: trust, confidence, effective communications, and strategic alignment in the overall marketing vision and goals, paired with the internal skill set and the external reach to match.

TABLE 13.6 Factors Determining Advertising Agency Selection and Termination	Factors for Selecting Advertising Agencies from Client's Perspective	Rank	Factors for Switching Advertising Agencies from Client's Perspective	Rank	Factors for Losing Clients from Agency's Perspectives	Rank
	Qualifications of personnel	1	Dissatisfaction	1	Change in client firm's size	1
	Fits the client's advertising	2	Disagreement over objectives	2	Poor communication performance	2
	Part of an international consortium	3	Insufficient attention by senior staff	3	Personnel changes	3
	Agency size	4	Time for a change	4	Change in client's strategy	4
	Past record	5	Decrease in sales, profits	5	Policy change	5
	Agency facilities	6	Not sure that ads were effective	6	Declining sales	6
	Recommendations	7	Key personnel left agency	7	Unrealistic demand by clients	7
	Advertising awards	8			Conflict in remuneration	8
	Reputation	9			Conflict of interest	9

Source: Adapted from: Yuksel, U., and Sutton-Brady, C. (2007), 'From selection to termination: An investigation of advertising agency/client relationships', *Journal of Business and Economic Research*, 5(1), pp. 31–9

PRACTICAL COMMUNICATIONS ACTIVITIES

The only way we can develop our products and brands is through effective communication. This will require consistency and teamwork in a company, empowered leadership, a clear understanding of communication principles, and consumer insight (Figure 13.7).

Inputs

The starting point for our communication process will always be the experiences that our consumers have with our brands. In 1964, the first "Unilever Plan for Great Advertising" proclaimed: "Good brand advertising builds up preference in the consumers' minds for one particular brand and thereby persuades them to buy it and continue to use it."[53] And this has remained true ever since. It is important that the whole **team** works on communications. Using its joint experience and skills, a team can deal with risks far more effectively than an individual. Very often, it is important to keep a team small and manageable, let's say four to five members at the most. The bigger the challenge, the better it is to keep the team small. In addition, it is important to have a clear **leader**, whose job is to initiate action and decide who is going to be involved. In short: those who decide, brief. Thus, a team leader must

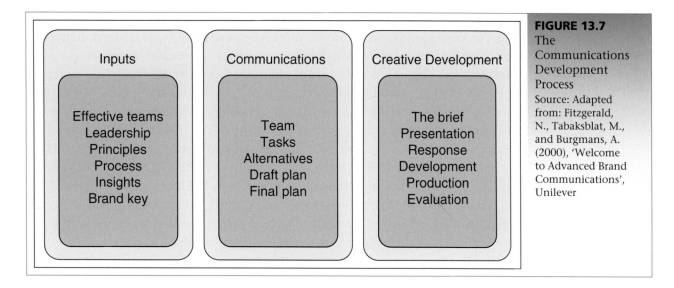

FIGURE 13.7
The Communications Development Process
Source: Adapted from: Fitzgerald, N., Tabaksblat, M., and Burgmans, A. (2000), 'Welcome to Advanced Brand Communications', Unilever

be the most experienced marketer involved in the project, usually the Marketing Director or the Head of Communications.

Many companies have developed a set of principles to help understand the objectives of advertising. For instance, Unilever states that there are several proven characteristics of great communication:[54]

- Communication is rooted in intimate knowledge of the consumer and assessed on the basis of how the consumer reacts to it. It must affect behavior.

- It has to contain a powerful discriminator for the brand. Not only should the communications strategy be distinctive, but also the ideas and channels the company uses to communicate it.

- It concentrates on strong ideas: a conceptual idea, which can work synergistically across time, and across different communications channels; and executional ideas, which add freshness and therefore impact to each element in the campaign.

- It is simple, in order to communicate clearly.

- It is credible and realistic, in order to convince.

- It involves consumers in a way that is enjoyable, so that their experience of the brand is positive.

- The idea and execution are recognizable; memorably and inextricably linked to the brand.

Process and insights: It is vital to have a clear process when developing communications. Typically it should involve positioning the company and the brand. Here the brand key is essential. Then you need to have a communications plan (final plan), a plan of how to deal with the customers (the brief), and make sure of how you respond to customer requests (response). The input into these processes comes from proper market research and from understanding the customer (see Chapter 6). The better your insights are, the better will be your relationships with the customer. In addition, successful marketers do not only understand their customers, they respect and empathize with them. An insight is often difficult to achieve. For instance, an insight into how children felt about ketchup and playing around with it led to the development of colored ketchup products by Heinz in October 2000, which included green (2000), purple (2001), pink (2002), orange (2002), teal (2002), and blue ketchup (2003).[55] These products were made by adding food coloring to the traditional ketchup. However, as of January 2006, products have been discontinued, which shows that consumer insight should never be regarded as stable. Insights can also go beyond products and include: a new category, a new communication idea, or a new use of media (e.g. posters).

In order to launch brand communication, the brand key is a useful tool (Figure 13.8). It consists of eight elements, which help to position the own brand vis-à-vis those of competitors.[56]

The individual elements of the brand key model can be described as follows by using the example of the Dove Bar:

1. **Competitive environment:** direct, indirect and potential competitors: The market and alternative choices as seen by the consumer and the relative value the brand offers in the market. Dove Bar bridges soaps and skincare. Many women consider it part of their beauty routines. It competes directly with premium soaps, such as Nivea and Olay.

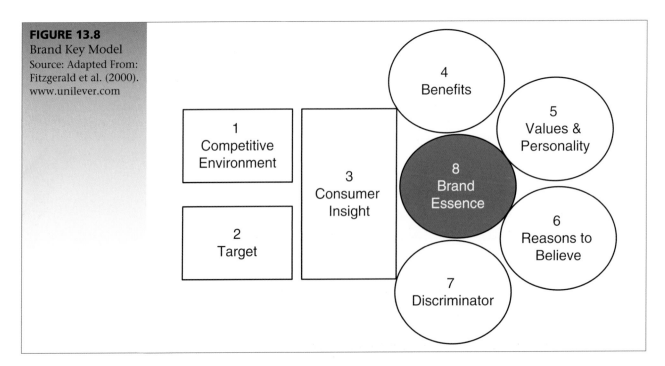

FIGURE 13.8
Brand Key Model
Source: Adapted From:
Fitzgerald et al. (2000).
www.unilever.com

2. **Target:** The person and situation for which the brand is always the best choice, defined in terms of their attitudes and values, not just demographics. Women who want to care for their skin; who want to look and feel their personal best; aged 35–50; beginning to feel the effects of dry skin.

3. **Consumer insight:** That element of all you know about the target consumer and their needs (in this competitive environment upon which the brand is founded). Soap leaves skin feeling dry and tight.

4. **Benefits:** The differentiating functional and emotional benefits that motivate the purchase. Won't dry my skin like soap can; makes skin soft and smooth; helps me feel more feminine.

5. **Values and personality:** The brand values—what the brand stands for and believes in and/or its personality. Honesty, purity, femininity, optimism, inner confidence.

6. **Reasons to believe:** The proof we offer to substantiate the positioning. Contains ¼ moisturizing cream; recommended by doctors; indicts other products with clinical proof; endorsed by users.

7. **Discriminator:** Single most compelling and competitive statement the target consumer would make for buying the brand. Dove won't dry my skin like soap can, because it contains ¼ moisturizing cream.

8. **Brand essence:** The distillation of the brand's genetic code into one clear thought. Femininity restored.

Communications Plan

In the next step, a communications plan needs to be developed that puts all of these insights into action. A good communications plan will provide a strategic framework to identify the different goals for brand communication—the tasks—and assign these to the channels which are likely to be the most effective; it is a blueprint against which campaigns in different communication channels will be briefed and evaluated; it is an aid to priority setting, and a check on how realistic brand objectives are; it is an overall work plan for the brand communication team, company, and agency.

Again, an effective team needs to be assembled (see earlier). Here, both people from the company marketing team and specialists from advertising agencies work together. Tasks need to be defined and prioritized, which involves answering the following questions:

- What is the brand's strategic role in the company portfolio?

- What are the tasks identified in the brand key?

- What is the level of priority for the planned activity?

- How will the activity be affected by the plans for other brand variants or other brands in the product category?

- What is the total budget for the brand?

- What was last year's investment?

Having defined the tasks, the next step is to evaluate the alternative communication channels available to help achieve them. Questions to be answered are:

- What are the options available?

- How could we use them?

- How does a specific target group regard and use different media?

- What opportunities are there to reach a specific target in specific situations, or at specific moments at which a purchase decision can be influenced, for example potential mobile phone buyers, in a taxi (in a traffic jam).

Finally, a draft plan needs to be put in place, agreed upon, and transferred into a final plan. For instance, it is a mandatory Unilever policy for a communication plan to be drawn up each year, for every brand, covering a twelve-month period.

Creative Development

For a marketing communications manager, briefing an agency is one of the most important things to do. How you brief determines what you get back. This is reflected in agencies having to say rather too often that: "clients get the work they deserve." What makes a good brief is founded on some basic principles, which can be applied to almost any briefing situation. There are three basic principles:[57]

- Be clear about what is needed.

- Provide the critical information necessary to complete the task.

- Inspire or motivate people to do their best.

Often with marketing communications we make it over-complicated and forget the basic principles ending up with the agency being unclear on what is required. In other areas of life we do things more instinctively and use the most efficient means of briefing—for example, it's sometimes faster and more accurate to brief a hairdresser by using a picture rather than a verbal description.

There are many different ways of creating a written briefing format for marketing communications. The format should reflect the company's beliefs about how communications work and therefore what is important enough to be included in the brief. Some advertisers may use versions of their agencies' creative brief formats as a basis for their own. Whilst this may initially look as if it is encouraging a collaborative way of working, it does demonstrate a lack of belief in the company's own practices. An agency's internal creative brief usually serves the fundamentally different purpose of inspiring their own creative people. A client marketing communications brief needs to inspire the whole agency team to deliver the best communications. Most briefs also act as a business process document to initiate a job start—in effect it's a purchase order and since large sums of money will be involved in both time and resources it needs to be taken very seriously. To provide a best practice guide to constructing a briefing format, the follow criteria may be observed:

- Where are we now?

- Where do we want to be?

- What are we doing to get there?

- Who do we need to talk to?

- How will we know when we have arrived?

These questions provide the logic for the thinking process for a brief. Often they are used as sub-heads to the broader section headers e.g. Target Audience (who do we want talk to?). This interrogative style acts as a form of tutorial for those writing the brief. It also becomes clear that most marketing communications briefs have three broad areas of headings; those that describe the background, the brief itself, and an implementation and process section (see Table 13.7 for an example).

Once the brief is finished and a new advertising idea is developed, it needs to be presented, which is always a time of tension. Therefore, it is vital that a few guidelines are observed: the whole core team should be present; but meetings should not be too large; it is better to have the meeting at the agency because they typically have better equipment for creative presentation; insist that the agency presents and explains its ideas before presenting the executions.

As a marketing manager, there comes the time when you need to respond to the agency. It is a critical moment, because a good idea may be killed. And a poor idea may be allowed to go forward. Both would be tragedies for the brand. For Unilever it is mandatory practice that the company's response to the agency proposal be put in writing. It needs to be done by the end of the next working day, while memories are still fresh, setting out clearly both the conclusions from the meeting and the actions required.

The final stages are development, production, and evaluation. If an idea is agreed upon, it takes more time to develop it further. Developing the idea needs the help of the consumer. And the developed idea needs to be checked as an execution. Research offers two different tools to help in those two tasks (see again Chapter 6):

1. Qualitative research for learning can be used to check whether the advertising idea works (is it understood? Is it relevant?) and then to grow and develop the idea into an outstanding execution.

2. Quantitative research for evaluation to check the execution and provide the diagnostic scores that enable a comparison against advertising norms.

TABLE 13.7 Example of a Brief	**The Background Headers Might Include:**

Background	Usually covers the business and marketing context and why the task is important.
Marketing or Sales Objective	This sometimes includes the business case for the activity.
Brand	Remarkably, this is often overlooked. It might include brand identity/brand capsule/brand vision/brand architecture/brand status/brand values/brand personality.
Previous Learning	Again a section, which is only used occasionally but may have wider potential.

The Main Communications Brief Section Headers Might Include:

Communications Objectives	Sometimes, they might be expressed as communications imperatives/challenges/barriers.
Target Audience:	Usually this section asks for more than simple demographics and specifically prompts for attitudes or other motivators.
Consumer Insight	Sometimes, specifically linked to the objectives.
Key Message/Proposition	Often phrased as the single-minded proposition/the one thing we want to say.

The Implementation and Process Headers Might Include:

Timing/Key Dates	May include project timelines as well as timing for response.
Budget	May specify if production is included or not.
Response Mechanisms	On relevant types of brief.
Evaluation/Success Criteria	A critical element for most disciplines.
Mandatories/Guidelines	May include what must be included and executional considerations.
Approvals	Signatures of both those issuing/approving the brief and the agency.

Source: Joint Industry Guideline. (2011), 'Briefing an agency', http://www.thegoodpitch.com/wp-content/uploads/2011/09/BriefinganAgency.pdf [Accessed: October 18, 2015]

Good production of the advertisement (whether for TV, print, poster, radio, or the Internet) will add value by leading to increased attention, better branding, and clearer communication. Conversely, poor production can weaken all three of these factors. Finally, advertisements need to be evaluated. The American Marketing Association provides a short video to help keep the evaluation process organized.[58] Others have provided more concrete measurement, suggesting the criteria of reach, resonance, and reaction.[59]

- **Reach**—The first job of any advertising campaign is to reach the right audience. How well is the brand doing at this? It is now possible to measure reach and frequency against a demographic target online just as you would in TV—on a daily basis. Early learnings show that advertisers could be saving 10–20 percent by simply optimizing reach against their target across sites—e.g. moving money out of weak sites and into strong ones.

- **Resonance**—Having reached the right audience, the next job of advertising is to get noticed. Breaking through is the most important job of advertising, because if it doesn't, nothing else matters anyway. But beyond breakthrough, advertising must communicate the brand and change how consumers feel about it. How well is the brand doing this—right now? The real news in the resonance space is the measurement of all of this in near real time. CMOs can use these in-flight insights to improve performance in market—and not wait till the next cycle. Optimizing creative unit rotation, media weight, programming, placement, and cross-platform exposure are all opportunities in the new world of optimization "on the fly."

- **Reaction**—Advertising exists to drive behavioral change. Usually this means increasing sales, but it can also mean getting consumers to search for the brand, go to your Facebook fan page, talk positively about your brand, etc. Measuring reaction is key to understanding if your advertising is going the final mile to cause behaviors that result in a positive ROI.

SUMMARY

- Integrated marketing communications strategies have gained in importance among multinational firms. Such a strategy enables the firm to not only plan communications on a regional or global basis, but also to immediately track performance.
- It is important to identify those products that are suitable to a globalized advertising campaign.
- When advertising messages are localized, there is increased use of local media. In addition, local customs, procedures, and legal regulations must be observed.
- Digital technologies have closed the gap between global and local advertising. They enable advertisers to obtain a global reach for their messages instead of communicating on a country-by-country basis.
- Global advertising agencies play an increasing role in coordinating campaigns across countries.
- Planning a communications campaign should be a very structured and coordinated process in which several parties are involved.

DISCUSSION QUESTIONS

1. How does an integrated marketing communications strategy differ from traditional marketing communications?
2. Why do you think direct marketing has become so important and where do you see its challenges?
3. When is a brand a global brand according to Interbrand definition? Would you agree that it is better to have a global brand than a local brand?

4. What trade-offs do marketers have to make when deciding whether to standardize or localize their global advertising and communications?
5. Keeping in mind that culture influences advertising practices, can you think of a commercial or an advertisement that you have seen recently that did not match your own cultural expectations?
6. What are some of the advantages that global advertising agencies offer to global companies?

EXPERIENTIAL EXERCISES

1. Create an outline of a digital advertising campaign for your consumer product of choice that can be targeted to the global segment of 18–34 year olds. Include:
   a. your selected geographic markets and the reasons you picked these countries or regions;
   b. provide websites for each of these countries or regions and justifications for them;
   c. proposed advertising methods and why;
   d. proposed frequency and why;
   e. proposed ROI metrics.
2. Identify a brand advertisement from the public press and try to retrospectively fill in the brand key model? What do you think the briefing for the agency looked like?

KEY TERMS

- Brand key
- Briefing an agency
- Communications development process
- Country-of-origin communication
- Culture-sensitive advertising
- Direct marketing
- Integrated marketing communications

- Legal issues in advertising
- Localized advertising
- Personal selling
- Promotional activities
- Public relations
- Standardized advertising

NOTES

1 Xerfi Global calculations. (2011), http://www.xerfi.com [Accessed: February 12, 2014].
2 Ibid.
3 Official website of L'Occitane en Provence: www.loccitane.com; Cookson, R. (2010). 'L'Occitane landmark IPO raises HK$5.5bn', *Financial Times*, April 30, 2010, http://www.ft.com/intl/cms/s/0/df4053dc-5411-11df-aba0-00144feab49a.html#axzz3ovgjKhvm [Accessed: October 17, 2014].; For the following also see Liu, X., Tan, Y., and Xuan, Y. (2012). *Market entry strategy for Fragonard in China*. [Master's thesis] EMLYON Business School.
4 L'Occitane. (2014). *Annual report 2014*. www.loccitane.com [Accessed: June 10, 2015].
5 Koschate-Fischer, N., Diamantopoulos, A., and Oldenkotte, K. (2012), 'Are consumers really willing to pay

more for a favorable country image? A study of country-of-origin effects on willingness to pay', *Journal of International Marketing*, 20(1), pp. 19–41.

6   Corporate website: www.loccitane.com

7   Businessdictionary.com. 'Integrated marketing communications (IMC) definition', http://www.businessdictionary.com/definition/integrated-marketing-communications-IMC.html [Accessed: December 15, 2014]; http://mkl.mmclearning.com/preview/?t=tutorials/marketingcommunications/c10t1.swf [Accessed: December 15, 2014].

8   Dictionary of Marketing Terms. 'International Advertising', http://www.allbusiness.com/glossaries/international-advertising/4962893-1.html [Accessed: December 15, 2014].

9   Public Relations Society of America. 'What is public relations?', http://www.prsa.org/aboutprsa/publicrelationsdefined/#.VK-je6Ufwll [Accessed: December 15, 2014].

10   Ibid.

11   Curtain, D. (2006), 'The challenges of international public relations', http://www.sagepub.com/upm-data/13709_Chapter1.pdf [Accessed: July 10, 2014].

12   'Coupon statistics', http://www.ilovecouponmonth.com/statistics/ [Accessed: December 20, 2014].

13   Jayasingh, S. and Eze, U. C. (2010), 'The role of moderating factors in mobile coupon adoption: An extended TAM perspective', *Communications of the IBIMA, 2010*, pp. 1–13.

14   The World Bank. (2012), 'Mobile phone access reaches three quarters of planet's population', http://www.worldbank.org/en/news/2012/07/17/mobile-phone- access-reaches-three-quarters-planets-population [Accessed: December 30, 2014].

15   McKinsey. (2014), 'Why marketers should keep sending emails', http://www.mckinsey.com/insights/marketing_sales/why_marketers_should_keep_sending_you_emails [Accessed: December 30, 2014].

16   Fine, L. M. (2007), 'Selling and sales management', *Business Horizons*, 50, pp. 185–91.

17   Euromonitor. http://www.marketresearchworld.net/content/view/1075/77/ [Accessed: December 18, 2014].

18   The Boston Consulting Group. (2010), 'The CMO's imperative. Tackling new digital realities', www.bcg.com [Accessed: December 18, 2014].

19   Dmitrijeva, K. and Batraga, A. (2012), 'Marketing paradigm: Transition from MC to IMC', *Economics and Management*, 17(3), pp. 1068–75.

20   Interbrand. (2013), 'Best Global Brands 2013', http://interbrand.com/best-brands/best-global-brands/2013/ranking/ [Accessed: October 18, 2015].

21   Interbrand. (2014), 'Financial applications for brand valuation', April, 2014, http://interbrand.com/views/financial-applications-for-brand-valuation/ [Accessed: October 18, 2015]; Entrepreneurial Insight. (2014), 'Top ten lessons from global brands', http://www.entrepreneurial-insights.com/top-ten-lessons-global-brands/ [Accessed: October 18, 2015].

22   The World Factbook. (2015), https://www.cia.gov/library/publications/the-world-factbook/docs/refmaps.html [Accessed: August 1, 2015].

23   Interbrand. (2014), 'Best global brands: Samsung', http://www.bestglobalbrands.com/2014/samsung/ [Accessed: October 18, 2015].

24   Baker, M., Sterenberg, G., and Taylor, E. (2003), 'Managing global brands to meet consumer expectations', *ESOMAR Global Cross-Industry Forum, Miami*, www.warc.com [Accessed: October 14, 2014].

25   Publicis Groupe's Zenith Optimedia. (2014), 'Advertising Expenditure Forecast', http://www.zenithoptimedia.com/wp-content/uploads/2014/12/Adspend-forecasts-December-2014-executive-summary.pdf [Accessed: June 1, 2015].

26   Gunelius, S. (2015), 'Kia rolls out brand positioning ad campaign', *Corporate Eye*, http://www.corporate-eye.com/main/kia-rolls-out-brand-repositioning-ad-campaign/ [Accessed: January 15, 2015].

27   Shankar, V. (2008). Strategic allocation of marketing resources: Methods and insights. In Roger A. Kerin and Rob O'Regan (eds.). *Marketing mix decisions: New perspectives and practice.* Chicago: AMA. (pp. 154–83).

28   Ibid.

29   Hussain, A. and Khan, S. (2013), 'International marketing strategy: Standardization versus adaptation', *Management and Administrative Sciences Review*, 2(4), pp. 353–9.

30 Onkvisit, S. and Shaw, J.J. (2004). *International marketing: Analysis and strategy*. New York: Routledge. (p. 455).

31 (2005), 'Managing brands in global markets: One size doesn't fit all', *Knowledge@Wharton*, June 1, 2005, http://knowledge.wharton.upenn.edu/article.cfm?articleid=1206 [Accessed: June 10, 2015].

32 Borden, J. (2008), 'Fitness for the everyday consumer', *Marketing News*, September 15, 2008, pp. 17–19.

33 De Mooij, M. (2005). *Global marketing and advertising*. 2nd ed. London: Sage. p. 8.

34 Hemlock, D. (2014), 'Businesses welcome new rules on Cuba travel, trade', http://www.sun-sentinel.com/business/fl-cuba-us-regulations-20150115-story.html#page=1 [Accessed: December 27, 2014].

35 Bryant, H. (2014), 'The importance of localization in advertising campaigns', http://translation-blog.trustedtranslations.com/the-importance-of-localization-in-advertising-campaigns-2014-05-16.html [Accessed: February 15, 2015].

36 Liu, R., Kramarczuk, R. and Megits, N. (2014), 'Consumers' perceptions of standardized advertising and localized advertising of multinational companies in the smartphone industry', *Journal of Eastern European and Central Asian Research*, 1(2), pp. 1–11.

37 Pinsent Masons. (2010), 'Consumer protection from unfair trading regulations', http://www.out-law.com/page-9050 [Accessed: December 10, 2014].

38 Doland, A. (2014), 'Authorities want to crack down on smoking and cigarette marketing, but it's an uphill battle', *AdAge*, http://adage.com/article/global-news/china-tobacco-brands-sponsor-schools/296061/ [Accessed: December 28, 2014].

39 Fam, K. (2008), 'Attributes of likeable television commercials in Asia', *Journal of Advertising Research,* 48(3), pp. 418–32.

40 IBM. 'Writing for an international audience', http://www-01.ibm.com/software/globalization/topics/writing/culture.html [Accessed: October 18, 2015].

41 B.C. (2014). 'Competing to be the real thing', *The Economist*, March 8, 2014, http://www.economist.com/blogs/erasmus/2014/03/religion-and-advertising [Accessed: September 8, 2014].

42 Ibid.

43 Ibid.

44 The Equal Rights Trust. (2012), 'Washing the tigers: Addressing discrimination and inequality in Malaysia', http://www.equalrightstrust.org/ertdocumentbank/Malaysia%20CR%201.pdf [Accessed: October 18, 2015].

45 Emarketer. (2014), 'Total US ad spending to see largest increase since 2004', http://www.emarketer.com/Article/Total-US-Ad-Spending-See-Largest-Increase-Since-2004/1010982#sthash.UOJYxzlo.RsD6OksX.dpuf [Accessed: October 18, 2015].

46 Avi, D. (2013), 'What are 10 great ad agencies of 2013, according to CMOs?' *Forbes,* http://www.forbes.com/sites/avidan/2013/12/04/ten-great-agencies-of-2013/ [Accessed: October 18, 2015].

47 Cuneo, A. Z. (2007), 'Visa teams with Wieden for soccer sponsorship', *Advertising Age*, June 28, 2007, http://adage.com/article/agency-news/visa-teams-wieden-soccer-sponsorship/118886/ [Accessed: October 18, 2015].

48 The World Factbook. (2015), https://www.cia.gov/library/publications/the-world-factbook/docs/refmaps.html [Accessed: August 1, 2015].

49 Coca-Cola. (2007, March), 'Brand profile', http://WARC.com [Accessed: October 18, 2015].

50 Madden, N. (2005), 'Home-field advantage? Toyota readies Lexus for its debut in Japan', *Advertising Age,* August 15, 2005, http://adage.com/article/news/home-field-advantage-toyota-readies-lexus-debut-japan/104188/ [Accessed: October 18, 2015].

51 Author Unknown. (2007), 'LG appoints new global advertising agency', *Cellular-news.com,* December 3, 2007, www.cellular-news.com/story/27823.php [Accessed: October 18, 2015].

52 Hall, E. (2008), 'Global media agency network of the year: Mediaedge:cia', *Advertising Age*, March 3, 2008, http://adage.com/article/special-report-media-agency-of-the-year/global-media-agency-network-year-mediaedge-cia/125401/ [Accessed: October 18, 2015].

53 Fitzgerald, N., Tabaksblat, M. and Burgmans, A. (2000). Welcome to Advanced Brand Communications. Unilever.

54 Ibid.

55 The Associated Press. (2005), 'Heinz unveils new blue ketchup', *USA Today*, April 7, 2003, http://usatoday30.usatoday.com/advertising/orbitz/orbitz-window-unldPop.htm [Accessed: October 18, 2015].

56 Fitzgerald, N., Tabaksblat, M., and Burgmans, A. (2000), op. cit.

57 Joint Industry Guideline (2011) 'Briefing an Agency', http://www.thegoodpitch.com/wp-content/uploads/2011/09/BriefinganAgency.pdf [Accessed: October 18, 2015].

58 American Marketing Association. (2014), 'Advertisement Evaluation Matrix', https://www.ama.org/resources/MarketingToolkit/BrandingAndMarketingEssentials/Pages/Advertisement-Evaluation-Matrix.aspx [Accessed: December 30, 2014].

59 Daye, D. (2012), 'Measuring advertising effectiveness', *Brand Strategy Insider*, http://www.brandingstrategyinsider.com/2012/05/measuring-advertising-effectiveness.html#.VLvRFaUfzFl [Accessed: December 30, 2014].

CASE 13.1   BRANDING ORLANDO FOR GLOBAL COMPETITIVENESS[1]

Ilan Alon, Jennifer Dugosh and Meredith Lohwasser wrote this case solely to provide material for class discussion. The authors do not intend to illustrate either effective or ineffective handling of a managerial situation. The authors may have disguised certain names and other identifying information to protect confidentiality.

Richard Ivey School of Business Foundation prohibits any form of reproduction, storage or transmission without its written permission. Reproduction of this material is not covered under authorization by any reproduction rights organization. To order copies or request permission to reproduce materials, contact Ivey Publishing, Richard Ivey School of Business Foundation, The University of Western Ontario, London, Ontario, Canada, N6A 3K7; phone (519) 661-3208; fax (519) 661-3882; e-mail cases@ivey.uwo.ca.

"We must promote Orlando as a business destination, as well as a tourist destination."
– Michael Schiffhauer, Enterprise Florida, May 2, 2012 at Enterprise Florida office

"Orlando." When the city was mentioned, most people intuitively thought of Disney, Mickey Mouse, Universal, SeaWorld and sun; Orlando was a brand known worldwide as a destination for tourism and sunshine. Over 50 million tourists visited the area each year and spent almost $30 billion.[2] Though Orlando was world renowned for its tourist industry, the Greater Orlando Area housed many other promising industries including technology, defense and simulation. Additionally, the area had a diverse community and a trade scene with vast potential. Orlando was a great place to do business and was one of the hottest markets in the nation for job growth. According to Diana Bolivar, vice-president of the Hispanic Chamber of Commerce of Metro Orlando, "People don't necessarily know how easy it is to do business here. We should be known as a great place to live and to work. We should be known as a business city."[3]

According to *Forbes* (as cited by the Pew Research Center), Orlando was one of the most popular cities in the United States because of its tourist attractions and beautiful weather; however, it was seldom recognized as anything else.[4] Despite its many industries, Orlando was absent from the list of the "World's Most Successful Cities." On this list of 26, five U.S. cities were included: New York, San Francisco, Chicago, Houston and Los Angeles.[5] CNBC's list of the world's most popular business cities included Paris, Dubai, Madrid, Beijing, Moscow, Shanghai, London, Tokyo, Singapore and Hong Kong.[6] Another source included only one U.S. city on its list of "Top 20 Destination Cities by International Visitors": New York City.[7] Why was Orlando overlooked for these types of designations? Orlando's brand was tourism, and as a result, the city was not recognized worldwide for anything else.

Why was the area not recognized as a great place to conduct business? Why was Orlando's reputation only tied to tourism? How could the city be marketed as a vibrant business destination in addition to a tourist destination? Many variables such as key industries, current international business presence, trade data and livability affected the brand and, therefore, perception of the city. What could be done to make Orlando more attractive and, through this, become a world city?

HISTORY OF ORLANDO

Orlando's history dated back to 1838 when the U.S. Army constructed Fort Gatlin in an effort to protect settlers from the Seminole Indians. The city was first known as Jernigan, named after the family who established the first permanent settlement. The community was named Orlando in 1856, and the Town of Orlando was incorporated nearly 20 years later in 1875.[8]

The citrus business encouraged development in the 1880s as improved transportation became a necessity. From 1910 to 1920, the population doubled, and the community became a major city.[9] Churches, roads and schools were built to accommodate the new arrivals. In the early 1920s, millions of immigrants, speculators and builders came to Central Florida looking for land. Land speculation soared rampantly, but the bubble burst in 1926. In 1929, the stock market crashed, ruining Orlando's economy, which was revitalized by President Roosevelt's New Deal programs, as well as the beginning of World War II. By 1950, Orlando had a population of over 50,000 and was visited by nearly 4.5 million tourists. In the 1960s, the government space industry helped to fuel the economy. In the early 1970s, Disney World opened, attracting 20 million visitors in its first two years alone. Additional attractions sprang up: SeaWorld in 1973 and Universal in 1990.[10] In 2010, the City of Orlando had a population of 238,300 making it the 79th largest city in the United States. Additionally, the Greater Orlando Area had a population of 2,134,411 and was the 27th largest metro area in the United States.[11]

ORLANDO'S BREAD AND BUTTER: TOURISM

On October 1, 1971, Walt Disney World's Magic Kingdom, along with two accompanying hotels, opened their doors in Orlando. As time passed and Disney's popularity grew, it expanded its operations to include additional parks. In 2011, Disney generated $18.2 billion in economic activity for Florida, 2.5 per cent of the state's gross domestic product (GDP); it was also responsible for one of every 50 jobs in Florida and represented 6 per cent of all jobs in the Greater Orlando Area. Tourists spent about $1.7 billion annually on expenses outside of the direct resort areas on hotels and lodging, food, retail purchases and transportation.[12] In addition to theme parks, cruise lines attracted a large portion of tourists annually. Port Canaveral, just an hour outside of Orlando, was the nation's second busiest cruise port.[13]

In 2010, 51.5 million visitors spent $28.3 billion in the Greater Orlando Area. There were 453 hotel properties with 116,534 rooms and $13.4 billion annual earned wages. Tourism accounted for over 216,000 direct industry jobs and 24.4 per cent of private employment (see Exhibit 1).[14]

EXHIBIT 13.1 ORLANDO VISITOR VOLUMES	Visitor Volumes (millions)	2007	2008	2009	2010	f2011	Change 11/10
	Total	48.745	48.888	46.583	51.455	54.29	5.5%
	Domestic	45.907	45.515	43.319	47.780	50.50	5.7%
	Leisure	35.334	35.282	33.992	38.263	40.46	5.7%
	Business	10.574	10.233	9.326	9.517	10.04	5.5%
	International	2.838	3.343	3.264	3.675	3.79	3.0%
	Canada	0.783	0.910	0.865	0.960	0.99	3.3%
	Overseas	2.055	2.433	2.399	2.715	2.78	2.3%
	U.K.	0.990	0.959	0.831	0.839	0.82	-1.85%

Source: Visit Orlando, "State of the Market," http://corporate.visitorlando.com/includes/content/ images/media/docs/State_of_the_Market_Apr2012.pdf, April 2012, accessed May 30, 2012.

BEYOND TOURISM: OTHER KEY INDUSTRIES IN ORLANDO

In addition to Disney World, Orlando was a center for many different kinds of businesses; however, the city was rarely seen as a destination for investment outside of the tourism industry. Jerry Ross, executive director of the National Entrepreneur Center, said, "Orlando is best known for Disney and tourism and it is recognizable worldwide. That shouldn't change. It's like attracting people with honey. It's what brings them here, and then they realize there is so much more."[15] This view was reinforced by Carmenza Gonzalez, president of CZA Inc., when she said, "Orlando should be known as a business destination. We have incredible business that even locals don't know about. Manufacturing is growing. Simulation and training is a large industry and healthcare is even bigger."[16]

- *Technology* — The Greater Orlando Area's second largest industry behind tourism was technology: there were 2,600 technology firms that employed over 42,000 people in sectors such as digital media and film; modeling, simulation and training; optics and photonics; aviation and aerospace; and information technology.[17]

- *Defense* — Defense companies such as Lockheed Martin, Siemens and Northrop Grumman located facilities in Orlando.

- *Health Care and Medical City* — Health care had a major presence in the Greater Orlando Area. Lake Nona Medical City was a $2 billion medical campus that included the University of Central Florida's medical school as well as numerous research laboratories and hospitals. Medical City was predicted to create 30,000 jobs and an annual economic impact of nearly $9 billion.[18] However, it was not the only health care entity in the Greater Orlando Area. According to Kenneth Mouradian, director of U.S. Commercial Service at the

U.S. Department of Commerce in Orlando, the area housed medical device manufacturers and pharmaceutical developers. Additionally, large hospital groups such as Florida Hospital, Nemours Children's Hospital and Orlando Regional Medical Center (ORMC) had established many operations in the area.[19]

- *Simulation and Training* — The simulation and training industry in Orlando was the largest cluster in the country, with over 100 companies, 12,500 direct employees and $3 billion in gross regional product.[20] Bolivar stated, "No one really knows, but we have spearheaded so many initiatives in the area of simulation. Simulation is Orlando's best kept secret."According to Thomas L. Baptiste, president and executive director of the National Center for Simulation, "Orlando and Central Florida are the epicenter for modeling and simulation. When you combine the power of the Research Park, close ties between a world-class university, industry and Team Orlando, you produce a synergy found nowhere else in the world. Companies who want to be serious players in the modeling and simulation industry need to consider focusing their efforts on Orlando and Central Florida."[21]

- *Space* — Located just east of Orlando in Brevard County, the John F. Kennedy Space Center was "the nation's gateway to exploring, discovering and understanding our universe."[22] Although the space program ended in 2011, which resulted in the loss of nearly 7,500 jobs,[23] Kennedy Space Center continued "to make history as America's spaceport," as it entered the new era of commercial space flight.[24]

INTERNATIONAL BUSINESS

Florida was a huge export state, one of the most active in the nation. Orlando and its surrounding counties, therefore, participated in a great deal of international business. Central Florida was home to three Fortune 500 company headquarters, all of which maintained an international business presence.[25] In addition, Orlando had many investment- and trade-facilitating organizations.

Trade

Orlando had a foreign trade zone, Zone 42, which sat off Interstate 4 near the Orlando International Airport (MCO), giving it access to both interstate and air transport. In the seven counties surrounding Orlando, there were three additional foreign trade zones located in Daytona Beach, Sanford and Cape Canaveral, zones 192, 250 and 136, respectively. These zones too sat close to at least one interstate highway.[26] This gave Orlando an advantage in the global marketplace and contributed to its international appeal.

There were 20 free trade zones (FTZs) in the state of Florida in Cape Canaveral, Daytona Beach, Fort Myers, Fort Pierce, Fort Lauderdale, Homestead, Jacksonville,

Largo, Miami, Ocala, Orlando, Palmetto, Panama City, Pensacola, Riviera Beach, Sanford, Sebring and Tampa.[27] According to Ross, Miami's FTZ was active and flourishing while FTZs in Central Florida lacked promotion and coordination, factors he believed deterred their success.

Exports

Florida exported $64.8 billion in goods and services in 2011, making it the fourth largest exporting state in the country only behind Texas, California and New York. In addition, Florida's trade surplus was the greatest in the nation. International business and foreign direct investment in Florida sustained approximately one of every six jobs, with exports expected to double by 2014.[28]

Foreign Direct Investment in Orlando

A foreign direct investment study conducted for the Greater Orlando Area revealed 312 foreign companies in 755 separate locations across the seven counties of Brevard, Lake, Orange, Osceola, Polk, Seminole and Volusia. The vast majority of these foreign companies were involved in the industries of manufacturing (88), services (64), wholesale trade (49) and retail trade (35).[29]

Over 30 countries were represented in the seven counties of the Greater Orlando Area. Of the 312 companies, over three-quarters were from the United Kingdom, Germany, Japan, Canada, France, Switzerland, Ireland, Italy and Sweden.[30]

Investment- and Trade-facilitating Organizations

Orlando had multiple organizations that worked to promote the Greater Orlando Area. These organizations — various chambers of commerce, MCO, VisitOrlando, Enterprise Florida, World Trade Organization of Orlando and the Metro Orlando Economic Development Commission — facilitated both investment and trade in and around the Orlando area. According to Ross, however, the various organizations often had their own competing agendas, which could present problems to the international business visitor. He explained, "If we could establish a single point of contact, one office or organization that is the coordinator for international inquiries in Orlando, it would allow us to compete more effectively! We need to get all the resources working together" (see Exhibit 2).

CULTURAL FACTORS OF ORLANDO

Diversity — The Greater Orlando Area was composed of a very diverse community. The Orlando Metropolitan Statistical Area (MSA) had a total population of 2,134,411. Of this, 10.45 per cent were from Latin America, 2.65 per cent were from Asia, 1.86 per cent were from Europe and 0.57 per cent were from Africa.[31] One out of every six people in Orlando was born in a country outside the United States, the majority of whom were born in Latin America. Hispanics, representing 22 per cent of the population in Orlando, brought over 20,000 Hispanic-owned business operations to the area.[32] In *Forbes* magazine's 2011 list of Best Cities for Minority Entrepreneurs, the Orlando-Kissimmee MSA ranked ninth.[33] According to Bolivar, "The role that our diaspora communities play in Orlando is absolutely positive. We no longer live in a local economy — it's now global. If you aren't looking to expand and diversify globally, then you are behind the curve. For these reasons, our diverse community is helpful." Schiffhauer agreed with Bolivar: "Our culturally diverse community makes us more attractive to expats who want to expand their companies here. For example, Germans will likely want to hire German-speakers, be it German-Americans, military personnel who know German or some other type of German speakers. It is easier. People gravitate first to their own cultures, not because of ethnocentrism, but because there are cultural affinities and language issues that play in. Look at Miami — it has driven business out of LA [Los Angeles, CA] exceedingly well. Export numbers for Miami are off the charts. In this way, our diversity is a strength to our community, not a weakness."[34]

Entrepreneurial hub — As home to key entrepreneurs such as Walt Disney, Orlando had a vibrant entrepreneurial scene. Orlando also had two exclusive entrepreneurial centers — the National Entrepreneur Center and the University of Central Florida Technology Incubator. The National Entrepreneur Center, originally a collaboration between the University of Central Florida, the U.S. Small Business Administration, the Orange County government and the Walt Disney World Company, was a public/private partnership dedicated to "the education, support, and development of our small business community . . . . Since inception, the center's service provider organizations have trained, counseled and assisted the small business community in record numbers." Since 2003, the National Entrepreneur Center facilitated $125,000 in loans, trained and coached 70,000 businesses and assisted in 700 new business start-ups. The UCF Technology Incubator was ranked one of the top incubators in America. These centers served as great resources for both entrepreneurs and innovative companies.[35]

Collaborative approach to business — Orlando was recognized for its willingness to collaborate and create partnerships, making the area an ideal place for companies that thrive on and need collaboration.[36] Bolivar confirmed this notion: "We are big on partnerships and collaboration. Collaboration is something you don't see too much anywhere else. We have been recognized for the amount of collaboration that we do here." Gonzalez saw a different reality: "We used to have great collaboration for many years, collaboration which was outstanding and recognized by other cities and states; however, in the last couple of years, that collaboration has been interrupted by unplanned situations. We were on track for positioning Orlando as an international business destination, but, for the last two years or so, that collaboration has been affected."

The Orange County Convention Center (OCCC), the second largest convention center in the nation, enjoyed international attendance of 15 to 20 per cent.[37] It was owned and operated by the county government and was a great asset to the Greater Orlando Area. Since its inception in June 1969, the convention center had earned a positive name for itself. It was named "One of the World's Best Congress Centers" by International Association of Congress Centres (AIPC). Additionally, a top online trade publication ranked the convention center as "The Number One Convention Center in the United States." The OCCC hosted several events each year, including trade shows, conventions, consumer shows, executive meetings and theater events.[38]

Livability — Florida was not called "The Sunshine State" for nothing. With year-round sunlight, Orlando was a desirable place to live. The weather went hand-in-hand with Florida's beautiful beaches, lakes, springs and parks. Combined with world-class entertainment and shopping, Orlando was a preferred place to live, work and raise a family.[39] Additionally, the city was inventing itself as one of the most sustainable cities in the south. A speech given at the Mayor's State of Downtown in early October 2012 was focused on sustainability. The mayor noted, "In 2007, with the support of many Downtown stakeholders, Orlando became one of the first cities in the southeast to adopt a comprehensive program designed to create a more environmentally friendly city — called GreenWorks Orlando." The mayor highlighted many successes in this area over a four-year span including reduction of energy consumption by 20 per cent by the city government and the addition of eight LEED certified buildings.[40]

Additionally, the Greater Orlando Area's urban design was remarkable. The area was full of lakes, parks, public art and many beautiful views — things that made a "picture of many shapes, textures and colors" — and the mission of the Urban Designs Division of Orlando was "to encourage sustainable development, protect existing neighborhoods and support the economic health of our community."[41] Orlando's city planning strategy was unique in that it positioned high-intensity developments involving concepts such as transit-friendly offices and multi-family residences at its core and surrounded it by lower intensity developments, single-family neighborhoods and parks, a design that made the City of Orlando the center of Central Florida, rather than just another city in the area.[42]

ADMINISTRATIVE FACTORS OF ORLANDO

Education — Florida had 2,676 elementary schools, 1,175 middle schools and 1,203 high schools, ranking fifth, fourth and fifth in the nation for number of schools.[43] Despite these numbers, the state received poor rankings in education quality. According to *Education Week* (as cited by the Florida Center for Fiscal and Economic Policy), Florida earned a D minus in national standardized testing scores,

EXHIBIT 13.2

INVESTMENT- AND TRADE-FACILITATING ORGANIZATIONS IN ORLANDO

Hispanic Chamber of Commerce	The Hispanic Chamber of Commerce, a product of two Hispanic chambers combined, started in 1993. Since its beginning, the chamber has made the promotion of the Greater Orlando Area as a business destination a priority. The organization had spearheaded many projects in this area with initiatives such as trade missions to Latin American countries. Bolivar explained, "I believe we are doing the right things. The trips are one of the best ways to educate foreign countries — it's grassroots."
African American Chamber of Commerce	The African American Chamber of Commerce offered tools and services such as mentoring, seminars and networking events to its members since its beginning over 65 years ago in 1945.
British American Chamber of Commerce	The United Kingdom represented the largest portion of international business in the Greater Orlando Area with over 400,000 British Americans in the area. The chamber facilitated relationships between the United States and the United Kingdom while also providing its members with innovative programs such as corporate, social, cultural and sports programs. It is also exploring postgraduate transatlantic educational opportunities.[1] Jason Edwards, president of the British Chamber of Commerce, mentioned the Orange County Convention Center as a missed opportunity to attract international business: "We have billion dollar companies meeting in our backyard. We don't have a format to pull them away from the convention and show them Orlando. Sure, the conventions are good for the local economy; there are blue-collar workers, but there are no white collar workers."[2]
Caribbean American Chamber of Commerce	In the early 1990s, many organizations emerged to represent several of the largest countries. In response, the Caribbean American Chamber of Commerce was founded in 1991. The chamber strived to create and build strong relationships between its U.S. members and Caribbean countries through workshops, seminars and other services.[3]
Asian American Chamber of Commerce	The Asian American Chamber of Commerce started in 1986 and served as the bridge between its members in the Greater Orlando Area and Asian American communities. Through support, leadership, encouragement and events, the chamber helped new and existing members to be successful with all business endeavors in the Greater Orlando Area.[4]
Indian American Chamber of Commerce	Since its inception, the Indian American Chamber of Commerce facilitated relationships and commerce between India and the United States. As the voice of the Indian American community in Central Florida, the chamber worked to enable Indo-American business and to promote the needs of business owners and professionals through initiatives such as the Indian American Expo and other events.[5]
Orlando International Airport (MCO)	Orlando International Airport was the 13th busiest airport in the country and the 29th busiest airport in the world.[6] It serviced 35.4 million passengers in 2011 and 5.7 million in the first two months of 2012 alone. MCO, with four parallel runways and 96 gates, was equipped to handle the largest aircraft. MCO was physically larger than Miami International Airport (MIA), Los Angeles International Airport (LAX) and John F. Kennedy International Airport (JFK) combined. Over 30 airlines, both domestic and international, resided at MCO.[7]
VisitOrlando	A major advocate of tourism, VisitOrlando's mission was to "market the area globally as a premier leisure, convention and business destination for the continual economic benefit of the community." VisitOrlando was officially recognized as the sales and marketing organization for the Orlando and Orange County area. It represented over 1,100 private tourist businesses to implement marketing programs to build a strong tourism industry.[8]

(Continued)

EXHIBIT 13.2 (CONTINUED)

Enterprise Florida Inc.	Enterprise Florida Inc. was a private/public partnership devoted to statewide economic development focused on many sectors including clean energy, life sciences, information technology, aviation and aerospace, homeland security and defense, financial and professional services and manufacturing. The organization provided many services through its offices located in Orlando, Tallahassee and Miami, as well as its international offices in Europe, Asia, South America, the Middle East and Africa.[9] From 2010 to 2011, Enterprise Florida funds were distributed to international trade, administration, business retention and recruitment, marketing and strategic intelligence and external affairs. Its return on investment (ROI) was measured using two factors: statewide economic effects of investments in business development projects and increased export sales. The results from the 2010 to 2011 fiscal year included "27,013 new and retained jobs related to Enterprise Florida programs and facilitated export sales; $1.9 billion added to Florida labor income through higher employment and export activity; $83.4 million added to state and local tax revenues because of economic growth; and new projects and assisted exports added more than $3 billion to Florida's gross state product; Ernst & Young ROI at 2.66:1."[10]
World Trade Centers	The World Trade Center Orlando, founded in 1970, was Orlando's branch of the not-for-profit organization dedicated to the establishment of world trade centers "as instruments for trade expansion." It brought together business and government agencies involved in international trade, provided services and worked to enhance the Orlando economy. "It is the goal of World Trade Centers to develop and maintain facilities to house practitioners of trade and the services they need to conduct business, creating a central focal point for a region's trade services and activities, or a 'one-stop-shopping center' for international business."[11]
Metro Orlando Economic Development Commission	The Metro Orlando Economic Development Commission was dedicated to creating a competitive economic climate in which businesses could thrive; as a result, it provided key services and support to the community. "Our charge is basically two-fold. To attract new business investment, we market the Orlando region worldwide as a top location for business. In addition, we work with local companies to assist them with expansion plans and other business concerns."[12] The mission of the organization was guided by a formula for the region's economic growth that included "a laser focus on generating strategic business and industry growth, resulting in high-quality jobs and investment; leveraging, studying, advocating for and shaping major regional assets to nurture competitiveness and economic growth; and engaging business, legislative and academic leaders to unite and collaborate on strategic economic opportunities."[13]
Orlando U.S. Export Assistance Center	The Orlando U.S. Export Assistance Center was the commercial section of U.S. diplomatic representations in 74 countries. The organization facilitated the sale of U.S.-origin exports in foreign markets and helped U.S. companies to defend their commercial interests abroad.[14]

Notes:

1 British American Chamber of Commerce, "Our Mission," www.britishamericanchamberorlando.com/content.aspx?id=1 accessed August 3, 2012.

2 J. Edwards, personal interview, July 26, 2012.

3 Caribbean American Chamber of Commerce, "About the Caribbean American Chamber of Commerce of Central Florida," www.caccf.org/about-caccf.html, accessed August 3, 2012.

4 Asian American Chamber of Commerce, "About the Chamber," www.asianamericanchambercfl.org/about.php, accessed August 3, 2012.

5 American Indian Chamber of Commerce, "Mission," www.iaccorlando.com/webroot/index.php?option=com_content&view=article&id=22&Itemid=29, accessed August 3, 2012.

6 World City Information, "Orlando," www.city-infos.com/orlando/, accessed June 27, 2012.

7 Orlando International Airport Report, 2012.

8 Visit Orlando, "About Us," www.visitorlando.com/about-us/ accessed June 4, 2012

9 Enterprise Florida, "About Us," www.eflorida.com/ContentSubpage.aspx?id=206 accessed June 3, 2012.

10 Enterprise Florida, "Enterprise Florida Annual Report 2010-2011," 2011, www.eflorida.com/Intelligence Center/download/AU/AR_2011.pdf, accessed June 3, 2012.

11 World Trade Center Orlando, "World Trade Centers Concept: A Fact Sheet," www.worldtrade centerorlando.org/wtcconcept.html, accessed June 4, 2012.

12 Metro Orlando Economic Development Commission, "About the EDC," www.orlandoedc.com/About-the-EDC/, accessed June 3, 2012

13 Metro Orlando Economic Development Commission, "EDC Annual Report 2011," www.orlandoedc. com/core/fileparse.php/1072/urlt/EDC%20Annual%20Report%202011.pdf, accessed June 3, 2012

14 K. Mouradian, personal interview, May 17, 2012.

Source: Created by authors.

an F for funding per student when compared to the national average and an F for college readiness. The same report noted that Florida's graduation rate ranked 45th in the country.[44] Despite these dismal rankings, Florida had implemented nearly all accountability and performance policies suggested by education reformers. This fact permitted the state to achieve a ranking of eighth in the nation for overall education in the same report. An additional source, U.S. News and World Report, which observed 21,776 high schools nationwide, included only 127 Florida schools on the list of best public high schools — less than 1 per cent of the entire list.[45] Bolivar expressed her view about the public school system in Florida: "Education is a factor — it is always a factor, especially because you usually think of the schools up north. In general, there are better schools up north. We have made strides in education over the years — it's changing. There are schools here in Florida that are as good as schools up north, but it's not advertised. It is a stigma . . . ." Further, trade education was an issue. According to Bolivar, "Trade education is a challenge that we have, probably more than other states — there is a skills gap. The unemployment rate is high, yet there are positions available. The problem is there is not enough skilled labor. Skill trade education is lacking."

Despite this negative image, public education was improving. According to a recent study, Florida ranked second in the nation behind Maryland for improved test scores. The study, conducted by Education Next, concluded that Florida had improved its test scores 3.2 per cent annually from 1992 to 2011 of a standard deviation, which used mathematics, reading and science performance data of students.[46]

Education in Florida at the university and college level was much more impressive. The University of Florida and the University of Miami were included in U.S. News and World Report's top 100 schools in the national university rankings of 2012, while Florida State University just missed this mark at the 101 spot.[47] Higher education in the Greater Orlando Area was also remarkable. It was home to the University of Central Florida, the nation's second largest university with over 56,000 students. Also in the Greater Orlando Area was Rollins College, the state's top-ranked MBA program and best regional university in the south, as well as Valencia College, Lake-Sumter Community College and Seminole State College, three of the state's best community colleges. Also in Central Florida were Embry Riddle Aeronautical University, the Florida Agricultural & Mechanical University School of Law and Barry University School of Law.[48]

Crime — Orlando had long been plagued by crime. It was ranked sixth on *Forbes'* list of "America's Most Dangerous Cities," with 845 violent crimes per 100,000 people.[49] While crime, both violent and property, was decreasing, it was still about double the state average, which in turn was higher than the national average.

Government — Government in the Orlando area was unique. The government of Orange County included the City of Orlando as well as a dozen other incorporated municipalities. Seven elected members served four-year terms on the

Board of County Commissioners, including the mayor.[50] Mayor Jacobs's initiatives included a prescription drug task force, one-stop permits for businesses, job-creating-tax abatement, public engagement, ethics, the 2011 Jobs Summits Series and the Youth Leadership Conference.[51] In 2012, Teresa Jacobs was the Orange County mayor and Buddy Dyer the City of Orlando's mayor. Mayor Dyer's most significant city programs included:

- *Strengthen Orlando* — The city's mission to build Downtown Orlando into an ideal location for corporate and division headquarters in the region.

- *Green Works Orlando* — The city's plan to protect its natural resources, encourage environmentally friendly lifestyles and business practices and engage the community in green efforts.

- *Public safety* — The city's mission to keep residents and visitors safe.

- *City Kidz/Children and Education* — The mayor's children and education initiative.

- *Pathways for Parramore* — The mayor's initiative to revitalize the Parramore Heritage District.[52]

GEOGRAPHIC FACTORS OF ORLANDO

Infrastructure — Orlando continued to need adequate product, or vacant buildings for potential foreign companies to occupy, according to Schiffhauer.[53] Companies looking to invest in the Greater Orlando Area could not wait to construct a building from scratch. Instead, companies, particularly smaller ones, needed built and vacant structures to begin operations. This remained an important factor for investors, both domestic and international. Additionally, nearly all traded goods in Florida required ground transportation at some point in the transport process; even product that arrived by air or port relied on supplemental transportation to move goods. According to Schiffhauer, Florida would need to expand its highway system to support much more trade activity than it was handling currently. The CEO of Orlando-based Tupperware brands, Rick Goings, agreed with Schiffhauer in this regard when he spoke to business leaders at MCO's 30th anniversary when he expressed his concern regarding Orlando's much-needed improvements to the transportation infrastructure.[54] Orlando did, however, have a multi-modal transportation system, complete with airports, deep-water seaports, highways and railways. Additionally, welcome stations, service plazas and weight stations were plentiful.[55]

Panama Canal Expansion Program — The widening of the Panama Canal in 2014, a project meant to significantly increase the capacity of trade, was a great opportunity for the state of Florida; however, it would compete for mega ships' activity. There were other ports — in Georgia, Virginia and New York in particular — that were also in the running. These ships, some of which carried as many as 12,000 steel cargo containers,[56] offered a lot to the selected state's economy. According to Mouradian, Cape Canaveral was planning to dredge to 45 feet, which depth does not accommodate Post Panamax ships. Miami was authorized to dredge to the requisite 50 feet, and Norfolk, the huge naval base that it was, was already equipped to house ships of this size. While other ports in Florida were prepped and ready, no port except Miami had received authorization and funding to dredge to that depth.

Both Ross and Schiffhauer believed the canal widening project could be a missed opportunity for the Orlando community if Miami did not get the ships. If the ships went to Miami, the secondary effects for Florida would be substantial. For example, Schiffhauer claimed that if Miami got the ships due to the expansion, Floridian exporting companies would see a 17 per cent reduction in shipping costs. However, if Georgia, Virginia or New York got the ships, the secondary effects would have a smaller impact. Further, Schiffhauer believed that Freeport, Bahamas was also a major contender and could very likely get the ships. He commented, "We'll be lucky if it [the increased shipping] hits Miami . . . . We are all hoping for Miami in 2014; however, even if Miami gets it, our roads are not currently set up for it. Imagine all that traffic! Our goods are transported mostly by truck, not train, which makes us that much more dependent on oil and highway. If you think it's crowded now, just wait. Our infrastructure, particularly the road system, is not setup for that. The highway system will need to be expanded to handle the additional product." Byron Sutton, president and CEO of the World Trade Center Orlando, was excited about the widening of the canal. He believed the project was a huge opportunity for the city, as it would position it as a trading hub for this hemisphere.[57] Additionally, he believed that Los Angeles would lose 100,000 jobs to Florida upon the canal's opening in 2014. Bolivar agreed with Sutton: "We have so many good ports — Jacksonville, Canaveral, Miami . . . . The widening of the Panama Canal will open up a world of opportunities for us."

Accessibility — Orlando was very accessible to the outside world by air, by land and by sea. The area had three major airports, two deep-water ports and ample road and rail networks.[58] Bolivar alleged that its accessibility and its unique geography in a state almost completely surrounded by water, were reasons for Orlando's appeal to foreign companies.

COMPETITORS

Tampa

Tampa, Orlando's nearest competitor, was the third largest city in Florida with a population of 335,709. Tampa, like Orlando, had a diverse community of people: 46.3 per cent were white/non-Hispanic, 23.1 per cent were of Hispanic descent, 3.4 per cent were Asian and 0.4 per cent were American Indian. The city was part of the

Tampa-St. Petersburg-Clearwater MSA, which was made up of four counties and 2.7 million residents.[59] Tampa had 480 foreign-owned companies in over 1,800 locations throughout the region. Major investment came from countries such as the United Kingdom, Canada, Germany and Japan.[60] According to the City of Tampa, the economy was founded on a base of industries including tourism, agriculture, construction, finance, health care, government, technology and its port.[61] Another source cited information services as a significant industry for investors looking to franchise their businesses.[62] *Forbes* (as cited by Pew Research Center) named Tampa one of the "Most Popular Cities" in the United States, noted for its weather, affordability and beach culture.[63]

Miami

Miami was the second largest city in Florida with a population of 399,457. Over 70 per cent of the population were of Hispanic descent, while 11.9 per cent were white/non-Hispanic, 1 per cent were of Asian descent and 0.3 per cent were of American Indian descent. Miami was included in the Miami-Fort Lauderdale-Pompano Beach MSA, which contained three counties and approximately 5.6 million residents.[64] Like Orlando and Tampa, Miami had an impressive international business presence, mainly through its natural connection with Latin America — major investments were by Latin American countries.

Miami was a leading U.S. center for international banking as well as a world fashion capital.[65] The healthcare and insurance industries were also significant. The city was considered "Latin America's Wall Street," with roughly $25 billion in foreign deposits. Many Latin American companies had operations in Miami, and the city had culturally adjusted to become more Hispanic — there was no other U.S. city that conducted as much business in Spanish on a daily basis. Exports were a huge part of Miami's economy, and trade activity was immense, given Miami's deep-water port. Many economists believed that trade activity was only going to increase with the improving economies of Central and South America.[66] Additionally, Miami's condominium market was coming back after it, like Orlando, was negatively impacted by the economic downturn. The housing market was experiencing an upswing primarily because of foreigners who accounted for nearly 80 per cent of condo sales.[67]

WELL-BRANDED CITIES: NEW YORK CITY AND BELFAST

City branding was growing increasingly popular in theory and practice. According to a study of 28 cities in 12 countries, the average per capita city marketing budget allocated for city branding was over $500,000 per city. Additionally, the number of published articles about city branding had exponentially increased from 1988 to 2009, illustrating the growth of the field over time.[68]

NEW YORK CITY, NY, USA

"The Big Apple." "The Empire City." "The City that Never Sleeps." These were just some of the many nicknames New York City (NYC) had acquired throughout its history. It was unarguably one of the world's greatest branded cities, known around the world for its many industries and attractions. Places such as Central Park, the Empire State Building, the Statue of Liberty, Rockefeller Center and the Museum of Modern Art enticed millions of visitors each year. The city's long-time title as a fashion capital of the world contributed to its pull. Nearly 51 million visitors came to New York City in 2011. Of these, 40.3 million were domestic visitors. Since 2001, the number of tourists to the city increased each year. Visitors spent billions of dollars annually, fueling the city's economy.[69]

The population of NYC, which included the five boroughs of Manhattan, the Bronx, Brooklyn, Queens and Staten Island, was 8,175,133 in 2010. The population was diverse: 44 per cent were white, 28.6 per cent were Hispanic, 25.5 per cent were African American, 12.7 per cent were Asian and 0.7 per cent were American Indian.[70] This racial diversity, engrained in history, afforded the city its reputation as a "melting pot."[71] Ellis Island, a small island in New York Harbor, was the gateway to the United States for over 12 million European immigrants from 1892 to 1954.[72]

KEY INDUSTRIES

Finance, entertainment and fashion, in addition to tourism, were huge industries for NYC. These industries were not only key to the city's economy, but, unlike the case in Orlando, they were synonymous with the city itself.

- *Finance* — Wall Street was the financial icon of the city and was home to the New York Stock Exchange, the world's largest stock with $9.57 trillion in market value.[73]

- *Entertainment* — Television and film production, composing almost 150 studios and stages, represented a growing industry for NYC, which was also home to three of the largest music recording companies in the world.[74] It was the birthplace to some of the country's (and the world's) most popular actors and musicians including Anne Hathaway, Adam Sandler, Ben Stiller, Robert DeNiro, Woody Allen, Mariah Carey, Neil Diamond and Jay-Z, to name a few.[75] Broadway entertainment was also a huge draw for the NYC tourist with plays, musicals and shows in over 40 theaters.[76]

- *Fashion* —NYC had long been recognized as a fashion capital. The industry employed 173,000 people, representing 5.7 per cent of the city's total workforce, and hosted over 75 fashion tradeshows, including Fashion Week. The city was also home to some of the best fashion schools and programs, including the New

York School of Design and the Fashion Institute of Technology. Finally, NYC was the flagship site of many famous department stores such as Macy's, Barney's New York and Bloomingdale's.[77]

"I Love NY" Campaign

Created by Milton Glaser in 1977 in the back seat of a taxi, the "I Love NY" icon was adopted by the state governor, Andrew Cuomo, who launched a $5 million advertising campaign to attract tourists in 2005. Somehow, the icon caught the attention of the world, and its immense popularity brought such great attention that it helped fuel the city's economy. Its design has been replicated all over the world, and it suited the city well since it is so multi-faceted and ever changing.[78] Travelers to New York spent an estimated $1.6 billion in 2005 in response to the campaign.[79]

NYC & Company

In 2006, the city under Mayor Bloomberg allocated an additional $15 million in annual funds and over $60 million in media and promotional assets to NYC & Company, one of the world's top municipal tourism, marketing and events organizations, in an effort to promote the city. Promotion existed nationally with bus shelters, television and radio advertisements and internationally with billboards and a retail merchandise website. Shortly after, NYC & Company opened several international offices for a total of 11 in 19 countries to promote the city worldwide and to increase tourism.[80]

Collaborative Approach

In addition to the city's alliance with NYC & Company, the NYC Economic Development Corporation and Empire State Development recently collaborated on a project to redevelop a site in the heart of Harlem, an effort that demonstrated the city government at its best. Collaborative ventures such as this helped NYC to be better all around and, ultimately, more attractive, fuelling growth through expansion and redevelopment programs that encouraged investment, increased tourism and reinforced the city's competitive position.[81] Investments in infrastructure, education and public transportation were vital for successful rebranding that would impact on economic change.[82] Given Harlem's shady reputation, rebranding initiatives, rather than branding, were appropriate.

BELFAST, IRELAND: A CASE OF REBRANDING[83]

Belfast was in a different situation than NYC. It had a history of over 30 years of civil conflict, so its challenge was to promote its positive offerings while changing negative perceptions through rebranding. In 2007, as conflict ended, Belfast City Council created a program to reinforce the city's brand through focus on factors such as business, skills, education, quality of life and tourism.

The Program Highlights

Collaboration — Marie-Therese McGivern, Belfast's director of development, believed that city branding was not just the responsibility of local government but instead was a collective duty to all with interest in the city's economic development

Inclusion of all stakeholders — Given the city's political and religious history, Belfast engaged all involved parties, both civil and commercial. These included all those with a long-term stake in the city: airlines, hotels, restaurants groups, ports, transportation networks and higher education institutions. Civilians, youth groups, local art representatives, business people and workers involved in tourism and hospitality were also hugely necessary and were engaged with the brand program through influential community groups.

Program Results

While sufficient time has not passed to positively correlate the brand program with a more positively perceived image, Belfast has enjoyed city improvements, such as:

- 143 per cent increase in day visitors to Belfast in 2008, a trend that continued into 2009.
- "Out of state" visitor numbers increased by 43 per cent.
- International visitors increased 3 per cent.
- The record number of 7.1 million tourists spent £436.5 million.
- Over the 12-month period of the brand program, noticeable positive changes in attitudes among the majority of stakeholders who played an active role in the program were noted.

ORLANDO: BEST-KEPT SECRET?

Orlando primarily had a branding problem. The city was an extremely accessible market, with three airports and two seaports in the area. It was an entrepreneurial hub and contained several promising industries in addition to tourism. The city also had an exceptional livability factor — perennial sunshine, proximity to beaches and excellent entertainment and shopping. Were most of these factors properly communicated to either the international or domestic marketplaces? Bolivar explained her chamber's efforts: "Branding is something we take very seriously here — trade missions are a way to educate the foreign community about Central Florida. We have been to Panama, Mexico, Puerto Rico and we are going to Colombia this year and bringing many impactful people to support the initiative of bringing more companies and businesses here. We want to spread the word and to educate. We are a great place to do business." Michael Latham, director of business intelligence of the Metro Orlando Economic Development Commission agreed: "Orlando is very young, even though we have this global brand. There is a great deal of growth and opportunity. I think today, we are known for tourism, *but* we have all these other growing industries. At some point, it will be that we are known for tourism *and* many other industries."[84]

In addition to branding, there were several areas that needed improvement in order for Orlando to become more attractive to business. The city was perceived as a tourist destination and nothing more. Elementary education, despite improvements over the years, was sub-par when compared to many other U.S. markets and that could have hindered the influx of domestic and foreign business. Free-trade consolidation, something that Orlando did not possess, was attractive to foreign investors. Finally, Orlando had many different international organizations operating individually and in many different sectors. As Ross said, "It's like an orchestra. Each player does well individually, but it would be better if they all pulled together, but not if they have been practicing different music. We need a conductor, and everyone must be willing to follow the conductor."

NOTES

1. This case has been written on the basis of published sources only. Consequently, the interpretation and perspectives presented in this case are not necessarily those of the City of Orlando or any of its employees.

2. "America's 10 Most Popular Summer Vacation Destinations," Daily Finance, www.dailyfinance.com/2011/07/15/americas-10-most-popular-summer-vacation-destinations/, accessed October 10, 2012.

3. D. Bolivar, personal interview, July 12, 2012. All further quotes from Bolivar in this case study come from this interview.

4. Forbes, "In-Depth: Americas Most and Least Popular Cities," www.forbes.com/2009/01/29/cities-top-ten-lifestyle-real-estate_0129cities_slide_3.html, accessed July 18, 2012.

5. The Atlantic, "The World's 26 Best Cities for Business, Life, and Innovation," www.theatlantic.com/business/archive/2011/05/the-worlds-26-best-cities-for-business-life-and-innovation/238436/#slide26, accessed July 18, 2012.

6. CNBC, "World's Most Popular Cities," www.cnbc.com/id/44084372/World_s_Most_Popular_ Business_Cities?slide=11, accessed July 18, 2012.

7. Yuwa Hedrick-Wong, MasterCard Worldwide Insights, http://newsroom.mastercard.com/wp-content/uploads/2012/06/MasterCard_Global_Destination_Cities_Index_2012.pdf, accessed July 18, 2012.

8. City of Orlando, "City of Orlando's History," www.cityoforlando.net/cityclerk/history.htm, accessed May 30, 2012.

9. City-Data, "Orlando: History," www.city-data.com/us-cities/The-South/Orlando-History.html, accessed May 30, 2012.

10. Frommers, "History," www.frommers.com/destinations/orlando/0022020044.html, accessed July 11, 2012.

11. World City Information, "Orlando," www.city-infos.com/orlando/, accessed June 27, 2012.

12. P. Ling, "Disney's Economic Impact on Florida," Uptake 2011, http://travel-industry.uptake.com/blog/2011/04 /25/disney-economic-impact-florida/, accessed June 2, 2012.

13. "A Proud History," Port Canaveral, http://www.portcanaveral.com/general/history.php, accessed October 10, 2012.

14. VisitOrlando, "State of the Market," 2012, http://corporate.visitorlando.com/includes/content/images/media/docs/ State_of_the_Market_Apr2012.pdf, accessed May 30, 2012.

15. J. Ross, personal interview, May 24, 2012. All further quotes from Ross in this case study come from this interview.

16. C. Gonzalez, personal interview, May 31, 2012. All further quotes from Gonzalez in this case study come from this interview.

17. Teresa Jacobs, "Doing Business with Central Florida," *Visión*, 2011.

18. Ibid.

19. K. Mouradian, personal interview, May 17, 2012. All further quotes from Mouradian in this case study come from this interview.

20. Metro Orlando Economic Development Commission, "Modeling, Simulation & Training," www.orlandoedc .com/Industry-Strengths/Modeling-Simulation-Training/, accessed June 3, 2012.

21. Ibid.

22. NASA, "About Kennedy," www.nasa.gov/centers/kennedy/about/index.html, accessed July 19, 2012.

23. CBS, "Space Workers Still Struggle a Year After Space Shuttle Mission Ended," www.cbsnews.com/8301-205_162-57472858/space-workers-still-struggle-a-year-after-space-shuttle-mission-ended/, accessed July 19, 2012.

24. Kennedy Space Center, www.kennedyspacecenter.com/, accessed June 28, 2012.

25. "Fortune 500 Companies: Florida," CNN Money, http://money.cnn.com/magazines/fortune/fortune500/2012/states/FL.html, accessed on September 11, 2012.

26. Enterprise Florida, "Florida's Foreign Trade Zones," www.eflorida.com/uploadedFiles/Why_Florida/International_Advantages/Foreign-Trade-Zones.pdf, accessed July 12, 2012.

27. Site Selection, "Guide to FLORIDA Free Trade Zones and Ports, www.siteselection.com/directories/indexTemplate2.cfm?start=1&G=FTZ&sort=city&type=FL, accessed July 12, 2012.

28. Enterprise Florida, "Florida's 2011 Merchandise Trade & Florida-Origin Exports," 2012, www.floridaworldtrademonth.com/sites/default/files/files/2011%20Florida%20International%20Business%20Highlights%20and%20Tables%20-%20March%202012.pdf, accessed July 12, 2012.

29. Research conducted by authors.

30. Ibid.

31. Metro Orlando Economic Development Commission, "Diversity in Metro Orlando," www.orlandoedc. com/core/fileparse.php/98857/urlt/Demographics_DiversityinMetroOrl_2010.pdf, accessed June 3, 2012.

32. Metro Orlando Economic Development Commission, "Orlando's Diversity Provides a Competitive Advantage," www.orlandoedc.com/News/2008/11/orlandos_diversity_provides_a_1.php, accessed June 2, 2012.

33. Joel Kotkin, "The Best Cities for Minority Entrepreneurs," March 31, 2011, www.forbes.com/sites/joel kotkin/2011/03/31/the-best-cities-for-minority-entrepreneurs/, accessed June 3, 2012.

34. M. Schiffhauer, personal interview, May 2, 2012. All further quotes from Schiffhauer in this case study come from this interview.

35. Ibid.

36. Ibid.

37. Orange County Convention Center, "Orange County Convention Center Voted #1 Facility in U.S.," www. occc.net/global/press/press_details.asp?page=pressreleases&ID=10261003, accessed November 29, 2012.

38. Orange County Convention Center, http://occc.net/default.asp, accessed July 17, 2012.

39. Teresa Jacobs, "Doing Business with Central Florida," Visión, 2011

40. B. Dyer, "The Mayor's State of Downtown," speech presented at The Amway Center, Orlando, Florida, October 4, 2012. LEED stands for Leaders in Energy and Environmental Design.

41. City of Orlando, "Land Development Studio," www.cityoforlando.net/planning/cityplanning/LDStudio.htm, accessed July 20, 2012.

42. City of Orlando, "City of Orlando Planning Division," www.cityoforlando.net/planning/cityplanning/PDFs/BROCHURES/City%20Planning%20Division%20BROCHURE_LATEST.pdf, accessed July 20, 2012.

43. Public School Review, "Florida Public Schools," www.publicschoolreview.com/public_schools/stateid/FL, accessed July 8, 2012.

44. Florida Center for Fiscal and Economic Policy, "Florida's Latest Education Ranking Deserves a Closer Look," www.fcfep.org/images/20100122-Florida's%20Education%20Rank%20Needs%20Another%20Look.pdf, accessed July 23, 2012.

45. U.S News and World Report, "Best High Schools in Florida," www.usnews.com/education/best-high-schools/florida accessed July 23, 2012.

46. Action News Jax, "Florida Ranks Second in the Nation for Test Score Improvement," www.actionnewsjax.com/content/topstories/story/Florida-ranks-second-in-the-nation-for-test-score/Q_Er1H0yr0-ojYREX7kdwA.cspx, accessed July 23, 2012.

47. U.S. News and World Report, "National University Rankings," http://colleges.usnews.rankingsandreviews.com/best-colleges/rankings/national-universities, accessed July 23, 2012.

48. Teresa Jacobs, "Doing Business with Central Florida," Visión, 2011.

49. Forbes, "America's Most Dangerous Cities," www.forbes.com/2009/04/23/most-dangerous-cities-lifestyle-real-estate-dangerous-american-cities_slide_11.html, accessed July 19, 2012.

50. Orange County Government of Florida, "About Us," www.orangecountyfl.net/?tabid=120, accessed July 20, 2012.

51. Orange County Government of Florida, "Mayor Teresa Jacobs Initiatives," www.orangecountyfl.net/BoardofCommissioners/MayorTeresaJacobs.aspx, accessed July 20, 2012.

52. City of Orlando, "Mayor Buddy Dyer's Initiatives," www.cityoforlando.net/elected/mayor/initiatives.htm, accessed July 20, 2012.

53. Information in this paragraph comes from the Schiffhauer interview noted above.

54. Sara Clark, "Tupperware Chief: Global Trade Requires Better Infrastructure," Orlando Sentinel, http://articles.orlandosentinel.com/2011-10-04/business/os-airport-infrastructure-rick-goings-20111004_1_rick-goings-tupperware-airport-security, accessed July 23, 2012.

55. Florida Department of Transportation, "Florida Department of Transportation Facilities," www.dot.state.fl.us/FacilitiesMap/FDOTFacilities.shtm, accessed July 23, 2012.

56. Rafael Gerena, "Panama Canal's Expansion," Visión, 2011.

57. B. Sutton, personal interview, May 9, 2012.

58. Teresa Jacobs, "Doing Business with Central Florida," Visión, 2011.

59. United States Census Bureau, "Tampa (City), Florida," http://quickfacts.census.gov/qfd/states/12/1271000.html, accessed June 28, 2012.

60. Tampa Bay Partnership, "2011 Tampa Bay Foreign Direct Investment Study," 2011, http://partnership.tampabay.org/documents/2011%20FDI%20STUDY.pdf, accessed May 9, 2012.

61. City of Tampa, "About the City of Tampa," www.tampagov.net/about_us/, accessed June 28, 2012.

62. Tampa Franchises, "Tampa Business," http://tampafranchiseopportunities.com/Tampa_Business, accessed July 18, 2012.

63. Forbes, "In Depth: America's Most and Least Popular Cities," www.forbes.com/2009/01/29/cities-top-ten-lifestyle-real-estate_0129cities_slide_2.html?thisspeed=25000, accessed July 18, 2012.

64. United States Census Bureau, "Miami (City), Florida," http://quickfacts.census.gov/qfd/states/12/1245000.html, accessed July 18, 2012.

65. Enterprise Florida, "Foreign Direct Investment," www.eflorida.com/ContentSubpage.aspx?id=358, accessed July 18, 2012; MSN Lifestyle, "The World's Top Ten Fashion Capitals," http://lifestyle.in.msn.com/gallery.aspx?cp-documentid=4276349&page=8, accessed July 18, 2012.

66. "Miami: The Capital of Latin America," *Time Magazine*, www.time.com/time/magazine/article/0,9171,162806,00.html accessed July 18, 2012.

67. BusinessWeek, "Foreign Buyers Heat Up Miami's Condo Market," www.businessweek.com/articles/2012-03-01/foreign-buyers-heat-up-miamis-condo-market, accessed July 18, 2012.

68. A. Lucarelli and O. Berg, *City Branding: A State-of-the-art Review of the Research Domain*, Emerald Group Publishing Ltd., Bingley, UK, 2011.

69. NYC Go, NYC Statistics, www.nycgo.com/articles/nyc-statistics-page/, accessed August 1, 2012.

70. Numbers do not equate to 100 due to cases where multiple races were reported; U.S. Census Bureau, New York (City), New York, http://quickfacts.census.gov/qfd/states/36/3651000.html, accessed August 1, 2012.

71. NYC 10 Best, 10 Best Nicknames for New York City, www.nyc10best.com/culture-history/10-best-nicknames-for-new-york-city/, accessed August 1, 2012.

72. Ellis Island Foundation, Ellis Island-History, www.ellisisland.org/genealogy/ellis_island_history.asp, accessed August 1, 2012.

73. Stock Trading Online, "World's Biggest Stock Exchanges," http://stocktradingonline.net/stock-trading-basics/worlds-biggest-stock-exchanges/, accessed August 1, 2012.

74. City Data, "New York Economy," www.city-data.com/us-cities/The-Northeast/New-York-Economy.html, accessed August 1, 2012.

75. Biography, "Famous People Born in New York," www.biography.com/people/groups/born-in-new-york/all?page=4, accessed August 1, 2012.

76. NYC Tourist, "History of Broadway in New York City, Broadway Theatre, Musical and Show History," www.nyctourist.com/broadway-theater-history.htm, accessed August 1, 2012.

77. NYC EDC, Fashion NYC2020, www.nycedc.com/industry/fashion, accessed August 1, 2012.

78. NBC, "'I Love NY': The Doodle that Became an Icon," www.nbcnewyork.com/news/local/The-Doodle-That-Became-an-Icon-156019055.html, accessed August 1, 2012; *The Guardian*, "Brand of Gold," www.guardian.co.uk/society/2008/oct/01/city.urban.branding, accessed August 1, 2012

79. Tourism Economics, "The Economic Impact of Tourism and the I Love New York Campaign," www.tourismeconomics.com/docs/ILNY_Impact_Executive_Summary.pdf, accessed August 1, 2012.

80. PR Newswire, "NYC & Company Expands International Marketing Reach to Promote New York City Worldwide; Unprecedented Financial, Creative Resources Elevate Campaign to New Level for Travel and Tourism Industry," www.prnewswire.com/news-releases/nyc--company-expands-international-marketing-reach-to-promote-new-york-city-worldwide-52132247.html, accessed August 4, 2012.

81. New York City Economic Development Corporation, "NYC and ESD Seek Proposals for Commercial and Cultural Development on 125th Street in Harlem," www.nycedc.com/press-release/nycedc-and-esd-seek-proposals-commercial-and-cultural-development-125th-street-harlem, accessed August 2, 2012.

82. Jim Northover, *A Brand for Belfast: How Can Branding a City Influence Change?*, Macmillan Publishers Ltd., NY, NY, 2010.

83. Ibid. Information in the section below comes from this source.

84. M. Latham, personal interview, June 6, 2012

PART IV

New Trends in Global Marketing

CHAPTER 14

Using Social Media for Global Marketing

Right now, a conversation is going on…"That conversation has your old customers talking to your former employees, while investors and prospective new customers review the conversation to help them make 'informed' decisions about what to do next. Are you engaged in that conversation?"

Das Global Media

LEARNING OBJECTIVES

After Reading This Chapter, You Should Be Able to:

* Understand what social marketing is and its use globally.
* Identify the major global social media networks.
* Understand how global marketing networks can be used as a promotional tool.
* Discuss how global social networks can be localized.
* Relate the difference between advertising on social media and traditional advertising.
* Discuss some of the privacy problems inherent in the use of social networks.

Elaine and Roz, two homemakers and friends, are connected to their Facebook, discussing a new refrigerator model that Elaine saw on Best Buy. They particularly like the idea of the three-door configuration and a number of other features. Two days later, they were joined in the Facebook conversation by twenty people who either had purchased the refrigerator or who heard comments about it. One person in particular was a good friend whose opinion was highly regarded. As a result of the discussion, Elaine decided that she should take another look at the refrigerator, pretty much convinced to make the purchase either on the Internet or in a retail store.

This scenario describes a trend that is occurring globally. Social media like Facebook, Twitter, and LinkedIn connect people with similar interests or likes. Through these media a marketer's message can be communicated to potential consumers; while on the other hand, marketers can learn how their product or service is evaluated in the eyes of the consumer. This two-way communication is the essence and importance of social media.

AN INTRODUCTION TO SOCIAL MARKETING

Kotler and Zaltman (1971) were the first to define social marketing as: "the design, implementation and control of programs calculated to influence the acceptability of social ideas and involving considerations of product planning, pricing, communication, distribution, and marketing research."[1] Kotler later defined social marketing as "[determining] the needs, wants, and interests of target markets and to deliver the desired satisfactions more effectively and efficiently than competitors, in a way that preserves or enhances the consumer's and the society's well-being."[2] A similar definition has been proposed by the Social Marketing Institute, as the planning and implementation of programs designed to bring about social change using concepts from commercial marketing.[3] Non-profit institutions, such as government agencies, charities, educational bodies (universities, schools), and ecology groups, adapt modern marketing techniques to advance social marketing objectives.

Social marketing later developed into what is called cause related marketing (CRM), which combines a cause (e.g. a charitable agency such as the London Children's Museum) with a for profit company (3M). The idea is to provide a synergy between the two that will result in raising money for the cause while promoting the sale of the company's products. One of the most noteworthy campaigns was the linking of American Express credit cards with the restoration of the Statue of Liberty in New York during 1983. For each purchase made with an American Express card, AMEX contributed one penny, and $1 for each new card issued. Within three months of the campaign, $1.7 million was raised for the restoration while the sale of AMEX cards rose by 27 percent. However, the major difference between social and cause related marketing is the absence of a continuing relationship between the two. CRM campaigns are limited to a given time cycle, while social marketing networks are long lasting. A definition of social marketing networks is proposed by Kaplan and Haenlein,[4] as a "group of Internet-based applications that build on the ideological and technological foundations of Web 2.0, which allows the creation and exchange of user-generated content."

SOCIAL MARKETING NETWORKS

Social marketing networks are synonymous with internet marketing. Marketing on the internet is accomplished through such methods as blogging, press releases, and social network websites. Social networks in particular have revolutionized the use of the Internet. Instead of just using the Internet to search for information, people are now connecting with others who have similar interests and habits. The connection is made via social network media such as Facebook, Twitter, Myspace, and LinkedIn. People can be connected not only locally but also regionally or globally. For example, MySpace and Facebook are utilized by those who are looking for friendships, LinkedIn (USA) is a professional network, while WELCOM: The

World Economic Leaders COMmunity, which was designed for world political and economic leaders to discuss global, regional, and industry agendas, is used for professional or business contacts. While Facebook, Orkut, LinkedIn, and MySpace are used to find people that you know, Twitter is used to find people that you don't know yet but have similar interests with. Orkut is truly global, it is headquartered in Brazil; forty eight percent of its users are from Brazil, followed by India with 39.2 percent and the United States with 2.2 percent. It is also popular in the Baltic States, especially Estonia. Facebook is the largest social global network, with over 900 million active users, 70 percent of which are outside the United States.

Table 14.1 shows the top social marketing website rankings in 18 countries. It is no surprise that Facebook is in first position in 20 of them. What is more surprising is that Twitter has moved to second place in 19 countries during 2014 compared to only 10 countries in 2002. Both have become truly global social networks. Why has Twitter become so popular even though it limits posting to only 140 characters? Twitter has most of the elements of Facebook but also allows texting with complete strangers. This element is interesting not only for the users but provides trending analysis for commercial and political users and analysts as well.

Two-thirds of the world's internet population connects to a social network or blogging site and the sector now accounts for almost 10 percent of all internet time. In 2010, Smith[5] found that digital communication via social networks had outpaced face-to-face communication. He reported that the average USA face-to-face network was 21.4 people compared to 49.3 people on social online networks. Social

December 2014 ALEXA				TABLE 14.1 Top Social Networking Websites
Countries	SNS #1	SNS #2	SNS #3	
Argentina	Facebook	Twitter	Linkedin	
Australia	Facebook	Twitter	Linkedin	
Belgium	Facebook	Twitter	Linkedin	
Brazil	Facebook	Twitter	Linkedin	
Canada	Facebook	Twitter	Linkedin	
Denmark	Facebook	Linkedin	Twitter	
Finland	Facebook	Twitter	Linkedin	
France	Facebook	Twitter	Linkedin	
Germany	Facebook	Twitter	Ask.fm	
India	Facebook	Linkedin	Twitter	
Italy	Facebook	Twitter	Linkedin	
Netherlands	Facebook	Twitter	Linkedin	
Norway	Facebook	Twitter	Reddit	
Portugal	Facebook	Twitter	Linkedin	
Sweden	Facebook	Twitter	Linkedin	
Spain	Facebook	Twitter	Linkedin	
United Kingdom	Facebook	Twitter	Linkedin	
United States	Facebook	Twitter	Reddit	

Source: Adapted from: World Map of Social Networks (2014), http://vincosblog.com

networking has followed the growth of internet availability and usage. However, while global internet accounts have increased by 88 percent from 2007 to 2011, social media adopters outpaced the Internet, growing by 174 percent.

Social Media and Television

The adoption and use of social media among consumers is transforming TV-watching into a more immediate and shared experience. As of June 2012, more than 33 percent of Twitter users had actively tweeted about TV-related content. Some 44 percent of US tablet owners and 38 percent of US smartphone owners

---

Box 14.1   People-in-Focus: Orkut Büyükkökten

While many people are familiar with the name Mark Zuckerberg, the founder of Facebook, not many are familiar with the name Orkut Büyükkökten, the founder of the social network, *Orkut*, named after him. Founded in 2004 while working for Google, as of 2013 *Orkut* had about 66 million users, about half located in Brazil and 39 percent in India. It became the third largest social network in the world. However, Google decommissioned the site at the end of 2014.

Explaining the decision, its engineering director Paulo Golgher wrote in a blog, "Over the past decade, YouTube, Blogger and Google+ have taken off, with communities springing up in every corner of the world. Because the growth of these communities has outpaced Orkut's growth, we've decided to bid Orkut farewell (or *tchau*). We'll be focusing our energy and resources on making these other social platforms as amazing as possible for everyone who uses it."

Orkut Büyükkökten, originally from Turkey, came to the United States to study for a PhD degree in Engineering and Information Science from Stanford University in California. He developed the concept for *Orkut* as a 20 percent independent project while working for Google. At the time, he was only in his mid-twenties. His goal was to "experience all the wildest things in life and never look back or regret about anything." He had achieved it.

Source: http://en.blog.orkut.com/2014/06/tchau-orkut.html.

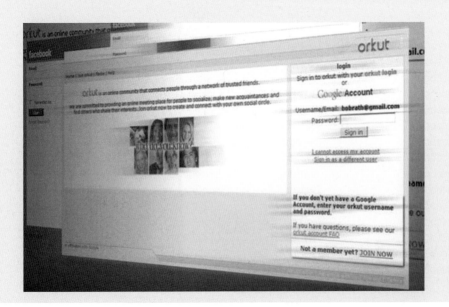

use their devices daily to access social media while watching television. In the Latin America region, more than 50 percent of consumers say they interact with social media while watching TV; in the Middle East/Africa region, more than 60 percent do. From global events like the Summer Olympics, to regional events like the Presidential debates in the US, consumers around the world use social media to engage with everyone from close friends to complete strangers, revolutionizing the television viewing experience.[6]

Behavioral Implications of Networks

Network analysis (social network theory) is the study of how the social structure of relationships around a person, group, or organization affects beliefs or behaviors. Network analysts believe that how an individual lives depends in large part on how that individual is tied into the larger web of social connections. Social networking often involves grouping specific individuals or organizations together. Social networking, of course, can be accomplished by face-to-face communication at a place of business, club, or place of worship, to name a few. However, face-to-face interactions are limited to a specific group and the network is largely static. The Internet has provided the opportunity to communicate with a much larger group that can be widened over time. While there are a number of social networking websites that focus on particular interests, there are others that do not. For example, LinkedIn mainly attracts professional and business people, while MySpace concentrates on music and entertainment. A more exclusive network was founded for delegates of the World Economic Forum, as mentioned earlier.

A network is composed of actors, represented as nodes in Figure 14.1, and the relations among them are represented as edges, or paths, while the links show relationships or flows between the nodes. Based on the six degrees of separation concept (the idea that any two people on the planet could make contact through a chain of no more than five intermediaries), social networking establishes interconnected internet communities. Assume that each node is a person. From the figure we can tell which two persons interact with each other and which person or persons is a leader (connects with more than one person). The leader in this case is person number 5, who is the central point in the network. Person 5 has the most influence on the behavior of the other nodes. Person number 6 has fewer connections than

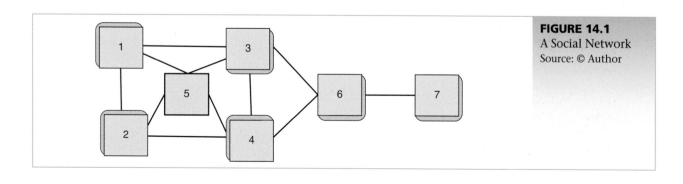

FIGURE 14.1
A Social Network
Source: © Author

number 5, but plays an intermediary role with connections 3 and 4 who are connected with persons 1, 2, and 5. An organization wishing to maximize its reach in a given social network would best identify the leaders or "influentials" and direct its message through them. As a result, many others in the network will be influenced as well. One of the implications of social networks is that people learn about and choose among behavioral options not only based on directly observing how others in their social circle engage in behaviors, but they also learn with whom their friends and associates connect with outside the network and then bring that information or those practices back to the immediate network.

What are the implications of social networks for marketers? Christakis and Fowler suggest that the world is governed by what they call "three degrees of influence"—that is, your friend's friend's friend, most likely someone you don't even know, who indirectly influences your actions and emotions.[7] Discussions among network participants about what products to buy, restaurants to frequent, places of entertainment, and what electronic and print media to watch and read are highly influenced by internet networks.

Motivations to Use Social Networks

What motivates people to use social networks?

A Nielsen Corporation global survey found that the three main reasons for using social media for personal use are:[8]

1. connecting with friends and family

2. reading social media content

3. connecting with like-minded people.

Based on their survey, NM Incite[9] determined that the main reason people use social media is to "find and maintain" relationships with family and friends, with 88 and 89 percent of users, respectively, saying they used social networking sites for this purpose. The next most popular activity is connecting with new friends (70 percent do this), followed by accessing product reviews (68 percent), and online entertainment (67 percent). Just 16 percent said they use social media for dating and less than a third reported using social networks to find a job.

In relation to the above motivations, R. Craig Lefebvres[10] suggests the following social marketing strategies:

1. Focusing on people with large numbers of connections within a network (connectors, influentials, or opinion leaders);

2. Reducing the density of a network in which risk behaviors are concentrated by introducing more boundary spanners or increasing social connections of members of the group outside of their immediate network;

3. Understanding the members of a network who are most attentive and responsive to the behaviors of others (or more easily influenced or persuadable) and providing them with protective or alternative behaviors to prevent adoption;

4. Enhancing the salience and attractiveness of the "out group" [positive deviants] by positioning these practitioners of desired behaviors in a way that attracts imitation or modeling.

Who Uses Social Media?

Table 14.2 shows that in all the countries surveyed the usage of social networking decreases with age. By far the heaviest users are in the age bracket 18–29 and the lowest in the age bracket 50+. These findings are confirmed in similar studies of media usage.

According to a study among a sample of 14,000 European and UK respondents by Forrester research, young people aged 13–19 are more active users of social media than older users.

Young Much More Likely to Use Social Networking				TABLE 14.2 Young Much More Likely to Use Social Networking
% That use social networking (based on total)				
	18-29 %	30-49 %	50+ %	Oldest youngest gap
U.S.	80	59	28	−52
Italy	91	52	13	−78
Poland	82	53	8	−74
Britain	94	66	22	−72
Greece	74	35	4	−70
Spain	91	58	24	−67
France	81	47	17	−64
Czech Rep.	87	57	25	−62
Germany	69	42	16	−53
Russia	84	59	20	−64
Lebanon	66	28	4	−62
Turkey	69	31	7	−62
Tunisia	64	25	7	−57
Egypt	50	22	18	−32
Jordan	35	35	6	−29
Pakistan	4	2	0	−4
Japan	71	41	10	−61
China	61	26	8	−53
India	12	3	1	−11
Mexico	63	29	7	−56
Brazil	62	43	12	−50

Source: Adapted from: 'Global Digital Communication: Texting, Social Networking Popular Worldwide', www.pewglobal.org/...'global-digital-communication-texting-social-networking-sites/ [Accessed: December 20, 2011], Pew Research Center

THE NETWORKED ENTERPRISE—BUSINESS USE OF SOCIAL NETWORKS

While it is generally assumed that social networks are used mainly by household consumers, there is growing use by business firms. A survey[11] by McKinsey & Company found that businesses gained benefits from utilizing social networking applications. These benefits are grouped into three categories: internal, customer-related, and working with external suppliers and partners. In both internal and external categories, the benefits include increasing speed of access to knowledge, reducing communication costs, increasing employee satisfaction and increasing satisfaction of suppliers, partners and external experts. Some of these applications allow management to see which employees are in contact with each other and what subjects they are discussing. Customer-related benefits include increasing the effectiveness of marketing, increasing customer satisfaction, and reducing marketing costs. Some firms emphasize one of the three applications, while about 3 percent of the firms surveyed are fully networked, utilizing all three applications. Most commercial firms are networked to Web 2.0 that is designed for them. They are similar in scope to Facebook but are not connected to the public domain and are protected behind a corporate firewall. Security is a main feature of these networks. Since both consumer- and business-based networks are used for collecting internal and external intelligence, there are privacy issues that have to be considered. We will consider these in a separate section later.

A global survey (Figure 14.2) of 3,025 executives by Social Media Examiner found that the most prevalent use of social marketing by business is external, to increase exposure and increase traffic. Other uses frequently mentioned were the acquisition of marketing intelligence and the development of customer loyalty.

Another global survey of 1,000 executives (Figure 14.3) by TMC.net™ Communications and Technology Industry Research found that the most prevalent use of social networks among all firms is to obtain information about other companies and industry updates. External marketing is the third most frequently mentioned use of networks. Following marketing, external and internal communications were used as a means to reach both customers and employees. A number of polls such as Online Social Networking and TopRank™ found that Facebook, LinkedIn, and Twitter (in that order), are the most used social networks by business firms.

An example of social network external marketing is illustrated by Regus, a global provider of virtual offices and meeting rooms. The company used a combination of social media such as Facebook and Twitter to enlarge their sales in New York. The campaign resulted in increased revenue of 114 percent compared to the same period the year before.[12] The campaign manager concluded that:

> Social media enables companies to engage directly with their target audiences...these audiences self-identify online as interested in specific topics, themes, products and/or

services…This type of focus is fertile ground for lead generation and driving revenue for business-to-business marketing.[13]

Using social media to reach consumers is by no means an easy task. It is similar to relationship marketing where the marketer responds to consumer dialog on the

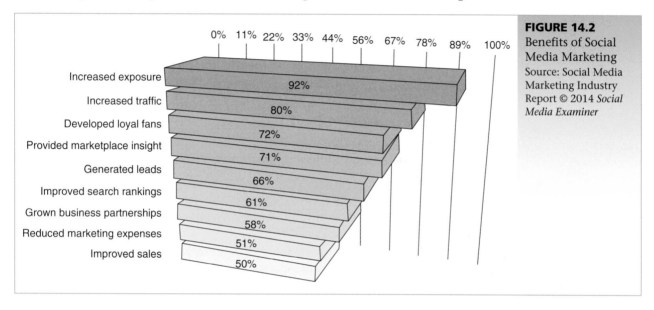

FIGURE 14.2
Benefits of Social Media Marketing
Source: Social Media Marketing Industry Report © 2014 *Social Media Examiner*

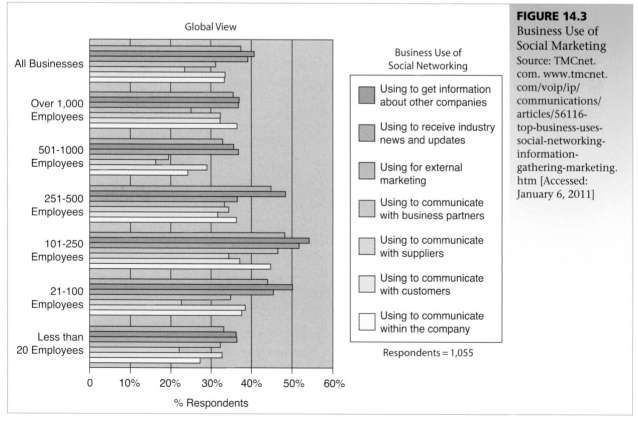

FIGURE 14.3
Business Use of Social Marketing
Source: TMCnet.com. www.tmcnet.com/voip/ip/communications/articles/56116-top-business-uses-social-networking-information-gathering-marketing.htm [Accessed: January 6, 2011]

media. This requires manpower dedicated to monitoring social media in order to determine what consumers have experienced with the company's products or services. The dialog between consumer and marketer is two-way: experiences with a brand are related by consumers and the marketer responds via the same social media. This two-way communication between consumer and marketer requires a shift in traditional advertising strategy. If done successfully, the return can be substantial. P&G, the largest advertiser in the United States decided at the end of 2010 to discontinue advertising on day-time television programs (so called "soap operas") after its success with a campaign for its brand Old Spice posted on YouTube. The campaign generated over a million Facebook fans.

Box 14.2   Company-in-Focus: Chilean Wines in China

Even though Facebook, Twitter, and YouTube have been blocked in China, the Chinese constitute the largest internet population in the world. However, there are several local social media networks in China that are permitted.

Chilean wine producers mounted a campaign to introduce their products to Chinese consumers. Social media were chosen to help establish a community where consumers would be able to discuss wine. Specifically:

- **Kaixin** – A social network site where wine fans could come together and share wine drinking tips.
- **Youku** – A video sharing site (like YouTube) where content was produced specifically about Chilean wine and this was uploaded for all to view.
- **Flickr** – Furnished numerous photos of Chilean wine, landscapes, and other activities by ProChile in China.

As a result of the campaign, Chilean wine became the fourth best selling wine in China.

Source: Information culled from Michael Darragh, 'Discovering Social Media in China', http://blog.ogilvy.pr.com/2009/11/discovering-social-media-in-china. [Accessed:January 13, 2011].

THE GROWTH OF GLOBAL SOCIAL MARKETING ADVERTISING

Advertising and promotion are other major uses of social networks by businesses. The amount spent on global social advertising was $5.5 billion in 2011 and increased to $10 billion in 2013 (Figure 14.4). Advertising expenditures on global media have increased annually at an average of 30 percent. The United States has accounted for about half of worldwide spending in social media, but other regions of the world, such as Europe and Asia are expected to increase their share of world spending.

Even in some of the BRIC countries, advertising in social media is extensive. For example, the social network/blog category reached 86 percent of active internet users in Brazil in 2010, while the number of social network users in China reached 245 million in 2009, up 34 percent over 2008.

According to The Nielsen Corporation, the social network/blog category reached 86 percent of active internet users in Brazil in 2010, and 78 percent of active users in Italy. By comparison, the percentage of active internet users in the United States during the same year was 74 percent.

Social networks are also on the increase in China. According to the Chinese Data Center, the number of social network users in 2009 was 245 million, an increase of

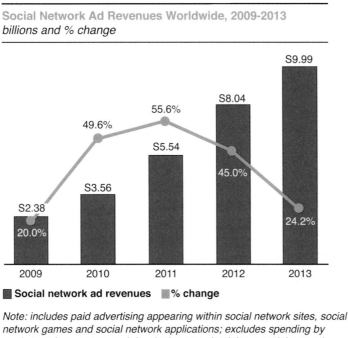

FIGURE 14.4
Social Network Ad Revenues Worldwide
Source: Adapted from: eMarketer.com

Social Network Ad Revenues Worldwide, 2009-2013
billions and % change

S9.99 — 2013
S8.04 — 2012
S5.54 — 2011
S3.56 — 2010
S2.38 — 2009

20.0% — 2009
49.6% — 2010
55.6% — 2011
45.0% — 2012
24.2% — 2013

■ Social network ad revenues   ■ % change

Note: includes paid advertising appearing within social network sites, social network games and social network applications; excludes spending by marketers that goes toward developing or maintaining a social network presence
Source: eMarketer. Sep 2011
132429
WWW.eMarketer.com

34 percent over the preceding year. Although the number of internet users in China reached approximately 500 million, there were almost 600,000 social network accounts.[14]

SOCIAL MEDIA USE IN THE BRIC COUNTRIES

Social media penetration in the BRIC countries has reached a level of usage that should be considered by marketing executives wishing to reach certain segments that we will discuss below.

Table 14.3 shows the relative use of social media in the BRIC countries. These figures show the percentage of social media accounts as a percentage of internet users. The figures should be used with some caution because they may change significantly over time in some countries like China and Russia where access is controlled by the government. For example, Facebook and Google have been blocked in China, but some internet users have succeeded to get around the government's firewall, while foreigners can gain access via a personal VPN account. As shown in the table, Facebook is the leading social media in Brazil and India, whereas in both China and Russia local media are dominant for the reasons mentioned previously.

What are the motivations to use social media in these countries? Taking the BRIC countries as examples of emerging countries, we have some answers from a survey (Table 14.4) of the GlobalWebIndex. The most important motivation to use social media in Brazil (69 percent of all respondents) and Russia (53 percent) was to "Stay up to date on news/events." In India the most important motivation was "Searching for work," 61 percent of all respondents. In China, "research/find products to buy" and "stay up-to-date on new/events" are listed as most important. Many people use social media to search for products to buy. Sixty-one percent did so in Brazil, 50 percent in India, followed by 46 percent in Russia and 40 percent in China. From these results and those shown in Table 14.5, we learn that social media usage differs by country. Both the relative importance of social networks as a source of information and influence, and the differences between countries must be taken into account when planning global advertising on social networks.

TABLE 14.3 Owners of Social Media Accounts as a Percentage of Internet Users	COUNTRY	FACEBOOK	TWITTER	GOOGLE	LINKEDIN
	BRAZIL	92	59	78	59
	RUSSIA	18	9	--	VKONTAKTE
	INDIA	94	64	53	62
	CHINA*	QZONE	SINA WEIBO	--	81
		100	60		

*Nearly all Chinese social media users connect via cellphone rather than via the Internet. Cf. Adapted from: www.forbes.com/sites/ciocentral/2012/10/25/5-things/you/need/to/know/about/Chinese/social/media/; Statista.com

(Percent Motivated)						TABLE 14.4
MOTIVATIONS	BRAZIL	RUSSIA	INDIA	CHINA		Motivation to Use Social Media
Research/find products to buy	61	46	50	40		
Promote something	27	11	32	16		
Find music	48	33	38	36		
Stay up to date on news/events	69	53	58	40		
To get inspired/new ideas	50	30	50	32		
Express myself	28	15	37	27		

Source: Adapted from: GlobalWebIndex.net

COUNTRY	FACEBOOK	TWITTER	YOU TUBE	LINKEDIN		TABLE 14.5
Brazil	40 million	2 million	20 million	500,000		Daily Visits to Social Media in the BRIC Countries
Russia	2.2 million	410,000	5 million	60,000		
India	12 million	300,000	7 million	600,000		
China	110,000	30,000	75,000	75,000		

Source: © Author

The difference between countries in the usage of social media means that a local rather than a standardized global campaign must be devised for most regions of the world.

Brazil

Social media in Brazil is increasingly used by companies as a strategic marketing tool. For example, the main use of social networks by companies in Brazil is for advertising their products and services, followed by brand monitoring and identifying sales opportunities. From a survey of 1,316 social media users in Brazil, 89 percent replied that Facebook was the site used most frequently, followed by Twitter (41 percent), Orkut (31.7 percent), and YouTube (21.7 percent). What are the shopping habits of Brazilians regarding social media? Seventy-five percent shop online, 45 percent search for information online, but do their shopping offline, 41 percent search for information, 40 percent use social media to give their feedback about products or services.

China

According to estimates, over 50 percent of the companies using social media campaigns in China were successful in broadening their customer base through digital media. China's digital usage, which is similar to that of the United States, skews toward instant messaging, social networks, gaming, and streaming video.

The popularity of mobile internet enables marketers to reach not only upper and middle class consumers, but also China's rural market and low income groups. With the country's increasing mobile penetration, more marketing budgets will be allocated for social media as mobile phone ads become more interactive and engaging. The launch of 3G and upcoming 4G services will further fuel the growth of social media marketing in the country. Increasingly, internet users in China are substituting digital media for traditional ones, with the potential for further cannibalization as digital consumption grows. This development has stark implications for advertisers and how they allocate future marketing budgets. Consumers, meanwhile, also use the Internet in their purchasing decisions. They are more influenced by recommendations from social-network contacts and friends than by traditional marketing messages or visits to company websites.

India

On average, Indians spend more than four hours a day consuming online and offline content. On PCs, often used in cyber cafés, Indians spend much time emailing and are heavy consumers of downloaded videos and music, as well as DVD movies. While Indian consumers use mobile phones predominantly for voice services, they also treat them as offline personal-entertainment devices, listening to radio stations or to downloaded music. There is significant pent-up demand for more convenient and personalized internet access—a void the mobile Web could fill.

There are about 110 million social network users in India. This includes users mainly accessing social networking sites like Facebook, Twitter, LinkedIn, and YouTube. Other new and upcoming social networking sites like Pinterest, Tumblr, and Foursquare are yet to take off in a major way in India. Facebook-user growth will come fastest from Asia-Pacific, where adoption rates in India, Indonesia, and

FIGURE 14.5
Objectives of Social Media Engagement
Source: Ernst & Young. 'Social Media Marketing India Trends Study 2013', http://www.ey.com/Publication/vwLUAssets/Social_Media_Marketing_India_Trends_Survey_2013/$FILE/EY-Social_Media_Marketing_India_Trends_Survey_2013.pdf

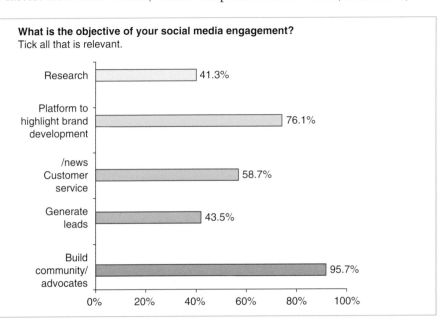

What is the objective of your social media engagement?
Tick all that is relevant.

- Research: 41.3%
- Platform to highlight brand development /news: 76.1%
- Customer service: 58.7%
- Generate leads: 43.5%
- Build community/advocates: 95.7%

Japan far exceeded the worldwide average growth of 28.2 percent in 2013. The Middle East and Africa and Latin America will also post higher-than-average growth rates going forward. Worldwide social network ad revenues are still going strong and set to grow nearly 54 percent.

Approximately $9.2 billion was spent on social network advertising worldwide in 2013, including paid advertising on social sites and on social games and applications but India's share was only 2.9 percent. However a higher portion of users in emerging markets are turning toward social media. The current set of web users in growing digital nations like India, behave like American youth. This is partly due to available technologies, commercial functions, and likely demographics of these young and urban users during this phase of adoption. India achieved a baseline of internet access in 2002, but its per capita income is only about US$ 3,600, and nearly 70 percent of its population is located in rural areas. There is not much potential for social media in that sector. Gender disparities, as defined by the gender gap index, are quite pronounced in India. While male internet penetration is around 10.6 percent of the overall population, the females' internet penetration in India is around 2 percent.

Russia

Internet availability in Russia is small resulting in low utilization of e-commerce websites. It is estimated that only 20 percent of the population has used the Internet to order goods and services. This however, doesn't happen by chance: the usage of e-commerce websites increases through the years—as users gain a better understanding of the Internet and its functions. Given that the Internet and social networking is in its premature stage (as contrasted to the UK or most Scandinavian countries) this is understandable. Russia is Europe's largest internet market by number of users. In the past decade, the number of monthly active internet users has risen from just 3.2 million in 2003, to over 66 million in the fall of 2013. In other words, Russia is experiencing somewhat of a digital awakening and quickly becoming a powerful online market.

CASE STUDIES OF GLOBAL SOCIAL MARKETING CAMPAIGNS

The Starbucks Fan Page

Starbucks has created a social network called a fan page on Facebook that is aimed mainly at people in the United States, but also is localized for foreign markets. As a result, Starbuck's fan page has become the largest on Facebook with six million in the USA and additional, but smaller numbers in other countries. Promotions and messages are localized for individual markets. A major advantage of such an approach allows Starbucks to not only aim its advertising globally where possible, but also to measure its effectiveness across target markets.

Bringing the "Like" Button into the Real World—Coca-Cola (Israel)

The Coca-Cola Village is a special summer experiential event in Israel. Every year Coca-Cola (Israel) invites 10,000 teenagers to the village, which is run on Facebook. Teenagers have to collect 10 Coca-Cola caps each, gather eight friends who did the same, and then register online through Facebook to gain exclusive entry. Arriving at the Coca-Cola Village, they are asked to wear a special wrist band, which securely holds their Facebook login/password, to swipe on a radio-frequency identification device (RFID) when starting each activity. The devices are installed at strategic places (swimming pool, dining room). Teenagers are then asked to place the bracelet alongside the RFID device signifying that the person "likes" the facility. This action automatically posts a Facebook message, keeping friends updated about the person's activities. Photos are taken by a photographer and these are also posted to the Facebook page. The village hosts some 650 participants daily with 35,000 postings or over 100,000 during the three days of the event. Thus, the Coca-Cola Village Facebook page has become the most "liked" in Israel and of course has generated hundreds of thousands of social media interactions.

Kraft Foods' Aladdin Chocolate Box

Aladdin chocolates have been sold in Sweden for 70 years and are a popular gift for Christmas. For Christmas 2009, Kraft planned to introduce a new type of praline chocolate to the box. Instead of advertising the new product, Aladdin arranged a community-voted competition wherein people would decide which praline would be eliminated to make room for the new entry.

Aladdin established a digital polling station four weeks before Christmas where consumers could cast their vote for their favorite chocolate. The largest newspaper in Sweden, *Aftonbladet*, reported extensively on the campaign. Organizers of the campaign designed a "personality test" on Facebook so that people could determine their personality based on their favorite chocolate praline. About 14,000 people took the test. The campaign generated more than 400,000 votes, which was more than the most voted for politician in the 2009 Swedish elections for representatives in the European parliament. The campaign resulted in an increase of both sales (26.5 percent) and market share (2.8 percent).

LEGAL ASPECTS OF SOCIAL MARKETING: THE PRIVACY QUESTION

Unwarranted access to private information is a concern to anyone who uses the Web. It is especially an issue when third parties gain access to information stored on social network platforms. In addition, most employees view their personal social media site pages as private. Employees are often unaware that personal information posted on these sites may be accessible by their employers and co-workers. If an

Box 14.3   Country-in-Focus: Egypt

Egypt has a population of 80 million, but only 13 million internet users. Nevertheless, when regulatory and social barriers (e.g. literacy, religious) are taken into consideration, the number of users becomes significant. Facebook, for instance, continues to gain ground in the social media arena in Egypt. There are 3 million Facebook users in Egypt, which is a little under 4 percent of the total population. Relative to 24 percent total online penetration, this is a relatively low percentage; however, user growth is measured at 7.63 percent. Sixty-two percent of Facebook users are men and 38 percent are women, and growth still favors the male element.

The majority of users are young, with 48 percent between the ages of 18 and 24 and 28 percent between the ages of 25 and 34. In late 2008, Nokia created a campaign that was built on the use of social media and user-generated content. The campaign utilized traditional and non-traditional mediums (TV, radio, print, social media) to encourage users to participate in a competition on Facebook. The campaign utilized popular Egyptian actor and rapper, Ahmed Mekky, who had a leading role in several popular Egyptian youth films. A music video with a catchy tune and colorful incidents that are locally insightful ("only-in-Egypt-type" scenarios) encouraged viewers to use their Nokia phones to create their own videos and upload them to the Nokia N96 Facebook group and enter the competition. Competition winners were listed on the website and their videos were posted on the group. Today, the group has more than 24,000 members and continues to be an active forum for users to share their content.

Source: Facebakers, April 2010 www.facebakers.com; Egyptian Information Bureau; http://Eccosocialmedia.files.wordpress.com/2010/04/Egypt/pdf.

organization monitors its employees' use of social media, it must inform them of the practice.

Examples of the information that is a privacy concern includes a customer's browsing and buying patterns, negative comments about brands or specific companies and products, and personal experiences. Are social network users aware of the privacy issue? While one cannot generalize, there are some indications from around the world that many users are not fully aware of this issue. For example, a survey by the Norwegian Consumer Council found that 66 percent of Norwegian internet users are using social networks and almost all (94 percent) said that it is important to have control over the personal information they provide online. In spite of this, users rarely read the terms and conditions governing their privacy and content they share on social networking sites.

A Canadian study reported that most of the 86 percent of the respondents who said they use social-networking sites "fail to perform the following basic security measures on a regular basis," including changing passwords, while 64 percent said they infrequently, or never, adjust privacy settings and 57 percent infrequently, or never, "inform their social network administrator on security issues."[15] On the other hand, a Pew Research Center study of American's use of social marketing networks found that two-thirds of all users claimed that they have changed the privacy settings for their profile to limit what they share with others online. Among users who worry about the availability of their online information, 77 percent have changed their privacy settings. However, even those who don't worry about such information are relatively active in this regard—59 percent of these less concerned users have adjusted their privacy settings in this way.[16]

Balancing privacy concerns with the benefits of social networking is not an easy task to achieve. Much of the adoption value in social network sites flows from social browsing, being able to see the "publicly articulated social networks" of others. The more private the profiles, the less valuable the social network site is to its users. *Orkut* users in Brazil, for example, were nearly unanimous in saying that, since profiles have become more private, it is "less fun" to use the site and people spend less time doing so. Yet, most users also want *Orkut* to give them more privacy options. In other words: they want to be able to see others' data, but they don't necessarily want others to be able to see theirs.[17]

THE USE OF CROWDSOURCING AS SOCIAL MEDIA

Crowdsourcing is defined as "the act of taking a job traditionally performed by a designated agent (usually an employee) and outsourcing it to an undefined, generally large group of people in the form of an open call" (Jeff Howe, 2009).[18] The basic idea is to tap into the collective intelligence of the public at large to complete business-related tasks that a company would normally either perform itself or outsource to a third-party provider. While crowdsourcing is considered to be a relatively new tool for reaching a company's target market, the concept has been around for some time, but not fully utilized. For example, the Wool Merchant Guild in Florence, Italy, held five contests to attract artisans in the building of the Duomo at the end of the thirteenth century. The aim of the contests was to recruit the best artisans such as masons, engineers, carpenters, and sculptors.[19]

Crowdsourcing has been applied in the survey research area as an innovative recruitment tool and data collection method. Crowdsourcing can be treated as a method by which to recruit respondents and build a panel similar to online recruitment, but extending beyond that. It is a method than can distribute questions and collect responses from a large sample of people; surveys are posted on crowdsourcing websites or smartphone applications and data is automatically collected and transferred to researchers once respondents fill in their answers. Eric Von Hippel, asserts that crowdsourcing is the biggest paradigm shift in innovation since the industrial revolution.[20] Social media is an essential tool of crowdsourcing because it has the ability to reach a wide audience faster, less expensively, and effectively.

One of the best examples of the use of crowdsourcing is Wikipedia. Most readers have utilized their website at one time or another. Given the amount of data available, you might think that Wikipedia employs a large workforce. Not at all. It has a staff of about ten, full-time workers, but millions of volunteers who supply the information viewed on its website.

Another example is the Samuel Adams beer company based in Boston, Massachusetts. The company asked consumers to concoct a recipe for what could be their favorite beer. Several were selected for possible brewing by the company.

Not only do consumers get to interact with the brand, but they get a tangible payoff in the end when they get to see (or if they're in the area, actually taste the brew) the end result. People want their voices to be heard, and having that payoff really helps. And since it's integrated right into social media, it's both easily accessible and allows fans to quickly get the word out to others.

CROWDSOURCING CAMPAIGNS AROUND THE WORLD

Ford Motor in India

In India, Ford Motor Company used social media to market its EcoSport car with an "Urban Discoveries" contest. Leading up to the launch, Ford India asked people to post a "cool place" in their city on the contest website, which attracted over 8,000 responses. Contestants promoted their posts through social media and the most popular posts were selected for the next round. Ford India narrowed the finalists down to 31 teams who were allowed to test drive the EcoSport while exploring urban India on video to be played on national television. A panel of judges then chose the best urban exploration video and awarded the team the grand prize of a new EcoSport.

Starbucks

Starbucks launched a crowdsourcing campaign more as a suggestion box than a contest called "My Starbucks Idea" for customers to suggest product ideas on their website. Even though the event offered no prize, in 2013, after five years, it attracted over 150,000 ideas. Fans were also allowed to vote on the best ideas, which added up to over 2 million votes. Some of these ideas that transformed into reality include digital rewards using Starbucks cards and being able to use free Wi-Fi at Starbucks stores. They've also used customer suggestions to add new coffee flavors and menu items such as skinny beverages and cake pop treats. The campaign has divided suggestions into product ideas, experience ideas, and involvement ideas.

Sony

Sony initiated a crowdsourcing contest to find a new name for their wireless speaker. A blog was posted on all their social media sites. Participants sent their suggestions by commenting on the post. More than 39 pages of suggested names were sent in less than three weeks. Sony executives selected the winner from the pool of names.

Unilever

Unilever employs one of the largest marketing research departments located at headquarters and in subsidiary companies. Yet, it discovered the value of crowdsourcing and seeks useful information from external contributors in such varied business areas as renewable energy, cleaning products, and reducing the quantity of sodium in food. Inputs from outsiders are invited through the company's "Open Innovation" portal (http://www.unilever.com/innovation/collaborating-with-unilever-challenging-and-wants/index.aspx).

McDonald's

McDonald's has used crowdsourcing in countries such as the United States, Canada, Australia, France, and Germany. In France, McDonald's logo is green, through a crowdsourcing graphic design and photo contest intended to communicate an image of sustainability. In Germany, the *Mein Burger* campaign asked people to design their own burger through a visual product configurator. The company received 116,000 burger ideas and 1.5 million votes for the best configuration.

Fiat Mio—The World's First Crowdsourced Car

The Fiat Mio Project started in August 2009. Fiat launched the website inviting people to help create a car for the future and design the world's first crowdsourced car. Fiat made the commitment to realize the ideas of the users in a futuristic concept car. More than 17,000 participants from around the world submitted more than 11,000 ideas. Users were stimulated to think in broad terms about traffic and life on-board. The ideas were studied and interpreted by Fiat and resulted in a briefing to build the Fiat Mio Concept Car, in Betim, Minas Gerais, Brazil, based on the ideas and needs of the users. The end result was summarized as follows: "A compact and agile car, comfortable and safe with innovative traffic solutions for big cities, a pollutant-free engine and the capacity to receive personalized updates, and changes in configuration, and having interface between car and user."[21]

However the people using the Mio website are likely distinct from the great majority of car buyers, and participants will probably be proudest if their input results in something that is obviously different from the norm. This is typically the case with crowdsourcing. The actual product resulting from the effort is something that will appeal to participants, but perhaps not much further.[22]

SUMMARY

- Social media has a global reach penetrating both developed and emerging markets. Two-thirds of the world's internet population visit social networking or blogging sites, accounting for almost 10 percent of all internet time.

- Social media networks are aimed at both consumer and B2B markets. Companies that will succeed in the twenty-first century will be social businesses, committed to forging deep and meaningful relationships with their customers. Its use is challenging traditional marketing media such as television advertising.
- Seventy-nine percent of the largest 100 companies in the *Fortune* Global 500 index are using at least one of the most popular social media platforms: Twitter, Facebook, YouTube, or corporate blogs.
- Companies based in the United States and Europe are more likely to use Twitter or Facebook than they were to have corporate blogs, while companies from Asia-Pacific were more likely to utilize corporate blogs than other forms of social media.
- Privacy has become an important issue regarding the protection that social media users have concerning their information which they place on the Web. Users of social networks are taking more precautions by upgrading their privacy settings.
- The most important factors for social media marketers is to know how to reach users in fast growing markets through both global and localization strategies taking into consideration cultural sensitivities, and online behaviors at the country level.

DISCUSSION QUESTIONS

1. How can a manufacturer of kitchen utensils best use social media?
2. What is the difference between social media marketing and cause related marketing?
3. Comment on the statement that social media is driven by people's need to create, share, discover, and participate.
4. While Facebook is the most popular social networking website in the United States and the UK, most people in India used *Orkut*. Why do you think this is so? Is it because of cultural differences? Other reasons?

EXPERIENTIAL EXERCISES

1. Now that the importance of social media has been reported, how can its effectiveness be measured? Use any available source and determine what measurement tools are available.
2. Compare two company fan pages on Facebook. Analyze the strategies used by both. What are the similarities and differences in their approaches?

KEY TERMS

- Crowdsourcing
- Internet networks
- Privacy problems
- Social marketing
- Social media

NOTES

1   Kotler, P. and Zaltman, G. (1971), 'Social marketing: An approach to planned social change,' *Journal of Marketing*, 35(3), pp. 3–12.

2   Kotler, P., Roberto, N., and Lee, N. (2002). *Social marketing*. 2nd ed. Thousand Oaks, CA: American Marketing Association.

3   The Social Marketing Institute is located at 1825 Connecticut Avenue NW, Suite S-852 Washington, DC 20009.

4   Kaplan, A. and Haenlein, M. (2010), 'Users of the world unite! The challenges and opportunities of social media,' *Business Horizons*, 53(1), pp. 59–68.

5   Smith, T. (2010), 'Global Web Index wave 2', http://globalwebindex.net/thinking.

6   A.C. Nielsen. 'The Social Media Report, 2012', http://www.nielsen.com/us/en/insights/reports/2012/state-of-the-media-the-social-media-report-2012.html [Accessed: July 30, 2016].

7   Christakis, N. and Fowler, J. (2009). *Connected: The surprising power of our social networks and how they shape our lives*. New York: Little, Brown and Company.

8   Social Media Across Cultures. http://zestnzen.wordpress.com/2010/10/01/social-media-usage-across-cultures/.

9   Ibid.

10 R. Craig Lefebvres. lefebvres_social2009/10/social_models_for_marketing_social_networks.html [Accessed: November 28, 2010].

11 www.mckinseyquarterly.com/article_print.aspx?L2=18&L3 [Accessed: December 16, 2010].

12 Swallow, E. '5 proven strategies for B2B social media marketing', www.mashable.com/2010/11/04/b2b-social-marketing-strategies/

13 Ibid.

14 Resonancechina.com

15 Bhandari, B. (2009), 'Internet users: Be aware of the dangers of social networking and community sites', http://gosecure.wordpress.com [Accessed: January 8, 2011].

16 Pewinternet.org/fact-sheets/social-networking-factsheet/ [Accessed: January 8, 2011].

17 Recuero, R. (2010), 'Privacy and social media sites: A growing global concern', www.dmlcentral.net/blog/raquel-recuero/privacy-and-social-media-sites-growing-concern [Accessed: January 13, 2011].

18 Howe, J. (2009). *Crowdsourcing: Why the power of the crowd is driving the future of business*. New York, Three Rivers Press.

19 King, R. (2000). *Brunelleschi's dome*. Winter Park, FL: Walker & Company.

20 Professor at Massachusetts Institute of Technology.

21 André Pinheiro. 'Fiat Mio, the world's first crowdsourced car', http://www.ideaconnection.com/open-innovation-success/Fiat-Mio-the-World's-First-Crowdsourced-Car-00273-html

22 Stephen Wunker. (2010), 'Can crowdsourcing uncover new markets?', http://www.newmarketsadvisors.com/blog/?tag=automotive [Accessed: November, 2010].

CASE 14.1   IN SEARCH OF BOOK SALES—SOCIAL MEDIA MARKETING AS A TOOL FOR SEARCH ENGINE OPTIMIZATION

In October 2008, Allen Kupetz was standing on a stage in the massive downtown Orlando, Florida public library for the official launch of his book, *The Future of Less – What the WireLESS, PaperLESS, and CashLESS Revolutions Mean to You*. In front of about 200 people, Kupetz joked about the irony of being in a library selling a book about going paperless. Most people there that night bought a copy of the book, but Kupetz knew he didn't have the time to do enough of these kinds of events to sell a lot of books. He needed direct and indirect distribution channels and in the world of books, this meant a relationship with Amazon.com. But how could he get people to Amazon.com to buy his book from them or directly from him, where he made more money. The answer seemed to be in using social media to increase his presence on the results pages of the various searches engines. This was not a get rich scheme for authors, but needed to be part of an overall marketing campaign that also included additional public events.

FIRST THINGS FIRST

Prior to the book launch, Kupetz bought the domains futureofless.com and thefutureofless.com, which he forwarded to futureofless.com to avoid having to build and maintain two sites. Although Google and other search engines have never confirmed that some sites must wait up to six months before appearing in search engine results, referred to as the Sandbox Effect, Kupetz wanted to get the sandbox clock ticking just in case. He knew it was not enough just to buy the domain and have an automated "Under Construction" page appear, so he put some relevant text about the upcoming book launch. Then Kupetz download the Google tool bar for his internet browser and installed the Page Rank button. He could then visit www.futureofless.com regularly and see when Google "had found it".

Kupetz also staked out his territory on the two most popular blog sites, blogger.com and WordPress. At no cost he obtained futureofless.blogspot.com and futureofless.wordpress.com. He also went to Twitter, a micro-blogging site, and reserved twitter.com/future_of_less rather than twitter.com/futureofless or twitter.com/foless, which was actually a mistake. Since Twitter limits users to

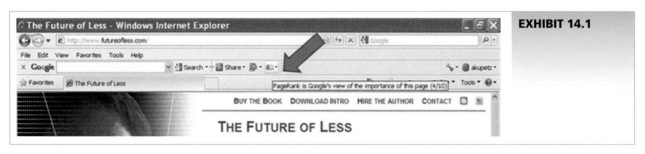

EXHIBIT 14.1

140 characters, at that time longer names limited the ability of others to retweet your long messages to others.

Blogs and Twitter were critical to Kupetz's search engine optimization (SEO) strategy since search engines prefer sites that are text based (it is difficult for search engines to evaluate photos or videos) and one where the content is updated regularly. Blogs and Twitter fulfill both of these requirements nicely.

The final step to tie all these seemingly disparate pieces together was to point all them to the website, www.futureofless.com. Kupetz knew that as his blog and Twitter sites grew in popularity and increased their own Page Rank, this would increase the Page Rank of www.futureofless.com. Kupetz also added his website, blog, and Twitter sites to his LinkedIn profile. And when he spoke before different organizations, he asked that they also include a link in the spear's bio section that pointed to www.futureofless.com. The strategy was to point everything to that site and the tactics were to use all forms of social media as pointers. Since Kupetz could not optimize Amazon.com, he optimized his site, which had a link to Amazon.com, as well as to his blog and Twitter accounts. Social media is about having a conversation, so Kupetz wanted people following his blog and Twitter to buy his book and for those who bought the book to comment about it on his blog and Twitter account. The goal was to create a buzz around the ideas of wireless, paperless, and cashless – interest in any of the three might motivate someone to buy the book.

LOOKING FOR AN INTERNATIONAL MARKET

When *The Future of Less* was published, Kupetz retained the international publication rights, meaning he could sell the right to translate, publish, and distribute his book in any country outside the United States. Given how far ahead most of Asia and Europe were in terms of wireless networks compared to the United States, he didn't find a lot of interest in these markets. But Kupetz used South Korea as an example in the book of successful private-public partnerships and found a South Korean publisher who wanted to translate the book into Korea and sell it. Although that publisher had an extensive and mature distribution network, Kupetz again chose to augment that with social media marketing (SMM).

Kupetz had an award-winning blog on Korea, www.koreality.com, which had a Page Rank of 2. Kupetz thought was pretty good for a narrowly-focused blog on a country that didn't get as much press as China or India. He had the publisher buy www.koreality.co.kr and point it at his blog. Then he created his own ads on the right side of the blog to buy the Korean-version of his book from Amazon.com and the four leading Korean online book publishers, Aladin, Interpark, Kyobo, and Yes24. The Korean-language version of the book sold over 1,500 in the first seven months it was available, May-Dec 2009.

MEASURING SUCCESS

With many SMM tools, it can be difficult to measure the impact of a campaign on revenue, or even less tangible things such as brand awareness and brand equity. The good thing about selling a product is that it is easier to discern the correlation and causation of SMM to sales because one can track the rate of book sales immediately after a social media tactic is used.

There are also several suites of tools to measure how many people are visiting your website, what site they were on immediately before arriving at your site, how long they are stayed on your site, how many pages they clicked on, and from what country they originated., Kupetz used Google Analytics (http://www.google.com/analytics/). In a corporate environment, this allows a Chief Marketing Officer to tell his boss specifically what is working, what is not, and start to calculate the return on investment of various SMM campaigns.

DISCUSSION QUESTIONS

1. Kupetz started his SMM and SEO strategies in 2008. What changes have occurred in social media since then that could be used today instead of – or in addition to – what Kupetz did in 2008?
2. As *The Future of Less* continues to mature – two years on the market is a long time for a book about technology with *future* in the title – what can Kupetz do to continue to sell books and keep his Page Rank and search results at current levels?
3. What sites do you visit the most often and what are the Page Ranks? Do you see a difference between domestic and more global sites, i.e., does yahoo.com have a higher Page Rank than yahoo.cn or br.yahoo.com? What are some of the variables the Google and other search engines use to rank a site or have appear on the first page of a search?

CHAPTER 15

Designing and Controlling Global Marketing Systems

The way you will thrive in a business environment is by innovating—innovating in technologies, innovating in strategies, innovating in business models.

Samuel Palmisano, CEO, IBM

LEARNING OBJECTIVES

After Reading This Chapter, You Should Be Able to:

- Understand the importance of selecting the optimum organization structure for a global business.
- Identify the differences between alternative organization structures.
- Discuss how a company's organization structure may have to be adapted to its internationalization process.
- Distinguish between a company's domestic and international organizational needs.
- Understand how globalization affects a company's organizational structure.
- Explain the difference between formal and informal control mechanisms.
- Understand the changing role of a chief marketing officer (CMO) and leadership requirements.

RESTRUCTURING FOR INTERNATIONALIZATION

"Cesca Therapeutics Inc. (Nasdaq: KOOL), an autologous cell-based regenerative medicine company, today (April 16, 2014) announced the restructuring of its sales, marketing, and technical support organization and the appointment of Tim Lee as Director of International Sales. The restructuring is aimed at further strengthening its cord blood business and new point of care and clinical commercial programs by providing more dedicated resource leadership to each discipline."[1]

The press clipping issued by Cesca, a leader in developing and manufacturing automated blood and bone marrow processing systems that enable the separation, processing, and preservation of cell and tissue therapy products, illustrates the challenges that many companies today face when they have to reorganize their global marketing departments.

In the newly formed role, Director of International Sales, Mr. Lee's primary focus is on global product sales and services, being directly responsible to the President, Ken Harris. Technical initiatives and customer support are organized by a specialist with extensive direct cord blood clinical and banking experience, who has leadership responsibility for the company's cord blood new product design and development programs, thereby providing maximum synchronization of these interdependent functions.

At Cesca Therapeutics Inc., all restructuring serves the purpose of maintaining its vision and quality standards: "We are committed to meeting our customers' expectations and requirements with high quality, reliable and safe products and services through open communication, effective processes, continuous improvement, and compliance with all applicable regulatory requirements."[2]

In addition to designing appropriate structures, successful leaders of global marketing organizations are often distinguished by their ability to deftly navigate the three functions we review in this chapter: organization, control, and leadership. These chief marketing officers (CMOs) shape the marketing organization within the context of the larger company and position it for success; they develop control mechanisms and methodically track performance; and they exude the leadership qualities that allow them to develop and implement their strategic vision, motivate their staff, and contribute to the overall success of the global organization by being champions for its customers.

In the latest IBM Institute for Business Value (IBV) study of more than 500 CMOs around the world,[3] the vast majority recognize that factors such as accelerating change in big data, cloud, social, and mobile technologies, which offers more potential for deeper customer insight than ever before, create a new competitive landscape and many opportunities to transform customer experience. Nearly all marketers plan to introduce predictive analytics platforms in this time, and 94 percent believe mobile will be a key to future success. However an increased number of CMOs revealed their organizations are underprepared to capitalize on the data explosion—82 percent compared to 71 percent three years before. There is a gap between aspiration and action and the challenge is to make sure it narrows rather than widens further, even if it does sometimes feel like permanent white water rafting. In many companies, the global marketing function develops organically, as the organization expands into more and more international markets. In the beginning, international marketing may be a function of the export department or, in bigger organizations, of the international division. As companies and their global marketing organizations (GMOs) evolve and grow, however, it is important that executives take the time to formulate and establish solid strategy, leadership, and cultural drivers. Research confirms that having these three building blocks not only leads to a more natural and efficient organizational structure, but also positively influences marketing and financial performance. As the authors point out, "[It] would be prudent for the senior leadership of a GMO to formulate a global strategy and to build an organizational culture, which should then pave the way for tackling structural issues and organizational routines."[4]

Traditionally, marketing organizations take one of the several established organizational formats: regional, functional, product-centric, or matrix. In the following sections, we'll review each of these formats. However, the world is changing so dramatically, that new approaches to designing marketing organizations have emerged that may completely change the way marketing is considered in an organization. We will highlight these trends and will also have a look into the future of global marketing organizations.

PRODUCT-BASED ORGANIZATIONAL FORMAT

MNCs, especially those marketing consumer products and those with very diverse end-user markets, commonly organize their global strategic business units based on products (Figure 15.1).

The Johnson & Johnson Family of Companies is organized into three segments (consumer healthcare, medical devices and diagnostics, and pharmaceuticals). The consumer segment includes a broad range of products used in the baby care, skin care, oral care, wound care, and women's health care fields, as well as nutritional and over-the-counter pharmaceutical products, and wellness and prevention platforms. The medical devices & diagnostics business segment produces a broad range of innovative products and solutions used primarily by health care professionals in the fields of orthopaedics, neurological disease, vision care, diabetes care, infection prevention, diagnostics, cardiovascular disease, and aesthetics. Finally, the Janssen Pharmaceutical Companies of Johnson & Johnson are dedicated to addressing and solving the most important unmet medical needs of our time, including oncology (e.g. multiple myeloma and prostate cancer), immunology (e.g. rheumatoid arthritis, irritable bowel disease, and psoriasis), neuroscience (e.g. schizophrenia, dementia, and pain), infectious disease (e.g. HIV/AIDS, Hepatitis C, and tuberculosis), and cardiovascular and metabolic diseases (e.g. diabetes).[5]

Since each unit is responsible for the worldwide marketing of a specific product line, it is able to focus on continuous innovation and improvement of the products to keep them competitive on a global scale. When combined with an efficient and globally positioned manufacturing and distribution operations, the product-based organizational structure provides companies with the flexibility to quickly respond to changing market needs and competitive pressures.

An organization based on product lines has certain drawbacks, however. It often results in duplication of resources and efforts among the different product teams. It may also prevent the organization from accumulating a common body of knowledge about shared markets, product design issues, or other areas where cooperation and coordination can produce long term benefits for the organization as a whole. Marketing, in particular, is very positively affected by shared know-how. Thus, integrating the marketing function by sharing information and market knowledge is

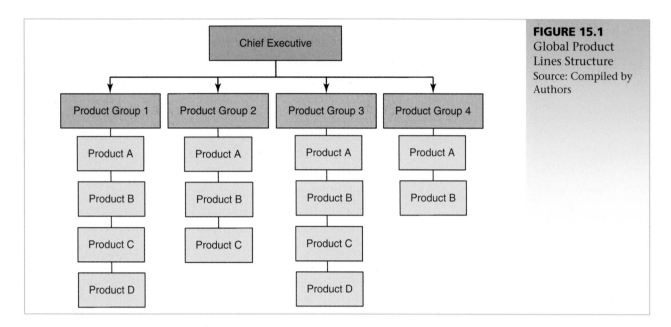

FIGURE 15.1
Global Product Lines Structure
Source: Compiled by Authors

seen as positive. Research that discusses the results of centralization versus decentralization[6] illustrates that many multinational firms have restructured their marketing organization on central global headquarters to guarantee better information transfer. In the phase of centralization, more tasks are being defined and handled by the central offices and there is a better alignment of marketing processes. It creates an increased competence level of the marketing organization and gives a better leverage of best practices. In addition, it increases synergies and a better addressing of strategic issues.

REGIONAL ORGANIZATIONAL FORMAT

In firms that base their organizational structure on the geographic areas which they serve, corporate headquarters usually becomes the hub for strategic planning, control, and coordination (Figure 15.2). The regions most often included are North America, South and Central America, Europe, Middle East and Africa (EMEA), and Asia-Pacific. However, regions may also be organized by other criteria, such as a common language or belonging to the same trade bloc such as the European Union or NAFTA. The boundaries of regions can be subject to considerable overlap and fluctuation depending on the context they are used in, which makes differentiation difficult. Regions are only social constructs and should not be understood as physical features defined by abstract, neutral criteria. For instance, the term "Eastern Europe" still encompasses most, or all, such European countries that until the end of the "Cold War" (around 1989) were under communist regimes or direct Soviet control, i.e. the former "Eastern Bloc." However, it is currently common to include many former "Eastern Bloc" nations in the categories of Southeastern Europe/Balkans, Central Europe, and Northern Europe.

The focus on specific geographies works to marketing's advantage, where knowledge of regional market conditions and cultural preferences helps with uncovering potential standardization opportunities in product design and promotion and can lead to economies of scale. Conversely, if individual markets within the region experience changing conditions or user needs, they can receive timely special attention.

Regional organizational formats work best for companies with a limited number of products and similar market segments throughout the world. This structure naturally requires a greater emphasis on marketing, price, and product design as the differentiating factors. One disadvantage of regional organizations is that they don't scale well. Should the organization decide to expand and diversify its products, the coordination of its product lines and regional and country units may become cumbersome and expensive. Also, regional divisions often become too focused on their own operations, hindering inter-divisional cooperation and transfer of knowledge and spurring unnecessary rivalry and duplication of efforts.

Meanwhile, companies have started to build regional headquarters and their role is evolving as business units that are repositioned to take advantage of cost efficiencies and more favorable labor supplies to better meet larger corporate objectives. The driving factor tends to be a combination of tax benefits and a business climate more conducive to successful and profitable operations. For instance Aon plc, the leading provider of risk services, announced in January the relocation of its global headquarters from Chicago, where it occupies one of that city's signature big-box skyscrapers at Aon Center, to London, where it will occupy that city's signature "Cheese Grater" building at Leadenhall. Aon Center will serve as the company's Americas headquarters with the addition of 750 jobs at that location. The move is largely seen as a play to improve its balance sheet with a more favorable taxation scheme than it enjoys in the "Windy City."[7]

Similarly, Heraeus, the leading precious metals and technology group, announced in October 2014 the opening of its Greater China Regional Headquarters in Shanghai. It is a strategic step of Heraeus toward its Vision 2020 and demonstrates its commitment to accelerating development in the Greater China region, one of its

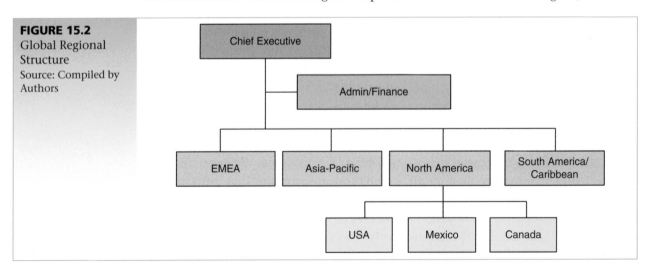

FIGURE 15.2
Global Regional Structure
Source: Compiled by Authors

key markets. Located in Caohejing Hi-Tech Park, Xuhui District of Shanghai, and with registered capital of US$30 million, the Greater China Regional Headquarters will provide strategic guidance, functional competencies, and shared services to nearly 20 Heraeus companies in the Chinese mainland, Hong Kong, and Taiwan. Including Greater China, Asia has been strategically important to Heraeus. In 2013, Asian markets contributed 51 percent of product revenue for the Heraeus Group.[8]

FUNCTIONAL ORGANIZATIONAL FORMAT

One of the classic organizational structures is the functional one. It is based on the processes performed by an organization, such as operations, finance, marketing, human resources, etc., and it involves building highly specialized teams that report to the respective division head—VP of Finance, VP of Marketing, and so on (Figure 15.3). This simple, and easy to grasp and navigate structure provides clear lines of communication and task management, which facilitate project coordination within the divisions.

Global functional structures are suitable when product/service range offered by both the parent and the subsidiaries are few resulting in undifferentiated production and marketing methods among them. For diversified entities offering different products/services this structure becomes cumbersome or less suited. At Westinghouse, which produces more than 8,000 different products in such diverse areas as real estate, finance, nuclear fuel, television production, electronics systems, and soft drink bottling, it is difficult to imagine that the production head knows intricacies of production of all the products. Oil and mineral extraction companies, such as Exxon use this structure, which is ideal when products and production methods are basically undifferentiated among countries. Under this structure, coordination is left to top management, with functional heads pursuing their responsibilities with tunnel vision orientation, unless otherwise advised by top management.

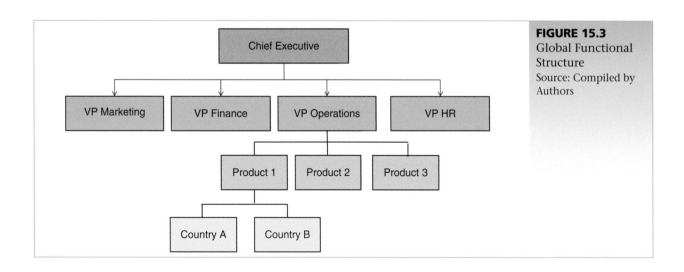

FIGURE 15.3
Global Functional Structure
Source: Compiled by Authors

Functional organizations are prone to develop "divisional silos" that interfere with cross-departmental communications and encourage an "us versus them" mentality within the departments. Such developments can slow down decision-making and impede problem-solving in today's fast-paced, competitive environment, where cross-functional solutions are often needed. Because of its limitations, the functional organizational format is often abandoned once companies reach a critical mass of diverse products and customers.

MATRIX ORGANIZATIONAL FORMAT

Some organizations have turned to the matrix structure (Figure 15.4) to avoid some of the drawbacks of the formats described earlier. Matrix organizations may include aspects of two or more of the product, geographic, or functional structures. They combine a product-based structure with key geographic regions, for example, or functional and geographic divisions.

The advantages gained in such hybrid structures may include improved communication and teamwork and better market coverage where both global and local perspectives are, presumably, integrated. Matrix organizations attempt to adapt to the multi-dimensional global business environment (Box 15.1).

The inherent duality of the structure may also cause problems, however. Many managers find it difficult reporting to two separate channels, and conflicts or confusion may become common. Decision-making also may become slower, as disparate objectives and priorities compete for attention and divisional overlaps often turn into turf battles. These issues have resulted in the gradual departure from the matrix organization among MNCs.

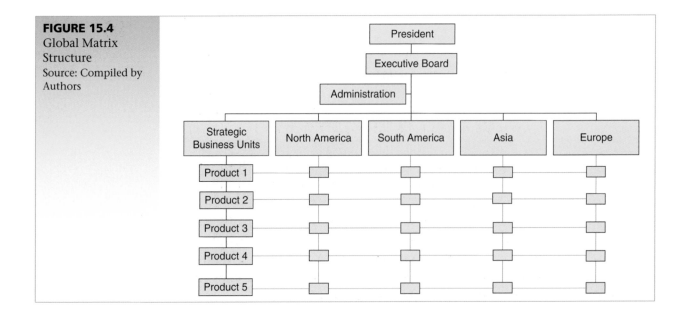

FIGURE 15.4
Global Matrix
Structure
Source: Compiled by
Authors

Box 15.1   Company-in-Focus: Allianz Global Corporate & Specialty

A True Matrix Organization

Allianz Global Corporate & Specialty (AGCS) services clients in more than 160 countries across the whole spectrum of marine, aviation, and corporate business—making it one of the leading global insurance companies. AGCS is a truly global company—a matrix organization designed to support complex risk management challenges worldwide. It offers a dynamic working environment in a global structure. It has grown quickly since it started out in 2006, now in 2014 operating in 28 countries on six continents. The company's staff is represented by more than 3,500 colleagues worldwide.

In all offices, there is staff from diverse countries and cultures and there is a lot of English being spoken around. Of course other languages are spoken as well but in order to collaborate on a global scale, English is used as the shared language.

How the matrix organization works: Similar to many of its global clients, Allianz Global Corporate & Specialty works in a matrix organization structure with functional teams on a global level as well as teams who implement the strategy locally. This approach is based on team work, shared decision-making, and trust, and has been developed to allow the company a flexible approach to both its challenges and those of its clients. Equally essential is a global mindset and a willingness to change when meeting new challenges.

With a fast growing company, of course this brings certain requirements. But this matrix organization structure also ensures that everyone can contribute directly to the overall success of the company. Client focus is the highest priority right across Allianz Global Corporate & Specialty. Clients need to be able to rely on their insurer at all times.

Sources: AGCS Corporate Website. (2014), http://www.agcs.allianz.com/careers/working-at-agcs/about-working-at-agcs/; 'Allianz announces new leadership team for combined Fireman's Fund, AGCS NA', http://www.insurancejournal.com/news/national/2014/12/12/349991.htm; http://www.versicherungsmagazin.de/Aktuell/Nachrichten/195/21948/AGCS-Neue-Sparte-fuer-mittelgrosse-Unternehmen.html [All accessed: December 30, 2014].

But as a recent Forbes[9] article titled "The matrix doesn't have to be your enemy," suggested, there may be potential benefits of matrix structures. Surely, it's a world of multiple bosses, endless relationships, and murky accountabilities. It's also a world of frustrated managers and employees, people who feel that they can't take effective action or deal with a customer without running into a series of organizational obstacles. But some form of matrix structure is essential for running any large company. A global consumer products company, for instance, must respond to local market needs and capitalize on global economies of scale. It needs organizations at both levels, and it needs to manage across those boundaries. To make this multifaceted system work—to turn it from a drag on performance into a source of support—a company needs to focus on its decision-making processes, not its organizational chart. The following few guidelines may be helpful:[10]

- Follow the money. High-performing companies know how each side of the business creates value and which decisions are key to unlocking that value. That helps them locate critical decisions at the appropriate points in the organization. For instance, telecom company Vodafone grew rapidly by acquisition. But then Vodafone saw opportunities for global scale advantage in three key areas—innovation, procurement, and the development of best practices in marketing. So it created a system with country-based businesses plus global functions in the three areas where the additional complexity actually added value.

- **Align people around key priorities and principles.** Most successful companies operate according to a set of core principles and priorities that supersede any matrix. These principles create a context enabling people anywhere in the organization to make appropriate trade-offs. For instance, at British American Tobacco several years ago, then-CEO Martin Broughton eliminated internal competition and established a handful of priorities that he believed would help BAT regain the top spot in its industry. BAT's new priority of growth in premium global brands, for example, allowed global marketers and local salespeople to focus their joint attention on decisions relating to this objective.

- **Assign clear decision roles.** People can have more than one boss, but decisions can't. The most common problem we find in matrix organizations is confusion over who should play which role in key decisions.

- **Help leaders set the right tone.** If leaders don't make good decisions quickly, others are likely to dither. If leaders don't collaborate across boundaries, others won't either. When Martin Broughton was leading BAT's restructuring, he brought 140 of the company's top leaders together in a three-day conference to kick off the new approach. The senior team then led a series of regional and functional conferences and sent videos explaining the changes to BAT's operations in more than 70 countries. Team members followed up with e-mail updates to reinforce their expectations.

- **Foster a performance culture.** This is the holy grail of decision effectiveness: an environment in which people naturally take responsibility for cross-boundary cooperation. It is critical for a smoothly functioning matrix as well. Everyone makes it their job to ensure that the right people are involved in every decision, that individuals debate honestly and listen to one another, that decisions are promptly made and implemented. All that becomes simply "the way we do things around here."

NEW MARKETING ORGANIZATION

The job of implementing a global marketing strategy within the context of the described organizational structures and their variations is not an easy one. The degrees of integration among the worldwide business units and headquarters or among various local and regional subsidiaries play a critical role in the success or failure of global marketing campaigns. In addition to their concern for strategic fit within the organization as a whole, marketing leaders are continuously challenged by the evolving nature of the marketing organization itself.

Further, the digital economy and the rapid growth of emerging markets are transforming the consumer products industry, and companies must make the best possible use of their limited resources to meet these new demands. It's time to rethink the traditional organization model for marketing in order to meet today's strategic challenges and cost pressures more effectively. What's needed is a leaner, more agile structure that can adapt more quickly to an increasingly dynamic, fast-paced world. At the same time marketing managers need to meet conflicting demands, which often are not reconcilable.

The scope of the change is profound: from rearticulating the role "marketing" plays across the business to changing how talent and performance is managed to redesigning structures, governance bodies and resourcing approaches. But a number of forward-looking companies are beginning to move boldly in order to define a new paradigm. The consulting company BCG has investigated new trends and offers the following guidelines that are more general and go beyond those mentioned before for the matrix organization:[11]

- **Delayer the organization.** The traditional marketing structure has too many management layers between the brand and portfolio levels—and these added layers tend to increase cost and complexity rather than value. Aim instead for fewer layers of management and greater spans of control.

- **Dynamically deploy resources.** To ensure that resources are allocated to the highest-priority work, they must be deployed and redeployed on a dynamic basis wherever they can add the greatest value across the portfolio. Although larger, more strategic brands benefit from the specialized knowledge and continuity of dedicated resources and brand managers, smaller brands are often better suited to dynamic deployment.

- **Ruthlessly prioritize work.** As noted earlier, marketing projects have a tendency to proliferate, and most add little value. Challenge teams to cut out 20 percent of their projects, and revisit this housekeeping exercise on an annual basis. The key is to identify and eliminate any projects that don't support the strategic priorities of the business.

Three significant developments accelerating this evolution have been the increasing power of the customer, the relentlessly growing global competition, and the uncertainty and unpredictability of the future which makes it impossible to implement strategies according to plan. Instead, marketers need to increase flexibility, the potential for change, and the way they are dealing with ambiguity and paradox. The following structures are answers to these requirements.

CUSTOMER-CENTERED ORGANIZATIONS

Marketing has been one of the first organizational functions to be affected by and to respond to the changing balance of power in favor of customers by advocating a fundamental shift to a more customer-centered organizational design. Such design is hailed as a way to avoid many of the limitations of the traditional organizational structures and to increase a firm's competitiveness by bringing better understanding of the markets' needs. As research indicates, the long and complex transition process may involve changes to specific management roles, such as those of the account, country, and product managers, as well as changes to the marketing function as whole, with marketing activities becoming more and more dispersed within the organization as it attempts to adapt itself to a more cross-functional, customer-centric perspective.[12]

For instance, Dell's business-to-business division recently underwent a major reorganization prompted by the desire to be more focused on its different customer segments rather than on its geographic coverage. It is now structured around Dell's three major segments of business clients: large enterprise clients, public clients (government, education, health care, and environment), and small and medium business clients. Such customer-based segmentation was first introduced in Dell's Global Consumer group, where it "has proved that an integrated business unit can move with greater agility to unleash innovation to respond to the changing needs of customers," according to the company's CEO, Michael Dell. Interestingly, Dell announced a change in marketing leadership at the same time. The outgoing CMO, Mark Jarvis, is retiring after completing the transformation of the company's brand and marketing organization with "new levels of marketing effectiveness and efficiency." The incoming CMO, Erin Nelson, will assume her new role after serving as VP of marketing for Dell's EMEA region.[13]

Other research has suggested to regard customers as evolving from passive consumers to active co-creators of value, irrespective of the structural marketing organization.[14] Customers become a vital part of the firm's value creation process like in Apple's recent customer involvement in the design and implementation of iTunes to facilitate individualized music selections. The overall approach of co-creation marks a shift whereby the customer is potentially involved in the creation and realization of collaborative innovation of several value chain functions.

Customization—Co-creation—Co-formation

Previous attempts at analyzing customer participation have mainly looked at selective up- or downstream functions of the global value chain. Involving the customer in the entire value chain suggests another level of collaboration, which goes beyond existing forms of co-creation in joint product development. It involves the customer in transforming traditional corporate practices, such as human resources, procurement, or even finance. Co-creation sparks interaction, increases engagement, and above all, generates additional value. Especially in transnational strategies, there is a huge potential for changing the role of customers from mere co-constructors to that of co-strategists as the selection of relevant firm locations is based on the extent of high-learning environments with best-practice potential for innovation. The customer is supposed to influence strategy at relevant touch points and to impact value chain functions, much like it is expected from internal experts.

Three variants of customer participation in a firm's strategy can be distinguished:[15] (1) customization: adaptation of processes based on aggregated customer input, (2) co-creation: joint value generation based on specific customer input, and (3) co-formation: large-scale customer participation in all or several strategic functions of the firm. In the last variant, increased connectivity between firms and customers across all value chain functions does not only enable innovation but more generally impacts strategy formation and implementation.

Customization—The Customer as Buyer

One of the most intuitive examples of involving customers into the firm's value chain function is to adjust offerings to their demands. Apart from adapting products, e.g. mi adidas shoes, the customer may also be involved in firms' sourcing policies. This is typically the case when firms capitalize on country-of-origin propositions and emphasize singular sourcing like, for example, Swiss-made watches or Whisky from Scotland.[16] Or, quite often, human resource functions of a firm organize selection and training of employees as a reply to customer expectations. This is a particularly pertinent issue when offering services like hospitality or private finance that are closely linked to the person providing it and human resource decisions impact service success. A last example can be found in corporate finance which may be impacted by customers, given the possibilities of choosing customized payment options, e.g. instalment sales with or without interest.

Co-Creation—The Customer as Value Creator

The involvement of customers increases in the next stage of participation, where they not only choose from a predefined customization portfolio, but also actively co-create the options and variants they are interested in. For example, customers may be involved in the content creation of major TV networks, such as Digg.com, and exert influence on what types of news or commercials are being transmitted. Customer roles are much more proactive and a tailored infrastructure allows them to have closer, faster, and more flexible input than before. One of the best examples is probably Wikipedia, which would not have come into existence without customers as producers who decide on the design of the platform, organize and reorganize content, and attract or deter other consumers by the soundness of information. But co-creation also relates to other value chain functions such as, for instance, human resources. Not least with the baby food scandal in the 1970s, customers required a larger involvement in environmentally and ethically sound practices of firms. As a result, many firms felt compelled to establish specific corporate units (corporate social responsibility, corporate communications) that explicitly dealt with these demands. Similarly, in the dramatic course of the Contergan scandal, consumer requests impacted different and more substantial monitoring and communication principles. Even though the creation of these internal functions was customer-driven, the implementation was under the auspices of the firm and changes incurred by the customer were largely implemented within the limits of firms' pre-specified guidelines.

Co-Formation—The Customer as Strategist

In the most elevated stage of participation, the customer becomes an equal partner in the strategy formation of a firm. This shifts perspective from co-creating single value chain functions to jointly formulating the future of the firm. Customer participation now relates to the governance of the firm for which both parties—customers and firm—mutually resume responsibility. Thus, the voice of the customer does not only transcend shared production activities but amounts to an enduring process of collaboration where customers assess the company's governance and performance as well as install required transformations.

Although this stage of customer participation has not yet been fully captured by current research, there are certain indicators that preview it. Firms have already started to invite customers to play a more important role in driving their business direction, i.e. in co-designing their future. Take for example, The Ladybank Company of Distillers Club, a members-only distillery, where consumers themselves produce whisky on a small and artisanal scale. Members have an active role in key decisions, such as product development, budgeting and other business matters, and each member has equal voting rights on the affairs of the firm. Other examples of customers forcing a change in corporate strategy can be found with fan clubs reinstating a particular chocolate brand of the UK confectionery manufacturer Cadbury that they planned to drop. Or with E.ON Nordic, as the first energy utility provider, which has institutionalized a customer ombudsman to look after customer interests and report directly to corporate management. Unlike earlier examples of co-creation, implementation is part of the customer's business. In the future, these trends may lead concerted actions on critical issues, such as violations of financial sustainability, industrial plagiarism, or child labor.

With respect to customer participation, reviewing, reversing, and relocating the value chain globally and adjusting structures becomes a pertinent issue, as customers start driving international location decisions and firms, in turn, need to reflect on the desired influence of customers.

GLOBAL MARKETING TEAMS

Cross-functionality and customer-centricity are seen also as a response to mounting global competition. Several companies have reacted to this challenge in the last couple of years and have restructured their marketing teams accordingly. For instance, Coca-Cola announced in 2010 that it was making changes to the leadership team of its global integrated marketing communications and capabilities organization. "It's recognition of a shift in the landscape," said Ms. Clark, senior-VP of integrated marketing communications and capabilities. "Increasingly, we understand the idea of a liquid and linked landscape. And perhaps we weren't structured for ultimate success within that landscape." Ms. Clark said that, previously, the organization had been more siloed and, in some ways, put more emphasis on paid media. It was a revelation to discover that of the 150 million views the brand has amassed on YouTube, only 25 million to 30 million of those views could be attributed to content Coca-Cola had put into the marketplace. "The organization was subsequently structured around the principles of content, connections and integration," she added.[17]

Some researchers also contend that multinational firms are adapting to the new reality by increasingly forming global task teams and, specifically, global marketing teams (GMTs), which "are taking on a strategic dimension that has traditionally been reserved for top management teams. [These GMTs] are acting as the key decision-makers and are identifying and implementing the means to build competitive advantage in multiple markets."[18] In addition, it has been suggested that global marketing teams should bring together talent with three kinds of focus: "think," "feel," and "do."[19]

More recent research[20] looks at the value of virtual teams as compared to face-to-face teams and finds that despite the attractiveness, virtual teams do face tremendous challenges, such as difficulty communicating and coordinating activities, misunderstandings, feelings of isolation, and poor team leadership. However, these teams are, more often than not, able to overcome such initial difficulties and still create sophisticated and sought-after products. For example, Boeing's SLICE rocket engine was created by a virtual team. Only five members of this team met face-to-face, and did this only once; all other communication between Boeing's experts and outside experts contracted to work on this project was carried out entirely virtually.

Companies have adopted these business practices for two main reasons. First, virtual teams have been linked with significant savings, due to reductions in travel expenses, meeting times, duplication costs, and other logistical expenditures. Second, virtual teams make organizations more flexible, allowing them to handle the pressures created by the increasing business globalization and competition, changing organizational structures, and growing customer demand for timely and efficient service. Because virtual teams are a cost-efficient business practice, and because they help increase organizations' competitiveness, organizations are likely to continue to use or to adopt virtual teams in the future.

However, one important question remains of how to staff global marketing teams. Should they be experts in the industry, marketing gurus, project managers, or natives that know about the culture of the target market? Questions of how to select global marketing teams become evident if you look at Figure 15.5, which depicts an advertisement in a Beijing shopping mall. It shows Western-style people posing for Aimer, which creates high-end lingerie products dedicated to women who love the exquisite, elegant, and confident inner garments and—apparently—live in China. Who may have designed these ads?

Similarly, an executive in the pharmaceutical industry experiences these difficulties in recruiting employees for market access. This director describes it as

FIGURE 15.5
Shopping Mall in
Beijing with an
Advertisement for
Aimer
Source: © Authors

"a mixture of arts and sciences" with multiple facets of both sides involved. The science side includes health economics, medicine, and an ability to work with the more scientific functions within the company. At the same time, it is beneficial to have someone who not only understands business, regulations and marketing, but also can develop relationships with people who help convince payers to reimburse a product. This director recognizes, however, just how incredibly rare a single person with such a diverse background can be, and that one person can't do it all.[21]

Very often, companies face these challenges in the form of paradoxes or ambiguities. Thus, going beyond the organization of global marketing teams, there is a need to also think about other different forms of organization.

AMBIDEXTROUS MARKETING

Global marketers are often faced with dilemmas: they are expected to consolidate their existing business while simultaneously finding new opportunities. They are torn between exploitation and exploration, or between alignment and innovation. Thus, implementing the right strategy is often difficult. Business development may be eager to sell new products that have not yet completed the research process. R&D may develop new product ideas, but fail to commercialize them. Firms are market-driven while market-driving firms are more conducive to innovations. And as if these tensions were not enough, marketing managers are also challenged to act locally but integrate globally, and to pursue differentiation but obverse low-cost strategies.

These examples underscore the existence of conflicting marketing strategies, which pose a dilemma for global marketing managers and require a balanced use of tools, procedures, resource endowments, structures, and supportive contexts. One such solution is ambidextrous marketing.[22] *"Ambidexterity" originally relates to "the power of using two hands alike" (Oxford English Dictionary).* In marketing it is used to refer to and reconcile to exploration and exploitation. *"Exploration"* implies experimentation with new alternatives, having returns that are uncertain, distant, and often negative. In contrast, *"exploitation"* describes the refinement and extension of existing competencies, technologies, and paradigms, exhibiting returns that are positive, proximate, and predictable.[23]

There are four different ways a company can make use of ambidextrous marketing, which the following framework (Figure 15.6) illustrates. It is based on the two dimensions of coordination level and coordination logic by which different approaches to ambidexterity are highlighted.

Structural Ambidexterity

Marketing strategists have typically resolved the tension between exploration and exploitation by separating them in two different parts of the firm (e.g. marketing versus sales; marketing versus R&D; marketing versus service). For instance, R&D and business development are given responsibility for new product development

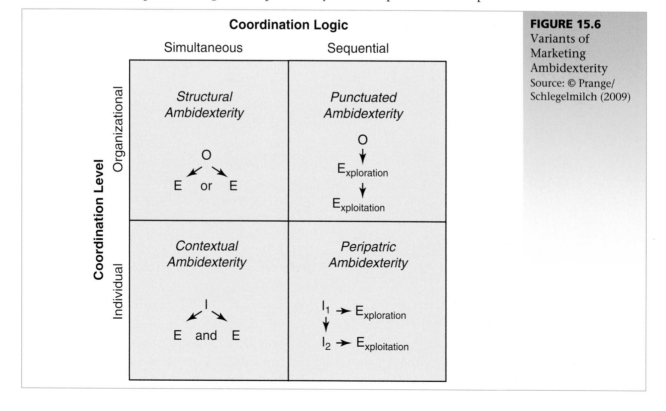

FIGURE 15.6
Variants of Marketing Ambidexterity
Source: © Prange/ Schlegelmilch (2009)

while the core business units focus on alignment and exploitation. In this vein, organizations use several structures simultaneously because the challenges they face are so dramatically different that they cannot be managed within one organizational unit.

Empirical research has further identified that structural separation usually occurs at different levels of the firm, e.g. between headquarters and subsidiaries or global teams and centres of excellence. Alternatively, structural separation can be achieved by separating functions of a multi-product firm or by creating functions with a particular orientation. For instance, R&D is more oriented towards exploration while production units normally focus on exploitation. Related to the overall balance of strategies, the most common tenet has been to structurally separate business units: some with a focus on explorative innovation and others specializing in exploitative innovation. For instance, structural separation is undertaken by most large software companies, which externalize specialist teams to develop revolutionary codes in distinct locations.

Punctuated Ambidexterity

Organizations may also disentangle different global marketing tasks by separating them over time. Major emphasis is placed on organizational units that focus on one type of strategy *one day*, and on a different set of innovations at another point in time. Thus, organizations temporally separate between exploration and exploitation. For instance, the same decision unit may use a mechanistic structure for making routine decisions and then shift to an organic structure for making non-routine decisions.

In the case of product development, temporal fluctuations may be best suited to cope with changes in technological jumps or breakthroughs, which are likely to interpenetrate long periods of incremental product development. These designs may differentially relate to information transfer and knowledge generation and, thus, have an impact on new product development rates. Occasionally, units or teams move from sales to service function or change from research-driven to commercial orientations. For instance, the RBC Financial Group in Canada is the largest bank as measured by assets and market capitalization and one of North America's leading diversified financial services. In order to become more competitive, RBC realized that some of their units had to become more market-oriented. Management started a process whereby, over time, employees sensed that the culture was fundamentally changing. Their ideas were given due consideration, and they were being rewarded for market-oriented activities.

Contextual Ambidexterity

The organizational literature also suggests that ambidexterity emerges when leaders in a business unit develop a supportive context. The resulting type of contextual ambidexterity, which was formally introduced by Birkinshaw and Gibson

(2004),[24] is seen as the behavioral capacity to simultaneously demonstrate alignment and adaptability. Indeed, contextual ambidexterity differs markedly from structural ambidexterity because it is a dual capacity woven into the fabric of an organization on the individual level. Instead of focusing on dual structures or on changing tasks for business units, organizations reconcile conflicting demands by building a set of processes, systems, or contexts that enable and encourage individual employees to make their own judgement as to how to divide their time between conflicting demands. For instance, marketing managers decide whether they engage in new business development, service, or sales activities, e.g. by involving customers with a need for ongoing incremental product development. Here, the contextual variant remains a set of stimuli that motivate marketing managers to act in a certain way.

Previous research has acknowledged the role of managers in enabling and developing conditions for ambidexterity.[25] Building predominantly on a leadership approach, studies have documented the importance of contextual leadership that helps to balance requirements posed by contradictory activities and, consequently, sustains business unit performance. Among scattered insights there is consensus on a few mechanisms that help to support contextual ambidexterity, e.g. internal processes that enable managers to handle large amounts of information and decision alternatives to deal with conflicts. Also, behavioral complexity, i.e. the capacity to adopt multiple leadership roles and change between them in selective contexts, is seen as primordial.

Peripatric Ambidexterity

While the previous types of separation are well anchored in the existing literature on ambidexterity, no explicit reference has yet been made to coordinating marketing strategies by exchanging the top management or founding team. For this variant, the notion of "peripatric ambidexterity," a term borrowed from genetics, has been introduced.[26] This approach specifies the formation of a new species during evolution and is often tied to the idea of a founder who develops a new population within an isolated niche. In the business world we can find some analogies, which emphasize the substitution of one "species" by another. Take the example of Nissan and Renault, now headed by Carlos Ghosn. The manager has instilled a vision of innovative and exploratory leadership at the two companies that his predecessors failed to achieve. However, people presently ask whether he might be better off in the saviour role rather than the consolidator and incremental adapter role. Thus, management may again have to change or evolve further. Similarly, when Goodyear was confronted by Michelin's introduction of the radial tire, Goodyear's senior management team first focused on the existing product and avoided radical challenge. When they finally introduced the radial tire, Goodyear completely shifted from bias-ply tires to radials. This strategic shift at Goodyear led to the creation of a new senior management team.

As executive behavior is supposed to be driven by past insights and experiences, previous career experiences shape the range of action that is available to formulate and implement strategies, i.e. engage in either explorative or exploitative behaviour. The peripatric version of marketing ambidexterity posits that it is difficult for individuals or teams to change behaviors. Once they surpass a critical size, only a few managers from the original founding team are normally able to manage the shift. Thus, a firm needs to exchange its top management if it intends to implement a drastic change in global marketing strategy.

AGILE MARKETING

Another new approach to organize global marketing originally comes from the domain of software development. The idea of agile organizations and methods dates back to 2001 and was originally used in software development.[27] "Agile" is

---

Box 15.2 Person-in-Focus: Mike Lawrie

The Ambidextrous CEO

In the fall of 2008, Mike Lawrie, the CEO of the London-based software firm Misys, asked his senior executives to prepare a plan for weathering the global economic crisis. When they reported back, at the top of their list of recommendations was to cut the company's annual $3 million investment in Misys Open Source Solutions, a venture aimed at developing a potentially disruptive technology in the health care industry.

It's a familiar story. Although most executives acknowledge the need to explore new businesses and markets, they almost always bow to the more-pressing claims of the core business, especially when times are hard. Innovations like Misys's Open Source face an uphill battle to secure a share of the firm's capital. They lack scale and resources and are usually underrepresented at the top table. At best, the leaders of the established business units ignore such projects. At worst, they see them as threats to the firm's core identity and values.

But firms only thrive when leaders embrace the tension between old and new and foster a state of constant creative conflict at the top. This is called *leading ambidextrously*. Three leadership principles help firms grow their core businesses even as they cultivate new offerings that will reshape their industries: (1) Engage the senior team around a forward-looking strategic aspiration. (2) Explicitly hold the tension between the demands of innovation units and the core business at the top of the organization. (3) Embrace inconsistency by maintaining multiple and often conflicting strategic agendas. When leaders take this approach, they empower their senior teams to move from a negotiation of feudal interests to an explicit, ongoing, and forward-looking debate about the tensions at the heart of the business.

When Mike Lawrie came to Misys, in 2006, he recruited a new management team to turn around the struggling software firm. The company, which served the financial services and health care industries, had been plagued by problems with quality, and it was losing customers at an alarming rate.

Despite the pressure to shore up the existing business, one of Lawrie's first moves was to create a stand-alone unit for open source technology, which was a key component of his vision for the company's future. He knew that open source was emerging as a serious disruptive threat in the software industry, especially in health care. It held the promise of seamless data exchange between the many players in health care delivery. Lawrie believed that Misys had an opportunity to get out in front and be the disruptor.

Sources: TIÊNG ANH THƯƠNG MAI. (2011), May 30, 2011, http://ceoenglishclub.blogspot.de/2011/05/ambidextrous-ceo.html [Accessed: March 10, 2014]; Probst, G., Raisch, S., and Tushman, M. L. (2011), 'Ambidextrous leadership', *Organizational Dynamics*, 40(4), pp. 326–334; Tushman, M.L., Smith, W.K., and Binns, A. (2011), 'The ambidextrous CEO', *Harvard Business Review* 89(6), June, 2011, pp. 74–80.

a set of values and principles, guided by self-directed, low-risk, and adaptable step-by-step-development for the delivery of IT projects. Instead of suffering from time-consuming, inflexible, highly complex and inefficient procedures, agile methods (such as Scrum or extreme programming) provide more flexibility to adapt to changes over time. An agile approach is different from traditional processes, such as the "waterfall approach" which follows a step-wise linear planning sequence; it is more iterative, focused on interaction, collaboration, and continuous responses to change.

Meanwhile, the term agile is used in a variety of settings. "Agile" is fundamentally about learning, people, and change, the three things organizations struggle with at the current time. Agile methods can be a powerful heuristic to transform companies into agile organizations that are better able to cope with the challenges of external stakeholders. For instance, the original Agile Manifesto has been applied to marketing and proposes the following guidelines:[28]

- **Validated learning over opinions and conventions:** Learning should be a non-linear, iterative process with a constant feedback loop between the company and their customers.

- **Customer-focused collaboration over silos and hierarchy:** Collaboration, focusing on the needs of the customer, produces better marketing than siloed, departmental turf wars and strict adherence to hierarchical decision-making.

- **Adaptive and iterative campaigns over big-bang campaigns:** A non-linear, adaptive approach, which involves starting with a little strategy, implementing it quickly, getting insight into it's success (or failure) with customers, adjusting and continuing to learn, is preferable to the conventional, linear big-bang campaigns, where big ideas are built, launched, and often either fail or are justified with metrics designed to tell a story.

- **The process of customer discovery over static prediction:** Customers' reactions are often unpredictable. Marketing is an act of customer discovery. Understanding customers is hard work, and it does require constant respect for the customer and consistent engagement.

- **Flexible versus rigid planning:** Plans must adapt to change. Planning by itself is not bad. As Dwight D. Eisenhower said, "Plans are nothing; planning is everything." But marketing is like war; just as no battle plan survives contact with the enemy, no marketing plan survives contact with the real, constantly changing market.

- **Responding to change over following a plan:** A company must build constant flexibility into its operations. Thus, processes are more important than structures.

- **Many small experiments over a few large bets:** As planning may not work, constant experimentation and play are important.

As illustrated by the Agile Manifesto for Marketing, it becomes more important for a company to change its mindset and processes than relying on structures only. Several managers and researchers have taken up the concept and have transferred it to their marketing operations. For instance, in early 2014, marketing strategy consultancy CMG Partners released the results of its sixth-annual CMO's Agenda, "The Agile Advantage," a qualitative survey assessing the role and responsibilities of the chief marketer.[29] The survey found that 63 percent of marketing leaders indicate agility as a high priority, but only 40 percent rate themselves as agile. Similarly, participants in a recent study of "The Marketing Organization of the Future" commented that they need to get prepared for something for which they cannot be prepared. Flexibility and agility are becoming the basic requirements for success.[30]

Most CMOs think of agile in terms of being nimble, being able to react quickly to the market. They understand that to achieve agility requires their organization to be data-driven, customer-focused, constantly prioritizing, and quick decision-makers. They also understand that this culture needs to be supported with process. Agile methods helps reinforce a culture of flexibility by providing structure that drives marketers to be iterative, customer-centered, and focused on priorities of high-value. Many CMOs are unfamiliar with the agile methodology used in software development and its application to marketing; agile is still a new concept in marketing (Box 15.3).

CONTROL MECHANISMS

Following agile ideas also implies rethinking traditional marketing control mechanisms in a company. Companies today are scrutinized on many different levels. Shareholders, regulators, customers, analysts, suppliers, and the general public can quickly form an opinion about a firm just by performing a quick internet search or

---

Box 15.3 Technology-in-Focus: Agile Marketing in Marketing Technology

Shift Communications is a marketing agency based in Boston with offices in New York and San Francisco. The company was founded in 2003, when the assets of former public relations firm Sterling Hager was acquired by three of its executives. In 2006, it created the first Social Media Release. The firm's primary practices areas are in the healthcare, technology, and consumer markets.

On a typical day, the agency's people encounter a hectic day-to-day work with multiple clients, diverging experiences, several projects, and numerous requirements to coordinate all at the same time. Every detail in every project is someone's responsibility and one missing piece of the puzzle can risk a client relationship. Often, changing requirements occur in the middle of a project and sometimes even contradict the initial briefing.

This is why at Shift, the marketing technology team has turned to the Agile development methodology to help keep track of what's going on teamwise, where people are stuck, where someone needs help and what questions they have, so that every day the company is able to go with the flow of changes that may come from any source. Agile marketing moves the company away from waterfall structures, where everything is planned in a linear way: the scope is set out upfront and then everybody works to implement details, get approval, and revisions, and then go do it for weeks or months at a time. When the project is done, it is reported back on how it went—and very often, there is a requirement that wasn't in the input gathering sessions, or the environment changed. For example, in a waterfall environment, the agency might design a yearlong Facebook marketing strategy, with a certain number of posts per day, a specific budgetary spend per day, etc. Midway through that year, Facebook changes the rules on everyone, and suddenly what started out as a well-designed strategy becomes a liability that one might not be able to change in a traditional waterfall organizational structure. At this point, the company started experimenting with Agile.

Setting up a story for each client is the way to do it. The company works through that by making sure everything is moving ahead. Cross-functional individuals of a team is what makes Agile work so well. One person may have more knowledge about paid media while another has more knowledge about social. The company keeps track of what individuals are working on with a 10–15 minute stand-up meeting per day in which three questions are answered: (1) What we've done. (2) What we're doing. And, (3) What's stopping us from moving forward?

And finally, Agile marketing puts the emphasis on acting. It avoids or reduces internal politics, takes us back to the client needs, and allows us to know when to say something isn't possible because it isn't what the client needs.

Sources: Wolverton, C. (2014), 'Agile marketing in marketing technology', http://www.shiftcomm.com/2014/09/agile-marketing-marketing-technology/; Shift Communications website: http://www.shiftcomm.com [Accessed: January 10, 2015].

accessing specialized information databases—all tools that are practically at their fingertips. In response to the need for increased transparency, many companies have implemented strong control practices for all of their business units and levels of management. In marketing, this trend has been met with even greater emphasis on planning and on establishing specific objectives, processes, metrics, and accountability measures that can prove marketing's impact on the overall profitability of the firm. However, given the lack of predictability, informal control mechanisms and self-organization have become even more important alongside the more formal approaches to controlling a marketing organization.

Especially with increasing amounts of data, it is clear that marketing executives have to delegate certain decisions to the local and regional levels of management, while retaining control over the consistency of the company brand across geographies, segments, and distribution channels. Achieving this balance between central control and local initiative is one of the main challenges for any global marketing executive.

Formal Control Mechanisms

By setting some specific long- and short-term plans, performance standards, and reporting structures, leaders can begin to align the global marketing organization for consistent, measurable operations. These mechanisms are planning, budgeting, and reporting.

Planning

At their best, strategic and operational plans are the road maps that explain why, how, when, and who will accomplish the tasks necessary to achieve marketing success. To be effective, the planning process should take into account the overall company goals and objectives, as well as the local and regional perspectives. Communications among all levels of the marketing organization are also very important to ensure that all those responsible for the realization of the plans are on board with the final goals and objectives, performance measures, and deadlines.

At Tektronix located in Beaverton, Oregon, United States (Geo Map 15.1), a global manufacturer of test, measurement, and monitoring devices, the incoming CMO faced the challenge of a marketing organization in disarray, where marketing initiatives—some 4,000 of them—were being executed with no connection to the company's (also numerous) strategic objectives, no performance metrics, and no relevance to the sales division. His "get well plan" entailed massive streamlining of all strategic objectives, realignment of the marketing activities to match both corporate and sales objectives, and a radical simplification of the marketing organization from ten to only three or four job levels. The CMO, Martyn Etherington, credits these "painful steps" as some of the reasons for Tektronix's continuous revenue growth and solid culture of accountability.[31]

Budgeting

Budgets are more specific answers to the "how" and "when" questions outlined in the planning stage. Usually established on a yearly basis, budgets are used to allocate funds across the marketing organization—from how much is allotted to regional offices and service providers such as PR agencies, to how much is spent on specific campaigns, sponsorships, and other marketing initiatives. Budgets are also one of the tools used to determine the performance of the marketing organization and its units. A recent Forbes article[32] notes that more than half of business-to-business marketers plan to increase their marketing budgets this year, with the

GEO MAP 15.1
Tektronix
Source: Adapted from: CIA Maps, The World Factbook[33]

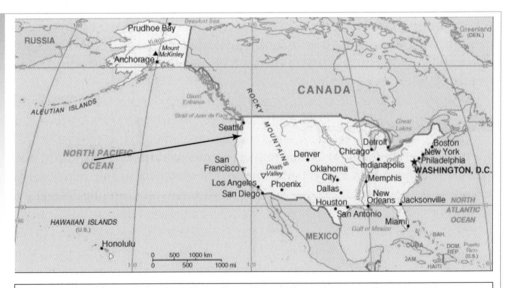

The headquarters of **Tektronix** is located in Beaverton, Oregon, United States.

average budget increasing by 6 percent, according to a new report by Forrester Research. The report, "Direct your 2015 B2B budget gains toward creating exceptional customer experiences," was based on a survey of 132 business-to-business marketers, conducted in the fourth quarter. It found that 51 percent of marketers plan to increase budgets this year, 30 percent plan to keep budgets flat, while 8 percent plan to decrease budgets. Marketing programs receiving the biggest chunk of the budget are in-person events (14 percent), followed by digital marketing (10 percent), and content marketing (9 percent).

Reporting

Proving marketing's value to the organization has been a historically contentious issue. Therefore, establishing metrics that show its impact and regularly reporting their performance has become one of the most critical issues for today's marketing leaders. The questions of how and what to measure in order to quantify return on marketing investment (ROMI) has plagued marketers since the dawn of the profession. As the ways of spending marketing budgets continue to increase (with the advent of Web 2.0, mobile marketing, etc.), new marketing mix models and other analytical tools to measure performance have emerged. It has become clear that using traditional metrics, such as market share or mass awareness is not enough; so much so that Jim Stengel, the now retired global marketing officer of P&G, has declared, "I believe today's marketing model is broken. We're applying antiquated thinking and work systems to a new world of possibilities."[34]

Current marketing thought is focusing on the customer instead of on the brand—the customer lifetime value (CLV) concept, quantified in the customer equity measure, is what should drive marketing strategy and budgets, argue many contemporary academics and practitioners. CLV is a metric that allows marketers to measure the overall effect of their marketing investment (Figure 15.7). As the authors of one of the most popular CLV and customer equity frameworks summarize it, "[C]ustomer equity provides an information-based, customer-driven, competitor-cognizant, and financially accountable strategic approach to maximizing the firm's long-term profitability."[35]

Many new tools are addressing the issue by providing better and easier ways to analyze marketing program performance. Powerful statistical software programs have made it possible to create so-called "marketing dashboards" where data can be tracked in real time, giving marketers unprecedented powers to adjust campaigns as they unfold (particularly in the digital domain). Such data availability and control options are very attractive to marketers who have to report bottom-line results.

However, some marketers caution against complete reliance on financial metrics for evaluating marketing performance. Rob Duboff, the author of *ROI for Marketing: Balancing Accountability with Long-Term Needs*, argues that intuition should still play a role in the field. Marketers can be "precisely wrong" by using only quantitative tools, when they should try to be "generally correct." Such an approach would still leave room for marketing tools that employ intuition, such as

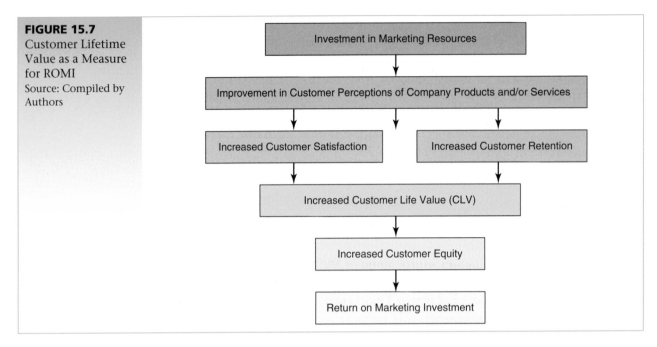

FIGURE 15.7
Customer Lifetime
Value as a Measure
for ROMI
Source: Compiled by
Authors

advertising, public relations, and sponsorships, while taking advantage of all the benefits that analytical tools can offer. Such a balanced approach would allow marketers to be " ... generally right and not oversell the precision of the tools we have. I also don't want us to blindly say, 'Believe me.'"[36]

For activities such as branding, advertising, or market research, the current corporate toolkit does not offer adequate means to quantify the value created by marketing. For example, although Google's brand was valued at an estimated $107.43 billion in 2014, the current financial reporting requirements for public companies do not allow the company to list it as an asset unless the brand is acquired. For acquired brands, mandatory brand valuations on balance sheets started life in the US. It was noted that intangible assets were accounting for an increasingly large portion of a company's worth—over 80 percent in the case of leading consumer brands such as Coca-Cola and Marlboro. Upon acquisition, all of this value was shoved into the black hole of goodwill where it was of no use to anybody; there was a complete lack of visibility. Breaking out the measurable and identifiable intangibles from this black hole has a number of advantages:[37]

- Royalty rates and transfer prices can be set more accurately from knowing and understanding the value of brands and other intangible assets.

- Knowing the value of a brand can help companies generate positive PR in financial markets which can, in turn, assist in boosting the share price.

- It is a highly effective benchmark of ROI (return on investment). Intangible asset valuation enables brands and other intangibles to be applied to the measure of return on investment, allowing management to be measured appropriately on what they drive through the application of the brands in their management.

- The share price can recognize the true value of brands in acquisitions—which can have the effect of the share price being raised.

- The actual process involved in putting brands on a balance sheet can throw up some useful insights. Among other factors it analyses the brand relative to the competition; it identifies potential opportunities, strengths and weaknesses of the brand; and consumer and market perceptions—an objective opinion can be extremely beneficial.

INFORMAL CONTROL MECHANISMS

By establishing a distinctive corporate culture and hiring and promoting managers with certain qualities, companies utilize some of the informal methods of exerting control on the organization. For global firms, these types of "soft" controls are often more important than formal ones, especially if they operate in many cultures where the data-driven management style favored in many Western cultures clashes with local social values that emphasize relationship-building, hierarchy, and social networks.

CORPORATE CULTURE

Certain corporations are known for their strong corporate culture. Johnson & Johnson, Wal-Mart, Sony, and many others have spent years instilling certain values and work ethic in their employees around the world in an effort to build cohesive, productive units that can perform to the company's standards regardless of their size, location, or national culture. Lenovo, the Chinese computer giant, has addressed the corporate culture issue head on, working hard to establish a truly global, inclusive culture. It has refused to establish an official central office. Its executives are stationed across Lenovo's worldwide offices on a temporary, rotating basis and even its chairman relocated his family to the United States in order to learn more about American culture and to perfect his English language skills. Development teams based in different countries often collaborate virtually; the marketing department is based in Bangalore. Company-issued tip sheets are used to foster cross-cultural understanding and cooperative spirit among employees. "In all situations: assume good intentions; be intentional about understanding others and being understood; respect cultural differences," reads one of them.[38]

MANAGEMENT SELECTION AND TRAINING

Management selection and promotion practices represent another informal control measure (see above for marketing team constellations). Managers are the primary conduit for the dissemination and maintenance of a company's mission, vision, and culture. By training and promoting managers who best represent its core values, a firm can do a lot to ensure that the desired corporate culture "lives" throughout the organization. This practice also facilitates collaboration and knowledge transfer among all business units around the world.

Consider the transformation of the Italian carmaker, Fiat (Geo Map 15.2). The first major initiative that Sergio Marchionne, the CEO responsible for the turna-round, embarked on was to identify and promote to positions of leadership a new crop of managers. He found most of them at Fiat's far-flung subsidiaries, where they have shown initiative and independence, unlike the senior managers at headquarters. Once he had the right people, Marchionne spent several months evaluating them on whether they had the right qualities needed to lead radical organizational change, such as the ability to handle more responsibilities and accountability. He also built a strong personal connection with each one. "If the organization can feel that kind of connection with its leadership, you're going to get a pretty sound culture aligned around strongly held common values," says Marchionne.[39]

GEO MAP 15.2
Fiat
Source: Adapted from: CIA Maps, The World Factbook[40]

The headquarters of **Fiat** is located in Turin, Italy.

LEADERSHIP

A recent article in the *McKinsey Quarterly* declared that "[F]ew senior-executive positions will be subject to as much change over the next few years as that of the chief marketing officer."[41] The authors of the article found several challenges for global CMOs, and identified a few key issues that will define marketing leadership in the near future including:

- balancing a global reach with a local touch;

- finding effective ways to reach the new, informed, and vocal consumer;

- learning to market effectively in the rapidly changing technology and media environment;

- redefining marketing's position as a strategic function that can shape a company's course with its knowledge of global markets and customers and stand accountable for the results.

There has never been a better chance for marketing to establish its central role, given the newly discovered importance of customer insight to the organization. To be successful, however, marketing leaders need the strength and skills to prove that marketing can be more than marketing services such as advertising, branding, or market research. They need to become change agents for the organization as a whole as well as corporate technologists. For instance, in 2012 the research and consulting firm Gartner predicted that by 2017, a company's chief marketing officer would be spending more on technology than its chief information officer was.[42] This claim already seems to be a reality today.

Top marketers can meet these higher standards for leadership and technology by taking specific actions, according to researchers. For example, the management consulting firm McKinsey contends that divisional and corporate organizations also play an important role in the success of consumer goods marketers. The firm's findings reveal that companies with high-performing brand portfolios tend to be the ones that allow divisional marketing heads to exert more control over marketing strategy and execution—a finding particularly relevant to global marketing organizations. At these companies, corporate marketing plays more the role of a disseminator of information and best practices to line marketers than a provider of marketing services or a manager of global branding campaigns.[43]

In addition, the role of the chief marketing technologist (CMT) is emerging. CMTs are part strategist, part creative director, part technology leader, and part teacher.[44] Acting as the connective tissue between different constituencies, these executives engage with different marketing responsibilities (Figure 15.8). The CMO is supported by ensuring technical capabilities. For instance, Joseph Kurian, Aetna's head of marketing technology and innovation for enterprise marketing, championed the use of "voice of the customer" software to collect user feedback. CMTs also facilitate

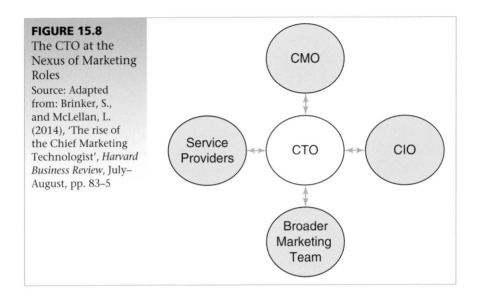

FIGURE 15.8
The CTO at the Nexus of Marketing Roles
Source: Adapted from: Brinker, S., and McLellan, L. (2014), 'The rise of the Chief Marketing Technologist', *Harvard Business Review*, July–August, pp. 83–5

and prioritize technology requests from marketing translating between technical and marketing requirements and making sure that the marketing's systems adhere to IT policies. Andreas Starke, the business information officer for global marketing at SAP, is the principal point of contact between the two functions and streamlines the planning and execution of marketing technology projects. The CMT also ensures that the marketing staff has the right software and training. Brian Makas, the director of marketing technology and business intelligence at ThomasNet, saw that field sales reps and support staff were inefficiently coordinating their activities through various Excel sheets. Instead, he introduced real-time views obtained through the company's CRM system, which increased efficiency. Finally, the CMT assesses how well providers' technical capabilities meet marketing's need. Shawn Goodin, the director of marketing technology at The Clorox Company, led the evaluation of six vendors for a platform that would optimize customer experiences across channels.[45]

The global executive search firm Spencer Stuart recently underscored how difficult it is to achieve the position of a true marketing leader today. From the managers they interviewed, both Mike Senackerib, senior vice president and CMO of Hertz, and Tom O'Toole, senior vice president and chief operating officer of United Airlines' Mileage Plus Holdings and former CMO of United Airlines, cited the shift from mass marketing to highly data-driven, highly targeted marketing and customer interaction as the biggest change during their CMO tenures. As Senackerib put it, "The ability to drill down to an individual customer level is becoming much more prevalent, driven by the way people consume media and get information." Noted O'Toole, "The rise in data-driven, real-time marketing and customer interaction is enabling us to change our marketing based on real-time events and operating dynamics."[46]

Spencer Stuart also conducted a study in 2014 that revealed that CMOs have some of the shortest tenures in the "C" level suites of large organizations. The average tenure for chief marketing officers of leading US consumer brand companies stayed at 45 months in 2013, remarkably, the same as the 2012 average. While turnover seems to have stabilized in the past year, average CMO tenure is now more than 21 months longer than in 2004 when Spencer Stuart began tracking CMO tenure. Data for the tenth annual CMO tenure study was based on an analysis of tenure of CMOs of the top 100 advertised brands. Spencer Stuart attributes some of this trend to the heightened visibility of the CMO and thus to the heightened expectations and accountability: "The fact that CMO tenure has been on the rise for the past seven years and has become relatively constant supports our belief that CMOs have truly become deeply rooted in management teams and are leading the charge for how their organizations interact with today's customers."[47]

As in past years of the study, CMO tenure varies widely across industries. Tenure is shortest in the automotive, communications/media, and restaurant sectors, averaging between 27 to 31 months. CMOs in technology companies, meanwhile, continue to enjoy the longest tenure, averaging 64 months—more than 1.5 years longer on average than CMOs overall. Average tenure is 56 months for CMOs of leading financial services firms and 52 months for consumer company CMOs.[48] While figures have been improving, tenure is still rather short, which reflects the increasing requirements posed upon jobholders: "Unless the CMO demonstrates the value that marketing is delivering and clearly shows the return on investment, the business owner, who is under pressure to deliver numbers, will pull funding," said Raja Rajamannar, MasterCard's chief marketing officer. "The CMO could find himself out of the job."[49] Clearly, more is expected today from marketing leaders than ever before.

SUMMARY

- There is no standard organizational control structure for global firms. An ideal structure depends upon the extent to which the firm has internationalized. Another factor that determines organizational structure is the extent to which the firm has integrated and coordinated its international operations.
- Most global organizational structures are either based on functional, product, or regional-area configurations. However, many advanced global firms have chosen a global-matrix structure.
- Many companies today are implementing new types of marketing structures, such as customer-centered, ambidextrous, or agile marketing organizations.
- Global firms must establish both formal and informal control systems. These systems take on greater importance as firms internationalize as the number of countries, consumer segments, distribution channels, and communication possibilities increase.
- The roles and responsibilities of CMOs have dramatically changed over time, including an increasing focus on technology.

DISCUSSION QUESTIONS

1. Why is the matrix form of organization difficult to implement for a global firm? Would such an organizational form be applicable to a domestic firm? Why or why not?
2. What are the different ambidextrous forms a company can adopt and do you think they are equally valid for firms operating in different industries?
3. What do you think are the personal and organizational requirements for agile marketing?
4. How does a corporate culture affect the choice of an organizational format?
5. How do you think a CMO of today should be best trained?
6. Do you think that the rather short tenure time of CMOs is good or bad?

EXPERIENTIAL EXERCISES

1. Visit the following website (http://www.strategy-business.com/article/rr00025?gko=4 89ba), learn about the different types of marketing organization and discuss how they are different from the marketing operations at a company you know. Write a short evaluation of a selected company profile and give your opinion on the strategic direction in which you believe the marketing department should move in order to achieve optimum results.
2. Select a company that you think can be better at marketing its products globally. Recommend an organizational structure that would be more suitable to improving marketing results. Provide the reasoning behind your recommendation: why do you think the new structure would yield better results? What are some of the potential pitfalls of this format? What are the advantages? Summarize your findings and recommendations in a PowerPoint presentation.

KEY TERMS

- Agile marketing
- Ambidextrous marketing
- CMO tenure
- Co-formation
- Control mechanisms
- Customer-focused organization
- Customization
- Functional organizational format
- Matrix organizational format
- Product-based organizational format
- Regional organizational format

NOTES

1 http://cescatherapeutics.com/wp-content/uploads/2014/06/Reorg_Lee-Appt-041614-Final.pdf
2 http://cescatherapeutics.com/about-us/mission-values/
3 IBM Institute for Business Value. (2014), 'Stepping up to the challenge', http://www.totalcustomer.org/2014/07/18/ibm-gives-insight-challenges-todays-cmos-face/ [Accessed: October 18, 2015].

4 Hult, G., Cavusgil, S., Kiyak, T., Deligonul, S., and Lagerstrom, K. (2007), 'What drives performance in globally focused marketing organizations? A three-country study', *Journal of International Marketing,* 15(2), pp. 58–85.

5 Johnson & Johnson. (2015), 'Company structure', http://www.jnj.com/about-jnj/company-structure [Accessed: January 12, 2015].

6 Bouwmester, R. (2014), 'Marketing organization. A view on centralization versus decentralization', http://www.batenborch.eu/wp-content/uploads/2014/02/Central-vs-de-central-marketing-organization-.pdf [Accessed: January 12, 2015].

7 Arend, M. (2012), 'Divisional headquarters role gain focus', http://www.siteselection.com/issues/2012/mar/regional-headquarters.cfm [Accessed: January 12, 2015].

8 Heraeus. (2014). Corporate Website. http://corporate.heraeus.com/en/presse/pressemitteilungen/pressemitteilungen_2014/141014_grand_opening.aspx [Accessed July 1, 2015].

9 Bain & Company. (2012), 'The matrix doesn't have to be your enemy', *Forbes*, December 9, 2012, http://www.forbes.com/sites/baininsights/2012/09/12/the-matrix-doesnt-have-to-be-your-enemy/ [Accessed: October 18, 2015].

10 Ibid.

11 BCG. (2012), 'Rethinking the marketing organization', *BCG Perspectives*, https://www.bcgperspectives.com/content/articles/consumer_products_organization_design_rethinking_the_marketing_organization/ [Accessed: January 3, 2015].

12 Gebauer, H. and Kowalkowski, C. (2012), 'Customer-focused and service-focused orientation in organizational structures', *Journal of Business & Industrial Marketing,* 27(7), pp. 527–37.

13 Hexus. (2016), 'Dell globalizes business groups around major customer segments', http://hexus.net/business/items/corporate/16720-dell-globalizes-business-groups-around-major-customer-segments/ [Accessed: July 30, 2016].

14 Grönroos, C. (2011),'Value co-creation in service logic: A critical analysis', *Marketing Theory,* 11(3), pp. 279–301.

15 Prange, C. and Ates, Z. (2010), 'Co-creation on a global scale – How customers impact firms' internationalization strategies', *Marketing Review St.Gallen*, April 2010, pp. 48–52.

16 Diamantopoulos, A., Schlegelmilch, B., and Palihawadana, D. (2011), 'The relationship between country-of-origin image and brand image as drivers of purchase intentions: A test of alternative perspectives', *International Marketing Review*, 28(5), pp. 508–24.

17 Zmuda, N. (2010), 'Coca-Cola restructures marketing communications team', *Ad Age*, 21 October 21, 2010, http://adage.com/article/news/coca-cola-restructures-global-marketing-team/146623/ [Accessed: January 3, 2015].

18 Kiessling, T. S., Marino, L. D., and Richey, R. G. (2006),'Global marketing teams: A strategic option for multinationals', *Organizational Dynamics,* 35(3), pp. 237–50.

19 Swaan, M.D., Van den Dries, F., and Weed, K. (2014), 'Marketing organizations need to get unstuck', *Harvard Business Review*, 92(10), October, p. 18.

20 Purvanova, R.K. (2014), 'Face-to-face versus virtual teams: What have we really learned?', *The Psychologist-Manager Journal*, 17(1), pp. 2–29.

21 Cutting Edge. (2013), '(eors and tails: Why is staffing market access teams so difficult?' http://www.cuttingedgeinfo.com/2013/staffing-market-access-teams/ [Accessed: October 18, 2015].

22 Prange, C. and Schlegelmilch, B.B. (2009), 'The role of ambidexterity in marketing strategy implementation: Solving the exploration-exploitation dilemma,' *Business Research*, 2(2), pp. 215–40.

23 March, J.G. (1991), 'Exploration and exploitation in organizational learning', *Organization Science,* 2(1), pp.71–87.

24 Birkinshaw, J. and Gibson, C. (2004), 'Building ambidexterity into an organization', *Sloan Management Review,* 45 (4), pp. 47–55.

25 Carmeli, A. and Halevi, M.Y. (2009), 'How top management teams' behavioral integration and behavioral complexity enable organizational ambidexterity. The moderating role of contextual ambidexterity', *The Leadership Quarterly,* 20(2), pp. 207–18.

26 Prange, C. and Schlegelmilch, B.B. (2009), op. cit.

27 Gorans, P. and Kruchten, P. (2014), 'A guide to critical success factors in agile delivery', Washington DC. IBM Center of Government, 2014, http://www.businessofgovernment.org/report/guide-critical-success-factors-agile-delivery [Accessed: October 18, 2015]; Schwaber, K. and Sutherland, J. (2013), 'The Scrum Guide ™', http://www.scrumguides.org/docs/scrumguide/v1/Scrum-Guide-US.pdf#zoom=100 [Accessed: September 19, 2014]; Beck, K., et al. (2001), 'Manifesto for agile software development', http://agilemanifesto.org [Accessed: September 19, 2014]; Leffingwell, D. et al. (2014), 'Scaled agile framework ™' http://scaledagileframework.com [Accessed: September 19, 2014].

28 http://www.agilemanifesto.org; guidelines adapted from: http://agilemarketingmanifesto.org [Both accessed: October 18, 2015].

29 Rooney, J. (2014), 'Applying agile methodology to marketing can pay dividends: Survey', *Forbes*, April 15, 2014. http://www.forbes.com/sites/jenniferrooney/2014/04/15/applying-agile-methodology-to-marketing-can-pay-dividends-survey/ [Accessed: October 18, 2015].

30 T-Mobile. (2014), 'Marketing organization of the future', http://www.t-systems.de/news-media/new-study-marketing-organization-of-the-future/1289096 [Accessed: October 18, 2015].

31 Economist Intelligence Unit. (2008), 'Future tense: The global CMO, September 2008', http://graphics.eiu.com/upload/Google%20Text.pdf [Accessed: October 18, 2015].

32 Maddox, K. (2015), 'B-to-B marketing budgets to increase an average 6%', *Forbes*, 22 January, 2015, http://adage.com/article/btob/b-b-marketing-budgets-increase-average-6/296688/ [Accessed: January 4, 2015].

33 The World Factbook. (2015), https://www.cia.gov/library/publications/the-world-factbook/docs/refmaps.html [Accessed: August 1, 2015].

34 Auletta, K. (2005). 'The new pitch', *New Yorker,* March 28, 2005.

35 Rust, R. T., Lemon, K. N., and Zeithaml, V. A. (2004), 'Return on marketing: Using customer equity to focus marketing strategy', *Journal of Marketing,* 68(1), pp. 109–27.

36 Krauss, M. (2007), 'Balance attention metrics with intuition', *Marketing News,* June 1, 2007.

37 Whitwell, S. (2004), 'Brands on the balance sheet for IFRS', http://www.intangiblebusiness.com/news/marketing/2004/11/brands-on-the-balance-sheet-for-ifrs [Accessed: January 14, 2015].

38 A bigger world. (2008). *The Economist* [special report], September 18, 2008, http://www.economist.com/node/12080751 [Accessed: October 18, 2015].

39 Marchionne, S. (2008), 'Fiat's extreme makeover', *Harvard Business Review,* 86(12), pp. 45–8.

40 The World Factbook. (2015), https://www.cia.gov/library/publications/the-world-factbook/docs/refmaps.html [Accessed: August 1, 2015].

41 BCG. (2010) 'The CMO's imperative. Tackling new digital realities', https://www.bcg.com/documents/file66995.pdf [Accessed: October 18, 2015].

42 Cited in: Brinker, S. and McLellan, L. (2014), 'The rise of the chief marketing technologist', *Harvard Business Review*, July–August, 92(7/8), pp. 83–5.

43 Crawford, B., Mulder, S., and Gordon, J. (2007), 'How consumer goods companies are coping with complexity [web exclusive]', *McKinsey Quarterly*, May 2007, www.mckinseyquarterly.com/article_page.aspx?ar=2004&pagenum=8 [Accessed: February 10, 2012].

44 Brinker, S. and McLellan, L. (2014), op. cit.

45 Ibid.

46 Kwong, C. and Nonan, J. (2011), 'The evolving role of the chief marketing officer', https://www.spencerstuart.de/research-and-insight/the-evolving-role-of-the-chief-marketing-officer [Accessed: October 18, 2015].

47 Spencer Stuart. (2014), 'Chief marketing officer tenure climbs to 48 months', [Press release], https://www.spencerstuart.com/who-we-are/media-center/chief-marketing-officer-tenure-climbs-to-48-months [Accessed: January 10, 2015].

48 Ibid.

49 Vranica, S. (2014), 'Average CMO tenure: 45 months (but that's an improvement)', *CMO Today*, March 23, 2014, http://blogs.wsj.com/cmo/2014/03/23/cmos-work-lifespan-improves-still-half-that-of-ceos-study/ [Accessed: January 10, 2014].

CASE 15.1¹   EVALUESERVE INC.: ESTABLISHING A KNOWLEDGE OUTSOURCING AND SERVICE MARKETING COMPANY

After viewing a presentation by his global sales team, Marc Vollenweider, CEO of Evalueserve (EVS), was walking back to his office. He was pleased with the presentation that had been both informative and impressive. Evalueserve is an industry leader in Service Marketing Outsourcing with around 1,500 employees, executing projects in 65 languages based on markets in more than 190 countries and undertaking more than 2 million hours of research per year for its clients. His mind travelled back almost six years in time to 2000 when Evalueserve had begun as a small four-employee firm. Within such a short time, Evalueserve had achieved the enviable status of becoming the undisputed industry leader in the Knowledge Process Outsourcing (KPO) domain and successfully placing India on the KPO map. However, Marc wondered if the company would be able to maintain its present leadership position and for how long. He realized that it was important to think of strategies to fight emerging competitors. Marc also recognized the need for expanding the company's reach so as to cover new geographical areas and new business lines. His mind furiously sought answers to each of these pressing questions. Yes, the time had not yet come to rest on past laurels.

COMPANY BACKGROUND

Marc had co-founded the company with Alok Aggrawal at a time when firms were outsourcing their non-core business functions to countries such as India to leverage the benefits of low cost, quality, better concentration on their core competencies. In fact, it was this concept that gave birth to many firms in India, in the Business Process Outsourcing (BPO) domain, which catered to the low-end needs of the outsourcing market. The success of the BPO industry had first prompted Marc and Alok to think of a potential business opportunity in catering to the high-end needs of the outsourcing market, thereby giving birth to a promising new industry – Knowledge Process Outsourcing (KPO) ². The KPO industry soon established itself as a critical provider of a range of high-end knowledge-based professional services, operating from offshore locations such as India, China, and Latin America, to clients located across the world. In 2003, it was estimated that the worldwide BPO and KPO markets were USD 7.7 billion and USD 1.29 billion, respectively. In 2010, these are expected to grow to USD 39.8 billion and 17 billion, respectively. **(See Exhibits 1, 2, 3)**

EVS was the brainchild of Alok Aggrawal, former director of IBM's research division – Emerging Business Opportunities, and Marc Vollenweider, former head of McKinsey Knowledge Centre. It was formed in 2000 and started operations from India. Its service offerings range from business research, market research,

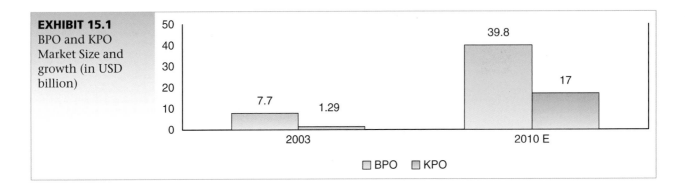

EXHIBIT 15.1
BPO and KPO Market Size and growth (in USD billion)

EXHIBIT 15.2
Opportunities in the KPO Market (2003–2010)
As the KPO industry is booming and expected to grow, it provides companies with many opportunities to tap diverse areas. The following table presents the various opportunities in the KPO industry.

KPO	FY 2003	FY 2010	CAGR (IN %)
Equity, Financial, Insurance Research	0	0.4	N/A
Data Search, Integration and Management	0.3	5.0	50
Research and Information Services in HR	0	0.2	-
Market Research and Competitive Intelligence	0.01	0.4	70
Engineering and Design	0.4	2.0	29
Animation and Simulation Services	0.1	1.4	46
Paralegal Content and Services	0	0.3	N/A
Medical Content and Services	0	0.3	N/A
Remote Education and Publishing	0	2.0	N/A
Biotech and Pharmaceuticals (CRO, lead optimization, and manufacturing processes)	0.28	3.0	40
Research and Development	0.2	2.0	39
Total (USD Billion)	**1.29**	**17.0**	**46**

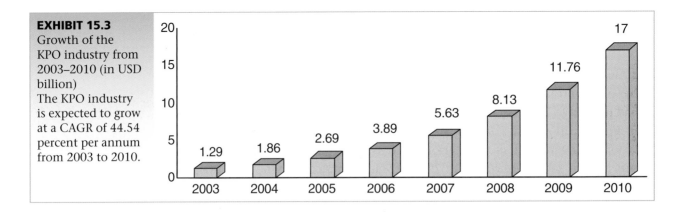

EXHIBIT 15.3
Growth of the KPO industry from 2003–2010 (in USD billion)
The KPO industry is expected to grow at a CAGR of 44.54 percent per annum from 2003 to 2010.

investment research, and intellectual property research to financial and data analytics. It also acts as a back-end knowledge aggregator for its clients. EVS focuses on helping clients take appropriate and timely decisions relating to strategy, value chain, marketing, investment, and numerous other issues that are of fundamental importance for global businesses.

Marc remembers EVS' growth from a four-employee company operating out of a single-room office in Delhi, India. He also recollects how difficult it was to sell the novel concept of KPO to clients. They were initially unwilling to back this untested concept and outsource research work, owing to strategic concerns such as data security, capabilities of EVS, etc. The founders of the company had to invest every bit of their vast experience, personal contacts, and communication skills to assure the clients that EVS would maintain the highest levels of confidentiality and deliver value-added results.

Within a span of six years, not only has EVS handled more than 500 clients across sectors ranging from Fortune 500 companies, market research companies, venture capital firms, and investment banks to small and medium enterprises, the company's operational philosophy has also witnessed a logical evolution. Initially, EVS concentrated on hiring client executives (CEs) with general experience; however, over time it decided to hire CEs with specialized sales experience across different service lines. The following figure illustrates the relationship between EVS, the CE's and the clients.

Client Executives sell EVS' services to clients worldwide, and they are critical for the company's success. They act as single points of contact between the company and clients and work as its brand ambassadors in the market. In 2006, the company has more than 40 CEs worldwide on its rolls, up from 8 in 2003. CEs meet with prospective clients and understand their research requirements. Subsequently, they chart out projects tailored to offer knowledge assistance to clients at competitive costs. They then convince clients about EVS' expertise and the value addition that it can offer them. They also complement EVS' research teams by offering suggestions on the methodology and content of projects. However, Marc believes that the role of CEs goes beyond client delight. CEs have to necessarily think of new initiatives whereby they establish an ongoing relationship with clients. Since EVS understands that CEs cannot meet their goals without adequate support from the company, EVS has already begun efforts in this direction. These efforts are mainly in the areas of building operational efficiency,

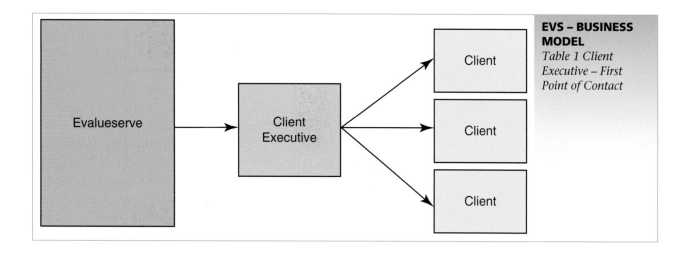

EVS – BUSINESS MODEL
Table 1 Client Executive – First Point of Contact

enabling global expansion, providing comprehensive solutions, and employing appropriate marketing efforts.

KEY DIVISIONS OF EVS

Business Research (BR): This division collects information through primary (i.e., interviews, phone) and secondary research (i.e., databases). It offers research expertise in the areas of market study and segment analysis, profiling and analyzing of companies/industries, product and value chain analysis, sector monitoring.

Intellectual Property (IP): The division's service lines include patent drafting, litigation, licensing, landscaping, prior art searching, asset management, and IP strategic consulting.

Market Research (MR): This business segment is involved in providing end-to-end market research services through designing questionnaires, identifying target respondents, and conducting interviews.

Investment Research (IR): This business division caters to big investment banks and other companies engaged in financial analysis. It also offers its research services from the point of view of buy side, sell side, corporate finance, and others.

Financial Analytics and Data Analytics (FA/DA). This particular division provides research services in the areas of data analytics, mathematical modelling, and financial analytics.

ORGANIZATIONAL EFFICIENCY

Over the years, EVS has built a successful operational model, clearly defining processes in a bid to help employees execute projects with minimum fuss. Standard procedures have been concretized for each and every operation, encompassing Requests for Proposal (RFP) to project closures. All operations are designed to be compatible with four sacrosanct values – Quality, Confidentiality, Flexibility, and Convenience, which are the main value propositions of EVS to its clients. To achieve the highest quality levels, EVS has developed a feedback/recovery mechanism to trace any abnormality in the quality of its deliverables. Performance benchmarking on a wide spectrum of issues forms an integral part of the company's operational schema. Further, it employs a four-step quality check process (self quality check, peer-to-peer quality check, project manager quality check, and finally, editorial quality check) for all documents. It also encourages its employees to attend various training modules and seminars. To maintain the confidentiality of client-specific data, EVS has put in place a mechanism called the EVS Confidentiality Management Systems (ECMS). This system encompasses various procedures relating to the operational, legal, and technical aspects of the organization.

This focus on building an innovative world class company is exemplified by the recognition EVS has received. EVS is the recipient of several awards, which include the NASSCOM Business Model Innovation Category Award and the Red Herring Top 100 Asia Award for 2006. It has also received ISO 27001 certification in the area of organizational security.

MARKETING EFFORTS

Although the company does not employ direct marketing efforts, it has been actively pursuing indirect marketing efforts. It regularly publishes white papers on promising businesses, venture capital scenarios, etc., and analyzes, dissects, and comments critically on these topics. These papers are widely circulated, quoted globally, and shared with EVS' clients. The company's Public Relations team organizes regular external communication initiatives, such as presentations by company executives at industry conferences and seminars, and focuses on disseminating word-of-mouth goodwill by highlighting the company's strict adherence to work ethics and quality.

GLOBAL EXPANSION PLANS

Evalueserve has been expanding its operations across various regions by setting up sales offices in North and South America, Europe, and the Asia Pacific, and doubling revenues each year. Initially, companies based in the US and Europe hired EVS' services to study the fast-growing East Asian economies, such as China, Taiwan, and Japan. To cater to such emergent needs, EVS set up its first delivery centre outside India in Shanghai, China. A combination of favourable factors made Shanghai the most appropriate destination for setting up an office. EVS Commercial Advisory Company (Shanghai) Ltd., China, started its operations in September 2005. To better align itself with different time zones and offer research services in multiple languages, the company opened another research centre in Chile in November 2006. To support its global growth, EVS has started adding international analysts to its workforce. **(Exhibit 4)**

CHALLENGING FUTURE

Unlike most other players in the KPO industry offering services in one, two, or three business lines, EVS offers services across five domains. Therefore, though some players exist in EVS' business segments, there are no players offering services across all the five business domains so for but this might change in the future. Some of the other players in the KPO industry are Adventity, Integreon, Progeon, Pipal Research and Inductis.

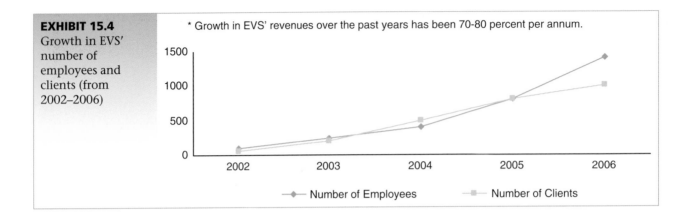

EXHIBIT 15.4
Growth in EVS'
number of
employees and
clients (from
2002–2006)

Evalueserve also plans to foray into new business lines such as Legal Processes Outsourcing (LPO). This business will revolve around services including document discovery, proofreading, administrative support, and asset management. Another future focus area of EVS is to expand its Marketing and Selling Operations (MSO), which consists of providing sales support, at competitive costs, to its clients in selling their services. The company plans to enter new markets either with its existing products or new products. The company's top management is also evaluating inorganic growth options and is likely to float an IPO in the next couple of years as it is confident that it can maintain its leadership position in the KPO domain.

Its confidence primarily stems from the distinct advantage India enjoys of having a large low-cost though skilled English-speaking workforce, as compared to most western competitors. For example, drafting and filing of patent applications in India costs less than 50 percent of that in the US, i.e., USD 10,000-15,000. This is primarily because of the substantial difference in salaries between similarly educated and skilled professionals in the western world and India. In spite of Indian salaries are rising by 15-20 percent per annum and western salaries by 5 percent, there will remain an immense gulf between the absolute numbers for a few years. The Indian wage scenario being thus, concerns regarding the country sustainable cost advantage may stay for a few years, thus EVS too will continue to maintain and sustain its cost advantage as a leading KPO player.

As Marc reminisces, he cannot escape the tide of mixed feelings over EVS' dizzying growth. It took fewer than eight months for the company to break even, and since then, it has witnessed unparalleled growth in revenues, clientele, and workforce. In fact, so far, it has emerged as the largest player in this growing market with almost no direct competitor matching its growth, size, and offerings. However, Evalueserve cannot afford to relax because of the "real competition" it is now facing. Marc is aware that the "pie" has attracted new competitors and might be shared with others. Other concerns were increasing competition, the possibility of some clients' in-sourcing research, sustaining its growth, and hiring the right employees. EVS will also have to work toward providing continuously superior quality as it enters new segments, offers new product lines and establishes offices in other markets.

SUMMARY

This case outlines Evalueserve, a company in the Service Marketing and more specifically in the Knowledge Outsourcing Industry, making its transition from a small start-up company to a global one in only six years. It presents an emerging industry, the Knowledge Operations Processing (KPO) industry, and shows how it has emerged a leader by exploiting its first-mover advantage. The case highlights the decisions/strategies that were employed to provide EVS with operational stability and sustainability thanks of having a cost-advantages due to it's location. It outlines the emerging challenges faced by EVS due to the growth witnessed by this industry and the ever-increasing competition. It outlines the strategic marketing options Evalueserve can follow in terms of market, segment, and product decisions.

POSSIBLE FRAMEWORKS

The case can be discussed within various frameworks such as SWOT analysis, Porter 5-forces, BCG Matrix, McKinsey 7-S framework, Ansoffs-Matrix, Market Entry Modes, Marketing Mix, Product Life cycle, among others.

POSSIBLE CASE QUESTIONS

1. Outline the competitive landscape of the KPO industry. Has the increasing competition harmed Evalueserve or helped it?
2. Over time, how sustainable is Evalueserve cost advantage of in the KPO industry?
3. Define 7 Ps of Service Marketing for Evalueserve; which is the most important P for the company?
4. What extra marketing effort should Evalueserve employ to maintain its leadership in the KPO industry?
5. Is Evalueserve's CE model the best way of selling its services?
6. In the BCG Matrix, where does Evalueserve lie and for how long will it be able to maintain its current position, considering the growth of the KPO industry, it's competitors. (See Exhibits 3 and 4)

NOTES

1   Authors: Dr. M. Fetscherin, Rollins College, International Business Department & S. Gupta, S. Gupta, G. Sharma, N. Seth, V. Suri Evaluserve Inc.

2   KPOs involve businesses outsourcing their high-end knowledge-intensive business processes to low-wage destinations, which require significant domain expertise in the areas of financial services, telecom, pharmaceuticals and bio-technology, energy, consumer products, etc. In comparison to BPOs (Business Process Outsourcing), which perform non core activities, KPOs deliver higher value to organizations that offshore their domain-based processes, thereby enhancing BPOs' traditional cost-quality paradigm. Since Os create value for their clients by providing business expertise rather than process expertise, KPOs entail carrying out processes that demand advanced analytical and technical skills as well as decisive judgment.

CHAPTER 16

Defining Ethics and Corporate Social Responsibility in the International Marketplace

"We need to address transparency, accountability, and institutional capacity. And let's not mince words: we need to deal with the cancer of corruption."

James Wolfensohn, President of the World Bank,
Annual Meeting 1996

"The unfolding financial crisis has shown us just how integrated the world's markets have become. Accountability must be guaranteed across borders, include improved risk management and reach all the way down a company's supply chain."

Cobus de Swardt, Transparency International, Managing Director.

LEARNING OBJECTIVES

After Reading This Chapter, You Should Be Able to:

- Understand what the ethics of doing business abroad are.
- Differentiate between the law and ethics.
- Determine whether there are universal ethical standards.
- Argue whether an MNC can be an ethical citizen.
- Determine what the social responsibility of an MNC is.
- Argue whether a company can afford not to be ethical.

You are the newly appointed manager of ABC (Ltd.) Company's subsidiary in Manila, the Philippines. Your company manufactures and distributes educational equipment for high schools, including audio-visual teaching materials. A large shipment worth about €50,000 has just arrived and is waiting to be released at customs. The customs authorities have informed you that there are "administrative delays" preventing the release of the equipment. After a week, you are told that "delays" are still in force. When you ask the customs official in charge when the equipment will be released, he replied that it is hard to say, but, if you would make a small donation to the union vacation fund, it would be possible to secure a prompt release. You know that the shipment is being stored in an unsecure place and theft is certainly a possibility. Also, many school children are in need of the educational equipment. Payments to government officials are frequent in this country in order to "prioritize" decision-making. They are not illegal here. However, you are also aware that your home government has anti-bribery legislation that could apply to this situation and possibly result in a fine for your company. What alternatives are there to this dilemma? What should you do?

Cases like the above occur only too frequently in international commerce. The solutions to such dilemmas are all the more difficult when both parties come from different ethical cultures. This chapter deals with providing a framework that will help with dealing with dilemmas in a global environment and provide a response that is acceptable to both sides. First, let us review some of the costs that accrue from unethical practices such as bribery and corruption.

THE COST OF DOING BAD BUSINESS

Taking the path of least resistance to requests for bribes, companies and individuals risk the chance of being caught and subjected to investigation, bad public relations, and if convicted, fines and even imprisonment. While there are many examples of firms and individuals being fined for illegal payments (Case #1), there are examples of fines being levied for lacking proper safeguards against such practices (Case # 2).

Case #1: An employee of CBRN Team, which is a UK consulting firm, and an official of the Ugandan government pleaded guilty to bribery charges stemming from a payment by the British firm in order to secure a contract to advise the Presidential Guard of Uganda. The UK Serious Fraud Office gave the CBRN employee a suspended sentence, while the Ugandan official was sentenced to serve a year in prison.
Source: Copyright © 2008 FBIC, www.badfaithinsurance.org [Accessed: May 10, 2009].

Case #2: A subsidiary of Aon Ltd. (UK) the world's largest insurance broker, was fined £5.25 million ($7.9 million) by Britain's Financial Services Authority for not having sufficient anti-bribery controls. Aon Ltd. allegedly made "suspicious payments" totaling approximately $7 million to overseas companies in countries such as Indonesia, Vietnam, Bahrain, and Burma from 2005 through 2007.
Source: www.growthbusiness.co.uk/channels/growth-strategies/legal-advice/ 996112/the-global-bribery- [Accessed: May 10, 2009].

These two examples show that there are regulatory agencies at the country level that monitor bribery and corruption behavior on the part of companies and individuals. As we will learn later, governments and multinational organizations such as the United Nations and the International Monetary Fund (IMF) monitor such activities. However, monitoring illegal and unethical activities starts at home. Companies have to monitor themselves, and many do. Bribery and corruption on a global scale are activities that cannot be ignored. According to the US Department of Commerce, bribery affected the outcome of 294 international contracts amounting to $145 billion over a five-year period from 1994 to 1999. In another area of the world, the Asian Development Bank estimated that the "corruption tax" in Asia cost governments approximately 50 percent of their tax revenues.[1]

These sums are equivalent to the GDP of developed countries such as the UK, Italy, and Canada! According to Transparency International, the cost of bribery alone amounts to $1 trillion annually.[2] The cost of corruption equals more than five percent of global GDP ($2.6 trillion) according to the World Economic Forum and the World Bank. In addition to paying fines and penalties, these costs may include lost business, reputational damage, and organizational turmoil.[3] There are no estimates of worldwide embezzlement of public funds. However, there are indications that Suharto embezzled between $15–35 billion in Indonesia, Marcos in the Philippines, Mobutu in Zaire and Abacha in Nigeria may have embezzled up to $5 billion each.[4] However, there are those who claim that some of these costs may be offset by the creation of firm value through corruption. Among detected and prosecuted bribery cases, Cheung et al. (2012) found that a $1 bribe payment creates $11 firm value.[5]

In one of the world's largest corporate bribery scandals in recent years, German industrial giant Siemens allegedly channeled millions of euros in bribes to customers in Nigeria, Russia, Libya, and other countries to win infrastructure contracts. The *Wall Street Journal* traces the unearthing of the Siemens case across four years of investigations in Switzerland, Liechtenstein, and Germany. After Liechtenstein rolled back banking privacy laws post-9/11, a flurry of transfers to and from offshore firms controlled by Siemens execs caught auditors' attention in 2003. The scandal ballooned as Liechtenstein froze €7.6 million in Siemens assets and German police raided Siemens' offices. Siemens has flagged €1.3 billion in suspicious transactions made from 2000 to 2006.

As shown in Table 16.1, the incidence of payments is greater in developing countries. Bribery and corruption hurt the poor disproportionately—by diverting funds intended for development, undermining a government's ability to provide basic services, feeding inequality and injustice, and discouraging foreign investment and aid.

More than one in four respondents (27 percent) to the *Transparency* bribery survey said they paid a bribe over the past 12 months when accessing key public institutions and services. Of those who reported paying a bribe, 40 percent said they did so "to speed things up," 27 percent said "it was the only way to obtain a service," while 21 percent said they paid a bribe "as a gift, or to express gratitude."

GEO MAP 16.1
Asian Development
Bank
Source: Adapted from:
CIA Maps, The World
Factbook[6]

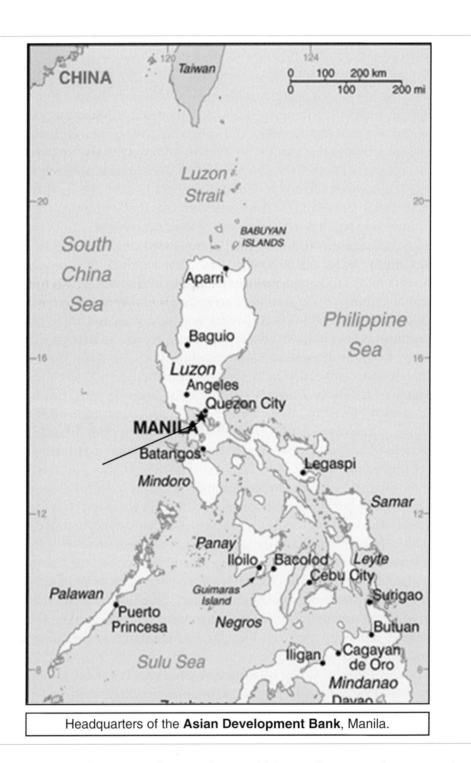

Headquarters of the **Asian Development Bank**, Manila.

The remaining 12 percent of respondents said it was "to get a cheaper service." Political parties are considered the most corrupt institution, followed by the police and the judiciary. Globally, religious institutions are seen as least corrupt. In Israel, Japan, Sudan, and South Sudan, however, religious bodies were perceived to be highly corrupt.

% of	60%+	Cameroon, Kenya, Liberia, Libya, Mozambique, Sierra Leone, Uganda, Zimbabwe, Yemen	**TABLE 16.1** Countries and the Prevalence of Bribery
Respondents Who Report Having Paid Bribes in the	46–60%	Afghanistan, Cambodia, Ghana, India, Senegal, South Africa	
	31–45%	Algeria, Bangladesh, Bolivia, Egypt, Ethiopia, Mexico, Mongolia, Nigeria, Taiwan	
Past Year to Any One of Eight Services	11–30%	Colombia, Cyprus, Czech Republic, Greece, Kosovo, Latvia, Turkey	
	5–10%	Bulgaria, Chile, El Salvador, Estonia, Hungary, Israel, Italy, USA	
	<5%	Australia, Belgium, Canada, Croatia, Denmark, Finland, Georgia, Japan, New Zealand, Norway, Slovenia, South Korea, Spain, Switzerland, UK	

Source: Adapted from: the Transparency International, Global Corruption Barometer, 2013

Bribery and corruption are not the only problems that managers face in a global world. Dishonesty, fraud, occupational health, safety, environmental concerns, and industrial espionage are also prevalent. Employee fraud alone costs firms $600 billion annually in the United States, which amounts to approximately six percent of GDP.[7] While many of these practices are monitored by laws and regulations, they are not uniformly enforced around the world. Therefore, managers of global corporations must have answers to questions like these:

- If ethical mores differ from society to society what rules do you follow?

- How do we do business with integrity in countries where bribery and corruption are widespread?

- How can we develop ethical norms that can guide global marketers and business people to act with integrity and accountability?

ETHICS AND THE LAW

Ethics are behavioral standards determined by society that stipulate how its members should act in a moral manner. Ethical standards vary from society to society, but individuals within the society are expected to maintain these standards. Laws are codes of conduct stipulating how members of a society are *required* to act and are enforced by relevant governance agencies such as the police and courts. Breaking the law carries penalties (fines, prison terms) while disregarding an ethical code may result in sanctions (losing one's job) that are short of criminal proceedings. Law and ethics overlap (Figure 16.1) and what is perceived as unethical may also be illegal (e.g. bribery). In other cases, they do not overlap. In some situations, what is perceived as unethical is still legal (polluting the environment, paying substandard wages), and in others, what is illegal may be perceived as ethical (using company equipment for personal use). In sum, a legal system may not cover all dilemmas concerning "right" and "wrong" (the left side of Figure 16.1). Therefore, the problem of how to behave in such situations falls on ethical codes (the right side of Figure 16.1). There are those who argue that right is synonymous with legal,

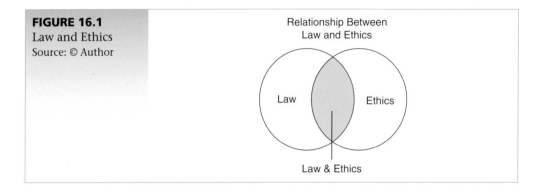

FIGURE 16.1
Law and Ethics
Source: © Author

Relationship Between
Law and Ethics

Law

Ethics

Law & Ethics

FIGURE 16.2
Home and Host
Countries Influence
Ethical Decisions
Source: © Author

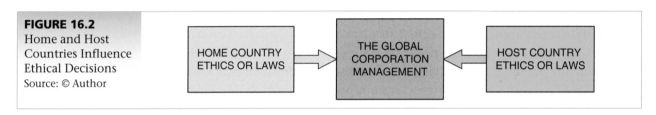

HOME COUNTRY
ETHICS OR LAWS

THE GLOBAL
CORPORATION
MANAGEMENT

HOST COUNTRY
ETHICS OR LAWS

TABLE 16.2
Ethical Philosophies
for Making Ethical
Decisions

Ethical Relativism	Ethical Absolutism	Ethical Universalism
No universal set of ethical standards	**Giving preference to one's own ethical values**	**A set of universally accepted and valid ethical standards**
The ethical nature of an action can only be determined relative to the moral norms of the particular culture where the action takes place. "When in Rome do as the Romans do."	"When in Rome, do what one would do at home."	The ethical nature of an action is independent of cultural settings.

Source: © Author

i.e. whether an action is ethical is not important as long as one does not break the law. In this case, it is the legal system alone that governs behavior. "If it is legal, it is ethical." However, when doing business globally, the question is whose law or whose ethics?

Is it the law in force where a transaction takes place, or the law of the home country? Is it the ethical standard of the home or host country that should be followed, especially in those cases when they differ from one another?

What happens when cultures collide? Whose standards do you follow, your home standards or those of the host country? There are three broad ethical philosophies or alternatives to choose from when doing business outside of one's home country (Table 16.2).

Ethical Relativists may plan globally, but act locally when it comes to ethics. They try to adapt the "When in Rome, do as the Romans do" adage. Ethical Absolutists (some call this Ethical Imperialism) "import" their ethical norms to the countries in which they operate. Generally, they believe that their norms are superior and therefore should be adopted by the host country. Ethical Universalists believe that there are enough universal standards that are found in cultures that vary from one another. These three frameworks suggest that there is no simple answer to the question of what is right and wrong when doing business across different national cultures. This debate leads to questions pertinent to the global community in which MNCs operate: are standards of good and bad relative to the culture and place in which they exist? Are values absolute or could they change over time with each new generation, or management structure, for instance? If they vary, whose ethics should prevail? Should social responsibility practices presuppose the existence of a universal set of values?

> "Companies must help managers distinguish between practices that are merely different and those that are wrong. For relativists, nothing is sacred and nothing is wrong. For absolutists, many things that are different are wrong. Neither extreme illuminates the real world of business decision-making. The answer lies somewhere in between."[8]

A typical dilemma of what to do in a seemingly ethical situation is exemplified by the example of gift-giving, a normal tradition in many non-Western societies. Sharing small gifts in Japanese culture, for instance, is an intrinsic part of business interaction, symbolizing reciprocity and relationship building, although it is commonly misconstrued as bribery by Western corporations and misinterpreted as wrong rather than culturally relative. This sort of dilemma illustrates the importance of context when evaluating different practices, while ensuring that they do not violate universal norms. The solution of a dilemma of this sort would depend on the material value of the gift. One should be able to differentiate between what is clearly a bribe and an acceptable gift.

THE MULTINATIONAL AS A GOOD CORPORATE CITIZEN

The ethical and social responsibility of the multinational corporation (MNC) is of concern to both host and home country. Because of their large size and economic power, the expectation is that their ethical and social behavior should go beyond what is required by law. Social responsibility is a concept of ethics that businesses should act in the interests of society at large, taking into consideration all of its stakeholders and not only stockholders. Thus, the multinational corporation has economic, ethical, legal, and social responsibility to its stakeholders. Therefore, the MNC should integrate core ethical and social responsibility values and goals into its strategic management process.

What is *corporate social responsibility* (CSR)? The European Union Commission defines it as a concept "whereby companies integrate social and environmental concerns in their business operations and their interactions with their stakeholders on a voluntary basis"[9] Likewise, the World Bank views

CSR as a contribution by business to "sustainable economic development working with employees, their families, the local community, and society at large to improve their quality of life, in ways that are both good for business and good for development."[10] The International Labor Organization sees CSR as a way in which enterprises give consideration to the impact of their operations on society and affirm their principles and values both in their own internal methods and processes and in their interaction with other actors.[11] In summary, these definitions imply that CSR goes beyond just being ethical and obeying the law in business practice. It assumes that businesses should contribute to the welfare of all its stakeholders beyond the goal of providing employment and making a profit (some of which should be shared by the community in which the firm operates).

An interesting example of the application of CSR is demonstrated by the following anecdote: the corporation that owned the Chicago Cubs (baseball team) refused to hold night games at Wrigley Field. Although holding night games would likely have increased attendance and profits, the president of the corporation, chewing-gum heir Philip K. Wrigley, believed that baseball should be a "daytime sport" and that installing 30 lights would disturb the peace of the surrounding neighborhood.

What are the CSR views of business management around the world?

While CSR activities and reporting are extensive in developed countries, they are less so in developing and emerging countries. Some of the adoption of CSR activities in non-developed countries is attributed to NGO organizations such as the Global Reporting Initiative and the International Labor Organization (GeoMap 16.2). The Global Reporting Initiative (GRI) is a large NGO, multi-stakeholder network of thousands of experts, in dozens of countries worldwide, who participate in GRI's working groups and governance bodies, use the GRI Guidelines to report,

GEO MAP 16.2
International Labor
Organization
Source: Adapted from:
CIA Maps, The World
Factbook[12]

Headquarters of the **International Labor Organization**, Geneva.

access information in GRI-based reports, or contribute to develop the Reporting Framework in other ways—both formally and informally.[13] Based in Amsterdam, the organization has developed a widely used sustainability reporting framework that has been adopted by 1,500 companies worldwide.

CSR in the BRIC Countries

A study by the Brazilian Institute of Applied Economics showed that about two-thirds of the 445,000 firms surveyed had invested in social programs, while half had intention to increase their involvement.[14] The adoption of CSR programs in Brazil has been attributed to the increase of NGOs operating in the country, a desire by companies to gain more legitimacy and increase customer loyalty, and to the rise of global codes. Some 950 Brazilian companies, which account for annual revenues of approximately 30 percent of the Brazilian GDP and employ roughly 1.2 million people, are members of a local organization, *Instituto Ethos*, a network of businesses dedicated to social responsibility. About 150 companies have signed the United Nations global compact, agreeing to adhere to fundamental principles in the areas of human rights, labor relations, protection of the environment, and the combat of corruption. Nevertheless, a study has shown that the impact of corruption in the public sector between 2002 and 2012 amounted to approximately Reais 40 billion.

Box 16.1 shows an example of the application of CSR in Brazil.

CSR in Russia

During the era of the Soviet Socialist Republics all industry was state-owned. The Soviet economy was based on large industrial plants that encompassed areas that included housing, schooling, and health and recreation facilities for employees and their families. Thus, the industrial complex was socially responsible for its employees. The breakup of the Soviet Union resulted in the privatization of many of these industries, while others remained state-owned. Thus, the industrial complex did not automatically take over the social welfare of employees; this task

Box 16.1 Country-in-Focus: Brazil

Project Plasma, a partnership between Klabin (paper), Tetra Pak (long-life packaging), Alcoa (aluminum), and TSL Ambiental (residue treatment) joined forces to solve a serious environmental problem in a creative and profitable manner. All three had an interest in recycling the three materials that make up long-life packaging (aluminum, paper, and plastic), used mainly for juices, milk, and other beverages. A unique plasma technology enables the total separation between the aluminum and plastic parts of the package. Before, the recycling process separated the paper, but the plastic and aluminum were still bonded together. Now, the three components can be recycled as three raw materials. This technology is a significant improvement on the current carton packaging recycling process. As a result, Brazil has become a world leader thanks to the development of this technology.

Sources: Alcoa, Klabin, Tetra Pak, and Alcoa press releases.

was now the responsibility of government which, because of budgetary constraints, found it difficult to provide aid for recreation, the environment, contributions to charity organizations and the like. To what extent did private business take over the social role of the government?

While Russian businesses have come to realize that CSR is crucial to their sustainability, most effort in this direction is done by large companies such as Norilsk Nickel, Lukoil, Novolipetsk Steel and Yukos (before its takeover by the government), and companies that serve western markets. Two main reasons that constrain the adoption of CSR practices in Russia is the lack of transparency of Russian business and a faulty definition of what CSR is all about. According to one observer, CSR is "thought by Russian top managers to be mainly a tool to managing non-financial risks and improve capitalization via better public image."[15] According to the Center for Political Technologies in Russia, the issue of corporate social responsibility can only be solved through the modernization of state institutions and the creation of civil institutions to monitor the interaction between businesses and the state.

CSR in China

CSR is a relatively new phenomenon in China and the government thus far has not actively promoted it. Chinese CSR initiatives include laws and regulations, governmental instructions and guidelines, and non-governmental standards and organizations. However, the large Chinese government bureaucracy hampers the realization of CSR programs.[16] There are more issues related to safety and intellectual property rights violations for Chinese products (81 percent) than for Indian products (6 percent).[17] China accounts for the largest percentage of all illegal products seized by the US Customs and Border Protection, whereas India is a distant second. However, the government has recently made efforts to improve the relevant laws and market regulations and to expand supervisory practices to decrease irresponsible corporate behavior. Environmental issues have received the most attention, while human rights issues, the least.[18]

The Chinese Federation for Corporate Social Responsibility was launched in Shanghai during 2007 by 13 foreign and domestic companies. China is only at the beginning of forming a viable CSR philosophy and governance. Examples of initiatives and guidelines include the Recommended CSR Standards for Chinese Corporations and the Compilation of Best Practices published by the Chinese Business Council for Sustainable Development as well as the Ministry of commerce guidelines for the preparation of CSR reports. However, CSR guidelines that require companies to address social and environmental considerations alongside the drive for profits remain unfamiliar to most Chinese businesses. The main cause of the Jilin City chemical explosion in 2005 that killed 6 people and wounded others was caused by improper handling of equipment by workers. In the same year another tragedy struck. This time it was the Dongfeng coal mine explosion that resulted in more than a hundred worker deaths. In this case, mine managers did not know about the central government's emergency instructions on mining safety and could not tell how many workers they dismissed immediately following the blast. Such ignorance of work safety, pollution, and educational needs—the underlying cause of thousands of tragedies—exists widely in Chinese industries.[19] Some people argue that it is too early for Chinese companies to embrace the CSR concept, since most businesses are still at the early stages of developing technological know-how and are struggling for their survival. However, as Gary Dirks, president of BP China, has noted, CSR goes beyond simply "charitable efforts" and addresses more fundamental questions of profit-making; therefore, it should be mainstreamed into a company's business model from the get-go, not considered a luxury to add on later. There are optimistic signs, however. The Chinese government and economic organizations are establishing Chinese standards and accreditation criteria of CSR reports and health and safety standards. Western companies operating in China should be aware of and promote CSR standards. Some of this optimism has borne fruit. In 2006, State Grid was the only company in China to file a CSR report. In 2012, 1,722 Chinese companies filed CSR reports. Indeed, almost a quarter of large state-owned enterprises in China filed CSR reports.

According to a survey by the US Department of Commerce, CSR will continue to develop in China, motivated by both government and by citizens, the latter mobilized through social media. As shown in Table 16.3, more companies in China perceive CSR as contributing to competitive advantage, especially among global companies that have to compete not only by formulating business strategy, but also by convincing consumers that environmental considerations are part of their business plan and practice. A case in point is Lenovo shown in Box 16.2.

CSR in India

Spirituality and CSR are deeply rooted in the Indian tradition. Therefore, CSR is not a new phenomenon, but rather it is linked to Indian culture and religion. Social duties and engagement in charity by Indian corporations were often implicit, but over time CSR has become more dominant and broader in scope. Corporate philanthropy is now part of normal business operations and is embedded in corporate activities.[20] India has a long tradition of paternalistic philanthropy. Big family-owned firms, such as Tata, are particularly active in providing basic services, such as schools and health care, for local communities. For example, organizations like *Bharat* Petroleum Corporation Limited, *Maruti Suzuki* India Limited, and *Hindustan* Unilever Limited, adopt villages where they focus on holistic development. They provide better medical and sanitation facilities, build schools and houses, and help the villagers become self-reliant by teaching vocational and business skills.

Table 16.4 shows some examples where CSR has paid dividends to Indian companies.[21] India became the first country to statutorily provide for CSR through The Companies Act (2013), the so-called "2 percent requirement," by inserting provisions on compliance, enforcement, disclosure, and auditing. States that

TABLE 16.3 The Shifting Landscape of CSR in China	Yesterday	What is changing?	Tomorrow
	CSR viewed by government as a **foreign-imposed requirement** with protectionist aims.	Government using CSR to encourage businesses to contribute to "scientific development" and a "harmonious society." Recognition of the limits of audit approach.	**CSR becoming a key factor determining competitive advantage** for companies in China and for China in the global economy. CSR in the area of manufacturing is more focused on **building capacity for environment health and safety (EHS) and HR management as well as local enforcement of environmental and labor laws.**
	Focus **on ensuring supply chain labor and environmental standards** through codes of conduct and audit.	Tightening domestic labor and environmental laws and maturing of enforcement. Partnership and capacity building for labor and environmental compliance.	
	Concern that many international standards initiatives represent **trade and investment barriers**, intentionally or otherwise.	Cautious endorsement and adoption of international standards. Learning and referencing international standards to construct China's CSR framework.	Development of **national standards that are in practice increasingly harmonized** with international standards.
	Multinationals tended to roll out global CSR practices and **signature programs**, while state-owned enterprises have viewed CSR as a matter of accountability to government.	Growing and confident consumers, non-governmental organizations, media, and other local stakeholder groups are making stronger demands on business responsibility.	Increasingly active and demanding consumers and civil society; developing and testing **bottom-up grievance and redress mechanisms.**

Source: Zadek, S., Forstater, M., and Yu, K. 'Corporate responsibility and sustainable economic development in China: Implications for business', Asia US Chamber of Commerce, March 2012, www.uschamber.com [Accessed: April 3, 2013]

Box 16.2 Company-in-Focus: Lenovo China

Lenovo China has been working with Lenovo International to launch their Environmentally Conscious Products program, which integrates environmental management systems with product specifications. It uses ISO 14001 as an environmental management system, which includes end-of-life management, supplier environmental performance, and greenhouse gas emission factors.

Yantai in Shandong Province aims to increase the number of green tourist hotels and economy hotels to promote energy saving and emission reductions. The term "green tourist hotel" refers to a hotel that can adhere to clean production, advocate green consumption, protect the ecological environment, and use resources in a rational way.

Source: Lenovo reports.

---

have companies with revenue of more than 1,000 crore,[22] or those with profits of more than 5 crore, or a net worth of more than 500 crore are required to spend a minimum of 2 percent of their net profits of the preceding three years on rural development and worker training, empowerment of women, promotion of the arts,

				TABLE 16.4
Boosting Profits	*Gujarat Ambuja,* one of the country's leading cement manufacturers, reports that "our efforts to achieve world standards in environment protection have …of substantially improving efficiency and profitability."			CSR in India
Cutting Costs	Reliance Industries energy conservation measures have saved the company 1150 million rupees per annum.			
Increasing Revenues	HLL's Project *Shakti* creates income-generating opportunities for the under-privileged rural women, while giving the company an enhanced access to hitherto unexplored rural areas.			
Strengthening Brand Value	Infosys was among seven international companies to be chosen in the first annual list of "Top Brands with a Conscience."			
Enhancing Reputation	The Oil and Natural Gas Corporation has found that its community development program has "generated goodwill and earned the company the reputation of being a company that cares."			
Improving Morale	*Tata* Steel believes that helping the community also provides a new perspective to its employees, thereby strengthening employee morale.			

Source: Company Reports

COMPANY	REVENUE[1]	AVERAGE PAT[2]	2% OF PAT	**TABLE 16.5**
Indian Oil Corporation	442,459	7,783	156	Ten Largest Companies in India (2012)
Reliance Industries	368,571	21,138	423	
Bharat Petroleum Corporation	223,315	1,438	29	
Hindustan Petroleum Corporation	195,891	1,118	22	
Tata Motors	170,678	8,437	169	
Oil & Natural Gas Corporation	151,121	23,660	473	
State Bank of India	147,197	13,056	261	
Tata Steel	135,976	3,895	78	
PNB Gilts	104,628	29	1	
Hindalco Industries	82,549	3,597	72	

[1] Revenue figures are indicative of the company's financial performance in financial year 2012. All figures are in Rs Crore and have been rounded off to the nearest decimal point.

[2] Average (last three years) profit after tax.

Source: http://forbesindia.com/article/real-issue/csr-report-card-where-companies-stand/34893/0#ixzz381c8jFXe [Accessed: March 4, 2013]

and road safety. A company falling in the above financial categories must appoint a committee to monitor its CSR activities and include its findings in the company's annual reports.[23]

Table 16.5 lists the ten largest Indian companies' revenues and net profit in 2012 (before the Companies Act of 2013). These companies would have had to allocate a total of 1684 crore for CSR if the Act was in place at the end of 2012. In any case, the example affords a glimpse of the amount of corporate contributions that will occur in following years.

CAN A COMPANY AFFORD NOT TO BE ETHICAL?

Maintaining an ethical stance in all situations may be difficult. An anonymous reader of a business magazine commented in the following way to an article supporting ethics in a global organization:

> Ethics do differ around the world. In some countries a bribe is required to do business and in others it is illegal. The only thing to do is follow your own country practices and live with the results.
>
> Source: www.getinternationalclients.com, May 15, 2009.

A study[24] of between 41 and 86 companies in the UK taken from the FTSE 350 for which full and comparable company data was available for the years 1997–2001 was divided into two cohorts: those who have had codes of ethics/conduct/principles for five years or more and those who explicitly said they did not. The results showed that:

- Regarding financial performance, from three of the four measures of corporate value used in this study (EVA, MVA, and P/E ratio) it was found that those companies in the sample with a code of ethics had, over the period 1997–2001, outperformed a similar-sized group who said they did not have a code.

- Companies with a code of ethics generated significantly more economic added value (EVA) and market added value (MVA) in the years 1997–2000, than those without codes.

- Companies with a code of ethics experienced far less P/E volatility over a four-year period, than those without them. This suggests that they may be a more secure investment in the longer term. Other research has suggested that a stable P/E ratio tends to attract capital at below average cost; having a code may be said to be a significant indicator of consistent management.

- The indicator that showed a different result pattern to the others was Return on Capital Employed (ROCE). No discernible difference was found in ROCE between those with or without a code for 1997–98. However, from 1999 to 2001 there was a clear (approximately 50 percent) increase in the average return of those with codes while those without a code fell during this period.

Some academic work has been done in the United States comparing the long-term added value of corporations with business ethics policies (e.g. codes of ethics) with those who do not have them. It indicated that there is a correlation between those with a reputation for integrity and the growth of long-term shareholder value. A 2006 study of nearly 100 research studies that investigated the relationship between corporate performance and ethics found:[25]

- In the 80 studies evaluating whether corporate social performance contributes to corporate financial performance, 53 percent of them point to a positive relationship. No relationship is identified in 24 percent of the studies, 4 percent find a negative relationship, and the remaining 19 percent of the studies yield mixed results.

- Of the 19 studies evaluating corporate social performance as an outcome of financial performance, 68 percent identify a positive relationship, with 16 percent showing no relationship, and 16 percent providing mixed results.

Obeua Persons[26] investigated two research questions: (1) what are characteristics of companies that have not adopted a written code of ethics for their principal officers such as the chief executive officer (CEO), and (2) what is an effect of not having such a code on these firms' financial performance? Analysis for the first question indicates that a firm with no ethics code had poorer financial performance; the analysis for the second question suggests that not having a code of ethics for principal officers could potentially increase a likelihood of poorer financial performance because stakeholders likely perceive having no ethics code as a negative reflection of the CEO ethical values.

Studies have found that ethical behavior has less impact on corporate performance in the short run than in the long run. An informal survey of a group of 51 employees of Hungarian companies from the fields of advertising, logistics, packaging, travel, recruitment and a few others, found that 67 percent of companies in Hungary that do business legally and ethically are more successful than other companies in the long term, but may be less successful in the short term.[27]

A study of firms in the UK examined the impact of ethical identity on their financial performance by comparing two dimensions of a firm's ethical identity: corporate applied ethics (CAE) and corporate revealed ethics (CRE). Since most companies have a revealed code of ethics, those companies who specifically provided training on their code of ethics to their employees were categorized as those with corporate applied ethics. It also tested whether business ethics has a stronger influence on accounting measures than on market measures. Corporate financial performance was measured using both accounting-based and market-based indicators over a five-year period (2001–5). It was found that in the short run, there was no significant difference between the financial performances of the companies in both categories, while in the long run; companies with CAE significantly outperformed those with CRE. Also, this study found an indication that accounting measures are more influenced by business ethics than market measures.[28] In effect, the ethics code is a policy statement that employees are expected to follow. However, a code in itself is not sufficient; it has to have monitoring features and someone who is responsible for overseeing that the code is implemented. The *Sarbanes–Oxley Act* requires a company to publicly disclose their code of ethics if their stock is traded under the auspices of the Securities Exchange Act of 1934.

SOCIAL RESPONSIBILITY PAYS

Being a socially responsible corporation can provide a number of dividends to the firm. In fact, the long-term survival of many firms depends on its contribution to society beyond the economic welfare of its stakeholders. If society collapses, so does the firm. From an economic perspective, there are many unmet needs in the market such as social and environmental challenges that can be addressed and solved with business solutions. Moreover, the reputation of the firm can be enhanced by being socially conscious. In addition, more and more consumers make their purchasing decisions partly on the basis of the social reputation of the

FIGURE 16.3
Who's Doing Well by Doing Good
Source: Adapted from: Pete Engardio, 'Beyond the green corporation', *BusinessWeek*, January 29, 2007, pp. 50–64. Reprinted with Permission

Who's Doing Well by Doing Good

SOME LEADERS What does it mean to say a company, its products, or its processes are "sustainable"? Here is a list of top-rated companies by industry:

AUTOMOBILES		COMMUNICATIONS EQUIPMENT	
TOYOTA	The maker of the top-selling Prius hybrid leads in developing efficient gas-electric vehicles.	NOKIA	Makes phones for handicapped and low-income consumers. A leader in phasing out toxic materials.
RENAULT	Integrates sustainability throughout organization. Has fuel-efficient cars and factories.	ERICSSON	Eco-friendly initiatives include wind- and fuel-cell-powered telecom systems in Nigerian villages.
VOLKSWAGEN	A market leader in small cars and clean diesel technologies.	MOTOROLA	Good disclosure of environmental data. Takes back used equipment in Mexico, U.S., and Europe.

COMPUTERS & PERIPHERALS		FINANCIAL SERVICES	
HEWLETT-PACKARD	Despite board turmoil, the company rates high on ecological standards and digital tech for the poor.	ABN AMRO	Involved in carbon-emissions trading. Finances everything from micro enterprises to biomass fuels.
TOSHIBA	At forefront of developing eco-efficient products, such as fuel cells for notebook PC batteries.	HSBC	Lending guidelines for forestry, freshwater, and chemical sectors factor in social, ecological risks.
DELL	Among the first U.S. PC makers to take hardware back from consumers and recycle it for free.	ING	Weighs sustainability in project finance. Helps developing nations improve financial institutions.

HEALTH CARE		HOUSEHOLD DURABLES	
FRESENIUS MEDICAL CARE	Discloses costs of its patient treatment in terms of energy and water use and waste generated.	PHILIPS ELECTRONICS	Top innovator of energy-saving appliances, lighting, and medical gear and goods for developing world.
IMS HEALTH	Places unusual emphasis on environmental issues in its global health consulting work.	SONY	Is ahead on green issues and ensuring quality, safety, and labor standards of global suppliers.
QUEST DIAGNOSTICS	Has diversity program promoting businesses owned by minorities, women, and veterans.	MATSUSHITA ELECTRIC	State-of-the-art green products. Eliminated 96% of the most toxic substances in its global operations.

OIL & GAS		PHARMACEUTICALS	
ROYAL DUTCH SHELL	Since Nigerian human rights woes in '90s, leads in community relations. Invests in wind and solar.	ROCHE	Committed to improving access to medicine in poor nations. Invests in drug research for Third World.
NORSK HYDRO	Cut greenhouse gas emissions 32% since 1990. Strong in assessing social, environmental impact.	NOVO NORDISK	Sells diabetes drugs in poor nations at deep discounts. Helps upgrade clinics, public education.
SUNCOR ENERGY	Ties with aboriginals help it deal with social and ecological issues in Canada's far north.	GLAXO-SMITHKLINE	One of few pharmas to devote R&D to malaria and T.B. First to offer AIDS drugs at cost.

RETAIL		UTILITIES	
MARKS & SPENCER	Buys local product to cut transit costs and fuel use. Good wages and benefits help retain staff.	FPL	Largest U.S. solar generator. Has 40% of wind-power capacity. Strong shareholder relations.
HOME RETAIL GROUP	High overall corporate responsibility standards have led to strong consumer and staff loyalty.	IBERDROLA	Since Scottish Power takeover, renewable energy accounts for 17% of capacity. Wants that to grow.
AEON	Environmental accounting has saved $5.6 million. Good employee policies in China and SE Asia.	SCOTTISH & SOUTHERN	Aggressively discloses environmental risk, including air pollution and climate change.

SOME LAGGARDS Concentrating on the bottom line makes companies postpone important changes. It can also lead to poor public relations. Here are a few companies that received lower marks:

ALLEGHENY ENERGY Reliance on coal poses risk if U.S. passes greenhouse gas rules.

BANK OF CHINA Hit by recent corruption cases, but bank says it has since improved governance.

GENERAL MOTORS Trails Toyota and Honda in fuel-efficient cars. High reliance on SUVs.

NINTENDO Slow to grapple with how emerging environmental, safety, and labor standards will affect offshore suppliers.

PETROCHINA Lacks transparent environmental programs. Safety record includes fatal gas leak and benzene plant explosion.

SURGUTNEFTEGAZ Plagued by shareholder suits. Lacks public environmental policy.

WAL-MART The mass retailer has made great strides with ambitious green initiatives, but the company's image remains tarnished by criticisms of labor and offshore sourcing practices.

Data: Innovest Strategic Value Advisors

Source: Adapted from Pete Engardio, "Beyond the Green Corporation," BusinessWeek, January 29, 2007, pp. 50–64. Reprinted with permission.

firm. Internally, a firm's good reputation will have an impact on its organizational culture and ethics.

Are Consumers Willing to Share in the Cost of Environmental Protection and Sustainability?

While business firms are being required to bear some of the cost of environmental and social programs (such as pollution controls) or to voluntarily absorb some of these costs, will consumers be willing to do their part by preferring the products and services of those firms whom they believe are carrying out a socially responsible program?

A survey carried out by the Nielsen Corporation consulting firm found that there is considerable willingness by consumers around the world to pay extra for products and services from environmentally-friendly firms. What is more surprising from the results is that respondents from Latin America, Asia-Pacific, and the Middle East-Africa had a higher rate of willingness than the global average and respondents from North America and Europe. This is an indication that social responsibility has become important in emerging economies as well as in developed countries.

ANTI-BRIBERY AGREEMENTS AND LEGISLATION

The Fight Against Corruption and Bribery

There are two major factors that motivate corruption and bribery: monetary gain and weak governance. While the monetary motive is difficult to remove, there is much that can be done to improve governance. There are three main organizations that have the resources to monitor and prevent corruption and bribery: governments, non-governmental organizations, and business firms. Before the 1990s there were few non-governmental agencies that dealt with these problems; since then some non-governmental organizations were formed like Transparency International, while conventions were enacted by existing bodies such as the OECD (Organization for Economic Cooperation and Development) and the UN. Table 16.6 shows some of these developments chronologically.

One major non-governmental organization is *Transparency International* (TI), a global network headquartered in Germany with more than 90 national chapters and chapters-in-formation around the world. These chapters bring together relevant stakeholders from government, civil society, business, and the media to promote transparency in elections, in public administration, in procurement and in business. TI's global network of chapters and contacts also use advocacy campaigns to lobby governments to implement anti-corruption reforms. TI publishes a number of surveys that measure the extent of corruption and bribery including the Corruption Perception Index (CPI), Bribe Payers Index and Global Corruption Barometer. The 2008 CPI ranks 180 countries in terms of perceived levels of corruption, as

TABLE 16.6 Anti-Bribery Organizations	**Anti-Bribery Organizations**	
	1993	Transparency International Established
	1995	Transparency International Corruption Perception Index
	1997	OECD Bribery Convention
	1999	Transparency International Bribe Payers Survey
	2001	Transparency International Global Corruption Report
	2003	UN Convention Against Corruption

FIGURE 16.4
2014 Corruption Perceptions Index
Source: Transparency International, Reproduced with Permission

determined by expert assessments and opinion surveys; the TI Bribe Payers Index evaluates the supply side of corruption—the likelihood of firms from the world's industrialized countries to offer or pay bribes abroad; while the Global Corruption Barometer is a survey that assesses general public attitudes towards and experience with corruption in dozens of countries around the world.

Figure 16.4 shows the 2014 CPI rankings. The three least corrupt countries are Denmark, New Zealand, and Finland, while the most corrupt are Afghanistan, North Korea, and Somalia. In the Bribe Payers Index, of the 22 countries surveyed, the firms least likely to bribe when operating abroad are headquartered in the Netherlands, Switzerland, and Belgium, in that order, while firms headquartered in Mexico, China, and Russia, are the most likely to bribe when operating abroad.

Note that companies operating in these countries are not necessarily owned by nationals but could also be affiliates of multinationals.[29]

The OECD Anti-Bribery Convention

The OECD Anti-Bribery Convention establishes legally binding standards to make bribery of foreign public officials in international business transactions a criminal offense and provides for a host of related measures that make this effective. The 34 OECD member countries and seven non-member countries— Argentina, Brazil, Bulgaria, Columbia, Latvia, Russia, and South Africa—have adopted this convention. The convention forbids payments to public officials, elected or appointed, in order to obtain business favors. Such payment is a criminal offense under the convention. Enforcement of the convention is the responsibility of the signatory countries that are expected to enact legislation dealing with such activities. While the OECD does not have the authority to implement the convention, it does monitor the effectiveness of legislation in force by member countries. This monitoring does have weight as exemplified by the United Kingdom's Serious Fraud Office. The UK Serious Fraud Office's decision to drop an investigation into BAE Systems over bribery allegations relating to a £43 billion arms deal with Saudi Arabia, and other alleged corruption cases, led to an investigation by the OECD that concluded that reform was urgently needed in the UK to address "systemic deficiencies" in the legal system.

The report sharply criticized the UK for failing to bring its anti-bribery laws into line with its international obligations under the *OECD Anti-Bribery Convention* and urged the rapid introduction of new legislation. Current UK laws made it very difficult for prosecutors to bring an effective case against a company for alleged bribery offenses, the OECD said. The criticism was a major factor in the enactment of the Bribery Bill, making it a criminal offense to offer a bribe at home or abroad.

UN Global Compact

The UN Global Compact is a strategic policy initiative for businesses that are committed to aligning their operations and strategies with ten universally accepted principles in the areas of human rights, labor, environment, and anti-corruption. By doing so, business, as a primary driver of globalization, can help ensure that markets, commerce, technology, and finance advance in ways that benefit economies and societies everywhere. Endorsed by chief executives, the Global Compact is a practical framework for the development, implementation, and disclosure of sustainability policies and practices. The Global Compact Principle 10 relating to corruption states that: "Businesses should work against corruption in all its forms, including extortion and bribery." The call to action is an appeal by the private sector to governments to promote anti-corruption measures and to implement policies that will establish systems of good governance. As of September 2014, 146 companies from 58 countries have signed the

TABLE 16.7 Examples of Signatories to the "Call"	Company	Country	Company	Country
		Developed		*Emerging*
	Daimler	Germany	Cementos Argos, S.A.	Colombia
	Danfoss A/S	Denmark	Finlay Limited	Bangladesh
	Dow Chemicals	USA	FLOR IBIS	Madagascar
	Nestle	Switzerland	Hashem Brothers	Egypt
	Sumitomo	Japan	Pain D'Or, S.A.	Bulgaria
	Walmart Stores Inc.	USA	SIVECO	Romania
	Whirlpool, S.A.	Brazil	Versopub Ltee	Mauritius

Source: https://www.unglobalcompact.org/docs/issues_doc/Anti-Corruption/call-to-action-global-development-agenda-signatories.pdf

"call." Examples of signatory companies from both developed and emerging countries are shown in Table 16.7.

Companies signing the call to action are expected, but not obligated to:

- integrate anti-corruption efforts into their business and operational strategies and organizational culture;

- adopt zero-tolerance of bribery and corruption;

- share good practices in the fight against corruption;

- engage with other businesses and stakeholders through the UN Global Compact;

- engage in policy dialogue to encourage more robust disclosure, transparency, and enforcement mechanisms.[30]

Has the UN Global Compact been effective in combating corruption? A major question about the effectiveness of the Global Compact is whether it should have more regulatory power to discipline companies that do not live up to its principles or is it more important to have a low requirement for participation so as to engage the maximum number of companies? According to *The Guardian* newspaper: "As with all voluntary corporate responsibility initiatives, the Global Compact is open to charges that …[it] is insufficiently transparent about participant performance … [however] for all its weaknesses and challenges, the UN Global Compact has changed the discourse on corporate responsibility forever and for the better."[31]

UN Convention Against Corruption

The UN Convention was adopted by the General Assembly of the United Nations on October 2003 and prohibits corruption in both the public and private sectors, although the prohibition concerning the private sector is not mandatory. One hundred and forty countries are signatories. The convention is the legal foundation for the Global Principle 10 mentioned before. The convention covers four areas: prevention, criminalization, anti-corruption policies, and coordination for implementation. Corruption also includes money laundering embezzlement. Embezzlement is a sensitive issue because it raises questions about public officials that live beyond their means in expensive housing and have egregious life-styles. However, the convention calls for an investigation whenever such asymmetries arise. International cooperation also calls for repatriation of assets that have been transferred illicitly to another country. The UN Convention has limitations. It does not cover bribery in the private sector, nor political corruption. Moreover, the UN does not have authority to enforce state compliance with the rules of the convention; it only serves as a watchdog agency that leaves enforcement to the countries involved.

Government Anti-Corruption and Bribery Enforcement

Governments have a key role to play in ensuring that foreign bribery is stopped at the source—and by making good on commitments to prevent and prosecute such practices. Some governments have enacted anti-corruption and bribery legislation in accordance with the OECD and UN conventions. Some examples follow.

US Foreign Corrupt Practices Act of 1977

The United States was the first country to enact anti-corruption legislation. The Foreign Corrupt Practices Act (FCPA) contains two major provisions. First, its anti-bribery provision makes it illegal to bribe foreign officials to retain or obtain business. Its second provision requires companies to make and keep books, records, and accounts that accurately and fairly reflect their transactions. Companies are also required to maintain a system of controls that can provide reasonable assurances of the propriety and legality of those transactions.

The FCPA began to take on a higher profile in the early 2000s. One key factor of this was the passage of the *Sarbanes–Oxley Act of 2002*, which emphasized greater corporate transparency, senior management accountability, enhanced control systems, and whistle-blower protections. The increased focus on *Sarbanes–Oxley* requirements and the additional resources dedicated to implementing them in many instances led to the discovery of improper payments and of control and compliance weaknesses that enabled such payments to go undetected. Moreover, companies sought to reduce their potential liability for violations found by voluntarily disclosing such conduct to the authorities and pledging to conduct thorough investigations, report the results of such investigations to the government, and remediate the gaps in their control structures.[32]

The number of FCPA investigations and cases brought by the Department of Justice and the Securities and Exchange Commission grew from 9 in 2003 to 79 in 2010. Similarly, corporate FCPA anti-bribery prosecutions and enforcement actions rose from 5 in 2004 to 8 in 2013.[33]

UK Bribery Act

The Bribery Act:

- Makes it a criminal offense to give, promise, or offer a bribe, and to request, agree to receive, or accept a bribe either at home or abroad. The measures cover bribery of a foreign public official.

- Increases the maximum penalty for bribery from seven to ten years' imprisonment, with an unlimited fine.

- Introduces a corporate offense of negligent failure to prevent bribery by persons working on behalf of a business. A business can avoid conviction if it can show that it generally has good systems in place to prevent bribery.

- Ensures that evidence from proceedings in Parliament can be considered by the courts in bribery cases by removing parliamentary privilege in the prosecution of an MP or peer.

Emerging countries have also passed anti-corruption and bribery legislation. Take Lithuania for example. Article 282 of the Criminal Code defines the *acceptance of a bribe* as accepting, promising to accept, or demanding of a bribe by a public official or a civil servant, for himself or herself or for anyone else, for him or her to act or refrain from acting, to make a decision, vote or express an opinion in favour of a bribe-giver, or the promise to do so. The Criminal Code also stipulates other corruption-related crimes. These include abuse of office, refraining from official duties (nonfeasance), fraud (related to document handling) in office (malfeasance), exceeding one's authority, commercial bribery, acceptance of undue remuneration.

Until 1911, the US Foreign Corruption Practices Act (FCPA) was the dominant anti-bribery legislation. Now, with the passage of the UK Bribery Act, global firms have to be aware of its procedures, which in some cases, are more robust than the FCPA. For example, firms may be prosecuted if they conduct business, or part of it in the UK, no matter where the bribe takes place. Another example is that the FCPA provides some justification for promotional expenses if it can be demonstrated that they were reasonable and bona fide. This is not allowed in the UK Act. Penalties and fines for violating the Acts also differ somewhat between both countries. For example, under the FCPA fines may reach up to $2 million for each violation, whereas under the UK Act, the fine may be unlimited. Potential imprisonment of executives found guilty of violation is up to ten years in the UK and five years in the US.

Anti-Corruption and Ethics Policy by Business Firms

One of the tools available to business firms is to compile a code of ethics. An ethics code is a set of guidelines that stipulates a set of acceptable behaviors. However, a written code is not sufficient unless it includes a mechanism for its enforcement, such as penalties for not adhering to the code and in some cases, rewards for following it. An ethics code needs the support of all top executives of the firm. A survey by Deloitte & Touche among 4,000 of the top publicly traded firms in the United States found that 83 percent of respondents had codes of conduct, but one-quarter of them were not enforcing them.[34] About one-half of the firms reported that ethics issues are taken up by the board of directors only when failure occurs.

In order to implement an ethics code, it is necessary to appoint an ombudsman; a manager who has the responsibility for coordinating ethical policy throughout the organization, and who serves as an advocate for employees and board members who report, or are involved in an ethical dilemma. If employees are expected to report what they observe as unethical behavior by their peers ("whistle-blowing"), they must be protected by the organization (and perhaps rewarded for their actions).

Attempts have also been made to motivate ethical behavior in a company's supply chain. An example of this is the Sedex non-profit organization based in London, UK, open for membership to any company anywhere in the world. Sedex is a knowledge management provider for measuring and improving ethical and responsible business practices in global supply chains. The organization enables member companies to manage efficiently the ethical and responsible practices of their global supply chains, generating transparency through the provision of a secure and user-friendly data exchange (Figure 16.5).[35]

ANTI-CORRUPTION LEGISLATION IN THE BRIC COUNTRIES

Brazil

Brazil is ranked 69 (out of 175 countries surveyed) on Transparency International's 2014 Corruption Perception Index.

A new anti-corruption law came into effect in 2014. It is believed to be stronger than either the FCPA or the UK Bribery Act, however, it is too early to judge whether the new law will have a significant effect on corruption. Fines imposed on firms can reach 20 percent of their gross annual revenue or, if turnover is hard to determine,

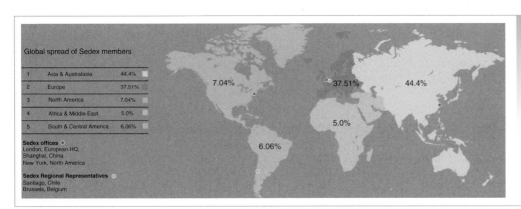

FIGURE 16.5
Global Spread of Sedex Members
Source: Reproduced with permission by the Social Media Examiner, 2014

60 million Reais ($25 million). Unlike America's FCPA, it requires no proof of executive intent or knowledge: so long as the charged firm benefits from corrupt acts committed by an employee (even acting through a subsidiary or a subcontractor).[36]

Penalties imposed on companies violating the new law include fines of up to 1 to 20 percent of the firm's gross revenues accrued during the year when the violation occurred. However, if it is not possible to make such a calculation, fines ranging from BRL60,000 and up may be imposed. Leniency is possible if the accused cooperates ("whistle-blowing") with the government investigation.

Russia

Russia is ranked 161 (out of 175 countries surveyed) on Transparency International's 2014 Corruption Perception Index.

The Russian Duma ratified legislation—the Anti-Corruption Law—which established the legal and organizational frameworks for combating corruption. The law prohibits giving a bribe to, or receiving a bribe from a public or foreign official, a corporate officer, or facilitating a bribe. It is also forbidden for a public official to accept gifts of any value. Receiving bribes by public or foreign officials may be fined up to 50 times the amount of the bribe and prohibition to be employed in government for a period of up to three years. Imprisonment is also a possibility given the severity of the bribe. Bribe givers in business may be subject to similar fines as public officials, while bribe takers may have to pay a fine up to 70 times the amount of the bribe. Imprisonment is also a possibility in these situations as well. As in the case of Brazil, there is a leniency provision for cooperation with the authorities.

India

India is ranked 85 (out of 175 countries surveyed) on Transparency International's 2014 Corruption Perception Index. Ratan Tata, chairman of the Tata Group observed that "If you choose not to participate in [corruption], you leave behind a fair amount of business."[37] The relatively low ranking of India above is compatible with the findings of a survey of managers of leading Indian corporations carried out by the consulting firm KMPG in 2011:[38]

- A majority of survey respondents felt that corruption in India will remain the same irrespective of new legislation;

- 68 percent believed that in many cases, corruption is induced by the private sector;

- 68 percent believed that India can achieve better GDP growth if corruption is controlled;

- 51 percent feared that rising corruption will make India less attractive for foreign investment.

Box 16.3 Company-in-Focus: Indian Institute of Management

The postgraduate programs at the Indian Institutes of Management have initiated an ethics program at the schools. One of their educators was quoted as saying: "Our social conditioning by and large makes us unethical vis-a-vis a lack of civic sense and concern for the environment. Management students are at an age when they are less vulnerable and can differentiate the right from the wrong. The subject has been introduced to sensitize students about ethical issues as and when they take up responsibilities later in their career."

The ethics course is compulsory for all students and it is joined by a course on social transformation in India, which focuses on the societal issues across the country. Such courses should help the students take sustainable decisions for the society when they graduate.

While India has a well-developed legal system based on British common law, its institutional framework is designed mainly to address the public, rather than the private sector. This makes it more difficult to monitor and prosecute business corruption.

Corruption is very costly to India. Reports from international organizations, including the UN Global Compact, estimate that corruption adds as much as 10 percent to the total cost of doing business globally, and as much as 25 percent to the cost of procuring contracts in developing countries.[39]

China

China is ranked 119 (out of 175 countries surveyed) on Transparency International's 2014 Corruption Perception Index.

Some progress has been made to root out corruption in China. Initiatives include the passage of laws and regulations, governmental instructions and guidelines, and the growth of NGO "watchdog" organizations.

Complaints of alleged corruption may be addressed to four government anti-corruption agencies (there are no independent non-government agencies in China): The Central Commission for Discipline Inspection (CCDI), The Supreme People's Procuratorate (SSP), the Ministry of Supervision, and the National Bureau of Corruption Prevention (NBCP). These agencies, especially the CCDI, deal with government officials suspected of violating party rules and regulations, including the abuse of power, bribery, and infringement on the people's economic, political and personal rights and interests.[40] The SSP is responsible for investigating the embezzlement of state property and bribery of public officials. The NBCP as its title suggests, is involved in corruption prevention through monitoring corruption legislation in force.

While the above agencies monitor government officials, what about foreign business investors operating in China? Amendment 8 to the People's Republic of China Criminal Law legislated in 2011 prohibits bribe payments to non-government officials. The Anti-Unfair Competition Law prohibits bribery in commercial transactions. The National Development and Reform Commission investigates antitrust violations including price fixing. Some recent examples of convictions include Chrysler Group China Sales was fined 31.6 million Yuan by the Shanghai government, equivalent to 3 percent of its previous year's sales in Shanghai. Three Chrysler dealers were fined 2.14 million Yuan. In another case, the Commission found (2014) twelve Japanese auto parts and bearings manufacturers guilty of fixing prices charged to Chinese factories of at least five automakers, and imposing fines totaling roughly $200 million.[41] Not only are foreign companies scrutinized. Two state-controlled alcoholic beverage companies, Kweichow Moutai and Wuliangye, were fined in February 2013 when regulators found them guilty of requiring retailers to charge a minimum price for their premium liquors. Kweichow Moutai was fined $40 million and Wuliangye $33 million.[42]

To sum up, corruption in the BRIC countries is relatively high compared to more developed countries as measured in the Corruption Perception Index. Brazil and India are somewhat of an exception showing improvement in their rankings. Some researchers attribute the difference in attitudes towards corruption of Eastern and Western countries to Kipling's adage: "…East is East and West is West, and never the twain shall meet." This may be an oversimplification, but cultural factors play an important role in the development and sustainability of ethics and social responsibility.[43]

What Can Be Done: Global Corporate Citizenship

Nations are interdependent in a world of globalization. Corporations operating in this world have the opportunity to build an international community of virtue and protection of basic human rights.[44] This task can be done by adhering to universal codes of behavior such as those promulgated by the United Nations, OECD, and relevant NGOs, such as Transparency International. Firms can promote basic, universal human principles, such as physical security, education, decent working conditions, and wages by practicing them in the workplace.

In addition to the Sedex organization, a group of business leaders from Europe, Japan, and the United States met in Caux, Switzerland, to develop "a shared perspective on business behavior acceptable to and honored by all."[45] The deliberations of the group led to the publication of seven general principles of behavior:

1. the responsibilities of businesses: beyond shareholders towards stakeholders;

2. the economic and social impact of business: toward innovation, justice, and world community;

3. business behavior: beyond the letter of the law towards a spirit of trust;

4. respect for rules;

5. support for multilateral trade;

6. respect for the environment;

7. avoidance of illicit operations.

These suggested modes of behavior contain both ethical (e.g. avoidance of illicit operations) and social responsibility (e.g. respect for the environment) principles that may be applied across nations.

A number of ethicists such as Richard De George,[46] Thomas Donaldson,[47] and Thomas Dunfee[48] have written broadly on the subject of moral values that corporations should follow when doing business abroad. All three educators have grappled with the problems that arise when home and host cultures differ, especially with respect to moral values. Business practices that may be considered unethical in one culture may be acceptable in another. The dilemma is how to act in a situation where what you consider being unethical at home is acceptable elsewhere. This situation is what Donaldson and Dunfee call *"moral free space."*[49] In this space there are no right answers, so managers must chart their own course of action, as long as they do not violate *core moral values*. Generally, these core values stem from a company's code of ethics. In the absence of such a code, or if the code does not fit the situation, then the manager must use his or her judgment. Donaldson suggests that most dilemmas that occur because of differences between two cultures are of two kinds: *conflict of relative development* and *conflict of tradition*. In the first conflict, a dilemma occurs because of a difference between stages of economic development. In this situation, it is suggested that managers ask whether the practice in question would be acceptable if his/her country was in the same stage of development. If so,

Bell Canada Enterprises	Bank of Montreal	General Electric	Nortel	TABLE 16.8 Moral Values and Principles of Selected Firms
Comply with applicable laws.	Do what is fair and honest.	Obey applicable laws and regulations.	Compete vigorously in the workplace.	
Work with integrity, honesty, fairness.	Respect the rights of others.	Be honest, fair, and trustworthy.	Treat others with dignity and respect.	
Foster environment of trust, respect, and open communication.	Work to the letter and the spirit of the law.	Avoid conflicts of interest.	Do what we say we will do.	
Maintain a safe and secure workplace and protect the environment.	Maintain the confidentiality of information.	Foster an equal opportunity atmosphere.	Be honest and obey all applicable laws.	
Sustain a culture where ethical culture is recognized, valued, and exemplified by all employees.	Avoid conflicts of interest.	Strive to create a safe workplace and protect the environment.	Committed to live out our values.	
	Conduct ourselves appropriately at all times.	Through leadership, sustain culture where ethical conduct is recognized, valued, and exemplified by all employees.		

Source: Adapted from: Schwartz, M. (2005). 'Universal moral values for corporate codes of ethics', *Journal of Business Ethics*, 59(1), p. 33.

then the practice would be ethical. The second case is one of traditional differences. The most prevalent situation is gift giving. In Asian and Middle Eastern countries it is customary to give business gifts. Here the problem is one of intent and magnitude. If the intention is to fulfill a cultural norm, then the gift may be considered ethical if its magnitude cannot be construed as being beyond the normal value of a gift in the context in which it is given.

SUMMARY

- As multinational companies expand globally and enter foreign markets, ethical conduct of the officers and employees assume added importance since the very cultural diversity associated with such expansion may undermine the much shared cultural and ethical values observable in the more homogeneous organizations.
- Unethical practices such as bribery and poor working conditions have negative effects on the firm in the long run in terms of lower profits and tarnished image.
- According to ethical absolutism, global firms need to develop and enforce their own codes of ethics wherever they operate specifically directed at the issues related to a multicultural, multinational business environment. However, there are those who believe that one should follow the ethical codes that prevail in the host country.
- Corporate social responsibility (CSR) in the international business environment is more challenging because there are many more diverse stakeholders of international business firms. MNCs are faced with wider CSR expectations, and MNCs are under increasing pressure for socially responsible behavior in their global operations.
- International monitoring of bribery and corruption is more widespread thanks to organizations such as Transparency International, the OECD, and the European Commission. Organizations such as these have led to the strengthening of anti-corruption domestic legislation in many countries, as well as multilateral agreements to curb these practices.
- CSR in the BRIC countries ranges from moderate in the case of Brazil and India to rather weak in China and Russia.

DISCUSSION QUESTIONS

1. In doing business in a foreign country, whose ethics should you follow, the norms of the foreign country or those of your country? Discuss.
2. Give three examples of corporate social responsibility in your state or city.
3. What can multinational corporations do to encourage corporate social responsibility among the companies with which they do business abroad?
4. Does a potential whistle-blower have a greater responsibility to the public, to the organization, to himself/herself?

5. How can American companies function in a country like India without having to resort to bribe payments?

EXPERIENTIAL EXERCISES

1. Obtain via the Internet the ethical codes of two American multinational corporations. Try to compare their codes to those of a French or British MNC (also obtained via the Internet). What similarities have you found in the company codes? Are there any differences?
2. Compare the anti-bribery legislation of the UK and the United States. Which legislation—in your opinion—will do the best job to prevent bribery?

KEY TERMS

- Conflict of relative development
- Conflict of tradition
- Core moral values
- Corporate social responsibility
- Ethical absolutists
- Ethical relativists
- Ethical universalists
- Ethics

- Ethics code
- Moral free space
- OECD Anti-Bribery Convention
- Sarbanes–Oxley Act
- Transparency International
- UK Bribery Bill
- UN Convention Against Corruption
- US Foreign Corrupt Practices Act of 1977

NOTES

1 'The global fight against bribery and corruption: U.S. law and policy', Speech by Ambassador Schneider at 'Transparency Unveiling Corruption', Deloitte & Touche, Amsterdam, October 1, 1999.
2 Transparency International: Gateway tools to measure corruption, www.Transparency.org. [Accessed: June 29, 2014].
3 (2014), 'The cost of corruption on global business', www.asil.org/event/cost-corruption-global-business/.
4 American Society of International Law, Asil.org. [Accessed: August 24, 2014].
5 Cheung, Y.L., Raghavendra, R., and Stouraitis, A. (2012), 'How much do firms pay as bribes and what benefits do they get? Evidence from corruption cases worldwide', NBER Working Paper Series, Paper No. 17981.
6 The World Factbook. (2015), https://www.cia.gov/library/publications/the-world-factbook/docs/refmaps.html [Accessed: August 1, 2015].
7 'The hidden costs of unethical behavior', Josephson Institute Reports, http://fliphtml5.com/sgqs/cfjc/basic/ [Accessed: July 30, 2016].
8 Donaldson, T. (1996), 'Values in tension: Ethics away from home', *Harvard Business Review,* September–October, pp. 47–62.
9 European Union Commission. (2001), '366 final green paper promoting a European framework for corporate social responsibility', http://eur-lex.europa.eu?lexuriserv/site/en/com/2001/com2001_0366en01.pdf [Accessed: May 24, 2009].

10   World Bank. (2003). *Corporate social responsibility practice: Strengthening implementation of corporate social responsibility in global supply chains*. Washington, D.C.: World Bank.

11   'InFocus initiative on corporate social responsibility (CSR), governing body, 295th session, Geneva, 2006', www.ilo.org/public/english/support/lib/resource/subject/csr.htm [Accessed: May 25, 2009].

12   The World Factbook. (2015), https://www.cia.gov/library/publications/the-world-factbook/docs/refmaps.html [Accessed: August 1, 2015].

13   Pagecargo.com/view/globalreporting.org/

14   Nascimento, A. (2004), 'Corporate social responsibility in Brazil: A comparative analysis of two paper companies', [Master's thesis] Massachusetts Institute of Technology, www.dspace.mit.edu/handle/1721.1/28800/ [Accessed: November 28, 2010].

15   Dayman, S. (2008), 'Russia in 2008: Corporate social responsibility in a post-socialist state', www.ecologia.org/isosr/sergey.html. [Accessed: June 21, 2009].

16   Lattemin, M., Fetscherin, M., Alon, I., Li, S., and Schneider, A. (2009), 'CSR communication intensity in Chinese and Indian multinational corporations', *Corporate Governance: An International Review*, 17(4), pp. 426–42.

17   Ibid.

18   Lin. L-W. (2010), 'Corporate social responsibility in China: Window dressing or structural change', *Berkeley Journal of International Law*, 28(1), p. 36.

19   Zinjung, L. (2005), 'Lack of corporate social responsibility behind recent China accidents', *World Watch Institute*, http://www.worldwatch.org/node/3859 [Accessed: May 25, 2009].

20   Lattemin, op. cit.

21   'The state of CSR in India 2004, acknowledging progress, prioritizing action', National seminar on corporate responsibility, November 10, 2004, New Delhi.

22   1 crore = 10 million rupees.

23   India Briefing. (2014), 'Key aspects of India's corporate social responsibility mandate clarified', June 25, http://www.india-briefing.com/news/key-aspects-indias-corporate-social-responsibility-mandate-clarified-8620.html/ [Accessed: July 30, 2016].

24   Webley, S. and More, E. (2002), 'Does business ethics pay', London: Institute of Business Ethics, www.ibe.org.uk

25   Margolis, J., Walsh, J., and D. Krehmeyer. (2006), *Building the business case for ethics*, Business Roundtable Institute for Corporate Ethics, Harvard Business School.

26   Obeua Persons. (2013), 'Characteristics of no ethics code firms and effect of having no ethics code on financial performance', *Journal of Academic and Business Ethics*, 7, June, pp. 1–14.

27   www.ethicalleadershipgroup.com/blog/2006/04/budapest_hungary_does_ethics_p_1.html [Accessed: May 18, 2009].

28   Ugoji, K. (2006). *Does business ethics pay? Ethics and financial performance.* [MSc thesis] Cranfield School of Management.

29   For an interactive map of the CI index, see http://www.transparency.org/research/cpi/overview [Accessed: July 30, 2016].

30   'The power of principles', https://www.unglobalcompact.org/what-is-gc/mission/principles [Accessed: July 30, 2016].

31   Hohnen, P. (2013). 'Is the UN global compact leadership an effective forum for change?', September 3, 2013, http://www.The guardian.com/sustainable-business/ungc-leaders-summit-forum-for-change.

32   Rial, E. (2009), 'Beyond reproach, why compliance with anti-corruption laws is increasingly critical for multinational businesses', *Deloitte Review*, April 17, 2009.

33   US Securities and Exchange Commission Actions: FCPA Cases, https://www.sec.gov/spotlight/fcpa/fcpa-cases.shtml [Accessed: July 30, 2016].

34   www.deloitte.com/us/ethicssurvey [Accessed: May 21, 2009].

35   "A" members include retailers and consumer products companies, "AB" members are agents, suppliers, manufacturers and importers.

36 (2014), 'Brazil's new anti-corruption law', http://www.Economist.com/blogs/Schumpeter/2014/01/brazil-new-anti-corruption-law/ [Accessed: July 17, 2016].

37 Anand, A., Cherian, K., Gautam, A., Majmudar, R., and Raimala, A. (2012), 'Business vs. ethics: The India tradeoff?', Knowledge@Wharton, http://knowledge.wharton.upenn.edu/article/business-vs-ethics-the-India-tradeoff/ [Accessed: September 9, 2014].

38 'EMA risk & compliance practice leaders meeting', April 4–5, 2011, Hotel Taj Mahal, New Delhi, report published February 14, 2011, www.in.kpmg.com.

39 Bajoria, J. (2011), 'Corruption threatens India's growth', Council on Foreign Relations, March 1, 2011, www.worldaffairsjournal.org/content/governance-india-corruption

40 (2012). 'CPC Discipline watchdog vows crackdown on corruption', *Xinhua*, November 19, 2012, www.china.org.cn

41 Bradsher, K. (2014). 'China fines Japanese auto parts and bearings makers in price rigging', *The New York Times*, August 20, 2014, http://www.nytimes.com/2014/08/21/business/international/china-fines-japanese-auto-parts-and-bearings-firms-for-price-rigging.html?_r=0 [Accessed: July 30, 2016].

42 Ibid.

43 See for example: Anand, A. et al. (2012). 'Business vs. ethics: The India tradeoff?', Knowledge@Wharton, http://knowledge.wharton.upenn.edu/article/business-vs-ethics-the-India-tradeoff/ [Accessed: September 9, 2014].

44 Rendtorff, D. (n.d.), 'Towards ethical guidelines for international business corporations aspects of global corporate citizenship', Proceedings of the fourth world congress, Capetown, South Africa, July 15–18, 2008, www.rucforsk.ruc.dk

45 *Caux Round Table Principles for Business*. (1994). The Hague, Switzerland.

46 De George, R. (1993). *Competing with integrity in international business*. New York: Oxford University Press.

47 Donaldson, T. (1989). *The ethics of international business*. New York: Oxford University Press.

48 Dunfee, T. (2003), 'Taking responsibility for bribery: The multinational corporation's role in combating bribery', In: Sullivan, R. (ed.). *Business and human rights: Dilemmas and solutions*. UK: Greenleaf Publishing.

49 Donaldson, T. (1996), 'Values in tension: Ethics away from home', *Harvard Business Review,* September/October, p. 44–52.

CASE 16.1   A CASE ON SERIOUS PROBLEMS IN CREATING A PARTNERSHIP IN RUSSIA

Tiia Vissak
University of Tartu (Estonia)
tiia.vissak@ut.ee

In the mid-1990s a medium-sized Baltic food producer BaltFoodEx (founded in the beginning of the 1990s)[1] decided to enter Russia because it felt that although its products were quite popular among its customers and had reached a relatively high market share in its home market, but also the other two Baltic countries and managed even to outcompete some well-known Western brands, the Baltic market did not offer it enough growth opportunities. The firm decided to enter Russia, not Scandinavia or Poland, because Baltic food had been quite popular among Russian and other ex-Soviet customers already in the Soviet time (especially in the St. Petersburg and the Moscow regions): there, many people saw the three Baltic countries as "almost real Western Europe" and the fact itself that a product originated from the West was a symbol of high quality. At the same time, Baltic food was not very familiar to Polish or Scandinavian customers as in the Soviet time, Baltic food had not been actively exported there (at that time, Soviet companies – including Baltic firms – could not select export markets themselves: the Planning Committee made such decisions and the main task given to Baltic firms was to supply the North-Western part of Russia and other Soviet Republics). Moreover, although the living standard was lower in Russia than in the three Baltic countries, its larger population (around 150 million at that time) made it an attractive market. Russia also had a larger market and a higher living standard (especially in the Moscow and St. Petersburg regions) than Belarus and the Ukraine that were also geographically close to the Baltic market and whose customers were quite well familiar with Baltic products. Thus, Russia was also preferred to these two countries. The geographically more distant countries – other Western European countries and other former Soviet Socialist Republics – were excluded almost from the start because of high transport costs, unfamiliarity with Baltic products (the former group of countries) or low incomes (the latter group). BaltFoodEx's managers' good Russian language skills[2] and their belief that Russian business practices should not be very different from their own (after all, they shared a common history) also influenced the firm's market selection.

BaltFoodEx could not enter Russia successfully by exporting because the country had high import duties on Baltic food products and the firm could not successfully compete with Russian lower-cost producers (it had tried to export there a year earlier but without considerable success: Russian consumers were quite price conscious while some of those who were not, preferred well-known "real" Western brands that had been inaccessible for them in the Soviet time). Even without the duties, the firm's products would have been more expensive than the Russian ones because of transportation costs and higher salaries in Baltic countries. So, BaltFoodEx decided to establish a production unit in Russia. The firm lacked funds for establishing such a unit in the country alone. Establishing its own subsidiary would have been also difficult because the company's owners and managers had not established close ties there and they also feared Russia's strict bureaucracy; moreover, they did not have enough knowledge of the Russian market as the firm was founded after the dissolution of the Soviet Union and the owners and managers had no business experience from this area of activities from that time. So, they decided to co-operate with a local enterprise. At a food fair, the company found a rather small Russian enterprise RusFoodProd that was already producing a similar type of products with quite a high market potential, but had relatively outdated technology. RusFoodProd lacked funds for updating its technology and increasing its production capacity on its own. So, it was interested in partnership with the Baltic food producer. The two firms discussed their future plans: they wanted to expand the Russian plant, add some Baltic products to its portfolio, increase its market share in Russia, start exporting to some neighboring countries in the near future and even consider opening a new plant in the Ukraine in the more distant future.

In the contract, BaltFoodEx and RusFoodProd agreed that the former would provide the latter with technology (it had recently acquired more modern machinery with a higher production capacity, so it did not need some of its old machinery any more, but it also agreed to acquire some additional machinery for the Russian partner) and with that, obtain a considerable share in the Russian enterprise. The Russian partner advised BaltFoodEx to save on customs duties by not declaring the machinery on the Russian border correctly. The Baltic firm agreed to follow the suggestion because the cost savings seemed to be substantial and the control at the Russian border was not very strict, so the risk of getting caught and paying the resulting fine was low; moreover, the Russian partner assured that they knew some right people at the border, so, even if the machinery were discovered, paying the fine could be also avoided at "just a little extra cost".

The machinery successfully crossed the border without anybody checking it and arrived at the Russian enterprise on time. When BaltFoodEx contacted its Russian partner and asked when it would obtain the share in RusFoodProd as it was agreed in the contract, the Russian firm claimed that the Baltic firm could not prove that it had ever sent the machinery to RusFoodProd as there were no documents showing that the machinery had crossed the Russian border or reached the enterprise at all. They also made some vague threats to their Baltic partners about knowing where their families lived and suggested them to send the machinery again or forget about the partnership. The owners of the Baltic firm decided to follow the latter suggestion although they could not be sure how realistic these threats were. So, BaltFoodEx lost a considerable amount of money without managing to obtain any share in RusFoodProd or getting the machinery back (it did not wish to admit to the authorities that it had not paid the customs duties properly and it also did not want to contact any "unofficial structures" as this could have caused even more serious problems; moreover, it was afraid that making the problem public would harm its image in the Baltic market and decrease its chances to enter other countries in the future). The only consolation for them was that they had not shared their recipes with their Russian partners yet. BaltFoodEx never completely recovered from this experience and it never entered Russia again. It also could not expand further on the Baltic market as it had planned: for example, it lacked funds for buying a local enterprise that it had promised to buy before facing problems in Russia. Because of financing problems, the company also failed to enter other foreign countries. Some years later, the firm was taken over by a larger Baltic food producer. This firm has not become active in Russia, either: it has decided to enter Scandinavia instead.

QUESTIONS FOR DISCUSSION

1. Was Russia the logical choice as a new target market for the Baltic firm?
2. List the reasons why BaltFoodEx was interested in co-operating with RusFoodProd and the other way round.
3. Explain why the co-operation between the two case firms failed.
4. Do you think that BaltFoodEx made the right decision to exit Russia without trying to get a compensation for the machinery or getting its share in the Russian enterprise? Was it a reasonable decision never to re-enter this country? Why?

RECOMMENDED LITERATURE

- CIA – The World Factbook (https://www.cia.gov/library/publications/the-world-factbook/); this site provides information about the countries' current economic state etc (the data are periodically renewed)
- Doing Business 2009. Country Profile for Russian Federation (http://www.doingbusiness.org/Documents/CountryProfiles/RUS.pdf)
- Doing Business in Russia: 2009 Country Commercial Guide for U.S. Companies (http://www.buyusa.gov/russia/en/market_reports.html)
- International Trade Administration, U.S. Department of Commerce (2004). Business Ethics: A Manual for Managing a Responsible Business Enterprise in Emerging Market Economies (http://www.ita.doc.gov/goodgovernance/adobe/bem_manual.pdf)
- PriceWaterhouseCoopers (2009). Doing Business and Investing in the Russian Federation (http://www.pwc.com/ru/globalisation/doing-business-in-russia-2009.pdf);
- The Library of Congress Country Studies (http://lcweb4.loc.gov/frd/cs/list.html); this source provides information about the countries' earlier history, society, economy etc.
- World Business Culture Cultural Compatibility Test (http://www.worldbusinessculture.com/compatibility/test/); answering the 25 questions in this test allows to measure cultural similarities and differences with people from 39 countries (including Russia) along seven dimensions.

NOTES

1 The Baltic market consists of three small countries: Estonia, Latvia and Lithuania with populations of 1.3, 2.2 and 3.6 million, respectively that all joined the European Union in May 2004. These countries restored their independence in 1991 when the Soviet Union dissolved (they were also independent for about two decades before the start of WWII). Because of the sensitive nature of this case story, the names of the two case enterprises were completely changed (so, the real names of these enterprises have nothing in common with Rusfood, Baltfood, Baltex, Rusprod or any others names of this type) and their exact area of activity and financial data were concealed in order to retain their anonymity.

2 Although in each of the Baltic countries, a different language is spoken, in Soviet time, all children studying in local-language schools had to learn Russian as their first foreign language; usually English or German came next; now, the first foreign language is usually English in local-language schools and the local language is taught first in Russian-language schools.

Index

Note: "F" after a page number indicates a figure; "t" indicates a table; "m" indicates a map.